Red Hat® Linux

INSTALLATION AND CONFIGURATION HANDBOOK

Red Hat® Linux

INSTALLATION AND CONFIGURATION HANDBOOK

Duane Hellums, et. al.

A Division of Macmillan USA
201 West 103rd Street, Indianapolis, Indiana 46290

Red Hat® Linux Installation and Configuration Handbook

Copyright © 2000 by Que Corporation

International Standard Book Number: 0-7897-2181-3

Library of Congress Catalog Card Number: 99-63852

Printed in the United States of America

First Printing: December 1999

01   00   99   4   3   2   1

Trademarks

Warning and Disclaimer

PUBLISHER
Dean Miller

ACQUISITIONS EDITOR
Gretchen Ganser

DEVELOPMENT EDITOR
Maureen A. McDaniel

TECHNICAL EDITOR
Brian Walters

MANAGING EDITOR
Lisa Wilson

PROJECT EDITOR
Tonya Simpson

COPY EDITOR
Krista Hansing

INDEXER
Heather McNeill

PROOFREADER
Juli Cook

TEAM COORDINATOR
Cindy Teeters

MEDIA DEVELOPER
Michael Hunter

INTERIOR DESIGNER
Anne Jones

COVER DESIGNER
Anne Jones

COPY WRITER
Eric Borgert

PRODUCTION
Stacey DeRome
Ayanna Lacey
Heather Hiatt Miller

Contents at a Glance

Table of Contents

IV Hardware

18 Installing and Configuring the Red Hat Linux Kernel   359

About the Authors

Duane B. Hellums (hellums@yahoo.com) is a systems analyst and program manager for a large software development firm in Montgomery, Alabama. He currently manages a multitude of Oracle and Web development projects. He has 10 years experience administering and maintaining mission-critical heterogeneous networks, servers, and workstations. He is an expert in various flavors of UNIX on numerous platforms, including Intel x86, Sun SPARC, HP 9000, and AT&T 3B15. He has experience as a lead programmer and tester of systems based in C/C++, Pascal, Assembler, UNIX shell scripts, and Access. He has developed or maintained many systems, including (but not limited to) an online account management system for a nationwide outsourced payroll and human resources firm, an enterprise circuit status reporting system for a telecommunication organization, a help-desk system for an engineering and construction firm, and a proprietary, fault-tolerant, real-time messaging system.

Duane became interested in Linux circa 1994 when he found out that he could have "UNIX" at home for virtually free. His writing gravitates toward UNIX-related topics, including Linux, networking, and the Internet. He was a contributing author for the UNIX portions (among others) of *FrontPage 2000 Unleashed*, the most recent in the extremely popular and successful series by William Stanek. He co-authored technical white papers on Microsoft's NT 4, Santa Cruz Operation (SCO) UnixWare and Open Server, and Sun Solaris 6. He also has written several articles for *Linux Journal*.

Duane earned his M.S. in Information Systems degree from Hawaii Pacific University and a Computer Science and Management degree from the University of Maryland. He owns a startup IT consulting company that has assisted the networking and computing efforts of several law offices, telecommunications firms, Boy Scout offices, and public schools. His company focuses primarily on Small Office Home Office (SOHO) needs in the areas of systems integration, online technologies, intranets, network and system administration (Linux, UNIX, NT, and Windows 95/98), databases, multimedia, and Web development.

Other than anything related to computers, Duane enjoys travel, golf, running, languages (he's fluent in Russian and Spanish), reading (Clive Cussler and Steven King), chess, photography, billiards, bonsai, swimming, diving, snorkeling, restoring his '67 T-bird (still looking for a nice Barracuda), model building, good movies, cooking, and the occasional TV sitcom. He hopes to someday have time to enjoy these hobbies and retire with his wife Michelle in Kentucky (with maybe a T1-equipped vacation beach house in Jamaica, Mallorca, or Sausalito.)

Kyle Amon is a principal of GNUTEC Information Technology Solutions and is currently engaged in writing. He has worked at IBM twice, as a UNIX Systems Administrator and Security Specialist, been Corporate UNIX Systems Administrator of Jabil Circuit, done writing and technical editing for Macmillan Computer Publishing, and established an e-commerce Web site in 1994. A member of USENIX, SAGE, ACM, ICSA, and CFUG, he has championed Free Software since Linux kernel discussion first hit Usenet. He skipped his senior year of high school, entered an early admissions program, and earned his B.A. (Eckerd College, 1988) in three years.

Max Cohan is a computer consultant specializing in Internet technologies with a focus on Perl and Linux. He dove into the telecommunications craze (BBS) at the age of 11, learned to program in C by the age of 13, and has been involved with the Internet in some form or another for more than 11 years and has been an independent consultant for more than five. His consulting has focused primarily on Internet technologies and specializing in working with Perl and Linux. However, in his consulting he has worked with C, VB, Windows NT, and many other environments, which keeps him on his toes and keeps the work fun.

He lives in San Diego with his fiance, Mary Whittington, and enjoys concerts, movies (there is a great Cinema Society here), and many other non-technical recreations. He can be contacted at mcohan@adnc.net.

Jim Henderson is a recognized expert in NetWare 4/NetWare 5 connectivity as well as Novell Directory Services, and is one of the volunteer SysOps on the Novell Support Connection. He is an avid Linux enthusiast with a background in various flavors of UNIX.

Neal S. Jamison is a consultant and author specializing in Internet technologies such as Web development and administration, intranets, and Linux and UNIX systems administration. As the director of the Internet Solutions Center for AnviCom, Inc., he researches and employs current and emerging Internet technologies for the benefit of his clients.

Neal holds a B.S. in computer science from Virginia Tech and an M.S. in information systems from Hawaii Pacific University. He lives, works, and writes in Falls Church, Virginia with his wife and son.

Jon Konrath first started using Linux in 1992, while a student at Indiana University. After several years of user support, technical writing, and teaching UNIX classes, he moved to Seattle and worked as a documentation engineer for Spry/Compuserve and WRQ, Inc. He has also written documentation for the Emacs-W3 browser, contributed to the WINE project, and was a technical editor for *Sams Teach Yourself Emacs in 24 Hours*.

When not writing technical documentation, Jon spends most of his time writing fiction. He's trying to complete his second novel and has made numerous appearances in zines and other small press journals. He recently moved to New York City, where he lives with his girlfriend Marie and their two cats. You can reach him at jkonrath@rumored.com.

Wade Maxfield is president of Central Telecommunications, Inc. CTI specializes in providing Internet service and software consulting. Past and current clients include GTE, Mobil Oil, RTEC Systems, Practitioner's Publishing Company, Aldus, Motorola, and others. For the last 20 years, Wade has practiced system software design and implementation for systems that include Macintosh, Windows 3.1, 95, NT, UNIX (Linux, HPUX, DGUX), VRTX, Psos, DOS, CP/M, and some custom designed operating systems. He has a son and a daughter (both aged 10), two dogs, three fish, and two birds. If he had spare time, he would enjoy traveling the world.

Kevin McPeake has been a six-year advocate and user of the Linux operating system. He has in-depth experience using Linux and Solaris in commercial enterprise environments and possesses an extensive personal collection of Linux and Solaris systems running on Sparc, Intel, and PowerPC hardware. Originally from Texas, he has relocated across the Atlantic more times than he personally cares to remember. Kevin now currently resides in the Hague, The Netherlands, where he is a chief security consultant for the Trust Factory (`http://www.trust-factory.com`). He can be reached at `kevin@mcpeake.net`.

Rob Napier (`rnapier@employees.org`) is an engineer with Cisco Systems in Research Triangle Park, North Carolina. He has been working with Linux since 1995 and is currently an officer for the Triangle Linux Users Group (`www.trilug.org`). He is the author of the "Finding the Answers in Linux" mini-HOWTO (`http://www.employees.org/~rnapier/linuxanswers.html`).

Rich Payne began working on Linux in 1994, while still a student at Keene State College in Keene, New Hampshire. He pulled his first distribution down over the Internet and put it on about 25 flop-pies for the install on his home machine. In 1998 he started `www.alphalinux.org` because he found there was a severe lack of information on the Alpha port of Linux out on the Web, and what was around was outdated. Since then, Rich has been working for Alpha Processor Inc. of Concord, Massachusetts. He recently co-wrote (with another `alphalinux.org` member) the Alpha appendix of O'Reilly's *Running Linux*.

John Ray is an award-winning Web application developer and network programmer for The Ohio State University. He holds a computer engineering degree from OSU and oversees network opera-tions for one of its colleges. There, he implemented a campuswide database for maintaining TCP/IP information for a wide range of networked computers. He has also created a beginning-level pro-gramming language known as Weaver, which is used in OSU Extension's news database, as well as several other high-end applications. For the past five years, John has used Linux exclusively for his programming efforts and has championed its use for projects inside and outside the university. He provides customized Linux and UNIX-based TCP/IP programming solutions to businesses nation-wide. His other publications include *Sam's Teach Yourself Linux in 10 Minutes*, Que's *Special Edition Using TCP/IP*, and the email server information contained in *Linux Maximum Security*.

Dedication

To Michelle, my best friend in the world and beautiful wife of 17 years, and Ellen Eisert, our wonderful exchange student and new "daughter" from Germany, for their boundless patience, support, and love.

Also to my family and close friends who have endured the lack of phone calls, letters, emails, and attention during the past few months (especially Moms in Texas and Kentucky, all my brothers and sisters, cousin Shani, and best friends Al and Rene).

Love you all. You're the greatest!

—Duane Hellums

Acknowledgments

You'd think writing a book would be a simple thing—all you have to do is a functional decomposition and then slap the words down on the paper, right? Unfortunately, it takes a lot more work by many hard-working people. I'd like to thank all the people at Que Publishing who brought this book from the conceptual to the actual. They were there every step of the way, and without each and every one of them, my words would have gone into an article and not a book—or worse, they would have stayed in my head instead of being offered up to help other Linux aficionados and newbies that need that extra ounce of help and encouragement when considering learning something new in such a rapidly changing technical field. Hopefully this book will help take some of the challenge out of installing and configuring Linux.

I'd specifically like to thank the contributing authors for pitching in their valuable and hard-earned knowledge and skills in many specialized areas. I also owe a great debt of gratitude to all the people who were patient with me during several unavoidable project slips, when it seemed like Murphy's Law was the rule, not the exception. I was lucky to be able to work with a top-notch crew of specialists, without whom the book would have gotten nowhere. This includes Gretchen Ganser, who worked with me from the very beginning to the very end, keeping me focused. I look forward to working with you again soon! Maureen McDaniel did an awesome job molding my writing style into the format appropriate for this series and keeping my eye on the needs of the target audience. Brian Walters provided a wealth of technical expertise that kept me on my toes and pointed out some great tips to include. Krista Hansing worked hard to make my English language considerably more readable than the form in which it was submitted originally. I especially enjoyed working with Tonya Simpson because that meant the book was almost finished! I didn't get an opportunity to work as close with the many graphics and index specialists that put those finishing touches on the book that the reader comes to expect (but they deserve no less credit!). Of course, the account managers and marketing specialists deserve great thanks for working so very hard to get this work high visibility on the shelves as soon as possible. You can't go wrong working with such a professional bunch of people!

Thanks also to all the developers who have worked to make Linux what it is today, from Linus Torvalds to anyone who has written a line of code in support of Linux since. A huge thanks to everyone at Red Hat for bolstering the business case behind Linux, including their focus on ease of installation and availability of support. I tip my hat to all the fine people at Schwarz Communication for providing boxed sets of Red Hat Linux 6.0 for me when they were so hard to come by in the early days following its release. Finally, thanks to people like Kernigan, Ritchie, Metcalfe, and Andreesen's team, without whose trailblazing we wouldn't be able to enjoy programming, networking, and the Internet (and by extension, UNIX and Linux) as the invaluable resources they are today.

—Duane Hellums

Introduction

by Duane Hellums

This book is geared toward the beginner, with some advanced but highly practical topics thrown in for the intermediate and adventurous reader. In this way, the first five chapters and the enclosed CD are essentially worth the cost of the book. These should serve to get Linux installed and configured for you as quickly and painlessly as possible, not to make you a UNIX guru or system administrator overnight (that'll take weeks!). The remaining chapters are "value-added" segments for the reader who wants to learn more about Linux or implement portions of it that typically are not covered in contemporary Linux books.

Specifically, each chapter is packed with procedural steps that are easy to understand and that help you reach your end goals quickly. This is accomplished without deluging you with page after page of lists or tables of infrequently used settings that duplicate the information contained in man or help pages. For example, entire books are written about sendmail, but it works fine for most computing environments right out of the box. That doesn't mean that the book shouldn't exist—just that the basic or intermediate reader doesn't need such detail; in fact, such detail could have a detrimental effect. This decision on what to include (and what to leave out) for clarity's sake was based solely on the authors' experiences installing and configuring many different versions and distributions of Linux. ■

Moving on.... Who would have thought even a few years ago that you would be able to run powerful Oracle databases off Linux servers and popular productivity suites on graphical,

multimedia-capable Linux workstations? Who would have thought that you would be able to connect a single PC or an entire company's network easily to the Internet using Linux, or seamlessly integrate a Linux workstation or server with a Windows, NetWare, or Apple network? Who would have thought that a small company could use a Linux server to provide file, print, email, and Web services for an entire intranet, including capabilities for employees to dial in from home or on the road? Who would have thought that Linux would be considered a viable alternative for Microsoft Windows on the desktop and Microsoft Windows NT on the server, and that Microsoft would find itself trying to find a way to market against it for control of their server market share? Who would have thought that Dell and Gateway would be selling desktop computers preloaded with Red Hat Linux?

Few people would have thought these things or given their probability very high odds, for several reasons. After all, this is UNIX—which is a little difficult and a lot different—which makes it the clear underdog fighting an uphill battle (except in vertical markets such as those with high-end graphics or scientific needs, or large shops that have dedicated information technology staffs, often with specialists in UNIX).

Yet Linux currently enjoys a healthy reputation as a reliable, powerful, high-performance, multiuser network operating system. It is estimated to be in use by more than 10 million users worldwide, and it arguably comprises the majority of the server base of the Internet infrastructure itself. Corporations, small businesses, and individuals by the droves are using it to solve their many computing challenges. Software firms are developing or porting major commercial applications to operate on Linux, often before they build the same applications for other, traditional versions of UNIX, such as those available from Hewlett-Packard, Sun, and Santa Cruz Operation (SCO). This all is made possible by Linux's reputation for scalability, reliability, affordability, native support for Internet networking protocols, and provision of such popular and critical applications as the Apache Web server and enterprise email services. Additions of user-friendly desktop environments such as GNOME and KDE have made Linux even more attractive as an alternative on the desktop.

So what are the reasons that might have prevented Linux from really grabbing hold? Well, unfortunately, Linux has a lingering reputation of being difficult to install and configure. This is a legacy reputation it earned in its infancy that is not as true today as it once was, as you will soon see in this book and hear echoed in the media. In its early stages of development, Linux did require ingenuity, luck, and even a considerable amount of UNIX and systems administration experience to install, configure, and use. At the time, it also did not have an extensive body of support available for people who didn't have such experience. Unfortunately, many Linux devotees at the time did not see this reputation as a problem. Conversely, these highly technical and capable experts wore this reputation as a badge of honor, something that reflected their prowess, expertise, loyalty, superiority, and ingenuity (because *they* were able to install and use it, after all). As a result, Linux long retained a reputation as a hacker system (with *hacker* referring to UNIX gurus who don't mind hacking or tweaking the kernel—not the type of hacker, usually called a *cracker,* who tries to break into systems). All these things had the end effect of stifling and holding back Linux from achieving its quick and rightful place in the operating system market.

At some point, Linux had to give in to the laws of supply and demand. This is primarily why Microsoft operating systems have thrived: They delivered a simple, affordable, multimedia-capable, graphical user interface that users thirst for on an inexpensive hardware platform (Intel), and this attracted users and developers in large numbers. This had a mushrooming or snowballing effect that has made Windows the industry-standard operating system on the desktop, with Macintosh (Mac) and UNIX workstations remaining firmly embedded in high-end graphics, publishing, scientific, production, and Internetworking organizations, and even on many desktops based on personal preference of the individual user. In exchange for afford-able, user-friendly, application-rich PCs, users (with the exception of Mac users) even forgave the Windows operating system and Intel architecture their many idiosyncrasies, inadequacies, and imperfections. (That's the closest this book will come to any level of Windows-bashing, given that UNIX has a few public relations problems of its own, and Mac has some marketing challenges despite its technical superiority.)

Given this analysis, the Linux industry had to focus on its weaknesses, not its many strengths. In other words, the focus had to shift to user-friendliness, ease of use, and support. Specifically, Linux had to become the following:

- Easier to install and understand.
- Easier to configure and manage.
- Graphical user interface (GUI)-centric (less reliant on the command line).
- Bundled with, or buttressed by, plentiful applications (productivity, games).
- Adaptable to more hardware configurations (drivers, drivers, drivers!).
- Supported by widespread interactive support channels (instead of just Internet newsgroups).

Luckily, Linux has evolved exactly along these lines. Red Hat has provided a setup program and package manager that has significantly improved the installation and configuration process. Maturation and improvement of desktop environments such as GNOME and KDE have made it even easier for inexperienced and experienced users alike to use, configure, and manage Linux. The installed user base for Linux grew steadily as a result, which drove the efforts of independent software vendors (ISVs) to focus extra attention on developing or port-ing applications to Linux. Software companies such as Oracle and Corel quickly jumped on board the Linux bandwagon. Sun even bought Star Division, the German company that developed the StarOffice application suite, which runs on numerous platforms. Game developers are beginning to sense a renewed market for Linux ports of popular games. Original equipment manufacturers (OEMs) decided to either develop Linux drivers for their peripherals or components, or just release their proprietary interface documentation to open source developers who could develop the necessary drivers for them. Hardware vendors such as Dell decided to offer affordable, robust, integrated Linux server and workstation solutions, preinstalled and preconfigured with Red Hat Linux (following the lead of trailblazers such as VA Research). Companies such as Red Hat increased availability of highly skilled technical expertise in support of their products, which is now available either bundled with distributions of their operating system or as single or multiple support packs.

That's not to say that everything is coming up roses. Some fragmentation and lively debate still circulates in the Linux development community regarding the best possible standards to follow. Despite major success in providing a GUI desktop environment and administrative utilities, there are still many things that are easier to perform (or must be performed) from the command line. There's also a lot of new development going on, and the maturity level of some utilities and applications is relatively low (but making good progress)—as a result, users may encounter some insignificant and infrequent hiccups. Keeping this in perspective, though, these are relatively small issues that more than likely will be resolved quite quickly, considering the current pace of Linux evolution. Anyway you look at it, it's an exciting time for all Linux lovers—there's a lot to look forward to!

Red Hat Installation

Preparing to Install Red Hat Linux

by Duane Hellums

In this chapter

Overview of the Linux Installation Process

Installing Red Hat Linux 6.0 is surprisingly similar to installing any other operating system. Depending on the hardware you have, the process can be easier or more difficult than that of other operating systems. By being prepared and providing a modicum of configuration information, you can have Linux 6.0 up and running in less than an hour, browsing the Web, downloading email, listening to a music CD, and editing a Microsoft Word document in Star Office's word processor.

This doesn't mean that it always goes this easy. Linux is a complicated, powerful, multiuser, multitasking, 32-bit operating system—as a result, it enjoys many of the same hardware compatibility issues and restrictions of competing products such as Microsoft Windows NT. In the long run, this just means that you need to do more up-front planning, information-gathering, and preparation before you begin your installation of Linux. This process takes only 5–10 minutes.

The more you prepare and plan, the easier the installation and basic configuration process will be and the higher your likelihood of success. If you do encounter snags in the installation, you will be better prepared to deal with them. The basic process you should follow includes the following steps:

1. Familiarize yourself with your system's hardware.
2. Familiarize yourself with Linux installation issues.
3. Prepare your system for accepting Linux software.
4. Create boot floppies if your system can't boot from CD-ROM.
5. Find a place on your system or network to place Linux software.
6. Start the installation and answer the questions you're asked.
7. Troubleshoot any problems that arise, and adapt as necessary.
8. Reboot your system, and enjoy the many benefits of Red Hat Linux 6.0.

You are not left to your own resources to complete the installation, either. Red Hat provides several very helpful tools to assist your Linux 6.0 installation and configuration efforts. They provide an Installation Guide, a Getting Started Guide, and a Linux Frequently Asked Questions (FAQ) document online at
http://www.redhat.com/corp/support/manuals/index.html at the Red Hat Web site. Printed versions of the Installation Guide and Getting Started Guide both are included in Red Hat's official two-CD boxed set of Linux 6.0. These useful documents are also included on most Red Hat Linux 6.0 compact discs, including the one distributed with this book.

Collecting System Information

The last thing you want to do right in the middle of an installation is try to determine what interrupt request (IRQ) your modem physically is configured for, or whether Linux will recognize and utilize your video graphics or sound card. If you spend a little time before you begin the installation, you will have all the information you need to answer a configuration question. This also will help later if you need to make changes or provide information to anyone trying to help you with a system problem.

Gather System Documentation

One of the first things you should do is round up all the technical manuals, specifications, schematics, and any other written products that document your equipment capabilities and settings. This even can be marketing information for your PC or peripheral that you find on your vendor's Web site (if applicable). Have all the information you can find in one place near you during the installation. That way, you won't have to go far to find the information you need to proceed with the configuration.

Document Hardware Configuration

You might not be able to find all your original documents that describe your hardware settings, though—you might not even have the original reference material. In this case, you will have to resort to other means of collecting information about your equipment.

N O T E　Keep in mind that you don't *have* to collect all this hardware information—Red Hat Linux autosenses quite a lot—but a bit of preparation goes a long way to preventing configuration problems later. For typical installations, the main things you really need to know are the manufacturer, model, and settings for your modem (at least COM port, but preferably IRQ and I/O in case it uses nonstandard settings), sound card (IRQ, I/O, DMA), network card (IRQ, I/O), and your video card and monitor (total RAM available, maximum resolution, and maximum/minimum vertical/horizontal synchronization rates). You also should have a good handle on your hard disk parameters (number heads, cylinder, sectors or tracks, master/slave, and location on primary or secondary cables). ▩

Many of your hardware devices, such as your modem, sound card, and local area network (LAN) card use a system of physical "jumpers" directly on the card that enable you to change hardware settings. These jumpers are nothing more than a small clip that connects two protruding wires on one side of the card, making an electrical connection and telling the electronics on the card to use a certain configuration option.

In the worst-case scenario, you can loosen the screws on your computer's case, remove the lid, take out the cards, and inspect them. If they do have jumpers, you can write down the settings for use during your Linux installation. However, some of your newer cards probably are

Plug-and-Play (PNP) devices, which means that they don't have jumpers but instead are automatically configured by a PNP-capable basic input/output system (BIOS) or operating system. As a result, it probably is worth going to these lengths only if you run into a problem during the installation and must terminate it, find out additional information, and begin the installation again.

> **CAUTION**
>
> Some hardware is not compatible with Linux (or any other flavor of UNIX, for that matter). In most cases, this is because the vendor will not develop the necessary operating system drivers and will not release specifications to developers so that they can, either. This is the case with a device called the Winmodem, which basically is a piece of stripped-down electronics that attempts to share some of the processing responsibilities with the operating system; it's called a Winmodem because the only operating system the manufacturer chose to allow to share with is Windows. When you run into really sticky problems, you should check the Red Hat hardware compatibility list for individual components or classes of components that are inherently problematic with Linux. This will save you much time trying to get an incompatible device to work.

There are other things you can do to determine system parameters and settings besides looking at documentation or directly at the hardware itself. Luckily, Red Hat Linux 6.0 has the capability of autosensing many standard devices and settings, but it might not be capable of determining every setting you need. Your only resort in these cases is to either use trial and error during your Linux installation and configuration, or to take a peek at the current configuration of such devices in Windows 95, 98, or NT (if you have access to these operating systems on your PC). This process takes only about 5–10 minutes (sometimes less). To do this, you should perform the following steps:

1. Right-click the My Computer icon of your Windows desktop, and then click the Device Manager tab in the System Properties window.

2. In the Computer Properties window, double-click Computer at the top of the list box. This brings up the Computer Properties windows.

3. Click View Resources and select Interrupt Request (IRQ). Write down all the devices listed under IRQ 3, 4, 5, 7, 9, 10, and 11. These should be your main configurable devices on your system, including your serial communications (COM) ports, sound cards, printer ports, modem, and possibly an Ethernet card.

4. Click Direct Memory Access (DMA) and write down any devices listed in the box, along with which DMA channel they currently are occupying.

5. In the Device Manager tab, click the plus signs next to such devices as your modem, COM port, line printer (LPT) ports, network interface cards (NIC), sound cards, and video cards. If there is more than one device in any category, double-click each device you think you will need or that you will be using with Linux as well. For each device,

write down any information related to Input/Output, DMA, or IRQ settings. You might need some of this information later.

Armed with this newfound information, you should be well equipped to handle the technical portions of the installation process. You'll probably be surprised at how simple most installations go, however. You might not need much of the information you've collected. Regardless, it is a good practice and a nice collection of information to maintain. Store your system documentation in a safe place so that you don't have to go through the process again later.

Understanding Installation Categories

You should have a good understanding of all the main options you will encounter during the installation. The menu-based installation is basically a decision tree, where your choices take you along different paths based on your particular system, environment, and situation. Sometimes you can navigate back and change your choices, while other times you won't be allowed to or will confuse the installation program logic and produce unrecoverable errors if you do. If the latter occurs, you likely will just have to begin the installation process all over again and re-enter your choices up to that point.

The following are the key things you should consider before you begin the installation process:

- Other operating systems needed on your PC
- Available hard drive space within your system
- Performing a workstation class installation
- Performing a server class installation
- Performing a custom class installation

Consider Storage and Dual-Boot Requirements

The optimum situation arguably is dedicating an entire system to Linux. This is "arguably" true because some people prefer to have "dual-boot" systems. This means that you have two or more operating systems on the same PC, on different sections (partitions) of your hard drive. Such arrangements are made possible by a small utility called a boot loader or boot manager that basically gives you a menu of operating systems to choose from. For example, across your desktop and laptop PCs you might have various combinations of Red Hat Linux 6.0, Slackware Linux, Windows 98, Windows 95, Windows NT, and Santa Cruz Operations (SCO) OpenServer. If you have only one PC, though, and want to use other operating systems such as Windows in addition to Linux, you won't have the option of a dedicated Linux solution.

Make sure you install all the other operating systems first, leaving sufficient space on additional partitions or drives for Red Hat Linux. Then when you are ready, you can install Linux and use its boot manager to make all the operating systems available on your PC during bootup. If you don't follow this basic rule, you could run into a situation where you install Linux properly and then have its boot manager erased and replaced by Windows 95 or 98, which doesn't have a boot manager that acknowledges or makes available any pre-existing operating systems.

Before you decide how to physically configure your system, you should consider how you will make sufficient hard drive space for Linux somewhere on your system. Depending on how much software you want to install, you might need from .5 to 1.5GB. It is highly recommended that you use a separate, additional drive (at least 2GB, around $120) on your system dedicated entirely to Linux. This ensures that you don't run into any problems storing Linux beyond the 1024th cylinder, which can be a problem with certain systems that don't properly map sector requests on large hard drives the way they should. It also reduces the probability that you accidentally could write over partitions and programs or data associated with your other operating systems.

 You also could purchase a removable hard drive bay and two removable cartridges (about $100 total) to store and boot each operating system on a primary drive all its own. If you choose this option, you will not be able to access data stored on your other operating system's disk space. If you need to do this, you should seek to add an additional drive for Linux or make sufficient space on your existing drive.

Linux coexists quite well with Windows 95 and 98, using the Linux boot manager. All you have to do is leave unformatted disk space available for Linux to format and install itself on. However, the process is a little different with OS/2 because it has its own boot manager to contend with. In this case, you likely will have to format the Linux partitions within OS/2 so that it can recognize the existence of that partition later. Formatting the partitions with Linux (outside of OS/2, as you do with Windows) might result in installation of a Linux boot loader that doesn't recognize your OS/2 partitions, or use of an OS/2 boot loader that doesn't recognize your Linux partition. If you use OS/2, you should consult your system documentation for instructions on handling such situations. You also should take more time to read all available instructions and help before beginning an OS-2/Linux dual-boot installation (especially the OS/2-related portions of the Official Red Hat Installation Guide on this book's CD-ROM).

CAUTION

Consult the documentation that comes with your other operating systems to determine how to repartition hard drives and free up disk space for Linux. If you are considering a dual-boot solution, it is important that you back up all your programs and data before you begin a Linux installation. This will enable a quick and painless recovery in case of problems. This is also one reason why a dedicated Linux or multiple disk solution is preferable. The DOS and Windows fdisk you must use before launching the Linux setup program (which uses its own version of fdisk) is not very intuitive or well documented. Refer to the Linux fdisk section in Chapter 2, "Installing Red Hat Linux on a Desktop PC," for basic guidelines on the functionality of this partitioning tool—the version shares similar commands and operates the same as the DOS/Windows version (although you should not use it to remove or modify DOS partitions).

After you have created sufficient disk space, either by dedicating an entire PC to Linux, making room on existing drives, or adding hard drives, you will have to decide which class of installation you want to pursue. There will come a time during the installation that you have to pick one of these three classes. Each has its advantages or disadvantages, naturally. You have three options available to you, each of which are described fully in the next few sections:

- Workstation installation
- Server installation
- Custom installation

N O T E After you decide which installation class you want to utilize, you might have to go back and reconsider your hard disk space allocations and plans. This is because certain classes write over some or all partitions, which might not suit your dual-boot requirements. Refer to the following sections for the necessary details. ▓

N O T E If you have anything other than a simple, single-disk, dedicated Linux configuration, you should also skim Chapter 19, "Installing and Configuring Hard Disks," before you decide what to do. Some restrictions govern the number of primary and logical partitions you have available on each disk. There also is a maximum number of disks that can go on each disk ribbon cable. Lastly, you must handle some specific hardware and BIOS settings for your system to properly recognize and address more than one disk. Linux will handle some of these issues, such as setting the bootable flag of your Linux sector, but it can't physically set jumpers on the drive for you or modify your BIOS settings. ▓

Install Linux Workstation

You need at least 600MB to perform a workstation class install. You should consider this a low estimate if you plan to install lots of applications on it, store large amounts of multimedia data (such as Web pages), or have multiple users. If you are planning a dual-boot configuration with Linux and other operating systems, this is the easiest and most appropriate installation method for you. This is especially the case if you don't have much experience with Linux (otherwise, the Custom installation might be more appropriate). The installation program makes lots of choices for you and simplifies the overall process. It will configure your boot loader automatically to manage booting from Linux or Windows.

If you have an existing partition with a different version of Linux and want to keep it, you will not want to use this method. This particular installation class is as tidy as a small tornado, removing any Linux partitions in its path (and any programs or data stored there), making this space available to itself for the new installation. If you don't mind or even want this tidiness (you don't have to manually remove the other Linux partitions), then the workstation class is very handy.

The workstation class creates three partitions on your hard drive(s). One occupies 16MB and is set aside for all the files and programs associated with your kernel (the core program that launches when you boot up in Linux, providing access to all your hardware and underlying technologies such as networking). Another is the "swap" space that occupies 64MB and serves the function of additional random access memory (RAM) for running your programs and storing in-use data. The remainder of the disk space will be made available to the operating system itself for storing all your Linux files.

Install Linux Server

You need about three times as much storage space (1.6GB) to perform a server class install. The same thing holds true regarding extra required space to support basic requirements that you can foresee in addition to the basic operating system—an additional 500MB to 1GB would not be out of order if you have an extra drive lying around. Note that not all software packages are installed on the server class because it is assumed that this type of PC installation will have different roles and need a different set of software than a workstation.

> **CAUTION**
>
> If you are planning a dual-boot configuration with Linux and other operating systems, do *not* proceed with a server class install, even if you plan to make the dual-boot system a server. This class will delete, remove, erase, and otherwise obliterate any existing partitions, programs, and data you have stored on all existing drives and partitions.

The server class creates six partitions on your hard drive(s). This is so that your system can better allocate portions of the operating system to different partitions for performance and administration purposes. For example, by creating a separate /home mount point (a place where a drive or partition is mounted and made available to the system as a directory), a server system is more scalable, meaning that it is easier to dynamically increase available space for additional users as the system grows. Backups are considerably easier as well.

The server swap and kernel partitions are the same size, but the root partition is reduced by 350MB to make room for the other partitions. The breakdown for server partitions is as:

- swap: 64MB
- kernel (/boot): 16MB

- root (/): 256MB
- user (/usr): 512MB
- home (/home): 512MB
- var (/var): 256MB

You need not trouble yourself unduly about what goes in each of these directories for a server installation, or what was behind the logic to break them down this way. Just keep in mind that all the user files are stored in the home directory, which is where administrators spend most of their time backing up, growing, shrinking, and so on.

Install Custom Linux

The custom installation can be the best of both worlds, if you are somewhat experienced at Linux or UNIX in general. It provides you a flexible menu to choose from, making all the decisions that are taken out of your hands with the other installation classes. However, many of the steps become manual and give you the smallest opportunity to make mistakes. Sometimes it is required though, such as when you are using an old hard drive that has large gaps between primary partitions (see Chapter 19). This is because the custom installation enables you to use the more flexible fdisk program to partition your hard disk.

You will have to choose how you want to divvy up your hard drive into partitions and what you want to put on them. You have the options of installing everything from the CD, installing a recommended subset of packages from the CD, or choosing from all the individual packages (a mix of the previous two options). You must specify what operating systems are available on your PC and how you choose to boot them. The amount of space required for a custom installation is somewhere between that required for a workstation and a server installation. As an estimate, 1GB is limiting, although it does allow for installation of most common applications and services. To prevent having to expand the system later, at least 2GB of space should be reserved for Red Hat Linux.

Understanding Installation Types and Methods

The class of installation isn't the only decision you will have to make. There are several decisions you need to make before you begin the installation and during the installation that you should be aware of before you begin so that you will be prepared for them. Basically, you will have to contend with the following options:

- Choosing a new installation or upgrade
- Installing from CD-ROMs with or without floppy disks
- Installing from a local or a network device

Choosing a New Installation or Upgrade

If you have an existing partition with Red Hat Linux installed on it, you will need to decide whether you want to upgrade it or replace it. There will come a time during the installation process when you have to pick, and you should give some thought beforehand what you want to do.

If you don't want to keep your existing applications or data, you can elect to perform a new installation. The setup program will just write over your existing partitions and applications. None of your current configuration settings will be kept or applied to your new installation of Linux. In effect, this is the same as deleting all your Linux partitions and information prior to the installation process.

If you want to upgrade, Red Hat will perform a search for applications on your hard drive. If you have some of the applications that are included on Red Hat Linux 6.0, then it will compare version numbers. If you have an earlier version, the setup program will flag the application for upgrade. It will do this for all the applications on the CD before beginning the upgrade of all the flagged applications only.

> **CAUTION**
>
> Be careful if you are performing an upgrade on a system that is highly customized and where you have made lots of small but important changes or modifications. The upgrade option is not perfect, and certain application upgrades require previous configuration files to be overwritten (such as when there are basic underlying changes to a program's functionality or configuration method, like the Apache or iBCS packages).
>
> If you have made such changes, you might want to back up these applications (to tape or to another location on the hard drive, for example) so you can compare old and new configuration files and settings after the upgrade. This necessarily requires a good understanding of the application. You might not be able to just back up the directory (/home/httpd) for example, if associated configuration files are located elsewhere on the system (/etc/httpd/conf).

Installing from CD-ROM With or Without Floppy Disks

You should evaluate your PC's capability to boot directly to CD-ROM instead of floppy disk. Newer PCs have BIOS systems that support bootable CD-ROMs. This means that you can boot to an operation system or program directly on a CD instead of forcing your system to look only on floppy or hard drive.

If your PC BIOS supports bootable CD-ROMs, then you will be able to avoid creating the standard boot floppy that Red Hat Linux 6.0 normally needs. Keep in mind that this relieves you only of the need to build the boot floppy—if you are using a laptop that needs PCMCIA card support to complete the installation, then you will still have to create that disk. Also, you will have access only to the normal boot image (boot.img) instead of the net-based boot image (bootnet.img). If you want to install over the network from a Web server or NFS network share, then you will still have to create the bootnet floppy (see "Creating Installation Floppies" later in this chapter).

To test for bootable CD-ROM capability, you must put this book's CD-ROM in your CD tray and reboot your system to see if you receive the blue screen of the Red Hat setup program. If you do, then your system supports bootable CD. You do not want to perform the installation yet, so cancel the installation by removing the CD-ROM and rebooting.

CAUTION

Be careful if you must edit your BIOS settings. The interface doesn't facilitate making an inadvertent mistake, but it doesn't prevent it either. It's possible you could change a setting you don't intend to and cause your system to behave in ways you won't appreciate. If you mess with some settings, you could even prevent your system from booting or operating properly. Don't be paranoid or afraid to enter the program—just make sure you change only what you need to, and nothing else. If at any point in the configuration you feel you have modified something you don't want to, but don't know how to change it back, your BIOS setup program always offers you an option to quit without saving changes.

If you don't see the blue screen, you must reboot and enter the setup program for your BIOS (check your system documentation to find out how to do this, or refer to the short list of BIOS setup program key combinations in Chapter 19). Navigate through the menus of your BIOS setup program looking for a boot sequence. You should have choices of floppy, hard drive, or CD-ROM. Make sure that the CD-ROM option is available and selected, and then move it to the top of the order (otherwise, you will just boot right into Windows, if it is installed).

 If your BIOS doesn't support bootable CD-ROM, you can try one last thing. If you have Windows 95 or 98 on your disk, boot up into DOS mode by typing F8 after the first beep during reboot, and then select to enter MS-DOS mode. You can get the same result by selecting Start, Shutdown, Restart in MS-DOS mode. When you get to the DOS prompt, type the command D:\autoboot.bat and press the Enter key to execute it. You should see the blue screen of the Red Hat Linux installation menu.

Installing from a Local or a Network Device

You do not have to install directly from a CD-ROM, although it is the most convenient option. In addition to installing from CD-ROM on your local PC, you have the option to install from a hard drive on your PC. You will have to copy the entire CD-ROM contents from CD-ROM to a hard drive on your system, but you might find this a better option than using a CD-ROM.

You also have two remote options that work with a properly installed and configured network. You can make Red Hat Linux 6.0 available for installation over a Web server. Simply share the

CD-ROM directory off your Web server, and then provide the path to it when prompted to do so by the setup program. For example, you can share it as `http://www.yourcompany.com/redhat/` (replacing `yourcompany` with the actual domain name of your server).

If you have a Network File Service (NFS) server handy, you can do the same thing. Simply share the CD-ROM off your NFS server and provide a pointer to it when prompted to do so during the Red Hat installation.

Creating Installation Floppies

The last step in your pre-installation of Red Hat Linux 6.0 is the creation of any floppy disks you will need for your installation. You can create four floppies, depending on your individual environment and needs. These disks and their capabilities are as follows:

- **Boot Image (`boot.img`)**—This is the normal setup program used to install Red Hat 6.0 Linux on a system's hard drive directly from that system's CD-ROM. This provides everything you need, including the basic kernel and any necessary module support, presuming that you are not performing a network-based installation and don't need PCMCIA support during the installation (to recognize a PCMCIA SCSI device or card). You will have an opportunity after you successfully install Linux to create a new custom (emergency) boot disk, which will be slightly different than this disk (it will have more configuration information specific to your system based on the options you chose during the setup).

- **Net Boot Image (`bootnet.img`)**—This is the disk you will need if you want the additional options on your installation menu to download the Red Hat Linux 6.0 files across your network off a Web or NFS server. The remainder of the setup program is the same as that for `boot.img`.

- **PCMCIA Support (`pcmcia.img`)**—You will need to create this disk if you are using a PC such as a laptop that is using a PCMCIA device during the installation itself (not just being added or built into the kernel later). Both the `boot.img` and `bootnet.img` disks will prompt you to determine whether you need PCMCIA support. If you answer yes, you will then be prompted to insert this disk (`pcmcia.img`).

- **Rescue Image (`rescue.img`)**—This image is not an installation disk in the strictest sense, although it can be used to support installation (especially if you run into problems that aren't easily cured). This provides a basic modular kernel as well as a RAM-based minimal root file system, including all the basic applications and configuration files you need to debug and repair problems with your newly installed Red Hat Linux system. The `rescue.img` disk serves the same purpose as the root disks that previous versions of Red Hat Linux used. It can be used in conjunction with the `boot.img` disk or the custom boot disk that you create during the installation. To mount this mini-Linux file system, type `rescue` at the boot: prompt and then, when prompted to "insert root floppy disk to be loaded into RAM disk," put the `rescue.img` disk in and press Enter.

To create these disks, you will need a clean, preferably unused, 3.5-inch DOS-formatted floppy. Put the floppy in the available drive. In Windows or MS-DOS, type (or graphically navigate to and click) `D:\dosutils\raawrite.exe` (where `D:` is replaced by the actual drive designator for your CD-ROM). This brings up an MS-DOS window and prompts you to enter the disk image source filename. Enter `D:\dosutils\images\<filename>.img` (where `<filename>` is replaced by the name of the actual image file, such as `boot`, `bootnet`, `pcmcia`, or `rescue`). You will be prompted to enter the target disk drive, at which point you should type the drive designator of your 3.5-inch high-density floppy drive (usually `A:\`). Finally, you will be told to insert a formatted floppy into drive A: (or other applicable drive) and press Enter. When you press Enter, the rawrite program will begin to copy the image from CD-ROM to floppy.

> **TIP**
>
> It is highly recommended that you just label four floppy disks boot, bootnet, pcmcia, and rescue, and then step through this process for all four floppies. You're already here, so it's easy to repeat the process, and you never know when you might need the floppies. You might find that you need a rescue disk even though you didn't plan on it originally. The extra time and disk resources expended here could save you lots of time rebooting and rebuilding floppy disks later.

After you have created all the installation floppies you think you will need, you are ready to proceed to Chapter 2 and start the setup, installation, and configuration of Red Hat Linux 6.0. You should consider reading all of Chapter 2 (and then Chapter 3, "Installing Red Hat Linux on a Laptop," if you are installing on a laptop) before beginning the installation. It is better to have a full understanding of the entire process from the start rather than trying to familiarize yourself with the process as you go along. ●

V6.0 CD use rawrite not raawrite. THIS IS LOCATED IN THE X:\dosutils DIRECTORY. THE IMAGES ARE IN THE X:\Images DIRECTORY. Also the DOS session will not accept the full long name of the file. Use the 8.3 equivalent.

Installing Red Hat Linux on a Desktop PC

by Duane Hellums

In this chapter

Double-Checking the Installation Environment

This chapter covers a typical Intel-based installation. Much of the material also applies to Sun, Alpha, and laptop installations because they all essentially do the same thing. However, there are a few peculiarities with each of these other installations, so these topics are broken off into Chapter 3, "Installing Red Hat Linux on a Laptop"; Chapter 4, "Installing Red Hat Linux on an Alpha"; and Chapter 5, "Installing Red Hat Linux on a Sparc." For maximum benefit, you should read this chapter and the appropriate individual platform chapter entirely before beginning the installation. This will give you a good overall picture of what is involved with a typical installation that encounters few problems.

By now, you should have read Chapter 1, "Preparing to Install Red Hat Linux," and followed the directions listed there. You should have created at least a basic hardware configuration list and checked it against the Linux hardware compatibility list (on Red Hat's Web page and this book's CD) to ensure that everything will work with Linux. If you have some irregular hardware or settings, you should have reviewed the appropriate chapters (for example, interface controllers, hard drives, modems, mice, keyboards, networking, sound, and game or video cards) regarding special instructions that you will need to pass to the kernel to make them work. Lastly, you should have made some basic decisions about what path your installation will follow.

For example, if you are performing a bootable CD-ROM installation onto a local system drive, with no PCMCIA support, you don't need to create any floppies. If you do need PCMCIA support, you should already have created a pcmcia.img floppy. If you plan to install remotely off a Web server or a Network File System (NFS) server, you already should have created the bootnet.img disk and the necessary network links and file-sharing permissions to make this possible and should know the appropriate address so that you can provide it to the Red Hat Linux installation and setup program when prompted.

Launching and Using the Installation Program

By this point, you should have either a bootable floppy in your disk drive or a bootable CD in your CD-ROM drive. If not, you should put one there now. This chapter follows the basic scenario of a typical installation from a boot floppy (boot.img) and a CD-ROM (or just a bootable CD-ROM with no floppy, if your system supports it) to a fresh, new 2GB hard drive dedicated entirely to Red Hat Linux 6.0 (all partitions will be removed, along with any pre-existing data and applications).

When you boot up, you will not see the typical LILO (Linux Loader) boot prompt, but rather a boot prompt with a color splash screen and a list of available help pages across the bottom. You can read any of these six screens (ALT+F1 to ALT+F6) that you feel apply to your installation (KickStart applies only to a small slice of the population that needs to install Linux on dozens of computers on a network, so you probably can skim or skip over that one very quickly). After reading these help pages, you should be familiar with the basic options you have available with regard to alternative boot methods and kernel interaction. When you feel comfortable with the information in all six information screens, you should type Linux and press Enter, or just press Enter. If you wait for too long on any single screen without pressing a key, the kernel will start loading and will bring you to the main installation menu screen. While you are using the installation menu, you should be aware of the following navigation and interaction features:

- **OK**—Tab to this button and press Enter to select it and accept the current choice before continuing on to the next configuration item.

- **Cancel**—Tab to this button and press Enter if you want to prevent the current action from happening and return to the previous step (note that you can't do this if you already clicked OK).

- **Back**—Tab to this button and press Enter if you want to return to the previous screen. Sometimes the installation program gets confused when you do this and will scrub (cancel) the installation, causing you to reboot and re-enter any data up to that point. Although this can be a nuisance, it's better than getting something you don't want or risking the loss of your dual-boot system data or programs.

- **Tab**—The Tab key navigates you between list boxes and option buttons.

- **Enter**—The Enter key selects the current choice and proceeds, just as if you had clicked on that particular button with a mouse.

- **Space**—The space key is used to highlight or mark the choice where the cursor is sitting in an option box or menu item.

- **Arrow keys**—Use the dedicated or numeric keypad arrow keys to navigate through the menu options until the cursor rests where you want it to.

- **Yes/No**—The Yes and No buttons are available at different times when you need to confirm explicitly what you want (usually after a warning message).

 TIP You can access some debugging information, if you need to, during the installation by typing ALT+F2, ALT+F3, ALT+F4, and ALT+F5. These functions will give you access to a shell prompt as well as a considerable amount of troubleshooting and error reporting that might indicate problems with the installation (such as sector overflows). Return to the main installation program by pressing ALT+F1, because it is always running on the first virtual screen.

Conducting the Installation Phase

At least six main steps occur during what is called the installation phase. Each one of these steps is addressed here, with appropriate comments to let you know what the best choice is for you under the circumstances:

1. **Welcome**—The Welcome screen is nothing more than a splash screen to make you feel comfortable during the installation program and to remind you to register the product. Press Enter or click OK to continue to the next screen.

2. **Language**—You have an option of choosing the language you want to use with Linux. The default is English, so most people simply must tab to the OK button and press Enter, or just press the Enter key while the cursor is already on the specific option.

3. **Keyboard**—You also can select the specific type of keyboard you have. (The default is us.) If there are no changes, just press the Enter key. An example of this window and the overall installation interface is pictured in Figure 2.1.

FIGURE 2.1
You can pick from many supported keyboard types.

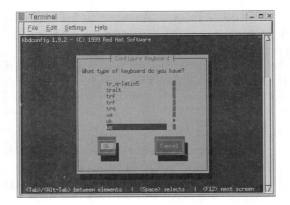

4. **Installation method**—You must specify whether you are installing from the local CD-ROM or hard drive (which is faster). This is the first place the installation program will branch off in another direction based upon your choices. If you are installing from the hard drive, you already should have copied the entire Red Hat disk to a place somewhere on that drive (and should know how to reference it by drive and partition—you can use any that are available to you). Refer to Chapter 19, "Installing and Configuring Hard Drives," for details on adding an additional drive to your system temporarily for this purpose. You can also use Windows to add a DOS partition that is big enough to handle the CD-ROM's contents. If you are installing from CD-ROM, like most people, you just need to press Enter. You will be prompted to make sure that your Red Hat Linux 6.0 disk is located in the CD-ROM drive; then press Enter on the OK button again to continue and initialize the CD-ROM.

NOTE   If you are using `bootnet.img` instead of `boot.img`, you will receive a different set of options here, including installation from Network File System (NFS), file transfer protocol (ftp), or hypertext from a Web site (http). Regardless of which one you choose, your network card and network will be involved and required, so the program skips ahead a bit and performs the network portions (steps 3–5) of the configuration phase (documented later in this chapter). When you have provided the network-related configuration items, you will be returned promptly to this part of the installation program for it to continue. ■

5. **Installation path**—You have a choice of selecting to upgrade your existing Linux operating system and applications or overwriting them with the newest, shiniest version of Linux. For this example, choose Install. Choosing Upgrade will cause the setup program to probe your system and determine a list of programs that need to be upgraded or installed (because they don't already exist on your current version).

6. **Installation class**—This is the last time during the installation phase that you will have the option of branching off the main program to an alternate set of tasks. You should have decided this already based on the discussion in Chapter 1 regarding the specific impacts of each option. If you have a dedicated disk with no other operating systems on it, you can just select Workstation or Server for a seamless installation involving very little manual manipulation of disk drive parameters. You do end up with a different set of applications on the server than on the workstation, however (so choose carefully based on your requirements).

CAUTION

You will be prompted several times with warnings about writing over and losing data if you choose Workstation or Server. Workstation writes over any existing Linux partitions (leaving Windows alone, allowing dual-boot scenarios), and Server removes everything on any drives on the system. If you are performing a custom installation, you should skip ahead and read the section later in this chapter on the details of that step because this is considerably more complicated than the automated Workstation and Server classes.

After you have completed all these steps, you will see several pop-up windows showing you the progress of your installation. You will see a message about scanning packages, followed by several messages about appropriate partitions being created on the hard drive and formatted for Linux. You then will see a note about the setup program finding overlapping files that it can write only once to disk, followed by a main status screen that stays up for the remainder of the installation. The status screen shows the total number of packages being installed, the number that have been completed (installed), and how many are left. A similar table is shown based on the size (KB, MB) of the installed files. Two status bars reflect the percentage of the entire installation that has been performed and the percentage of the current package that has been installed. The installation takes from 10 minutes to an hour, depending on how fast your machine is and which class of installation you chose.

Conducting the Configuration Phase

After the installation program finishes formatting the hard drives, gathering the packages it needs to install, and copying them to all the appropriate disk partitions, it will begin a series of tasks aimed at initially configuring your installed system for use. This is called the configuration phase of the installation program, to differentiate it from any manual configuration you do immediately after the program has run its course (or any administrative configuring you do over the lifecycle of your system).

At least a dozen main steps occur during this configuration phase. Similar to the installation phase, each one of these steps is addressed here, with appropriate comments to let you know what the best choice is for you under the circumstances:

1. **Mouse**—As shown in Figure 2.2, the installation program will attempt to probe your system to find an available mouse and attempt to guess its type. If the probe fails, you will be asked to manually select the mouse. You can also change the probe-based selection, if it is incorrect. Click OK after the probe is complete to see what it found. Highlight an appropriate mouse from the list if the probe selection is incorrect. Tab to and check the Emulate 3 Buttons box using the Spacebar if you have a two-button mouse and want to be able to simulate having a third button (by clicking the right and left buttons at the same time). This is recommended because it will be a valuable shortcut for pasting text as well as accessing certain desktop environment menus.

FIGURE 2.2
Linux supports all industry-standard serial, PS/2, and glideport mice from Microsoft, Logitech, and other vendors.

2. **Network**—Select Yes if you want to configure your local area network (LAN). You then will see a series of Probe windows informing you of what network interface cards were found on your system, if any. You can choose any of the supported cards, regardless of what the probe results were.

3. **Boot Protocol**—Some networks provide a single server that passes out Internet Protocol (IP) addresses to client machines on the network from a pool of available IP addresses. Two protocols for accomplishing this task are BOOTP and DHCP (Domain Host Control Protocol). If you select one of these, the installation program will perform a request over the network, looking for the networking information it needs. If it doesn't find this information, or if you don't have these types of IP naming services on your network, you will be able to set static IP address information.

4. **Configure TCP/IP**—If you have to manually configure IP networking on your Linux PC, here is where you will enter the necessary information. You should be able to get the information from your network administrator. You must provide the IP address (for example, one machine on a private network might be 192.168.1.1), netmask

(255.255.255.0 for smaller networks), default gateway (192.168.1.1, for example, if your Linux PC will be your router to the Internet when you are done), and a primary name server (192.168.1.1 also, if your Linux PC eventually will be running Domain Name Service [DNS] for your entire LAN). Your settings will be different based on your individual environment, of course.

5. **Configure Network**—This window gives you the opportunity to provide a few more mandatory network-related items, as well as a few optional items. You should enter your network's domain name (such as `hconsulting.com`) and your PC's host name (such as barracuda, which ends up translated into `barracuda.hconsulting.com` automatically; you could also enter www here if you wanted to be able to address the Linux Apache Web server in this manner, but it makes more sense to add that alias later). If they apply, you have the option of adding a second and third name server address here, just in case the first and second go down for some reason. That way, you'll still be able to access sites on the Web by their host and domain name (`www.redhat.com`) instead of their IP address, which is much harder to remember and often not documented anywhere because it is subject to change at a moment's notice.

6. **Configure Time Zones**—Select the time zone that applies to your geographical location, and use the Spacebar to choose Hardware Clock Set to GMT, if you need that functionality (it will set your PC's internal clock to Greenwich Mean Time, which will be several hours ahead of or behind your actual local time). The default time is US/Eastern, although you can change this, as indicated in Figure 2.3.

Part

I

Ch

2

FIGURE 2.3
You can set your system clock separate from your local time, if you need to, or keep them the same.

7. **Configure Printer**—If you have a local or network printer, now is your chance to at least do a minimal configuration of it. Note that you will not be able to configure a network printer if you performed a Workstation installation because this doesn't install the necessary Windows and NetWare protocol suites needed for network printing. For local printers, you will have to provide the name of the print queue (the default of lp is fine) and the spool directory where printed files are temporarily stored while they await

printing (the default of /var/spool/lpd/lp is also fine). Select OK to confirm that /dev/lp0 (for example) was detected during the probe for parallel printers. Choose an appropriate print driver from the list, and select OK. Set the paper size and resolution as necessary, and check the Fix Stair-Stepping of Text option if you're using a standard Windows-based printer. This appends a carriage return to Linux's line feed during prints, which wraps the text to the beginning of the next line (where you want it). Select OK to verify the chosen printer settings.

8. **Root Password**—Enter the root password twice for verification, and select OK to lock it into the system. You will need this password any time you want to log on as root either from the login screen or using the su command from a normal user account.

9. **Boot Disk**—Place a DOS-formatted 3.5-inch disk in the disk drive, and press Enter to select Yes and begin the creation of an emergency boot disk.

10. **PCI Probe**—The setup program will attempt to autoprobe and detect your video graphics adapter and will install the necessary Xfree86 drivers for it, as necessary. Figure 2.4 shows the results of one sample probe.

FIGURE 2.4
Red Hat Linux auto-probes the majority of today's industry-standard video cards but doesn't strip you of the flexibility of changing settings or using less capable drivers.

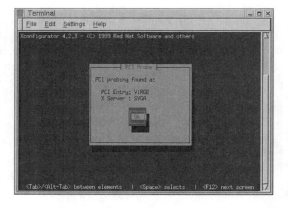

11. **Monitor Setup**—You should choose from the list of supported monitors. Refer to your monitor's documentation here, especially with regard to maximum pixel capabilities (such as 1280×1024; see Figure 2.5), its horizontal and vertical phase or refresh rates (such as 30–70KHz and 50–120Hz). If you can't find one that suits your exact hardware configuration, you should pick custom. Do not try to guess if one of the drivers is close to your hardware designator; that's a dangerous test that could result in the destruction of a video card, a motherboard, or even a monitor. Pick an appropriate graphics mode that you are accustomed to (such as Super VGA at 800×600 pixels, for example). You have the option of changing the default resolution for different bit depths (the number of possible colors), but this isn't recommended because the function can fail during installation. You are probably better off just getting your system up and running, and then tweaking the video settings to your liking later.

FIGURE 2.5
You can pick the type of monitor resolution that meets your needs.

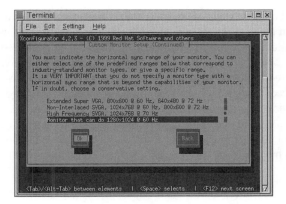

12. **XFree86 Test**—The XConfigurator portion of the installation and setup program will attempt to probe your display and video card, and then have you confirm that the settings it has captured actually work. If this is successful, you will see a nice graphical desktop with a crisp little box in the middle asking you to confirm that you can see it. If this is unsuccessful, you'll never see the box, or you'll see junk characters or screen garbage—either way, you'll have the opportunity to go back to the monitor setup or to skip this portion of the configuration phase. Try various combinations that you feel might work with your equipment (see Figure 2.6). However, keep in mind that in dozens of installations, this part of the installation might not work properly. If you see the box OK, then X is configured properly and you will have the option of making it the default login interface (which also is recommended, unless you know that the machine will be used strictly as a server that won't use the graphical desktop very often).

N O T E   More than anything else, your video graphics card (and your knowledge of its physical parameters) will be key to a successful XFree86 installation and configuration. XFree86 provides good support for most video cards, but it does not support them all. You might find that it supports your card, but not all features of it. ■

FIGURE 2.6
You can set specific resolutions for each available bit depth your monitor is capable of.

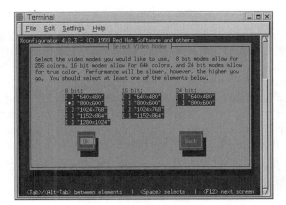

Congratulations! If all went well, you've successfully negotiated the entire installation and basic configuration phases. You should now take any bootable floppies and CDs out of your disk drives and reboot when prompted. After you reboot, you should see a graphical login followed by the GNOME desktop environment. If the X portions of your configuration phase failed, you will have to reinitiate this step and try to get it working. You can do this using several configuration commands, including Xconfigurator and xconf, or you can directly edit the /etc/X11/XF86Config file. Be forewarned that manual modifications are not very easy and come with some risk if you enter the wrong settings. This section doesn't go into detail on how to massage this configuration file to get X working for you—there are just too many cards out there to try to address the special needs and requirements of each of them in any appreciable way.

To solve the problem, you should consult Chapter 9, "Installing and Configuring Video Cards, Monitors, and Mice," and Chapter 10, "Updating the X Window System," before proceeding. Additionally, you should check a few applicable Internet resources to see if there are any document problems, solutions, or words of wisdom with regard to getting your hardware to work with Linux, or vice versa. Recommended sites are http://www.xfree86.org and http://www.redhat.com/support, at a minimum. These have good compilations of known problems and solutions, as well as configuration steps to take for getting around problem cards. You can also turn to Internet newsgroups or Red Hat support if you just can't figure it out based on known documentation.

Performing a Custom Installation

When you elect to perform a Custom Installation, you follow a somewhat more complicated installation path in exchange for more flexibility and customization of your new Linux system. This portion of the installation is closest to the way most Linux installations went. For example, you are in total control of how your drives and partitions will be divided up and used by Linux. You also have total control over what packages get installed and which ones don't. If you don't look forward to this type of decision-making or headache, you're probably best off choosing a Workstation or Server installation.

If you continue with a Custom installation, you follow a path to configure the following items:

1. **SCSI Configuration**—Although the default Linux kernel included with the CD supports and therefore can autosense Integrated Drive Electronics (IDE) drives, it must dynamically load support for Small Computer Systems Interface (SCSI, pronounced "skuzzy") devices (identified in Linux as /dev/sd?, where the question mark is replaced by a separate number for each device or partition) using modules riding on top of the kernel. This window offers you the opportunity to help that process and indicate whether you have any SCSI adapters (and associated devices). If you do, you will have to pick from among a list of supported adapters from numerous vendors; Linux will then try to autosense that card based on known configuration settings for it. If this

process is successful, you will continue with the installation, with the added support for any SCSI devices you have attached to your SCSI adapter. Consult Chapter 19 for additional information on using SCSI hard drives.

2. **Disk Setup**—You will have an option of choosing between Disk Druid (a Red Hat disk administration utility) or the conventional fdisk program. Both of these disk partitioning and formatting utilities are discussed in better detail in Chapter 19. You can also refer to the documentation that comes with this book's CD regarding how to use both these programs. Basically, the process involves manually creating, editing, deleting, and modifying the necessary and available partitions on your system's hard drives. You must determine how many partitions you will need, how big each should be, what type of partition it will be (Linux swap, Linux native, DOS, and so on), which part of the file system it will be mounted on or used with, which partitions should be primary partitions (maximum of four) and which logical drives in an extended partition (maximum of four additional), which partition will be bootable (such as Linux boot, which contains the kernel), and whether the format program should look for bad blocks during the format of each partition.

3. **Select Packages**—Unlike Workstation and Server installations, that have predefined what software packages will be installed, you must perform all this analysis and selection yourself manually if you choose Custom installation. You will be prompted with a menu that displays all the available groups of packages, and you can toggle them on or off depending on whether you want to install them. You can also check the box marked Select Individual Packages to receive a long list of Red Hat Package Manager (RPM) packages to choose from. In general, you should stick with the group-based installation from the first option screen.

4. **Services**—You can pick the standard services (or daemons) that run on your workstation or server by default. For example, if you don't want to run a Web server off your machine, you would deselect the httpd service. You can do the same for other services such as the advanced power management daemon (apmd). Figure 2.7 shows a sample of some services that are turned on (marked with an asterisk) and turned off (the remote services, which are known security weaknesses).

FIGURE 2.7
You have full control over what services can and cannot run on your Linux PC.

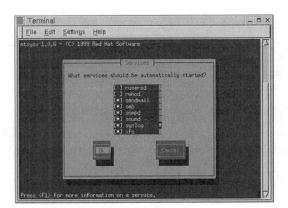

5. **Authentication**—Many people prefer to use Shadow and MD5 passwords to increase system and user-level security. This increases the protection of the /etc/passwd file by hiding it because it is a common target of hackers. NIS is a distributed authentication system historically used in UNIX environments. You can use this option, displayed in Figure 2.8, only if you have a domain and server name that is already functional and supplying NIS services.

FIGURE 2.8
You can enable Network Information Service (NIS) and also use more secure modes of user password protection.

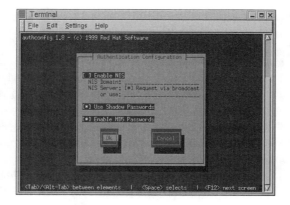

After you have partitioned the hard drives, formatted them accordingly, and chosen the software components you want to install, you will be back at the latter stages of the installation phase. Packages will begin flowing from your CD-ROM to your hard drive while you view the status of the overall and individual package installations.

Performing Quick Basic System Administration Tasks

You will want (and need) to accomplish several system administration tasks as soon as you log in as root. Many of these tasks are discussed throughout the many chapters of this book. However, some are included here in quick synopsis form for people who are fairly comfortable with maintaining computers and who want to get up and running as soon as possible. These steps are all optional, of course, but they might help familiarize you a little more with your system and some of its common controls and might help you get a lot of the small configuration steps out of the way at the same time.

Some of the first things you might want to do include the following:

■ **Users**—Create a user account for yourself via the main menu and System, Linuxconf, User Account, Normal, User Account, Add. Enter the login name (duane, for example) and full name (duane hellums, for example). In the Privileges tab, check

Granted/Silent for all the available options on all four underlying tabs. This gives you superuser capabilities for almost everything on the system. Enter a password twice, and then back out of the program by clicking Quit and Activate the Changes. Generally accepted practice is to pick passwords that are not in the dictionary or easy for other people to guess, so you should avoid names, nicknames, or favorite sports teams; a good hint is to include some numbers in the middle of a password, such as mint87xyz. Of course, do not write it down and do not pick one that is hard to remember, otherwise you might not be able to log in if you forget it.

Part

I

Ch

2

- **Sound**—Click the monitor icon on the main GNOME menu bar, which brings up an X terminal. Type `sndconfig` on the command line, and click OK until you get to the point where you can choose the specific sound card you have (or whatever compatible one is listed). Enter the I/O port, IRQ, and DMA channel that you recorded in Chapter 1 (for example, 220, 7, and 1). Click OK to overwrite and OK to proceed with the test. You should hear a sample audio file of Linus Torvalds pronouncing Linux. If you did hear it, confirm this in the pop-up window. Repeat the same process for the MIDI sound that plays immediately afterward. If you had the correct settings for your sound card, your Linux system should be capable of emitting sounds now.

- **Music CD**—You'll want to make sure that the `/dev/cdrom` and `/mnt/cdrom` symbolic links were properly created. Pop a music CD into your CD-ROM player, and then click Start, Multimedia, and CD Player. Click the Play arrow and confirm that the music is playing over the speakers or headphones you have available. Leave the music playing, and familiarize yourself with the other controls, or stop the music with the Stop button and retrieve your CD with the Eject button.

- **Desktop Sound**—Click the toolbox in the main GNOME menu bar. Under Audio, click Enable. This allows your system to make sounds when events occur. The individual events are customizable, when you find the time. This window contains many other configurable items (such as left-handed mouse settings). If you want, check them out now or come back and experiment with them later.

- **Netscape Communicator**—Netscape generates some licensing and error messages, and now is as good a time as any to clear them up and get your system a little closer to the way you will see it every day. Click the N icon of the main GNOME toolbar. Click Accept on the license agreement and OK for the two Netscape informational error messages. Unless you chose a Workstation class (or elected in Custom class not to run the Web server), you can test your local Web server now by entering `http://localhost/` or your configured IP address in the location text box. Close Netscape by clicking the small X in the top right corner.

- **GIMP**—If you use lots of graphics, you probably will be using GIMP, which has some installation steps you can step through quickly now. Click the main GNOME menu button, Graphics, GIMP. Click the Install button on the Installation window, click Continue on the Installation log window, and then watch it install. Check to make sure that no error messages occur, and then click Close.

■ **Enlightenment**—You can tweak a few things in E to make using your desktop more intuitive and enjoyable. Click simultaneously with both your left and right mouse buttons on a blank spot of your desktop (or use your middle mouse button if you have a three-button mouse) and select Enlightenment Configuration. Under Basic Options, click Sloppy Pointer (you'll probably prefer it to the alternatives). Under the Behavior group's Advanced Focus tab, click All New Get Keyboard Focus and Send Pointer When Moving with Keyboard. These both provide functionality that is a little more intuitive (and less frustrating) for most users. Under Audio, check the box named Enable Sounds in Enlightenment, and then click OK. This will provide additional sound support to your desktop events. As with the GNOME toolbox, you can customize and personalize your Linux experience (now or later) with plentiful configuration items in this section.

■ **Printer**—One of the problems with the setup program is that it doesn't set one of the main features of common DOS-based printers. If you print pages right now, you probably will not get a page eject at the end of a page, which will leave the print platen right in the middle of the page (where the next page will start printing). To correct this, from the main GNOME menu, select System, Control Panel, Printer Configuration. Click OK to clear the Samba and ncpfs errors (if you used a Workstation installation class, which doesn't install these networking components). Click lp, then Tests on the menu bar, and Print ASCII Test Page. Click OK on the info box, confirming that the print was OK. If your page didn't eject, click Edit, Select, Send EOF After Job to Eject Page, OK, and OK. Remove the printed page. Highlight printer lp again, and then click Tests, Print PostScript Page, and OK in the info box. Confirm that the final page printed and ejected properly. Close the Print System Manager window.

Troubleshooting Desktop Installations

The main thing that can go wrong during an installation is that sometimes the setup program gets confused if you use the BACK button to go back several steps. This could cause the installation process to stop and initiate a reboot, in which case you must start all over again and re-enter all your configuration data. The best way to prevent this is to make sure you're well prepared for the installation from Chapter 1, which will reduce your odds that you'll have to change your decisions in midstream.

X Window (XFree86) can be a little challenging if you have a card that requires some tweaking. All you can do in these cases is to seek out the solution and determine what you need to modify. Refer to the Web pages mentioned earlier in this chapter for that, and be patient. You might want to perform the installation at a time during the day or evening when you have access to a second computer that has Internet access, even if it is through a friend or neighbor. This will prevent problems from forcing you to terminate an installation and start all over again later.

If you run into other peripherals that aren't correctly autosensed or that aren't listed any-where on a list, check the chapters in this book that deal with those types of peripherals (such as modems and sound cards). There might be some additional detailed information there that can help you debug the problem. ●

## CHAPTER 3

Installing Red Hat Linux on a Laptop

by Duane Hellums

In this chapter

Understanding Laptop Installation Challenges

The interesting part of installing Red Hat Linux 6.0 on a laptop is that you might not need this chapter at all. This is because some of the new laptops that are coming out have almost all the features and capabilities of a normal desktop PC. For example, I installed Red Hat Linux 6.0 on a Compaq Presario 1255 and didn't have any special problems or challenges. The only problem I ran into was that it had a WinModem, which is basically a crippled modem and doesn't work with Linux (along with other modems designed especially for Windows, such as Mwave modems). However, I easily inserted an old PCMCIA modem and configured it for use with Linux.

TIP One of the most significant factors that made Red Hat Linux 6.0 so easy to install on my Compaq was the availability of both a CD-ROM and a floppy drive. Another factor was bootable CD-ROM capability in my BIOS, which precludes the need for a floppy anyway. My laptop had Linux-compatible hardware components, with the exception of the modem. Lastly, having a PCMCIA network card on my laptop made it possible to install from a Linux desktop across my local area network (LAN), which precludes the need for a CD-ROM and floppy. If you have one of these scenarios, your installation should be much easier than if you don't. Adding to my good fortune was the fact that the vendor provided me with two partitions, one of which I easily used for Linux (there was some Windows recovery stuff on the second partition, but nuking it didn't cause any problems).

All laptop installations don't go that easy, unfortunately. Laptops pose several challenges to the installation of Linux—most of these challenges don't exist to the same degree on desktop PCs. For example, laptops contain some hardware components that are atypical for desktop PCs, such as batteries, PCMCIA (PC card) devices, and infrared devices. Laptops traditionally have had more restrictive hardware, such as less memory, LCD panels, smaller hard drives, and floppy drives that share the same bay as a removable CD-ROM. Some manufacturers don't provide the information developers and users need to determine how to make a piece of equipment work with Linux, if it is even possible. You should familiarize yourself with all your laptop's components (more so than with desktop installations), and read through this entire chapter (and possibly considerable amounts of http://www.cs.utexas.edu/users/kharker/linux-laptop) before actually beginning your laptop installation—this will increase your chances for success.

If you have the opportunity to buy a new laptop, you should consider all the hardware components individually to make sure they are Linux-compliant. The vendor might or might not want to talk Linux-compatibility issues with you because vendors often have relationships and contracts with Microsoft that prevent them from doing so (Compaq wouldn't discuss Linux issues with me, for example). You might even want to consider one of the many vendors that sell laptops preloaded with Linux. This can save you all the compatibility considerations and save you all or most of the installation and configuration work; the additional cost of installed and configured Linux is negligible considering the few challenges and headaches you risk by doing it yourself.

N O T E This chapter will not help all people install Linux on every kind of laptop. Too many combinations of proprietary, undocumented hardware require special treatment to get them to work with Linux. Red Hat admits on its support page that laptops are the most problematic of all installations and that tech support often must refer people to the Linux laptop page at http://www.cs.utexas.edu/users/kharker/linux-laptop. This chapter addresses the special installation methods common with laptops as well as the configuration steps that are peculiar to laptops. ▨

Understanding the Laptop Installation Process

If you already have a laptop and want to install Red Hat Linux 6.0 on it, you first should follow all the instructions from Chapter 1, "Preparing to Install Red Hat Linux," and document your hardware settings (to the extent possible). Then you should try to determine how you will have to install Linux on your laptop. Basically, you have the following options:

- **CD-ROM only**—This option is normally the best, easiest, and fastest, if your system supports a bootable CD-ROM.

- **boot.img floppy and CD-ROM**—This is the next best option, if your system doesn't support a bootable CD-ROM but you're lucky enough to have a laptop that has both a CD-ROM and a floppy drive in it (without having to swap them).

- **boot.img floppy and hard drive image of CD-ROM contents**—This enables you to just make an image of the CD-ROM on one of your hard drives, an extra partition, or an extra hard drive. This circumvents the need for having both a CD-ROM and a floppy drive.

- **bootnet.img floppy and NFS-shared CD-ROM**—This method uses Network File System as a transport medium to install Linux over the network. This is a good option when you have a floppy drive on your laptop (but don't have a bootable CD-ROM and can't access your floppy simultaneously with your CD-ROM). You need a boot floppy, a PCMCIA card on your laptop, a functional network, and a Network File System server.

- **bootnet.img floppy and Web-shared CD-ROM**—This is the same as the previous option (NFS), except that you share the Red Hat Linux CD-ROM over the network using a Web server. Network requirements are the same, except you need a Web server instead of an NFS server.

- **bootnet.img floppy and FTP-shared CD-ROM**—This is the same as the previous two options, except it uses anonymous File Transfer Protocol and requires an FTP server.

Part

I

Ch

3

Installing Red Hat Linux 6.0 on a Laptop

If your laptop has a bootable CD-ROM (enabled in your BIOS), the installation method should be a no-brainer, as it was with mine. If not, the installation still will be easy if you have a CD-ROM and a floppy drive that you can use simultaneously (you don't have to swap out in the same port, in other words). However, if you can't get to your CD-ROM locally by one of these two methods, then you will have to consider the other options.

If you have a local area network, then you can use the bootnet.img installation method. This requires your laptop to have either an internal Ethernet device or a Linux-compatible PCMCIA card. You also need a PC on your network configured as an NFS server, a Web server, or an FTP server. If you have a Linux desktop configured somewhere on your network, NFS or HTTP are probably the simplest methods to share your Linux installation CD (and are the two methods documented in this chapter).

If you don't have a LAN, you will have to use the boot.img floppy and choose a local hard drive installation, assuming that you have copied all the necessary files from CD to your hard drive. Installing from a hard drive is a good alternative installation method for a desktop, but not so much for a laptop—few laptops have additional hard drives or hard drives large enough to store Windows, a copy of the Red Hat Linux CD-ROM, and your new Linux partitions.

Performing a Network Installation

As mentioned previously, you have the option of sharing your Red Hat Linux 6.0 CD-ROM (included with this book) on Network File System (NFS) server, a Hypertext Transport Protocol (HTTP) Web server, or a File Transfer Protocol (FTP) server. Your best bet is to have Linux or another version of UNIX installed on another PC (acting as the server) to perform this. Windows doesn't have native NFS and FTP server capability, and some Web servers such as Microsoft Personal Web Server are not fully compatible with the installation program's HTTP client (although they seem to work fine with lynx and Netscape Communicator).

 TIP Use a Server or Custom installation on any Linux network servers that you plan to use to share a CD. If you use a Workstation installation, you will not have certain services, such as the Apache Web server, installed by default.

You also will need the pcmcia.img floppy disk, an internal Ethernet device or external PCMCIA network card, and the necessary network cabling and hubs. If your desktop PC has a network card but you don't have all the network hardware (such as an Ethernet hub), you can get by with a simple Ethernet crossover cable, which is built to directly connect two PCs with a single cable (without needing a hub). Of course, you don't need a hub if you're using BNC connectors and coaxial cable instead of RJ-45 connectors and twisted-pair cable. One of the best places to find information on how to create a crossover cable and where to buy one can be found at the http://www.gcctech.com/ts/doc/crossover.html home page.

Installing from an NFS Server   Performing an NFS installation is fairly simple. The basic procedure involves sharing your Linux CD on a network PC running the NFS server software and booting your laptop up on the network using the `bootnet.img` floppy disk and the `pcmcia.img` floppy disk. Chapter 1 provides the procedures for creating these disks. Consult your Windows and NFS documentation if you are using Windows as the server instead of Linux for this type of installation. Specifically, you should perform the following steps:

1. On the Linux server, insert the Red Hat Linux 6.0 CD in the CD-ROM. Mount it by typing `mount -t iso9660 /dev/cdrom /mnt/cdrom`. You can replace `/dev/cdrom` with any other appropriate name for your CD-ROM, such as `/dev/hdc` or `/dev/sdc`.

2. On the server, edit the `/etc/hosts` name resolution configuration file, and add a line identifying your laptop PC name and IP address. For example, I added the line `192.168.1.2 cuda70` to my server's `/etc/hosts` file.

3. On the server, edit the `/etc/exports` NFS configuration file, and add a line identifying that you want to share your mounted CD with the Linux laptop. For example, I added the line `/mnt/cdrom cuda70(rw)` to my server's `/etc/exports` file (`/mnt/cdrom (ro, no_root_squash, insecure` also worked). Resolution of the cuda70 reference will work because I already associated the name with an IP address in the previous step. Alternatively, you can select System, Linuxconf, Config, Networking, Server tasks, Exported file systems (NFS) from the main GNOME menu, if you prefer a graphical configuration process. You will have to select Add and then enter `/mnt/cdrom` in the Path to Export text box; check only the Root Privileges box below that to achieve the previously mentioned (`ro, no_root_squash, insecure`) entry in the exports file.

4. On the server, type `exportfs -rva` to enable the NFS share you just created (unless you accepted and activated the graphical changes you made, in which case the changes have already been applied for you). NFS clients, such as the one used by the Red Hat Linux 6.0 installation program, now will be capable of accessing the Red Hat Linux CD.

5. On the laptop, insert the `bootnet.img` floppy disk, and boot up your computer. The program steps you through the same installation procedures documented in Chapter 2, "Installing Red Hat Linux on a Desktop PC," except that you will have different procedures for handling the PCMCIA Support and Installation Method screens (as outlined in the next few steps).

6. When asked if you need PCMCIA support, confirm Yes and replace the `bootnet.img` floppy disk with `pcmcia.img`. Confirm OK to load the PCMCIA module in your kernel. Look for signs that the PCMCIA module loads correctly and recognizes your Ethernet card. If not, consult Chapter 27, "Installing and Configuring TCP/IP Network Support," and Chapter 18, "Installing and Configuring the Red Hat Linux Kernel" (and possibly `http://www.cs.utexas.edu/users/kharker/linux-laptop`) to determine whether your PCMCIA drive and Ethernet card are supported. If they are, you might have to find out what boot parameters you will have to pass to the kernel to enable your network card.

Part
I
Ch
3

TIP You should receive an audible double-beep confirming the PCMCIA support module was loaded, and see the LEDs lighted up on your Ethernet connector (if it provides such capability). When you identify your IP address and computer name in later steps, you can `ping` your laptop from another PC to ensure that the card is working properly. If your IP address is 192.168.1.1, for example, you can type `ping 192.168.1.1` from a shell prompt or X terminal in Linux or from an MS-DOS prompt or Start, Run in Windows. You can use Alt+F3 to look at the kernel messages also (you might see something like `pcmcia_core.o`, `i82365.o`, and `ds.o` modules being loaded with no errors, although you might see different modules based on your hardware configuration), followed by Alt+F1 to return to the main installation screen. Alt+F4 shows another screen that should indicate that the card manager services were started.

7. At the Installation Method screen, select NFS Image (the default option) and OK to begin configuring your laptop for networking to allow it to connect to the NFS server and start installing from the mounted CD there. Fill out the necessary networking information (Boot Protocol and Configure Network windows) according to the instructions from Chapter 2. In my case, I configured my laptop as host name `cuda70` and IP address `192.168.1.2`—you should recognize this from the server's `/etc/hosts` file settings discussed previously.

8. After configuring your laptop and network IP settings, you will see the NFS Setup screen. You will have to provide the IP address of your Linux NFS server and the directory name of your Linux installation CD. Select OK to continue. For my situation, I entered `192.168.1.1` as the NFS server name and `/mnt/cdrom` as the Red Hat Directory. If your PCMCIA card is properly installed, if your laptop network configuration was properly completed, if you have the necessary network connectivity (cabling, hubs), if your NFS server configuration was correct, and if there are no name resolution problems in DNS or the `/etc/hosts` file, then you should see the Installation Path window; the rest of the installation from this point on will be the same as from a local CD-ROM. If not, you will receive a few error messages and will have to go back and debug why the installation failed.

9. In the Installation Path window, you will have to choose Install or Upgrade. At this point, you are finished with the laptop-specific portions of the installation and can continue with the remaining installation steps as documented in Chapter 2.

Installing from an HTTP (Web) Server The process for installing over an HTTP or Web server is very similar to NFS installations. Actually, it's a little bit easier, even though performance might not be as crisp and quick as the NFS method. Luckily, you do not have to perform any major configuration file updates or worry about name resolution. To configure your Web server easily to share your Linux 6.0 CD over the network for your laptop installation, perform the following steps:

1. On the Linux Apache Web server, insert the Red Hat Linux 6.0 CD in the CD-ROM drive. Mount it by typing `mount -t iso9660 /dev/cdrom /mnt/cdrom`. You can replace `/dev/cdrom` with any other appropriate name for your CD-ROM, such as `/dev/hdc` or `/dev/sdc`.

2. On the server, change to the Apache server's root directory by typing `cd /home/httpd/html` (assuming that you have not changed the default—enter the appropriate directory if you did).

3. Create a link on your Web server's root directory by typing `ln -s /mnt/cdrom cdrom`. This creates a file named `cdrom` that can be accessed from any network browser by referencing `http://<server-name>/cdrom` (where `server-name` is replaced by your Linux Web server name). This assumes that you have not made any configuration changes to your Apache Web server to disable browsers from following symbolic links on the server; in such a case, you will have to modify settings for the `FollowSymLinks` variable in your Apache configuration files (see Chapter 30, "Configuring the Apache Web Server").

 TIP If you performed a Workstation or Custom installation, you might not have installed Apache Web server. In this case, install it easily using `rpm -i /mnt/cdrom/RedHat/RPMS/apache-1.3.6-7.i386.rpm` from an X terminal or shell command line. If you prefer to use the graphical method, select System, GnoRPM from the main GNOME menu button (see Chapter 11, "Installing and Managing RPM Packages").

4. On the laptop, insert the `bootnet.img` floppy disk and boot up your computer. The program steps you through the same installation procedures that are documented in Chapter 2, except that you will have different procedures for handling the PCMCIA Support and Installation Method screens (as outlined in the next few steps).

5. When asked if you need PCMCIA support, confirm Yes and replace the `bootnet.img` floppy disk with `pcmcia.img`. Confirm OK to load the PCMCIA module in your kernel. Look for signs that the PCMCIA module loads correctly and recognizes your Ethernet card. If not, you will have to consult Chapters 27 and 18 (and possibly `http://www.cs.utexas.edu/users/kharker/linux-laptop`) to determine whether your PCMCIA drive and Ethernet card are supported. If they are, you might have to find out what boot parameters you will have to pass to the kernel to enable your network card.

6. At the Installation Method screen, select HTTP and OK to begin configuring your laptop for networking to allow it to connect to the Apache Web server and start installing from the mounted CD there. Fill out the necessary networking information (Boot Protocol and Configure Network windows) according to the instructions from Chapter 2. In my case, I configured my laptop as host name `cuda70` and IP address `192.168.1.2`.

Part
I

Ch
3

7. After configuring your laptop and network IP settings, you will see the HTTP Setup screen. You will have to provide the IP address and directory name of your Linux Apache Web server and Linux installation CD. You also might have to provide proxy server information on the off chance that your laptop is located behind a proxy or a firewall. Because my laptop was located directly on the LAN (not behind a proxy), I entered 192.168.1.1 as the Web site name and cdrom as the Red Hat directory. If your PCMCIA card is properly installed, if your laptop network configuration was properly completed, if you have the necessary network connectivity (cabling, hubs), and if your Apache Web server configuration was correct, then you should see a few pop-up windows indicating that the second-stage ram disk (stage2.img) file is being retrieved and loaded. Then you will be at the Installation Path window, and the rest of the installation from this point on will be the same as from a local CD-ROM. If not, you will receive a few error messages and will have to go back and debug why the install failed.

8. In the Installation Path window, you will have to choose Install or Upgrade. At this point, you are finished with the laptop-specific portions of the installation and can continue with the remaining steps, as documented in Chapter 2.

Performing a Hard Drive Installation

To perform a hard disk installation, you will have to install all the applicable Linux 6.0 installation files on a hard drive or a partition on your laptop. This will take approximately 50–60MB. If you don't have an extra hard drive to use, you will have to perform a backup and then use the DOS/Windows fdisk.exe program to repartition your existing drive and restore your Windows files on a partition. Consult Chapter 19, "Installing and Configuring Hard Drives," for details on how to do this. To install the Red Hat installation files on a laptop drive or a partition, perform the following tasks:

1. Assuming that you are installing the files on the C: drive (otherwise, replace with your actual drive in these instructions), create one directory (RedHat) and two subdirectories (base and RPMS) off of C:, either from an MS-DOS prompt using the mkdir command or using the graphical interface (double-click My Computer and C:, and then File, New, Folder from the menu bar). When you are finished, you should have three directories: C:\RedHat, C:\RedHat\base, and C:\RedHat\RPMS.

2. Copy the contents of the appropriate Linux directories from the installation CD (assume here that it is the d: device on Windows) to their counterparts on Windows (the directory and subdirectories you just created). The best way to do this is to bring up an Explorer window for D:\RedHat and another Explorer window for C:\RedHat. Select all the files in D:\RedHat except for the translation file (which won't copy well), and then drag and drop them onto the C:\RedHat directory. Perform the same task for the two subdirectories.

3. On the laptop, insert the boot.img floppy disk, and boot up your computer. The program steps you through the same installation procedures that are documented in Chapter 2, except that you will have different procedures for handling the Installation Method screen (as outlined in the next few steps).

4. When asked if you need PCMCIA support, select No for most situations, unless you need it to access SCSI adapters and hard drives during the installation, perhaps. If you do have SCSI adapters and hard drives, you also will have to answer Yes to the SCSI Configuration window to take you to a screen that enables you to pick a Linux-supported SCSI adapter.

5. In the Select Partition window, you are asked to provide the (local) partition and directory name where your Red Hat Linux 6.0 installation files are located. Unless you have a very customized Windows configuration, you most likely have Windows installed on the first partition of the IDE or SCSI drive. Because you installed the RedHat directory right off the main directory in Windows (C:\RedHat) and not in a subdirectory, you effectively installed the files on the root directory, or the / directory, as Linux calls it. Therefore, you would select the first device (/dev/hda1 [IDE] or /dev/sda1 [SCSI], by default) and leave / as the directory. Click OK to continue. If you copied the files to the folders properly, and if you are referencing your local drive partition correctly, then you should see a few pop-up windows indicating that the second-stage ram disk (stage2.img) file is being retrieved and loaded. Then you will be at the Installation Path window, and the rest of the installation from this point on will be the same as from a local CD-ROM. If not, you will receive a few error messages and will have to go back and debug why the install process failed.

Configuring Red Hat Linux 6.0 for Laptops

After you install Red Hat Linux 6.0 using one of the installation methods previously discussed, there are still a few things you should do. For example, because you will not be plugged into electrical outlets all the time, you will need to have ways of managing your battery power. You will need to monitor your current battery level so that you'll know approximately how much longer you can use your laptop before you need to plug back into electrical power. You also will need a way of suspending power instead of turning your laptop entirely off; this will prevent you from wasting power the next time you reboot because Linux will still be running in the state it was in when you suspended work.

Red Hat Linux comes with a suite of Advanced Power Management (APM) tools and utilities to perform these power-conservation functions. The apmd-3.0beta5-7.i386.rpm package is installed by default with all installation methods. Many of these tools depend on a correct implementation of the APM standard in the laptop's BIOS.

TIP If you need to minimize power consumption, evaluate /etc/inetd.conf and /etc/inittab to determine which daemons or processes you can disable (and don't need). You can reduce the clock speed of your CPU in the BIOS setup program; processing will be slower (which might be fine for what you're doing) but will consume much less memory. Peripherals are power drains, so remove PCMCIA devices you don't plan to use on battery power, and don't use modems, CD-ROMs, a network device, or your floppy drive unless absolutely necessary.

Enabling the Battery Monitor

To enable and configure a monitor that lets you quickly see how much power you have remaining on your laptop battery (when not plugged into electrical power), perform the following steps:

1. Right-click a GNOME panel and select Add Applet, Monitors, Battery Charge Monitor. The monitor appears on the appropriate panel (although you can move it to another one later, if you want).

2. To toggle between numerical and graphical displays of battery charge levels, click the battery power monitor directly on the GNOME panel.

3. To change the monitor's settings, right-click the monitor icon in the panel, and select Properties. This brings up the Battery Monitor Settings dialog box (see Figure 3.1).

FIGURE 3.1
You can easily change the applet icon size and period between battery checks.

4. In the General tab, select the time in seconds that you want the monitor to update (the default is reasonable). In the Applet Mode section, select Readout or Graph to view numerical or graphical displays.

5. In the Readout and Graph tabs, you can click the color boxes and select different colors that you want displayed when you are disconnected from power or attached, and whether you are running low on battery power. You can also change the direction that the graphical bars flow as you discharge or recharge your battery.

6. In the Battery Charge Messages tab, check the boxes indicating whether you want to receive a low battery warning or full-charge notification (see Figure 3.2). Most importantly, this is where you set the lowest level your battery can go before displaying a

warning about the need to charge the battery or turn off your computer to risk loss of data. Be sure to leave yourself enough time to save all your data, close your applications, and shut down your computer. Click OK to save and apply your changes.

FIGURE 3.2
You can set alarms to activate when the battery reaches certain levels (high or low).

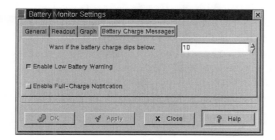

Configuring the Linux Suspend Functions

Your laptop BIOS might support a form of suspend that you can use, independent of any operating system installed or in use on your laptop. For example, if I press the power button on my Compaq Presario 1255 just once, for less than a second, the BIOS will save the current memory status of the system and turn off the power. To resume where I left off, without having to reboot, all I have to do is press the power button again. To actually turn off the power, the BIOS requires me to hold the power button down for at least 4 seconds. These types of functionality are configurable within your BIOS, normally.

Even if your BIOS doesn't support this type of suspend and resume operation, a Linux laptop can activate a similar function itself internally. To create a Suspend launcher, perform the following steps:

1. Right-click a GNOME panel and select Add New Launcher. This brings up the Launcher Properties window, shown in Figure 3.3.

FIGURE 3.3
Create a launcher as a graphical shortcut to the suspend utility.

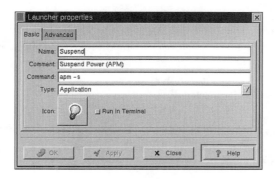

Part

I

Ch

3

2. In the Basic tab of the Launcher Properties window, enter a name and comment for your Suspend button (the comment you enter is the "tooltip" text displayed.

3. Enter apm −s as the command that you want the launcher icon to execute when you click it.

4. Click the Icon box to bring up the Choose an Icon window, which enables you to associate a graphic icon with your Suspend button.

5. You don't need to make any changes to the Advanced tab entries. Just click OK and then check to see if the icon was created properly on the panel.

 You might be able to use the hdparm command to "spin down" your laptop's hard drive. Normally—when plugged into power, for example—a laptop will keep a hard drive spinning for quite a while, waiting for your next read or write. If you want hdparm to turn off your hard drive after 60 seconds of activity, for example, type hdparm −S12 /dev/hda (or /dev/sda, if SCSI drive and it works with hdparm). Notice that each hdparm tick is equal to 5 seconds of delay. You might have to run the command again after you use the apm suspend and resume functions, though. You also can use hdparm −g to view drive geometry and hdparm −C /dev/hdd to check the current power mode status of the disk.

Troubleshooting Linux Laptops

You might run into problems configuring XFree86 with your laptop because monitors and video cards are inherently more restrictive. If you run into problems, you can try a little trial and error, but be careful. Read over Chapter 9, "Installing and Configuring Video Cards, Monitors, and Mice," on XFree86 configuration to see if there's something that can assist you there. Then, go to the Linux laptop page located at http://www.cs.utexas.edu/users/kharker/linux-laptop. If you don't find anything on that site related specifically to your problem, then you should check the XFree86 Web site for anything that might help you.

If you absolutely can't find anything that helps, contact Red Hat directly (if you have a support contract). It's better to try to solve the problem yourself before asking for assistance because that is the only way you will learn and improve your troubleshooting abilities. Lastly, subscribe to an appropriate Linux Internet newsgroup and read over past messages to see if anyone else has had your problem. Otherwise, post a note providing plentiful technical details and asking if someone can help you with it.

If your modem won't work, it's probable that you have some sort of crippled modem. These types of modems have had specific hardware components removed (to reduce price) and have passed their tasks off to Windows. Unfortunately, the manufacturers haven't supported development of such programs for other operating systems. Examples of these types of modems, which are strictly incompatible with Linux, are the WinModem and the Mwave modem.

You might know that your system supports bootable CD-ROMs, but you boot straight into Windows, even with your Red Hat CD inserted. If so, there's a chance that your system supports bootable CD-ROM but that the hard drive (and possibly the floppy drive) is selected as a higher boot priority. In such a case, you will have to enter your BIOS setup program. If your computer prompts you during normal bootup with the specific key combination needed for entering BIOS setup, reboot and use this key combination to launch the setup program. Otherwise, consult your user's manual to determine how to bring up the BIOS setup program. If you can't find anything explaining how to do this, refer to Chapter 19, which includes a tip box containing popular methods for launching your BIOS setup programs used by different manufacturers; you might find one that gets you in.

After you enter the right key combination and enter the setup program, look for an item under one of the menu bar categories that enables you to change the bootup sequence. The method for changing these settings is BIOS-dependent, but you should have a way of adding CD-ROM as a boot option (if your BIOS supports bootable CD-ROMs). You also can move the CD-ROM up in the priority or sequence to prevent your system from launching straight into the hard drive or floppy disk bootup before looking to see if you have a bootable CD such as Red Hat's installation CD.

One thing to remember is that you'll need to change this setting back after the CD-ROM installation, otherwise you or someone else that powers up the PC later with the Red Hat installation CD in it will encounter the installation menu. If this happens, it is no real problem, you will just have to remove the CD and reboot. But, you don't want a coworker or family member installing Linux and wiping out all your work, right? ●

Part
I

Ch
3

## CHAPTER 4

Installing Red Hat Linux on an Alpha

by Richard D. Payne

In this chapter

Introduction and Background

The Alpha processor was first started at Digital Equipment Corporation (DEC) in mid-1989 to provide a high-performance upgrade path for VMS users. In March 1992, the Alpha was announced to the world as the first 64-bit RISC processor.

In 1998, Compaq Computer Corporation Inc. merged with Digital Equipment Corporation, making Digital a wholly owned subsidiary of Compaq. Today, the Alpha is still owned by Compaq and production is done by Compaq and Samsung (an Alpha technology licensee).

The Linux port to Alpha was started by several engineers within Digital, and it has taken several years for the kernel code to become 64-bit clean. Starting with the 2.1 kernel versions, the Alpha tree was included in the kernel, so the 2.2 series has proven to be much more reliable and easier to use than the 2.0 series.

Currently, you can choose from four Linux distributions for Alpha. Red Hat (`http://ww.redhat.com`) was one of the first to produce an Alpha port, followed by Debian (`http://www.debian.org`) and SuSE (`http://www.suse.com`). As of this writing, both Stampede (`http://www.stampede.org`) and TurboLinux (`http://www.turbolinux.org`) are in the process of bringing their distributions to Alpha as well. The directions and tips provided in this chapter are based on a Red Hat install, although most of the information should apply equally to the other Alpha distributions available.

Understanding Alpha Challenges

Installing Linux on an Alpha system can be a little more challenging than installing on an i386 (Intel, AMD, Cyrix) system. The first main difference is the system console (also known as the BIOS). Alpha systems have several different system consoles, used for bootstrapping different operating system. These consoles are as follows:

- **SRM (System Reference Manual)**—This was originally designed for booting either OpenVMS or Tru64Unix (previously Digital Unix). Linux can be booted from SRM with the assistance of the aboot secondary boot loader.

- **ARC (Advanced RISC Console)**—This was originally designed to boot Microsoft Windows NT but can be used to boot Linux with the help of MILO. On later systems, the ARC Console (known as AlphaBIOS) has been made more user-friendly.

- **ARCS Console**—This is used only on machines based on the 164UX (also known as the Ruffian) motherboard. The UX was not a Digital/Compaq design, so it has its own console and cannot use either SRM or ARC (AlphaBIOS).

The console you use will depend on several things. First, some machines can hold both consoles (SRM and ARC/AlphaBIOS) in their flash memory; others can take only one at a time. Some systems come with AlphaBIOS, and SRM is available only for a price. The thing to remember is that most machines with SRM can boot Linux, and machines with AlphaBIOS can also boot Linux with the help of MILO. Those that have AlphaBIOS but not MILO can usually be changed over to SRM for booting Linux.

The various Alpha BIOS systems are much more advanced than their PC counterparts. For example, AlphaBIOS includes the capability to partition and format disks, set up a boot selection menu, and report on the hardware installed in the machine. All this is done in a menu-based environment.

SRM is much more a command-line console. It also can report on the hardware installed in the system, but it does not have the capability to set up a boot menu as AlphaBIOS does. However, SRM does allow certain variables to be set to automate booting.

Validating Hardware Compatibility

To decide whether Linux will run on a certain piece of hardware, you must examine two components: the Alpha motherboard and the peripherals contained in the machine.

Most Alpha-based systems in existence today are capable of running Linux. The main exceptions are the early TurboChannel-based machines, known as the DEC3000 series of machines. Work is being done to enable Linux on these systems, but it is yet not usable for an everyday system.

When it comes to peripherals, most of those supported under i386 Linux will work under AlphaLinux, with some exceptions. The best place to start with peripherals is to look at the hardware compatibility lists published by the distributions. Red Hat's compatibility list is available at `http://www.redhdat.com/corp/support/docs/hardware.html`, and SuSE has a hardware database available at `http://www.suse.com`.

Part
I

Ch
4

Understanding Installation Differences for Alpha

The main differences for installing on an Alpha-based machine revolve around the BIOS. When the distributions' installation process has started, you will see little difference, but starting the installation can be a little tricky at times.

The way in which the installation is started depends on the BIOS used on the system. Installing from AlphaBIOS (ARC Console) and ARCS BIOS is basically the same, so those two will be handled together. Installing from SRM will be handled separately.

Installing from AlphaBIOS

Installing and booting from AlphaBIOS requires the use of MILO, the AlphaLinux Mini Loader that loads and starts the Linux operating system and provides the necessary PALcode for Linux to run. The MILO used is specific to the machine type on which the installation is being done, and not every machine has a MILO available (when no MILO exists, installation must be performed from SRM Console).

Table 4.1 shows system types and their respective MILOs.

Table 4.1   MILO System Table

Family/Model	Aliases	MILO
ALCOR		xlt-alcor
AS 600	ALCOR	
AS 500 5/3xx	MAVERICK	
AS 500 5/5xx	BRET	
XL-300	XLT	
XL-366	XLT	
XL-433	XLT	
XL		xl
XL-233	XL	
XL-266	XL	
AVANTI		avanti
AS 200 4/*	MUSTANG	
AS 205 4/*	LX3	
AS 250 4/*	M3	
AS 255 4/*	LX3+	
AS 300 4/*	MELMAC	
AS 400 4/*	AVANTI	
Personal Workstation		miata
PWS 433a or 433au		
PWS 500a or 500au		
PWS 600a or 600au		
NONAME		udb-noname
AXPpci33	NONAME	
UDB	MULTIA	
EB64+		
EB64+	EB64+	eb64p
AlphaPC64	CABRIOLET	cabrio
AlphaPCI-64		
PC164		
AlphaPC164	PC164	pc164
AlphaPC164-LX	LX164	lx164
AlphaPC164-SX	SX164	sx164

Family/Model	Aliases	MILO
EB164	EB164	eb164
EB66+	EB66+	eb66p
EB66	EB66	eb66
TAKARA	TAKARA	takara
Ruffian	164UX	ruffian

The MILO file should be placed on a DOS format floppy (also know as FAT format) with the `linload.exe` file. These files should be available with any AlphaLinux Distribution, and you can put these files on the floppy in several ways.

The first method is by just copying the two files (`linload.exe` and the relevant MILO) onto a DOS floppy; the MILO file itself must be renamed from whatever it is called on the CD-ROM to `milo`.

The second method involves using the floppy images the distributions provide. In the case of Red Hat, the MILO files and `linload.exe` file are found in the `/milo` directory of the CD-ROM; images are located in the `/milo/images` directory but can be directly written to a floppy using the commands described in the following sections.

Under Windows/DOS Use the rewrite utility, found in the `/dosutils` directory, to write the image to the floppy. For example, if the CD-ROM drive was drive D: and the floppy drive was drive A:, the following would create the MILO floppy for a Noname/Multia machine:

```
d:\rawrite.exe d:\milo\images\udb-noname.img a:\
```

Under Linux (or Other UNIX System) Use the `dd` command that comes with most UNIX systems.

Assuming that the CD-ROM drive is mounted under `/mnt/cdrom` and the floppy device is `/dev/fd0`, enter the following on one line:

```
dd if=/mnt/cdrom/milo/images/udb-noname.img of=/dev/fd0 bs=1440k
```

When this step is complete, the installation can be started.

With the floppy just created in the machine's floppy drive and the CD inserted into the CD-ROM drive, the machine can then be set to boot from the floppy. Press F2 while AlphaBIOS is initializing to enter setup. When setup is started, go to the Utilities menu item and choose the OS Selection Setup item. Then press the Insert key to add another selection. The new boot selection should look similar to this:

```
Boot Name: Install Linux
 Boot File: A:     \linload.exe
 OS Path: Disk0 Partition 1    \
OS Options:
```

Press the Enter key when finished to allow this selection to be saved. AlphaBIOS might report the error The OS Path: Disk 0, Partition 1 \ not found. This can be safely ignored because this variable is not used during the install.

When the selection is set up, press F10 to save the changes to the flash ROM, and press the Esc key to exit AlphaBIOS setup. At this point, a boot menu should appear. One item should be the Linux Install selection added previously. Use the arrow keys to highlight this selection, and press Enter to start MILO.

When MILO has finished booting, the MILO> prompt will be displayed. From here the installation is started. The command should be something like this (for Red Hat 6.0):

```
MILO> boot hda:/kernels/generic.gz root=/dev/hda
```

This assumes an IDE CD-ROM; if the machine has a SCSI CD-ROM, the command should look something like this:

```
MILO> boot scd0:/kernels/generic.gz root=/dev/scd0
```

At this point, MILO will load and start the Linux kernel, which will in turn invoke the distribution's installation process. From here on, the Linux installation is the same as on an i386-based machine, with one exception. During the disk partitioning, a small (about 5MB) DOS (FAT) partition should be made on the disk. This holds the MILO and linload.exe files when installation is complete. If one of the standard Red Hat configurations is chosen (Workstation or Server), this partition will automatically be created. If for some reason it is not possible to create this partition, Linux can still be booted using the MILO floppy, but the boot process will take a little longer because floppy disks are slower than hard disks.

When the installation is complete, Linux must be booted to copy the contents of the floppy onto the small DOS partition. The installation process returns the system to the MILO prompt. To boot the newly installed operating system, use a command like this:

```
MILO> boot sda2:/boot/vmlinuz-2.2.5-16 root=/dev/sda2
```

This assumes that sda2 (SCSI disk 1, partition 2) is the root file system. This will need to be changed to reflect whichever disk partition contains the root file system (this was set during the install).

When the system is booted, log in as root, using the root password set during install, and copy the contents of the floppy to the small DOS partition. Assuming that the partition is sda1 (SCSI disk 1, partition 1), the command would be the following:

```
dd if=/dev/fd0 of=/dev/sda1
```

All that remains to be done now is to set up the boot selection within AlphaBIOS to start Linux. To set up AlphaBIOS, press F2 during AlphaBIOS initialization, and select Utilities, OS Selection Setup. Use the arrow keys to select the Linux Install item added earlier, and press Enter to edit that selection. Change the values to look like this (substituting the correct root file system and disk partitions):

```
Boot Name: Linux
 Boot File: Disk 0, Partition 1      \linload.exe
 OS Path:   Disk 0, Partition         \
 OS Options: boot sda2:/boot/vmlinuz-2.2.5-16 root=/dev/sda2
```

Press Enter to commit the changes, and then press F10 and Enter to save the changes to the system; finally, press Esc to exit. At this time, the boot menu should be present and you can choose the Linux option to start Linux.

N O T E   Some copies of the official Red Hat CD-ROM are not made properly, and the previously described procedure might fail after being started from MILO. In this case, use the same procedure to create to two more floppy disks: one from the /images/generic.img file, and the other from the /images/ramdisk.img file. These can then be used instead of the CD-ROM to boot the installation. The following would be the boot command:

```
MILO> boot fd0:vmlinux.gz root=/dev/fd0 load_ramdisk=1
```

If this also fails, you should obtain the updated ramdisk image and use this instead of the original. The update image is available from http://www.redhat.com/errata.

Installing with SRM

Part
I
Ch
4

In contrast to installing and booting from AlphaBIOS, using SRM is much simpler. SRM itself does not understand disk partitions or file systems. In the case of Linux, SRM relies on the aboot secondary boot loader to start the Linux kernel. However, unlike the MILOs, only one aboot exists, and it works for every Alpha machine that supports Linux and SRM.

Installation from SRM can also be done by either booting from the CD-ROM or booting from floppies, as with AlphaBIOS. To boot using the CD-ROM, first you must find out what SRM calls the CD-ROM device. The best way to do this is to use SRM's show dev command. This outputs the list of devices that SRM has detected in the machine. The device will probably be either dqa0 (for IDE CD-ROMs) or dka0 (for SCSI CD-ROMs). The device name might be slightly different than these—for example, if it's the second IDE device on controller 1, it would be dqa1. Usually, there is a short description of the device in the right column of the show dev output.

The command to start the installation should be the following:

```
P00>boot dqa0 -fi /kernels/generic.gz -flags "root=/dev/hda?
```

Again, the correct devices need to be substituted for dqa0 and /dev/hda, depending on the machine's configuration.

This should successfully start the installer for a Red Hat 6.0 release. The installation can now progress, with one exception. When partitioning the disks, fdisk must be used as the hard disk and must be set up with BSD disk labels; Disk Druid cannot do this. To create the BSD disk labels, select fdisk as the partitioning tool, and immediately change fdisk into BSD mode using the b command. When partitioning in BSD mode, you must remember a few things:

■ Partition c should be left as the whole disk. This will not be used by Linux.

■ The first partition should start on at least cylinder 2 or 3. This leaves room at the start of the disk for aboot.

■ Sometimes fdisk will falsely report the number of cylinders available in the disk. The number it reports is usually one higher than what is actually available. In this case, just make sure that the last partition ends on the number of cylinders reported, minus one.

When this is complete, the install can be completed like any other install.

After the installation process has finished, Linux must be booted via the CD-ROM one more time to enable the aboot boot loader to be written to the disk. Assuming that the second partition of the first SCSI disk contains the root filesystem, the command would look like this:

```
P00>boot dqa0 -file kernels/generic.gz -flags                ?root=/dev/sda2"
```

This boots the Linux kernel on the CD-ROM but uses the root filesystem that was just installed. The kernel will report several errors during this boot, but you can safely ignore these. When Linux has started, log in as root using the password specified during install, and use the following command to set up aboot:

```
/sbin/swriteboot /dev/sda /boot/bootlx -f3
```

This writes aboot to the first SCSI disk and enables you to boot the hard disk directly from SRM.

Then you can shut down the machine and set up SRM to boot the Linux directory. From the SRM prompt, you can set the following environmental variables to allow Linux to boot:

■ **bootdef_dev**—This defines the boot device. In the case of IDE disks, it is dqa0, dqa1, dqb0, and so on. In the case of SCSI disks, it is something like dka0, dka1, and so on.

■ **boot_file**—This is the name of the kernel that aboot will try to load.

■ **boot_osflags**—This is a list of any parameters that should be passed to the kernel at boot time.

■ **auto_action**—This defines what SRM should do after it has finished its tests. Setting this to halt forces SRM to wait at the P00> until the user tells it what to do. Setting this to boot forces SRM to automatically try to boot whatever has been set up using the environmental variables previously discussed.

To set up SRM to boot Linux for the install just described, the code would look like this:

```
P00> set bootdef_dev dka0
P00> set boot_file 2/boot/vmlinuz-2.2.5-16
P00> set boot_osflags ?root=/dev/sda2"
P00> set auto_action boot
```

These three boot variables can always be overridden by the command-line flags. The —file option takes precedence over the boot_file value, and —flags takes precedence over the boot_osflags value.

N O T E Some CD-ROM vendors who copy the official distributions do not always make their CD-ROMs bootable by SRM. In this case, an SRM bootable floppy must be created from the `/image/generic.img` file on the CD-ROM. ■

Troubleshooting Alpha Installations

After AlphaLinux is installed, you should watch for a few things that can cause trouble. Some of these are serious problems, whereas others are just annoyances that could potentially cause problems over time. It's always a good idea to keep up with any new versions of software released by the distributions.

Clock Wrong by 20 Years

This problem stems from the fact that SRM and AlphaBIOS/ARC store the system time in different formats. The usual way to fix this is to edit the `/etc/sysconfig/clock` file and make sure that the line `'ARC=true'` is there. Red Hat also has now added this to the installer so that this can be set when the time zone is selected.

Unaligned Traps

Unaligned traps are caused by memory accesses that are not naturally aligned. The message comes from the kernel fixing the problem so that the end user process can continue. These are not dangerous, so you can ignore them because they cause only a small performance loss.

0>0>0>0>0> When Trying to Start MILO

This happens because, by default, MILO echoes its output to the first serial port as well as the screen. Chances are that a modem on the first serial port is talking back and confusing MILO. The best thing is to move the modem to a different serial port.

Booting the kernel hangs on a Ruffian: The original MILO and `ldmilo.exe` for the ruffian (164UX) machines face a problem in loading large kernels. The easiest way around this is to go to the Compaq ftp site (formerly the Digital ftp site) and download an updated version of each. The URL is `ftp://ftp.digital.com/pub/DEC/Linux-ALpha/Kernels`, and the files are `milo-ruffian-981020` and `ldmilo-ruffian-981020`.

Further Resources

The very nature of Linux is that it changes rapidly. With thousands of people all over the world constantly using and improving the software and its documentation, it's always a good idea to keep an eye on what's going on. This section lists some other sources of information that can help when installing or running Alpha Linux.

Part

I

Ch

4

Web Sites

The following are several Web sites that provide information either for Alpha Linux or for just the Alpha architecture in general:

- **The Alpha Linux Organization**—This is the official Alpha Linux Web site:
  `http://www.alphalinux.org/`

- **The Digital Alpha OEM site**—This is home to a lot of information about Alpha OEM products (including technical information):
  `http://www.digital.com/alphaoem`

- **The Compaq AlphaLinux Web site**—This site supports documents for running Linux on Compaq Alpha products, as well as information on the new Compaq optimized compilers for AlphaLinux:
  `http://www.unix.digital.com/linux`

- **The Alpha Processor Inc. Web site**—Alpha Processor Inc. was set up in June 1998 to promote the Alpha architecture and has recently started building Alpha motherboard for its own design:
  `http://www.alpha-processor.com`

Informational Mailing Lists

Mailing lists enable users to send email to one address and it will be sent to the entire list. Most of the lists will allow users to subscribe or unsubscribe automatically without human interaction. They are usually an excellent resource for new users and experienced users alike.

- **Red Hat's axp-list**—Send email to `redhat-axp-request@redhat.com` with *subscribe* as the subject line.

- **Debian debian-alpha list**—Send email to `debian-alpha-request@lists.debian.org` with *subscribe* in the body of the message.

- **SuSE's suse-axp list**—Send email to `majordomo@suse.com` with *subscribe suse-axp* in the body of the message.

Archives of the lists are available at `http://www.alphalinux.org/archives`.

Installing Red Hat Linux on a Sparc

by R. Kevin McPeake

In this chapter

Understanding Sparc Challenges

Installing Red Hat Linux on a Sparc can seem like a formidable challenge if you are new to the Sparc platform. Although certain considerations must be taken into account for the Sparc hardware, the installation should be no more difficult than counterpart platforms, such as Intel or Alpha. If you have previously worked with Sun hardware before, especially if you have ever installed Sun Solaris on a Sparc system, you should find installing Linux on Sparc, a relatively smooth task. This chapter walks you through a general installation of Linux on Sparc and gives you enough direction to explore more advanced technical configurations on your own. The aim of this chapter is not to teach you the inner details of Sparc Hardware or OpenBoot. For more information on these details, see the appropriate reference manuals or various sites on the Web that document this.

- **Sparc**—Introduced in 1989 by Sun Microsystems, the original Sparc (Scalable Processor Architecture) processor is a 32-bit RISC (Reduced Instruction Set Computer) CPU. The more recently released UltraSparc processor is a 64-bit RISC CPU. While the *Sparc* name is used loosely to refer to the entire range of Sparc platforms, to avoid confusion when discussing issues specifically pertaining to the 32-bit or 64-bit Sparc platforms, the terms Sparc32 or Sparc64 will be used for the remainder of this chapter.

  Sparc systems come in a wide variety of configurations, ranging from a single Sparc32 CPU workstation, to 64 Sparc64 CPUs on a single server (yes, that's 64 separate CPUs on a single server, with each CPU being a 64-bit design). With the advent of the new 2.2.x Linux kernel, you can even install and run Linux in these largest of Sun Sparc64 servers.

- **OpenBoot**—During the startup of your Sparc system, your system first executes the firmware stored in the boot Programmable Read Only Memory (PROM). This firmware, which is often known as OpenBoot, provides initial kernel loading and execution as well as hardware diagnostics and kernel debugging features. OpenBoot is standard across all Sparc platforms, so once you know how to work with OpenBoot on one type of Sparc system, you will know how it works on other systems.

- **SILO**—On an installed Linux system, OpenBoot will load SILO, which is nearly identical to LILO in configuration and functionality. It should be noted that while you can configure SILO to dual-boot Linux on Sparc and another OS (for example, Solaris), this cannot be done during the install of Red Hat Linux and must be performed after the installation is complete.

- **Kernel implementations**—The default setup of Red Hat Linux for Sparc will install the 32-bit version of the kernel, which is compatible with both Sparc32 and Sparc64 architectures. After installation, it is possible to install precompiled kernels, which support either multiple processor systems (SMP) or Sparc64 implementations, or both (multiple Sparc64 CPUs). Most Linux applications are compiled for 32-bit CPUs, but they still can take advantage of the speed increase provided by 64-bit CPU and SMP kernels.

Validating Hardware Compatibility

Before you begin installing Linux for Sparc, it is wise to know whether your hardware will actually support and run Linux. Although you can expect better configuration compatibility than commonly found on Intel platforms—that is, you won't be required to change interrupts, DMA assignments, and so on—not all Sparc hardware is fully supported yet by the available ports of Linux for Sparc. Furthermore, it should be noted that not all Sun systems are actually based on the Sparc CPU design; some are based on the Motorola 68000 or the Intel 386 CPU instead. These were some of the earliest systems produced by Sun and, as such, are not planned for support by Linux anytime in the future.

For a full list of currently supported hardware, check with the Red Hat Linux Hardware Compatibility Lists at http://www.redhat.com/.

In addition to being a currently supported Sun Sparc or Sparc-compatible clone listed on the Hardware Compatibility Lists, Red Hat Linux for Sparc also requires the following configuration:

- **Hard drive space**—At least 32MB for swap partition and 120MB for basic installation. For a typical installation, at least 800MB is advisable; for the full installation of everything, you will need at least 1GB.
- **RAM**—16MB minimum.

At least one of the following interfaces must be present to run and configure the system during installation:

- Monitor and keyboard
- Remote serial terminal (for headless installations)

At least one of the following is required for bootup of the installation program:

- Floppy drive (3.5-inch high-density)
- CD-ROM
- Network Adapter (and another system on the network capable of serving the Red Hat Linux installation files via FTP, NFS, or SMB [Win32 file share])

Part

I

Ch

5

Preparing Hard Drives

If you are planning to use Linux as your sole operating system, not too much preparation is required in most cases for using your disks under Linux. However, there are some basic things to remember.

- Linux makes use of ext2 (Second Extended File system) as its native file system format, while SunOS/Solaris makes use of UFS (UNIX File System) format. Although Linux can mount, read, and write to UFS partitions, you cannot install Linux onto a UFS-formatted partition.

- If you plan to use Disk Druid to format your disks, do not delete your SunOS/Solaris disk labels. Disk Druid can partition and format disks under Sparc, but it cannot initialize disk labels. Therefore, you will be required to create these using fdisk's 's' command during the Linux installation process to create the standard disk label.

- During the install of Linux, it is recommended that you verify that there is a partition defined as "Whole Disk" spanning from Cylinder 0 to the end of the disk, under partition 3. It shouldn't be used or assigned to anything, as this partition is a reserved partition for the system to access this drive. If you have had to relabel your disks, it might be necessary to recreate this partition.

- Most importantly, before you do anything else, be sure to back up any files you desire to keep for later use.

 TIP It is possible to set up Sparc for Linux to co-exist with SunOS/Solaris or other operating systems and configure SILO to prompt at system startup which OS to boot.

CAUTION

If you plan to create a dual-boot system on a single hard drive and then use Disk Druid to create your Linux partitions before creating your partitions for the alternate OS, you might find that you have no free disk space after creating your Linux partitions. This is because Disk Druid defines all contiguous free space as an Extended (DOS) partition, and then creates ext2 partitions within the space of the Extended partition. Any disk space not used by ext2 partitions simply gets left as wasted space. As a workaround, either use fdisk to define your partitions under Linux, or simply install the alternate OS first, making sure to leave enough space for you to later install Linux.

Understanding Installation Differences for Sparc

The biggest difference between installing Red Hat Linux for Sparc and installing Linux for Intel is that a basic understanding of OpenBoot is required to successfully boot the Sparc installation program. Fortunately, because most of the recent Sun systems have OpenBoot 2.0 or greater installed, this will make your installation much easier. However, if you have a version prior to 2.0, then it might take you a little more work to determine what the proper boot arguments are. If you're unsure of which version you have, you can usually tell by the prompt itself. If the prompt is displayed with ok, then you have a version 2.0 or later of OpenBoot. If the prompt is a > character, then most likely you have an older version.

To boot a newer version, the command is boot followed by one of the following device aliases: floppy, CD-ROM, or net. To boot an older version of the PROM, instead of the device aliases, you must specify the boot device literal name in the following format: $xx(a,b,c)$, where xx is the device type (such as sd for SCSI), a is the controller number, b is the device's unit number, and c is the (slice) partition number. Refer to the appropriate manuals included with your system if you need more information.

As is the case with the Intel platforms, you can perform a boot of the installation software either from a CD-ROM or from a floppy disk. Unlike the Intel platform, you can also perform a Net boot of the installation boot disk, which is stored elsewhere on a remote server on the network as a disk image file. Net booting is useful for systems that have hard drives installed but have no CD-ROMs or floppy drives, or where multiple machines on the same network are to be installed simultaneously.

Roughly, the Net boot process is described as follows. When OpenBoot is given the command to perform the Net boot, it requests an IP number from another server on the network, which is responsible for assigning it an IP number. Once the Sparc system is assigned an IP number from the remote server, it then proceeds to use that IP number to connect to the TFTP server process on the same or different server on the network, where the disk image is stored and waiting to be downloaded by the Sparc. After the disk image is downloaded, it is loaded into RAM and is invoked by OpenBoot. After being invoked, the Linux kernel takes over from OpenBoot and mounts the disk image currently loaded in RAM, as a RAM disk. When it has successfully booted, the Red Hat Linux for Sparc installation program starts and then you are prompted through the install process.

To boot from the CD-ROM or floppy, you must give the appropriate command and arguments to OpenBoot. When it starts to boot from either of these two devices, the installation program loads and the resulting program is very similar to the Intel-based version.

CAUTION

Some models of the UltraSparc systems contain a bug in the OpenBoot firmware, which prevents booting from the floppy device. If this is the case for your system, you may still install using either the Net boot or the CD-ROM boot options.

Part

I

Ch

5

Creating Installation Disks

If you are not capable of booting via CD-ROM or Net boot, then you might have to create the installation disks so that you can begin the install process. For this you will need two new or freshly formatted 1.44 floppy disks and a computer running either DOS/Windows, Linux, or SunOS/Solaris to transfer the disk images to the floppies. The boot image file you must use to create the first floppy boot disk depends on what architecture you are using to install Linux— use boot32.img for sparc32 platforms, or boot64.img for sparc64 platforms. For the second floppy disk, you must use the same disk image file (ramdisk.img) regardless of architecture.

To make the installation boot disks on a PC under MS-DOS, you will need to first obtain the utility named `rawrite.exe`, which can be found on the Red Hat Linux CD-ROM. This program is located in the directory named `dosutils` and can be run directly from the CD-ROM or copied to the local hard drive of the PC. When you run `rawrite`, it will prompt you for the path to the image file, and then what drive letter your floppy is on. The following is an example of how to use the `rawrite` command:

```
C:\>rawrite
Enter disk image source file name: D:\images\imagename
Enter target disk drive: a
Please insert a formatted disk into drive A: and press -ENTER- :
C:\
```

After you have entered in the necessary information, it will then transfer the contents of the image file to the floppy disk, thus producing a bootable installation disk.

To use the SunOS/Solaris environments to create the floppies from the disk images, it should be pointed out that there is a difference in commands that must be issued depending on whether you have SunOS or Solaris without Volume Manager or Solaris with Volume Manager. Listed here are the actual commands that you will need to use, depending on the type of system you are building the floppy disks from. Be sure to use the appropriate command for your respective system only. Also, the term *imagename* in the following commands should be replaced with the name of boot image file—`boot32.img` or `boot64.img`—depending on your destination architecture.

For SunOS system and Solaris systems without Volume Manager (vold) running, use the following:

```
dd if=imagename of=/dev/rdiskette bs=1440k
```

For Solaris systems with Volume Manager (vold) running, you must use this:

```
volcheck
dd if=imagename of=/vol/dev/aliases/floppy0 bs=1440k
eject floppy0
```

Repeat the process for the second floppy disk, this time using the name of the second floppy disk image filename: `ramdisk.img`.

To create the installation disks using the Linux environment, you will either have to be logged in as the root user or will need permission to write to the floppy disk drive. After you have permission to write to the floppy drive or are logged in as the root user, you can insert the disk into the floppy drive, but do not mount the disk with the `mount` command. Change to the directory where you have the necessary floppy disk images, `boot32.img` or `boot64.img`, and then issue the following command at the prompt:

```
dd if=imagename of=/dev/fd0 bs=1440k
```

Repeat the process for the second floppy disk, this time using the name of the second floppy disk image file name: `ramdisk.img`.

Preparing for Net Boot Installation

If you cannot boot from a floppy or CD-ROM, or you are deploying multiple Linux installations at once, you will find net booting quite useful. Net booting will enable you to perform multiple installations at once, and can make your administration of re-installs easier over the long term. However, preparing for a network boot can be a lengthy exercise if you have not set up the prerequisite environment. This is discussed in the following sections.

The RARP Server

This is required for assigning an IP address. The RARP server is a remote machine on the local network that answers requests by the machine that broadcasts its Ethernet address as a lookup query for an IP address.

Before you can begin to set up the RARP server, you must know the Ethernet address of the machine that will be served by the RARP server. This Ethernet address (also called a *MAC address*) can usually be found printed on the back or bottom of your Sparc machine, printed on the Ethernet card itself, or displayed on the screen by OpenBoot during initial system bootup. This address is in the format of six hexadecimal numbers, each separated by a colon, such as 31:07:03:62:06:84.

The first step in setting up the RARP server under Solaris is to make sure that the Ethernet address is in the ethers database, which is stored in /etc/ethers or in NIS/NIS+ databases. The format for the /etc/ethers file is similar to the one that follows:

```
00:80:5f:95:65:10      supernova
00:08:c7:fa:a1:c4      supernova-2
08:00:20:88:84:21      darkstar
31:07:03:62:06:84      blackhole-sun
```

The second step in setting up a RARP server under SunOS/Solaris is to add the entries for the machines you want to net boot into the /etc/hosts file. This is used by the RARP server to cross-reference the hostname of the new machine with the IP number it should be assigned. The format for the hosts file under Solaris is as follows:

```
127.0.0.1      localhost
192.168.2.2    supernova loghost
192.168.2.3    supernova-2
192.168.2.4    darkstar
192.168.2.5    blackhole-sun
```

For information on how to build the ethers and hosts databases in NIS/NIS+, consult the appropriate reference materials with SunOS/Solaris.

The final step in setting up the RARP server under Sun/Solaris is to make sure that you are running the RARP daemon. If you are not running it, simply start it with this line:

```
/usr/sbin/in.rarpd -a
```

If you want to use a Linux machine, on the other hand, your job is a little simpler. To do this, first make sure that the new IP number and hostname are entered into the /etc/hosts file, and then populate the kernel's RARP table with the following commands:

```
/sbin/rarp -s blackhole-sun  31:07:03:62:06:84
/sbin/arp -s 192.168.2.5  31:07:03:62:06:84
```

N O T E If the RARP server does not seem to work, try changing the MAC addresses so that it does not have the padded zeros.

For example, changing 31:07:03:62:06:84 into 31:7:3:62:6:84 might resolve the problem with some RARP caches. ■

The TFTPboot Server

This is required for downloading the boot kernel file. The Trivial File Transfer Protocol (TFTP) server will answer specific requests for the boot image file by TFTP clients and then will transfer that file to the client.

The first step in creating the TFTP boot server is to edit the /etc/inetd.conf file and uncomment the line that refers to the tftpd daemon. If you modify the /etc/inetd.conf file, be sure to send the SIGHUP (kill HUP inetd) signal to the inetd process so that it reloads the configuration file. Then you will need to create the /tftpboot directory and copy the appropriate file listed here into the /tftpboot directory.

If you have 16MB of RAM or more, copy the following file for your architecture to the /tftpboot directory.

```
/images/tftp32.img — for Sun4c and Sun4m
/images/tftp64.img — for UltraSparc
```

If you have less than 16MB of RAM, you will have to use an NFS-mounted root disk. For this you must use the following respective kernel file for your architecture class.

```
/kernels/vmlinux32 — for Sun4c and Sun4m
/kernels/vmlinux64 — for UltraSparc
```

Next, you will need to make a pointer file, or a symbolic link, to identify the server to be booted to the TFTP daemon. The convention for doing this is hexIP.archname, where hexIP represents the IP address (in hexadecimal format) and archname represents the architecture of the system.

An easy way to determine the IP address in hexadecimal is to use Perl, an interpreted programming language that is installed on a majority of Unix systems. To do this, you can use the following command; just replace the address of 192.168.2.5 with your own address.

```
perl -e 'printf "%02x"x4 ."\n",192,168,2,5;' | tr "[:lower:]" "[:upper:]"
```

In this example, this produces the following output:

```
C0A80205
```

Now you can create the symbolic link using this hexadecimal number as the first part of your name; the second part of the name will be based on the machines hardware name (class), such as sun4u or sun4m. In this example, sun4U is used. Create the link, using all uppercase characters, such as follows:

```
ln -s /tftpboot/tftp64.img /tftpboot/C0A80205.SUN4U
```

 TIP Some versions of OpenBoot contain a bug that actually makes requests to the TFTP server that specify only the hexadecimal IP address, not the architecture class. If your machine does not begin to load the image file via TFTP, try making another symbolic link without the architecture class specified, such as `ln -s /tftpboot/tftp64.img /tftpboot/C0A80205.`

The NFS Server (Optional)

This is required when your Sparc machine has less than 16MB of RAM and cannot load the entire root file system partition into memory as a mounted RAM disk. In this case, the booting system must mount an exported NFS file system from a remote server, which contains the Red Hat Linux for SPARC CD-ROM file system, which will function as the root file system partition during the installation phase.

To set this up, you will need to mount the CD-ROM under an operating system that is capable of exporting the CD-ROM drive as an NFS shared resource. For Solaris, this is accomplished with the following command:

```
share -F nfs -o ro /cdrom/cdrom0
```

For Linux, you must edit the /etc/exports file and create the following entry to refer to wherever you mounted the CD-ROM.

```
/mnt/cdrom          (ro,no_root_squash)
```

For other operating systems, refer to your reference guide on how to share/export a mounted file system.

Booting Linux

To boot your Sparc system with Linux, you must first tell OpenBoot the medium you have selected to boot from. To do this, you must first get to the OpenBoot command prompt. If your system is still running SunOS/Solaris, reboot it. If it's turned off, turn it on. When the monitor powers on and you see that the system is initializing memory, press the combined keys—Stop+A—at the same time. (Depending on the type of keyboard you have, you might have a key labeled L1 instead of the Stop key. In this case, use the combination L1+A

Part

I

Ch

5

simultaneously.) At this point, the boot process is halted, and you should have dropped into the OpenBoot command prompt. If this was successful, your screen should look like the following representation:

```
Sun Ultra 2 UPA/Sbus (2 X UltraSPARC-II 296MHz), Keyboard Present
OpenBoot 3.11, 256 MB memory installed, Serial #0112267
Ethernet address 31:07:03:62:06:84, Host ID: 12752252.

Initializing Memory /
{0} ok _
```

NOTE Remember, if your OpenBoot prompt displays a > instead of the ok, then you have a version prior to 2.0 of OpenBoot, and your commands will vary from the newer version commands. Refer to "Understanding Installation Differences for Sparc," earlier in this chapter for more information. ▨

Floppy Boot

To boot OpenBoot 2.0 versions and greater from the floppy drive, be sure that the boot floppy is in the appropriate drive, and then simply type the following command:

```
boot floppy
```

For versions before 2.0 of OpenBoot, issue this command:

```
b fd()
```

After you have issued the boot command, you will be presented with the SILO boot: prompt. If you take no action, SILO will time out and continue the default boot process. To get a listing of additional boot options, press the Tab key.

CD-ROM Boot

To boot OpenBoot 2.0 versions and greater from the CD-ROM, be sure that the boot CD-ROM is in the appropriate drive, and then simply type the following command:

```
boot cdrom
```

For versions before 2.0 of OpenBoot (assuming that your CD-ROM is at SCSI-ID #6), issue this command:

```
b sd(0,6,0)
```

NOTE Most Sparc systems prior to OpenBoot release 2.0 might not be capable of booting from the CD-ROM. If this is the case, you will have to boot the system using floppy disks or the net boot option. ▨

After you have issued the boot command, you will be presented with the SILO boot: prompt. If you take no action, SILO will time out and continue the default boot process. To get a listing of additional boot options, press the Tab key.

Network Boot

To boot OpenBoot version 2.0 and greater from the network, be sure that you have fulfilled the prerequisites under "Preparing for Net Boot Installation," earlier in this chapter, and then use the following command to boot your system:

```
boot net
```

If you plan to use an NFS mounted root partition, use the same command, but with the following argument format:

```
boot net linux nfsroot=192.168.2.5:/cdrom/cdrom0
```

Systems with older PROM versions can use this command for booting:

```
b hme()
```

Or, in the case of mounting the root partition via NFS, use the following:

```
b hme() linux nfsroot=nfs.server.IP.address:/cdrom/cdrom0
```

Managing the Installation Process

When the boot is successful for whatever option you chose, your Sparc system's screen should change from the default white background with black characters to the standard Linux black background with white text while the kernel loads. After it has successfully loaded, the kernel will begin the installation program, which will launch with the blue background and a character-based menu program.

Part

I

Ch

5

Navigation

To navigate the installation menus, use your Tab key to move forward from one element to the next, and use Alt+Tab to move backward through the elements. To make selections within the elements, use your up-arrow and down-arrow keys on your keyboard/keypad and the spacebar to actually select an option. The Enter key is to be used when you are finished making your selections and are ready to continue to the next screen.

Welcome

The first screen should simply welcome you to the Red Hat Linux for Sparc installation. If you see this screen, congratulations—the hardest parts are over. Press Enter to continue to the next screen.

Choose Your Language

On the next screen, the installation program gives you the opportunity to choose what language should be used during the installation process. While this has no effect on what language version of software is installed, it can make your initial setup easier if your native language is something other than English. Use your up-arrow and down-arrow keys to choose a language, and press the Enter key when you have made your selection.

Choose Your Keyboard

The next screen enables you to choose the keyboard mappings that you wish to use for your keyboard. This is important if you have a non-U.S. keyboard layout and you want to have your keys mapped to what is actually labeled on the keycaps. If you're not sure what type of keyboard you have, you can check on the underside of the keyboard, where you should find a label indicating the model and language layout. If you are still not sure, then try the default selection sunkeymap.

Choose the Installation Method

Next, you are presented with a choice of what source media options are available to you for installing the remainder of the Linux software:

- **Local CD-ROM**—If you have a local CD-ROM drive and the Red Hat Linux for SPARC CD, then you may use this option. If you booted from the CD-ROM, this is the only valid option for you.

- **NFS image**—If you have the Red Hat Linux for Sparc files on an exported or shared NFS file system and you want to install them via the NFS mounting mechanism, then you will want this option.

- **Hard drive**—If you have the files on a local second hard drive and they are stored on that hard drive on an ext2 Linux file system, then you may mount that hard drive with this option and copy them across.

- **FTP**—If your files are accessible on an FTP server on your local or remote network, you can proceed with this option, which logs in to the FTP server and copies all the files needed to install Linux, and then uncompresses and installs them.

- **HTTP**—If your files are accessible via a Web server on a local or remote network, you can use this option, which downloads and installs all the files for your Linux installation from the Web server.

If you are installing from a CD-ROM or a hard drive, you can skip to the section "Installation Path (All Installs)" because the following information is relevant only for network installs.

Boot Protocol (NFS, FTP, or HTTP Installs Only)

On this page, you will need to instruct your system on how it will gain its identity on the network to gain access to the network resource of your choice that is serving the installation files. The choices are manual assignment of static IP numbers, or automatic assignment of IP numbers from a BootP, or DHCP server located on your network. If you are unsure of what any of this means, contact your network administrator for more information.

Configure TCP/IP (NFS, FTP, or HTTP Installs Only)

This screen will display only if you have chosen the static IP address option on the previous screen. If you are unaware of what the following values are, contact your network administrator for this information.

Here, you will be prompted for the following information:

- **IP address**—This is the TCP/IP network address that will be assigned to this machine. An example of this would be 192.168.2.5.

- **Netmask**—This is the netmask assigned to the local network, and should look similar to a value of 255.255.255.0. This value is used to determine the address of the network itself and the broadcast address of the network, thus defining the size of the local TCP/IP network or subnetwork.

- **Default gateway**—This is the address of a router or server that acts as a gateway to other networks or subnetworks.

- **Primary nameserver**—This is the IP address of a server that translates domain names (such as www.linux.org) to IP numbers, and vice versa.

Configure Network (NFS, FTP, or HTTP Installs Only)

This screen might or might not appear, depending on whether the install process was capable of determining your host name, domain name, and additional DNS servers on your network:

- **Domain name**—Here you will need to specify the domain name that this computer resides in. An example of this would be mcpeake.com.

- **Host name**—This is the actual name that will be assigned to the host. The installation program of Red Hat Linux will automatically append the domain name specified in the previous field to the hostname you enter here to build what is commonly known as the Fully Qualified Domain Name (FQDN). In this example, if entered in the hostname of supernova, the fully qualified domain name of supernova.mcpeake.org will be displayed here.

- **Secondary nameserver (IP)**—If you have secondary DNS servers on your network, you should enter the IP address of one of them here. This is vital for domain name resolution when the primary DNS server fails or is slow to respond.

Part

I

Ch

5

■ **Tertiary nameserver (IP)**—If you have a DNS server that is external to your organization, such as those provided by your Internet Service provider, you can put the IP address of such a server into this field.

NFS/FTP/HTTP Setup (NFS, FTP, and HTTP Installs Only)

The next screen that will appear might vary slightly depending on your install method, but it is basically the same as this:

■ **Site or server name**—This is the name of the server where the files are stored. You may use either an IP address or the hostname of the server you are installing from. If you are specifying a server external to the domain that you are currently in, be sure to use the FQDN in this location.

■ **Directory**—This is the full directory path, as offered by the network resource server to the directory that contains the Red Hat subdirectory (not the Red Hat directory itself).

■ **Proxy settings**—If you are installing from an FTP or HTTP server that is external to your local network and you must access a proxy server to be able to get data from the external networks when using these protocols, you can enter specific information about your proxy server here. In addition, for FTP installs, you can enter your login information to the FTP server, if the FTP server is not an anonymous server.

Installation Path (All Installs)

At this point, you will be given a choice between upgrading a previous system and installing a new system. Unless you are installing Linux for the very first time on this system or want to delete your previous installation of Linux, be sure to choose Upgrade.

Installation Class (New Installations Only)

On this screen, you can choose between a standard workstation installation and a server installation, in which case a set of predefined software programs for use with the respective role you plan to use this machine for will be installed. These two choices will also cause the installation program to evaluate your disk size and determine automatically how they should be partitioned and formatted. These choices are especially recommended for beginning Linux users.

For more advanced users, or for those who wish to have more control over what is installed, you can choose Custom to install packages based on specific functionality groups. (such as graphic design or C/C++ development). You will also be required to manually determine the placement of the various partitions required by Linux. While you will have the choice of using one of two tools provided by the Install package, if you are not familiar with how the Linux file system is structured, it is recommended that you take one of the two previously mentioned options.

Creating File Systems

Creating the file systems is a crucial step in any Linux installation because how you plan to use your Linux system will have direct bearing on how you will want to lay out the partitions on your hard drive. Linux, like its UNIX cousins, uses a distributed file system, which allows separate file systems to be mounted onto mount points (often other directories) of an existing file system. This enables an administrator to segregate separate functions of a file system from other functions, while preserving a single contiguous hierarchical directory structure. For example, a Linux system might have its / directory on one partition, while /usr might exist on a separate partition, and /usr/local exists as a third mount point for another partition. This allows each separate file system to be addressed just as an ordinary directory but separates the file systems for the purposes of file system integrity or load distribution. This could be useful in spreading the load of a database server across multiple hard drives or ensuring enough drive space on a partition for system logs, regardless of the available space on other partitions.

The increased functionality and flexibility of the distributed file system, however, does have a minor trade off. It requires some planning and considerable forethought into the creation of the base partitions, as this has direct results on both capacity and intended use of the file system.

Managing Disk Setup (Custom Installations Only)

Here, you have the choice of using one of two tools to partition your hard drives: Disk Druid and fdisk.

Disk Druid is a text menu-based partitioning utility that can make the installation process easier in most cases because it can perform the most common partitioning functions. You can specify the mount points and also decide how that partition should be used (for example, as a root file system or as a swap partition). This is the tool of choice for most users, whether beginning or advanced.

fdisk, on the other hand, is a far more powerful partitioning tool. Unlike the MS-DOS partitioning tool by the same name, fdisk gives you almost full control over the partition tables of your hard drive. It also enables you to create and manage partitions from almost any other operating system. However, the user interface of fdisk is less intuitive than Disk Druid. Unless you have some special partitioning requirements that require the functionality of fdisk, you should find that Disk Druid will handle most of your partitioning needs.

Partitioning Disks (New Installations Only)

In partitioning your disk, you should remember that the Linux file system is almost identical to other UNIX file systems in that it utilizes what is known as the Distributed File System architecture. With this, you can mount other disk devices onto directories and subdirectories rather than the standard DOS drive devices such as C: and D:. In other words, your first drive is always mounted as the root directory, which is /, while your second drive or partition could be mounted on /usr, and your third drive could be mounted on /home.

Within a short time of using Linux, you will begin to see the usefulness and flexibility this provides. If your /home directory becomes full with files, you can archive everything in that directory, install a new disk, mount the new disk to /home, and unarchive everything back into that directory. Your paths and various data links will remain unaltered, and no further modifications to installed libraries are necessary. The drive structure becomes transparent, and you are required as a user only to navigate directories, not hard drives. As an administrator, however, you must take the planned use of the directories into account during the partitioning of your drives. For example, if this system is to have a large number of multiple users, then it is best to leave enough room for those users in the /home file system. If you are planning to install a lot of additional software, it is best to give the partition you dedicate to the /usr file system enough room so that you can add programs to it later.

At a minimum, all Linux systems must have the root file system /. However, it is preferable on medium to large installations of Linux to split up the file systems. This is due to the fact that, with the exception of the /home, /usr, and /var directories, most of the files just off the root / directory are not written to by the hard drive after initial bootup. By splitting up the root file system onto its own dedicated partition (which is often less than 50–100 MB), you can achieve better resiliency against damage to the necessary files required for a bootup if the system crashes or a disk error occurs on partitions that are being constantly written to. By protecting the root file system in this manner, you can more often than not ensure at least a boot into single user mode, which is often crucial to recovering the remaining file systems and data.

To help you understand the basic common directories on Linux, the following is presented as a rough guide to assist you in deciding how to partition your own system. These are not recommendations, but merely an example based on a single 1GB hard drive, which has 130MB reserved for a swap partition:

```
/        - root file system - 100 MB - files for basic system booting
/usr     - user file system - 500 MB - files required for full operating system
/var     - var(iable) file system - 50 MB - System logs, file locks
/usr/local  - local file system - 320 MB - additional & customized software
```

You might not have the need or desire for all these partitions, and you may rather allocate only a / partition and a /usr partition. In such cases, you must remember that your "var" directory will be located on the / partition, and your "local" directory will be located in the /usr partition, and thus you should be sure to allocate the necessary space to both of these directories to compensate.

N O T E   Many GNU-based and commercial server programs install to default subdirectories located in /home, /opt, or /var. If you choose to use such a program that will be writing large amounts of data to the hard drive or placing the hard drive under heavy load—such as MySQL, Oracle, or Lotus Notes—it is highly recommended that you create a dedicated partition, mounted on that particular subdirectory path, on which to store the databases. This will help protect the other partitions from problems if such an application experiences or causes write-errors on that partition.

Furthermore, by configuring database servers to use a total different partition on which to store their data, the overall risk of data corruption is reduced because specific file systems are created and responsible for specific functions. For example, the /var directory is preserved for system logs and accounting.

To further ensure data protection in the case of drive failure and increase performance of such an application, consider installing a second (or more) drive dedicated to the purpose of storing this data.

The previous example mentioned the use of a swap partition, but this wasn't included in the listing. That is because swap space is a part of the file system that has been allocated to act as a type of virtual RAM. This virtual RAM is not part of the file system that will directly be accessible for your use, but the system instead uses it when it has run out of all available free space in actual physical RAM. This is useful for systems with less than enough actual physical RAM to properly run programs. It is recommended that you allocate a minimum of twice the actual physical RAM you have installed on your system. Thus, if you have 32MB of RAM installed, you should allocate a minimum of 64MB of RAM to your swap partition.

Linux refers to both your hard drives and the individual partitions on your hard drives by specific device nodes located in the /dev directory. These device nodes are the means by which Linux refers to the actual hardware stored on your system. As such, these device nodes have names that bear some resemblance to what they perform. For example, your first IDE-based hard drive on your system will be represented by a node in the /dev directory called hda, while your second IDE hard drive would be represented hdb. Alternatively, a SCSI drive would be represented by the sd prefix and a letter behind it to refer to its numerical position in the SCSI chain—for example, a SCSI drive with the SCSI ID jumper set to 3 would be reflected in the /dev directory as sdc.

As you allocate one or more partitions to your hard drives, Linux assigns each individual partition its own device node, in the order that the partitions are assigned. For instance, if you assign the root partition to your first SCSI drive on the SCSI chain, it will end up with the device node of /dev/sda1. If you assign the /var partition to your second SCSI drive on the chain and then the /usr partition to the same drive immediately after that, those partitions will be assigned the nodes of /dev/sdb1 and /dev/sdb2 respectively.

After you have assigned these partitions, you may continue with the installation process.

Part

I

Ch

5

Granting Active Swap Space

Here you are presented with a screen that enables you to decide whether to use the allocated partitions as swap space. Be sure to check that this is the actual device node you meant to be assigned for use as a swap partition. It is recommended to select the option to check for bad blocks on your drive, as this will mark any bad blocks as unusable for later use and will help prevent this from causing errors during normal Linux operation.

Using Partitions for Format

Here again, you are prompted for final confirmation to format the listed partitions. If all listed partitions are newly created partitions, it is required that you format them. If the partitions such as /home or /opt or /usr/local already exist from a previous installation and their partition values have not been changed, it is not necessary to reformat these drives if you wish to preserve the data and files on them.

It is recommended to also check these newly formatted partitions for bad blocks.

Choosing Software to Install

After you have selected which partitions to format, you can then select which components of the operating system to install. These so-called components are basically groups of various applications defined by the functionality they provide to the end user. If you want to use your Linux installation as a desktop focused toward graphic design, you might want to choose components such as X multimedia support and Graphics Manipulation, as well as GNOME and KDE window managers.

If you are not sure of what you want and you have more than 1GB of space allocated to the /usr partition, you can select the Everything option at the bottom of the list, in which all components and packages are installed to your hard drive.

If you want more than the predefined components but do not want to install everything, you can also choose the option at the bottom to select individual packages, in which case you will have total control of what programs and services are installed onto your Linux system. To get information about a particular package and what it contains, you can highlight it with your cursor, and then press the F1 key.

After you select the components and packages you want to install, select OK and continue with the install. The installation program then proceeds to format your selected partitions on your hard disks and then begins the installation process of all the selected software.

Configuring the Operating System

Now that the installation program has completed, you must make a final configuration of the operating system so it is ready to run when it reboots. This is necessary because you might be deploying your system on another network than the one you originally installed, or you need to configure whether you want a graphical user interface or a text-based console interface at boot up. By making the final changes to your configuration during the installation process, you can expect to start using Linux sooner than you would if you had to configure the system after the initial bootup.

Network Configuration

If you have previously chosen to install Linux from an NFS, FTP, or HTTP server, you will be prompted for the opportunity to keep your current network settings, reconfigure your network settings, or deactivate your network settings. The choice you make here often depends on whether your network environment will remain the same as it was during the install process or if it will change.

If you performed the installation from a CD-ROM or a local hard drive, then you will now be prompted for the opportunity to set up your permanent network settings.

Here, you will be prompted for the following information:

- **IP address**—This is the TCP/IP network address that will be assigned to this machine. If for example, your machine is on the network address of 192.168.2.0 and your netmask is 255.255.255.0, then your machine could be assigned any IP address, but not including 192.168.2.0–192.168.2.255. An example of this would be 192.168.2.5.
- **NetMask**—This is the NetMask assigned to the local network, and it should look similar to a value of 255.255.255.0. This value is used to determine the address of the network itself and the broadcast address of the network, thus defining the size of the local TCP/IP network or subnetwork.
- **Default gateway**—This is address of a router or server that acts as a gateway to other networks or subnetworks.
- **Primary nameserver**—This is the IP address of a server that translates domain names (such as www.linux.org) to IP numbers, and vice versa.

For more information on TCP/IP protocols, *Internetworking with TCP/IP, Volume 1: Principles, Protocols and Architecture*, by Douglas E. Comer (Prentice Hall, Third Edition, 1995) is an excellent source of material on the subject.

Part

I

Ch

5

Configure Network (NFS, FTP, or HTTP Installs Only)

This screen might or might not appear, depending on whether the install process was capable of determining your hostname, domain name, and additional DNS servers on your network.

- **Domain name**—Here, you will need to specify the domain name that this computer resides in. An example of this would be mcpeake.com.

- **Hostname**—This is the actual name that will be assigned to the host. The installation program of Red Hat Linux will automatically append the domain name specified in the previous field to the hostname you enter here to build what is commonly known as the Fully Qualified Domain Name (FQDN). In an example, if entered in the hostname of supernova, the fully qualified domain name of supernova.mcpeake.org will be displayed here.

- **Secondary nameserver (IP)**—If you have secondary DNS servers on your network, you should enter the IP address of one of them here. This is vital for domain name resolution when the primary DNS server fails or is slow to respond.

- **Tertiary nameserver (IP)**—If you have a DNS server external to your organization, such as those provided by your Internet service provider, you can put the IP address of such a server into this field.

Configure Time Zones

Select the time zone that best reflects your location. You also have the option of standardizing on Greenwich Mean Time.

Services

Now you have the choice of selecting the various daemons, or server processes, that will automatically start during bootup of the Linux system you have just installed. Several of these services include functionality such as serving email or allowing other users to mount your hard drives remotely.

If you're not sure what a particular service is in this list, use your arrow keys to move the cursor to the service in question, and then press the F1 key to display the appropriate description of that service.

Configure Printer

If you plan to print from your Linux system, you may configure your printer in the following screens. If you choose to, you will be prompted on the various screens for configuration information such as whether it is a local or remote printer and, if it is a remote printer, what type of network resource is acting as the printer server. You also must provide the necessary login information for that printer server, printer queue name, and so on.

Select Printer Connection   On the Select Printer Connection screen you will need to choose one of the four following options to define how your printer is connected to your system:

- **Local**—The printer is connected directly to your system by means of a parallel printer cable.

- **Remote lpd**—Your Linux system will connect to another UNIX or Linux host that services print requests to the printer connected to it, via the lpd (Line Printer Daemon) service.

- **SMB/Windows 95/NT**—Your Linux system will connect to a Windows-based system or a server running the SMB server protocol (such as a UNIX host providing Windows file and print services via Samba), which services remote print requests for its locally connected printer.

- **NetWare**—Your Linux system will connect to a Novell NetWare-based server or a server running NetWare services that services remote print requests for its locally connected printer.

Standard Printer Options   The Standard Printer Options screen enables you to define the name of the printer queue that Linux will use and in which directory on your file system those queued files will be stored until they are sent to your printer for processing.

Local Printer Device   If your printer is connected to the applicable port, the installation program will attempt to autodetect it. If this is not successful or not correct, change this to the correct setting. Keep in mind that Linux device names begin with a numerical index of 0, as opposed to the DOS standard of 1. This means that if your printer is LPT1 under DOS, then you will need to assign this under Linux as /dev/lp0. However, because this is a Sparc machine, you probably weren't running DOS anyway before you installed Linux, were you?

Remote lpd Printer Options   For the remote hostname, you must provide the hostname of the UNIX/Linux server that is handling network print requests via its lpd service. You will also need to specify the name of the queue on the remote server. An example of this is lp.

SMB/Windows 95/NT Printer Options   To print to a remote printer serviced by a Windows-based machine, you will need to provide the following specific information about the appropriate Windows network. If you are unsure about the following information, check the Network Properties of the Windows machine providing the services, or in the case of a Samba server, check the smb.conf configuration file on the server:

Part
I

Ch
5

- **SMB server host**—This is the NetBIOS network name of the host providing the print services. This sometimes is the same as the TCP/IP hostname, but not always.

- **SMB server IP**—This is the TCP/IP Address of the host providing the print services.

- **Share name**—This is the actual name of the shared resource on the remote server. If you shared the printer on your Windows system with the designated name of lp, you would need to type lp in this field.

- **User name**—If a username is required to connect to this share (and it often is), you must input what you will connect as.

- **Password**—The appropriate password for the user account with which you are connecting (not always required).

- **Workgroup**—The name of the workgroup or NT domain in which the remote printer server resides. This is usually always required.

NetWare Printer Options To print to a remote printer serviced by a Novell or IPX-based server, you will need to provide the following specific information about the appropriate Novell network. If you are unsure about the following information, check the network configuration of the Novell server providing the print services.

- **Printer Server**—The name of the server providing Novell- or IPX-based print services. This might or might not be the same as the TCP/IP hostname.
- **Print Queue Name**—The name of the queue being serviced by the remote server.
- **User name**—The remote user name on the Novell server under which all remote print requests will be queued.
- **Password**—The appropriate password for the username you entered.

Configure Printer Scroll down the displayed list of printers until you find your printer, and select it. This will present you with specific options for your printer on the next screen.

Now you can make specific choices about your printer's configuration, such as resolution and paper size. If your printer does not automatically produce a carriage return after each line, you will need to check the Fix Stair-Stepping of Text option so that Linux will send this carriage return at the end of each line.

Verify Printer Configuration If all the information displayed is the correct configuration for your computer, select OK. If not, use the Back button to return to the previous screens and make the appropriate changes to your configuration.

Root Password

Now comes the critical part: selecting the password for the root user. It is important that you carefully select a good password for your system, that cannot easily be guessed by someone wanting to gain access to your system. This is especially true for systems that will be in environments where the data stored on the system is sensitive in nature.

Because the characters you type are not echoed back to the screen, you will need to type in the root password you have selected twice, to ensure that you did not make a typographic error.

Authentication Configuration

If your network makes use of Sun's Network Information Services (a.k.a. YP domains) for storing and managing systems and user accounts, you can enable your Linux system to connect to such servers and make use of NIS authentication services.

Shadow passwords is the name given to a more secure version of the old standard password databases used in older releases of Unix systems. Shadow passwords help increase system security by maintaining the password information in a separate database from the user information. This separate password database has increased security by means of restricted file permissions, and it prevents normal users from copying the database of encrypted passwords. However, some older legacy applications that depend on the functionality of the authentication mechanisms of the OS are not capable of properly working with Shadow passwords, and you might need to turn this off to run those applications.

For the majority of users, this is best left on. Regardless of your choice here, you may use the pwconv and pwunconv commands after installation to convert to or from using shadowed password files.

It is also highly recommended to leave the MD5 password option enabled because this enables you to use more than eight characters for your passwords.

SILO Installation

Here you are prompted to install the boot loader for Linux. SILO works very much like the Intel version of Linux's LILO, can mostly be configured in the same way, and can prompt at boot time to boot different operating systems, such as Linux, SunOS, Solaris, and BSD.

SILO is most often best installed at the master boot record of your hard disk unless you plan to use a different mechanism for deciding what operating system to boot at startup.

If Linux is the only OS on this system, your only choice will be to install it on the master boot record.

If you need to pass additional arguments to the Linux kernel during boot, you can enter these now.

SILO Boot Loader

In this section, you can configure the SILO boot loader to launch other operating systems. However, in Red Hat release 6.0, this functionality doesn't work, and you must configure this after you have completed the installation.

The configuration of SILO is similar to LILO on the Intel platform. The following example configures SILO to present an option to boot either Solaris or Linux at boot time. This example also makes the assumption that the Solaris root partition is on /dev/sda1.

The format for an entry for Solaris into the /etc/silo.conf file is as follows:

```
image = 1/kernel/unix
    label=solaris
    literal="-s" (optional)
    solaris
```

Part

I

Ch

5

The `image` tag defines the path to your `unix` image. This is relative to the `/platform/`*`your_platform_name_here`*`/` on your Solaris root partition. The number 1 tells SILO that this is stored on your `/dev/sda1` partition of your hard drive. So in another example, if you were configuring SILO on an Ultra2 Sparc and the Solaris root partition was on the fifth partition of your first drive, you would need an entry like `image = 5/kernel/unix`. SILO then would automatically determine that this is relative to the `/platform/sun4u/` directory on the fifth partition.

The `label` flag defines the name of the boot option you want to be prompted with for this configuration. In this example it is defined as `solaris`.

The `literal` tag will hand over additional arguments at boot time to the Solaris kernel. This is useful if you want to have more than one Solaris option, each one configured for a specific boot flag. In this example, the flag for single-user mode is defined.

The last tag, `solaris`, defines a mode of special handling for SILO to boot Solaris. This is required for all Solaris boot entries in SILO.

After the additions have been made into `/etc/silo.conf`, it is not necessary to rerun the `silo` command like it is to run `lilo` on the Intel platform. SILO can read and understand the ext2 file system at boot time and will reread the boot parameters in `/etc/silo.conf` at boot.

X Windows Configuration

On this screen, Linux attempts to identify the particular graphics card/frame buffer that you have installed on your system, and then immediately installs the necessary X windows server for that card. After this has installed, Linux configures it for the maximum graphic options and prompts you to test the configuration. When you have a successful X Windows test, you will be prompted for the choice of having X Windows start at bootup too. If you choose yes to this option, X Windows will begin at bootup and will present you with a graphical-based login manager screen. If not, you will be given a text-based console login at bootup; after login, you may start X Windows with the `startx` command.

Note that it is often desirable not to have X Windows start up by default at boot time on systems destined for use as servers. Because X Windows is network aware, this is especially true for systems providing a public service, such as a Web, FTP, or mail server on an unprotected network like the Internet. On the flip side of the coin, if the system is to be used as a desktop client on a private network, then running X Windows at bootup will help enhance the end user experience by providing the user with an easy-to-use graphical interface.

For more information on X Windows and the various security issues surrounding it, *Practical Unix & Internet Security*, by Simson Garfinkel and Gene Spafford (O'Reilly, 2nd Edition, 1996) is an excellent source of information.

Congratulations, Your Installation is Complete

At this point, you should have an installed and configured Linux operating system on your Sparc system. Here you can select OK on your screen, and the install program will cease to run after giving the command to reboot the system. If you have a CD-ROM in the drive bay, remove it.

Almost immediately after OpenBoot loads, you should see the SILO boot prompt, which will time out after approximately 5 to 10 seconds. Before this time out, you can use the Tab key to get a list of available boot labels, if SILO is configured for more than one. If you type nothing and wait for the time out, or if you hit the Enter key, your newly installed system should begin to load the Linux kernel and begin the boot process. You'll be able to tell this is working when the monitor inverts to white text on a black background and you are presented with the icon of the Linux penguin logo at the top of your screen, as the rest of your OS loads.

If you see this, you're on your way. Happy Linux-ing!

Troubleshooting Sparc Installations

Due to the constraints placed on manufacturers of Sun and Sun-compatible hardware, various bugs with Linux on Sparc are not as prevalent as on other platforms. Still, a few can trip up what should be a painless installation.

Known Caveats/Problems

The following is a listing of discovered bugs with Red Hat 6.0 for Sparc.

■ **`/platform/kernel/unix` not found at boot**—After installation, this problem might arise with booting from OpenBoot. To resolve this, reboot the system and use the Stop (or L1 key)+A key combination to stop the boot, and enter the OpenBoot PROM prompt. Use the `printenv` and `setenv` commands to change the entry for `boot-file`. Either delete the entry for this reference, or replace the current line with the word *linux*.

■ **Networking doesn't seem to work after boot up**—If networking doesn't seem to work, you might have enabled support for pcmcia. To disable pcmcia, use the following commands:

```
rm -f /etc/sysconfig/pcmcia
/etc/rc.d/init.d/network stop
/etc/rc.d/init.d/network start
```

■ **I want to perform a serial installation, but everything still outputs to the screen**—You may resolve this by one of two ways. Either disconnect the keyboard from the Sparc system and then power on the system, or use the following two commands at the boot prompt to redirect all input and output to the serial port. Be sure to note which serial port you are connected to, and use the appropriate argument (ttya or ttyb) for the respective port (serial A or B).

```
setenv input-device ttya
setenv output-device ttyb
```

Make sure your terminal emulator or device is set for 9600bps 8,n,1. Boot the machine, and you should see the system boot OpenBoot and then the operating system or the Installation boot disks.

■ **SILO doesn't timeout at bootup**—Execute the following commands in OpenBoot to correct this problem:

```
setenv boot-file linux
setenv auto-boot? True
```

■ **SILO doesn't show my SunOS/Solaris installation after installing Linux**—This is a known problem with SILO, and work is underway to fix this. You still can configure SILO to prompt you for a choice of Linux and other operating systems, but you must configure this after installing and rebooting into Linux. See the "SILO Boot Loader" section in this chapter for more information on how to configure SILO to recognize your SunOS/Solaris partition.

Find a New Problem?

Various other troubleshooting information, as well as the latest in bug fixes and upgrades, can be found on the Errata pages of Red Hat's Web site (http://www.redhat.com/), the UltraLinux Web site (http://www.ultralinux.org/), or in the /usr/doc directory of your Linux installation. ●

Installing the Linux Loader (LILO)

by Duane Hellums

In this chapter

Understanding LILO

When you first power up (boot) your PC, your computer system must follow a predefined sequence of events before you can actually use it. You must understand this sequence before you can properly and safely configure how to integrate Red Hat Linux 6.0 with your system. For simple systems, this entire process might be transparent to you, in which case you might need this chapter only in case of an emergency or if you eventually decide to expand or modify your boot sequence.

For example, Linux might be the only operating system you use with your PC, and you might never need to reconfigure your kernel to support specific or additional hardware. In such a case, you can continue to use the default boot sequence and emergency boot disk that you created during the initial installation. However, if you do need to access other operating systems, or if you modify your kernel and need to enable it properly, you will need to know about the boot loader.

Most modern operating systems provide a *flexible boot loader*, or a *boot manager*, as it is sometimes called. A boot loader is simply a small utility that enables you to choose which operating system to boot when you power up your PC. If you have multiple copies of the same operating system installed on a hard drive, a boot loader also enables you to choose which one to boot. The Linux Loader (LILO) is the boot loader currently used by the Linux community, and this loader is installed by default on your Red Hat Linux 6.0 system.

Understanding the Boot Sequence

When your PC is powered on, it immediately gets basic instructions from the basic input/ output system (BIOS). BIOS is nothing more than a chip located on your PC's motherboard that stores critical information about available hardware and user-defined configuration settings, such as the current date and time.

You interface with the BIOS through a setup program that you can access during the initial part of the boot sequence, if the security settings of your PC have this feature enabled. The look and feel of the BIOS setup program differ for each manufacturer, as does the method of accessing BIOS setup. Typically, you are prompted very early in the bootup process with a message about pressing the Del or F1 key to run the setup program. Most vendors provide a manual with new PCs that documents the motherboard features.

LILO does not store information in the BIOS, but Linux does need information that is stored there. For example, Linux must know the current date and time, how many hard drives you have, and what their parameters are (number of heads, cylinders or tracks, and sectors). The BIOS also is important because this is where you initially configure the boot sequence, independent of any boot loaders or operating systems that are installed on your PC.

For example, in one place in your BIOS you must define which hardware you can boot from, and in what order. I have configured my system's BIOS to boot from the CD-ROM, the floppy drive, and then the hard drive (your settings could be different). As a result, if a bootable CD (such as the one included with this book) is in the CD-ROM drive, the BIOS will perform all the functions it needs to and then will hand off control of my system to the initial instructions stored on the CD. If I don't have a bootable CD in the drive, the BIOS will proceed to look for a bootable floppy, and then a bootable hard drive. Some systems don't have bootable CD-ROMs and might choose not to allow booting from the floppy drive (for security reasons). In such a case, the system can be configured to boot directly to the hard drive when the BIOS initialization is complete.

Understanding How LILO Works

The LILO boot loader takes over control of the boot sequence only after the BIOS has performed its job and LILO receives control of the system's processing. This process is made possible by something called the Master Boot Record (MBR), which consists of information and instructions stored in the first sector of a disk (where your BIOS expects it). When properly configured and installed, LILO resides on a drive's MBR as a very small set of instructions that control the boot sequence according to the settings you have chosen.

Disk drives also can be split into smaller divisions, called *partitions*, which enable you to install different operating systems (or even multiple copies or versions of Linux) on a single system. Each partition has a boot record of its own, so LILO can reside on an individual partition's boot record. This can be very useful if you want to use a boot manager other than LILO that is already installed and configured on your MBR. All you have to do is add a boot option in your other boot manager that points to your Linux partition; when selected, this option will launch your LILO boot loader seamlessly.

> **CAUTION**
>
> To effectively use LILO and prevent problems with booting your system, you should become very familiar with all the hard drives, partitions, and operating systems currently on your system, if you're not already. Chapter 19, "Installing and Configuring Hard Drives," provides details on how to do this.

Part

I

Ch

6

One last thing to understand is that the LILO boot loader controls not only which drive and partition you can boot from, but also which Linux kernel (if you have more than one on a partition) is involved. A Linux *kernel* is the underlying set of instructions that provide all the basic components and functionality of your Linux system, including such things as support for hardware and networking. The kernel is extended further through the use of modules, which can be loaded during runtime (without rebuilding the kernel or rebooting). Chapter 18, "Installing and Configuring the Red Hat Linux Kernel," provides detailed information about Linux kernels and modules.

Installing and Accessing LILO

The LILO program is located in the sbin directory (/sbin/lilo), and its configuration file is stored in the etc directory (/etc/lilo.conf). You access and configure LILO using the Linux configuration tool, or LinuxConf. To ensure that the LILO and LinuxConf packages are installed, perform the following steps:

1. As the root user, select System, GnoRPM from your main Gnome menu and panel. You will see the Gnome RPM window.

2. Select Packages, System Environment, Base from the Gnome RPM window, and confirm that lilo-0.21-6 is listed in the package listing on the right.

3. Select Packages, Applications, System from the Gnome RPM window, and confirm that gnome-linuxconf-0.22-1 is listed on the right.

4. (Optional) If you want or need to use the text-based LinuxConf interface, select Packages, Applications, System from the Gnome RPM window, and confirm that linuxconf-1.14r4-4 is listed.

5. If LILO and LinuxConf aren't installed, you should follow the instructions outlined in Chapter 11, "Installing and Managing RPM Packages," to install them from this book's CD.

After you make sure you have the LILO and LinuxConf packages installed, you can proceed to launch LinuxConf, which will enable you to graphically configure LILO. Using LinuxConf, you no longer have to manually edit the /etc/lilo.conf configuration file and run the /sbin/lilo command to install LILO to the appropriate boot records. The steps to use LinuxConf are relatively straightforward:

1. As the root user, select System, LinuxConf from your main Gnome menu and panel. You will see the gnome-linuxconf window. As an alternative, you can run the command-line interface by typing /bin/linuxconf at the shell prompt.

2. Select Config, boot mode, Lilo from the gnome-linuxconf window. You will see six submenus, as shown in Figure 6.1 (note that the submenu LILO defaults [Linux boot loader] has been selected as well).

3. Click the specific LILO submenu you need to configure. One or more tabs will appear to the right in the LinuxConf window.

4. Make the appropriate changes to the available options (described later in the "Changing LILO Defaults" section), and click either the Accept button (to make changes) or Cancel (to ignore any changes made).

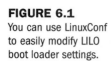

FIGURE 6.1
You can use LinuxConf to easily modify LILO boot loader settings.

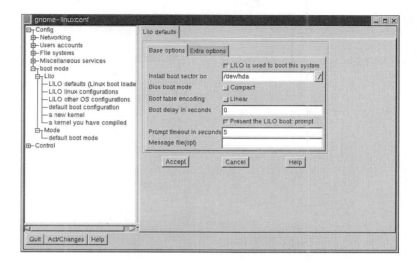

Booting to Other Operating Systems

One of the strengths of LILO is its capability of booting from multiple operating systems stored on hard drives and partitions throughout your PC. To use such an advanced feature with an operating system (OS) such as Windows 95, you normally must purchase a third-party utility. With LILO, you can have Windows 95, Windows NT, and Linux all on the same system, and you have the choice of booting up to any of the three you choose. You also can boot to OS/2 and other flavors of UNIX.

> **CAUTION**
>
> Boot managers for some operating systems are not as friendly and sensitive to your needs as Linux. For example, if you install or reinstall Windows 95 on any partition, that system automatically overwrites your MBR to boot the active partition (Windows 95) and ignores any boot manager options configured there previously. This effectively prevents you from accessing your Linux boot loader, operating system, and files—unless you have an emergency boot disk or choose to install a third-party boot manager and re-create all your configuration settings. I highly recommend that you keep an up-to-date emergency boot disk to preclude this type of problem.

Part

I

Ch

6

To configure additional operating systems in your `/etc/lilo.conf` configuration file, perform the following actions:

1. Select Config, boot mode, Lilo, LILO other OS configurations from the gnome-linuxconf window. You will see the tab pictured in Figure 6.2, which depicts a Windows 95 operating system installed on the second primary partition on the first IDE interface (`/dev/hda2`).

FIGURE 6.2

Viewing other operating systems currently available during the bootup sequence.

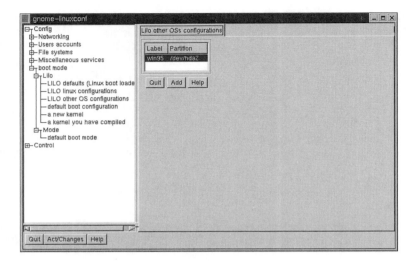

2. To change or delete an existing OS label or partition, click the OS you want to modify. You will see an Other Operating System Setup tab that enables you to type in a different label or partition. Make your necessary changes, and then click either Accept (to activate your changes), Cancel (to ignore changes), or Del (to remove the LILO option of booting to the currently selected OS).

3. To add another OS to your boot options, click the Add button. You will see the Other Operating System Setup tab mentioned in the previous step, but no label or partition will be shown. You can choose from a list of available hard drives and partitions by clicking the arrow beside the text box labeled Partition to Boot. Make the necessary additions, and click Accept, Cancel, or Del.

TIP If at all possible, you should set up your drives and partitions in advance to meet your requirements, and then install any other necessary operating systems first. Keep in mind that the other operating systems have their own preferred installation order as well—Windows 95 should be installed before Windows NT, for example. Whether you're using one drive or several, make sure you determine exactly how many partitions your system will need for Windows and Windows NT. If you don't (and later have to add a DOS partition to any available drive), a legacy MS-DOS convention for numbering (naming) hard drives will cause some of your Windows applications and file pointers to point to the wrong drive or partition. Linux will not be affected, however.

Creating a LILO Boot Floppy Disk

When you first install Red Hat Linux 6.0, the installation program installs the LILO boot loader to the hard drive by default. However, it is possible that you could make changes to LILO and subsequently be unable to boot your system for some reason. If this happens, you will not be able to boot to Linux or your other operating systems on the drive.

TIP It is good practice to install your LILO changes to floppy disk and test all the boot options first; then go back into gnome-linuxconf and install LILO to your hard drive. This is especially true if you have a complicated configuration, such as multiple operating systems, drives, and partitions. The floppy boot disk you create can serve as a backup in an emergency (such as when a reinstallation of Windows 95 writes over your MBR). This can save you a trip to your Linux emergency boot floppy and associated floppy rescue images.

After the initial installation process, LILO enables you to install the boot sector on any appropriate device, including your floppy drive. After you've configured LILO to your liking (see the "Changing LILO Defaults" section later in this chapter), it is relatively simple to store LILO to a floppy disk. From the main gnome-linuxconf window, select Config, boot mode, Lilo, LILO defaults (Linux boot loader). This will bring up the Lilo defaults tab you see in Figure 6.3.

FIGURE 6.3

LILO can boot from a floppy drive so that you can retain your current hard drive MBR settings.

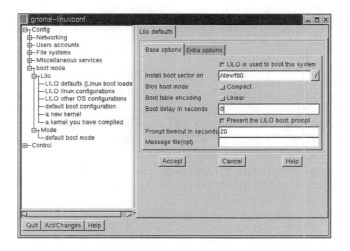

If you have only one hard drive, and if Linux is the only operating system on it, you are probably booting from the MBR of that drive. In such a case, the device name will be /dev/hda for an IDE drive or /dev/sda for a SCSI drive. You should see this device name listed in the Install boot sector on text box of the Lilo defaults tab (look ahead to Figure 6.5). Click the Install Boot Sector on arrow, and you will see a pop-up menu that will enable you to click the disk drive of your choice—in this case, that will be either /dev/hda or /dev/sda, depending on the interface type of your hard drive. If you prefer, you can also click in the text box and type in the device name instead of using the mouse. The other settings in the Base and Extra Options tabs are explained fully in the later section "Changing LILO Defaults." Make your changes, and click Accept to save your changes to the /etc/lilo.conf file. Click Cancel if you made changes but decide that you don't want to install them.

Part

I

Ch

6

If you clicked Accept, you will see an Activating LILO configuration tab to warn you that LILO affects the way your system boots. You are given an opportunity in this tab to not save your changes by clicking No (to not activate changes) or to continue with the LILO floppy disk installation by clicking Yes (to activate the changes). To activate your changes, label a floppy disk with an appropriate name (such as "LILO boot disk"), place it in the floppy disk drive, and then click the Yes button.

Keep in mind that you can use any floppy disk—regardless of whether it is formatted for a DOS or Linux file system—because LILO installs the boot loader only to the MBR, which is the first sector of the disk and not part of the floppy disk file system itself. LILO also will not write over any of the data stored on your floppy disk.

Enabling New Kernels

In some instances, the basic modular kernel that you inherit during the initial installation of Red Hat Linux 6.0 is not sufficient to meet your needs. For example, you might need hardware or networking capabilities that are not supported by the default kernel. In such a case, you might have to first build a new kernel that enables you to define exactly which components your system will support and then recompile those options into a new kernel. Chapter 18 fully describes this process.

If you build a new kernel, you must create a pointer to it from LILO so that your system will know how to boot that particular kernel, in addition to the default kernel and any other kernels that you have configured in LILO. You typically place the kernel file either in the / directory or in the /boot directory (which could also be a mounted disk partition). You can name newly created kernel files anything (as long as it doesn't duplicate any other filename in the directory you're storing it), but the convention is to store kernels in these directories with a filename beginning with vmlinuz.

 TIP If you have just completed a new compilation of a kernel configuration, you can dispense with the manual installation of that kernel into LILO. Instead of choosing Config, boot mode, Lilo, a new kernel, you can choose Config, boot mode, Lilo, and then a kernel you have compiled. The gnome-linuxconf utility will find your recently compiled kernel and bring up the Adding a New Kernel to LILO tab, with certain information already supplied in two fields. The Kernel Image File field will have your new kernel's path and filename (for example, /usr/src/linux/arch/i386/boot/zImage). Also, the Where to Copy the Kernel file field will have the default kernel name and version number (for example, /kernel-2.2.5). You can change the kernel path and name in this field, if you want (for example, /boot/new-kernel)—the kernel image will be copied to that directory with that name.

If, for example, you were to follow the instructions in Chapter 18 to create a new kernel named vmlinuz-new and then store it in the /boot directory, the LILO boot loader would enable you to add that new kernel to your boot configuration easily. Follow these steps:

1. Log in as root, and launch gnome-linuxconf from the main GNOME menu and panel. You will see the gnome-linuxconf window.

2. Select Config, boot mode, Lilo, LILO Linux configurations. You will see a tab named Lilo Linux Configuration, which has a table listing the currently enabled kernels (including the kernel name, the partition on which it is located, and the label LILO offers you to choose during the boot prompt).

3. Click the Add button. You will see the Linux boot configuration tab with an empty record (see Figure 6.4).

FIGURE 6.4
Linuxconf enables you to add, modify, and delete multiple Linux configurations.

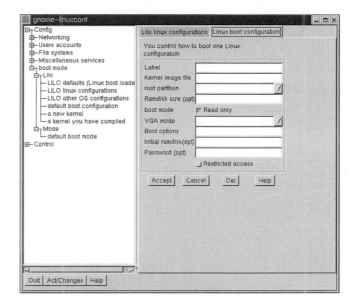

4. Fill in at least the text boxes identifying the label, kernel image file, and root partition. For the current example, I used New, /boot/vmlinuz-new, and /dev/hda5, respectively.

5. Click the appropriate radio button that indicates whether you want to add the new kernel to your existing configuration and make it the default (new default bootable setup), to overwrite the existing default settings (replace the current bootable setup), or merely to add this option to your boot menu (selectable setup).

6. Click Accept to save your new Linux boot configuration, or click Cancel to revert to the previous configuration and ignore the changes you just entered.

   If you choose Accept, you will be warned that the changes you made will affect your boot sequence, and you will have another opportunity to select Yes (to continue) or No (to cancel changes) before proceeding. If you choose Yes, your changes will be saved and you will see a new record listed in the table on the Lilo Linux Configuration tab.

Part
I

Ch
6

You also will be able to access your new kernel during the LILO boot menu by selecting New.

7. If this is the only kernel image that you want to add at this time, click Quit to close the Lilo Linux Configuration tab.

Changing Default Settings

Numerous places in gnome-linuxconf enable you to modify default settings for LILO and to determine how your system behaves during the initial and subsequent bootup sequence. For example, you can enable or disable the LILO boot menu, modify how long the LILO boot menu is displayed before automatically booting to the default kernel configuration, and specify whether you are presented with a graphical or text-based login prompt.

Changing LILO Defaults

This is where you have the opportunity to control most of the core functionality of LILO. For example, you can choose to display a menu during the early stages of the boot sequence, when your BIOS passes control to the MBR of your floppy or hard drive (which contains LILO, in this case). You also can customize the message displayed with the boot menu, set an amount of time before the menu is displayed, and control how long the menu is displayed before proceeding automatically with the boot sequence.

To configure LILO defaults, log in as root and launch gnome-linuxconf from the main GNOME menu and panel. From the gnome-linuxconf window, select Config, boot mode, Lilo, LILO defaults (Linux boot loader). You will see two tabs, labeled Base Options and Extra Options, as shown in Figure 6.5.

FIGURE 6.5
You can configure exactly how you want LILO to behave when it gets control from the BIOS.

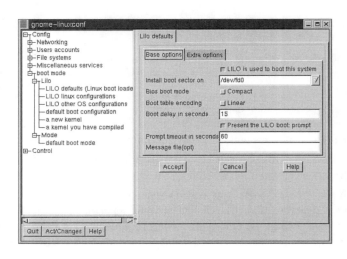

Changing Base Options   Using the Base Options tab, you can enable LILO, change where LILO installs the boot loader, enable the LILO boot prompt, and specify how long this prompt will be available during bootup. You can configure several text boxes and check boxes in the Base Options tab:

- **LILO is used to boot this system**—Keep this box checked if you want to use LILO instead of a boot loader provided by another operating system or a third-party vendor.

- **Install boot sector on**—This option changes the location where LILO installs the boot loader. Type (or pick from the pop-up menu) the name of the appropriate disk drive or partition in this text box. The process for installing the boot loader to a floppy was described earlier in this chapter.

- **BIOS boot mode**—This option enables you to select Compact mode for a BIOS boot. You should not check the Compact check box unless it has been determined that you absolutely need it and that this mode will work with your system's hardware.

- **Boot table encoding**—Checking this box can help you deal with some disk geometry problems some people might encounter (although you normally don't need to check it). In some instances LILO has problems using the default disk mapping style (Cylinders, Heads, and Tracks). This is the case with some SCSI disks, or if you try to install LILO with a kernel image that is outside the 1024 cylinder limit (kernel and its configuration files normally must be installed on a block lower than 1024).

- **Boot delay in seconds**—Enter 0 if you want to see the boot menu immediately after the BIOS initializes the hardware and passes control to LILO. Otherwise, enter the number of seconds you want the system to pause before showing you the menu.

- **Present the LILO boot: prompt**—Check this box if you want to see the actual prompt during bootup. Uncheck it if you want the prompt to be available (with the Tab key) but invisible. The word "LILO" will still be displayed, and you still can activate the boot prompt by pressing the Tab key.

- **Prompt timeout in seconds**—Enter the amount of time that you want the boot prompt (if enabled, or activated with the Tab key during bootup) to be active before automatically loading the default operating system. Enter 0 here if you want to force an interactive boot process where an operator must choose from one of the available boot options.

- **Message file**—Enter the path and filename of a plain text file that you want to be displayed immediately before the boot prompt (such as basic instructions and descriptions of the available options).

If you have changes to make to fields in the Extra Options tab, click that tab and continue making changes. If not, click Accept to save any changes you made to the base options, or click Cancel to revert to the previous settings and ignore the changes you just entered. If you choose Accept, you will be warned that the changes you made will affect your boot sequence, and you will have another opportunity to select Yes (to continue) or No (to cancel changes)

Part

I

Ch

6

before proceeding. If you choose Yes, your changes will be saved to the /etc/lilo.conf configuration file, and /sbin/lilo will install the boot loader as configured to the drive or partition you chose.

Changing Extra Options   When you click the Extra Options tab of the Lilo Defaults window, you will see the options shown in Figure 6.6. Within this tab, you can configure several different fields, including the location of the root partition (where most of your system and user files usually are stored) and any boot parameters you need to pass to the kernel during bootup (such as hardware-specific settings).

FIGURE 6.6
You must tell LILO which hard disk partition contains your root directory and whether the kernel needs additional parameters (Boot Options).

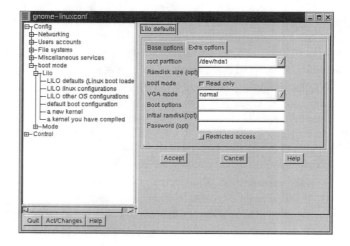

Several text boxes in the Lilo Defaults tab are listed as optional (opt), so leaving them empty should not cause you any problems. You must enter at least a root partition, however. In addition, you can configure several other items to meet your needs:

- **Root partition**—Type (or select from the pick list) the path and filename of the device representing the hard disk partition that stores your root directory and most of your system and user files. This example shows the first main partition on the first IDE interface (/dev/hda1), although your settings might be different. Chapter 19 contains details on device naming conventions for hard disks and partitions.

- **Ramdisk size (opt)**—This text box specifies the size of the ramdisk, if it is used. You can enter 0 in this text box to disable ramdisk use, or you can just leave it blank to default to the settings in the kernel. You are probably safe just leaving this setting blank (the default).

- **Boot mode**—You should leave this box checked to enable Linux to perform diagnostics properly during bootup and to prevent files accessed during bootup (including system configuration files) from receiving a new modification date every time you boot up your system.

- **VGA mode**—You can leave this text box empty or select normal.

- **Boot options**—If your kernel requires boot-time parameters, you should enter them here. For example, certain hardware devices, such as SCSI and PCMCIA (PC-card), require that you inform the kernel about their existence and location using a boot option. You can also enter the boot option as an append to the boot prompt.

- **Initial ramdisk (opt)**—You can leave this text box empty and should experience no problems. This setting informs the kernel which device should be used to store a basic root file system during the initial bootup process, before the actual root file system is loaded.

- **Password (opt)**—Enter a password in this text box, if you want.

- **Restricted access**—Check this box if you want to limit access to your system by other people. If you select this option, other users would have to supply the necessary password to use the system.

Just as you did with the Base Options and many other gnome-linuxconf LILO settings, click Accept to save any changes you made to the Extra Options, or click Cancel to revert to the previous settings and ignore the changes you just entered.

Changing the Default Boot Configuration

If you have only one kernel installed, it will be your default boot configuration. However, as you add different kernels, kernel configurations, and operating systems, you might find the need to force your system to default to one of these. For example, you might want to boot automatically to Windows 95 in the event that you do not choose manually to boot from one of your Linux configurations before your LILO boot menu times out (if it is enabled). To change the default boot configuration on your system to another configured drive or partition, perform the following steps:

1. Select Config, boot mode, Lilo, default boot configuration from the gnome-linuxconf main window. This will bring up the Default Boot Configuration tab (see Figure 6.7).

2. Click the radio button of the operating system or Linux kernel you want to boot from by default. In this case, I have selected Windows 95 instead of the original kernel installed with Red Hat Linux 6.0 or the new Linux kernel we configured earlier in this chapter.

3. Click Accept to save these settings, and then click Yes to confirm. If you change your mind and don't want to save these settings, click either Cancel in the Default Boot Configuration tab or No when you are asked to confirm activation of your changes.

Part

I

Ch

6

FIGURE 6.7
You can select to boot from any operating systems or Linux kernels that you have configured with LILO.

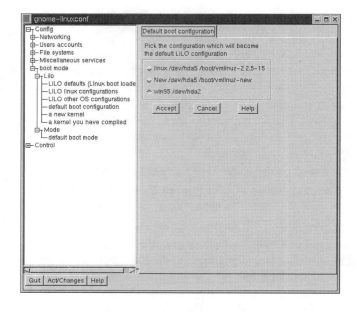

Changing the Default Boot Mode

You also can change the way your system behaves after LILO boots your system and passes control to your initialization processes, which in turn loads your kernel and numerous other startup processes and daemons. For example, you can control whether you want to see and use a text-based login prompt or a graphical login screen. Follow these instructions to perform this action:

1. Log in as root, and launch gnome-linuxconf from the main GNOME menu and panel. You will see the gnome-linuxconf window.

2. Select Config, boot mode, Mode, default boot mode. You will see a tab named Boot Mode Configuration and three groups of options (see Figure 6.8).

3. If you want to see a graphical interface when you log in, press the Graphic & Network radio button. Otherwise, press the Text Mode & Network button to view a standard, text-based login prompt (followed by a shell and a command-line interface). Keep in mind that this particular option is not specific to LILO, even though it is related to the bootup process (only at a later point). The changes actually are made to /etc/inittab rather than /etc/lilo.conf.

4. Click Accept to save your boot mode configuration, or click Cancel to revert to the previous configuration and ignore the changes you just entered. If you choose Accept, your changes will be saved and will take effect the next time you reboot.

FIGURE 6.8
You can choose to log in graphically or from a text-based interface.

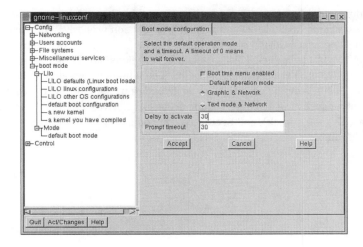

Troubleshooting LILO

Because BIOS controls the initial boot sequence, you must make sure that the settings in it are correct. For example, if your BIOS is configured to boot from a CD-ROM or a floppy before the hard drive, you must make sure that you don't have a bootable CD or a floppy in either drive. If you installed the LILO boot loader on the MBR of a floppy instead of your hard drive, you must make sure that your BIOS is configured to boot from the floppy (before the hard drive) and that the floppy you created is in the appropriate drive. You very easily could be making changes to LILO and saving the boot loader to your hard drive, but accidentally booting from an old LILO boot floppy that does not have the updated changes you expect.

LILO and gnome-linuxconf come with their own set of warning messages to help you troubleshoot any problems you encounter. For example, if you don't have a floppy disk in your drive, you will be told that errors occurred and will be asked if you want to check the logs. If you try to install to a device that doesn't exist, you will get an error message saying that your choice will yield a non-bootable system.

You might find that sometimes gnome-linuxconf unexpectedly closes its main window right after you perform an action. For example, this sometimes happens after deleting a previously configured operating system. In the event that this occurs, all you can do is proceed to the main GNOME panel and menu to launch gnome-linuxconf again (although your recent changes should be reflected). Additionally, sometimes when you bring up two instances of gnome-linuxconf and then close the most recent one, you might not be able to make changes to the first one you launched. In this case, close the first window as well, and then restart a single gnome-linuxconf.

Part

I

Ch

6

If your hard drive is very large, or if you are using several drives, you might experience problems trying to install LILO and getting it to function properly. When using LILO, the Linux kernel and its associated files (all located in the /boot directory) must reside entirely below the first 1,024 cylinders. This is especially true if you are using a single / partition and have recompiled the kernel (which might put it on a higher numbered cylinder behind your other files). This restriction might not apply if you are using a third-party boot loader from another operating system or software vendor. Some SCSI drives also don't understand the popular Head, Cylinder (track), and Sector table encoding. In such a case, you should try using linear block number encoding under Base Options. ●

The X Window System

Installing and Configuring GNOME

by Duane Hellums

In this chapter

Why GNOME?

GNOME and Enlightenment are critical parts of the Red Hat 6.0 experience. Without them, we would not have all the bells and whistles that we've come to expect from a contemporary operating system environment. Alternatives exist for each, but none currently offers the seamless, efficient, and polished qualities that you see when you first log in graphically to your Red Hat Linux system. This explains why Red Hat included the combination as the default configuration during installation.

Figure 7.1 shows the desktop environment that you start with after a fresh Red Hat Linux 6.0 installation. As you can see, Red Hat Linux 6.0 is very graphical, and it hardly is the "green screen" and command-line monster that some fear Linux is because of its UNIX roots.

FIGURE 7.1
The GNOME desktop environment and Enlightenment window manager.

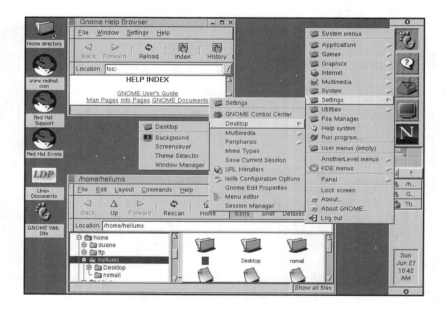

NOTE The desktop in Figure 7.1 was rearranged a little from what you will see to facilitate showing off the startup applications, default icons, and exploded menu options. Basically, the only differences between what you will see and Figure 7.1 are that the Help Browser and File Manager windows are resized and moved, a few submenus are shown selected, and the panel is depicted here on the right instead of the bottom. No configuration files were modified to achieve this; it just requires a few mouse clicks and drags.

Understanding Your Desktop Environment

The graphical user interface (GUI) in Linux is a little more complicated than what you might be accustomed to in the Windows or Macintosh world. Believe it or not, this is a good thing because an open system provides more choices and more flexibility than a proprietary, controlled system.

You benefit from the development efforts and friendly competition of many different organizations and groups of people, who all have a slightly different view of how Linux should look. With open systems, however, you don't get locked into a certain model because the building blocks are designed to be highly interoperable and interchangeable.

Understanding XFree86

XFree86 provides the basic GUI tools that you need to support use of a graphical desktop, mouse, windows, icons, and menus. This is an important building block because it provides the core components that you need, including hooks to device drivers for your video card and tools for changing the configuration settings for your monitor.

XFree86 is basically an X Window clone developed by the XFree86 Project. It operates on many different makes and models of UNIX, and it is freely distributable. XFree86 is an integral part of Linux, so the most current version of XFree86 is included on the CD. You can find out more about XFree86 at the `http://www.xfree86.org/` Web site.

Understanding Enlightenment

Enlightenment (or, *E*, as it is sometimes called), is a window manager that enables you to extend the basic functionality of XFree86. With Enlightenment, you efficiently can change the way your windows and a few other desktop components behave. This is the default window manager for Red Hat Linux, but you can use other popular managers, such as Ice, Window Maker, or FVWM. However, some window managers are only partially GNOME-compliant, so certain components of GNOME (such as drag-and-drop, session management, and pager functionality) might not work with them as effectively as they do with Enlightenment, which is 100% compliant. You can find out more about Enlightenment at the `http://www.enlightenment.org/` Web site.

Understanding GNOME

The GNU Network Object Model Environment (GNOME) works hand-in-hand with Enlightenment to provide a user-friendly GUI. The easiest way to understand these programs' Linux roles is to think of them merely as additional building blocks that are part of your Red Hat Linux system. A Linux system is composed of many layers that basically include kernels, drivers, source code, compilers, shells, applications, and the XFree86 graphical interface. Enlightenment and GNOME sit on top of all this, and each can be extended further through the use of such things as themes and GNOME-compliant applications.

Part

II

Ch

7

GNOME is a desktop environment that rides on top of Enlightenment and XFree86 to provide the desktop that you see and use when you first log in graphically to Red Hat Linux 6.0. You can get drag-and-drop functionality between applications and your GNOME desktop with any Motif or GNOME-compliant applications and window managers. GNOME provides an additional layer of functionality, but it has additional building blocks sitting on top of it, such as the many GNOME applications that take full advantage of all the lower-level components discussed so far. Keep in mind that you easily can use other popular environments as well, such as the K Desktop Environment (KDE) or the Common Desktop Environment (CDE), which are included with Red Hat 6.0.

Putting All the Pieces Together

When you stand back and look at your Red Hat Linux 6.0 open system, you should see the basic Linux kernel bolstered by a multitude of drivers, networking components, and basic applications; this, in turn, is extended by the XFree86 GUI, the Enlightenment window manager, and the GNOME desktop environment. Topping all these off are the many utilities and applications Red Hat has developed to provide additional functionality and to improve the installation, configuration, and system management process, not to mention their strong support structure.

Installing Enlightenment and GNOME

Enlightenment is included on the CD as `/RedHat/RPMS/ enlightenment-0.15.5-32.rpm` and is installed by default with the Red Hat Workstation and Custom installation methods. If for some reason you don't have it, or if you must reinstall it, you should consult Chapter 11, "Installing and Managing RPM Packages," which steps you through the necessary paces.

GNOME also is included on the CD and is installed by default. If you must install it using RPM, you can find the package on the CD as `/RedHat/RPMS/gnomer-core-1.0.4-34.rpm`, along with supporting packages such as the `control-center-1.0.5-20.rpm` and `gnome-audio-1.0.0-6.rpm` (as well as associated GNOME games, editors, utilities, linuxconf, and so on).

Configuring Enlightenment

Enlightenment is still under development, so you might see many slight changes in the interface during the next few months—and definitely during the next few years. This is a complex application that has many bells and whistles that you will discover as you use it. However, I wouldn't dream of covering every little aspect of E here—there simply isn't enough space. What I do cover here is the basics of installation and configuration that will enable you to use the basic functions of E.

You could probably get by without ever changing the default settings within Enlightenment because most of the desktop environment settings are changed in GNOME. However, some basic settings (mouse behavior) and a few advanced settings (themes) will improve your desktop experience if you change them a little bit in E.

One of the things to keep in mind is that, in effect, GNOME sits on top of E, so GNOME will override some of the settings that you make in E when the desktop environment comes up during login. For example, consider what happens when you bring up the Enlightenment configuration tool and set or change the background. The background looks fine during your current session, but when you log in again, you will see your E background for a few seconds before the default GNOME background will be displayed.

 TIP For most situations, I recommend changing only those settings within E that do not compete with GNOME, such as those that control window, desktop, and mouse behavior. In other words, steer clear of the background and theme settings (which can be set from GNOME). That should prevent any confusion.

Accessing the E Configuration Tool

You can launch the E configuration tool either from the desktop or from a hook inside the GNOME configuration tool. To launch it from the desktop, go to any clean space on your desktop and click with the center mouse button; you should see the pop-up window pictured in Figure 7.2. If you have a two-button mouse and enabled three-button emulation during installation or setup of XFree86, you can achieve the same result by clicking simultaneously with the left and right mouse buttons.

FIGURE 7.2
The Enlightenment menu.

This menu can be a nice shortcut when you don't feel like moving your mouse to one of the panels. Most of the applications located in the GNOME system menus are available from this pop-up menu. You can also change themes from this screen, but as I mentioned before, I recommend that you make it a habit of changing themes from within the GNOME configuration tool, to prevent confusion between the window manager and the desktop environment.

If you click the Help menu item, E brings up a nice document viewer that displays a small slideshow about E. It's worth reading, if you want to know a little bit more about E's current state of development and how themes and backgrounds can be configured.

Part
II

Ch
7

From the pop-up desktop menu, select Enlightenment Configuration; the E configuration tool will launch. You can also use the GNOME configuration tool (Control Center) to launch the E configuration tool. Select Desktop, Window Manager from the Control Center, and then click the button labeled Run Configuration Tool for Enlightenment.

Whether you launch the E configuration tool from the pop-up desktop menu or from the GNOME Control Center, you will be presented with the Enlightenment Configuration Editor window pictured in Figure 7.3. The program's interface has a small window in the top-left corner, right above the E logo, where you can select from the available configuration groups. As you click each group's icon or label, the right half of the window changes to show the specific configuration options related to that group. You then just have to make the changes you want and click Apply before proceeding; you can also wait until you are finished with all the groups, and then click OK to activate the changes.

FIGURE 7.3
Enlightenment
Configuration Editor.

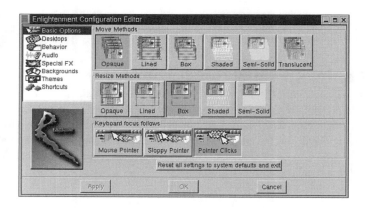

 TIP   You should immediately notice the button at the bottom of the main window marked Reset All Settings To System Defaults And Exit. You should use this button when you find that you don't like the settings you've made, or when E is misbehaving and you feel that your configuration changes are to blame. If you click this button, any configuration changes you have made will be removed, and E will be returned to the way it was installed originally.

Configuring E Basic Options

When you first bring up the E configuration editor, the Basic Options group is the default group displayed in the configuration window. In this window, you have the option to change the way windows appear to you while you move them around the screen or to resize them. Opaque (the default) and Box are both nice methods, but you should try different options to see which you prefer. Opaque moves the entire color window around, whereas Box only shows you an outline of the window as a guide (which is nice if you have slow processor or graphics capabilities).

The keyboard focus options enable you to control window focus with your mouse. If you select Pointer Clicks (the default), you must click a window before your keyboard typing will work in that window. Personally, I don't like this method because when I bring up an X terminal (shell prompt), I must physically move the mouse there and click it before I start typing. So, the first thing I did was to change this setting to Mouse Pointer, which enables me to just move the pointer over the window rather than force a click. Sloppy Pointer goes a step further and enables you to keep typing in a window even if you bump the mouse off the window (as long as it doesn't move over another window, of course). You might want to tweak some other automated focus settings in the Behavior group as well.

Configuring E Desktops

You have the option of configuring your desktop to be larger than the finite graphical real estate available on your screen. When you bring up a few applications, it becomes pretty difficult to keep them positioned on your desktop in such a way that you get maximum use out of them without your screen looking cluttered. Select the Desktops group; the desktop items shown in Figure 7.4 appear.

FIGURE 7.4
Creating virtual and separate desktops.

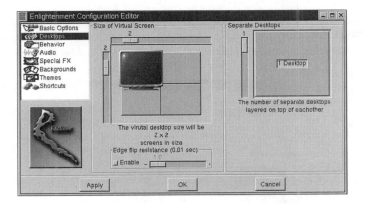

You can increase your available desktop space in two ways: by using multiple (separate) desktops overlaid on top of each other, or by creating several virtual screens. Virtual screens are the preferred method and will cause you the least grief and misunderstanding. However, if you choose to have multiple, separate desktops, use the vertical sliding bar on the right side of the window to select from 1 to 32 desktops.

If you choose to maintain a virtual desktop, use the horizontal and vertical sliding bars to choose from 1 to 64 (8×8) screens. You will probably find that the default of 4 (2×2) screens is a good setting.

N O T E The virtual screens picked here interact with the GNOME pager on your main panel. Don't confuse virtual screens with the virtual terminal capabilities of Linux (accessed by Alt+F1, Alt+F2, and so on, from a command-line prompt or by Ctrl+Alt+F1, Ctrl+Alt+F2, and so on while in the X interface). You should notice that, immediately after you apply changes to the number of virtual screens, your pager window changes to reflect the new setup. ■

The last item you can configure in this window is the edge flip resistance. This is nothing more than a way of forcing your mouse to pause for a short period of time before you are whisked into the neighboring window (if there is one in the direction you're moving your mouse). If you don't press the Enable button, your mouse will seamlessly move across virtual screen boundaries without pausing. This can be a handy setting if you enable and configure it, because sometimes trying to resize or move a window can be difficult if you keep getting moved into another screen just because you got too near the edge. I have found that settings of between 50 and 60 are a nice tradeoff between speed and convenience, but you will have to find your own resistance level that feels natural.

Configuring Advanced E Focus Behavior

In the Advanced Focus tab of the Behavior configuration window, you can change the way the keyboard and mouse automatically interact, even more so than the manual settings configured in the Basic Options window discussed earlier in this section (see Figure 7.5).

FIGURE 7.5
Configuring mouse, keyboard, and application focus behavior.

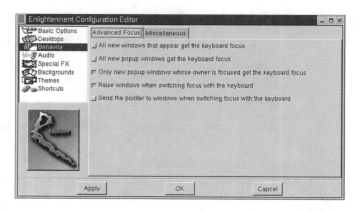

If you click a launcher icon somewhere on your desktop, or if you select a menu item that opens a program, you normally have to either move your mouse to that window or click on that window (depending on your Basic Options settings) before you can begin typing in your new window. Clicking the first radio button (all new windows that appear get the keyboard focus), you can immediately start typing in the new program, as if you had moved your mouse to it or clicked it. I recommend turning on this feature (it is off by default) because you might find that it gets tedious pointing to the application you just brought up.

If a program you are using generates a pop-up window, such as a dialog box or a warning, you would normally have to move your mouse to that window to click the OK button or possibly type an answer in a text box. If you select the second button labeled All New Pop-up Windows Get The Keyboard Focus, you will be able to respond to and use the keyboard with such pop-up windows immediately, without using the mouse. I don't recommend turning on this option, however, because it could have adverse effects. For example, a pop-up window that wants your attention and a decision might immediately take your typing (such as an Enter key) as input, even though you didn't mean for it to happen that way.

The third button, the Only New Popup Windows Whose Owner Is Focused Get The Keyboard Focus button, is a partial compromise meant to prevent some problems of the second option. If you select this button, programs running in the background won't accidentally get input from your keyboard. Only warnings and dialog boxes created by the program you are actually using will receive the focus automatically.

The fourth radio button on this screen is very useful if you are accustomed to switching applications using the keyboard instead of the mouse. For example, you can press the Alt+Tab key combination to switch from one open application to the next. If you do, the window of the application you switch to will immediately come to the top of the screen so that you can see where you are typing. I recommend using this option unless you have a reason not to.

The fifth and last radio button has a similar effect as the fourth, but it automatically moves the mouse pointer to the application that is now active (that has the focus). That way, you can immediately begin using the mouse as well as the keyboard with your current application. I recommend that you keep this option enabled (it is off by default) so that your mouse, keyboard, and application focus all work together seamlessly.

Configuring Miscellaneous E Focus Behavior

Enlightenment can provide ToolTips so that you can get some brief instructions when you have the pointer over a window border or a title bar. This feature is turned on by default, with a time delay of half a second, as indicated by Figure 7.6. In other words, if the object you are pointing at has the focus for half a second, the ToolTip pop-up window will appear. You can disable this feature so that no E ToolTips are used, or you can use the horizontal sliding bar to change the amount of time that passes before the pop-up window appears.

Default E behavior normally requires you to right-click a window that is underneath another for it to rise to the surface so that you can see the entire window. You can also use the GNOME panel to hide or show an application. However, the Miscellaneous tab enables you to get E to move to the foreground any window that you have the mouse over, even if only a small portion of the application is visible from under many others. If you enable this function, you can use the horizontal sliding bar to set the amount of time that you want E to delay before bringing the application to the top. I recommend that you enable this option and try it for awhile, with maybe a setting of 1 second or so; you might find that it saves you some time.

Part
II

Ch
7

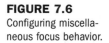

FIGURE 7.6
Configuring miscella-
neous focus behavior.

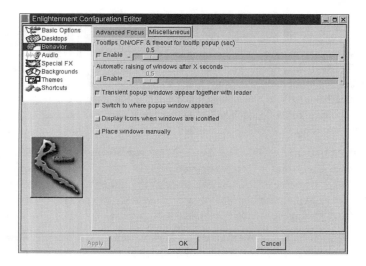

The other buttons on the Miscellaneous tab enable you to change how pop-up windows appear in relation to their owner, to display icons when an application is iconified (minimized), and to manually place windows on your desktop. I advise against changing any of these settings unless you find that you have a problem with default E behavior.

N O T E   The only item in the Audio group is a button by which you can enable sounds in Enlightenment. Because sound can be controlled in the GNOME desktop environment, there is normally no need to enable it in E. However, if you want to, you can enable it in this window (not pictured here). The basic difference is that certain E themes (try Shiny Metal, for example) have event sounds that you might want to hear, and these will be audible only if you enable E sounds. ■

Configuring E Special Effects (FX)

By default, the E window manager will just pick a place to position your application's window and then will draw that window there. Some people prefer a more stylistic, multimedia approach to window placement and behavior. If you want to give it a try, you can click the Animate Menus button, enable each option in Figure 7.7 individually, and experiment with different settings using the horizontal sliding bars.

 TIP   You probably will find that Opaque window sliding (the default) and settings of about 3500 on each special effect bar have a fairly pleasing effect.

FIGURE 7.7
Configuring sliding
window special effects.

FIGURE 7.7
Configuring sliding
window special effects.

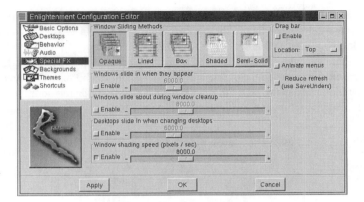

Configuring E Desktop Backgrounds

The interaction between E and GNOME desktop backgrounds can be a little tricky. If you have only one desktop with several virtual screens, you can change your background with either the E or the GNOME configuration tools. However, GNOME takes precedence over E settings when you log in again. As mentioned previously, you will see your E background for only a very short period of time, just after E starts and before GNOME takes over. If you fall into this category, it is probably best that you just use the GNOME desktop background selector.

However, if you are using multiple (separate) desktops, each with its own lot of virtual screens, then you can use the E configuration editor to your advantage. The reason for this is that the GNOME Control Center enables you to change background settings only for the main (first) desktop, while E enables you to set backgrounds independently on each desktop (see Figure 7.8). In this manner, you can set the background for Desktop 0 (as indicated here) using GNOME and can set the background for any additional desktops with E. This could be a convenient way of reminding yourself which desktop you're on at any given time, such as in the case where two people share the same computer but don't have separate logins.

FIGURE 7.8
Configuring E desktop
backgrounds.

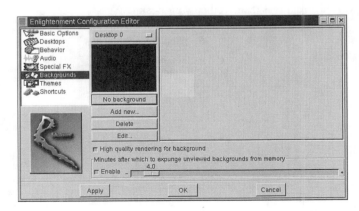

Part

II

Ch

7

Any available backgrounds are shown in the large empty window frame to the right of the preview window. To change the background graphic for Desktop 1, you should click the Desktop 0 button at the top of the window, at which time you will have the option of picking any of the available desktops. If you pick Desktop 1 (your second desktop, actually, because your first is numbered 0), that will be displayed on this button. Then click the Add New button, which divides the panel to the right to make room for the additional background and then brings up the window pictured in Figure 7.9.

FIGURE 7.9
The solid color background selection tab.

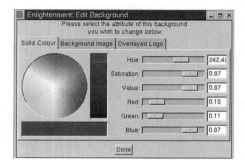

If you prefer a solid color, you can just use the Solid Colour tab instead of the other two. If you want a blue background, for example, you will have to click on an appropriate section of the blue portion of the circle, and then click one of the hues in the vertical rectangle immediately to the right of it. You should see two elements: a small circle to mark what color you chose, and a thin line showing what hue and saturation you picked. This puts your chosen color in the horizontal rectangle underneath the circle. If you click the Done button, your solid color will become your selected background for the chosen desktop (Desktop 1, in this case).

If you prefer an image for your background, however, you should click the Background Image tab, which brings up a typical text box and browse button (see Figure 7.10). The Browse button on this window enables you to navigate through your file system directories and pick the picture or graphic of your choice. You can also toggle the four buttons to modify the way the graphic is displayed on your desktop.

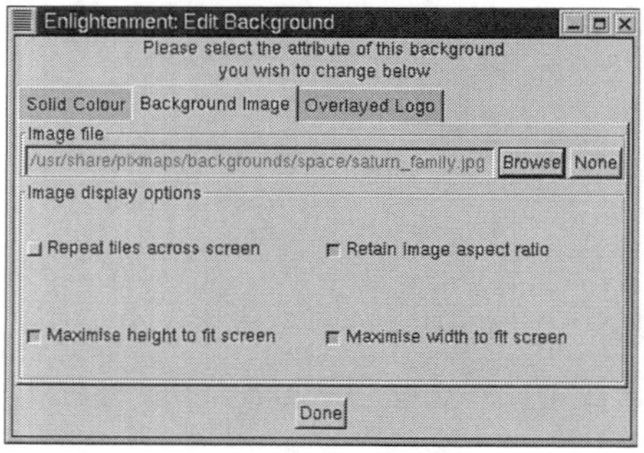

FIGURE 7.10
The image background selection tab.

For small pattern graphics, you might select Repeat Tiles Across Screen, which fills the screen with your pattern. For pictures, however, you would normally choose to Retain Image Aspect Ration and Maximize Height and Width to Fit Screen. That makes your picture as large as possible and centers it in the middle of your screen without distorting the image.

Click Done to save your new setting. This should return you to the main background editor window, where you will see your newly selected color or image listed as an available background to choose from. Click the background you want to see; it will be shown in the preview window. If you are satisfied with the look, click Apply or OK to change your background.

Configuring E Themes

Enlightenment defaults to the rather conservative, clean-cut theme called ClearBig. This provides a relatively simple set of window borders, controls, and event sounds. But variety is the spice of life, so you can choose from several E themes available. Figure 7.11 shows you the Themes window in the E configuration editor, where you make the changes.

FIGURE 7.11
E themes selection window.

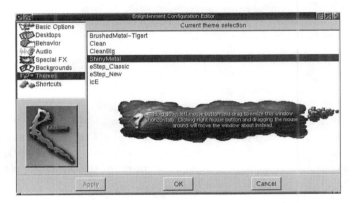

This window lists the available themes as well as the effect that changing themes will have on your interface. You can readily see the difference between ShinyMetal and CleanBig, I'm sure. The ToolTips pop-up window that you see is an example of the different effects window actions can have with other themes; in this case, I moved the cursor over the right edge of the window, preparing to resize it. You can also see the different shading on the title bar as well as the stylistic window controls.

Configuring E Shortcut Keys

E shortcuts are basically hot keys that enable you to use modifiers (the Shift, Ctrl, and Alt keys) in conjunction with regular keys to perform a specific action. For example, Alt+Tab moves from one open application to another. Alt+F1 takes you to the top-left corner of your virtual desktop (also known as linear area number 0). You don't have to live with the default settings, however, and you can create your own to suit your needs. You can define or modify shortcuts with the window shown in Figure 7.12.

Part
II

Ch
7

FIGURE 7.12

E shortcut key definition window.

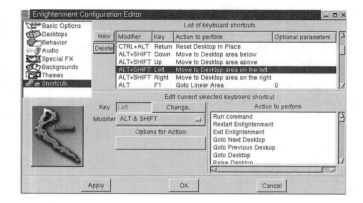

If you want to change the default shortcut for an action, you must scroll to it in the list of keyboard shortcuts and then click to highlight it. A corresponding highlight will occur in the Action to Perform window. You can click a different action, and the keyboard shortcut will be updated in the other window. You can choose from many actions, and most of them are standard E window manager functions.

If you want to keep the function and change the associated shortcut key, first find and select the action that you want to modify in the list window. Then click the Change button; this brings up a window asking you to press the specific key that you want to associate with the desired action. For example, if you wanted to change Cleanup Windows from Ctrl+Alt+Home to Ctrl+Alt+c, you would highlight Cleanup Windows in the list window, click Change, and then press the C key. If you wanted to change it from Ctrl+Alt+Home to Shift+Home, you would then click the button next to the Modifier selector (instead of Change) and choose Shift from the options listed. Clicking Apply or pressing OK would activate your changes.

Last, but not least, you have the capability to delete any existing shortcuts (select a shortcut, and then click Delete) or even create your own shortcuts for your most popular applications. This prevents you from having to go to a menu, panel, file manager, or desktop to launch an application. For example, if you wanted to use Alt+e to launch the GNOME Notepad editor (gnp), you would click the New button, which would default to the Run command action (that you'll have to specify) with no selected modifier or key. This also would highlight the Options for Action text box. In this case, you would type gnp in the Options for Action box, click the button next to Modifier and choose Alt, click the Change button, and then type the letter e. After saving the changes with the Apply or OK button, you could press Alt+e any time you wanted to bring up the editor. Note that you can't use capital letters because that would take the Shift key as an actual key before you typed the capital letter you wanted; this also would create a possible conflict with other shortcut keys.

Configuring GNOME

GNOME comes out of the box preconfigured with settings that you probably will enjoy and will not need to modify very much. However, you can easily tune many different parts of the GNOME desktop environment to your liking. With the Enlightenment plus GNOME combination included with Red Hat 6.0, Linux finally has a robust, user-friendly graphical interface that supports the demands for popular features such as support for multimedia, drag-and-drop, and point-and-click technology.

GNOME has many components that you can configure to meet your needs. These components primarily include menus, panels, and drawers, but you will find that you can configure the desktop itself as well as the GNOME file manager and session manager. This section does not tell you how to modify every possible preference and setting in GNOME tools; you will have to learn some of those on your own, if necessary. However, this section covers all the information you need to know so that you can customize and personalize your desktop interface for maximum efficiency, ergonometry, and visual impact.

Getting Help with GNOME

One of the complaints about earlier versions of Red Hat Linux was that GNOME was a powerful but insufficiently documented desktop environment. If you buy the official boxed set of Red Hat Linux 6.0, you receive a 288-page book titled the *Getting Started Guide*. The first 14 chapters of the book include the official GNOME User's Guide and a little documentation on Enlightenment, while the last four chapters provide a useful introduction for new Linux users who might need an introduction to the shell and command-line interface of Linux.

The GNOME User's Guide is distributed with this book's CD, and you can access it from the GNOME help system; it is listed directly under the GNOME logo in the Help Browser that comes up when you first log in. The User's Guide is also available at `http://www.gnome.org/users-guide/index.html` on the official GNOME Web site.

Finding GNOME-Compliant Applications

The Web site `http://www.gnome.org/applist/listrecent.phtml` contains a very useful GNOME software map, from which you can see a current list of GNOME-compliant software for downloading. For example, version 4.5.33 of the GNU Midnight Commander (file manager) is available there and can upgrade version 4.5.30, which is distributed with this book's CD-ROM and the official Red Hat 6.0 boxed set. Files are listed in reverse chronological order based on the date they were made available, so you can just check every few weeks or months to see GNOME application changes that are available.

Be sure to consider the release and version numbers of packages before you install them. Anything beginning with a zero should be used with some degree of caution, whereas you can have a little more faith in applications with a number such as 1.3 or 2.1 because these numbers indicate maturity and the number of bug fixes that have taken place over time.

Part
II

Ch
7

Using the GNOME Configuration Tool (Control Center)

GNOME provides its own configuration tool that enables you to easily change the settings for the many components of your desktop environment. For example, you can change the look and feel of your desktop by selecting from a wide range of backgrounds, screen savers, themes, and window managers. You can also choose a default editor, associate applications with specific filename extensions, and configure the sounds you hear when you use your desktop and window controls.

Configuring Desktop Settings   The GNOME configuration tool is also known as the Control Center. This tool enables you to manipulate all the different parts of your desktop to enhance your multimedia windowing experience while using Linux. To access the Control Center, click the toolbox icon that comes standard with your default main panel; it should be labeled GNOME Configuration Tool, and you can see the title as you hold the mouse pointer over the icon for about a second.

Selecting Backgrounds   When you bring up the Control Center window, you will see that it is split into two portions, including a menu selection area on the left (looks like a file tree) and a display area on the right. When you click Background from the Desktop group on the left, you will see the window pictured in Figure 7.13. To change the wallpaper as I have in this figure, click the Browse button. You will see a Wallpaper Selection window with three buttons, a directory listing, a file listing, a small preview area, and a text box that indicates your current selection.

FIGURE 7.13
Selecting a background image in the Control Center.

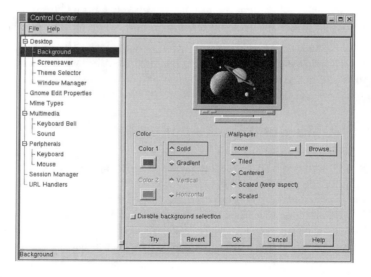

Navigate through the directories in the left window frame with your mouse until you get to the directory you need. Select a file from the window frame in the middle by clicking on it. You should see a depiction of the image in the Preview area. The path and filename of the selection will also be updated in the text box at the bottom.

A good selection of images is located in the `/usr/share/pixmaps/backgrounds` directory, in three subdirectories named Propaganda, space, and tiles; however, you can use any favorite image you have stored on your system. Clicking OK makes the change and returns you to the Control Center, while clicking Cancel ignores any changes or selections that you have made. You will have to click Try or OK from the Control Center to actually activate your changes.

You have the option to stretch the image to fit the desktop, center it in the middle of the screen, or duplicate it as many times as it will fit onscreen (horizontally and vertically). You do this by clicking the buttons labeled Scaled, Centered, or Tiled, respectively. If you want the image to fill as much of the screen as possible without being distorted, select Scaled (keep aspect). For images that don't fill the entire screen, you can select an additional background color (solid or gradient). Clicking on the disable button temporarily inactivates the currently selected background.

Selecting Screen Savers   Clicking Screensaver brings up several settings that you can manipulate in the right window frame of the Control Center. Most of the options are self-explanatory. The list box labeled Screen Saver enables you to click the screen saver you want to try, which will then be displayed in the Demo frame immediately to the right. The default is random, which changes frequently among the screen savers you have installed. If you click a specific screen saver, you can also click the Settings button to the left of the Demo window to try different settings (each individual screen saver has its own set of options, based on its functionality and capabilities).

Under Screen Saver Settings, you can specify how long your system should delay before it turns on the screen saver when you aren't using your system's keyboard or mouse. If your monitor has advanced power management capabilities, you can also choose the option to turn off your monitor after the screen saver has been on a certain amount of time. Click the Help button if you want to know more about the Control Center's options.

Selecting Themes   One of the really nice things about GNOME is its capability to customize your desktop environment so that windows look, feel, and function differently. Themes enable you to benefit from the efforts many individuals and developers have put into creating a pre-configured set of styles, colors, behaviors, and appearances for your windows. Several themes are available by default when you install Red Hat Linux 6.0, but you also can download others from the Internet and add them to your system.

Click Theme Selector, and you will see a list of currently installed themes that you can choose from. In addition, you can click the Preview button to see what effect the chosen theme will have on your desktop controls. Look in the small rectangular frame at the bottom of the Control Center when you change themes and preview them; there you will see what the window control tool set looks like so that you can decide whether you want to activate that option or go back and try others. If you have downloaded a theme and it is not listed in the Available Themes scroll box, click Install New Theme; you can access a file browser to find the theme you want to add to your list. Finally, you can change the default user font by clicking Use Custom Font and selecting your favorite font.

Part

II

Ch

7

N O T E It might seem a little confusing that there is an E and a GNOME background image selection. You might notice the same thing in Windows, where you see a certain splash image during the initial boot-up sequence, and then another image when the individual user logs in. The E background image is shown shortly when X initially starts, but is replaced by the GNOME background during the boot-up sequence.

Selecting Window Managers   GNOME does not require the use of any specific window manager, although it benefits from window managers such as E that are 100% GNOME-compliant. This improves the interaction between the two applications. You can add, edit, and delete additional window managers by clicking Window Manager from the Control Center. When you add or edit a theme, you will see a dialog box that enables you to specify the window manager title, the filename of the command that launches the manager, and the filename of the configuration tool.

If the window manager you're adding or editing is session-managed (meaning that GNOME can save your desktop settings so that your next session will look exactly the same as the one you most recently quit), you should check the box to indicate that. When you have several window managers listed in this window, you will be able to choose among them. You also can click the Run Configuration Tool button at the bottom, which brings up an application by which you can customize the highlighted window manager.

Configuring Editor and MIME Types   You might not want to use the Emacs editor, which is set as the default for GNOME. If not, clicking GNOME Edit Properties brings up a window that enables you to pick from many different editors, including basic ones such as gnotepad or gedit. The editor you choose is the application that will be launched automatically when you right-click a document on your desktop or in your file manager and then choose Edit.

A similar functionality is available to you by configuring Multimedia Internet Mail Extension, or MIME types. These are standard descriptors for different types of files that enable specific client applications to be launched when you try to view such a file. MIME is based on file extensions. For example, you might have the xpdf application installed to enable you to manually open and view documents stored as Portable Document Format (PDF) files. However, if you want this application to launch automatically when you double-click a file on the desktop or file manager, you will have to make sure that a MIME type is specified for the .pdf file extension.

Click Mime Types to see the list of predefined MIME types in the right window frame. From this list, you can add a file type or select an existing file type and then edit or delete it. If you choose to edit one, or if you just want to check the applications associated with a certain MIME type, double-click the file type or highlight it, and click the Edit button. This brings up the pop-up window shown in Figure 7.14.

FIGURE 7.14
Editing MIME types
and associated
applications.

In this case, files stored in the PDF format, as indicated by the extension .pdf, are associated with the application xpdf. If you double-click on such a file, the system will try to open the file and will therefore run the xpdf command and bring up the file you choose to open. If you right-click a file and select View or Edit, nothing will happen in this particular example because you haven't selected a Mime Type Action for View and Edit. Copy the command that is in Open down to the other two boxes if you want to enable such functionality.

If you know where the launcher application is but you can't remember where it is located, just click Browse to bring up a file browser that you can use to find the application in your file system. You also can click the No Icon button at the top of the pop-up menu to bring up a handy icon selector for you to choose an image to associate with such files when they are displayed on your desktop, menu, or panel. After you've made the changes, you can click Try to see what they look like, OK to save the changes and continue configuring the Control Center, or Revert to ignore the changes you just made and return to the previous settings.

Configuring Multimedia   You can make two simple configuration changes in this section. First, you can change the way your system bell sounds, or activate system sounds and change the sounds associated with certain system or application events. Second, you can modify the pitch and duration of the default system bell and click Test to hear what the new settings sound like.

In the General tab of the sound menu, you will be able to enable or disable GNOME sound support and event sounds. In the Sound Events tab, you can associate specific sounds that will occur when certain events occur within your applications. In addition to the typical Try, Revert, OK, Cancel, and Help buttons, you will see a Play button that enables you to hear the sound associated with any event that you have highlighted in the Events window frame. Additionally, you can change the sound file that plays for any event by clicking the Browse button, navigating your file system, and selecting an audio file of your choice.

Configuring Peripherals   The peripherals section enables you to change the default settings for your keyboard and mouse. For example, you can disable or enable auto-repeat, which enables you to hold down a key and have the system continue to generate that key in your application as if you were pressing it over and over again. You can also enable and set the volume of the keyboard click, which makes a small clicking noise when you press a key.

The mouse section enables you to set the mouse for left-handed or right-handed operation, depending on your preference. It also lets you set the acceleration speed and threshold (delay) settings of the mouse; some people like the mouse pointer to move rapidly across the screen when they move the mouse, while others prefer a slow motion.

Configuring GNOME Session Manager The GNOME Session Manager gives you the capability to log out of your system while you still have applications running and located across your desktop or minimized on your panel. When you log back in, session management enables you to view your desktop as it looked when you logged out (as if you brought all the applications back up and repositioned them the way you like them). This feature is not the same as a laptop's suspend and resume feature—the applications do not store and recall any data you have active in them. You can recall only the active applications and their locations on your desktop, not the data contained in them. This automatic function works only for applications that are capable of being session-managed, however. If you want to launch non-session-managed applications on startup, you will have to add them to the list using the Add button. You also can delete or edit a highlighted application.

If you click the Prompt On Logout button here, you will have to select Save Current Setup when you log out; your desktop environment will not be saved automatically. If you want your settings to be saved automatically, click instead the Automatically Save Changes To Session button. If you have lots of applications running, you can click the Browse Currently Running Programs option to view a list of applications that can be session-managed. If one of the applications that you have up is not listed, you must manually add it to the startup list.

TIP GNOME comes with a built-in emergency and recovery mechanism, just in case you change your GNOME desktop environment settings in such a way that you can't properly log in and access your desktop. To do this, hold down the Ctrl and Shift keys simultaneously while you are logging in. This will give you a pop-up window, where you can choose either to start with default programs (ignore session-specific settings from previous logout saves) or reset all user settings (restore all GNOME configuration settings to the defaults that existed when you first installed). Of course, you should use the latter with extreme caution and only in dire emergencies, unless you absolutely can't avoid it and don't mind configuring GNOME all over again.

Configuring GNOME Panels

The first thing you will notice and want to learn how to use is the default GNOME panel (see Figure 7.15). The default panel is divided into several parts, consisting of the hidebuttons on each side, several applets (including the main menu on the far left and the GNOME pager in the middle), a clock on the far right, and a blank section in the middle where running and minimized (iconized) applications are listed. In this case, you can see the GNOME Help Browser listed and visible on the desktop.

FIGURE 7.15
Configuring and using the GNOME panel.

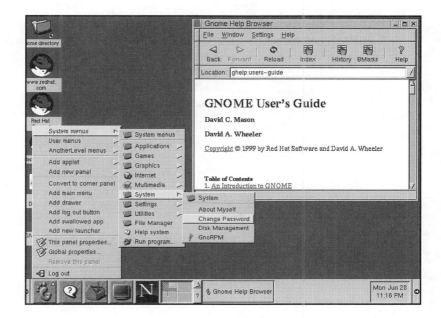

You can access the main configuration tool for this panel (and any other) by right-clicking the hidebuttons or any blank area of the panel. Right-clicking any of the applet icons brings up a different pop-up menu that enables you to remove them from the panel, move them around on the panel, or edit their properties (such as name, ToolTip comments, icon, and associated command or application). You can see a similar set of panel configuration options by clicking the Panel option of the GNOME main menu button.

In Figure 7.15, I have expanded a few menus to show you that this action gives you access to many of the system and user menu items available from the main GNOME menu (the GNOME footprint icon in the bottom-left corner, with the arrow that indicates the menu expands). However, it provides additional configuration choices that are not available from the main menu, such as the capability to edit panel properties, convert the panel type, and add panel menus, drawers, applets, and launchers.

Editing Global Panel Properties Selecting the Global panel configuration item enables you to change the appearance and behavior of the default panel and any new panels you create. For example, you can disable or change animation settings in the Animation tab. Four tabs enable you to disable or change tile characteristics of panel buttons, such as the background image and border width of launcher icons, drawer icons, menu icons, and the logout icon. The default settings on the first five tabs of the Global Panel Configuration window are very suitable to normal operations and can be easily modified—feel free to experiment with different settings to see which you prefer.

Part

II

Ch

7

In the Miscellaneous tab, you want to change several settings to extend and enhance the functionality of all your panels (see Figure 7.16). Any settings you change here will automatically be applied to any existing or newly created panels on your desktop.

FIGURE 7.16
Miscellaneous tab of GNOME global panel properties.

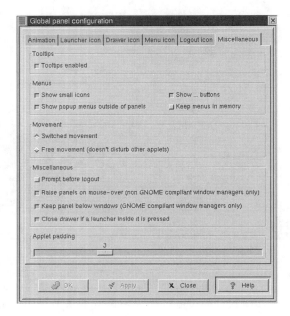

For example, this is where you can disable the ToolTips that pop up when your cursor remains over a panel button for a short period of time. Select the Show Small Icons button if you want to see little icons alongside menu item names. Select Show Buttons if you want to use a left mouse click to access a few special shortcuts associated with menus and launchers when clicking the ... icon. (These shortcuts are normally accessed by right-clicking these items.) The shortcuts enable you to add the selected item quickly and easily to another menu or panel.

TIP The Help button at the bottom of the Global Panel Configuration window brings up a very comprehensive help file in your Netscape Communicator browser. This not only provides a convenient online help function, but the file also can provide some additional configuration information not provided here.

Select the Show Pop-up Windows Outside of Panels option if you don't like the default behavior of pop-up windows (normally, if you right-click on the bottom or outer edge of a corner or edge panel or applet icon, the pop-up window will overlap and cover part of your panel). Select Keep Panels Below Windows if you want your applications to have priority over the panel for display. This can be a difficult tradeoff to determine because enabling it means that you can always access the buttons at the bottom of applications that extend vertically across the entire virtual screen, but you will sometimes have to move your application window to access panel buttons and menus.

Select Close Drawer If a Launcher Inside It Is Pressed if you don't like having to manually close a drawer after selecting an application within it; this is a nice feature that can save you a little time if you use drawers often. The vertical scrollbar at the bottom of the tab enables you to set the amount of space that is automatically placed and kept between icons and buttons as you add, remove, and move them around on your panel.

Converting Panel Types   GNOME provides for two different types of panels: You can choose to use either edge or corner panels. The default panel is an edge panel, and it behaves somewhat differently than a corner panel. For example, if you click a hidebutton on either end of an edge panel, the panel closes and becomes an icon in the corner where you clicked the mouse. If you click the hidebutton immediately afterward, the panel opens back to its original position.

However, a corner panel acts differently. A corner panel does not stretch to occupy the entire edge of a virtual screen, but it grows and shrinks as you add icon buttons, launchers, and menus to it. If you click the hidebutton in the corner, an open corner panel will behave similarly to an open edge panel and will close toward that corner. If you click the opposite end of an open corner panel (the hidebutton that is somewhere in the middle of a screen's edge), on the other hand, a corner panel will not close in the direction of that hidebutton. Instead, it will slide the open corner panel over to the other corner. You will then have to click on that same hidebutton again to get the corner panel to close in the corner to where you just repositioned it.

The style of panel you use is purely up to you, based on the action that feels natural. Selecting Convert to Edge (or Corner) Panel from the Configuration pop-up menu will allow you to try the opposite type of panel. You can also have more than one panel, such as one of each, strategically placed along your desktop. For example, I store my CD, modem, clock, and monitor applets conveniently in a corner panel in the top-right corner of the screen; this keeps my edge panel at the bottom relatively uncluttered.

Editing Individual Panel Properties   Converting between corner and edge panels is useful, but you also probably will want to know how to place the panels in different corners or on other edges of your screen. You can configure placement of your panels by clicking the This Panel's Properties option from the Panel Configuration pop-up menu. The window and tabs shown in Figure 7.17 now appear.

FIGURE 7.17
Changing individual panel properties.

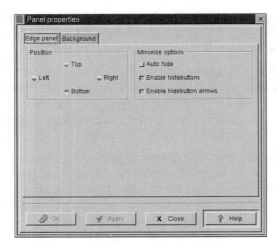

As you can see, there are relatively few items to configure for individual panels, in comparison to the global panel properties described previously. In the first tab, you can determine by the tab title whether the panel you are configuring is an edge or corner panel. In the Position section of the window, you will be able to pick between four different corners (depicted as geographical locations based on North, East, South, and West for corner panels) or four different sides (depicted as top, bottom, left, and right for edge panels, as shown in Figure 7.17).

In the Minimize Options section of both edge and corner panels, you will be able to enable or disable autohide, which specifies whether the panels will always be visible or whether they will implode when the mouse pointer is not directly over them. You can experiment with the autohide function to see if you like it. This feature comes in handy to keep your desktop tidy, and it always grants you access to your application's entire window; sometimes, however, it is a pain when you try to resize a window or move to another virtual screen and the edge or corner panel keeps popping up to complicate what you're trying to do. In this section, you also have the ability to disable hidebuttons and the arrows that are displayed on them.

One other difference exists in configuring edge and corner panel properties, and that is the orientation section associated with the Corner Panel Properties window. This additional section provides the capability for you to dictate not only which corner to position the panel, but also along which edge the panel is located and along which the panel slides back and forth when you click its hidebuttons. For example, you would select Northeast position and Vertical orientation if you wanted a corner panel to start out in the top-right corner and stretch across the right side of the screen.

N O T E   When you move an open corner panel to another corner by clicking the hidebutton opposite the corner where it is located, the panel properties will be updated automatically. For example, if you click twice on the lower (southern) hidebutton of an open, northeast-vertical corner panel, you will notice that the panel properties show that it now has become a southeast-vertical corner panel. This might seem a little complicated, but it will become clear as you experiment with it a little and come to understand the odd panel terminology. ▪

Adding and Removing Panels   You probably will find that a panel quickly can become cluttered and unwieldy to use. In this case, you will want to add another panel. You do this simply by right-clicking any panel or hidebutton background and selecting Add New Panel from the pop-up panel configuration menu. You will have the choice of creating a new corner or edge panel. GNOME will create a new panel for you and will place it automatically, but this panel will be empty and ready for you to add functionality to it manually.

Removing a panel is just as easy. Bring up the pop-up panel configuration menu by right-clicking it, and select Remove This Panel. The panel will be removed immediately. Keep in mind that you must always have at least one panel, otherwise you would not be able to access your default main menu and pager applet. As a result, if you have only one panel, the option to Remove This Panel will be ghosted out so that you cannot select it.

CAUTION

No warning or confirmation window pops up if you choose to remove a panel, even if you have placed several drawers, menus, and launchers in it. Make sure that you avoid the menu item labeled Remove This Panel if you don't want to re-create and reconfigure the panel again if you accidentally delete it!

Configuring Panel Applets   You can add an applet to a panel simply by clicking Add Applet on the panel configuration pop-up window. Applets are grouped in several different menus, and you can select one from any of the categories that you need, such as amusements, monitors, multimedia, network, or utility.

After you've added an applet to a panel, you can move it around on that panel. To move an applet, right-click it and select Move Applet. Your mouse pointer will change to a crosshair (depending on your selected theme). Move that crosshair cursor to the new position on the panel, and left-click where you want the applet to remain.

Some applets, such as the GNOME terminal, have properties that you can edit. These settings differ for each applet, so they all can't be discussed or shown here. However, if your applet has properties that you can edit, you can do so by selecting the Properties option from the applet configuration pop-up menu that appears when you right-click it. Other applets, such as a CD player, have an option to run the applet; this is just a different functionality coded into the applet, and it serves the same purpose and result as double-clicking on the applet's button. A few applets, such as the GNOME pager, have an About option that you can choose to view a small pop-up window that gives some basic information about what the applet does and who developed or distributed it.

Removing an applet from a panel is just as easy. All you have to do is right-click on the applet to bring up the applet configuration pop-up menu; then select the Remove From Panel option. Unfortunately, no confirmation window or warning appears before you remove an applet, so be careful and make sure that you want to remove an applet from a panel first.

Part
II

Ch
7

Configuring Panel Launchers   Let's say that you have an application or utility that you often run, and you want to create a shortcut to it on one of your panels. You have two primary methods of accomplishing this. The absolute easiest way is to bring up the GNOME File Manager, navigate through the file system until you find the application you need, and then drag and drop it onto your panel with the mouse. You will then have the opportunity to specify a title and comments for the launcher (see Figure 7.18). You also can dictate whether the launcher should run the application silently or within a shell so that you can interact with it or view the output.

FIGURE 7.18

Creating an application launcher on a panel.

For example, Figure 7.18 shows the pop-up window that appears when you drag and drop the /bin/date file from the File Manager to the default panel. In this case, I added the name and comment and selected Run in Terminal (otherwise, the command would run, but I wouldn't see the output). Clicking OK, without selecting an icon, places a generic GNOME icon and button on the panel; clicking the button will run the date command and display the output in a pop-up window.

The other method of creating a panel launcher is to select Add New Launcher from the panel's pop-up configuration window. This will bring up the same window and enable you to type in the specific information that you need to launch the application. The difference with this method is that the window provides no browse capability to assist you in finding an application or utility (unlike other properties windows, such as those that occur with icon selection). Unlike dragging and dropping with the File Manager, you will have to know and type the exact full path and filename of the application.

N O T E   The Create Launcher Applet dialog box pictured in Figure 7.18 is similar in appearance and function to the Launcher Properties window you see when you select Properties after right-clicking a panel launcher. The primary difference, other than the name, is that you have two additional buttons (Apply and OK) that enable you to save any changes you make to the properties while you're viewing and editing them (the two buttons are enabled only if you make changes). ■

TIP GNOME gives you a handy shortcut to add a logout function to your panel. Just select Add Logout Button from the panel configuration pop-up window, and an extra launcher/applet button will appear on your panel. Clicking this button will have the same effect as selecting Logout from the main GNOME menu.

Configuring GNOME Drawers

A drawer is a convenient mechanism GNOME provides you to store application launchers and menus (which contain groups of launchers) on your panels. In effect, a drawer is basically a panel that is contained within other panels but is displayed as a drawer with its own icon. You can delete a drawer from any panel by right-clicking it and selecting Remove From Panel. Adding a drawer to a panel is equally easy. To create an empty drawer on a panel, right-click the panel background and select Add Drawer. You can then add application launchers to that drawer by dragging and dropping them from your desktop or file manager.

NOTE You can even edit a drawer's properties just as you can those of a panel. However, when you bring up the Properties window, you will not be able to configure the position and orientation settings like you can with a drawer. To move a drawer, you must select Move Applet after right-clicking it. ■

To add a menu or group of launchers from your main menu or submenus to your panel as a drawer, you have two options. The main method is to right-click the launcher you want (the CD player, for example) and select Add Launcher to Panel. Then right-click the launcher and select Move Applet to move it where you want on any panel's open drawer. However, if you enabled the Show Buttons option in the Miscellaneous tab of the Global Panel Properties window, you can click the ... button next to a launcher on a menu and then select Add Launcher to Panel.

You can also add an entire menu or submenu of application launchers to a panel and make them available in a drawer. To do this, go to the menu or submenu you're interested in, and either right-click the launcher or click the ... next to it (if enabled) and select Add This As Drawer to Panel. All the launchers contained in the chosen menu or submenu will now be listed as icons inside a new open drawer on the panel where you accessed the menu in question. You can then close and open the drawer by clicking the hidebuttons.

Configuring GNOME Menus

The main method of configuring your menus and submenus in GNOME is through the menu editor that you can access from the main menu. Select Settings, Menu Editor; you will see the application window pictured in Figure 7.19. This application enables you to expand rolled-up menus (indicated by the plus sign) to see the launchers and submenus underneath them. You can also right-click a menu (as depicted here) to add or delete a launcher, create a new submenu, or move and sort the menus to your liking. Many menus can be edited only by the root user.

Part
II

Ch
7

FIGURE 7.19
Using the GNOME
Menu Editor.

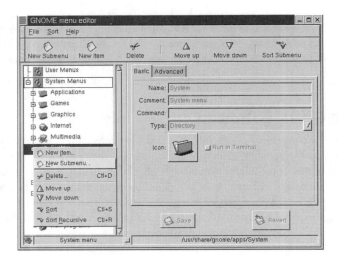

You will see two tabs in the menu editor: Basic and Advanced. Under Basic, you have the capability to edit the name of a menu, submenu, or menu item (launcher), as well as the comment (ToolTip-related), command (filename of application, if applicable), and type (menu/directory or application). If an item's details are ghosted out and you can't modify them, this is because you don't have appropriate permissions to change these items. If you want a different icon than the default, click the button next to the Icon text label. If you want the command to run in an xterm command-line shell, click Run in Terminal. Some applications require this; otherwise, you won't be able to interact with them or view the output. Click Save or Revert if you want to activate or ignore any changes you made while in this editing mode.

As with everything else in Linux, however, you have a little more flexibility than just using the Menu Editor. For example, you can add a system menu item (launcher) directly to a user or personal menu by right-clicking (or clicking the item's ... button, if it's enabled) a menu or submenu item and then selecting Add This to Personal Menu. The application launcher you just chose will now be visible off the main menu under User Menus. In this manner, you can duplicate an entire system submenu onto your user menu by performing the action previously described on a submenu.

Finally, you can make a few changes to your main menu (the one with the GNOME footprint logo on your main panel) by right-clicking it and selecting properties. This brings up the screen shown in Figure 7.20. The menu type section reflects that it is a main menu, which provides all the additional functionality you need. Under the Main Menu section, you can toggle buttons to disable (turn off and not display) any available menu. You can also choose to make the menus listed appear either directly on the main menu or in a submenu.

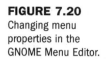

FIGURE 7.20
Changing menu
properties in the
GNOME Menu Editor.

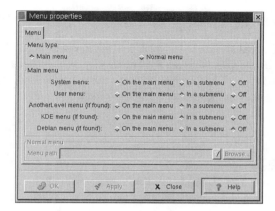

For example, the user menus are usually shown directly on the main menu. In Figure 7.20, I changed the default setting to force User Menus to be shown as a submenu. When you do this, the user menu will be displayed as a single menu item with a small arrow icon to the right, enabling you to click it and bring up an exploding menu beside it to choose launchers (similar to the way the KDE and AnotherLevel menus work by default). This can be a powerful tool if you find that some of your user menus and submenus are taking up too much real estate and cluttering your main menu.

Configuring the GNOME Desktop

Don't forget that you also have a lot of real estate available on your desktop to supplement the functionality of your panels, menus, and drawers. You might want to store frequently used directories, files, and application launchers directly on your desktop for quick access. This capability can be an even greater asset when you take into account that you can create and use multiple desktops and multiple screen areas. That way, you can have different desktops preconfigured with the tools you need at different times, but you can always keep one nice and clean desktop for general computing.

One of the most powerful features of Red Hat 6.0 with GNOME and Enlightenment is the drag-and-drop functionality it creates for you right out of the box. To drag and drop a favorite application, folder, or document (and its associated icon, defined in MIME types discussed earlier) onto your desktop, just select the file from your File Manager and hold down the Ctrl key while you drag and drop the file onto your desktop area.

CAUTION

Be sure to keep the Ctrl key pressed while you drag and drop files around your system. If you don't, the default action is to move the file, not copy it or create a shortcut (symlink).

Part

II

Ch

7

Another way exists by which you can add launchers and directories to your desktop. Just right-click a blank portion of your desktop, and select New, Launcher or New, Directory. If you choose to create a new desktop directory, you will have the opportunity to enter its name in a pop-up window. If you elect to create a new launcher, you will see a pop-up equivalent to that shown in Figure 7.18 that enables you to enter the command's filename, requirements to run from a terminal, and ToolTip comments to describe it.

Summary

GNOME and Enlightenment provide a robust, user-friendly, flexible desktop environment that is easy to configure. You should familiarize yourself with all the major options and capabilities of each application so that you can use them to your advantage. You will enjoy your Linux experience more if you customize the way your desktop appears, behaves, and sounds.

Red Hat Linux 6.0 includes all the graphical tools you need to configure GNOME and Enlightenment to your liking. No need exists to use command-line configuration tools that were the only option in the early days of Linux development. The GNOME and Enlightenment Configuration tools can be accessed easily from your main panel, the main menu, and your desktop background. ●

## CHAPTER 8

Installing and Configuring the KDE Desktop

by Robert Napier

What Is KDE?

The *K Desktop Environment (KDE)* is a UNIX desktop, which means it provides a user-friendly GUI that can be integrated with applications. KDE offers features similar to what the Macintosh and Windows interfaces provide. It also provides a framework for developers and a way for applications to communicate with each other. Figure 8.1 shows KDE in action.

FIGURE 8.1
KDE provides many of the same features that you find on Macintosh and Windows machines—and many features that you don't.

From a user's point of view, KDE provides many features, such as the following:

- **Files directly on the desktop**—In KDE, just as in a Macintosh or Windows machine, you can drag files to the desktop and store them there as icons. Applications can be automatically launched by links placed on the desktop as well.

- **Session management**—Session management means that applications can remember the state they were in when you logged out and can restart the application in exactly the same state when you log back in. For example, you can restart in the same file you were working on and at the same point where you were in the file.

- **Desktop panel**—The desktop panel provides quick access to applications by providing the Application Starter (or K-Menu) and panel buttons to start your favorite applications. You can also *swallow* applications, which means that what looks like a button can actually be a running application. This capability is very useful for programs such as xbiff, which checks for new mail.

■ **Taskbar**—The taskbar shows all the currently available windows, which enables you to quickly switch between applications, even if they're minimized.

■ **Pager**—A *pager* enables you to maintain several desktops and easily switch among them. For example, you might put your mail program on one desktop, all your programming tools on another, and a game of Solitaire on a third.

From the user's point of view, the most important parts of KDE are kwm, kpanel, and kfm. First, kwm, the KDE Window Manager, provides all the normal window manager functionality, such as displaying, minimizing, moving, and resizing windows. The kpanel tool provides a convenient panel, usually at the bottom of the screen. It has quick-launch buttons, menus, a clock, and much more. In addition, kpanel provides the taskbar, usually at the top of the screen. It shows all the currently open windows and enables you to switch among them easily. Finally, kfm is the KDE File Manager, which not only provides access to your files, but also acts as a Web and document browser.

Installing KDE

Red Hat 6.0's default desktop is GNOME, so you need to make some modifications to install KDE.

Table 8.1 lists the KDE packages for Red Hat 6.0.

Table 8.1 KDE Packages	
RPM	**Purpose**
qt	(Required) Qt toolkit.
kdesupport	(Recommended) Various non-KDE libraries that KDE requires.
kdelibs	(Required) KDE shared libraries.
kdebase	(Required) The core of KDE, such as the window manager.
kdegames	(Optional) Several games.
kdegraphics	(Optional) Various programs to view and draw graphics.
kdeutils	(Optional) Calculator, editor, and similar utilities.
kdemultimedia	(Optional) CD player and other multimedia applications.
kdenetwork	(Optional) Internet applications, including a mail reader and a news reader.
kdeadmin	(Optional) System administration programs.
kdetoys	(Optional) Fun programs that aren't games. For example, kmoon puts the phase of the moon on your panel.
korganizer	(Optional) Personal organizer.

The required and recommended packages should be installed in the order listed using `rpm` (the Red Hat Package Manager):

```
$ su
Password: <root password>
# cd /mnt/cdrom/RedHat/RPMS      (or your local directory if
➥you have downloaded updated RPMs)
# rpm -i qt*
# rpm -i kdesupport*
# rpm -i kdelibs*
# rpm -i kdegames* kdegraphics* kdeutils* kdemultimedia* kdenetwork*
➥kdeadmin* kdetoys* korganizer*
```

> **N O T E** The version of KDE that ships with Red Hat 6.0 is 1.1.1 pre2. This is a prerelease beta of version 1.1.1, and you should upgrade to the released version to avoid known bugs. You can get updated RPMs from `ftp://ftp.redhat.com/`. ■

Using the *switchdesk* Tool for Red Hat 6.0

The easiest way to switch to KDE is to use the `switchdesk` tool. This tool might not be installed by default, so you might have to install the `switchdesk-1.7.0-1` package by using `rpm`:

```
$ su
Password: <root password>
# cd /mnt/cdrom/RedHat/RPMS
# rpm -i switchdesk-1.7.0-1.i386.rpm
```

After you've installed `switchdesk`, launching it is simple:

```
$ switchdesk
```

This command produces a dialog box asking whether you prefer GNOME, KDE, or AnotherLevel. Click KDE, choose OK, and then log out. When you log back in, your default desktop will be KDE.

Choosing KDE Without *switchdesk*

If you'd rather not use `switchdesk`, you can make KDE your default desktop by modifying your `$HOME/.Xclients-default` as follows:

```
$ echo exec startkde > ~/.Xclients-default
```

Configuring KDE

KDE is extremely configurable, but only in specific ways. Much like Windows 98, KDE can be configured to perform only tasks that the developers thought you might like to do. Although KDE is still more configurable than Windows 98, tasks as simple as removing the clock from the panel (or replacing it with your own) can be very difficult or impossible. The developers thought that everyone would want a simple digital clock with the date on the right side of the panel.

Templates

The Templates folder on your desktop contains various *kdelnk* files that you can use to create new objects on your desktop or in folders. A kdelnk file (pronounced "K-D-E link") contains information about another file or location and is similar to a Windows shortcut. All the entries in the Root menu's New menu come from the Templates folder (except Folder, which is built in). To create a new instance of the template, right-click the background to pull up the Root menu. Then click New and the item you want to create. The following sections describe items that can be created.

Folder   Folders are directories and can hold other files or folders. You can use spaces or punctuation other than the slash (/) in the folder names. In KDE, this is a special character and cannot be put into a folder name. If you use spaces, note that you will have to put the whole name in quotation marks to refer to it on the command line. For example, to change into a folder called My book on the command line, you would need to type

```
$ cd "My book"
```

To create a folder, follow these steps:

1. Open kfm (for example, click the Home icon on the panel).
2. Right-click the background of kfm to get the local menu.
3. Click New, Folder.
4. Enter the name of the folder and press Enter.

File System Device   Using the File System Device, you can mount devices such as CDs or floppies directly from the desktop. Before you can create this kind of link, you must make sure that you are able to mount the device.

When you are able to mount the device normally, here's how to create a File System Device link:

1. Open kfm (for example, click the Home icon on the panel).
2. Right-click the background of kfm to get the local menu.
3. Click New, File System Device.
4. Enter a name for the device. For example, you could call your CD-ROM drive `CD-ROM.kdelnk`.
5. Select the Device tab.
6. In the Device field, enter the device name (such as `/dev/fd0` or `/dev/cdrom`) as the Device.

7. If the device should be read-only, select the Readonly check box.

8. Click the Mounted Icon to select the icon that appears when the device is mounted. Select Unmounted Icon to select the icon that appears when the device is unmounted. Icons of floppy disks and CDs with and without small green lights beside them are available for your convenience. To select an icon, simply click it and then click OK.

9. Finally, click OK to close the dialog.

URLs URLs include FTP URLs, Internet addresses (URLs), and World Wide Web URLs. The only difference among them is their icons.

To create a URL, follow these steps:

1. Open kfm (for example, click the Home icon on the panel).

2. Right-click the background of kfm to get the local menu.

3. Click New.

4. Click the type of URL you would like (FTP URL, Internet Address, or World Wide Web URL).

5. Enter a meaningful name for the URL.

6. Click the URL tab.

7. Enter the URL in the URL field.

8. If desired, click the icon to choose a new icon. Select the icon you want, and click OK.

9. Click OK to close the dialog box.

MIME Type *Multipurpose Internet Mail Extensions (MIME)* originally was intended to encode files in email messages, but it has moved on to handle a wide variety of tasks. KDE now uses normal MIME mechanisms to identify and handle files. If KDE applications need new MIME types, the applications install them. Generally, you set up your own MIME types to associate a type of file with a non-KDE application.

Following are instructions on how to create a MIME type. In this example, we'll create the MIME type `image/x-xcf`. The `image/` indicates the category, `x-` indicates that this is a non-standard MIME type, and `xcf` indicates that this is for `.xcf` files, which are the native file format for the GIMP (an image manipulation package for Linux).

1. Open kfm (for example, click the Home icon on the panel).

2. Click Edit, Mime Types.

3. Click the `image/` folder.

4. Right-click the background of kfm to get the local menu.

5. Click New.

6. Click Mime Type.

7. Name the Mime Type `x-xcf.kdelnk`. The name should be the MIME Type followed by `.kdelnk`.

8. You will receive an error that says `The mime type config file <config filename> does not contain a MimeType=...` `entry`. This is completely normal because you haven't configured this MIME Type yet. Click OK.

9. A MIME Type dialog box will appear. Click the Binding tab.

10. In the Pattern field, enter the filename patterns that indicate this type of file. In this example, enter `*.xcf;*.XCF;`. Leave the trailing semicolon. Notice that lists of filename patterns are separated by semicolons.

11. In the Mime Type field, enter `image/x-xcf`. This is the MIME Type.

12. In the Comment field, enter `GIMP image file`. This is just a comment to explain what the MIME Type is.

13. In the Default Application field, select The GIMP if The GIMP is installed. If The GIMP isn't installed, leave this blank for now and see the "Application" section for information on installing new applications.

14. Click the icon of the question mark and select a good icon for this MIME Type. In this example, select the paint can (`image.xpm`) and click OK.

15. Click OK to save the new MIME Type.

Application KDE must know about the applications that you have installed in order to match data files to the appropriate application. For example, if we want to use The GIMP to view xcf image files, KDE must know that you have The GIMP installed and how to run it. Application kdelnk files provide this information.

In this example, we will associate The GIMP with various image files. This example assumes that you have already installed The GIMP from the Red Hat 6.0 CD. Follow these steps:

1. Open kfm (for example, click the Home icon on the panel).

2. Click Edit, Applications.

3. Click the Graphics folder. These folders help organize your application links.

4. Right-click the background of kfm to get the local menu.

5. Click New, Application.

6. Name the application `gimp.kdelnk`.

7. An application dialog box will appear. Click the Execute tab.

8. In the Execute field, enter `gimp`. This is the program to execute to launch this application.

9. Click the gear icon to choose an icon for The GIMP. If the icon gimp.xpm is available, choose that. Then click OK.

10. For this example, you don't need the Swallowing on Panel or Run in Terminal boxes. You will learn about these options later in this section.

11. Click the Application tab.

12. For Binary Pattern, enter `gimp;`. This is a semicolon-separated list of possible names for the executable.

13. For Comment, enter `GNU Image Manipulation Program`. This is just to let you know what program this is.

14. For Name, enter `The GIMP`. This is the name that will show up in local menus (the menus that pop up when you right-click on a file). This can also be used as the window title if the program does not provide its own title.

15. In the list of MIME Types in the lower-right corner of the dialog box, select the following MIME Types if they are listed and press the left arrow button for each one: jpeg, png, tiff, x-pcx, x-xbm, x-xcf, x-xpm. This will indicate that The GIMP can handle each of these MIME types, which will add The GIMP to the local menu for any files of these types.

16. Click OK to finish.

The Execute tab has several useful options. The following sections provide detailed explanation of each field.

Execute   This is the command line that will be executed when this application is launched. For most KDE applications this should be the following:

```
executable %i %m –caption \"%c\"
```

For example:

```
kfract %i %m –caption \"%c\"
```

The letters following the percent signs are variables. KDE will expand these before executing the command line. The preceding standard command line tells KDE to set the icon for this program to the user-specified icon (the icon you chose in the icon selection box). It also sets the mini-icon (the icon used on the taskbar or Application starter) to the smaller version of the user-selected icon. Finally, it tells KDE to set the caption (the text printed on the title bar) to the user-specified title of the application.

The following is a more complete explanation of the percent variables:

`%c`	This expands to the language-specific name given in the Name field of the Application tab.
`%d`	This expands to the path of the data file without its filename. For example, if you have associated xcf files with The GIMP, and you click `mypicture.xcf` in the `/tmp` directory, then `%f` will be `/tmp/`. `%d` and `%n` together are the same as `%f` (see `%n` later in this table).

%f   This expands to the full local filename of the data file including its path. For example, if you have associated xcf files with The GIMP, and you click `mypicture.xcf` in the `/tmp` directory, then `%f` will be `/tmp/mypicture.xcf`. If you click on a file that is not on your local machine, KDE will first download the file to a temporary location and then substitute that temporary location for `%f`.

%i   This expands to `-icon` `usericon.xpm`, where `usericon` is the icon you chose on the Execute tab. KDE will look for this icon in `$HOME/.kde/share/icons` and then `$KDEDIR/share/icons`. This icon is used on the desktop and in `kfm` directory listings.

%k   This expands to the location of the configuration file that was used to launch this application. When you use the Application dialog box, KDE creates a configuration file to store your preferences. `%k` expands to the full pathname of this file. This is generally used only for advanced features when you are modifying the configuration file by hand.

%m   This expands to `-miniicon` `usericon.xpm` where `usericon` is the icon you chose on the Execute tab. KDE will look for this icon in `$HOME/.kde/share/icons/mini` and then `$KDEDIR/share/icons/mini`. This icon is used on the taskbar and on the Application Starter.

%n   This expands to the filename of the data file without its path. For example, if you have associated xcf files with The GIMP, and you click on `mypicture.xcf` in the `/tmp` directory, `%f` will be `mypicture.xcf`. `%d` and `%n` together are the same as `%f` (see `%d` earlier in this table).

%u   This expands to the URL of the data file. For example, if you have associated xcf files with The GIMP, and you click on `mypicture.xcf` in the `/tmp` directory, then %f will be file:`/tmp/mypicture.xcf`. This allows you to select files that are on remote machines. For example, if you visit `ftp.redhat.com` and select `/pub/README`, %f will expand to `ftp://ftp.red-hat.com/pub/README`.

Swallowing on Panel   When the panel "swallows" an application, the application actually runs on the panel. This can be very useful for small programs like xbiff, which check your mailbox and change their icon when new mail arrives. Follow these steps to add the xeyes amusement program to the panel:

1. Open kfm (for example, click the Home icon on the panel).
2. Click Edit, Applications.
3. Right-click the background of kfm to get the local menu.
4. Click New, Application.
5. Name the application `xeyes.kdelnk`.
6. An application dialog will appear. Click the Execute tab.

7. In the Execute field, enter `xeyes`. This is the program to execute to launch this application.

8. Click the gear icon to choose an icon for xeyes. If the icon xyes.xpm is available, choose that. Then click OK.

9. In the Swallowing on Panel section, enter `xeyes` for both the Execute field and the Window Title field. The Execute field tells KDE what to run when this is put on the panel. The Window Title field tells KDE what window to "swallow." This should be the title that the application puts on its title bar.

10. You don't need to select Run in Terminal for this example.

11. Click the Application tab.

12. For Binary Pattern, enter `xeyes;`. This is a semicolon-separated list of possible names for the executable.

13. For Comment, enter `xeyes`. This is just to let you know what program this is.

14. For Name, enter `xeyes`. This is the name that will show up in local menus (the menus that pop up when you right-click on a file). This can also be used as the window title if the program does not provide its own title.

15. Click OK to finish.

16. Finally, click the xeyes icon that you've just created and drag it to the panel. You'll see two eyes on the panel that watch your mouse as it moves around the screen.

17. To remove xeyes, right click the eyes and click Remove.

Run in Terminal   For command-line applications, select Run in Terminal. KDE will launch a terminal to display the application. Follow these steps to make a link to the mail program elm:

1. Open kfm (for example, click the Home icon on the panel).

2. Click Edit, Applications.

3. Right-click the background of kfm to get the local menu.

4. Click New, Application.

5. Name the application `Elm.kdelnk`.

6. An application dialog will appear. Click the Execute tab.

7. In the Execute field, enter `elm`. This is the program to execute to launch this application.

8. Click the gear icon to choose an icon for elm. Then click OK.

9. Leave the Swallowing on Panel entries blank.

10. Click Run in Terminal.

11. For Terminal Options enter `-caption "Mail"`.

12. Click the Application tab.

13. For Binary Pattern, enter `elm;`. This is a semicolon-separated list of possible names for the executable.

14. For Comment, enter `Elm Mail Reader`. This is just to let you know what program this is.

15. For Name, enter `Elm`. This is the name that will show up in local menus (the menus that pop up when you right-click a file). This can also be used as the window title if the program does not provide its own title.

16. Click OK to finish.

The following options are commonly used for Terminal Options:

`-caption "Text"`	This makes the window title Text. The window title is printed on the title bar.
`-nowelcome`	When new terminal windows are opened, the title is usually set to Welcome to the Console for a few seconds before the title you set with `-caption` is displayed. To avoid the Welcome to the Console message, use `-nowelcome`.
`-vt_sz CCxLL`	This sets the terminal size to *CC* columns by *LL* lines. For example, to open an 80-column by 25-row terminal, use `-vt_sz 80x25`.

Adding Programs to the Application Starter

The Application Starter, or K-Menu, provides quick access to many applications, as shown in Figure 8.2. The Application Starter has three sections: the default menu, the personal menu, and the administrative menu.

FIGURE 8.2
The Application Starter, or K-Menu, offers a great way to organize your applications.

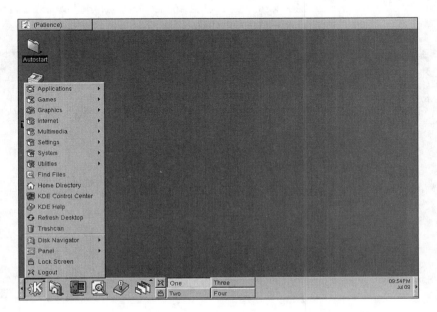

The Application Starter has three sections:

- The default menu is the same for all users on the system; it can be modified only by root.
- The personal menu is unique to each user and can be modified by that user.
- The administrative menu contains items that cannot be modified at all.

Each of these sections can contain one or more of the following elements:

- **Separator**—This thin horizontal line separates one part of the menu from another. This can make grouping related applications easier, without having to create submenus.
- **Submenu**—This is a menu within the menu. You can nest menus as deeply as you like, but more than two or three levels can become unwieldy. In Figure 8.2, Applications is a submenu. A small triangle to the right of the name shows you that it is a submenu.
- **Application**—An application is the most common thing to put on the Application Starter. This entry launches an application.
- **Link**—This is a URL, either local or remote. A link enables you to put your favorite Web sites or local documents right on your Application Starter.
- **Device**—This provides access to a physical device, such as a CD-ROM or floppy drive. See the section "File System Device," earlier in this chapter, for full details.

All Application Starter entries are kdelnk files, just like templates. In fact, the same files can be used to create desktop icons and Application Starter entries.

Menu Editor   The easiest way to modify the Application Starter is to use the Menu Editor. To launch the Menu Editor, click the Application Starter (K-Menu), Panel, Edit Menus. The Menu Editor is shown in Figure 8.3.

FIGURE 8.3
The Menu Editor provides a graphical way to modify your Application Starter.

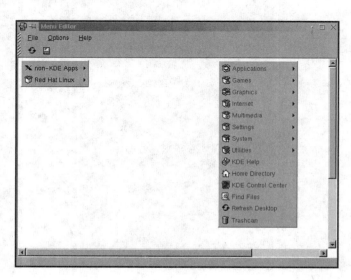

The menu on the left is the personal menu. The menu on right is the default menu. Notice that the default menu's items are grayed out. This indicates that you do not have permission to modify the system menu. If you run the Menu Editor as root, then you can modify this menu as well.

Navigating the Menu Editor The Menu Editor interface is not like most other interfaces, so it can take a little while to get used to. The following tips should help you get around:

- To open or close a submenu, left-click the menu name.
- Right-clicking an entry brings up a local menu of actions.
- To copy an item from one menu to another, click and drag it to the new menu. It will always appear as the last element of the new menu. You can copy submenus this way as well.
- To move an item within a menu, click and drag with the middle mouse button.
- To move an item from one menu to another, copy it as stated previously, and then right-click the old copy and click Delete. Alternatively, use the Cut and Paste functions from the local menu.
- To add a new item, right-click the item below your desired placement, and click New. If you wish to add a new item at the end of the menu, you will have to create it and then move it.
- To move an entire menu (not a submenu) around the screen, right-click any of the items in that menu and click Select Menu for Moving. The cursor will change to crosshairs. Click and drag the menu to another place on the screen.

Adding a new entry to a menu is very similar to creating templates (see the section "Templates," earlier in this chapter). Right-click above where you wish the new entry to be, and click New. Select the Type (Separator, Submenu, Application, Link, or Device). For Separator, nothing else is needed. Submenu just needs a name to display. The rest of the items are filled out exactly like templates. The reason this is so similar to templates is that both mechanisms use the same kdelnk files to store the information.

When you have finished changing the menus, select File, Save. This saves your menus and restarts kpanel so that your changes take effect.

Here's an example of creating a Graphics submenu for your local menu and adding The GIMP to it:

1. Right-click the Application Starter (K-Menu) and click Properties to start the Menu Editor.
2. The left-most menu is the local menu. Right-click the last entry in it and click New.
3. Select Submenu for Type.
4. Type Graphics for File Name and Name.

5. Click the gear icon to select an icon. Pick your favorite icon from the list and click OK.

6. If the icon you chose has a mini-icon associated with it, the mini-icon will appear in the mini-icon box. If no icon appears, or if you want a different mini-icon, click the mini-icon box and select a new mini-icon. Then click OK.

7. Enter Graphics for Comment.

8. Click OK to finish adding the submenu.

9. Click your new Graphics submenu. A menu will appear with EMPTY in it.

10. Right-click Empty and click Change.

11. Leave Type as Application.

12. For File Name, enter gimp.kdelnk. This is the name of the configuration file you are creating.

13. For Name, enter The GIMP. This will appear on the menu.

14. Click the gear icon to select an icon. Select gimp.xpm and click OK.

15. gimp.xpm has a mini-icon associated with it, so you don't have to select a mini-icon.

16. For Comment, enter GNU Image Manipulation Program. This will be the pop-up help that appears when you leave the mouse pointer over the menu entry.

17. For Execute, enter gimp. This is the program that should be executed when this menu entry is selected.

18. Click OK to create your new menu item.

19. Click File, Save to save your new menu.

20. Click File, Quit to quit the Menu Editor.

Bookmarks

Any file in KDE can have a bookmark pointing to it. From within kfm, right-click the file or folder, and select Add to Bookmarks. A bookmark to the file or folder is then placed in your Bookmarks menus, both on the Root menu which is displayed when you right-click on the background, and in kfm.

To edit or remove bookmarks, click Bookmarks on the kfm toolbar, and then choose Edit Bookmarks. When you do so, you open another kfm window looking at your bookmarks. All normal kfm functions work here. To give the bookmark a more convenient name, right-click the bookmark and click Properties. Then change the filename to whatever you would like it to be. Changing the name doesn't affect the file the bookmark points to in any way.

 TIP Remember that KDE doesn't care if a file is local or remote. If you view a Web page using kfm, you can right-click the background of the Web page and select Add to Bookmarks. The same is true of files on an FTP server or any other network resource.

Customizing the Panel

The panel is a central part of KDE and one of the most configurable aspects. It contains your most used applications, status indicators, the desktop pager, and much more. Configuring your panel to work the way you do is one of the best ways to improve your productivity.

Default Panel Components   Before configuring the panel, first take some time to look at its default configuration. Figure 8.4 shows a very common default panel configuration.

FIGURE 8.4
The default KDE panel provides the most critical functions, but not everything you'll want.

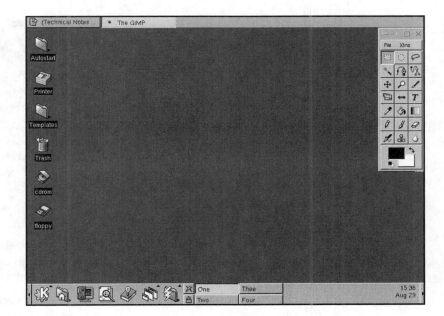

Your default panel will have the following:

- **Application Starter**—The Application Starter, which is also called the K-Menu, holds links to all your programs and configuration menus. It is similar to the Windows 95 Start menu. Press Alt+F1 to open the Application Starter. See the section "Adding Programs to the Application Starter," earlier in this section, for information on customizing this menu.

- **Home Directory**—The Home Directory launches the file manager on your home directory. You can also put other directories on the panel, as we'll discuss later.

- **KDE Control Center**—Using the Control Center, you can configure various parts of KDE, including the window manager, file manager, keyboard, sound, and much more.

- **Find Utility**—KDE has a powerful tool for finding files. You can search by name pattern, modification time, file type, size, or contents. This tool is modeled very closely on Microsoft Windows 98's Find utility.

■ **Help Browser**—If you're a new KDE user, the Help Browser can be a great asset. This is essentially a simple Web browser. In fact, the help files are written in HTML, and hyperlinks in the help system may point to Web pages on the Internet. Links outside the help system are not displayed in the same window, though. The Help Browser can launch kfm to handle those requests.

■ **Window List**—The Window List provides instant access to all your current windows, no matter what desktop they are running on. Being able to access these windows can be a real time-saver when you have many windows open across numerous desktops. You can also get the Window List by clicking the middle mouse button on the desktop.

■ **Disk Navigator**—This provides quick access to your disks and recently accessed files. Via cascading menus (just like in the Application Starter), you have quick access to the root directory, the KDE directory, your CD-ROM drive, your home directory, and your desktop.

■ **Logout**—Logout logs you out of KDE and returns to the login screen.

■ **Lock**—KDE provides various screen savers that activate after a configurable time of inactivity. If you want to start the screen saver immediately, you can press the Lock button. To unlock the screen, you need to enter your login password. The screen saver is configurable through the Control Center (see the previous point on the KDE Control Center).

■ **Pager**—Each of the four buttons in this block provides you with a completely different desktop, each displaying different windows.

■ **Clock**—The clock appears on the far right side of the panel.

■ **Panel Hide**—On either side of the panel is a textured tab with an arrow on it. When you click one of these buttons, the panel slides off the screen in the direction indicated.

Arranging the Default Panel Components   The Application Starter, Pager, Logout, and Lock cannot be removed from the panel, but they may be moved around. The clock cannot be removed or rearranged. All the other items on the panel can be added, removed, or moved around to suit your needs.

To move an item within the panel, click and drag it with the middle mouse button. It may take a little practice to get used to how the buttons move. The other buttons may rearrange themselves to accommodate your move in ways you didn't expect.

Adding New Panel Components   Most panel components are simply kdelnk files, as described in the section "Templates," earlier in this chapter. To add these to the panel, first create them as described in the "Applications" section, earlier in this chapter. Then drag them to the panel. For example, to add The GIMP graphics program to your panel, follow these steps:

1. If you have not already, create gimp.kdelnk as described in "Applications" earlier in this chapter.

2. Open kfm (for example, click the Home icon on the panel).

3. Click Edit, Applications.

4. Click Graphics to enter the folder.

5. Click and drag the GIMP icon from `kfm` to an unused section of the panel. Release the mouse button.

6. If you want to move the icon you've just put on the panel, click and drag it using the middle mouse button.

If the link is already on your Application Starter, you can click Application Starter, Panel, Add Application, and then select the application from the menu.

The Window List and Disk Navigator are special. To add or remove them, click the Application Starter, Panel, and then select either Add Disk Navigator or Add Windowlist. A small block beside the option indicates whether it is currently active.

Removing Panel Components   To remove components, right-click a component and click Remove. Remember that the Application Starter, Pager, Logout, Lock, and Clock cannot be removed.

Configuring the Panel Appearance   The panel's appearance is very configurable. You use the KPanel Configuration dialog box to control the appearance of the panel. To access the KPanel Configuration dialog box, right-click the panel in an unused area, and click Configure.

The Panel Tab   The Panel tab determines the location and style of the task bar and panel.

The Location box sets the location of the panel. You can choose the Top, Left, Bottom, or Right edge of the screen.

The Style box sets the size of the panel. You can choose Tiny, Normal, or Large.

The Taskbar box sets the location of the taskbar. You can choose Hidden, in which case there is no task bar. Top or Bottom will display the task bar horizontally across the top or bottom of the screen. Finally, Top/Left will display the task bar vertically in the upper-left corner of the screen.

The Options Tab   The Options tab determines the panel and task bar's behavior.

Selecting Show Menu Tooltips will pop up descriptions of menu and panel entries when you point the mouse pointer to them. The Delay slider sets how long you have to leave the mouse pointer pointed to the item before the description pops up.

Auto Hide Panel will cause the panel to "slide" off the bottom of the screen when you are not using it. To access it again, point the mouse pointer to the panel's screen edge (usually the bottom of the screen, unless you reconfigured it). The Delay and Speed sliders determine how soon and how quickly the panel slides on and off the screen.

Auto Hide Taskbar is the same as Auto Hide Panel, except it works on the task bar.

Animate Show/Hide determines whether the task bar and panel slide off the screen, or if they just disappear and reappear. The Speed slider determines how fast the animation runs if it is turned on.

Personal Menu Entries First moves the personal menu to the top of the Application Launcher. By default, the system menu is first. See the "Menu Editor" section, earlier in this chapter, for more information on the personal and system menus.

Menu Folders First will move all submenus on the Application Launcher to the top of the menu.

Clock Shows Time in AM/PM Format causes the clock to show time in 12-hour format with AM and PM designations. Clearing this selection displays time in 24-hour ("military") format.

Clock Shows Time in Internet Beats causes the clock to show time in *beats*. Beats are a time standard proposed by Swatch, A.G. It divides the day into 1000 beats. This is generally seen as a marketing ploy on the part of Swatch, A.G., but if you're interested, visit http://www.swatch.com for more information.

Configuring Virtual Desktops   KDE enables you to have multiple *virtual desktops*. Virtual desktops are entire screens onto which you can separate your applications. For example, you could run your mail program on one virtual desktop, your editor on a second, and a game on a third. Because you can use the entire screen for each desktop, your screen can be much less crowded.

You select which virtual desktop to display by using the *pager*. The pager is the block of buttons to the right of the logout and lock buttons. In Figure 8.4, these buttons are labeled One, Two, Three, and Four. You select the virtual desktop to display by clicking one of these buttons.

Virtual desktops are highly configurable. To configure your desktops, click the Application Starter, Panel, Configure to bring up the KPanel Configuration dialog box (see Figure 8.5). Click the Desktops tab to configure your desktop.

FIGURE 8.5
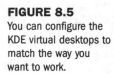
You can configure the KDE virtual desktops to match the way you want to work.

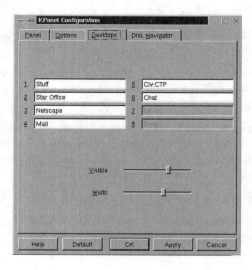

The numbered fields in this dialog box determine the names of the desktops. To change the names of the desktops, just change the values in these fields. You should name them meaningfully so that you can remember what is on each desktop. The Visible slider sets the number of virtual desktops available. You can have two, four, six, or eight desktops; four is the default. The Width slider sets the width of the virtual desktop buttons on the panel. You should set the buttons wide enough to see the names you have chosen but narrow enough not to take up unneeded space on the panel. KDE remembers your desktop names between sessions.

TIP If you want to change only the name of a desktop, you don't need to use the KPanel Configuration dialog box. Just click the desktop button to go to that desktop, and then click it again. You then are presented with a standard I-beam text cursor to change the name.

Configuring the Disk Navigator

The Disk Navigator is very useful for getting to common files quickly. Because the files are displayed as cascading menus, you can get to any file on the system after you have access to the root directory. Generally, however, you don't want to go through four or five levels of menus to get to the file you want. To make this easier, Disk Navigator enables you to set where the tree will start. You can have as many trees as you like—remember, though, that having too many can make it hard to get to what you need quickly, which was the whole point of the Disk Navigator.

Disk Navigator consists of three sections: Shared, Personal, and Recent. The Shared section can be modified only by the superuser and will be used by all users on the machine. The Personal section can be modified by each user and will be used only by that user. The Recent section lists files and applications that you have recently accessed through KDE.

To configure the Disk Navigator, right-click it and click Properties. This brings up the Disk Navigator configuration panel, shown in Figure 8.6. Note that this is identical to the Disk Navigator tab shown in Figure 8.5.

FIGURE 8.6
Disk Navigator enables you to define your own most-used directories.

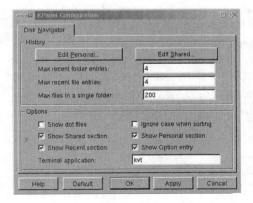

The following are the Disk Navigator options:

- **Edit Personal**—This option determines which directories are listed in the Personal section. Selecting this brings up a kfm window. Simply place links here to the folders you would like to be included. See the section "Templates," earlier in this chapter, for more information on creating links.

- **Edit Shared**—This option is the same as Edit Personal option, except that it manages the Shared section. This can be done only by root.

- **Max recent folder entries**—This option sets how many recently accessed folders will be displayed. The default of 4 is generally a good choice. Setting it much higher can make the disk navigator too large.

- **Max recent file entries**—This option sets how many recently accessed files will be displayed. The default of 4 is generally a good choice. Setting it much higher can make the disk navigator too large.

- **Max files in a single folder**—This option limits how many files can be shown in a folder. If more than this setting is present, the message "Too Many Files" will be displayed. For performance reasons, it is best not to set this value much higher than its default (200).

- **Show dot files**—In Linux, files that begin with a period are considered hidden files. These are generally configuration files that you don't want to see anyway, so it is usually best to leave this option unset.

- **Ignore case when sorting**—This sets the sorting order to "A," "a," "B," "b" rather than the usual Linux sorting method of "A," "B," "a," "b." Note that this isn't exactly "ignoring" case.

- **Show Shared section**—With this option, you can toggle whether the Shared section is displayed.

- **Show Personal section**—This option enables you to toggle whether the Personal section is displayed.

- **Show Recent section**—With this option, you can toggle whether the Recent section is displayed. Note that when this option is turned off, the list of recently accessed folder and files is not updated at all. Some users see this as an improvement of privacy.

- **Show Option entry**—This option enables you to toggle whether the Options entry is available on the Disk Navigator. If you turn this off, you will have to go through the main kpanel configuration dialog box to configure Disk Navigator.

- **Terminal application**—If you Shift+click a folder's Open Folder entry in the Disk Navigator, a terminal will be launched in that directory. This option determines what terminal program to use.

Making It Pretty

You can customize KDE in many ways to make your desktop more attractive. Few of these changes will boost your performance, but they may make you happier while you're working. All the settings described in the following sections are found on the KDE Control Center under Desktop. Follow these steps to customize your desktop's appearance:

1. Click the KDE Control Center on the panel.
2. Click the small plus to the left of Desktop to expand the option list.
3. Select the desired option (Background, Borders, and so on).

Background One of the most personal things about a desktop is the background. Some users like simple, flat backgrounds, whereas others like textures or even images. KDE supports all of them.

Each desktop can have its own background, so you need to select which desktop you're working on. Having different backgrounds can be very useful in helping you determine which desktop you're on at any time.

The One Color option does exactly what it sounds like: You select the color bar to open a color chooser. The Two Color option enables you to blend two colors or create various patterns based on two colors. You can find the two colors used on the color bar under One Color and the color bar under Two Color.

Wallpaper is also fairly obvious if you're used to other desktops. KDE has a wide selection of arrangement types such as tiled, centered warp, and symmetrical tiled. Just experiment with them to see which works best with your image. KDE also can modify your background as you work. To use this feature, select Random; after a set time, KDE switches images based on a list that you provide (or just all images in a directory). This feature can really break up the monotony; it can also be distracting, depending on your mood.

The Dock Into the Panel selection puts an icon on the right side of your panel that you can use to quickly bring up this dialog box. If you're using the Random selection just described, clicking this icon cycles you to the next background without waiting for the timeout.

TIP

It is possible to use a screen saver as your background. This takes up some CPU resources, but it can look quite good on a fast machine. Just run the screen saver with the -inroot parameter. For example, from the command prompt, type the following:

```
$ kmatrix.kss -inroot
```

For a list of all the available screensavers, type

```
ls ${KDEDIR}/bin/*.kss
```

Colors If you just want another color scheme, KDE provides a wide variety. If you like changing the colors, check out the section "Using Themes in KDE," later in this chapter.

Fonts   Using the Fonts feature, you can set your default fonts, which will be honored by most KDE applications and some other apps. One of the best uses of this feature is to set a larger font size for really high-resolution screens on small monitors.

Screen Saver   What modern desktop would be complete without 20 or so screen savers? Select the screen saver you want from the Screen Saver list and preview it in the preview window.

In the Settings box, set Wait for X Minutes to the number of minutes of idle time to wait for before starting the screen saver.

Require Password requires that you type your login password to turn off the screen saver.

Show Password as Stars will obscure your password as you type it (if you selected Require Password). This is a very good idea.

The Priority slider determines how much processor time the screen saver will get. If your machine is generally idle when you aren't there, you can set the screen saver priority to High so the screen saver will run smoothly. If you have long-running processes that are using the CPU when you're not there (ray-tracing, for example), set priority to Low to prevent the screen saver from stealing CPU time from your real work.

Some screen savers have options of their own. To set these, click Setup.

The Test button runs the screen saver immediately so you can see what it looks like.

TIP   Screen savers that include (GL) in the name use a 3D rendering system called OpenGL. These screen savers will run much faster with 3D accelerator cards.

Using Themes in KDE

Using themes is perhaps one of the most fun parts of using window managers. Themes enable you to define the look and feel of KDE in a central, consistent way.

KDE comes with four themes, which are not nearly enough for a real theme lover. So, you can start by going to the source of KDE themes: `http://kde.themes.org`. At this time, KDE has 80 themes available. Just select the theme you want from the gallery, and download it. The file is saved as a `tar.gz` file. Theoretically, themes are supposed to use a new `.themerc` file format, but I've never seen this format except in the stock themes. Generally, you need to use `kinstall` by Dmitry Zakharov (`dmitry_z@iname.com`), from `http://kde.themes.org/php/downloads.phtml`. After you have your theme file and `kinstall` installed, type the following at the command line:

```
$ kinstall theme
```

The *theme* entry here is the name of your theme file (including the `tar.gz`). You don't even have to restart KDE. Your theme comes up immediately.

TIP The themes available are of variable quality; kde.themes.org rates themes from –2 to +2. From the theme gallery, select the lowest rating that you wish to see, and you will remove a lot of the less interesting themes. If you prefer to make your own decisions, though, set the filter down to –2 so that you can see everything. You can also submit and read comments on the themes.

Getting More Desktop

KDE offers many options for maximizing your available screen real estate. If you're interested in reorganizing your desktop, try some of the following:

- **Make your panel smaller**—From the Panel tab of the KPanel Configuration dialog box, click Tiny.

- **Move the panel off the screen by clicking the left or right hide buttons**—KDE puts the Application Starter, Window List, and a disk navigator on your taskbar whenever you move panels off the screen.

- **Autohide the panel and the taskbar**—From the Options tab of the KPanel Configuration dialog box, click Auto Hide Panel and Auto Hide Taskbar. Choosing these options causes the panel and taskbar to hide until you touch the mouse cursor to their borders. For example, when you move the mouse cursor to the bottom of the screen, the panel reappears.

- **Get rid of the taskbar altogether**—You don't really need the taskbar because the Window List provides similar functionality. From the Panel tab of the KPanel Configuration dialog, select Hidden.

Troubleshooting KDE

When you get KDE configured the way you want it, there isn't a lot that is likely to go wrong. Getting KDE installed and configured, however, can sometimes be tricky under Red Hat.

If your problem isn't covered in this section, you should consider joining the KDE users-helping-users list, at kde-user. To subscribe, send a blank message to kde-user-request@kde.org with a subject of subscribe <email address> (replace <email address> with your email address). Before posting a question, be sure to check the archives at lists.kde.org.

Problems Installing KDE

Installing KDE from RPMs generally goes very well. If you have problems, however, this section might be able to help.

Using kfm to contact ftp.redhat.com, I receive the message Could not login for ftp.redhat.com. Perhaps wrong password.

The Red Hat FTP server is often overloaded. Using ncftp, ftp, or Netscape, you will receive a helpful message: 30 Anonymous Full, Please try http://www.redhat.com/mirrors.html. Unfortunately kfm doesn't display this message. Note that mirrors generally are updated at most once per day, and some are updated less frequently.

RPM complains that prerequisites are missing.

Make sure you're installing KDE RPMs in the correct order: qt, kdesupport, kdelibs, kdebase, and then all other packages.

If you are installing KDE on Red Hat 5.2 or earlier, KDE packages are not included in your distribution, so you will need to download them. Make sure that you download version 1.44 of Qt because Qt version 2.0 is not compatible with KDE 1.x.

$KDEDIR isn't set when I log in.

If you've installed the RPMs, verify that kdesupport is properly installed with the following command:

```
$ rpm -Vkdesupport
$
```

If any errors print, you will need to reinstall kdesupport. The file that sets $KDEDIR is /etc/profile.d/kde.csh (for csh and tcsh shells) or /etc/profile.d/kde.sh (for almost everything else). If you're uncertain which shell you use, you almost certainly use bash, which uses kde.sh. Both these files belong to the kdesupport package.

If you installed KDE from source code and use any csh shell but csh or tcsh (type echo $SHELL at the command prompt to verify), you can duplicate the RPM way of setting $KDEDIR (which is a good, standard way to do it). Just create /etc/profile.d/kde.sh with the following contents:

```
# KDE initialization script (sh)
MYKDEDIR=<your KDEDIR>
if [ -z "$KDEDIR"  -o  "$KDEDIR" != "$MYKDEDIR" ] ; then
        KDEDIR=$MYKDEDIR
        if [ "$KDEDIR" != "/usr" ] ; then
            PATH="$KDEDIR/bin:$PATH"
        fi
fi
export   KDEDIR PATH
```

Replace <your KDEDIR> with your KDEDIR value. Usually, this is /usr or /opt/kde. If you use csh or tcsh, create /etc/profile.d/kde.csh with the following contents:

```
# KDE initialization script (csh)
if ( $?KDEDIR ) then
        if ( $KDEDIR == "/usr" ) then
        exit
        endif
```

```
endif
setenv KDEDIR /usr
setenv PATH "${KDEDIR}/bin:${PATH}"
```

Replace all occurrences of /usr with your KDEDIR.

I've downloaded the source code distribution from ftp.kde.org, and all the files have a bz2 extension.

These are compressed with bzip2 instead of gzip. To uncompress them, you will need to install bzip2 from your Red Hat CD:

```
$ su
Password: <root password>
# cd /mnt/cdrom/RedHat/RPMS
# rpm -i bzip2*
```

After you've installed it, you can extract these archives by typing this at the command prompt:

```
$ bzip -cd filename.tar.bz2 ¦ tar xvf -
```

Replace filename.tar.bz2 with the file you would like to extract.

Problems Configuring KDE

I rearranged the panel haphazardly, and now it's a complete mess. I want to get back to the default.

Remove your kpanelrc file and restart the kpanel:

```
$ cd $HOME/.kde/config
$ rm kpanelrc
$ kwmcom kpanel:restart
```

Problems with KDE Applications

My kfm occasionally crashes.

It does that. Hopefully version 1.1.2 will be more stable.

On older versions of Red Hat, the clock on the panel is always in GMT.

This was a problem with Red Hat 5.0 and has been fixed in later versions. To fix it, type this at the command prompt as root:

```
# ln -s /usr/share/zoneinfo /usr/lib/zoneinfo ●
```

Installing and Configuring Video Cards, Monitors, and Mice

by Jon Konrath

In this chapter

The X Window system, also called X11 or X, is a windowing system that was developed at the Massachusetts Institute of Technology (MIT) to provide a universal desktop for a variety of different hardware platforms. Along with most other flavors of UNIX, Linux uses X for its graphical user interface (GUI) because of its power, flexibility, and portability. X is based on a client-server system, in which client applications communicate with an X server that does all the low-level work involved with drawing windows, displaying dialog boxes, moving the mouse pointer, and the like. This means that if an application is written for X (and there are hundreds of them on FTP servers across the Internet), there isn't an overwhelming amount of work involved in porting it from one platform to another. In fact, many applications will run under Linux, BSD, IRIX, and many other UNIX platforms with a simple recompile of the source code.

Another example of the power of X is the flexibility of the user interface. With many other operating systems, the GUI is part of the OS. You can configure some items, but if you don't like that silly toolbar at the bottom of the screen, you're stuck with it. In X, a program called a window manager handles the appearance of the interface. The window manager typically manages things such as toolbars, menus, window behavior, and general desktop properties. Several different window managers are available for Linux, ranging from old UNIX standbys such as twm and fvwm to more involved environments such as GNOME and KDE. And each one is fully configurable, so you can customize any part of the GUI.

Several different X servers are available for Linux, both free and commercial. As with most other Linux distributions, Red Hat Linux 6.0 uses XFree86, a free version of the X11 windowing system developed specifically for PC-based UNIX systems. XFree86 includes generic servers for monochrome, VGA, and SVGA video cards, plus accelerated servers for S3, Mach8, Mach32, 8514/A, and other video cards. Red Hat Linux 6.0 also includes a full range of X applications, including development and productivity software, Web browsers, and games.

Verifying Hardware Compatibility

A complete X Window installation can be one of the most hardware-intensive components of a Red Hat Linux 6.0 installation. The suggested setup for XFree86 under Linux is a 486 or better, with at least 8MB of RAM and 16MB of swap space. However, if you plan on using X, a current window manager, and several memory-intensive applications at the same time, you should probably have a Pentium and at least 32MB of RAM. The X server and X applications can each take up a great deal of RAM, so adding memory is one of the best ways to improve performance of your X setup.

You can configure X to work with almost any video hardware, including VGA, SVGA, Hercules, and Monochrome cards and built-in hardware on many laptop and desktop models. However, for quicker performance, you should use an accelerated video card, such as one with an S3, Mach8, Mach32, 8514/A, or other hardware-accelerated chipset. Also, cards with more DRAM support higher screen resolutions and enable you to use 16 and 32 bit-per-pixel modes, in addition to the default 256-color mode. Video cards with supported chipsets work on all bus types, including VESA Local Bus and PCI.

You'll also need a monitor that works with your video card. Most monitors will work at the standard VGA resolution of 640×480, but if you plan to have a few programs open at the same time, look for something that will work smoothly at 1024×768. In addition to a monitor, you'll also need a pointer device, such as a mouse or trackball. X supports many different protocols of two- and three-button mice, as well as touchpad and trackball hardware.

Installing the X Window System

The easiest way to install X is during the Red Hat Linux 6.0 installation. When choosing components to install, make sure to select X Window System. At the end of the installation procedure, the Xconfigurator utility is run to test your video card and configure X. This procedure can usually configure most monitors with little or no difficulty. However, if you skipped this step during the installation, or if Xconfigurator did not correctly detect your hardware, you might need to reconfigure X or change some settings manually.

The first step in installing X manually is to make sure that the X Window components have been installed. All the components are installed by default with the Red Hat Workstation and Custom installation methods. The easiest way to install all the X software is to re-run the Red Hat Linux 6.0 installer by booting with the install floppy, perform an upgrade of the system, and select only the X Window System components. This will also run the Xconfigurator utility and configure X for your hardware setup.

If you want to install X manually, you should add the X11R6-contrib, XFree86, Xconfigurator, XFree86-libs, and xinitrc packages. You will also need a font package such as XFree86-75dpi-fonts and the XFree86 package that corresponds to your video card. If you are not sure, install XFree86-VGA16, the generic 16-color VGA server. You should also consider installing some of the other items in the X11 RPM group, including applications and games. Consult Chapter 11, "Installing and Managing RPM Packages," for more help with updating the software.

Installing X Servers

Although the base XFree86 components are used with every X installation, Red Hat Linux 6.0 comes with several X servers to support different types of video hardware. This enables the X server to take advantage of the graphics acceleration features of many different popular video cards. When you install Red Hat Linux, the Xconfigurator utility determines whether you have a video card with an accelerated chipset and installs the correct X server. However, if you didn't run Xconfigurator at install, or if you finally tossed that Oak 256K VGA card you bought for $25 back in 1991 and bought a brand new 128-bit card with 32MB of SDRAM, you might need to install a new X server manually.

Here's a list of the X servers included with Red Hat Linux 6.0:

RPM Name	Description
XFree86-3DLabs	3D Labs GLINT and Permedia chipsets.
XFree86-8514	Older IBM 8514 cards and compatible cards such as ATI.
XFree86-AGX	AGX-based cards, such as Boca Vortex, Orchid Celsius, Spider Black Widow, and Hercules Graphite.
XFree86-I128	#9 Imagine 128 and similar cards.
XFree86-Mach32	ATI Mach32 chipsets, including ATI Graphics Ultra Pro and Ultra Plus cards.
XFree86-Mach64	ATI Mach64 chipsets, including Graphics Xpression, GUP Turbo, and WinTurbo cards. Note: This server is known to have problems with some Mach64 cards.
XFree86-Mach8	ATI Mach8 chipsets, including ATI 8514 Ultra and Graphics Ultra cards.
XFree86-Mono	Monochrome two-color VGA cards.
XFree86-P9000	Weitek P9000 chipset, including most Diamond Viper cards and the Orchid P9000 card.
XFree86-S3	The S3 chipset, including most #9 cards, many Diamond Stealth cards, Orchid Farenheit cards, Micros Crystal 8S cards, most STB cards, and some motherboards with built-in accelerated chipsets, such as the IBM ValuePoint line.
XFree86-S3V	The S3 ViRGE chipset, including some Diamond Stealth 3D cards.
XFree86-SVGA	Most simple framebuffer SVGA devices, including ET4000 chipsets, Cirrus Logic chipsets, Chips and Technologies laptop chipsets, Trident 8900 and 9000 chipsets, and Matrox chipsets.
XFree86-VGA16	The generic 16-color VGA. Use this server if you're having problems with other servers.
XFree86-W32	ET4000/W32 chipsets, including Genoa 8900 Phantom 32i, Hercules Dynamite, LeadTek WinFast S200, Sigma Concorde, STB Lightspeed, TechWorks Thunderbolt, and ViewTop PCI cards.

TIP If you rushed out and bought a Creative Labs 3D Blaster card before realizing that it wasn't fully supported in Red Hat Linux 6.0, don't fret. Creative Labs has released a beta driver for the Savage and Banshee cards. It's available for download at http://developer.soundblaster.com/linux/.

The default X server that is called when you start X is /etc/X11/X in Red Hat Linux 6.0. This is actually a symbolic link pointing to the actual server executable in /usr/X11R6/bin. If you install a new X server, you must change this link. For example, if you just installed the S3V server and need to fix this link, issue the following command:

```
ln -sf ../../usr/X11R6/bin/XF86_S3V /etc/X11/X
```

Configuring the X Window System

After you've installed all the software you need, the next step in getting X to run is configuring it. This sounds easy, but getting a working configuration file for an X server is the toughest part of any X install. After all, this one file must be configured exactly for your video card, monitor, mouse, and keyboard. Luckily, Red Hat Linux comes with some tools to greatly simplify this process. And if that doesn't work, you can always change your configuration by hand.

The XF86Config File

When the X server is launched, it reads a file of settings to customize things such as your video card, monitor, keyboard, pointer, and other settings. Traditionally, this file is located at /usr/X11R6/lib/X11/XF86Config. In Red Hat Linux 6.0, this is a link to the real configuration file, which is located at /etc/X11/XF86Config. In the past, it took a great deal of skill to manually configure this file and get X to start. Now, there are automated ways to generate an XF86Config file according to your hardware and preferences. However, it's possible that you might need to manually change a setting.

The XF86Config file has a standard layout, divided into sections for each item it configures. If you don't have XF86Config for some reason, an example is at /usr/X11R6/lib/X11/XF86Config.eg. The following sections are used in Red Hat Linux 6.0:

- **Section Files**—Pathnames to binary files and fonts
- **Section Keyboard**—Keyboard configuration
- **Section Pointer**—Mouse configuration
- **Section Monitor**—Monitor configuration
- **Section Device**—Video card configuration
- **Section Screen**—Video modes (optimal resolutions and color depths)

The Keyboard, Pointer, Monitor, Device, and Screen sections are described briefly in the following sections. For more detailed information on XF86Config settings, read the XF86Config man page.

TIP If you're manually editing your XF86Config file, make a backup first. For example, if your configuration works for the SVGA server but you're trying to change it to work for the P9000 server, do this first from the /etc/X11 directory:

```
cp XF86Config XF86Config-svga
```

That way, if you destroy your XF86Config while trying to configure it, you can always copy back the other one and go back to SVGA.

Using Xconfigurator

When you choose to install the X Window System components during the Red Hat Linux 6.0 installation, the Xconfigurator utility is run at the end of the installation. This configures X for your video card, monitor, and mouse. You can also run Xconfigurator outside of the installation program. Make sure you are not running X, and type Xconfigurator at the shell prompt.

When you run Xconfigurator, it first tests to see what kind of video hardware you have installed on your system. It probes your video card and tries to match it with a list of known video cards. If that doesn't work, a list of video cards is displayed. If your video card is on this list, select it and press Enter. If your video card is not on the list, you can configure it by hand by choosing Unlisted Card. See the next section, "Installing Video Cards," for more information.

After your video card has been selected, Xconfigurator automatically installs the appropriate XFree86 server. If you're running Xconfigurator manually, make sure that you have the Red Hat Linux 6.0 CD mounted so that the new software is accessible.

N O T E If you're running Xconfigurator manually and you either installed manually or previously installed an accelerated X server, Xconfigurator will probably exit with an error at this point. This happens if you don't have the XF86_SVGA server installed because Xconfigurator uses that server by default to probe your system later. You'll need to install it in addition to your accelerated server to continue.

Next, Xconfigurator asks you to select your monitor type from a list of known monitors. Make sure to select a monitor that matches yours exactly. For example, MAG MPX-17F and MX-17H may have similar names, but they are different monitors; using the wrong one could overclock your monitor and damage or destroy it. If your monitor is on the list, select it and press Enter. If your monitor is not on the list, you can select Custom and enter its horizontal sync and vertical refresh range. See the section "Installing Video Monitors," later in this chapter, for more information before attempting this.

After you select a monitor, Xconfigurator will ask for the amount of video memory on your video card, if it wasn't capable of figuring this out by itself. Consult your video card documentation to determine this. If you enter the wrong amount, it won't hurt anything, but it may prevent the X server from starting.

Xconfigurator may also ask about the type of video clockchip in your video card. It's usually best to leave this at No Clockchip Setting because X can usually autodetect your clockchip.

Next, Xconfigurator probes your video hardware and determines the optimal video mode for you. Don't be alarmed—this causes your display to blink on and off several times. You are presented with an optimal video mode setting (color depth and resolution). You can accept this setting or select other video modes you wish to use. These are the resolutions used at various color depths. To select a mode, highlight the mode by moving the cursor over it with the cursor keys, and then press the space bar. You can select more than one video mode.

Xconfigurator then tries to start X, with no window manager or other applications, as a quick test of your settings. When X is running, a small dialog box appears, asking if you can see it. Use the mouse to select yes if everything's working. If your mouse isn't working, you can press Enter to dismiss the dialog box. If you can't see anything, press Ctrl+Alt+Backspace to exit X.

If your quick test-drive works, Xconfigurator writes the XF86Config file and then give you an option to run X when you reboot. If you think that you might have trouble with your X setup, it's best not to check this, or to keep a rescue disk handy.

Now, you're ready to start X and see how everything works. Skip to the "Starting the X Window System" section, later in this chapter, and try it out. If you have problems, or if Xconfigurator was incapable of getting everything configured, the following sections give some specific information on video cards, monitors, and mice.

Installing Video Cards

Video card configuration is probably one of the most automated parts of installing X for Red Hat Linux 6.0. Because Xconfigurator probes and tests your video card, it can usually figure out everything it needs to configure X automatically. However, if your video card is either very old or very new, the Xconfigurator utility may not be capable of detecting it. This section helps you configure your video card manually.

Determining Video Card information

Before you start, you must know the following things about your video card:

- The make and model of the hardware
- The chipset used by the video adapter
- The amount of video memory (SDRAM)
- The video adapter's clock frequencies, also called "dot clocks"

The easiest way to get this information is to RTFM (Read The Fabulous Manual) that came with your video card or computer. However, sometimes systems don't have great documentation, and it's possible that the manual went straight in the trash five minutes after you got your new machine. In that case, you'll have to do some detective work. One or more of the following techniques may get you the information you need:

- Go to the manufacturer's Web site, and look for any manuals, FAQs, or other information on your video card.

- Contact technical support for the manufacturer of your computer or video card.

- Do a Web search on the make and model of video card to see if it's mentioned on a third-party Web page or support forum.

- Sometimes SuperProbe (see the section "SuperProbe," later in this chapter) can detect part of your setup but not the rest. So, you may be able to find out your dotclock, but not your video memory, for example.

- Carefully read the startup screen when you boot your computer. Sometimes built-in video cards will display their chipset or manufacturer or card type.

- Open your computer (be careful!) and look at your video card. Usually, at least the make and model will be on the card itself.

- Post a message to the Usenet newsgroup `comp.os.linux.x`, and see if somebody else has configured hardware like yours for XFree86. If you can't get Usenet from your ISP, try a Web-based news service such as `http://www.deja.com`. Don't forget to do a quick search first to see if anyone else asking the same question already got an answer.

- Contact Red Hat support to see if they have a configuration for your card.

- If you know the card type but can't figure out what server you need, go to `http://xfree86.org/cardlist.html` for a very comprehensive list of video cards and the servers they use.

Xconfigurator Custom Video Card Configuration

The Xconfigurator utility will let you select an Unlisted Card option if it cannot properly detect your video hardware. This doesn't do much, aside from give you an option to select an X server. If you know you have an accelerated card and you know the chipset, you can select the corresponding server. If you aren't sure, select the 16-color VGA or SVGA server for now. After you run Xconfigurator, you will possibly need to change your XF86Config file manually.

XF86Config File Device Settings

The Device section of the XF86Config file deals with the video adapter on your computer. You can configure several different cards, as long as they have unique Identifier strings. Here's an example of the generic VGA card:

```
Section "Device"
    Identifier      "Generic VGA"
    VendorName      "Unknown"
```

```
      BoardName  "Unknown"
      Chipset    "generic"
#     VideoRam  256
#     Clocks    25.2 28.3
EndSection
```

Identifier is a string used later in the Screen section of the XF86Config file to refer to a specific video card. VendorName, BoardName, and Chipset entries are optional identifiers for organizational purposes. Note that you can comment out optional lines with a #.

Several different optional settings are supported in the Device section. Most of these are optional because X scans the hardware for them. However, with some configurations, X can't figure something out with a hardware probe, or the probe itself can crash the hardware. In those cases, you can configure these settings yourself. Some of these settings include Clocks, VideoRam, Ramdac, Dacspeed, and ClockChip. For more information on device settings, see the XF86Config man page.

SuperProbe

If you're trying several different video cards in your machine, or if you are in the depths of a manual installation that requires probing the video hardware scores of times, you're probably finding the many screens of XConfigurator to be a hassle. If you want to just probe the video hardware, you can also use SuperProbe.

SuperProbe is a program included with XFree86 that Xconfigurator uses to scan your video hardware. It can also be run manually on the command line. SuperProbe can determine the chipset, memory, and RAMDAC for most video cards. SuperProbe -info will display all the video hardware it can detect.

> **NOTE** Running SuperProbe can lock up your machine! SuperProbe executes instructions to identify unique registers in certain video cards, which can sometimes lock up other cards. This won't cause damage, but it will require you to reboot your machine. Make sure that nobody else is using your machine, and save data in other applications before trying SuperProbe. ▪

Installing Monitors

Although the capabilities of your video card contribute greatly to the performance of X, another important factor is your monitor. Although it's easy to set your monitor to the default generic VGA 640×480 mode (where a single xterm takes up the entire screen), it can sometimes be more difficult to find a more optimal, high-resolution setting. Many times, Xconfigurator can find the exact make and model of your monitor in its monitor database. However, if you have an older computer, a laptop, or a monitor built by one manufacturer and resold by another, it can take some guesswork to get the proper setting. This section will give you some information to help manually configure your monitor optimally for X.

Determining Monitor Information

In a perfect world, every monitor would have a make and model stamped on its case that you could easily find in Xconfigurator's monitor list. But, if that isn't true with your system, you'll need to do your homework to find some information about your monitor. At the least, you'll need to know the following:

- Your monitor's horizontal sync and vertical refresh frequencies. Vertical refresh is usually measured in Hertz (Hz), usually between 50Hz and 150Hz. Horizontal sync is measured in Kilohertz (kHz), usually between 31kHz and 135kHz.

- Your monitor's video bandwidth, measured in Megahertz (MHz). This ranges from 25MHz for 640×480 displays to upwards of 185MHz for 1600×1200 displays.

Note that monitor performance information is highly arbitrary and varies by manufacturer. Almost every vendor claims that its monitor will work up to 1280×1024 or some other high resolution, but, in reality, performance varies, especially if you want a readable display.

To find solid technical data on your monitor, you'll need to dig around with the same techniques described in the previous section. Find the manufacturer's Web site, search the Web, call technical support, and, above all, try to find someone who has invented X settings for the same monitor. There's a somewhat outdated database of monitors at `/usr/X11R6/lib/X11/doc/Monitor`, and similar lists are available all over the Web. Unlike video cards, monitor settings are much more qualitative, and there's not always one right answer on configurations.

 TIP If you're searching the Internet for information on your monitor, there's a list of several Internet sites with monitor configurations in the XFree86 FAQ, located at
`http://www.xfree86.org/FAQ/index.html#MONITORS`.

Xconfigurator Custom Monitor Configuration

Xconfigurator can recognize many types of monitors during configuration. If your monitor isn't listed and you're not feeling adventurous, the easiest thing to do is choose a generic setting close to your monitor setting. But you can also select the Custom monitor from the list and enter the horizontal sync and vertical sync information about your monitor.

After you enter a custom monitor, Xconfigurator finishes the X installation and tests X for you. If your settings didn't work, either you'll need to go back and run Xconfigurator again with new settings, or you'll need to configure the XF86Config file manually.

XF86Config File Monitor and Screen Settings

The `Monitor` section starts out simply enough with an identification subsection that looks like this:

```
Section "Monitor"
    Identifier  "FooBar Superscreen 2000"
    VendorName  "FooBar"
    ModelName   "Superscreen 2000"
```

These strings are just for identification and don't actually tell X anything about your hardware. If Xconfigurator wrote your XF86Config file, the VendorName and ModelName are probably Unknown.

The next subsection configures the horizontal sync and vertical refresh rate. A typical configuration looks like this:

```
# HorizSync is in kHz unless units are specified.
# HorizSync may be a comma separated list of discrete values, or a
# comma separated list of ranges of values.
# NOTE: THE VALUES HERE ARE EXAMPLES ONLY.  REFER TO YOUR MONITOR'S
# USER MANUAL FOR THE CORRECT NUMBERS.

    HorizSync   30-70
# VertRefresh is in Hz unless units are specified.
# VertRefresh may be a comma separated list of discrete values, or a
# comma separated list of ranges of values.
# NOTE: THE VALUES HERE ARE EXAMPLES ONLY.  REFER TO YOUR MONITOR'S
# USER MANUAL FOR THE CORRECT NUMBERS.
    VertRefresh 50-160
```

Change HorizSync and VertRefresh to match your monitor. Do not use the values given here!

The next section, which covers modes, is more complex. Modes tell X which dotclock and timings to use for different resolutions. A typical monitor configuration contains several mode configurations for each resolution it supports. There are two ways to write modes in an XF86Config file. The first is a multiline format:

```
Mode "1024x768i"
    DotClock   45
    HTimings   1024 1048 1208 1264
    VTimings   768 776 784 817
    Flags      "Interlace"
EndMode
```

You can also write the same thing on one line, a method used in most automated installers, such as Xconfigurator:

```
ModeLine "1024x768i" 45 1024 1048 1208 1264 768 776 784 817 Interlace
```

If mode configuration seems daunting, it is. Most of the time, the five values you plug into a Mode or ModeLine setting are things that you find on the Internet and that aren't generated by hand or experimentation. Be careful with the values you use, and don't edit this part of the configuration unless you know what you're doing.

Part
II

Ch
9

Another related section you might need to configure is Screen. This puts everything together and declares different screens that use a combination of Device and Monitor settings. A typical Screen section looks like this:

```
Section "Screen"
    Driver      "vga16"
    Device      "Generic VGA"
    Monitor     "ViewSonic G773"
    Subsection "Display"
        Modes       "640x480" "800x600"
        ViewPort    0 0
        Virtual     800 600
    EndSubsection
```

The Driver string determines which X server uses this combination of video card and monitor. Possible values are Accel, Mono, SVGA, VGA2, and VGA16. This configuration specifies that the Generic VGA video card and ViewSonic G773 monitor are used by the 16-color VGA server.

The Display subsection specifies display-specific parameters. In this example, two video modes are defined. This means that the X server will start in 640×480 mode. If you press Ctrl+Alt+Keypad Plus, the X server switches to 800×600 mode.

Other Display parameters enable you to configure different color depths or larger virtual displays. For more information, see the XF86Config file.

Installing Mice

An important part of the X Window user interface is the mouse, especially because you can't do much in a GUI without one. X supports several different types of mice and most mouse-like devices (trackballs, tablets, and pointers) that behave like mice. The mouse is configured in the Red Hat Linux 6.0 installation, but you can reconfigure it in case it's not working yet. In general, you must know two things about your mouse to configure it: its interface and its protocol.

The mouse interface is the method by which it physically connects to the computer, and that's pretty easy to figure out. Most computers have a serial mouse that plugs into a serial port. Otherwise, you probably have a bus mouse, also commonly referred to as a PS/2 mouse. A bus mouse connects to an interface card or a special port with a nine-pin mini-DIN connector. In addition to IBM computers, bus mice are also manufactured by Logitech and ATI (used on some Gateway computers), and some laptops use the bus mouse protocol for their trackball or touchpad pointers.

A mouse protocol is a method in which mouse movement is sent to the computer. Many conflicting and competing mouse protocols exist, and it can be very difficult to determine which one a mouse speaks, especially with older hardware. These protocols include Microsoft,

Mouse Systems, Mouseman, PS/2, Thinking Mouse, Logitech, and at least a dozen others. A fortunate side effect of the Microsoft monopoly is that most new mice all use the Microsoft protocol, removing some of the guesswork.

During installation, Red Hat Linux 6.0 attempts to configure your serial mouse as /dev/mouse, which is a pointer to ttyS[0-3], depending on which one is your mouse. If you have a serial port conflict, try linking /dev/mouse to a different port. If you have a bus mouse, it will be installed as /dev/inportbm, /dev/logibm, or /dev/psaux.

About mouse-test

If you don't know what kind of mouse you have, you can easily test it with the program mouse-test. Run mouse-test to determine the location and protocol of your mouse. If this utility has difficulty locating your mouse and you know on which port it is installed, run it with the command-line option of your mouse location (for example, mouse-test /dev/mouse); mouse-test will ask you several questions and will ask you to move the mouse and press buttons several times. When it is finished, it should give you a mouse type, or one of two or three options.

Using mouseconfig

To configure your mouse, use the mouseconfig utility. It will first ask you for your mouse type. Choose a mouse protocol from the list, or choose Generic if you have a mouse that uses the Microsoft protocol. There is also an option to emulate three buttons. When this is selected, you can simultaneously press the left and right buttons on your mouse to use the middle mouse button. If the middle button of your three-button mouse doesn't work, you can sometimes select this option to enable it.

Next, mouseconfig will ask you for the location of your mouse, if you have a serial mouse. Enter the serial port in which your mouse is connected. After you've configured your mouse, you will be asked if you want to change your XF86Config file settings to reflect these changes. If you are satisfied with your changes, save them and start X to test your mouse.

XF86Config File Pointer Settings

You can also configure your mouse settings manually by editing the XF86Config file. A typical Pointer section looks like this:

```
Section "Pointer"
    Protocol    "microsoft"
    Device      "/dev/mouse"
# When using XQUEUE, comment out the above two lines, and uncomment
# the following line.
#    Protocol    "Xqueue"
# Baudrate and SampleRate are only for some Logitech mice
#    BaudRate    9600
```

```
#     SampleRate    150
# Emulate3Buttons is an option for 2-button Microsoft mice
# Emulate3Timeout is the timeout in milliseconds (default is 50ms)
#     Emulate3Buttons
#     Emulate3Timeout    50
# ChordMiddle is an option for some 3-button Logitech mice
    ChordMiddle
EndSection
```

The important settings are `Protocol` and `Device`. Set Protocol to the type of mouse protocol your mouse uses. Device should point to the device to which your mouse is connected; you usually use `/dev/mouse` for serial mice.

If you want your two-button mouse to emulate a three-button mouse, uncomment the `Emulate3Buttons` line. After you do so, you can press the left and right buttons and emulate a middle button press. There is also a timeout value, `Emulate3Timeout`, to configure how close together you must press the two buttons for them to emulate the middle button. If you have a Logitech mouse or another brand with three buttons that uses the Microsoft mouse protocol, skip `Emulate3Buttons` and uncomment `ChordMiddle`. This enables your middle mouse button.

For more information on Pointer settings, see the XF86Config man page.

Starting the X Window System

After you've configured X, it's time to try it out. Later in the book, you'll learn how to use the KDE and GNOME environments with X. Both of these can be configured to run right after your system boots. But, for the purpose of testing your configuration, you should start X by hand. If you misconfigure X and configure it to run at startup, you'll be stuck out of your system when it crashes. It's much easier to start X by hand so you can easily kill it, make small changes to your configuration, and then restart it.

About *startx*

The easiest way to start X from the shell prompt is with the `startx` command. This is a simple script included with XFree86 and other X distributions. Its job is to start the X server and then start the window manager and any other default X clients that should run at startup. For starters, `startx` looks for configuration files in the user's directory; then it looks at default configuration files.

First, `startx` looks for an `.xinitrc` file in your home directory. This contains a list of programs to be run when X is started. Red Hat Linux 6.0 also looks for an `.Xclients` file, which does the same thing. Here's a simple example of an `.xinitrc` file:

```
xterm  -geometry  +5+5   -ls &
emacs  -geometry  +60+20 &
xclock -geometry  -20+20 &
exec   fvwm
```

This starts an `xterm` window, Emacs, a clock, and the fvwm window manager. Note that everything but fvwm is run in the background. X will continue to run until fvwm is closed down, usually by the `exit` command from the menu.

If `.xinitrc` or `.Xclients` isn't in your home directory (neither is, by default), startx uses `/usr/X11R6/lib/X11/xinit/xinitrc`. In Red Hat Linux 6.0, this is linked to `/etc/X11/xinit/xinitrc`. This script runs the programs in `/etc/X11/xinit/xinitrc`. In Red Hat Linux 6.0, this launches the GNOME environment with the Enlightenment window manager.

To exit GNOME, select the GNOME foot on the panel bar, and select Log Out from the menu. If something goes wrong with your configuration and you can't see the screen, you can kill X by pressing Ctrl+Alt+Backspace. This closes everything with no confirmation, so make sure that you've saved any data, if possible.

Troubleshooting X Windows and Peripherals

If you can't get things to work, the best thing to do is reconfigure your X setup to use a standard VGA card and a generic 640×480 monitor. If that works, you can go back and try gradually increasing the resolution and trying different cards.

If you can't get something to work and you want to read the stream of messages X produces, you can always do something like this:

```
X > /tmp/x.out 2>&1
```

This starts X without a window manager. To exit, press Ctrl+Alt+Backspace. The messages will be written to the file `/tmp/x.out`.

Also take a look at the following common questions and problems with X setup:

Q. My image looks fine, but it runs off the edge of the screen.

A. Try adjusting the horizontal/vertical size and position controls on your monitor. Sometimes, even if the display looks fine in text mode, the image may run off the edge of the monitor while in X.

Q. Is there any better way to experiment with my video settings?

A. A tool called xvidtune lets you interactively change video settings such as vertical and horizontal sync, and then print the changes in the same format as the XF86Config file. It's extremely easy to crash your system, damage your video hardware, and cause incredibly complicated problems when using xvidtune. Unless you've really researched your monitor and know what you're doing, don't use this program.

Q. I simply can't get XFree86 to run with my hardware. Do I have any other options?

A. Yes, if you're willing to spend some money. XFree86 is just one implementation of X11 for Linux; several other commercial options are available. One example is the Metro-X server, available at `http://www,metrolink.com` for prices as low as $39. Commercial X servers generally have support for more hardware, better installation programs, and more comprehensive technical support. On the other hand, they don't always come with source code, and you can't download the new version from the Internet as you can with XFree86.

Q. Where can I find more information on configuring custom monitor settings?

A. There's an excellent HOWTO on the subject that goes into much more detail about how a monitor works and what you must know to calculate optimal video settings. If you installed the HOWTO files on your Red Hat Linux 6.0 system, this is located at `/usr/doc/HOWTO/XFree86-Video-Timings-HOWTO.` ●

## CHAPTER 10

Updating the X Window System

by John Ray

In this chapter

Upgrading Your X Window Software

Keeping your X Windows software up-to-date is important for maintaining compatibility with the latest versions of desktop software as well as keeping security risks to a minimum. X Windows is different from other windowing environments that you might have used before.

X Window's Network Heritage

Unlike MS Windows or the Mac OS, X Windows works as a server-based system. The server software—in this case, Xfree86—runs on the computer that you wish to display the windows and accepts requests from a client computer to draw windows, menus, and similar components. The terminology might seem a bit backward (the "server" seems to be the client, and vice versa), but it actually does make sense. The server contains all the information necessary to draw windows, fonts, and other components. The client (a program such as Netscape) makes requests to the server for tasks to be completed. Because of this structure, X Windows opens itself up to network attack. The server software does not necessarily have to be running on the same computer that has the client. It is entirely possible to run a copy of Netscape on the other side of the world and have its output (windows, menus, and so on) displayed on your computer. For a quick demonstration on how to do this, try the following procedure (this requires two Linux machines):

1. Start X Windows on one of the two Linux machines.

2. Telnet into the second machine. For the sake of this example, we'll use the IP address 192.168.0.5 to represent the first machine and 192.168.0.10 to represent the second.

3. Type `xhost +192.168.0.10` (or whatever the appropriate IP number is for the second machine) into a terminal session on the first.

4. On the second computer, type the line `export DISPLAY=192.168.0.5` and press Enter. Then type `xterm &` and press Enter.

5. Within a few seconds, a command window should appear on the first system. This program is actually running from the second machine but is being displayed on the first. This is X Windows in action.

Furthermore, you don't even need a Linux computer to run an X Windows server. A popular server available for Mac OS (as freeware) and Windows (for $25) can be used on either of those systems to display and control applications that you are running on your Linux machine. This software is available from `http://tnt.microimages.com/freestuf/mix/download.htm`.

This rather complex way of operating is what makes X Windows vulnerable to outside attack. Keeping your software current and keeping track of the posted vulnerabilities (`http://www.XFree86.org/security/`) is important for keeping your system stable and secure.

Downloading the XFree86 Update

The easiest way to update your X Windows distribution is to download any errata releases directly from Red Hat. These releases will be in RPM format and very simple to install. For example, on September 7, 1999, Red Hat issued a security patch for version of XFree86 that comes with Red Hat 6.0 (`http://www.redhat.com/corp/support/`).

Choosing the Right Files to Download   Looking at this page, you might be a bit overwhelmed by the number of different files that have been updated. The complete XFree86 distribution is available for download:

```
XFree86-100dpi-fonts-3.3.5-0.6.0.i386.rpm
XFree86-3.3.5-0.6.0.i386.rpm
XFree86-3DLabs-3.3.5-0.6.0.i386.rpm
XFree86-75dpi-fonts-3.3.5-0.6.0.i386.rpm
XFree86-8514-3.3.5-0.6.0.i386.rpm
XFree86-AGX-3.3.5-0.6.0.i386.rpm
XFree86-FBDev-3.3.5-0.6.0.i386.rpm
XFree86-I128-3.3.5-0.6.0.i386.rpm
XFree86-Mach32-3.3.5-0.6.0.i386.rpm
XFree86-Mach64-3.3.5-0.6.0.i386.rpm
XFree86-Mach8-3.3.5-0.6.0.i386.rpm
XFree86-Mono-3.3.5-0.6.0.i386.rpm
XFree86-P9000-3.3.5-0.6.0.i386.rpm
XFree86-S3-3.3.5-0.6.0.i386.rpm
XFree86-S3V-3.3.5-0.6.0.i386.rpm
XFree86-SVGA-3.3.5-0.6.0.i386.rpm
XFree86-VGA16-3.3.5-0.6.0.i386.rpm
XFree86-W32-3.3.5-0.6.0.i386.rpm
XFree86-XF86Setup-3.3.5-0.6.0.i386.rpm
XFree86-Xnest-3.3.5-0.6.0.i386.rpm
XFree86-Xvfb-3.3.5-0.6.0.i386.rpm
XFree86-cyrillic-fonts-3.3.5-0.6.0.i386.rpm
XFree86-devel-3.3.5-0.6.0.i386.rpm
XFree86-doc-3.3.5-0.6.0.i386.rpm
XFree86-libs-3.3.5-0.6.0.i386.rpm
XFree86-xfs-3.3.5-0.6.0.i386.rpm
```

Luckily, there isn't a need to download everything. You should always download the packages that are part of the base distribution along with the server that supports your video card.

For example, if you have an S3 card, you'd want to download this set of files:

```
XFree86-100dpi-fonts-3.3.5-0.6.0.i386.rpm
XFree86-3.3.5-0.6.0.i386.rpm
XFree86-75dpi-fonts-3.3.5-0.6.0.i386.rpm
XFree86-S3-3.3.5-0.6.0.i386.rpm
XFree86-XF86Setup-3.3.5-0.6.0.i386.rpm
XFree86-Xnest-3.3.5-0.6.0.i386.rpm
XFree86-Xvfb-3.3.5-0.6.0.i386.rpm
XFree86-cyrillic-fonts-3.3.5-0.6.0.i386.rpm
XFree86-devel-3.3.5-0.6.0.i386.rpm
```

need XFree 86 - VGA16 as well   XF86 Setup depends on it .

```
XFree86-doc-3.3.5-0.6.0.i386.rpm
XFree86-libs-3.3.5-0.6.0.i386.rpm
XFree86-xfs-3.3.5-0.6.0.i386.rpm
```

If you have a very slow connection, don't worry about downloading the font files—chances are, there are no updates in these files. Many times packages are simply reposted under modified version numbers so that the versions remain consistent across all the files for that package. Rather than having "100dbi-fonts" version 3.3.5-0.3.0, it makes sense to repost an updated version of that file along with the rest of the program.

Determining which X Server You're Using   If you can't remember the type of X Server that you are using on your machine, you easily can check to see what is currently installed. The X -showconfig command will display the currently configured server along with all the drivers that it supports.

For example, I'm using an S3 Virge+ card in my computer. If I don't remember installing the initial server on my machine, I might think that this card uses the S3 server. In fact, as X -showconfig reports, it does not—it uses the SVGA driver that supports many different video card drivers:

```
[root@pointy updates]# X -showconfig

XFree86 Version 3.3.3.1 / X Window System
(protocol Version 11, revision 0, vendor release 6300)
Release Date: January 4 1999
        If the server is older than 6-12 months, or if your card is newer
        than the above date, look for a newer version before reporting
        problems.  (see http://www.XFree86.Org/FAQ)
Operating System: Linux 2.2.5-15smp i686 [ELF]
Configured drivers:
  SVGA: server for SVGA graphics adaptors (Patchlevel 0):
      NV1, STG2000, RIVA128, RIVATNT, ET4000, ET4000W32, ET4000W32i,
      ET4000W32i_rev_b, ET4000W32i_rev_c, ET4000W32p, ET4000W32p_rev_a,
      ET4000W32p_rev_b, ET4000W32p_rev_c, ET4000W32p_rev_d, ET6000, ET6100,
      et3000, pvga1, wd90c00, wd90c10, wd90c30, wd90c24, wd90c31, wd90c33,
      gvga, ati, sis86c201, sis86c202, sis86c205, sis86c215, sis86c225,
      sis5597, sis5598, sis6326, tvga8200lx, tvga8800cs, tvga8900b,
      tvga8900c, tvga8900cl, tvga8900d, tvga9000, tvga9000i, tvga9100b,
      tvga9200cxr, tgui9400cxi, tgui9420, tgui9420dgi, tgui9430dgi,
      tgui9440agi, cyber9320, tgui9660, tgui9680, tgui9682, tgui9685,
      cyber9382, cyber9385, cyber9388, cyber9397, cyber9520, 3dimage975,
      3dimage985, clgd5420, clgd5422, clgd5424, clgd5426, clgd5428,
      clgd5429, clgd5430, clgd5434, clgd5436, clgd5446, clgd5480, clgd5462,
      clgd5464, clgd5465, clgd6205, clgd6215, clgd6225, clgd6235, clgd7541,
      clgd7542, clgd7543, clgd7548, clgd7555, clgd7556, ncr77c22, ncr77c22e,
      cpq_avga, mga2064w, mga1064sg, mga2164w, mga2164w AGP, mgag200,
      mgag100, oti067, oti077, oti087, oti037c, al2101, ali2228, ali2301,
      ali2302, ali2308, ali2401, cl6410, cl6412, cl6420, cl6440, video7,
      ark1000vl, ark1000pv, ark2000pv, ark2000mt, mx, realtek, s3_virge,
      AP6422, AT24, AT3D, s3_svga, NM2070, NM2090, NM2093, NM2097, NM2160,
      NM2200, ct65520, ct65525, ct65530, ct65535, ct65540, ct65545, ct65546,
```

```
ct65548, ct65550, ct65554, ct65555, ct68554, ct69000, ct64200,
ct64300, mediagx, V1000, V2x00, p9100, spc8110, generic
```

X reports that I'm using the SVGA server and that it is version 3.3.3.1. The version that Red Hat has posted is 3.3.5, so I definitely must upgrade.

Upgrading the Red Hat RPMs

After you've determined the files that you need for an upgrade, go ahead and download the files from Red Hat's update FTP site (ftp://updates.redhat.com/) or one of the many mirror sites. You can then install the files all at once using rpm -Uvh *.rpm, upgrading your software to the latest versions. In-depth instructions on using the RPM system are available in Chapter 11, "Installing and Managing RPM Packages."

For example, you might collect all the files you need to update your system in your updates directory and might be ready to run rpm -Uvh *.rpm. You must be logged into your system as root to install the XFree86 RPM updates:

```
[root@pointy updates]# rpm -Uvh *.rpm
XFree86-100dpi-fonts ##################################################
XFree86               ##################################################
XFree86-75dpi-fonts  ##################################################
XFree86-SVGA          ##################################################
XFree86-XF86Setup     ##################################################
XFree86-Xnest         ##################################################
XFree86-Xvfb          ##################################################
XFree86-cyrillic-font##################################################
XFree86-devel         ##################################################
XFree86-doc           ##################################################
XFree86-libs          ##################################################
XFree86-xfs           ##################################################
```

After this is installed, you can immediately verify that you're running the new version of X by using X -showconfig again. If you're currently running an X session, you'll need to reboot or restart X Windows for the update to actually take effect.

```
[root@pointy updates]# X -showconfig

XFree86 Version 3.3.5 / X Window System
(protocol Version 11, revision 0, vendor release 6300)
Release Date: August 23 1999
        If the server is older than 6-12 months, or if your card is newer
        than the above date, look for a newer version before reporting
        problems.  (see http://www.XFree86.Org/FAQ)
Operating System: Linux 2.2.5-22smp i686 [ELF]
```

That's all there is to performing an update. If you happen to switch to a new video card, you might have to change the type of server you're using. The list of supported video cards and the server that is needed to drive them is available at http://www.XFree86.org/. If you happen to find a video card that is supported via a patch to the XFree86 server, you might need to compile XFree86 from scratch. The process of compiling XFree86 is discussed later in this chapter.

Now that X Windows is up and running, you might want to customize it a bit. The first thing to take a look at is the installation of new fonts on your system.

Working with Fonts in XFree86

Before installing fonts, you need a bit of background on X Windows font support. X Windows names fonts a bit differently than other operations systems. A font name is based on the "X Logical Font Description," which is made up of several different pieces of information.

The X Windows Font Naming Convention

To choose a particular font, it is possible that each of these pieces of information also must be specified:

- **fndry**—The creator of the font, called the foundry.
- **fmly**—The font family. This is the name you're probably accustomed to calling the font, such as Times.
- **wght**—The weight of the font, such as bold.
- **slant**—The slant of the font, such as italics.
- **sWdth**—Font width, usually grouped with wght and slant on other operating systems. Some sWdth values are normal and extended.
- **adstyl**—Additional style information for the font.
- **pxlsz**—The height of a character in pixels.
- **ptSz**—Point size of the text. This is the same as font size on other platforms.
- **resx**—The horizontal resolution.
- **resy**—The vertical resolution.
- **spc**—Kerning information.
- **avgWidth**—The average width of the characters in the font.
- **rgstry**—The registry that the font is a part of.
- **encdng**—The nationality encoding of the font.

Depending on how specific you have to get to uniquely identify a font (you usually don't have to specify all these fields), you might see fonts identified in X Windows configuration files that look like this:

```
-adobe-helvetica-bold-o-*-*-15-*-75-*-p-80-iso8859-1
```

Most fonts, however, do not need quite so much information specified to be uniquely identi-fied, so the font strings that you see most commonly will probably be much shorter and will also have any range of unspecified parameters replaced with a single "*". To get a better idea of what is going on, try running the program xfontsel inside of X Windows. This program will let you choose a particular font and style and identify it by its proper name.

Both GNOME and KDE offer their own versions of xfontsel. KDE's font browser is called Font Manager and is located under System from the main KDE pop-up menu. GNOME's browser is called Font Selector and can be found under Utilities in the GNOME's main sys-tem menu. These applications are similar to xfontsel, but with an interface more comparable to traditional desktop operating systems. You should have no problem looking through the fonts on your system.

Using xfontsel to explore font names

Run the xfontsel utility from inside any X Windows session. Within a few seconds, a window should appear that looks very much like the one in Figure 10.1.

FIG. 10.1
The xfontsel utility enables the user to explore the available fonts and font naming conventions.

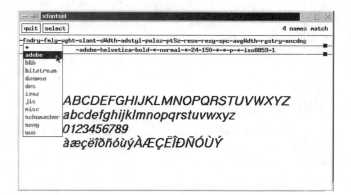

Each field in a font name is represented by its name, as was defined earlier. Each of these field names is actually a drop-down menu. By configuring as few or as many menus as you want, the derived name for the font being displayed is shown in the Window. You can use this value to configure X Windows font settings in .Xdefaults, or through the font selection set-tings that are available in some applications.

Creating Font Aliases

If you find a particular font that you like, but you don't want to type its long name repeatedly, you can create an alias for the font. This enables you to use any word you'd like to call up a particular font. To create an alias, you must edit the alias file that is appropriate for your font. Depending on the physical location of the font on your system, you'll need to edit one of these files:

```
/usr/X11R6/lib/X11/fonts/misc/fonts.alias
/usr/X11R6/lib/X11/fonts/100dpi/fonts.alias
/usr/X11R6/lib/X11/fonts/75dpi/fonts.alias
/usr/X11R6/lib/X11/fonts/cyrillic/fonts.alias
/usr/share/fonts/ISO8859-2/misc/fonts.alias
/usr/share/fonts/ISO8859-2/100dpi/fonts.alias
/usr/share/fonts/ISO8859-2/75dpi/fonts.alias
/usr/share/fonts/ISO8859-2/Type1/fonts.alias
/usr/share/fonts/ISO8859-9/misc/fonts.alias
/usr/share/fonts/ISO8859-9/100dpi/fonts.alias
/usr/share/fonts/ISO8859-9/75dpi/fonts.alias
```

This is just a tiny snippet of the entire file. If you wanted to add the font `-adobe-helvetica-bold-o-*-*-15-*-75-*-p-80-iso8859-1` to the list under the name prettyfont, you would just add this line to the appropriate `fonts.alias` file:

```
prettyfont    adobe-helvetica-bold-o-*-*-15-*-75-*-p-80-iso8859-1
```

In the case of this particular font, it is located in `/usr/share/fonts/ISO8859-2/75dpi/`, so you would edit `/usr/share/fonts/ISO8859-2/75dpi/fonts.alias`.

After the edit is made, you'll need to tell the X Server what has changed. To do this, issue the following two commands, substituting the appropriate font directory where necessary:

```
[root@contempt jray]# mkfontdir /usr/lib/X11/fonts/misc
[root@contempt jray]# xset fp rehash
```

The alias should now be ready to use anywhere a full font name was previously specified.

Adding Type 1 Fonts

Adding fonts to X Windows can be a bit of a chore. Bitmap font sets are mostly useless in today's world of ornate, scalable fonts. Luckily, XFree86 supports two other font standards. The first standard is the postscript Type 1 font, which is widely used in the typesetting and publishing world. Commercial distributions of Type 1 fonts can be quite expensive, ranging in the thousands of dollars. Type 1 fonts are not as popular as they once were, but you can still find them, with a bit of searching, on the Internet.

Using a Type 1 font is simple. First download the fonts you want and make sure that they are named with a .pfb extension. Next, move them into your system's default Type 1 directory `/usr/X11R6/lib/X11/fonts/Type1`. Finally, you must edit the file `fonts.scale` in the Type 1 directory to include information about your new fonts. The `fonts.scale` file looks something like this (your file will probably already be larger than the example file):

```
[root@contempt Type1]# more fonts.scale
3
c0582bt_.pfb -bitstream-courier-medium-i-normal—0-0-0-0-m-0-iso8859-1
c0583bt_.pfb -bitstream-courier-bold-r-normal—0-0-0-0-m-0-iso8859-1
c0611bt_.pfb -bitstream-courier-bold-i-normal—0-0-0-0-m-0-iso8859-1
```

The first line is the number of fonts listed, and the subsequent lines are the font filenames, followed by the official X Windows font name to be used for that font. Add the necessary information for the Type 1 font that you've installed, increment the font count, then save the file.

As a final step, you'll need to do the exact same thing that you did when you made a font alias:

```
[root@contempt jray]# mkfontdir /usr/lib/X11/fonts/Type1
[root@contempt jray]# xset fp rehash
```

The fonts should become available immediately, although you might need to restart X Windows first.

Adding TrueType Fonts

A more popular font format is introduced in Red Hat 6.0: TrueType fonts. The TrueType font format was created by Apple for the Mac OS and then later was adopted by Microsoft for Windows. As a result, thousands of fonts are available in TrueType format. As with Type 1 fonts, TrueType fonts are scalable and look good at any size.

The Web site http://www.1fonts.com/ is an excellent source for free TrueType fonts. You'll probably run into lots of .zip files containing the fonts, but you can use Red Hat Linux's unzip command to decompress the zipped files. After uncompressing these files, make sure that the font file is stored as a lowercase filename with no spaces that ends in .ttf. If you are trying to use TrueType files from a Macintosh, you'll need to use TTConverter, which translates between Mac style fonts and Windows .ttf font files. TTConverter is available from ftp://ftp.visi.com/users/thornley/TTConverter1.5.sit.hqx.

If you have some .ttf files ready to install, follow these steps to have them recognized by your system. You must be logged into the system as root:

1. Make sure that the X Font Server (xfs) is running on your computer. You can verify that it is added to your runlevel with chkconfig -add xfs.

2. The default installation of Red Hat 6.0 doesn't install a TrueType directory, so you must create one using mkdir /usr/X11R6/lib/X11/fonts/TrueType.

3. Next, copy the TrueType font files into your new TrueType directory
cp /yourtruetypefiles/*.ttf /usr/X11R6/lib/X11/fonts/TrueType.

4. Now you must generate the scale file for the fonts. You do this with the /usr/sbin/ttmkfdir program. Cd into the TrueType font directory, and then run this command: /usr/sbin/ttmkfdir fonts.scale. The fonts.scale file will contain the long X Windows name for each font.

5. You now must tell the system to read in the configuration files. Type mkfontdir /usr/X11R6/lib/X11/fonts/TrueType, followed by chkfontpath -add /usr/X11R6/lib/X11/fonts/TrueType.

6. Finally, restart xfs. This will happen when you reboot your computer, or you can manually restart the server with /etc/rc.d/init.d/xfs restart.

Your TrueType fonts should now be accessible from within X Windows.

Listing Available Fonts

If you'd like to generate a list of the fonts that are accessible on your system, you can use the xlsfonts utility to display fonts being served by xfs. You must be running X Windows before using this command.

KDE's Font Manager also offers this functionality. Launch the Font Manager by clicking the main KDE pop-up menu and choosing System and then Font Manager. The Raw X11 Font List tab will display all the recognized fonts currently installed on the system. Figure 10.2 shows Font Manager in action.

FIG. 10.2
Font Manager displays all fonts installed on your system.

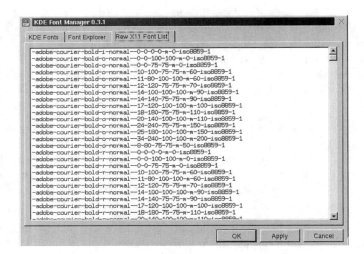

Configuring Colors and Fonts in *.Xdefaults*

With all the new fonts that you have installed, you might want to configure some of your X Windows applications to use the fonts. Applications in KDE and GNOME are controlled by the default settings from within the respective desktop environment. Applications such as xterm and xemacs do not have a way to configure them from directly within the X environment. Instead, these applications pull their default fonts from the .Xdefaults resource file that is located within your home directory. You'll also notice that other resource settings, including colors and window sizes, are configured in the file. Let's start by taking a look at the .Xdefaults file's configuration information for xemacs. Lines beginning with ! are comments:

```
[jray@pointy jray]$ more .Xdefaults
! Parts (C) 1996 By Greg J. Badros <gjb@cs.duke.edu>
! You may use this file as specified under the GNU General Public License
```

```
!!!!!!!!!!!!!!!!!!!!!!!!!!!!!!!!!!!!!!!!
! emacs, xemacs

emacs*Background: DarkSlateGray
emacs*Foreground: Wheat
emacs*pointerColor: Orchid
emacs*cursorColor: Orchid
emacs*bitmapIcon: on
emacs*font: fixed
emacs.geometry: 80x25
```

The configuration file is very easy to understand. The majority of the lines configure the color of the various xemacs elements. The standard X colors are listed in the file /usr/X11R6/lib/X11/rgb.txt. The colors are defined as RGB values and a color name:

```
[jray@pointy doc]$ more /usr/X11R6/lib/X11/rgb.txt
! $XConsortium: rgb.txt,v 10.41 94/02/20 18:39:36 rws Exp $
255 250 250          snow
248 248 255          ghost white
248 248 255          GhostWhite
245 245 245          white smoke
245 245 245          WhiteSmoke
220 220 220          gainsboro
255 250 240          floral white
255 250 240          FloralWhite
253 245 230          old lace
253 245 230          OldLace
250 240 230          linen
...
```

You can set any of the color settings in the .Xdefaults file with the values from this file. If you want to browse the files, you can use GNOME's Color Browser program. To access Color Browser, click the main GNOME popup menu and choose Color Browser from the Utilities menu (see Figure 10.3).

Now, on to the fonts. In the Emacs configuration that you've been looking at, you'll see the line emacs*font: fixed. This tells Emacs to use the font alias called fixed for its display. The fixed font alias points to a nonproportional font that is used to display program source code (Emacs is a heavy-duty editor that is mainly used for programming). If you'd rather have a different font used in Emacs, all you must do is exchange the fixed alias with either a full font name or another alias.

You can do the same with other X Windows applications. Reading the man pages for the application that you want to configure will help you determine what settings you can configure. If you can't find any information, it is completely reasonable to guess what you must set. For example, <program name>*font: <font name or alias> should work for many programs that don't have obvious configuration options.

Part
II

Ch
10

FIG. 10.3
The GNOME Color Browser offers a friendly interface to browsing the standard X Windows colors.

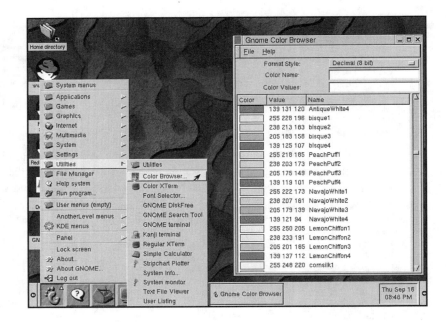

Recompiling X Windows

Sometimes you might want to recompile an X Server distribution rather than work with the supplied Red Hat upgrades. The XFree86 distribution is updated frequently, and a beta release might support a video card that you need to use. In other instances you might need to patch the X Server with additional features. For example, a product called VMware (available from http://www.vmware.com) allows your Linux computer to run Windows and other operating systems inside a window. VMware includes modified X Server software for a variety of different cards, but not all of them. If you have one of the cards that isn't supported with the X Servers distributed with VMware, you can download a patch file that will modify the standard XFree86 source code so that you can compile your own copy of the server.

Downloading the XFree86 Source Code

The XFree86 distribution can be downloaded from ftp://ftp.xfree86.org/pub/. If you are using a dial-in connection, downloading these files will take a while—there are currently four files that make up the distribution, totaling roughly 35MB in size. For the current 3.3.5 source code, these are the steps needed to compile and install X Windows on your computer. If you are installing a later release, however, be sure to read the README.INSTALL file for the source code. There is no guarantee that these instructions will work for future revisions.

It might be a good idea to skip ahead to Chapter 12, "Installing and Managing Linux Software," before reading this section. The process of installing the XFree86 software is very similar to that for other standard Unix distributions. You might better understand the following process if you understand the standard procedures for installing non-RPM based software on your computer. Follow these steps:

1. Download the source code files for the distribution.

2. Assuming that you've retrieved a gzipped distribution, uncompress the files with this command: `gunzip *gz`.

3. Unarchive each of the resulting tarfiles. These will create a master source code directory called `xc`:

```
[root@contempt XFree86]# tar -xf X335src-1.tar
[root@contempt XFree86]# tar -xf X335src-2.tar
[root@contempt XFree86]# tar -xf X335src-3.tar
```

4. If you have downloaded any patches for the X Windows system, now is the point at which you would install them. Most patches are easily installed by placing the patch file in the same location as the `xc` directory and issuing the following command: `patch -p0 < patchfile`. It's impossible to guess what useful patches you might find on the Internet, so always read the instructions for any patch you find. These directions should apply in most cases.

5. Edit any preferences that you might want in the `xc/config/cf/site.def` file. This contains local configuration information for your machine, including the directory in which the distribution will be installed. Linux installs XFree86 in `/usr/X11R6`, which is the default for the XFree86 distribution as well. At this time, there is no real need to modify these preference files.

6. When you're ready to start compiling, type `make World`, and the process will begin. This can take quite a while, depending on your machine. On a dual Pentium Pro, the compilation takes well over an hour:

```
[root@contempt xc]# make World

Building Release 6.3 of the X Window System.

I hope you checked the configuration parameters in ./config/cf
to see if you need to pass BOOTSTRAPCFLAGS.

Fri Sep 17 08:50:17 EDT 1999

cd ./config/imake && make  -f Makefile.ini BOOTSTRAPCFLAGS="" clean
make[1]: Entering directory `/home/jray/XFree86/xc/config/imake'
rm -f ccimake imake.o imake
rm -f *.CKP *.ln *.BAK *.bak *.o core errs ,* *~ *.a tags TAGS make.log
➥\#*
```

Part
II

Ch
10

```
rm -f -r Makefile.proto Makefile Makefile.dep bootstrap
make[1]: Leaving directory `/home/jray/XFree86/xc/config/imake'
make  Makefile.boot
make[1]: Entering directory `/home/jray/XFree86/xc'
cd ./config/imake && make -w -f Makefile.ini BOOTSTRAPCFLAGS=""
make[2]: Entering directory `/home/jray/XFree86/xc/config/imake'
making imake with BOOTSTRAPCFLAGS= in config/imake
cc -o ccimake   -O -I../../include -I../../imports/x11/include/X11 ccimake.c
cc -c   -O -I../../include -I../../imports/x11/include/X11
➥`./ccimake` imake.c
cc -o imake   -O -I../../include -I../../imports/x11/include/X11 imake.o
make[2]: Leaving directory `/home/jray/XFree86/xc/config/imake'
rm -f ./config/makedepend/Makefile.proto
./config/imake/imake -I./config/cf  -s
cd ./config/makedepend && rm -f -r Makefile
➥Makefile.dep makedepend *.o bootstrap
cd ./config/makedepend && make -f Makefile.proto bootstrap
...
make[1]: Leaving directory `/home/jray/XFree86/xc'

Fri Sep 17 10:32:12 EDT 1999

Full build of Release 6.3 of the X Window System complete.

[root@contempt xc]#
```

7. If the conclusion of the "make World" process does not end in a successful `Full build complete` message, you must go back and reread the compilation instructions. Do not attempt to install a version that has not fully compiled successfully.

8. After the system has compiled, all you must do is install it. Use `make install` to complete the installation. You might want to log the installation process to a file for later reference with this command: `make install > install.log`.

```
[root@contempt xc]# make install
make -f xmakefile install
make[1]: Entering directory `/home/jray/XFree86/xc'
installing in ./include...
make[2]: Entering directory `/home/jray/XFree86/xc/include'
+ install -c -m 0444 DECkeysym.h /usr/X11R6/include/X11
+ install -c -m 0444 HPkeysym.h /usr/X11R6/include/X11
+ install -c -m 0444 Sunkeysym.h /usr/X11R6/include/X11
+ install -c -m 0444 X.h /usr/X11R6/include/X11
```

```
+ install -c -m 0444 XWDFile.h /usr/X11R6/include/X11
+ install -c -m 0444 Xalloca.h /usr/X11R6/include/X11
...
```

9. As a final step, you must link the appropriate X Server binary to /usr/X11R6/bin/X. By default, XF86_SVGA, the SVGA server, will be automatically linked. If that's the server you want, you're done. Otherwise, check http://www.XFree86.org/cardlist.html for the appropriate server filename for your card; then link that file to X. For example, if your card is a Diamond Stealth 64 Video 3200, you must use the XF86_S3 server, so you should issue this command:

```
[root@contempt xc]# ln -fs /usr/X11R6/bin/XF86_S3 /usr/X11R6/bin/X
```

You're finished! You can configure X Windows as discussed in Chapter 9, "Installing and Configuring Video Cards, Monitors, and Mice."

Part
II

Ch
10

Installing VNC, the Virtual Network Computing Package

Earlier in this chapter you learned about the network nature of X Windows and how you could remotely connect to a machine and use a local X Windows Server to display programs that are running on the remote machine. This is fine for many situations and offers the benefit of seamless integration with the X Windows desktop on your computer: You won't be able to tell the difference between a program running on your computer and one on a remote machine. The only difference is speed. Unfortunately, speed is sometimes a big deal. If you have to wait several seconds for a menu to draw, using the program is going to become extremely painful.

Another problem is that an X Windows Server is big. Usually, the servers come with the standard X Windows font distributions and are several megabytes in size. An X Windows server is *not* a thin client, and it is not easily installed on workstations. Linux is a fantastic network operating system, and would greatly benefit from a system through which you could view the desktop anywhere, on any machine, at any time. If it has this capability, it could easily compete with products such as Microsoft's NT Windows Terminal server and Cytrix WinFrame products. Luckily, such a product exists, and it is entirely free. VNC is a Virtual Network Computing platform that is available for many different operating systems. Arguably, it is one of the best additions you can make to the Red Hat Linux X Windows system.

VNC enables you to share Linux desktops with other Linux machines, or machines running other operating systems. Best of all, each user on the system can have an individual desktop made available simultaneously, without interfering with anyone else's machine. By installing a single high-powered Linux machine, VNC can serve GNOME or KDE desktops to an entire office. The client machines can be reasonably low-powered computers running Windows. In fact, a VNC Linux distribution is available that provides a single bootable floppy that will enable an x86 PC to contact a VNC server—with no hard drive necessary. If you're on the road and must access your Linux desktop for emergency purposes, versions of VNC run on Windows CE and the Palm Pilot as well.

VNC can also work the other way around. Rather than serving Linux KDE/GNOME desktops to other machines, you can also view remote desktops on your computer. This can come in quite handy if you're migrating from a Windows/Mac OS-based computing environment to one with Linux desktops. If you still have applications that must be used on the previous operating systems, there are VNC servers for Mac OS and Windows 95/98/NT that enable the user to remotely access their old desktops from their new Red Hat Linux computers—all for free.

The VNC software is under active development and is provided free of charge from AT&T. The VNC Web site is `http://www.uk.research.att.com/vnc/`. The software is provided precompiled for the Linux system, so all you must do is download and install it. As with the X Windows installation instructions, refer to Chapter 12 for more information about the instructions that follow:

1. Download the VNC server software. It is available in several different archive formats, but this section assumes a gzipped tarfile.

2. Uncompress and unarchive the VNC server archive using `gunzip *gz` and `tar -xvf` *filename.tar*:

   ```
   [jray@pointy vncstuff]$ gunzip vnc-3.3.3_x86_linux_2.0.tgz
   [jray@pointy vncstuff]$ tar -xvf vnc-3.3.3_x86_linux_2.0.tar
   vnc_x86_linux_2.0/LICENCE.TXT
   vnc_x86_linux_2.0/README
   vnc_x86_linux_2.0/Vncviewer
   vnc_x86_linux_2.0/Xvnc
   vnc_x86_linux_2.0/classes/
   vnc_x86_linux_2.0/vncpasswd
   vnc_x86_linux_2.0/vncserver
   vnc_x86_linux_2.0/vncviewer
   ...
   ```

3. Install the binary files in the appropriate location. The README file suggests the following: `cp vncviewer vncserver vncpasswd Xvnc /usr/local/bin`. This should be fine for your system.

You might want to take the time to download a viewer program while you're at the VNC Web site. As already mentioned, viewer software is available for a wide variety of platforms. If you have a Windows or Macintosh desktop, you should follow the instructions for that platform. Directions on configuring the vncviewer for Linux follow at the end of this chapter.

That's all there is to it. VNC Server is now ready to run on your computer. Before starting it, however, there are a few changes that you'll probably want to make.

Changing the VNC Server Display Modes

The VNC viewer can serve virtual displays with many different bit depths and sizes. By default, it will serve your virtual desktop using 8-bit color (256 colors) at a resolution of 800×600. If you prefer to look at your desktop at a higher color depth and a lower resolution, for example, you must edit the /usr/local/bin/vncserver script. This script calls Xvnc, which is the actual server process.

Look for the following lines in /usr/local/bin/vncserver:

```
#
# Global variables.  You might want to configure some of these for your site.
#

$geometry = "1024x768";
$depth = 8;
$desktopName = "X";
```

The geometry is the virtual screen resolution. If you'd like to run at 800×600, just replace the 1024×768 configuration. The same goes for the bit depth. To change to 16- or 24-bit color, replace the 8 with the number that you prefer. Setting the bit depth higher than your client computer can handle, however, isn't going to be useful. Finally, if you'd like to name your desktop, you can change the X to whatever you'd like, such as Johns Desktop. After the changes, your configuration should be similar to this:

```
$geometry = "800x600";
$depth = 16;
$desktopName = "Johns Desktop";
```

Starting VNC for the First Time

After making the changes you want, you can (finally) start vncserver. Type vncserver from any command line to start the server. You'll be prompted to set a password that will be used to connect to your shared desktop. Choose a password and enter it twice. The server should then start, giving you the hostname and display number that you'll use to connect, for example:

```
[jray@pointy jray]$ vncserver

You will require a password to access your desktops.

Password:
Verify:

New 'X' desktop is pointy.poisontooth.com:1
```

Part
II

Ch
10

```
Creating default startup script /home/jray/.vnc/xstartup
Starting applications specified in /home/jray/.vnc/xstartup
Log file is /home/jray/.vnc/pointy.poisontooth.com:1.log
```

If you have a client machine, you could connect to the remote server, but you'd notice that your desktop of choice wasn't running. That's because VNC sets up its own startup files that don't start KDE/GNOME. So, before connecting for the first time, it's best to kill the server and then edit the startup files so that your usual desktop appears.

Stopping VNC

Kill the server now by typing `vncserver -kill :<display number>`, for example:

```
[jray@pointy jray]$ vncserver -kill :1
Killing Xvnc process ID 7264
```

This is the same way that you would kill the server at any time. Just use `vncserver` with the `-kill :` option, followed by the display number that you want to kill, such as 1. If you do not cleanly exit the vncserver program, you might need to delete temporary files in the `/tmp` or `~/.vnc` directories.

Configuring the VNC Server Startup File

The VNC Server startup file is located in the `.vnc` directory, which is created in your home directory the first time you run the server. This file, named `xstartup`, is a shell script that will be run when the VNC server starts. The default `xstartup` file does nothing but attempt to read the X defaults, set the background to gray, and then start an xterm:

```
#!/bin/sh

xrdb $HOME/.Xresources
xsetroot -solid grey
xterm -geometry 80x24+10+10 -ls -title "$VNCDESKTOP Desktop" &
twm &
```

If you'd like the KDE environment to start by default when running vncserver, just substitute the following file in place of `xstartup`:

```
#!/bin/sh

xrdb $HOME/.Xdefaults
startkde &
```

For those who prefer GNOME, the process is just as simple. Replace `xstartup` with the following:

```
#!/bin/sh

xrdb $HOME/.Xdefaults
gnome-session &
```

When you've replaced the `xstartup` file with the shell script you'd like, you can restart vnc-server and the new settings will take effect. The second (and subsequent) times that you run vncserver, it will no longer ask for a password:

```
[jray@pointy jray]$ vncserver

New 'X' desktop is pointy.poisontooth.com:1

Starting applications specified in /home/jray/.vnc/xstartup
Log file is /home/jray/.vnc/pointy.poisontooth.com:1.log
```

If you have a viewer configured, you can connect to your server and see your desktop from anywhere in the world. What makes this even more exciting is that other users can log into the Linux machine and start vncserver in their accounts and simultaneously connect to their remote desktops as well. The vncserver sessions remain active even after the clients discon-nect, until the `vncserver -kill` command is used or until the machine reboots. This means that clients can work on an application, disconnect from the server, reconnect, and be exactly where they left off.

Changing the Password for Your Desktop

If someone can guess the password to your desktop, that person can control your VNC ses-sion. If you happen to be running a VNC desktop as root, that could be a very bad thing. Keeping a secure and updated password is essential for keeping VNC safe.

If you'd like to change the password that you have set for the VNC server, just use the `vncpasswd` command, as in the following:

```
[jray@pointy jray]$ vncpasswd
Password:
Verify:
```

Any subsequent connections you make to vncserver will use your new password. This does not affect any other passwords on your system; in fact, it is wise to keep this password differ-ent from the password that you use to log into the system.

Using the VNC Viewer on Linux

The VNC viewer is very easy to use under Linux: You can invoke it at the command line under Linux as `vncviewer`. You will be prompted for the server name, which should be entered in the format `<fully qualified hostname>:<display number>`. Press Enter, and you'll be asked to enter the password for the connection. Within a few seconds, you should be connected to the remote display.

If you'd like to speed up the process, you can invoke vncviewer with the hostname and display as parameters to the command. You'll be prompted for the password, and then the remote dis-play will be drawn. Figure 10.4 shows a Windows NT desktop being displayed on a Red Hat Linux computer running vncviewer.

Part

II

Ch

10

FIG. 10.4
The vncviewer can be used to display remote Windows, Mac OS, and other Linux desktops.

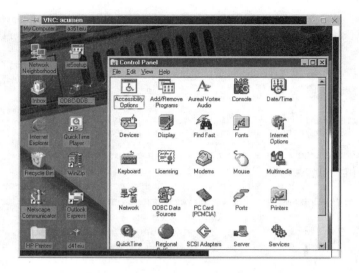

Using the VNC system will liberate your Linux machine from needing a display. With VNC installed, you can remotely control your Linux computer from any machine on your network. This is one of the best (and first) additions you should make to your preinstalled Red Hat X Windows software.

Troubleshooting

Maintaining a current and secure version of X Windows is very important in keeping your machine stable and protected. Upgrading the RPMs is as simple as downloading from Red Hat's site and using the rpm command to perform the upgrade. If you want to install from the XFree86 source distribution to gain added video card support or extra features, this chapter hopefully shed some light on the process. For those who must access other desktop computers remotely, the VNC server software works with your X Windows applications to create a very fast (and free) network computing environment. For more information, check out the following:

Q. I've upgraded the XFree86 packages and can no longer start X Windows; what happened?

A. Chances are, you installed the wrong X Server for your video card. Check the cardlist: http://www.xfree86.org/cardlist.html. You must re-install the appropriate server that supports your video chipset.

Q. I'm sure I have the appropriate server installed, but X Windows still doesn't start. What can I do?

A. Try running XF86Setup and reconfiguring your video board, as discussed in Chapter 9, "Installing and Configuring Video Cards, Monitors, and Mice."

Q. I've added fonts to my system, but they aren't showing up. What do I do?

A. Be sure that you've run mkfontdir and xset on the directory where you added the fonts. If you don't tell the system there has been a change, it won't recognize it automatically.

Q. I've installed and compiled the XFree86 source code but it doesn't seem to recognize my new video card, despite claims of being supported by the new server. What's wrong?

A. Check to make sure that the server you're compiling is being copied or linked to /usr/X11R6/bin/X. There's a good chance it has been installed elsewhere and you're still running an old server.

Q. VNC server is no longer starting up with display 1 as the default. Why not?

A. VNC sometimes leaves files lying around that shouldn't be there. To prevent this, always kill vncserver with vncserver -kill :<display name>. If the problem still exists, be sure that any .pid files are removed from your .vnc directory and that there aren't any .X11-* files that belong to you in the /tmp directory. If there are, delete them, and then try vncserver again.

Q. I've tried to update X Windows and now I can't get anything to work. HELP!

A. If everything fails, go back and reinstall the base XFree86 RPMS from your Red Hat CD distribution. Rest assured that you can go back if something goes wrong. ●

Part

II

Ch

10

Software

Installing and Managing RPM Packages

by Duane Hellums

In this chapter

Understanding Gnome Red Hat Package Manager (GnoRPM)

Before Red Hat came along and decided to make Linux a little easier to install, configure, use, and manage, we all had to use some arcane and far-from-intuitive interfaces (inherited from UNIX) for installing and configuring software applications on Linux. Primarily, this involved using something along the lines of the gzip/gunzip compression and tar archiving utilities. Chapter 12, "Installing and Managing Linux Software," explains how to install software that still is distributed the old way (pre-Red Hat).

Red Hat first developed the Red Hat Package Manager (RPM) to facilitate efficient bundling of software files and easy installation. This was a text-based interface launched from the shell and command-line interface. Red Hat later improved on this with the glint program to provide an intuitive, graphical user interface for RPM software.

N O T E Although developed by Red Hat, RPM is an open, freely distributable standard. As such, it can be used as a model for distributing software that can be installed easily on any Linux operating system that supports it.

Although you can still use all these methods, the GNOME desktop comes with a very powerful graphical utility that uses Red Hat's RPM library functions and that serves as a graphical front end to Red Hat's RPM: GnoRPM (depending on where you look, you also might see it called Gnome RPM). Figure 11.1 shows the main GnoRPM window (version 0.8) on a fully installed and configured system, with a few of the groups conveniently expanded to show the different categories in each. This utility provides a standard graphical interface, including a menu bar, a toolbar, and windows displaying what appear to be directories, subdirectories, and files (which are actually groups, categories, and packages).

N O T E You will need to perform routine system administration functions on your Linux system, just as you would with any system. One thing that might be different for you, if you are new to the UNIX world, is the concept of the superuser or root account. This user has special privileges that allow it to make system-level modifications that other, normal users can't because of file and directory permissions and ownerships restricting modifications to the root user. Because you wouldn't want any user to be able to install applications on your system, GnoRPM requires that you be logged in as root.

Keep in mind that this package is not supported by Red Hat, although it is bundled and installed by default with the GNOME desktop. (*GNOME* stands for the *GNU Network Object Model Environment*, which uses *Common Object Request Broker Architecture* [CORBA] technology to provide seamless interoperability among multiple software programs.) If X Window is not working on your system and GnoRPM is therefore unavailable, you should skip to the "Using RPM" section at the end of this chapter.

FIGURE 11.1
The Gnome RPM (GnoRPM) window is intuitive and flexible.

Installing GnoRPM

GnoRPM should have been installed by default. If it wasn't, for some reason, you might have to use RPM to install it. The file is located on the Red Hat installation CD in the RPMS directory, with a filename of gnorpm-0.8-5.i386.rpm. You can find out how to use RPM by using the GNOME consolidated help system (look under administration) or by typing man rpm from an X terminal command line. The basic syntax of an RPM installation would be the following:

```
rpm -i /mnt/cdrom/RedHat/RPMS/gnorpm-0.8-5.i386.rpm
```

(However, you should consult the help pages before using rpm.) Of course, your directory path might be slightly different if you have the CD installed on a different mount point.

If you get an error message saying that GnoRPM is already installed, you just might be lacking a shortcut to the program on your desktop, panel, menu, or submenu. You can either create a shortcut somewhere or type gnorpm from the shell and command-line interface.

Configuring GnoRPM

GnoRPM comes preconfigured to behave just as the text-based rpm does from the command line. However, just as you would with rpm, you might want to change the way GnoRPM behaves. You access the main configuration tool by selecting Operations, Preferences from the menu bar. This brings up the Preferences dialog box you see in Figure 11.2. Unfortunately, GnoRPM is still in its infancy, so the Help button is inoperable at this time—look for it in future releases, though.

Part
III

Ch
11

FIGURE 11.2
You can change the way the GnoRPM interface looks and responds.

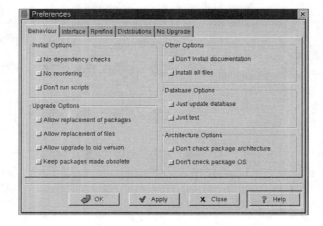

Configuring GnoRPM Behavior

The first tab in the Preferences dialog box, named Behaviour (this is the British spelling, not incorrectly spelled, by the way), is broken into several sections that cover options related to installs, upgrades, database, architecture, and other functions. Because GnoRPM is basically a front-end to RPM, it is no surprise that each of these options equates to one of the flag options that can be passed to RPM from the command line. For example, the Don't Install Documentation button has the same effect as adding the `--excludedocs` option to an `rpm -i` command string.

You can leave these options as is, and you should experience no real problems. However, when you become more familiar with GnoRPM and RPM in general, you may decide to change some of these advanced settings to cause a specific behavior or to prevent installations from negatively affecting your Linux system. For example, you might not have the space to support installation of documentation, so you might depress the Don't Install Documentation button. You might want to revert back to a previous version of a software package (as I did with Windows 95 from Windows 98), which GnoRPM prevents by default and tries to protect you from yourself. In such a case, you would depress the Allow Upgrade To Old Version option button.

Configuring the Interface

The only two things you can change in the Interface tab are the default RPM path and the manner in which the packages are listed in the GnoRPM window (see Figure 11.3). Click the View As List option if you want to see file system details about each package; or, click View As Icons if you prefer a more graphical view of the group package contents. You can either type in the full path to where your RPM packages are stored, or you can click the Browse button to navigate there graphically. On my system, the RPM path is `/mnt/cdrom/RedHat/RPMS`, but it could be different on your system, especially if you typically install from a local or network hard drive.

> **NOTE** If your CD is not already mounted, you will have to mount it. As mentioned earlier, you should be root to do this. You can mount the CD simply by selecting System, Disk Management from the main Gnome menu. Click the Mount button to mount the CD. If it is already mounted, you will see an Unmount button instead. From the command line, you can type `mount -t iso9660 /dev/cdrom /mnt/cdrom` (or simply `mount /dev/cdrom` if your CD-ROM information is configured in `/etc/fstab`). ▨

FIGURE 11.3
You can change GnoRPM default directory locations and display formats.

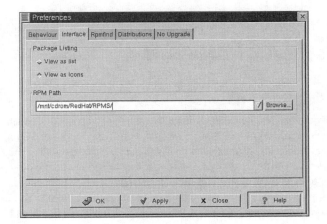

Configuring Rpmfind

Most of the information in the Rpmfind tab is filled in for you based on previously established system and network settings, such as your local hostname. However, as you can see in Figure 11.4, you can—and should—control a few settings here. Most importantly, you should identify the directory where you want to install metadata server database files (I chose /mnt/net, a directory I created, although this directory might have been installed for you already; you must be root to create this directory, of course). These files are stored as a cache on your Linux system for the time specified in the Cache Expire box, which you also should set. GnoRPM is preconfigured to use the Red Hat server, but you are welcome to change the site to another server if you know the address for one.

If you are behind an HTTP or FTP proxy server, you should identify the name or network address so that you will be able to access the Internet to download the files. You can also specify exactly what vendor or distribution you want to limit your searches to by modifying the Vendor and Distrib text boxes. Finally, you can select whether you want the most recent versions and any source code. You do this by pressing the Want Sources and Want Latest Version buttons.

FIGURE 11.4
You can change how
your system stores
downloaded packages
and how long it keeps
them.

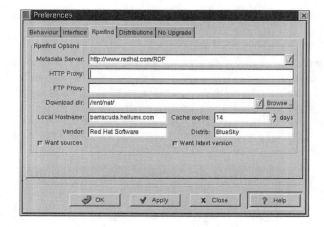

Configuring Distributions

There is no way Red Hat could include all the software you need on a single CD, and even if it could, new programs come out that you might want (that were not available when the CD was created and distributed). Mirror sites are Web servers that provide a mirror image of all the content located at another site; this provides a way to reduce traffic on a popular site and allow people to effectively download files (especially when you might be downloading an entire operating system, like the newest version of Red Hat Linux). You can identify preferred mirror sites for downloading RPM packages in the Distributions tab, shown in Figure 11.5. That way when you want to look for new software packages, your system will know where to go. To do this, type the network name or address of the mirror in the Preferred Mirror text box, and click Change. If you have more than one mirror specified, you can use the arrow on the side to scroll down and select a different one. A good starting point is the list of mirrors at http://www.redhat.com/mirrors.html.

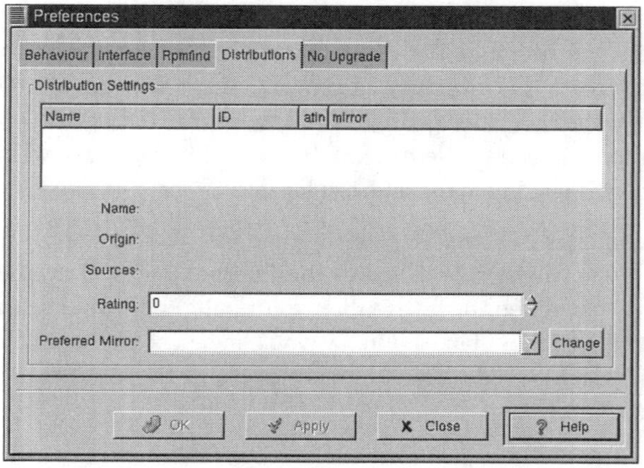

FIGURE 11.5
Creating a list of pre-
ferred sites for down-
loading new software is
easy with GnoRPM.

Configuring Upgrade Options

In the No Upgrade tab, you have the option of telling GnoRPM to not upgrade certain packages (see Figure 11.6). For example, by default GnoRPM does not upgrade the libc, glibc, and shlibs libraries—if it allowed this, you might get new functionality at the expense of creating problems for some of your existing applications. To prevent damaging your system, you should not override this setting unless you are very familiar with these program libraries, what they do, how they affect your system, and why you need to upgrade them. If you have some applications on your system that you absolutely do not want to upgrade (such as a Web server or Oracle database server that must be a specific version to interface with specific clients), you should add those package names here as well.

FIGURE 11.6
Tell GnoRPM if you
don't want certain
applications or libraries
upgraded by new packages (for compatibility
purposes, for example).

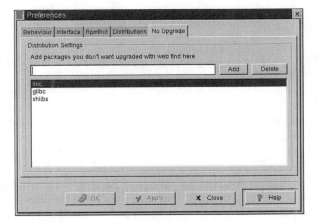

Part

III

Ch

11

Installing Software with GnoRPM

The GnoRPM interface initially shows you which RPM packages and software applications you currently have installed on your Linux system, under the Packages tree in the main window. This can be useful to let you know what you have that you might not be using. All software that you install is not automatically reflected in shortcuts or links on your desktop, panel, menu, or submenu. Also, all software packages included on the CD are not installed by default. At some point, you will probably want to install some additional or new software packages.

Installing New Software Packages

You install new packages by clicking the Install button on the toolbar or by selecting Operations, Install from the menu bar. This brings up the Install dialog box, shown in Figure 11.7.

N O T E Don't get confused or led astray by the Remove From List button. This button essentially
is useful and feasible only in the current version if you have one or two packages
selected. If you try to remove a single item from a long list of selected packages, you will have to
click each and every package before clicking Remove, followed by clicking all the remaining packages again before pressing Install. All you really have to do is click the package you do not want to
install, which takes the highlight off it. Then when you click Install, it will ignore the fact that the package is listed in the window. ■

FIGURE 11.7
You can see a list of all
the packages you cur-
rently have selected for
installation in the
Install dialog box.

The Install dialog box is initially empty until you click the Add button and select one or more
packages to install in the Add Packages dialog box (see Figure 11.8). In this case, one has
already been selected. As you can see, after you've selected a package for installation, the
package name is listed in the Install dialog window and is highlighted.

N O T E The Add Packages dialog box is almost exactly the same in appearance and function
to the Upgrade dialog box, so it is not discussed at length here. Basically, the
functionality is the same for both of these boxes, except that Upgrade Packages is used for packages
that you already have installed, whereas Add Packages is for new applications (not already on your
system). ■

FIGURE 11.8
The Add Packages dia-
log box allows you to
pick individual pack-
ages to install.

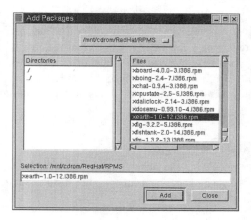

In the Add Packages dialog box, the directory from which you are installing is listed at the top of the window. You can navigate through the directories, if there are more than one, in the Directories window on the left to get to the directory you want. Double-click the packages you want to install in the Files window frame on the right (this double-click functionality does not work with all mice hardware configurations, however). Alternatively, you can click once to insert the package name in the Selection text box at the bottom, and then click Add. After you've selected all the packages you want, click the Close button to return to the Install dialog box. There you should see a complete list of all the packages you selected.

> **CAUTION**
>
> Be careful that you don't select the same package more than once, which GnoRPM enables you to do in the current version. If you do, you will have to come back later and remove one of the duplicate references.

Look over the list one last time, and make sure that you have no duplicates or incorrect packages. If you know that a certain package depends on other packages, such as certain libraries, you should select those packages also. However, if you don't, GnoRPM will notice the problem later in the process and will offer you an opportunity to install the other packages.

> **CAUTION**
>
> The Check Sig(nature) button enables you to check the pgp (Pretty Good Privacy) signature of the packages you want to install. This verifies that the file comes from an authenticated source and that the file and its programs have not been modified. You don't need to do this with the Red Hat CD-ROM, but you might want to do this if you were installing packages given to you on a CD-ROM someone created, or that you downloaded from the Internet. If you don't verify the authenticity and integrity of such programs, you could create a security problem, allow unauthorized access to your system, or cause damage to your system (if the programs have been modified to do such things). However, if you don't have PGP installed, GnoRPM has a bug that causes it to crash (the application itself, not your system). If this happens, you will have to restart GnoRPM and reselect your packages. Avoid this button unless you need to use it and have PGP installed.

As a precaution, you can click the Query button, which brings up a Package Info dialog box with tabs for each package you're planning to install (only one tab is shown in Figure 11.9). You can then read the descriptions of the packages and look over the filenames and installation directories, if you feel you need to. You might find one or two packages that you didn't intend to install or that do something different than you originally thought they did. If you're happy with your selections, click Install to continue.

Part
III

Ch
11

FIGURE 11.9
The Package Info dialog box provides a general description of the applications you want to install, along with a list of files included in the package.

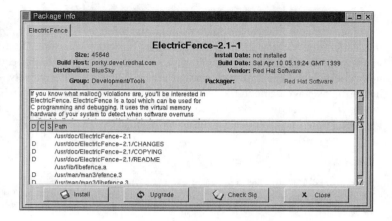

If all goes well, you will see an Installing pop-up window, similar to the one shown in Figure 11.10. This window shows you an installation progress bar along with the time remaining and the total number of packages and megabytes being installed.

FIGURE 11.10
You will see an Installing progress dialog box that lets you know how much of your selected applications have been installed.

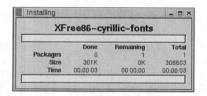

However, sometimes all does not go as planned. For example, you might see an Information dialog box appear indicating that the installation of several items failed. The failure is likely to be because of two things: you are trying to install a package that is already installed (did you want to upgrade?) or the package can't be installed because it depends on other packages that are not installed. When either of these problems occur, you have two options. You can ignore the warning and continue installing your currently selected packages (and risk possible erratic consequences), or you can go back and correct the problem. This can be done in two different ways.

Installing Packages That Are Already Installed

If GnoRPM recognizes that you are trying to install a package that already exists on your system, it normally will warn you about it and let you correct the problem. If this happens, you should perform the following steps:

1. In the Installation Problems pop-up window, read the error messages and decide what you want to do. If you want to ignore the warning and perform the installation anyway, click Yes. Be aware that the system is warning you that Linux or your applications might become unstable if you ignore these warnings. You are better off to click No and try to correct the underlying problem in GnoRPM.

2. If you decide (wisely) to go back and correct the problem, note the packages that had problems (write them down if there are many or you don't think you can remember). Click No so that GnoRPM halts the installation of the currently selected packages. Click OK on the information box that tells you the package installations failed. You will now be back in the Install window.

3. The packages currently selected for installation are highlighted. If you decide not to install a package (because it is already installed and you don't want to upgrade or over-write it, for example) click the package name in the Install window; it should change background color to white, indicating it is no longer selected for installation (even though it is still in the window). Do this for all applications you have decided you don't want or need to install (for example, the ones that generated error messages). When you are ready, click Install again. If you removed all the offending programs, you should see an Installing window with a progress bar showing that the applications are being installed.

 TIP   To deselect packages, I advise against using the Remove from List button unless you have only a few packages to install. If you click the package in question and then click Remove from List (the intuitive behavior many people would expect), GnoRPM will remove all remaining highlighted packages; this could force you to go back and select them all over again.

Installing Packages That Have Dependencies

Some of the packages you try to install are very complex. Many of them require shared libraries or other programs to function properly. Before RPM and GnoRPM, it was up to you to determine these dependencies and fix them manually. Now you don't have to worry about reading all about each individual package and determining the dependencies yourself—GnoRPM does this tedious work for you.

Normally you will select packages for installation in the Add Packages dialog box and then try to install them using the Install button. If these packages need other packages, you will see a Dependency Problems dialog box pop up on your screen. This dialog box will list any packages that you're trying to install and what other packages they need.

For example, if you try to install tetex-dvips-0.9-17.i386.rpm (and didn't have it installed already), you will be warned that it needs tetex 0.9. An analogy would be grocery shopping; if you put chocolate frosting in your shopping cart, you should also have a cake mix or the appropriate fixings for a cake in your cart too (if not, you'll have to go back, right?). If you receive a Dependency Problems error message, you should perform the following tasks:

Part
III

Ch
11

1. In the Dependency Problems pop-up window, read the error messages and decide what you want to do. If you want to ignore the warning and perform the installation anyway, click Yes. However, because the program doesn't have the underlying support files and programs that it needs, it probably will not work. You are better off to click No and try to correct the underlying problem in GnoRPM.

2. If you decide (wisely) to go back and correct the problem, note the package that had problems. Click No so that GnoRPM halts the installation of the currently selected packages. Click OK on the information box that tells you the package installations failed. You will now be back in the Install window. Do not deselect the package that had a dependency problem unless you just decide not to install it.

3. More than likely, you will want to add the dependent package to your list of currently selected files, so click Add. You will see the pop-up Add Packages window. Choose the additional package that you need (which was displayed in the error message when you tried to install) by double-clicking it or clicking it and pressing Add. This package will be added to the Install window in the background.

N O T E Unfortunately, you will have to solve dependency problems one file at a time, moving back and forth between the error messages (generated by the Install button) and the Add Packages window; GnoRPM does not give you a single, comprehensive list of all the files that your package needs. For example, `tetex-dvips` requires `tetex-0.9` and `dialog-0.6-14` (but you won't be warned of them both at the same time). ■

4. Make sure the Install window reflects all the packages you now want to install, and click Install. If all is well, the installation process will continue. However, you might receive additional error messages if you still have dependency problems or are trying to install packages that are already installed. In these cases, repeat the appropriate process discussed in this section.

Upgrading Software with GnoRPM

When you bring up GnoRPM, you will see an Upgrade button on the toolbar. You also can get to this function by selecting Operations, Upgrade from the GnoRPM menu bar. The Upgrade button enables you to install a new package and perform an upgrade of an application that you have installed on your Linux system previously. This is different from the Install button, which should be used only for new programs that you haven't previously installed (you will receive an error message otherwise).

Because of the similarity between installing and upgrading packages, you will find that many windows are almost exactly the same as those you see when using the Install button. The major difference is that you will see Upgrade at the top of the windows instead of Install. For example, clicking Upgrade will bring up a window with the same buttons as those displayed in Figure 11.7.

However, the upgrade functionality isn't exactly what you might expect. When you select or highlight a package in the main GnoRPM window and click Upgrade, you might think that it would go to the RPM directory on the CD and check to see whether the package needs to be upgraded. Instead, GnoRPM ignores the file you have highlighted and takes you directly to the Upgrade window. There you can add packages to upgrade, just as you did with the Install feature. The difference is that Install should be used for packages you do not have installed on your system, and Upgrade should be used for packages that you do (for example, if you have Apache version 1.1.3 from a previous Red Hat installation and want to upgrade your installed version to 1.3.6). Upgrade will remove all existing versions of the application on your system. In effect, this has the same function as the `rpm -U` command.

> **N O T E** Keep in mind that software development of Linux applications flies along at a quick clip.
> It is likely that there are likely newer versions of most of the applications even at the time
> you install them from CD. You don't have to upgrade necessarily. Few people will have to upgrade at
> all unless they are running Web servers, ftp servers, and so on and need to have the most current
> version for security purposes or for additional functionality not provided by the current version. You
> probably just can wait until the next major release of Linux to update many of your programs. ▨

Querying and Verifying Software with GnoRPM

Part III
Ch
11

Querying and verifying go hand in hand because they are both debugging tools that enable you to find out information about the packages you have installed. Unlike the Install and Upgrade functions previously discussed, which primarily reference packages found on a CD or the Internet, the Query and Verify button items focus on the software already installed on your system.

The Query menu button enables you to find out basic information about your installed software packages: who packaged them, when, and what files are included. The Verify button enables you to test the installed files for integrity; missing or corrupt files are identified so that you can re-install, if necessary. To pick files from the main GnoRPM window pictured back in Figure 11.1, perform the following steps:

1. Navigate through the Package groups and subgroups in the left window frame, and select the packages in the frame on the right that you want to query or verify.

2. To select (or deselect) multiple files, hold down the Ctrl key while you click the desired packages. You do not have to hold the Ctrl key when you click groups in the left frame, though; that's only for packages. If you have one package selected within a frame and you hold down the Shift key while clicking another, all packages between the two will also be highlighted. If you click one file in a group that has multiple files selected without holding down the Ctrl key, all files will lose their highlight, and the single file you clicked will be selected (all packages selected in other groups will still be highlighted, however).

3. After you have chosen all the files you want to query or verify, you can proceed by various routes. You can click either function in the toolbar, or you can choose Packages, Query or Packages, Verify from the main menu. If you have multiple files selected but want to check only a single file for some reason, you can right-click that file and select Query or Verify. This will ignore all your other selections for now, although they will still be highlighted.

If you select Query, the Package Info dialog box appears. You can see basic information about all the files, conveniently separated by tabs labeled with the package name. You also have the option of clicking the Verify button at the bottom of this dialog box.

If you select Verify, GnoRPM will check the files in the selected packages and make sure there are no errors. You will see a Verifying Packages window. If there are no problems, the window will remain empty and you can click Close to return to the main GnoRPM window. If GnoRPM finds problems with any of the package files, it will give you a short description of the problem in the Verifying Packages window. Different problems will require different solutions, or possibly no action at all (as long as the applications are working OK). If there are problems you want to fix, you probably need to install the package again or upgrade the package. Keep in mind that you will want to back up any configuration files or data associated with any such package before you do so, however.

Uninstalling Software with GnoRPM

Compared to the tedious gunzip and tar methods, uninstalling software with RPM and GnoRPM is extremely easy. If you decide you need to remove a package from your system (to make room for user data or more applications, for example), follow these steps:

1. Launch the GnoRPM application by going to the main Gnome menu and selecting System, GnoRPM. You will see the main GnoRPM window with a directory tree menu (with application groups) on the left and an individual package listing on the right.

2. In the directory tree menu on the left, navigate to the application group where your package is located (for example, the Apache Web server is located under Packages, System Environment, Daemons) by clicking on the plus signs by each group.

3. In the package listing on the right, select the package or packages that you want to uninstall by clicking them. To select multiple files, refer to step 2 in the previous section on querying and verifying software.

4. (Optional) If you want, you can select Query before you uninstall the selected packages. This will bring up the Package Info screen, which also has an Uninstall button at the bottom. This provides you the basic information you need about each selected package to determine whether you really want to Uninstall it.

5. When you are sure that you have selected all the files you want to uninstall, just click Uninstall, either in the Package Info dialog box or directly on the toolbar. You can also choose Packages, Uninstall from the menubar. After you have started the uninstall process for the selected files, you will see a progress bar indicating how many applications are being uninstalled and how many kilobytes or megabytes remain until the process is finished.

Finding Software with GnoRPM

Determining which packages rely on other packages can be pretty difficult. You might also want to know which programs are in certain groups or what the name of the package is that has the application named xpdf, for example. That is why GnoRPM includes the Find function. To use the GnoRPM Find function, follow these steps:

1. Click the Find button on the toolbar. The Find Packages dialog box appears.

2. Click the drop-down menu box and select Are In the Group from the list of choices.

3. For this example, enter Amusements/Games in the text box next to the Find button at the top right (see Figure 11.11).

FIGURE 11.11
GnoRPM provides the capability to find currently installed packages and files.

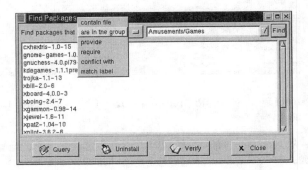

4. Click the Find button.

5. The packages contained in the Amusements/Games group are then listed in the main window. You can now click any of the files listed to highlight the file; then press Query, Verify, or Uninstall.

As you can see from the options in the drop-down box, you can also find packages that require another package, that conflict with other packages, or that contain a specific file you found on your system. If you select Match Label, you can enter the program name—such as xboing, trojka, xpdf, or gedit—and find out what the full package name is (if it is not installed, nothing will show up in the Find Packages window). This includes the version number and other things that you are unlikely to remember off the top of your head. This can save you some time guessing and digging through the package groups in the GnoRPM main window to find a certain program.

Finding RPMs on the Web with GnoRPM

The Webfind button on the toolbar brings up the Rpmfind dialog box, which integrates with a Web-enabled database at Red Hat to enable you to find RPM packages that you might need or want to upgrade after your initial CD-ROM or network-based installation of Linux (see Figure 11.12). Webfind and Rpmfind are essentially synonymous terms, although you will see each of them in different places within the application. To use Rpmfind, perform the following steps:

FIGURE 11.12
The Rpmfind dialog box can be used to find Red Hat packages on the Internet to upgrade your Linux system components.

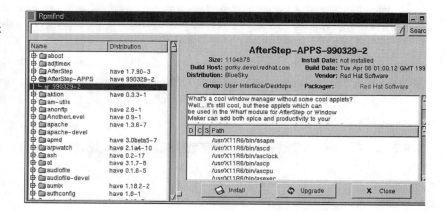

1. As root, select System, GnoRPM from the main GNOME menu. This will bring up the main GnoRPM window.

NOTE Notice when using programs such as GnoRPM and a few others, that the windows default to a size of 800×600 pixels, assuming everyone has nice, large monitors and X Window configured to handle that size. Unfortunately, if you have an older monitor that is not capable of this high resolution, or you have X set to 640×480 pixels, sometimes it is hard to view the entire application window or even click buttons that are located at the bottom.

If this occurs and you are not using multiple virtual screens (pages), you should consult the chapters in Part II of this book, which covers configuration of your video card, monitor, X Window, GNOME, and Enlightenment. You might find that just making a few changes recommended in Chapter 2 (such as changing the mouse behavior) to Enlightenment, and then saving your changes, will force GNOME and E to interface properly when you reboot, enabling you to scroll across virtual screens and get to the buttons you need (although you still will have to change your resolution size to see the entire screen).

2. Click Webfind on the toolbar. The first time you enter this screen it will connect you to Red Hat's Web site and download the index of applications. You will see an Rpmfind window split into two sections. The section on the left is a directory tree similar to the one you are accustomed to using with the main GnoRPM window. There are two columns in this section: Name and Distribution. Name lists the applications you currently have installed on your machine. If there are any new versions of a program, you will see a comment in the Distribution column, indicating that an update is available.

3. For example, if you have the `xtrojka` game version 1.2.3-6 installed, and there is an update available (version 1.2.3-7), you will see `have version 1.2.3-6` next to `xtrojka`. Click `xtrojka`, and the tree will expand to show you available versions, which will include both your current version and the new software (or possibly older versions). Click the new version you are interested in. On the right side of the window, you will see a description of the application, a listing of files included with the package. There are also Install and Upgrade buttons.

4. If there is a program that you don't have installed on your system, you can click Install and GnoRPM will begin the download and installation. You will see a pop-up window confirming the site where the file will be downloaded from and asking your permission to continue. Click Yes to continue or No to stop the download. All other functionality is similar to what you encountered in the section "Installing New Software Packages." GnoRPM will download the information it needs to perform dependency checks and look for existing (duplicate) packages, and then it will prompt you once again to see whether you want to download the packages (select Yes or No again).

5. If you want to upgrade software already installed on your system, like the current `xtrojka` example, click Upgrade. You will see a pop-up window confirming the site where the file will be downloaded from and asking your permission to continue. Click Yes to continue or No to stop the download. The functionality then will be the same as that described in the section "Upgrading Software with GnoRPM."

Using Command-Line RPM

You might find that you run into a problem that prevents you from bringing up X Window. You might be able to fix the problem from the command line by modifying configuration files or running text-based X configuration programs. However, suppose your X Window software is totally malfunctioning and you need to reinstall or upgrade it. Because you can't bring up X, you can't bring up GnoRPM, which is the main way you have to install and upgrade software from your Red Hat installation CD.

Luckily, because GnoRPM is just a front end to the `rpm` command, you do have the option of just using `rpm` directly from the command line in these types of instances. Because this should be a rare occurrence, not much detail is needed here; you should keep in mind that rpm is a very robust package with many different options you will never use. The `man rpm` command provides help on using this command during special circumstances (for example, if you need to send it additional, infrequently used command-line parameters). To use `rpm` to perform basic functions from the command line, perform the following tasks (some are optional, depending on your needs):

1. From the command-line prompt, type `man rpm` to see the help file on the command if you need it. Using the command improperly could cause you to lose data or overwrite programs you don't want to, so you should become familiar with the command's functionality if you are not already.

2. Mount your CD (if it is currently unmounted) by using the `mount /mnt/cdrom` command; you might have to use the `mount -t iso9660 /dev/hdc /mnt/cdrom` command if you do not have the correct CD filesystem configured in `/etc/fstab` (this assumes your CD is the third IDE device (the first device on your second IDE interface controller), but you should replace `hdc` with the appropriate designator for your CD-ROM if necessary, such as `sdb` for the second SCSI device, `hdd` for the fourth IDE device, and so on).

3. You might want to navigate to that directory with `cd /mnt/cdrom/RedHat/RPMS` (so you can do file listings and see what you are working with). You will have to know the exact name or filename of the application you want to work with. For example, if you want to query, upgrade, install, or uninstall `xpdf`, you will have to use `xpdf` or `xpdf-0.80-4.i386.rpm` (for the Intel platform; extensions are different for Alpha and Sparc architecture). Type `ls -al xpdf*` (or `*xpdf*`) to see a listing of the xpdf-related files. You should something like the long file mentioned previously.

4. To query this package and find out if it is on your system, type `rpm -q xpdf`. If it is installed, `rpm` will print out the long filename of the package. If it is not, `rpm` will say that `xpdf` is not installed.

5. If `xpdf` is installed and you want to uninstall or erase it, type `rpm -e xpdf`. The package will be removed from your system.

6. If `xpdf` is installed and you want to verify its integrity, type `rpm -V xpdf`. Note the capital V, which is different than the small case parameters used with previous options.

7. If an earlier version of `xpdf` is installed and you want to upgrade it to a newer version, type `rpm -Uvh /mnt/cdrom/RedHat/RPMS/xpdf-0.80-4.i386.rpm`. Note the capital U again. Because you are entering the entire pathname associated with the file, keep in mind that you can install from other directories as well (such as an Internet download directory if you downloaded the newer version of `xpdf` off the Internet). All you really need is `-U` to upgrade, but the `vh` options provide a verification of the upgraded files and print out a convenient progress bar (useful for large packages). If the package you are trying to upgrade is not installed already, the `-U` option will react the same as if you were performing an installation instead of an upgrade.

8. If `xpdf` is not installed and you want to install it, type `rpm -ivh xpdf-0.80-4.i386.rpm`.

Troubleshooting GnoRPM

GnoRPM should not cause you too many problems. This is a fairly efficient front-end program to RPM, which has in turn been widely tested.

If you can't find a package that you know is on your system, you might check that you have the right spelling and case. Linux and GnoRPM are case-sensitive, so text boxes such as the Search box in the Find Packages dialog box can be problematic if you don't know whether certain letters are capitalized (for example, xboard and xBoard will not have the same result). If you can't get to the Red Hat metadata server from Web Find, you should make sure that you have the necessary proxy server addresses properly configured in the Rpmfind tab of the Preferences dialog box.

If portions of GnoRPM become corrupted, you may not be able to recover by using GnoRPM to recover files because GnoRPM has control of the RPM database and may not be capable of writing over parts of itself. In such a case, you may have to use the RPM command-line tool, which is also relatively simple if you browse through the man page (help file) for it.

If you can't install parts or all of a package, or certain files within the package, you more than likely have either a space or a permissions problem. Usually, it is a permissions problem; security permissions on a file or directory might have been changed to a setting that prevents you from writing to the resource in question. If you suspect that this is the case, you will have to check permissions on all directories and subdirectories above the file or directory you're trying to access with the `ls -al` command. You can find the permissions on the left side of your screen as three groups of permissions: (r)ead (w)rite, and e(x)ecute.

Part III

Ch 11

You might find that a file has owner, group, and other permissions of 664 (rw-rw-r--), which enables everyone to read a file but not execute it. In this case, change the permissions using `chmod 775` followed by the directory or filename (read, write, and execute permissions are cumulative, with values of 4, 2, and 1 respectively, so a value of 444 is read-only for everybody, whereas 750 is read/write/execute by the owner, read/execute by the group, and no access by everyone else). If you want to change the owner or group association of a file or folder, use the `chown` and `chgrp` commands (for example, `chown root /etc/testfile` or `chgrp users /etc/testfile`).

The Getting Started Guide in the `docs` directory of your Red Hat CD-ROM contains important information about these types of commands, and you should become familiar with the material as soon as possible after installing Red Hat Linux.

You should also check your amount of free disk space using one of GNOME's monitors (gdiskfree, for example) or the `df` command from an X terminal. You might be running out of disk space for your larger applications. You probably also should make sure that you have at least 25% available disk space, to provide the flexibility you need to manage your system programs and have sufficient storage space left over for your data. ●

## CHAPTER 12

Installing and Managing Linux Software

by John Ray

In this chapter

Understanding Linux Software Applications

Getting the most out of Linux means taking advantage of software that isn't specifically packaged for your system. Thousands of UNIX applications are available that will compile on your Linux computer.

Before you start compiling and installing Linux applications, you need to understand the methods in which the software is delivered to your system and how you can turn the software into a usable form.

Distribution Method: Binary and Source

Linux and Unix differ from traditional desktop operating systems in the way that software is distributed. Software will arrive on your computer in one of two forms:

- **Binary distributions**—These programs are ready to run out of the box. A binary distribution means that the software has been compiled for your system and will run immediately. A drawback to a binary distribution is that it can be specific either to the type of processor you are using or even to the version of Linux you are running. Some risk also is associated with running any software that is precompiled and lacking source code—you don't know (and can't find out) exactly what the software will do. Before installing a binary distribution, make sure that you are downloading from a trusted source.

- **Source distributions**—Instead of creating machine-specific distributions of software, some developers prefer to distribute the source code of the application. The end user is given the responsibility of compiling the software on his computer and preparing it for use. Installing a source distribution is generally very easy, but the extra steps needed can be confusing to first-time Linux users. Most source code can be compiled and installed with one or two easy steps, but some programs require the user to actually edit source files to configure options for their computer. As with binaries, make sure you download from a trusted source—someone could have modified the code you're about to compile!

To add an extra layer of complexity to the software distribution problem, there is also the matter of software distribution packaging. You probably are aware that programs rarely arrive as a single file—especially in the case of source distributions, which might be made up of hundreds of files. Archiving software combines these files into a single archive file that can be handled more easily. Software distributions can also be rather large, so a method of compressing the final archive file is necessary as well. Unfortunately, all these different possibilities for distributing, archive, and compressing software can lead to a surprising number of different combinations. Let's take a look at some of the more common methods of distributing software and how to prepare them for installation. Don't worry if this is a little overwhelming. You'll soon be introduced to a Linux-specific method of software distribution that is growing in popularity and that is as easy to use as any Windows or Mac-based software installation wizard.

Archiving Formats: tar and zip

The most popular archiving program under Linux or Unix is tar. This program simply takes several files and outputs them as a single archive. It does not incorporate any sort of compression; the resulting file will be slightly larger than the combined size total of the input files. You can recognize tarfiles by the .tar extension they are commonly given.

 TIP

If you have a filename that has .tar in it but that is followed by something else (.gz, .Z, .bz2), then it is a compressed tarfile and must be uncompressed before you can work with it. Skip ahead to the "Compression Formats: compress, gzip, and bzip2" section in this chapter for more information on uncompressing common file formats.

To unarchive a tarfile, use the command `tar xvf <filename>`. The options x, v, and f refer to extracting files, verbosely showing what is being done, and specifying the name of the archive to extract. You might want to create a new directory and move the archive into it before you start extracting files; otherwise, you might end up with hundreds of files being created in a directory that you hadn't intended to use.

See the following for an example:

```
[jray@contempt]$ tar -xvf kmysql-1.1.1c.tar
kmysql-1.1.1c/AUTHORS
kmysql-1.1.1c/COPYING
kmysql-1.1.1c/ChangeLog
kmysql-1.1.1c/INSTALL
kmysql-1.1.1c/Makefile.am
kmysql-1.1.1c/Makefile.dist
kmysql-1.1.1c/Makefile.in
...
kmysql-1.1.1c/missing
kmysql-1.1.1c/mkinstalldirs
kmysql-1.1.1c/po/
kmysql-1.1.1c/po/Makefile.am
kmysql-1.1.1c/po/Makefile.in
kmysql-1.1.1c/po/kmysql.pot
kmysql-1.1.1c/stamp-h.in
```

The archive `kymsql-1.1.1c.tar` has been extracted into a `kmysql-1.1.1c` directory. The program is now ready to be compiled and installed.

Another popular archiving method that you might already be familiar with is zip. Zipfiles are common on Windows/DOS platforms and combine the capability to archive and compress simultaneously. Linux/Unix distributions rarely use zip as a packaging method, but sometimes it is useful to be able to access the same zipfiles under Linux that you can under Windows. To extract and uncompress a zipfile, simply type `unzip <filename.zip>`, as in the following example:

```
[jray@contempt]$ unzip setistuff.zip
Archive:  setistuff.zip
  inflating: README
  inflating: setiathome
 extracting: lock.txt
  inflating: nohup.out
  inflating: outfile.txt
  inflating: state.txt
  inflating: temp.txt
  inflating: user_info.txt
  inflating: version.txt
```

Nothing to it, huh? If this isn't working on your system, make sure you've installed the rpm unzip-5.40-1.i386.rpm (or something similar) from your Red Hat CD-ROM.

Compression Formats: compress, gzip, and bzip2

Linux and Unix offer many different ways to compress a file or archive. The most popular method is with gzip. You can recognize a gzip file by the extension .gz. To uncompress a gzip file, just type gunzip <filename.gz>, and the original file will be recreated without the .gz extension. Sometimes tarfiles that have been compressed with gzip have the extension .tgz. You have two different options for uncompressing and unarchive these files. You may run gunzip on the .tgz file and then subsequently run tar to extract the archive (as seen in the previous section), or you can accomplish both tasks at once using a special option in the tar command: z. To perform both tasks with a single command, use this form of the tar command: tar xvzf <filename.tgz>.

An older compression format is that of the compress command. You will rarely see compress files anymore, but occasionally they still pop up. You can tell a file has been compacted with the compress utility by the .Z extension in the filename. To uncompress such a file, use uncompress <filename.Z>, and the original file will be recreated. As with gzip files, you might occasionally run into a file that is tarred and compressed. You can uncompress and untar these files in a single step. Instead of the z option used with gzip files, try Z: tar xvZf <filename.tar.Z>. You'll usually see .Z compression used on files that are not specific to a particular distribution of UNIX.

Finally, a new compression utility is creeping into the limelight. Bzip2 is gaining popularity rapidly in the Linux community. Bzip2 archives are denoted by a .bz2 filename extension and are uncompressed by simply typing bunzip2 <filename.bz2>.

RPMS: Some Difficulties

In the previous chapter, you learned about the Red Hat Package Management System. Even with all the strengths of RPMs, there are some reasons why you might sometimes run into trouble. For beginners, RPMS can sometimes prove to be frustrating. The extensive dependency checking of RPMS often leads to situations where upgrading software fails due to errors while replacing in-use files. There are ways to force installation of files, but adding an option such as `-force` to a command line can be a bit frightening.

Another problem is that with the rapid development of Linux, you might end up downloading an RPM that was compiled with an early version of the operating system libraries that doesn't work quite correctly with the version of the OS that you are running. You should pay close attention to clues given in the filename. If you are faced with installing a file with `libc5` or `glibc6` in the filename, you'd want to choose `glibc6`, which is the appropriate libc version that is packaged with Red Hat 6.0. Some packages might include the Red Hat version in the filename, such as `rh5.2` or `rh6`. Be sure that the package you're downloading is the appropriate RPM for your CPU type and distribution; otherwise, you might run into difficulties. Downloading and compiling source files will always result in a proper binary file for your Linux distribution. As you're about to see, the process isn't nearly as daunting as you might think.

The Process of Unarchiving in KDE and GNOME

KDE and GNOME both recognize .tar archives and will show a special icon for these types of files. If you want to unarchive either file, simply click the icon, and it will be extracted.

KDE   In KDE, the unarchiving operation is handled by a piece of software that is part of the basic KDE installation: kArchive.

To start using kArchive, just click the archived file, whether a bzip2-compressed tarfile, a gzipped tarfile, or another file compressed with a similar compression utility. Almost instantly, you will be presented with a list of the files that can be extracted. The operation of kArchive is very similar to Stuff-It on the Macintosh and WinZIP on the Windows platform. To extract specific files from within the archive, you can select a range of files and then choose Extract from the Edit menu. You will then be asked what files you want to extract (all files, or the selected files). Then you have the option of specifying a directory that will contain the extracted files (see Figure 12.1). When you have decided what you want and where you want it, just click the OK button; the files will be extracted.

GNOME   GNOME's default graphical archive manager does not handle gzip or bzip2 files transparently, as kArchive does. You must first uncompress the packages using a different technique, as discussed earlier. When you have a simple .tar tarfile to work with, it's easy sailing. Double-click the tarfile, and you are presented with a directory representation of the tarfile that you will be able to navigate through as if it were any other directory on your system. To extract files, just drag them to the destination you'd like using the same techniques you already use to interact with GNOME. To extract all the files, just drag the entire tarfile directory wherever you want it. GNOME presents you with a dialog box as it moves the files from a temporary storage location to your destination.

FIGURE 12.1
kArchive provides a graphical interface to the unarchiving process.

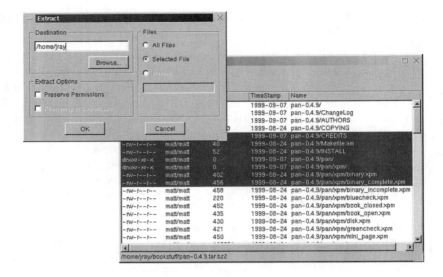

Installing and Compiling Linux Source Code Distributions

Before you can compile a program, you must obtain its source code. You might have both GNOME and KDE on your system, so the following sections show examples of downloading and installing software for both desktop systems. Software for these systems is most commonly distributed in source format for the sake of hardware independence, but it is usually very easy to install.

Installing a KDE Application

Take a look at the KDE Web site http://www.kde.org. Under the applications section, you will find a few hundred programs that are under active development and are ready to be installed. Everything from games to network traffic monitors is there.

Imagine that you have decided to download a Pac-Man clone called kzacman, which is stored on your system as kzacman-1.0.tar.gz, a gzipped tarfile. This section goes through the steps of preparing this file to be compiled and installed. Although you could uncompress and untar the file in a single step, the process is demonstrated here in two steps. Tar's capability to work with gzip is a nicety, but it is not available for all compression formats. It's a good idea to get used to dealing with things like this by hand.

First, uncompress the archive:

```
[jray@pointy kzacman]$ gunzip kzacman-1.0.tar.gz
[jray@pointy kzacman]$ ls -al
total 987
drwxrwxr-x   2 jray     jray        1024 Sep 11 12:34 .
drwxr-xr-x   3 jray     jray        1024 Sep 11 12:33 ..
-rw-r--r--   1 jray     jray     1003520 Sep 11 12:18 kzacman-1.0.tar
```

Now you have a single tarfile ready to be unarchived. Use the `tar` command to unarchive the file:

```
[jray@pointy kzacman]$ tar -xvf kzacman-1.0.tar
kzacman-1.0/
kzacman-1.0/README
kzacman-1.0/INSTALL
kzacman-1.0/Makefile.am
kzacman-1.0/Makefile.in
kzacman-1.0/acconfig.h
kzacman-1.0/acinclude.m4
kzacman-1.0/aclocal.m4
kzacman-1.0/config.guess
kzacman-1.0/config.h.bot
...
kzacman-1.0/src/kzacman.h
kzacman-1.0/src/gamewindow.h
kzacman-1.0/src/gamewidget.h
kzacman-1.0/src/scoredialog.h
kzacman-1.0/src/newscoredialog.h
kzacman-1.0/src/kzacman.xpm
kzacman-1.0/src/mini-kzacman.xpm
kzacman-1.0/src/kzacman.kdelnk
```

Looks good so far. Now you have created a kzacman–1.0 directory, and all the files needed to compile the application are sitting in the directory. Notice that there are two files that look rather important in the directory listing: README and INSTALL. These are rather typical file-names that you will see when downloading files. It is recommended that you read both files before continuing the installation; they might contain important information about running the application on your computer. Rather than guess the installation procedure, and end up with errors, it's better to check the instruction files that are included.

In the case of kzacman, the README file simply says this:

```
[jray@pointy kzacman-1.0]$ more README
See the HTML documentation in the doc/ subdirectory.
```

If more information is needed, you can always look in the doc subdirectory for program documentation. The INSTALL document, however, almost certainly contains detail instructions for compiling and installing the software. A portion of this document appears here. This is very typical (and probably identical) to many applications that you'll find. This is because modern software distributions use an automated configuration system that identifies the type of computer you are running, the operating system, and the installed features on your computer that can be used:

```
Basic Installation
==================

   These are generic installation instructions.

   The 'configure' shell script attempts to guess correct values for
various system-dependent variables used during compilation.  It uses
those values to create a 'Makefile' in each directory of the package.
It may also create one or more '.h' files containing system-dependent
definitions.  Finally, it creates a shell script 'config.status' that
you can run in the future to recreate the current configuration, a file
'config.cache' that saves the results of its tests to speed up
reconfiguring, and a file 'config.log' containing compiler output
(useful mainly for debugging 'configure').

   If you need to do unusual things to compile the package, please try
to figure out how 'configure' could check whether to do them, and mail
diffs or instructions to the address given in the 'README' so they can
be considered for the next release.  If at some point 'config.cache'
contains results you don't want to keep, you may remove or edit it.

The simplest way to compile this package is:

  1. 'cd' to the directory containing the package's source code and type
     './configure' to configure the package for your system.  If you're
     using 'csh' on an old version of System V, you might need to type
     'sh ./configure' instead to prevent 'csh' from trying to execute
     'configure' itself.

     Running 'configure' takes a while.  While running, it prints some
     messages telling which features it is checking for.

  2. Type 'make' to compile the package.

  3. Optionally, type 'make check' to run any self-tests that come with
     the package.

  4. Type 'make install' to install the programs and any data files and
     documentation.

  5. You can remove the program binaries and object files from the
     source code directory by typing 'make clean'.  To also remove the
     files that 'configure' created (so you can compile the package for
     a different kind of computer), type 'make distclean'.  There is
     also a 'make maintainer-clean' target, but that is intended mainly
     for the package's developers.  If you use it, you may have to get
     all sorts of other programs in order to regenerate files that came
     with the distribution.
```

The process is clearly spelled out in these instructions, so follow along:

First, cd into the directory containing the source distribution. This is the main kzacman distribution directory:

```
[jray@pointy kzacman]$ cd kzacman-1.0
[jray@pointy kzacman-1.0]$
```

Next, run the configuration script. This might take a while on your system; it depends on what the script checks for and the speed of your processors and disks. You'll see output during the entire process. Don't be alarmed by messages saying that a particular function or library is missing; it doesn't mean that the software won't compile:

```
[jray@pointy kzacman-1.0]$ ./configure
creating cache ./config.cache
checking how to run the C++ preprocessor... g++ -E
checking for a BSD compatible install... /usr/bin/install -c
checking for X... libraries /usr/X11R6/lib, headers /usr/X11R6/include
checking whether build environment is sane... yes
checking whether make sets ${MAKE}... yes
checking for ranlib... ranlib
checking for main in -lcompat... no
...
checking for extra libs... no
checking for kde headers installed... yes
checking for kde libraries installed... yes
checking for KDE paths... done
checking for sleep... yes
updating cache ./config.cache
creating ./config.status
creating Makefile
creating src/Makefile
creating data/Makefile
creating wav/Makefile
creating doc/Makefile
creating doc/en/Makefile
creating config.h
```

In the last few lines of the configuration process, you'll notice that several files are created: Makefiles and a config.h header file. These are the files that are necessary to build the software for your particular system. They take into account the location of your KDE distribution and other specifics of your configuration. Because of this, you cannot expect to move this preconfigured source code tree to another machine and have it compile; if you modify the configuration of your machine (moving the KDE installation directory, for example) it might have trouble compiling as well. For now, however, the software is ready to be compiled, so move on to the next step: compiling the software.

Part

III

Ch

12

N O T E With very few exceptions, the process of compiling software on your computer will be identical, no matter how the package is distributed. All you need to do to start the process is type make in the main source directory. The make command calls the makefiles that were created during the configuration process. In some software distributions there is no configuration phase, and you move directly to running make. Makefiles contain all the information necessary to run the compiler software on the source code files and produce programs that you can run. They manage dependencies between different pieces of code. For example, for a particular portion of the program to be compiled, the system relies on a different part of the program already existing. Makefiles instruct the compiler which files need to be compiled first, how to compile them, and what to do with them when they are compiled. As a final step, Makefiles can also contain information on how to install the resulting compiled program and its documentation on your computer for systemwide use. ■

Typing make runs the main makefile (and the makefiles that were created in the other subdirectories). This will be the most lengthy step of the installation. Depending on the size of the program and the speed of your computer, you might want to take a coffee break, eat lunch, or take a brief nap:

```
[jray@pointy kzacman-1.0]$ make
make all-recursive
make[1]: Entering directory '/home/jray/bookstuff/kzacman/kzacman-1.0'
Making all in data
make[2]: Leaving directory '/home/jray/bookstuff/kzacman/kzacman-1.0/data'
Making all in src
make[2]: Entering directory '/home/jray/bookstuff/kzacman/kzacman-1.0/src'
g++ -DHAVE_CONFIG_H -I. -I. -I.. -I/usr/include -I/usr/include/qt -
    I/usr/X11R6/include  -O2 -Wall -c main.cpp
g++ -DHAVE_CONFIG_H -I. -I. -I.. -I/usr/include -I/usr/include/qt  -
    I/usr/X11R6/include  -O2 -Wall -c gamewindow.cpp
...
g++ -DHAVE_CONFIG_H -I. -I. -I.. -I/usr/include
    -I/usr/include/qt -I/usr/X11R6/include
    -O2 -Wall -c newscoredialog.cpp
/bin/sh ../libtool --mode=link g++ -O2 -Wall -s -o kzacman
    -L/usr/lib -L/usr/X11R6/lib
    -rpath /usr/lib -rpath /usr/X11R6/lib main.o gamewindow.o
     gamewidget.o scoredialog.o
     gamewidget.moc.o gamewindow.moc.o newscoredialog.o -lkfm
     -lkdeui -lkdecore -lmediatool
    -lqt -lXext -lX11
g++ -O2 -Wall -s -o kzacman -L/usr/lib -L/usr/X11R6/lib main.o
    gamewindow.o gamewidget.o
    scoredialog.o gamewidget.moc.o gamewindow.moc.o newscoredialog.o
    -lkfm -lkdeui
    -lkdecore -lmediatool -lqt -lXext -lX11 -Wl,--rpath
    -Wl,/usr/lib -Wl,--rpath
    -Wl,/usr/X11R6/lib
make[2]: Leaving directory '/home/jray/bookstuff/kzacman/kzacman-1.0/src'
make[1]: Leaving directory '/home/jray/bookstuff/kzacman/kzacman-1.0'
```

Depending on the software being compiled, you might notice warnings during the compilation. Warnings are non-fatal errors that occurred in the compilation process; they are generally harmless and are the result of the compiler trying to help the programmer find potential problems in the source code. The most common cause of a warning message is when a programmer casts a particular variable to a different type. For example a long int holds large integer numbers, and an int holds smaller integers. If the programmer copies the contents of a long int into an int, a warning will be generated. Most of the time, this is harmless and is precisely what the programmer intended.

The last step of the compilation process is the installation of the compiled software. Again, the make command is used, this time with the install option:

```
[jray@pointy kzacman-1.0]$ su
Password:
[root@pointy kzacman-1.0]# make install
Making install in data
make[1]: Entering directory '/home/jray/bookstuff/kzacman/kzacman-1.0/data'
/bin/sh ../mkinstalldirs /usr/share/apps/kzacman/data
mkdir /usr/share/apps/kzacman
mkdir /usr/share/apps/kzacman/data
/usr/bin/install -c -m 644 ./arrow-down-mask.bmp
    /usr/share/apps/kzacman/data/arrow-down-mask.bmp
/usr/bin/install -c -m 644 ./arrow-down.bmp
...
/bin/sh ../libtool  --mode=install /usr/bin/install -c kzacman /usr/bin/kzacman
/usr/bin/install -c kzacman /usr/bin/kzacman
/bin/sh ../mkinstalldirs /usr/share/applnk/Games
/usr/bin/install -c -m 644 kzacman.kdelnk /usr/share/applnk/Games
/bin/sh ../mkinstalldirs /usr/share/icons
/usr/bin/install -c -m 644 kzacman.xpm /usr/share/icons
/bin/sh ../mkinstalldirs /usr/share/icons/mini
/usr/bin/install -c -m 644 mini-kzacman.xpm /usr/share/icons/mini/kzacman.xpm
make[1]: Leaving directory '/home/jray/bookstuff/kzacman/kzacman-1.0/src'
```

When running make install, there is a very good chance that you will need to be logged into the system as the root user for the software to be moved to the KDE application directory. In this example, su is used to become root for the rest of the installation process. If you do not have root access, ask your administrator for help, or check the README/INSTALL files for more information on changing the installation directory. Most likely, you will need to explicitly specify a destination when running the configure program. For example, the INSTALL file in this distribution says this:

```
Installation Names
==================

   By default, 'make install' will install the package's files in
'/usr/local/bin', '/usr/local/man', etc.  You can specify an
installation prefix other than '/usr/local' by giving 'configure' the
option '--prefix=PATH'.
```

Part

III

Ch

12

You might want to run ./configure —help for more information on the options that you can pass to the configuration process.

That's all there is to it! The kzacman application is now installed on your Linux machine. KDE packages are extremely nice in that the makefiles for most KDE applications will actually install the files so that they show up in the appropriate place in the KDE pop-up application menus. If you haven't booted into KDE yet, check the KDE-Games menu, and you will see a Zacman icon just waiting to be clicked. If you're already running KDE, you must right-click the KDE launcher bar and then choose Restart from the KDE contextual menu. Figure 12.2 shows the newly installed piece of software.

FIGURE 12.2
Zacman is successfully compiled and installed.

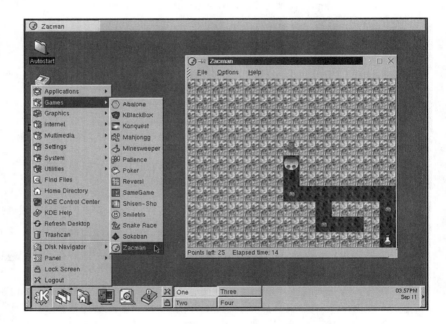

Installing a GNOME Application

Now turn your attention to the GNOME environment and see how to install a new GNOME application. As with KDE applications, GNOME applications are popping up on a daily basis. The GNOME Web site (http://www.gnome.org/applist) has a software map with download links to all the known GNOME software. Imagine that you have chosen to download a piece of Internet software for GNOME called pan. As with the previous example installation, the first step will be to unzip and uncompress the file:

```
[jray@pointy bookstuff]$ gunzip pan-0.4.9.tar.gz
[jray@pointy bookstuff]$ ls -al pan-0.4.9.tar
-rw-r--r--   1 jray     jray      870400 Sep 11 12:18 pan-0.4.9.tar
```

Now, unarchive the tarfile. You can use the command line or double-click the pan tarfile in the GNOME file manager:

```
[jray@pointy bookstuff]$ tar -xvf pan-0.4.9.tar
pan-0.4.9/
pan-0.4.9/ChangeLog
pan-0.4.9/AUTHORS
pan-0.4.9/COPYING
pan-0.4.9/CREDITS
pan-0.4.9/README
pan-0.4.9/Makefile.am
pan-0.4.9/INSTALL
pan-0.4.9/pan/
pan-0.4.9/pan/xpm/
pan-0.4.9/pan/xpm/binary.xpm
pan-0.4.9/pan/xpm/binary_complete.xpm
pan-0.4.9/pan/xpm/binary_incomplete.xpm
...
pan-0.4.9/uulib/uunconc.c
pan-0.4.9/uulib/uuscan.c
pan-0.4.9/uulib/uustring.awk
pan-0.4.9/uulib/uustring.c
pan-0.4.9/uulib/uustring.h
pan-0.4.9/uulib/uuutil.c
```

In this archive, you might want to take a look at a few files: AUTHORS, COPYING, CREDITS, README, and INSTALL. For now, the INSTALL file is the most important file. As with the KDE installation, the INSTALL file contains all the information necessary to compile and install the software on your computer. For pan, the INSTALL file contains these rather terse instructions:

```
[jray@pointy pan-0.4.9]$ more INSTALL
To install try this:

./configure
make
make install
```

Although the INSTALL file is a bit less verbose than in the last example, you should note that the instructions are exactly the same. Run configure, followed by make, and then make install:

```
[jray@pointy pan-0.4.9]$ ./configure
creating cache ./config.cache
checking for a BSD compatible install... /usr/bin/install -c
checking whether build environment is sane... yes
checking whether make sets ${MAKE}... yes
checking for working aclocal... found
checking for working autoconf... found
checking for working automake... found
checking for working autoheader... found
checking for working makeinfo... found
...
```

Part

III

Ch

12

```
checking for io.h... no
checking for sys/time.h... (cached) yes
checking for gettimeofday... yes
checking for tempnam... yes
checking for strerror... yes
checking for stdin... yes
checking version number... 0.5pl13
updating cache ../.config.cache
creating ./config.status
creating Makefile
creating config.h
```

Again, the makefile is created, and you're ready to compile by running the `make` command:

```
[jray@pointy pan-0.4.9]$ make
Making all in uulib
make[1]: Entering directory '/home/jray/bookstuff/pan-0.4.9/uulib'
gcc -c -O2 -I.   -DHAVE_CONFIG_H -DVERSION=\"0.5\" -DPATCH=\"13\" uulib.c
gcc -c -O2 -I.   -DHAVE_CONFIG_H -DVERSION=\"0.5\" -DPATCH=\"13\" uucheck.c
gcc -c -O2 -I.   -DHAVE_CONFIG_H -DVERSION=\"0.5\" -DPATCH=\"13\" uunconc.c
gcc -c -O2 -I.   -DHAVE_CONFIG_H -DVERSION=\"0.5\" -DPATCH=\"13\" uuutil.c
gcc -c -O2 -I.   -DHAVE_CONFIG_H -DVERSION=\"0.5\" -DPATCH=\"13\" uuencode.c
...
gcc   -g -O2 -I/usr/lib/glib/include -D_REENTRANT -I/usr/include
    -DNEED_GNOMESUPPORT_H
    -I/usr/lib/gnome-libs/include -I/usr/X11R6/include -I/usr/lib/glib/include
    -o pan  article.o articlelist.o date.o db.o groups.o
    gui.o guru.o log.o nntp.o pan.o
    post.o props.o qmanager.o queue.o server.o sockets.o text.o
    util.o ../uulib/libuu.a
    -lpthread -lgdbm  -L/usr/lib -lgthread -lglib -lpthread -rdynamic -L/
usr/lib -L/usr/X11R6/lib -lgnomeui -lart_lgpl -lgdk_imlib -lSM -lICE -lgtk
    -lgdk -lgmodule
    -lXext -lX11 -lgnome -lgnomesupport -lesd -laudiofile -lm -ldb1 -lglib -ldl
make[1]: Leaving directory '/home/jray/bookstuff/pan-0.4.9/pan'
make[1]: Entering directory '/home/jray/bookstuff/pan-0.4.9'
make[1]: Nothing to be done for 'all-am'.
make[1]: Leaving directory '/home/jray/bookstuff/pan-0.4.9'
```

Finally, the `make install` stage moves the software into its default destination directory. Here, you should temporarily `su` to the root account so that `make` can install the software in protected system directories:

```
[jray@pointy pan-0.4.9]$ su
Password:
[root@pointy pan-0.4.9]# make install
Making install in uulib
make[1]: Entering directory '/home/jray/bookstuff/pan-0.4.9/uulib'
make[1]: Nothing to be done for 'install'.
make[1]: Leaving directory '/home/jray/bookstuff/pan-0.4.9/uulib'
Making install in pan
make[1]: Entering directory '/home/jray/bookstuff/pan-0.4.9/pan'
make[2]: Entering directory '/home/jray/bookstuff/pan-0.4.9/pan'
/bin/sh ../mkinstalldirs /usr/local/bin
```

```
   /usr/bin/install -c  pan /usr/local/bin/pan
make[2]: Nothing to be done for 'install-data-am'.
make[2]: Leaving directory '/home/jray/bookstuff/pan-0.4.9/pan'
make[1]: Leaving directory '/home/jray/bookstuff/pan-0.4.9/pan'
make[1]: Entering directory '/home/jray/bookstuff/pan-0.4.9'
```

Unlike the KDE software installation, this pan did not install itself in the GNOME system menu; it simply installed the pan binary in /usr/local/bin (you can see this in the previous output). You can add the application to the GNOME menus manually by running Menu Editor from Utilities under the main GNOME pop-up menu. Alternately, you could make a shortcut to the application by navigating to the /usr/local/bin directory, clicking the center mouse buttons (or both buttons simultaneously, if you are emulating a three-button mouse) and dragging the icon to the desktop. When you have chosen a spot for the icon, let up on the center mouse button and choose Link Here to create a symbolic link (similar to a Windows shortcut or a Macintosh alias) to the file. You can then use this icon to run the software. Figure 12.3 shows the compiled pan application up and running.

FIGURE 12.3
Pan is compiled and running.

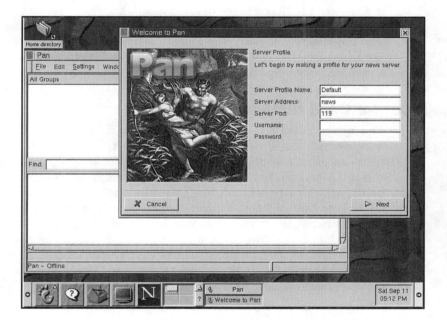

Part
III

Ch
12

As you can see, the process of installing source code and compiling applications is not terribly difficult; the process is generally the same for most of the files that you will find on the Internet. Any variation in the procedure will almost certainly be documented in the README or INSTALL files.

Understanding KDE and GNOME Compatibility

You might be thinking to yourself, "What if I want to run GNOME as my desktop environment but I find a KDE application that I want to compile and run (or vice versa)?" Don't worry—KDE and GNOME are essentially a set of programming APIs and customized window managers for the X Windows System. If both KDE and GNOME are installed on the system, you can run software from either environment in either environment. The only exception to this is if a piece of software uses a specific function of the KDE window manager or expects a piece of support software to be running that isn't. For the most part, you can run anything anywhere. In fact, you'll notice that GNOME's main system menu displays a menu of the installed KDE applications for your convenience.

Managing Linux Software Applications

Managing software on your Linux computer is often more of an art than a science. Part of the beauty of the Red Hat package management system is that it takes the responsibility of keeping track of what files go where and places it on an operating system utility rather than on the user. Unfortunately, as you've seen in this chapter, the software is not always available as a Red Hat package. So, how do you go about managing the programs you've installed? The next sections examine this issue in greater detail.

Choose a Good Installation Directory

First, wisely choose an installation directory. Much of the software you find will automatically install itself in the appropriate directory for use by KDE or GNOME. Other software will give you an option of an installation directory. You might be tempted to install software in /usr/bin, where much of the system software is located, but this might lead to confusion later. If you wish to remove software that you've installed, trying to weed through /usr/bin will be quite difficult. You also risk accidentally replacing utilities that came with the operating system with ones that you have compiled. A popular place to install added software is /usr/local/bin. Installing your software in this location allows you to immediately see what has been installed. The /usr/local directory is also often created as a separate partition from the other system partitions, which allows software and files to be written to it without fragmenting or hurting the system partitions.

Keep a Copy of the Source

Second, keep a copy of the source files in /usr/local/src. Keeping a copy of the source code can often save you in emergency situations. A system that performs dial-in authentication for several thousand people recently suffered from several corrupted files after a severe crash during a lightning storm. As luck would have it, the backup system was completely toasted. All that needed to be done to bring the system back online was to reinstall the software that handled the user authentication, but the source code had not been kept on the machine. I downloaded a new version of the software, compiled it, and installed it—it didn't work. The new version of the software used a different format for the user account files and refused to read the data. Because other systems depended on the user account file, I couldn't upgrade the file to the new format; instead, I had to go looking for an older version of the source code for the authentication system.

Searching for old software is not a situation you want to be in—it took well over a day of downtime to locate the author and get a copy of the older version. If you keep a copy of the source code in /usr/local/src already configured, all you need to do is type make and make install, and your applications will be recompiled and reinstalled exactly as they had been. The best way to do this is to compile your software and then move the entire directory to /usr/local/src when the program is installed. Before moving it, however, you can save yourself a bit of space by cleaning out temporary binary files that the compiler created while generating the program. To do this, type make clean inside the source directory, as in the following example:

```
[jray@pointy pan-0.4.9]$ make clean
Making clean in .
make[1]: Entering directory '/home/jray/bookstuff/pan-0.4.9'
make[1]: Nothing to be done for 'clean-am'.
make[1]: Leaving directory '/home/jray/bookstuff/pan-0.4.9'
Making clean in pan
make[1]: Entering directory '/home/jray/bookstuff/pan-0.4.9/pan'
test -z "pan" ¦¦ rm -f pan
rm -f *.o core *.core
make[1]: Leaving directory '/home/jray/bookstuff/pan-0.4.9/pan'
Making clean in uulib
make[1]: Entering directory '/home/jray/bookstuff/pan-0.4.9/uulib'
rm -f [Xx]deview gif2gfp
rm -f *.o *.a *.so core *~ TAGS
make[1]: Leaving directory '/home/jray/bookstuff/pan-0.4.9/uulib'
```

Be sure to have a feasible uninstall plan.

Third, keep track of what files the software installs on your system. This is probably the most difficult part of managing your installed software base. While the binary portions of software will typically install themselves in typical directories such as /usr/local/bin, configuration and support files tend to spread themselves out over the system. The /etc directory is a very common place for support files and directories to be created. If you're lucky, the makefile for the application you're installing also includes uninstall options. This is a nicety that is not always included in makefiles:

```
[root@pointy kzacman-1.0]# make uninstall
Making uninstall in data
make[1]: Entering directory '/home/jray/bookstuff/kzacman/kzacman-1.0/data'
   list='arrow-down-mask.bmp arrow-down.bmp arrow-up-mask.bmp
   arrow-up.bmp back1.bmp
   back2.bmp back3.bmp back4.bmp back5.bmp back6.bmp wall1.bmp
```

```
    wall2.bmp wall3.bmp
    wall4.bmp wall5.bmp wall6.bmp zacman-down.bmp zacman-left.bmp
    zacman-right.bmp
    zacman-up.bmp zacman-potion-down.bmp zacman-potion-left.bmp
    zacman-potion-right.bmp
    zacman-potion-up.bmp zacman-down-mask.bmp zacman-left-mask.bmp
    zacman-right-mask.bmp
    zacman-up-mask.bmp monster-down-mask.bmp monster-down.bmp
    monster-left-mask.bmp
    monster-left.bmp monster-right-mask.bmp monster-right.bmp
    monster-up-mask.bmp
    monster-up.bmp balloon-ouch.bmp balloon-ouch-mask.bmp balloon-chomp.bmp
    balloon-chomp-mask.bmp balloon-exit.bmp balloon-exit-mask.bmp point.bmp
    point-mask.bmp potion.bmp potion-mask.bmp pause.bmp bg.bmp';
      for p in $list; do \
  rm -f /usr/share/apps/kzacman/data/$p; \
done
...
rm -f /usr/share/applnk/Games/kzacman.kdelnk
rm -f /usr/share/icons/kzacman.xpm
rm -f /usr/share/icons/mini/kzacman.xpm
make[1]: Leaving directory '/home/jray/bookstuff/kzacman/kzacman-1.0/src'
```

TIP As with the `install` command, you'll need to be logged into the system as root for the process to complete successfully. Running as an unprivileged user account won't hurt anything, but it will display an error message each time the process attempts to uninstall a protected file.

Unfortunately, pan didn't include this option in the software, so only an error message is returned when you try to uninstall it. In the case of software such as pan, you might want to create a log of the installation process that you can later use to determine what files were installed and where they were installed. If you eventually must remove the files by hand, at least you'll have a good idea where to start.

To generate an installation log, simply redirect the output of the make `install` command to a log file. For example, if you were installing kzacman, and it didn't have an uninstall procedure, you could do this:

```
[root@pointy kzacman-1.0]# make install > install.log
```

Now you have a log of what the installation process did, so you could undo it, if necessary:

```
[root@pointy kzacman-1.0]# more install.log
Making install in data
make[1]: Entering directory '/home/jray/bookstuff/kzacman/kzacman-1.0/data'
/bin/sh ../mkinstalldirs /usr/share/apps/kzacman/data
 /usr/bin/install -c -m 644 ./arrow-down-mask.bmp
   /usr/share/apps/kzacman/data/arrow-down-mask.bmp
 /usr/bin/install -c -m 644 ./arrow-down.bmp
   /usr/share/apps/kzacman/data/arrow-down.bmp
...
```

These logs can be a bit difficult to read, so a quick-and-dirty piece of Perl code is included to provide a list of files and directories that must be deleted for the software to be removed from the system. Because different makefiles install software in different manners, this code might not always work; for the majority of software distributions (those that rely on `install` and `mkinstalldirs`), however, it should be fine:

```perl
#!/usr/bin/perl
# 1999 by John Ray
#
# This program may be modified and distributed freely.

if ($ARGV[0] eq "") {
    print "\nUsage: installcheck.pl <install.log>\n";
    exit 1;
}

if (!(-f $ARGV[0])) {
    print "\nFile \"$ARGV[0]\" doesn't exist!\n";
    exit 1;
}

$installlog=`cat $ARGV[0]`;
while ($installlog=~s/mkinstalldirs (.*)//i) {
    $directories=$1." ".$directories;
}
while ($installlog=~s/usr\/bin\/install.*?\s+([^\s\n]+)\n//) {
    $files=$1." ".$files;
}

$dircount=@dirlist=split(/\s+/,$directories);
$filecount=@filelist=split(/\s+/,$files);

print "\n----------------------------------------\n";
print "Total files installed: $filecount\n";
print "Total directories created: $dircount\n";
print "----------------------------------------\n";
print "The follow directories MAY have been created by the installation\n";
print "process.  Some may have existed prior to being installed, so be wary\n";
print "when removing.\n\n";
for ($x=0;$x<@dirlist;$x++) {
    print $x+1,". $dirlist[$x]\n";
}
print "----------------------------------------\n";
print "These files were installed:\n\n";
for ($x=0;$x<@filelist;$x++) {
    print $x+1,". $filelist[$x]\n";
}
print "\n";
```

Feel free to use this sample code in any way that you see fit. If you are feeling adventurous, for example, you could add the line `unlink $filelist[$x];` immediately after the line `print $x+1,`. Likewise, you could use `$filelist[$x]\n;` to automatically erase the installed files when the program is run.

To install `installcheck.pl`, simple type it into a text editor as it appears in the book text, and then save the file as `installcheck.pl`. As a last step, type `chmod +x installcheck.pl` at a command line so that the program is given the necessary permissions to execute. Running `installcheck.pl` on the `install.log` file you created earlier, yields these results:

```
[root@pointy kzacman-1.0]# ./installcheck.pl install.log

----------------------------------------
Total files installed:
Total directories created:
----------------------------------------
The follow directories MAY have been created by the installation
process.  Some may have existed prior to being installed, so be wary
when removing.

1. /usr/share/icons/mini
2. /usr/share/icons
3. /usr/share/applnk/Games
4. /usr/bin
5. /usr/share/doc/HTML/en/kzacman
6. /usr/share/apps/kzacman/wav
7. /usr/share/apps/kzacman/data
----------------------------------------
These files were installed:

1. /usr/share/icons/mini/kzacman.xpm
2. /usr/share/icons
3. /usr/share/applnk/Games
4. /usr/bin/kzacman
5. /usr/bin/kzacman
...
```

As you can see, managing the software that you have installed on the system is mainly up to you. You may develop techniques that are better suited for your environment than what is covered here. A first-time Linux user might be a bit overwhelmed by the amount of software that is available for the system; as such, this user will certainly be tempted to try installing things. Reckless installation can lead to disk space being filled up on important system partitions and files being created in places that are impossible to track. Six months after it's installed, who is going to remember what software application uses the file `libargu.5.3.a`?

Test Before Deploying

If you are using Linux as a server rather than as a personal workstation, it is *extremely* important to keep a test machine for the purpose of installing programs and testing how they interact with the services that the machine must provide. Using a single machine for both providing services and testing software can have serious consequences. Time and time again, servers malfunction because of inappropriate software that has been installed and forgotten on the computers. Some software installation procedures are complex enough that they modify configuration files on your computer, perhaps eliminating services altogether.

A particularly nasty piece of security software has caused several headaches over the past few years. This particular program monitors the computer's network connection for potential port scans, a possible indication of attack. Unfortunately, the software also seems to suffer from a memory leak that eventually causes the computer to come to a grinding halt.

If you have only a single computer and *must* provide services from that machine *and* want to install software on it, be sure to research the software and search Usenet newsgroups before installing it. A quick peek at http://www.deja.com/ takes only a few seconds but can save you hours of headaches later. Also be sure to keep accurate logs of what is installed and where. If you are attempting a delicate operation such as patching the Linux kernel, back up all files that risk being replaced before you attempt the installation.

Troubleshooting Linux Software Applications

As with managing your software installations, troubleshooting is more of an art than a science. This goes for almost any operating system. If a program goes awry under Windows, you might try twiddling some registry entries or an .INI file. On the Macintosh, you would open the System preferences folder and delete the preference file for the application giving you trouble. Linux is no different—it's a matter of trial and error.

Keep Your Software Up-to-Date

Although this seems very logical, it can be very difficult to do. Keeping your system current is very important. Rather than issuing service packs or system updates, Red Hat releases updates to individual applications and services as soon as they become available. These are available as RPMs from the Red Hat update site (ftp://updates.redhat.com/). Unfortunately, if you installed the software yourself, you must also keep track of the versions by yourself. A good resource that tracks Linux software packages is LinuxApps.com (http://www.linuxapps.com/). The site maintains a software database that is constantly being updated.

As critical components on your Red Hat system are updated, you'll need to pay close attention to their effect on other software components. If shared libraries are updated, they might break programs that depend on them. Be sure to read all the errata information on Red Hat's Web site before committing yourself to upgrading a particular package—some upgrades are not friendly.

If You Don't Mind Behaving Like a Windows User...

If you feel like taking the direct approach to fixing a problem, you might want to take the Windows approach: Reboot your system. If a background process that your software depends on has failed for some reason, your application might just stop functioning. For example, KDE starts up several background processes the first time it runs that handle interactions with the operating system. If one of these processes quits in the middle of your KDE session, the computer might start acting strangely. In these cases, a reboot wouldn't hurt. To reboot your machine, you can type /sbin/reboot or the preferred /sbin/shutdown -r now at a command line. If you're not in a graphical environment, you can also use Control+Alt+Delete to safely reboot the machine.

Maintain a Reasonable Amount of Free Space

After reading these tips, you'll probably feel very comfortable diagnosing software problems because you've almost certainly done the same thing on other operating systems. This tip is no different. Be sure that you maintain a reasonable amount of free space on your partitions. Linux applications often write temporary files to the drive as they are running (cache files, lock files, temporary files, and so on). If a program cannot create a lock file (a file that tells the system not to use a particular resource), there is a good chance that the program will fail completely. Use the df command to get a quick overview of the space left on your drives:

```
[jray@pointy jray]$ df
Filesystem        1k-blocks      Used Available Use% Mounted on
/dev/sda1          1918622    1181413    638034  65% /
/dev/sdb           4116087    3654363    248744  94% /mnt/storage
```

This computer has a rather simplistic partition layout, but you can see that there is plenty of free space on the root (/) partition and that /dev/sdb is close to running out of space.

Delete Renegade Temp Files

Sometimes programs create files that get left behind if the application unexpectedly quits. This can create further problems when the software is restarted. The most common place for files to be created is in the /tmp directory. If you have a piece of software that is failing to start, first see if you have any related files in the /tmp directory. Software that you use will most likely save its temp files under your user ID and group.

Take a look at this example:

```
[jray@pointy jray]$ ls -al /tmp
total
drwxrwxrwt   8 root    root        3072 Sep 11 18:40 .
drwxr-xr-x  21 root    root        1024 Sep 11 14:57 ..
drwxrwxrwt   2 jray    jray        1024 Sep 11 15:42 .ICE-unix
-r--r--r--   1 jray    jray          11 Sep 11 15:12 .X1-lock
drwxrwxrwx   2 jray    jray        1024 Sep 11 16:59 .X11-unix
-r--r--r--   1 jray    jray          11 Sep 11 16:59 .X2-lock
drwxrwxr-x   3 jray    jray        1024 Sep 11 15:31 ark.985
drwx------   2 jray    jray        1024 Sep 11 14:54 kfm-cache-500
```

Here, you can see that several lock files exist in the /tmp directory. If the system is giving you problems, quit to a text-prompt, stop any processes you have running, and then remove the /tmp files that you own. In many cases, this will do what you need to get back up and running.

KDE and GNOME Are Failing: Can't Even Load the Desktop, Configuration File Corruption

Programs often create directories and configuration files under your home directory. Often, your desktop software won't show these directories and files because they begin with a period (.), which hides the file/directory in a standard file listing. Here's a sample of the hidden files in a home directory:

```
[jray@pointy jray]$ ls -al ¦ more
total 4976
drwxr-xr-x  40 jray     jray         2048 Sep 11 19:07 .
drwxr-xr-x   8 root     root         1024 Aug 30 11:23 ..
drwx------   2 jray     jray         1024 Jul 13 21:32 .e-conf
drwx------   3 jray     jray         8192 Sep 11 16:59 .enlightenment
drwxr-xr-x   9 jray     jray         1024 Sep 11 17:13 .gnome
drwxrwxr-x   2 jray     jray         1024 Sep 11 17:13 .gnome-desktop
drwx------   2 jray     jray         1024 Jul  8 20:23 .gnome_private
-rw-rw-r--   1 jray     jray          263 Jul 13 21:42 .gtkrc
drwxr-xr-x   3 jray     jray         1024 Jul  7 01:07 .kde
-rw-r--r--   1 jray     jray         1029 Sep 11 15:54 .kderc
drwxrwxr-x   2 jray     jray         1024 Sep 11 17:03 .mc
drwxr-xr-x   2 jray     jray         1024 Sep  3 11:14 .ncftp
drwx------   5 jray     jray         1024 Aug 16 15:57 .netscape
-rw-rw-r--   1 jray     jray         3505 Jul  7 01:07 .screenrc
drwxr-xr-x   2 jray     jray         1024 Sep 11 16:59 .vnc
drwxr-xr-x   3 jray     jray         1024 Jul 14 23:50 .x11amp
...
```

Many of these hidden files should look very familiar to you. There are configuration directories for GNOME, the GNOME window manager Enlightenment, KDE, X11Amp (an X Windows-based MP3 player), and Netscape, among others. If you haven't configured any settings (this includes icon placement in the desktop environments), you can rename these directories, run the software that was failing, let it recreate its configuration files, and see if that clears up your problems. This technique is usually necessary only if a configuration file is corrupted. Make sure you don't have any important custom setting files saved in these directories before you delete them—the result of deleting the KDE or GNOME directories, for example, is identical to resetting the configuration to the same state it was in when you first installed Red Hat Linux.

Monitor Your Log Files

Log files are mainly reserved for system-level processes, but they might contain information that can help you figure out why your software is misbehaving. The main system log file is /var/log/messages. You can search the messages program for the name of the program that is misbehaving, as the system logging functions include the name of the process generating the logged error.

Part
III

Ch
12

For example, you could configure several virtual hosts on your Apache Web server. Sometimes, at boot, the hosts might not work as intended. In this case, you could search the messages file to see if Apache (httpd) is logging anything to the system when it tries to start. You will need to have root access to read the log files, for example:

```
[root@pointy log]# grep "httpd" /var/log/messages
Sep 11 14:57:57 pointy httpd: [Sat Sep 11 14:57:57 1999] [error] Cannot resolve
host name www.poisontooth.com --- ignoring!
Sep 11 14:57:57 pointy httpd:
Sep 11 14:57:58 pointy httpd: [Sat Sep 11 14:57:58 1999] [error] Cannot resolve
host name www.brevardmpo.com --- ignoring!
Sep 11 14:57:58 pointy httpd:
Sep 11 14:57:58 pointy httpd: [Sat Sep 11 14:57:58 1999] [error] Cannot resolve
host name brevardmpo.com --- ignoring!
Sep 11 14:57:58 pointy httpd:
Sep 11 14:57:58 pointy httpd: [Sat Sep 11 14:57:58 1999] [error] Cannot resolve
host name icbins.poisontooth.com --- ignoring!
Sep 11 14:57:58 pointy httpd:
Sep 11 14:57:58 pointy httpd: httpd startup succeeded
```

From these messages, you can see that the virtual hosts are not working because their names are not being resolved correctly by the computer. This would point you toward a problem with the network configuration rather than a problem with the Web server itself.

By default, the /var/log/messages file is set to log what the system considers important messages. However, this isn't all the information that can be logged. You can also request that the system log debug information, which can be voluminous and is not necessarily something that you'd want to do continuously. To set up the system to log debug information for any process that can, just add this line to the file /etc/syslog.conf:

```
*.debug                                    /var/log/debug
```

After adding the line, you can either reboot the machine for the changes to take effect, or restart the syslog daemon, like this:

```
[root@pointy log]# /etc/rc.d/init.d/syslog restart
Shutting down kernel logger:                          [  OK  ]
Shutting down system logger:                          [  OK  ]
Starting system logger:                               [  OK  ]
Starting kernel logger:                               [  OK  ]
```

Depending on the software that you are running, it might or might not log errors in the syslog. At any rate, this is a powerful tool for seeing the messages that your system considers important.

Start X Windows Applications from a Terminal Session

Another place that messages might be showing up (and you might be missing) is on the standard output and standard error of graphic-based applications. Even though you start an application by clicking on it in a desktop environment, the system might still be sending out messages that you can't see. To view these messages, simply bring up a command prompt and run the program manually by typing its path and name at the command prompt. The program will run as it normally does, but the command window will remain open; and any messages that the program sends to standard out/error will appear in the window. Typically, you will see complaints about configuration files and errors writing to files that don't exist or that have inappropriate permissions.

If All Else Fails...

If you cannot find the reason for an apparent malfunctioning program, and if you happened to save the source code, you can always re-install. This is a viable option only if the program or its base configuration files have become corrupted, which is generally a very rare occurrence.

The most successful way of fixing misbehaving software is to delete any temporary files that the program has created and remove any personal configuration files or directories, if needed. With experience, you will find that Linux is more forgiving than Windows when it comes to trying to fix software problems. You don't have a registry to deal with, and the software configuration files are generally very easy to deal with. If you end up getting nowhere, tap into the extensive Linux support community. Thousands of Linux users all over the world—who are just like you—would be more than willing to help out. Also look at the software documentation: There is a very good chance that you can email the author directly and get his take on the problem. For an operating system that is criticized for it's lack of a support structure, I assure you that you will have no problems getting support for the applications that you install.

Summary

One of the greatest strengths of Linux is its capability to compile and run UNIX software. Thousands of software packages are just waiting to be downloaded and installed. Unfortunately, installing a non-Red Hat-specific program requires a bit more hands-on effort than simply using the Red Hat package manager.

However, this chapter showed you that the process is actually quite simple and, in most cases consists of running three simple commands: `configure`, `make`, and `make install`. You should now also be aware of the dangers of installing software on your system without keeping track of where it is being installed. The Red Hat package system keeps track of this information for you, but as soon as you enter the world of do-it-yourself software, you must also take responsibility for keeping track of how the software affects your system.

Finally, this chapter demonstrated a few simple techniques for determining what could be causing problems with applications you have installed. As with traditional desktop operating systems, Linux also requires trial and error to determine what is causing a problem. ●

## CHAPTER 13

Installing Adobe Acrobat

by Duane Hellums

In this chapter

The Importance of PDF

Nothing seems more frustrating than needing to access data that is stored in a format that your software doesn't recognize. I'm sure I'm not the only one who has received email back from someone asking that I save a word processing file in another format so that the recipient could read it. This is especially true when you're publishing to the Web, adding multimedia to your files, or moving data among multiple operating systems as well as applications.

To help reduce the impact of this problem, Adobe created what it calls the Portable Document Format, or PDF. You've probably run across this data format already. This format can be used to encapsulate text, hyperlinks, and high-resolution graphics from any document source and store them in a standard format. Freely distributed Adobe Acrobat readers and viewers are available for every major operating system and Web browser, so content providers can rest assured that there's no reason why any recipient shouldn't be able to view a PDF document. Most importantly, recipients won't have to buy an expensive software application just to view data otherwise stored in a proprietary format.

So why is this important to Red Hat Linux? Primarily because you will run into this format extensively on the Internet—many Web site administrators provide product documentation and catalogs in PDF format. For example, if you need to download tax forms from the Internal Revenue Service, you need an Acrobat reader. You'll also find that help files are sometimes stored in PDF format for distribution with software applications that you will install on your Linux system.

Installing xpdf

If you don't feel that you will need to view PDF files very often, you might be able to get by with the xpdf program that is distributed with Red Hat 6.0 and other versions of Linux. The xpdf application, shown in Figure 13.1, is a simple viewer for Adobe Acrobat files. xpdf uses standard X fonts and was written by Derek Noonburg, not Adobe. You can find out more about the program—and check on the latest versions to download—by visiting Derek's Web site at `http://www.foolabs.com/xpdf/`.

As you can see, unlike the more powerful Adobe Acrobat Reader, xpdf allows only basic functions, such as searching for text, navigating through pages, zooming in and out, rotating the document 90° at a time, and exporting or saving to a PostScript file. The rotate feature is not available as a button on your main screen; you must right-click the document itself and choose Rotate left or Rotate right from the pop-up menu. The resulting PostScript file can then be opened for printing with gv, a PostScript file viewer based on GhostView.

For the most part, the program's icon controls are standard and self-explanatory. The single arrows advance one page forward or back, while the double arrows fast-forward to the beginning or end (as displayed by the page counter to the right). The magnifying glasses with plus and minus signs perform zooming in and out, respectively. The binoculars perform searching for text strings. The printer icon is actually used to convert the PDF file to a PostScript file. The question mark icon brings up a basic information file about the application, and the Quit button enables you to close the program.

FIGURE 13.1
The xpdf PDF file viewer can read documents from the IRS, among others.

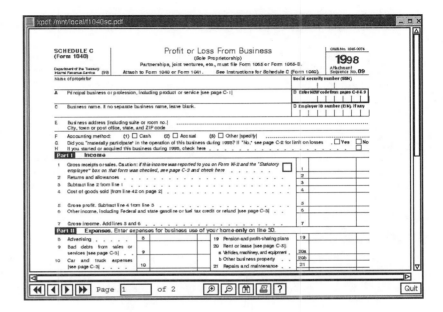

Version 0.8, the latest version, is included as a package on the CD-ROM with a filename of `xpdf-0.80-4.i386.rpm`. If you didn't select xpdf for installation initially, you can use the Red Hat Package Manager (RPM) or GnoRPM (the graphical equivalent) to install the package. Chapter 11, "Installing and Managing RPM Packages," provides details on how to do that. If you have xpdf installed, you should see it in GnoRPM within the Applications group, under the Publishing category.

You can launch xpdf by double-clicking any file with a `.pdf` extension (from within a Midnight Commander file browser, for example). By default it will attempt to bring up the xpdf application to view the file. You can launch xpdf from the command line (in a shell) by typing `xpdf` or `/usr/bin/xpdf`. However, it is recommended that you add the program to a GNOME menu, submenu, panel, or desktop. See Chapter 7, "Installing and Configuring GNOME," for an explanation of how to do this.

Part
III

Ch
13

Downloading Adobe Acrobat Reader

Although xpdf might meet some of your needs, you might need something a little more powerful. In this case, you should go directly to the source and use Adobe's Acrobat Reader.

TIP If you have a choice, you should always try to download and install an RPM file instead of the older `tar.gz` file. The download size is very similar, but RPM installation and package management is significantly easier. See Chapter 11 to better understand this process.

The current version of Acrobat, version 4.0, can be downloaded from many mirror File Transfer Protocol (FTP) sites as a package named `linux-ar-40.tar.gz`. You can download the 5.7MB file by going to `http://www.adobe.com/prodindex/acrobat/readstep.html` and filling out the required form. Although the Acrobat Reader is free, you will need to provide some information about yourself, including your email address and how you use Acrobat and PDF files in general.

CAUTION

Make sure you change the default to Linux in the Platform text box of Step 1 before submitting the Adobe Acrobat Reader download form; otherwise, you'll end up with a Windows 95 version.

Installing Acrobat Reader

If you're using a downloaded `tar.gz` file, the first thing you'll have to do is decide where to store the archive on your hard drive. Because you probably will be installing Acrobat as root, you can just use the `/root` directory; but you can use others, such as the `/usr/local/src` directory. After you find a place for the package, you will have to uncompress and unpackage the Acrobat reader, unless you are lucky enough to be using an RPM file. Currently Adobe does not support the RPM format, but if it changes this practice and policy, you might find an RPM package for Acrobat on the Internet or a CD. If you do, you should use it instead of the tar.gz file, which is considerably more difficult to use.

Uncompressing and Unpackaging Acrobat Reader

As you can tell from the `tar.gz` file extension, you will have to uncompress and unpackage the archived files in this package. Unfortunately, the process is not as easy as with RPM or GnoRPM, and it normally involves two steps—even worse, this is one of the few times you must use the shell and command-line interface with Red Hat Linux 6.0. You can use either an X terminal or a standard virtual terminal for this. Follow these steps:

1. First, you can uncompress the files with the `gunzip` (GNU unzip) command (see the Tip in this section before you do so, however). For example, after changing to the directory to where you downloaded or copied the compressed archive, you would type the following:

   ```
   gunzip linux-ar-40.tar.gz
   ```

This changes the 5MB compressed file into a 14MB uncompressed file named linux-ar-40.tar (the .gz extension falls off because the file is no longer compressed).

2. If you manually uncompressed the tar.gz file, you can restore the archived files back to the hard drive's file system using the tar command, as follows:

   tar xvf linux-ar-40.tar

 TIP You can perform both actions in a single command by typing tar xvfz linux-ar-40.tar.gz (although some people try not to use the z option with tar because it is not supported on all versions of UNIX). You can also type zcat linux-ar-40.tar.gz ¦ tar xvt, which uncompresses the data on the fly (leaving the original file intact) and then immediately sends it through a system pipe to the tar command for unarchiving. If you use just the gunzip command, you will have a 14MB uncompressed file that you'll have to clean up later, instead of 5MB of data. If you have limited space on your hard drive or limited system memory (RAM) and don't want any more clutter than necessary, you should use the tar xvfz command.

Nothing will happen to your archive (.tar) file, but you will see a few lines of output on your terminal. Unless you see error messages, this should indicate that the tar command successfully restored files into a new subdirectory named ILINXR.install in your current directory.

 TIP If you didn't use tar -xvfz and you have limited space on your hard drive, you can compress the tar file back to its original size (5MB) by typing gzip linux-ar-40.tar in the directory where you downloaded and uncompressed the file. You could just remove the file, but this isn't recommend—especially if you haven't completed the installation successfully yet, or if you downloaded the file off the Internet and don't want to have to do that again at a later date.

Running the Installation Script

You should move (cd) into the ILINXR.install directory and read the installation help file named INSTGUID.TXT. You can edit this file directly from the graphical user interface by opening it with an editor, or you can type gedit INSTGUID.TXT (assuming that you installed gedit) on the command line to achieve the same goal. You also could just use the more INSTGUID.TXT command to read the file a page at a time. When you know where you plan to install Acrobat Reader and are ready to proceed with the installation, follow these steps:

1. As root, type the command . ./INSTALL (you can replace the periods with the full pathname of the ILINSR.install directory, if you prefer) to begin the installation script. You will be presented with the Adobe license agreement.

2. Keep pressing the Enter key (single line scroll) or the Spacebar (full page scroll) to proceed to the end of the end user license.

3. If you accept the licensing terms, type accept and press Enter to continue with the installation. You will then be prompted for a specific installation directory, although the default of /usr/local/Acrobat4 is fine. You can create this directory beforehand or confirm during the installation that it is OK to create the directory for you.

After the installation is over, you should create a link in a common directory so that you don't have to modify your path and environment variables. To create a symbolic link to your Acrobat Reader, type the following:

```
ln -s /usr/local/Acrobat4/bin/acroread /usr/bin/acroread
```

Using Acrobat Reader

You can launch Acrobat Reader from the command line (in a shell) by typing `acroread` or `/usr/bin/acroread` (`/usr/local/Acrobat4/bin/acroread` if you chose to install to the default location and didn't create a link). However, I recommend adding `acroread` to a GNOME menu, submenu, panel, or desktop. Chapter 7 explains how to do this.

TIP If you installed xpdf, xpdf might be listed as the default viewer for PDF files, which means that xpdf will be launched when you double-click a PDF file from the File Manager. If you want Acrobat Reader to be the default viewer, you can edit the MIME types under the Gnome Configuration Tool or Control Center. You can also select MIME Types from the Settings System Menu. Edit the application/pdf MIME type, and change xpdf to acroread. You can do the same thing with gedit or gnotepad for `.txt` type files, such as the previously mentioned license and installation help files that come with Acrobat Reader.

One of the first things you might want to do is familiarize yourself with Adobe Acrobat Reader, if you haven't done so already. The best way to do this is to browse the Guide that came with the Reader. If you used the default installation path, the file is located at `/usr/local/Acrobat4/Reader/help/reader.pdf` (see Figure 13.2).

FIGURE 13.2
The Adobe Acrobat Reader comes with a convenient help file, in .pdf format.

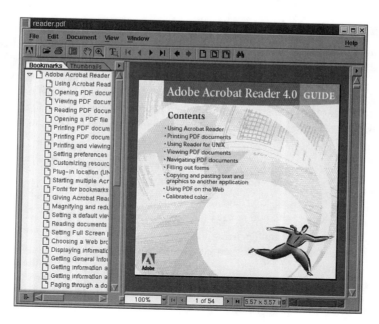

If you view the Guide with xpdf, you will notice that only the page itself is visible. When you view the Guide with acroread, you should notice the Bookmarks and Thumbnails tabs on the left, which serve as a nice index for quickly finding help in the areas you want to know more about or are having trouble with. This is a small example of the benefits that you will enjoy from installing Acrobat Reader instead of sufficing with xpdf.

Creating PDF MIME Types

If you want to make Acrobat Reader your default PDF file viewer, you can do so at two levels: within your GNOME interface and as a helper application in Netscape Communicator. The first will allow you to bring up Acrobat Reader when you double-click a PDF file from within a Midnight Commander file browser, whereas the latter will launch Acrobat Reader to view any PDF files that you point to from within Netscape (on the Internet, for example). This is done by configuring the MIME (Multimedia Internet Mail Extension) types for PDF files as an application/pdf that is associated with Acrobat Reader.

To add support to GNOME for the Acrobat Reader application/pdf MIME type, perform the following steps:

1. As root, go to the main GNOME panel and click the toolbox that launches the Control Center. If you have a Midnight Commander file browser up, you also can select Commands, Edit MIME Types from the menubar. Either way, you will see the Control Center with a directory tree menu on the left. Click MIME Types, which will bring up two columns on the right with MIME Types and Extensions.

2. Browse through the list of MIME Types and see if you have one called application/pdf. If you do, it probably is associated with Extension .pdf and the xpdf application. Click the application/pdf entry, and then click the Edit button. This will bring up a Set Actions for Application/pdf window.

3. Click the icon button at the top of the window if you want to select an icon graphic that will appear alongside any `.pdf` filename.

4. In the Open text box of the MIME Type Actions frame, type `acroread %f`. Don't enter the entire path, just the filename, and your file must be in `/usr/bin` or you must have a symbolic link there to your Acrobat Reader (see the `ln -s` command described earlier in this chapter). Click OK to save your changes and return to the Control Center window.

5. You can save the changes temporarily by clicking Try (which enables you to click Revert if it doesn't work). Click OK to save your changes or Cancel to ignore any changes made while you were in this window.

6. If you don't have a MIME type for application/pdf listed in the MIME Types column, you will have to create one. Click the Add button to do this. You will see an Add MIME Type window. Here you will have to add the text `application/pdf` in the MIME Type

Part
III

Ch
13

text box and `pdf` in the Extension text box. Click OK to save your changes and create the application/pdf MIME type. When it is created, you can click it in the MIME Type column, and then click Edit to associate the Acrobat Reader command with this type of file. See the previous paragraph on how to do this.:

Netscape Communicator works a little differently. By default, for security reasons, Netscape segregates itself from your operating system, so it can't launch external programs without your explicit permission. You give it this permission by creating what Netscape calls a helper application, which also uses the application/pdf MIME type, just like GNOME does. To do this for Acrobat Reader in Netscape, perform the following steps:

1. Launch Netscape Communicator from your GNOME panel and select Edit, Preferences when it comes up to the default home page.

2. You will see a Netscape Preferences window that has a directory tree menu on the left labeled Category. In this area, click the arrow next to Navigator, and then click Applications when the tree expands.

3. You will see two columns on the right, labeled Description and Handled By. Basically, you'll want to add an entry into this table that reads `Portable Document Format handled by /usr/bin/acroread %s` (your directory path to the Acrobat Reader executable can vary, depending on where you installed it, but at a minimum you should have a symbolic link in `/usr/bin` to wherever `acroread` is actually located).

4. To add Acrobat Reader as a helper program for Netscape, click the New button. You will see the Netscape Application window with four text boxes that you will have to fill in.

5. In the Description text box, type `Portable Document Format`, or something like `Adobe Acrobat` if you prefer (it is only a label).

6. In the MIME Types box, type `application/pdf`. This says that you want to associate PDF files with an application. In the Suffixes box, type `pdf`. This indicates that any files ending in `.pdf` are assumed to be PDF files.

7. Now all you must do is specify what application should be launched when you try to download or view a PDF file. To do this, click the Application check box in the Handled By section. In the text box next to it, type `/usr/bin/acroread %s` (note that Netscape uses `%s` for the filename, while GNOME uses `%f`; this is not a problem, just different. Netscape also uses full filenames, whereas GNOME doesn't).

8. Click OK to return to the Netscape Preferences window, and then click OK to save your changes (or Cancel to ignore the changes you made while in this window, if you think you did something wrong, for example).

If everything went well, you will be able to use Adobe PDF files seamlessly with Red Hat Linux. If you are using Midnight Commander or another GNOME-compliant file browser, you will see the PDF files with the icon you configured for it (if applicable), and double-clicking it will immediately launch Acrobat Reader. This is easier than manually bringing up Acrobat

Reader and selecting File, Open and browsing for your PDF file. You also can seamlessly use PDF files that are on the Internet or a local Web server because clicking a link that contains a PDF file will cause Netscape to immediately launch its helper application, Acrobat Reader, for you to view the file.

Configuring Acrobat Reader

You won't find much to configure within Acrobat, other than display, font, and printer settings. The Acrobat configuration options are accessible from the menu by selecting File, Preferences. The four submenu options are as follows:

- **Annotations**—The Annotations dialog box merely lets you pick the font style and size that you want to use for marking up (annotating) documents.
- **Full Screen**—The Full Screen dialog box creates a slide show format, enabling you to navigate through all pages in a document automatically or by clicking any key.
- **Weblink**—The Weblink dialog box enables you to choose how Acrobat Reader handles hyperlinks within PDF files. Through this box, you also can determine how the Reader ties in with your Netscape browser (you must designate the path to /usr/bin/netscape, for example).
- **General**—You can change most of the default viewing parameters by choosing File, Preferences, General. This brings up the pop-up window shown in Figure 13.3. The defaults are fine for most people, but you might want to tweak them some. For example, you can change the default page layout to Continuous, or the default zoom to Fit Page (displays the entire page on your screen, so you don't have to scroll). This is also where you can toggle off the display of the Adobe splash screen when you start Acrobat Reader, or you can choose to immediately bring up a dialog box that prompts you to open a file.

CAUTION

Your configuration settings for Acrobat Reader are stored in your home directory ($HOME) in an .acrorc file. If you are upgrading from a previous version of Acrobat Reader, you should remove or rename this file so you have a copy of it, just in case. Acrobat Reader 4 will create a new file with recommended default settings that you can then modify.

Part III
Ch 13

You might also want to change your Print Settings, using the pop-up window displayed in Figure 13.4. You will see this pop-up window when you select File, Print from the menu or click the printer icon on the toolbar to print the file currently being viewed. You have the option of printing to a file or to the default printer (a network printer controlled by the /usr/bin/lpr program, in this instance). As indicated, you can choose to print all pages, a range of pages, or odd and even pages within any range, in forward or reverse order. These settings apply only during your current Acrobat Reader session; they will be restored to the defaults if you close acroread and launch it again.

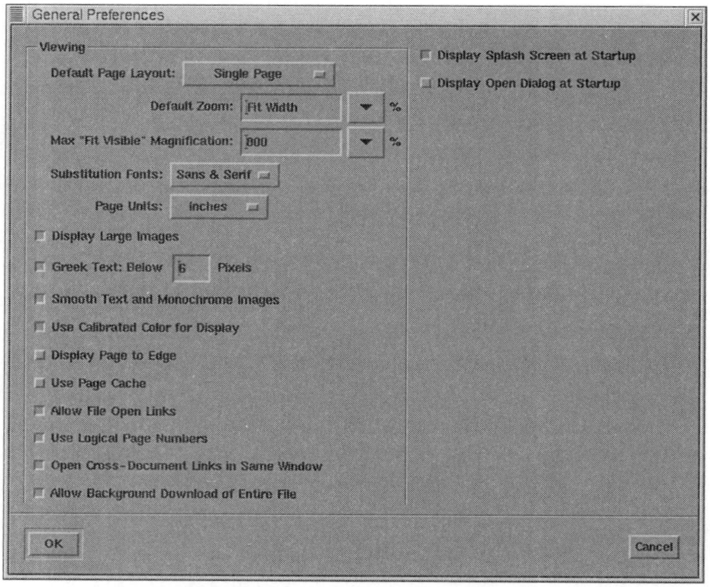

FIGURE 13.3
You can change default Acrobat Reader behavior easily by modifying the default settings (general preferences).

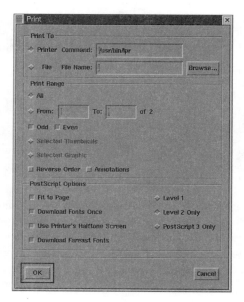

FIGURE 13.4
Acrobat Reader print properties.

N O T E If you change the print settings to some format that your printer can't recognize, Linux prints a warning message to let you know what is wrong. For example, when I changed my PostScript options to PostScript 3 Only, I was informed that I had to make my settings reflect Level 2 Only because my Windows printer won't recognize PostScript 3. ■

Using Acrobat Reader from the Command Line

You might find a need to use the Adobe Acrobat Reader from the shell or command-line interface. This can come in handy if you want to automate an otherwise tedious task by writing a shell program that converts a list of Acrobat files to PostScript, for example. You can find out all the flags to send Acrobat by typing `acroread -help` or `acroread -helpall` for basic and advanced options, respectively (of course, you will have to type `/usr/local/Acroread4/bin/acroread` if you didn't create a link).

For example, if you wanted to convert a file named `f1040sc.pdf` to a PostScript file named `f1040sc.ps`, you would type the following:

```
acroread -toPostScript -pairs f1040sc.pdf f1040sc.ps
```

If you wanted to convert three PDF files (for example, `one.pdf`, `two.pdf`, and `three.pdf`) in a directory to PostScript files in a subdirectory called `postscript`, you would type the following:

```
acroread -toPostScript one.pdf two.pdf three.pdf postscript
```

Many other command-line options are available, but their use depends on your requirements. These options include, but are not limited to, options that enable you to scale the files to your page size (`-shrink`), set printing options for landscape format (`-landscape`), and convert starting with page 2 (`-start 2`).

Troubleshooting Acrobat Reader

If you can't get Adobe Acrobat Reader to work, the most likely thing wrong is that you are referencing an invalid path or filename. All you can do is confirm your information and try again. If you still can't access the file, your problem might involve security permissions. In that case, go through your path recursively, looking for any anomalies such as directories or files that you don't have permission to read or access. You might also be trying to open a newer PDF file than your system is capable of handling. In the event that Adobe comes out with a newer version of Acrobat Reader, the file format might not be backward-compatible, so you will have to upgrade to the newest version. ●

Part
III

Ch
13

Installing and Configuring Netscape Communicator

by Duane Hellums

In this chapter

About Netscape

Netscape offers two different Web browser products: Communicator and Navigator. Communicator includes a Web browser (Navigator), a Web page editor/publisher (Composer), an emailer (Messenger), and an Internet newsgroup reader (Messenger). Navigator consists only of a Web browser. Both products are included on this book's CD and the Official Red Hat 6.0 CD. In addition to basic Web browsing, it is likely that you will be using at least email, so you should plan to install Netscape Communicator, if you have the disk space.

Installing Netscape Communicator

Both Communicator and Navigator share certain files, which are included in a Red Hat Package Manager (RPM) package named `netscape-common`. If you install Communicator, you will need to install both the `netscape-communicator` and the `netscape-common` packages. Communicator should have been installed whether you chose a custom, workstation, or server installation (unless you deselected the package during a custom installation).

Verifying Installation of Communicator

You should have a Netscape icon on your GNOME panel that is linked to your Communicator executable. To confirm that this icon is installed, you can try clicking it to see if Netscape Communicator launches. If the program doesn't launch, for some reason, perform the following steps:

1. Select System, GnoRPM from the main GNOME menu. Alternatively, you can bring up an X terminal or text-based shell prompt to run the `rpm` utility.

2. In GnoRPM, look under Packages, Applications, Internet. If you see the Communicator package (`netscape-communicator-4.51-3.rpm`) and Common package (`netscape-common-4.51-3.rpm`), then all the Netscape components are already installed.

3. (Optional, command-line only) From the shell prompt, type `rpm -q netscape-common` and `rpm -q netscape-communicator` to verify that you receive messages saying that both are installed (you will see either the name of the installed package or a note that the package is not installed).

Completing the Communicator Installation

If either Communicator component is not installed, you can install it by performing the following steps:

1. Click the Install button on the GnoRPM toolbar, which should bring up an install window.

2. Make sure you have a Red Hat CD mounted in your CD-ROM drive. Click Add, which brings up an Add Packages window (if it is configured properly to look in the RedHat/RPMS directory of your mounted CD, usually /mnt/cdrom).

3. Scroll down in the files window and then double-click the netscape-common -4.51-3.i386.rpm file, or click it and then click Add; it should appear in the Install window. If the file does appear, repeat the same procedure for the netscape-communicator-4.51-3.i386.rpm package.

4. Then click Close on the Add Packages window, and click the Install button on the Install window.

5. (Optional, command-line only) From the shell prompt, you should type rpm -ivh /mnt/cdrom/RedHat/RPMS/netscape-common-4.51-3.rpm and rpm -ivh /mnt/cdrom/RedHat/RPMS/netscape-communicator-4.51-3.rpm to install them (assuming that you have your CD-ROM mounted at /mnt/cdrom; otherwise, you should replace that with the mount point of your CD-ROM).

N O T E If you get a Dependency Error message, you might have tried to install Communicator without the underlying Common files. Go back and select both Common and Communicator, and then click Install. Chapter 11, "Installing and Managing RPM Packages," provides additional information on using GnoRPM and rpm, especially if you encounter problems installing and need to troubleshoot. ◼

Launching Communicator

When you first launch Netscape, you will quickly see two error message dialog boxes and then a Netscape License Agreement dialog box. If you accept the terms of the agreement, click Accept. This brings up the main Netscape Communicator window, but it leaves the two error messages. Don't let the label scare you—these are not really error messages, but just informational dialog boxes stating that your cache and archive directories have been set up under your current user home directory (/root or /home/login-name). Just highlight each error message window and then click the OK button to make them go away. You do not need to take any action unless you want to change the settings of these directories, which is described later in this chapter.

If the installation was successful and no other problems arise, you should see the window shown in Figure 14.1. This is the main Communicator browser window. It defaults to a Red Hat documentation page, which can be very useful for you to familiarize yourself with Red Hat Linux 6.0. For example, you can read soft copies of the Red Hat Linux Installation Guide and Getting Started Guide that are included with the Official Red Hat Linux 6.0 boxed CD set.

Part
III

Ch
14

N O T E If you did not install the Installation and Getting Started Guide, you should adapt the procedures mentioned earlier in this chapter to install `rhl-Install-guide-en-6.0-2.noarch.rpm` and `rhl_getting-started-guide-en-6.0-2.noarch.rpm`. ■

FIG. 14.1
The main Netscape Communicator window shows Web content and provides a convenient menu bar, toolbar, and status bar.

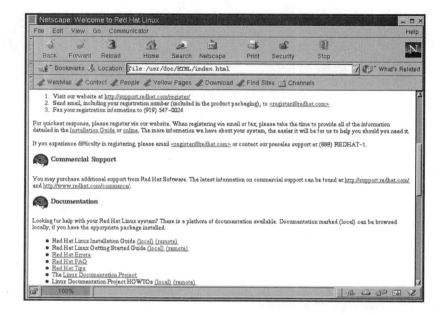

To view Red Hat 6.0 documentation, click one of the guides that are listed halfway down the first page; you should click the link marked (local), unless you have already configured your Internet connection and want to connect to the (remote) guide stored on Red Hat's Web server. Chapter 33, "Configuring Access to the Internet," discusses this in more detail. You may want to read some of the documentation (such as errata) on Red Hat's (remote) home pages because it may be more current than the information distributed with this book's CD.

Testing Your Browser and Web Server

If you installed the Apache Web server, you can also test it at this point by entering `http://localhost/` in the Location box of the Location toolbar. If the server is running and configured properly, you will see a default Apache home page that provides links to Apache and Red Hat's home pages, as well as Apache documentation installed on your local drive.

The default Apache home page that is installed with your Web server is stored as `/home/httpd/html/index.html`, and you can edit it or replace it with whatever content you wish to actually serve from your PC.

Testing Composer and Modifying Your Local Home Page

To see how easy it is to maintain your local Web pages with Communicator and Composer, choose File, Edit from the main menu bar. This brings up the Netscape Composer window shown in Figure 14.2. Composer is a completely graphical, WYSIWIG (What You See Is What You Get), HTML (Hypertext Markup Language) editor. You can make any changes you want and then click the toolbar's Save button to record your modifications (you will have to tell Composer where you want to store the file, such as /home/httpd/html/index.html). Note that you can modify this home page only if you are logged in as root or if you su to root. You should be able to see your changes by clicking the Reload button of the Netscape Communicator toolbar.

FIG. 14.2

Netscape Communicator comes standard with Netscape Composer, a powerful HTML editor for creating and modifying Web pages.

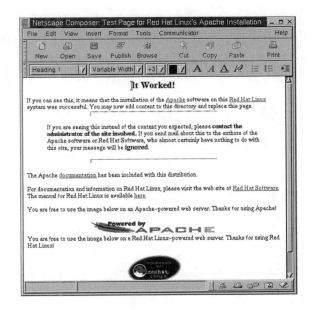

After you have installed Communicator, configuring it is fairly simple because the parameters all can be performed graphically from a few simple menu choices. Specifically, you can edit the following groups of parameters:

- Appearance preferences
- Navigator preferences
- Mail and newsgroup preferences
- Roaming user preferences
- Composer preferences

Part

III

Ch

14

■ Advanced preferences

■ Digital certificate preferences

Configuring Appearance Preferences

You can change the look and feel, as well as the basic functionality of Communicator. By default, you will see only your browser when you first launch Communicator. To change this, select Edit, Preferences, Appearance from the Netscape Communicator menu bar. You should see the Preferences window pictured in Figure 14.3.

FIG. 14.3
You can have Communicator automatically launch several components as soon as you launch it.

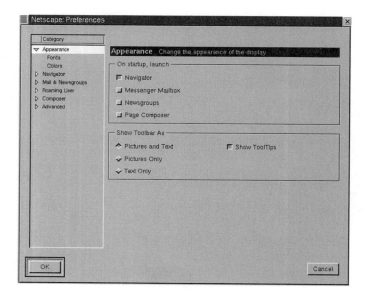

In the first frame, marked On Startup Launch, you can select one or more of the four following choices:

■ **Navigator**—Click this to see a browser window after launching Communicator.

■ **Messenger Mailbox**—Click this to automatically bring up your inbox window.

■ **Newsgroup**—Click this if you also want to have Internet news available.

■ **Page Composer**—Click this if you want the HTML editor to bring up an empty Web page.

You also can change the way your toolbar appears. In Figure 14.1, you can see that the toolbar uses both icons and text to describe your options. If you want more space for your content, or if you just prefer text instead of icons, you can specify exactly how the toolbar selections are presented to you. In the Show Toolbar As frame, you can choose to view text, pictures, or both—you also can choose to show ToolTips, which are the little descriptions that pop up when you hover your mouse over a toolbar icon.

Configuring Fonts

Underneath the Appearance category, you can choose to modify the fonts that Communicator uses. Click Fonts, and you will be able to modify the following options:

- **Fonts and Encodings**—You can select the default variable and fixed width fonts that your browser will display for certain character set encodings.

- **Size and Scaling**—Select the default font size you want to see, and indicate whether scalable fonts will be allowed.

- **Document-specified Fonts**—Choose the way you want your browser to either handle or ignore documents that specify certain fonts.

Configuring Colors

When you visit a Web page, your browser keeps track of it. As a result, it can change the colors of different links on a page so that you know whether you've already visited it or not. Web page designers can dictate these colors directly in their Web pages so that they can provide you a consistent look across an entire site. However, as discussed in the previous section on fonts, you can also set your browser to override a page's settings and consistently display the colors you want.

To configure your Netscape color settings, select Edit, Preferences, Appearance, Colors. This brings up a window with three frames in it. You can change the following items:

- **Colors**—Click Text and Background to bring up a color picker, where you can choose the color you want your page and fonts to look like. If you don't like your current settings, click Use Default to revert back to the original settings.

- **Links**—Click Unvisited Links and Visited Links to bring up the color picker again and choose a different color for links. In addition, you can depress the Underline Links button to have link descriptions appear in an underlined font so that they're easier to spot.

- **Always use my colors**—Depress this button to override a Web page's settings and always view the color layout you've just picked instead.

> **N O T E** Color and Font settings you choose under Preferences will apply across all components of Netscape Communicator, including Composer and Messenger (email and news). ▇

Part

III

Ch

14

Configuring Navigator Preferences

You can modify many different settings to change the way your Navigator browser behaves. You do this by launching Communicator from the GNOME main panel or menu and then clicking Edit, Preferences, Navigator. This brings up the configuration window you see in Figure 14.4. In this main window, you can change the following options:

- **Browser starts with**—Choose Blank Page if you don't want anything to come up when you start Navigator. Choose Last Page Visited if you want to continue where you left off during your previous session. Click Home Page if you want a certain page to load every time.

- **Home page**—If you selected Home Page in the previous step, you should type in the hypertext link that you want to see every time you launch Communicator. Click Browse to select a previously stored bookmark, or click Use Current Page to store the hyperlink currently listed in your Location bar.

- **History**—Your browser keeps a history of pages you've visited so that you can easily visit them again. Enter the number of days that you want this information stored on your system (enter 0 if you don't want it stored). Click Clear History if you want Communicator to purge these records.

FIG. 14.4
You decide which components Communicator displays—and how long it should record your site visits—when you launch it.

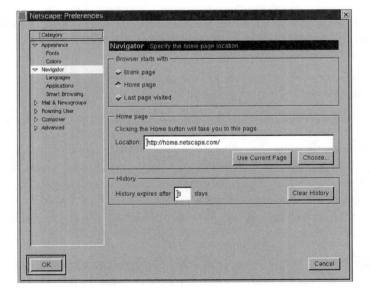

N O T E If you are not connected almost full-time to the Internet, or if you often browse local files before connecting, you should consider defaulting to a blank page or to your localhost Web page (`http://localhost/`). This will prevent a very lengthy delay when you launch Communicator, which waits almost forever to time out on a Domain Name Service (DNS) request. This process is normally required to map a name such as www.netscape.com to an Internet Protocol (IP) address such as 201.168.15.7, which your browser needs to locate the site. ▓

Configuring Language Support

With Communicator, you can enable or disable support for additional languages if you browse international Web sites. This way sites that offer more than one language will know which languages you prefer to view. Underneath the Navigator category, choose the Language subcategory. This brings up a frame with several configuration options. To configure language support, perform the following steps:

1. Select Edit, Preferences, Navigator, Languages.

2. To add a language, highlight the spot on the list where you want to add the new language (if you already have more than one language listed). Click the Add button to select the language you want to enable from the pop-up list. Click OK, and the language will be inserted immediately above the language you had highlighted.

3. To delete support for a certain language, highlight it in the list and click the Delete button.

4. To change the order of any language in the list, highlight the language and click the up or down arrow.

Configuring Application Support

Typically, Web browsers natively support common Internet file types, such as HTML, plain text, graphics, and some multimedia files. However, as the Internet evolves, you might find that you are downloading files for which your browser does not have support (at the current time, anyway). To extend your browsing capabilities, Communicator enables you to add helper applications by specifying a Multimedia Internet Mail Extension (MIME) type and associating it with an executable program or script on your Linux PC. For instance, if you download a picture with a .GIF extension, the MIME type is `image/gif` and Netscape is configured to be the default application to view it. To configure support for an external helper application, perform the following steps:

1. Select Edit, Preferences, Navigator, Applications. You will see two columns describing the file type and the program that handles it when you access it within Netscape Communicator.

2. To edit an existing file type, highlight a MIME type and click Edit. You can change the description, MIME Type, and filename extensions (for example, .htm, .html, .jpg, .jpeg).

Part
III

Ch
14

You also can select a helper program by clicking Application and Choose; this brings up a file browser. Alternatively, you can depress buttons that force Netscape to handle supported file types, save the file to disk, or interactively prompt you each time you access the selected file type.

3. To remove support for an existing file type, highlight it and click the Delete button.

4. To add support for a new or previously unsupported file type, click the New button. This brings up the same window you see when editing an existing application. However, you will have to type in at least a description and suffix before choosing how to handle the file.

5. If you choose to download files to disk, you can set the default directory for storing these files by typing the path in the Download Files To box, or by clicking Choose to pick a directory from the file browser.

N O T E   Chapter 7, "Installing and Configuring GNOME," provides additional information and methods for configuring MIME types from the GNOME interface, which also uses MIME for point-and-click functionality.

Configuring Smart Browsing

Netscape has provided an interface between your Netscape Communicator browser and the Netscape Netcenter Web site. This interaction enhances your browsing activities by introducing a Smart Browsing capability. If you enable this functionality, Netscape can help you find the sites you are looking for with a minimum amount of hassle. To configure Smart Browsing, perform the following steps:

1. Select Edit, Preferences, Navigator, Smart Browsing. This brings up a frame with two groups of items: What's Related and Internet Keywords.

2. To enable What's Related and be able to find other sites or pages that deal with similar topics to the one you currently are viewing, depress the Enable What's Related button. If you select this, you also must specify whether you want What's Related to automatically load all the time (Always), on After First Use, or Never.

3. To enable Internet Keywords and be able to enter plain language terms in the Location box (instead of domain names or IP addresses), depress the Enable Internet Keywords button. You can then enter `Charmin toilet paper` or `Atlanta Braves Tickets`, and Netscape will automatically do the necessary searches and provide you a list of categories or sites to choose from.

 TIP   To activate What's Related, depress and hold the What's Related button for a few seconds. This brings up a list of similar pages and categories that you can choose from.

Configuring Mail and Newsgroup Preferences

While Navigator enables you to efficiently browse for information on the Web, you likely will want to communicate with other people using email and Internet news. As a result, one of the first items you will probably configure in Communicator is the window pictured in Figure 14.5. Specifically, this is where you can provide the necessary information regarding your identity, account names, and servers for both mail and newsgroup messaging.

FIG. 14.5
You can tell Communicator where your mail and news servers are located, and you can provide the names of your accounts.

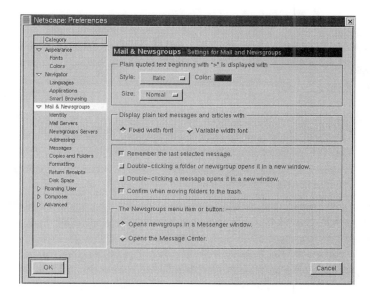

One of the things you can do is change the way your mail and newsgroups messages look and react when you use them. For example, you can change the color, style, and size of characters in your messages, or you can bring up additional windows to view individual files or folders. To configure these basic settings, perform the following steps:

1. Select Edit, Preferences, Mail & Newsgroups. This brings up a frame with four groups of items.

2. Click the Style button to pick Plain, Bold, Italic, or Bold Italic. Click the Size button to pick Normal, Bigger, or Smaller text. Click the Color box to bring up a Color Picker and choose a font color. These steps effectively change the appearance of text that is included or quoted in messages you send or receive so that you clearly can distinguish original text from quotes.

3. If you use plain text messages instead of HTML, choose whether you want to view such text in a fixed-width font or a variable-width font (whichever you find more appealing and easier to read).

Part
III

Ch

14

4. Choose one or more of the appropriate check boxes to tell how Netscape Messenger should behave in certain instances or events. You can choose to remember the last selected message (on startup); bring up a new window when you double-click a folder, newsgroup, or message; and bring up a confirmation box when you try to send messages to the trashbox (just in case).

5. Select the appropriate radio button indicating whether you want to bring up the Messenger window or the Message Center when you launch Newsgroups from the menu or toolbar.

Setting Your Identity for Email and News Messages

Your email and news client needs to know some basic information about you so that it can properly format a message. Recipients of your messages will then be able to determine who sent the message and how they can reply back to you. To enter or change your identity, perform the following steps:

1. Select Edit, Preferences, Mail & Newsgroups, Identity. This brings up a frame with several text boxes for you to complete.

2. Provide your name or nickname that you want recipients of your mail to see in their From field.

3. Enter your complete email address, including your account name and server/domain name. If you don't know this information, you should contact your Internet service provider.

4. (Optional) If you want your recipients to respond to your messages at an address other than the account you're using to send mail, enter the Reply-to Address in the same format you did for Email Address.

5. (Optional) Enter the name of your organization, if applicable.

6. (Optional) If you have created a file on your local hard drive that contains your signature block (name, address, phone and fax number, and so on), click Choose to bring up a file browser and include the text contained in that file in any outgoing messages. This can save you time from having to enter this information manually for every message.

7. (Optional) Instead of including plain-text personal information in the Signature File block, you can include a vCard attachment in all your outgoing messages. Check the Attach Personal Card box, and click Edit Card to enter your personal data. This properly formats an industry standard .vcf file that mail recipients can download and insert automatically into their address book or personal information manager (PIM).

Identifying Your Email Servers

Now that you have your mail and news clients configured to behave the way you want and to recognize you, you will have to configure Netscape to recognize and use your email server.

Netscape Messenger recognizes and interfaces with both Post Office Protocol (POP) and Internet Mail Protocol (IMAP). To configure your mail servers, perform the following steps:

1. Select Edit, Preferences, Mail & Newsgroups, Mail Servers. This brings up a frame with three sections for configuring incoming mail servers, an outgoing mail server, and a local mail directory.

2. To delete settings for an existing incoming mail server, highlight a server in the list and click the Delete button.

3. To edit the default POP server, click Pop and then the Edit button. Alternatively, you can delete the default pop account and click the Add button to start fresh. You can have only one pop server identified, so you must either edit or delete the default pop settings. You can have more than one IMAP server configured, however.

4. When editing or adding an incoming POP email server, select POP from the Server Type list in the General tab. Provide the domain name or IP address of your email server and your email account name (User Name). Check the Remember Password box if you want Netscape Messenger to remember your password and not make you enter it every time you check mail. Specify how often, in minutes, you want to check your mail. Check the last box if you want Messenger to immediately download any new messages as soon as you log in and launch Netscape Messenger. In the POP tab, check the box Leave Messages on Server if you don't want to remove the remote files after downloading and viewing. Check the other box if you want to remove the remote files only after deleting them locally (some people need to do this if they check mail from different machines, such as from work and home).

5. When editing or adding an incoming IMAP email server, select IMAP from the Server Type list in the General tab. This disables the Server Name field, removes the POP tab, and adds an IMAP and Advanced tab. Configure the other fields in the General tab similarly to the previous POP instructions. In the Advanced tab, enter your IMAP server directory and namespaces for yourself and other users. If you don't know this information, you can get it from your ISP or network administrator. You can also specify how you want the IMAP server to react to your settings and display folders when you log in. In the IMAP tab, check the appropriate box if you want to use Secure Socket Layer (SSL) during transmission of your email messages. Check the radio button specifying whether you want the IMAP server to delete, flag for batch deletion, or immediately remove files that you delete. Lastly, check the last two boxes if you want the IMAP server to clear your inbox and empty your trash folder when you log out.

6. Highlight your main email server and click Set as Default. Anytime you check mail, this is the server Netscape Messenger will use to download messages.

7. In the Outgoing Mail Server section, enter the domain name or IP address of your outgoing mail server and your email account name. An outgoing mail server uses the Simple Mail Transport Protocol (SMTP) to send your email to other servers. This server may or may not be the same as your incoming server (both protocols can be

Part
III

Ch

14

supported on the same machine, on different ports). Select the radio button indicating that you want to use secure transmission (SSL) always, never, or when possible.

8. (Optional) Click the Choose button to bring up a file browser and identify the directory where you want to store your mail files, if you don't want to use the default directory.

NOTE IMAP email servers offer many advantages over POP servers. Primarily, you have the ability to access your IMAP folders and files virtually, storing and managing (moving, deleting) your messages centrally on the server; you download small headers and only the entire messages you want. Most ISPs support only POP servers, though, so you may not be able to benefit from IMAP functionality. ▪

Configuring Your News Servers

News servers are very similar to IMAP news servers in functionality. You must identify where your server is located; subscribe to the newsgroups you want, need, or find interesting; and then download message headers. If a header looks interesting, you can download the entire message. To configure your news servers, perform the following steps:

1. Select Edit, Preferences, Mail & Newsgroups, Newsgroup Servers. This brings up a frame that enables you to add, edit, and delete newsgroup servers and specify where your news messages are stored locally on your machine.

2. To edit existing settings, highlight a server and click Edit. This brings up a pop-up window showing the name and IP port of the server. You also can select to be prompted for your username and password every time you access news or just when necessary.

3. To delete existing settings, highlight a server and click Delete. The settings for that server will be removed.

4. To add a server, click the Add button. In the pop-up window, enter the Server domain name or IP address, followed by the IP port number (if the default is not correct, which it probably is). Your Internet service provider or network administrator can provide this information for you, if necessary. Select the appropriate check boxes indicating whether you want to use secure (SSL) connections and always use your username and password (if required by your news server).

5. If you have more than one newsgroup server configured, highlight the one that you will be using the most, and click Set as Default.

6. Check the available box, and enter the maximum number of message headers you want to receive in a single newsgroup download.

7. (Optional) Click the Choose button to bring up a file browser and pick the directory where you want to save your downloaded messages (if you don't like the default directory).

Configuring Message Addressing

You might or might not know all the email addresses of people you want to send email to. If you are writing an email message to someone who has an email account registered with Netscape Netcenter, you can configure Messenger to use those centralized address records in addition to your locally stored information. To configure the way your email client interfaces with these address databases, perform the following steps:

1. Select Edit, Preferences, Mail & Newsgroups, Addressing.

2. In the Pinpoint Addressing section, check the boxes specifying whether you want to use your local address books or the directory server; pick a directory server from the available list.

3. Select a radio button indicating whether you want a pop-up list to appear when you reference a name that has multiple entries in the chosen database stores.

4. (Optional) If you chose to use a directory server, in the next box you have the option of telling Messenger to use the address in your address book and ignore the directory server.

5. In the last box, select your preferred method of displaying names by clicking the appropriate radio button.

Configuring Message Parameters

You might not want to use Messenger's default behavior and message format when editing messages. For example, you can choose to forward messages as attachments or plain text, and you even can change the length of your lines. To configure these message parameters, perform the following steps:

1. Select Edit, Preferences, Mail & Newsgroups, Messages. This brings up a window frame with three sections.

2. In the top section, check the box if you want the originator's text to automatically be quoted in your response. Click the button and select whether you want the originator's text (in forwarded messages) to be included as quoted plain text or an attachment.

3. In the middle section, Message Wrapping, give the maximum line length (number of columns) you want to appear in your messages before text automatically wraps around to the next line. Also click the box if you want incoming messages to be wrapped to fit in the current window.

4. In the bottom section, select the radio button that determines if your outgoing messages will be allowed to use 8-bit characters. You will have to base this decision on whether or not your messages are being properly received on the other end because some servers and email clients cannot understand certain methods. You should leave this as the default setting unless you know for a fact that your server or recipients have problems.

Part
III

Ch
14

Configuring Copies and Folders

You might want some information available to you offline so that you don't have to connect to the Internet every time you work with your email or news. By default, Netscape stores a copy of your templates, draft messages, and sent messages on your local system. However, you can change these defaults if you're low on space or just don't want this functionality. You can also tell Netscape to provide copies of all outbound messages automatically to a specific email address or a group of people. To configure these copy and folder settings, you should perform the following steps:

1. Select Edit, Preferences, Mail & Newsgroups, Copies and Folders. This brings up a window frame with three sections in it.

2. In the top section, check the box and click the Choose Folder button to pick a folder in your local email directories where you want a copy of outgoing email messages to be stored. If you don't select this box, no local copies will be kept of outbound messages. Click the other boxes in this section to send automatic copies of all sent mail to your default email address or any other individuals you specify in the text box (separated by commas).

3. In the middle section, perform the same steps, but this time for newsgroup messages (instead of email).

4. In the bottom section, click the Choose Folder buttons and select directories from your local email system where you want to store templates and draft messages.

Configuring Message Formats

Contemporary email clients no longer are restricted to boring, plain-text fonts and characters. You can spice up your messages and include word processor-like quality in your email messages. Netscape does this by enabling you to use HTML inside your messages. However, not all people you send mail to will have compatible email clients, so you must tell Netscape Messenger how to deal with such situations. To configure message formatting, perform the following steps:

1. Select Edit, Preferences, Mail & Newsgroups, Formatting. This brings up a window frame with two sections in it.

2. In the top section, pick whether you want to use the HTML or text-based editor when composing messages. If you find that most of the people you send mail to can't receive HTML email properly, or if you just prefer to use plain text, there is no reason to continue using an HTML editor, for example.

3. In the bottom section, choose a radio button to tell Messenger how you want it to handle a message you're sending to a person that isn't indicated as being able to handle HTML—in your address book entries, you can choose a check box to record the fact that a person has an HTML-capable email client. In this lower section, you can choose to be prompted, to ignore the warning and send HTML anyway, to convert the message

format to plain text (and lose the font and color settings, of course), or to send the message as both plain text and HTML; this last option is the best if you just want to make sure the recipient can read the message either way, and you don't care too much about the additional storage space required for duplicating the text in every message.

Handling Return Receipts

Sometimes you must know whether your addressees received a message you sent them. Unfortunately, the way Internet mail works, getting a return receipt can occur in several different ways. For instance, you may consider the message received if the addressee's email server received the file correctly, or you might need to know exactly when the addressee downloaded it off the email server with the local client. Unfortunately, only some email servers and clients support this feature, and the recipient always can turn off the feature. In other words, just because you ask for the receipt or acknowledgement doesn't mean you will get it. To change the way Netscape Messenger uses incoming and outgoing receipts, perform the following tasks:

1. Select Edit, Preferences, Mail & Newsgroups, Return Receipts. This brings up a window frame with three sections in it.

2. In the top section, select a radio button to indicate whether you want to know when the server receives the outgoing email message (DSN), when the recipient downloads (and presumably reads) your message (MDN), or whether you want to be informed of both, just to be sure.

3. In the middle section, tell Messenger whether you want it to store message receipts you get back in your Inbox or move them to the Sent Mail folder.

4. In the lower section, you have the option of telling Messenger whether it should generate a receipt when you download mail messages that the originator flagged for a return receipt (from you). Select Never Return a Receipt if you don't want the originators to know that you have obtained the message, or click the other radio button and the Customize button if you want to specify some rules of how to handle such instances. The Customize button brings up a window that enables you to force Netscape to prompt you, never send such a receipt, or automatically (always) send a receipt—you can set these options for different message categories, depending on if the message was addressed to you by name, if the message originated locally (in your domain), and for all other messages.

Managing Message Disk Space

If you have limited space, or if you just don't want to waste it unnecessarily, you can restrict the amount of mail or messages that are processed or stored on your system. You can choose to limit messages based on size, or you can choose to purge stored messages after a specific period of time. To change the disk space settings in Netscape Messenger, perform the following steps:

Part
III

Ch
14

1. Select Edit, Preferences, Mail & Newsgroups, Disk Space. This brings up a window frame with two sections in it.

2. In the first section, there are two check boxes. Check the first box to limit the size of files your system will store locally, and enter the amount (in kilobytes). Check the second box if you want Messenger to automatically compact a folder, followed by the minimum amount of space Messenger calculates that it will be capable of saving if it were to compact the folders.

3. In the second section, there are a number of check boxes related to the amount and type of Newsgroup messages routinely stored on your system. The default is to keep all messages, but you can check the first box and select the number of days' worth of messages you want to keep on file (before they are aged off and deleted). You can choose the third box and specify the total number of recent messages you want to keep handy (regardless of their size). The fourth box allows you to keep only unread messages, deleting files that you have viewed previously. The last box should be used if you want the message body (not the header) of older messages to be removed after a number of days that you also specify.

Configuring Roaming User Preferences

While you're using Netscape, it stores a considerable amount of useful information in local configuration files and folders that you need and use on a routine basis. Normally, if you move to another computer, these personalized and useful settings and information are not available to you because they are stored on your local machine and because your machine has no standardized way of exporting the data to any other machines you operate.

Luckily, Netscape supports a technology known as roaming user profile servers; this enables Netscape to store your configuration settings and certain browser-related data in such a manner that you can access it from any machine that you use with Netscape. Not only can you access it from another PC, but when you're done with a session on that PC, your changes will be saved back to the roaming access server for future use (from your original PC or another). Your Internet service provider or network administrator will be able to tell you if your servers support this useful functionality. To modify your roaming user settings, perform the following steps:

1. Select Edit, Preferences, Roaming User. This brings up the window frame pictured in Figure 14.6.

2. Click Enable Roaming Access for this profile if you want to use it and you have a server that supports it.

3. Enter your Roaming Access server account or username. Check the box below User Name if you want Netscape to remember your Roaming Access account password so that you don't have to provide it every time you use it.

FIG. 14.6
If your server has Roaming Access capability, your Netscape configurations and data will be available to you regardless of which machine you use to browse the Web.

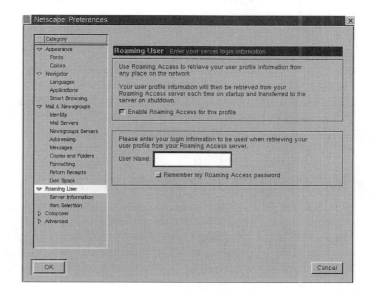

Setting Roaming Access Server Information

Just as you had to provide technical information about your email and newsgroup servers, you must let Netscape know all about your Roaming Access server. For instance, you must let Netscape know if your settings are stored on a directory server or a Web server. To provide or change your server information, perform the following steps:

1. Select Edit, Preferences, Roaming Access, Server Information.
2. If you know (or if your Internet service provider or network administrator tells you) that your Roaming Access information is stored on a directory server, select the LDAP Directory Server button. Provide the address of the server, followed by your specific user directory name on that server.
3. If you determine that your Roaming Access information is stored on a Web server, click HTTP Server, followed by the uniform resource locator (URL) address of that server.

Selecting Specific Roaming Access Services

After you've told Netscape all about the Roaming Access server, where it's located, and what your account name is on it, you can continue and select one or more standard services that Roaming Access servers can provide to multiple computers. To pick the specific services you want to be able to access from any computer, perform the following steps:

Part
III

Ch
14

1. Select Edit, Preferences, Roaming Access, Item Selection.

2. In the first column, you can select or deselect Bookmarks, Cookies, Mail Filters, and your Address Book.

3. In the second column, you can select or deselect User Preferences, History, Java Security, and Certificates and Private Keys. By default, only User Preferences is selected in this section (for security purposes because some people don't want to share security-related information from their local machine to a remote machine on the Internet). If you feel that you need to share the remaining items, select them as well.

Configuring Composer Preferences

Composer has a few settings that you can configure to optimize your HTML editing and Web page creation activities. For example, you can set default templates, colors, and background images for your Web site; automatically save edited files periodically; specify helper applications for editing HTML or images; and provide information needed to transfer your files to a Web site. To modify general preferences for Composer, perform the following steps:

1. Select Edit, Preferences, Composer. This brings up the window you see in Figure 14.7.

FIG. 14.7
You can set some basic defaults regarding the author, templates, and third-party editors.

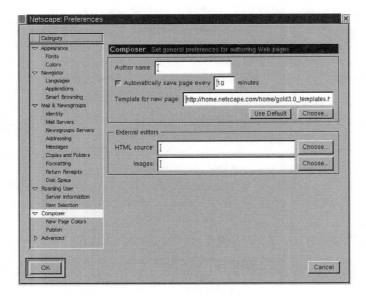

2. Enter your name in the Author Name field. This information will be stored with any HTML files that you create.

3. In the first section, click Automatically Save Pages if you want your work to be saved on a routine basis to prevent loss of data. Also provide the number of minutes you want Composer to delay before saving again.

4. If you don't like the default template, click the Choose button to bring up a File Browser and pick a different template to be used with all your Web pages. If at a later date you decide to change back, click the Use Default button.

5. In the bottom section, click Choose to bring up a file browser and select an external HTML and Image editor, if applicable to your Web creation environment. You can also type the pathname and filename directly in the text boxes.

Setting New Page Colors

Just as you could change the default type, size, and colors of fonts used in your email messages, you can select the look and feel of documents you create with Composer. You also have the ability to set page-specific options, such as the ability to use the default color schemes of the client-side Web browser, overriding any colors you previously formatted in Composer. To change color settings, perform the following steps:

1. Select Edit, Preferences, Composer, New Page Colors. This brings up a window frame with two basic sections, labeled Document Colors and Background Image.

2. Click Use the Browser's Color Settings if you don't want to personalize the look and feel of files you create with Composer. Alternatively, you can click Use Custom Colors, which enables the rest of the items in this section.

3. (Optional) If you chose to use custom colors, click the color boxes next to each Composer page category. This brings up a Color Picker, where you can choose the color you want (graphically in the Swatches tab or numerically using the RGB settings tab) to associate with the Composer object in question. You will be able to preview the changes dynamically in the box to the right.

4. If you prefer to include a default background image on all your pages created with Composer, click the Use Image and Browse for File buttons in the bottom section. You can then select an image file from the file browser that launches. This file will be used as the background for all newly created Web pages.

Modifying Publish Settings

Although contemporary tools make Web page and site creation much simpler than in years past, there are still some tricky parts of the process—you're probably well aware of this due to the many broken hyperlinks and missing pages or file components that you encounter when browsing the Web. Composer provides some convenient general settings that aim to prevent that from occurring. Composer also provides an easy, automated way for you to publish your Web pages directly to a Web site with the least amount of manual intervention,

Part
III

Ch
14

which would only slow the process. To change your publish settings in Composer, perform the following steps:

1. Select Edit, Preferences, Composer, Publish. This brings up a window frame with two basic sections, labeled Links and Images, and Default Publishing Location.

2. In the first section, click Maintain Links if you want hyperlinks to continue pointing to files located on your local computer even after you publish the page to your Web site; this will prevent the duplication of data on both machines. Click Keep Images with Document if you want to publish all hyperlinked files along with your HTML documents to your Web site.

3. In the lower section, enter the default URL where you want to publish or browse Web files in Composer.

Configuring Advanced Communicator Preferences

You can modify several security-related, cache, and proxy settings within Netscape Communicator. You do not have to make any of these changes, as the default settings should meet the vast majority of most people's needs. However, you may be in an environment in which you don't want to enable Java, for example, or you may be located behind a corporate firewall protecting your local area network from the Internet. You also may have performance or hard disk space restrictions that require attention. To change these advanced preferences, perform the following steps:

1. Select Edit, Preferences, Advanced. This brings up the Advanced window shown in Figure 14.8.

2. Deselect the Automatically Load Images button if you want to browse in text mode, with no multimedia support. This will speed up your browsing considerably, but you will not be able to use advanced capabilities that depend on graphics, such as imagemaps or hyperlinks that don't provide alternate descriptions.

3. Deselect the Enable Java and Javascript buttons if you are concerned about security and do not want to execute a site's Java code when browsing. This will make certain parts of a Web site unavailable to you, however.

4. Click Enable Style Sheets if you want to be able to share common components of certain pages with other pages that you are downloading. This will increase performance and ensure a consistent appearance within a Web site.

5. Click Send Email Address as Anonymous FTP Password if you want to access file transfer protocol (FTP) sites that require a username and password; such sites usually accept "anonymous" as the username and your email address as the password.

6. Cookies are used to temporarily store information about your browsing session on your local machine so that a Web site doesn't have to ask repeatedly for it. In the lower section, select the radio button indicating whether you want to disable cookie use, accept

cookies that originate with the currently visited Web site, or accept all cookies. If you select either of the latter two options, you can elect to receive a warning each time a cookie is used by clicking Warn Me Before Accept a Cookie.

FIG. 14.8
Netscape Communicator needs to know what security level you need, how you want to store temporary Internet files, and whether your network has a proxy you must go through to access the Internet.

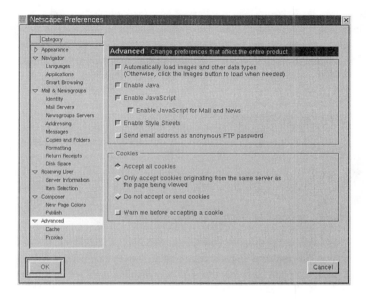

Modifying Cache Settings

If you're using a modem, you're probably concerned about transmission speed. Caching is one of the techniques Communicator uses to minimize the amount of information you download over slow bandwidth links. Files from a Web page are stored directly in memory and physically on your hard drive for ready access when needed. You can change the way Communicator creates and uses these information caches. To change cache settings, perform the following steps:

1. Select Edit, Preferences, Advanced, Cache.

2. Click Clear Disk Cache or Clear Memory Cache if you want to remove your local copy of files in memory and on your hard drive.

3. Enter the amount, in kilobytes, of hard drive and RAM resources you want to dedicate and reserve for Netscape Communicator use.

4. Click Choose to bring up a file browser to pick a different cache folder than the default.

5. Click a radio button indicating how often you want Navigator to compare locally stored (cached) files against the referenced source documents. Choose Never if you want to always use your offline copy of any files, if available (even if they may be out-of-date). Choose Once Per Session (the default) if you want to use locally cached files during the

Part
III

Ch
14

current login session. Click Every Time if you are more interested in making sure that you have updated information than you are in network bandwidth or modem download speed.

TIP When you click the Reload button, your browser normally reads its files from the cache, if they're available. If you instead want to reload information from the network or Internet, regardless of what's stored in the cache, hold down the Shift key while you click Reload. This is useful in cases such as Web development, in which you make changes frequently and want to confirm them in your browser interactively.

Modifying Proxy Settings

If you are using a personal standalone or networked Linux workstation at home, you do not have to worry about configuring this section of Communicator. However, if you are in a corporate setting, your Linux machine may be located behind an Internet firewall. If so, you will have to provide some basic information regarding this arrangement so that Communicator knows to ask for Web pages directly from the proxy rather than from the site. To add or change proxy settings, perform the following steps:

1. Select Edit, Preferences, Advanced, Proxies.

2. If you don't need or have a proxy, click Direct Connection to the Internet. Information downloaded will not pass through any proxies, and you will be reflected as the network node that requested the information.

3. (Optional) Click the Manual Proxy Configuration box and then click the View button (it is actually an edit function, however). This brings up a dialog box that enables you to enter the applicable URL or IP addresses and port numbers of the proxy servers supporting certain IP network traffic (for example, FTP and HTTP). Your network administrator will be able to provide this information, if you need it and don't know it already. If local traffic doesn't need to pass through the proxy, enter the network addresses in the No Proxy For box. If you have a SOCKS host, enter its address and port number at the bottom of the screen.

Troubleshooting Communicator

For the most part, Netscape Communicator is a fairly robust and dependable program. However, like any software package, it will act up from time to time. If you absolutely can't get Communicator to clear up a problem you encounter, you may have to close and relaunch Communicator. You might also have to log out and back in, or even reboot, but this should be a rare occurrence.

One of the problems you are most likely to encounter is a Netscape lock file. This problem sometimes occurs when Communicator crashes or misbehaves while you are using it. A lock file is used to flag the fact that certain Communicator resources are being used by an instance of the Communicator program (which may not be running any longer). If you launch Communicator and receive a lock file warning, you have two choices. You can continue with the launch of Communicator and work without resources such as the disk cache and history. Or, you can remove the lock file. To remove the lock file, navigate to the hidden directory in your home directory named `.netscape` (`/root/.netscape`, in the case of the root account). Delete the file named `lock` in this directory. You can use the GNOME File Manager for this, or you can use an X terminal command line (`rm -rf /root/.netscape/lock`, in this instance). ●

## CHAPTER 15

Installing StarOffice

by Duane Hellums

In this chapter

Understanding StarOffice

StarOffice is a complete suite of Web-enabled office automation tools. This suite is especially unique because it works cross-platform, supporting a standardized interface and file format across Linux, Windows 95/98/NT, Sun, Macintosh, and OS/2 platforms. It also is available in English, German, French, Italian, Spanish, Swedish, Dutch, and Portuguese. Figure 15.1 shows the many features available in StarOffice.

FIGURE 15.1
StarOffice provides an Explorer, a Beamer, and a desktop to facilitate creation and management of your office documents.

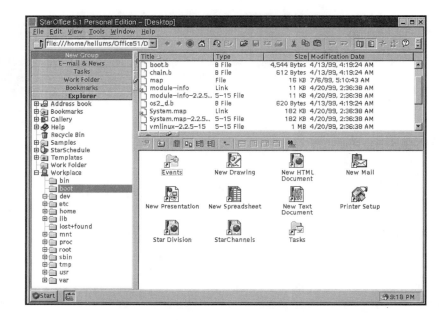

You probably will find the installation of StarOffice relatively easy, assuming that you have sufficient hard drive space and are at least a little familiar with the shell and command-line interface. On the other hand, maximizing your productivity within StarOffice and configuring it to your liking is a little more difficult. This is based on the sheer amount of suite components and modules that you must learn to use and individually configure. This chapter does not aim to teach you how to use application modules (StarWriter or StarBase) or components (Explorer, Beamer, desktop); it does aim to help you configure the most commonly configured items that you will need for normal operations. After accomplishing these basic steps, you will be prepared to more easily learn how to use StarOffice and make more advanced changes to the StarOffice interface.

You can download StarOffice 5.1 Personal Edition for free off the Internet for personal, educational, and non-commercial use. For $39.95, you can purchase Personal Edition (PE) Deluxe, which comes complete with a CD and an Installation and User Guide. The suite requires

32MB of RAM and 90–150MB of hard disk space. This version also includes some handy tools, such as a help agent and AutoPilot feature that assist you with complex tasks. Included in both packages are the following components and modules:

- **StarDesktop**—A graphical workspace built to interface with the KDE desktop environment. (It also works with GNOME, but not as well, in my experience.)
- **StarWriter/Web**—A powerful WYSIWYG (what you see is what you get) Web-enabled word processor, with all the industry-standard bells and whistles.
- **StarBase**—A full-featured Open Database Connect (ODBC)-compliant database engine.
- **StarCalc**—A capable spreadsheet program.
- **StarChart**—A program for quick creation and manipulation of data charts.
- **StarSchedule**—A calendar and task-management and planning tool.
- **StarImpress**—A presentation graphics tool for building slide shows.
- **StarDraw**—A vector graphics drawing program.
- **StarImage**—A drawing program for bitmap graphics.
- **StarMath**—A program for creating mathematical formulas.
- **StarMail**—A mail client capable of using standard mail protocols and storage/retrieval methods.
- **StarDiscussions**—A news reader client for participating in Internet newsgroups.
- **StarChannel**—A program that enables you to use Internet push technology to automatically receive Web content (software upgrades, news, stock quotes).

If you're willing to shell out $169 (a fairly good bargain, compared to the competition), you can get StarOffice Professional Edition. The Professional Edition comes with additional printed documentation and 60 days of technical support for installation. It also extends the functionality of StarOffice by providing more templates, import/export filters, drawings, pictures, and fonts.

Installing StarOffice

Unfortunately, StarOffice Personal Edition is available only as an archive (.tar) file, if you download it over the Internet. Because this version is not compressed (gzip), the entire program is 70MB, which can take quite a while to download. After you download it, you will have to follow a few steps to install it properly, depending on whether you're installing in a network or a standalone PC environment.

Downloading StarOffice

Star Division provides a mechanism on its Web site for downloading StarOffice Personal Edition 5.1. However, the application itself actually is downloaded off servers located throughout the world, but you must go through Star Division's registration process to get your registration number. If you are directly connected to a local area network (LAN) that has Internet capability, the download should last only a few minutes for you. If you don't have LAN access to the Internet and don't have your modem, point-to-point protocol (PPP) networking, or Netscape Communicator installed and configured, you should do this now.

It is possible to download the file using a browser on another operating system (Windows, for example) and file system. However, this would require additional steps and a more complicated process, such as mounting an MS-DOS or vfat file system and copying the files over, or using file-sharing, Windows networking, and Samba to access them over your network. You'll probably want to connect to the Internet anyway, so I recommend downloading directly to your Linux workstation. To download StarOffice, you will need to perform the following steps:

1. Go to the Star Division Web site at `http://www.stardivision.com/`, and click StarOffice 5.1—Download for free! (assuming they haven't changed the name yet).

2. After the first few paragraphs describing StarOffice, you should see several operating systems listed, including Windows, OS/2, Linux, and Sun Solaris; you should click the Linux link.

3. After reading the comments regarding the Linux version, click the link StarOffice 5.1 Personal Edition Download (70MB), which will bring up the license agreement. Click I Accept to proceed.

4. On the registration page, you will have to provide the operating system and platform (Linux Intel is default), language (English is default), your first and last name, street address, city, zip code, state (US only), country, and email address. Phone and fax numbers are optional, and mandatory fields are marked with an arrow.

5. After you fill out the registration information and click Submit, you will have to confirm your choices or go back and make changes, as necessary. If the form looks correct, click Confirm to continue.

6. Print the registration form you see because you will need the personal information and registration key data listed there when you install StarOffice later (you'll also receive the data via email, but the numbers won't be underlined to differentiate between zero and O, or eight and B, for example).

7. Click the continue button (right arrow) or the downloading hyperlink at the bottom of the page; you will now see a list of sites and can begin your download by picking the site nearest you. I recommend using FTP sites because the protocol is faster than HTTP, and you usually can resume downloads if you lose connection during the file transfer.

The remaining steps you perform will depend on your browser and the way you have it configured to download different file types. You should be prompted to save the file to disk or to open it from its current location; you should pick Save the File to Disk. You will also have to provide a directory path indicating where you want to install the archive file. If the directory you name doesn't exist, most browsers prompt to create it for you, in which case you'd select Yes. When you have provided this information, the download process will begin and will last for four to eight hours, depending on your modem speed and your Internet service provider's bandwidth and network activity (assuming 56K or 28K modems, anyway).

> **N O T E** Unfortunately, StarOffice doesn't provide a Red Hat Package Manager distribution of their product yet, and neither does Red Hat. So, you will have to do a little bit of command-line work to install StarOffice. Chapter 12, "Installing and Managing Linux Software," provides additional details, if needed. ▨

After you have downloaded StarOffice 5.1, you must decide how you want to install it. You have the choice of installing locally for a single user, or installing on a shared directory for a multiuser or networked environment. If you are the only one using your Linux workstation, you can follow the directions for installing locally; you have to run setup only once, and all configuration changes you make will be saved in your home directory. If you have several family members or co-workers using the same PC or accessing the server over the network, then you should follow the network instructions. Each individual needing StarOffice will have to run the setup program to install the necessary configuration files, and only about 2MB is stored on any additional PCs. However, each person will be able to use the application and store local configuration settings in his own directories.

TIP Unless you're cleaning up files as you go along, the .tar archive and the temporary installation directories will use up valuable storage space very quickly. You should check how much free disk space you have by launching Utilities, GNOME Diskfree from the main GNOME menu and panel, or by running df (disk free) from the command line. The df command might be better because it lists the amount of free megabytes. You should make sure you have at least a few hundred megabytes to prevent running out of space during the installation.

Installing StarOffice for Single-User Operations

This example assumes that you downloaded the StarOffice archive file so51_lnx_01.tar to the /tmp directory. If you installed it elsewhere, you should replace /tmp during the installation with the actual path you used. To perform a typical single-user instance of StarOffice, perform the following steps:

1. Assuming that you downloaded the file to the /tmp directory, you need to change to that directory (or the one you chose yourself) as the root user from an X terminal window. Type cd /tmp to change directories to where you will expand the StarOffice installation files and directories (temporarily).

2. Type tar -xvf so51_lnx_01.tar, and press Enter. This begins the process of creating necessary directories and unarchiving the appropriate installation and setup files and programs. You will see a list of filenames flash across your screen as the process continues.

3. Type cd so51inst from the /tmp directory, and browse the readme file (more readme or gedit readme) to learn about glibc2 and Java requirements. You already have glibc2 installed with Red Hat Linux 6.0, and you don't need Java installed to run StarOffice. The file has some important instructions for verifying required libraries and installing necessary components (for some systems).

4. Type cd office51 from the /tmp/so51inst directory, and type ./setup to run the main installation program, which moves the core StarOffice files to your final destination directory, among other things.

Several stages are involved in the installation process, and from this point on it is all graphical in nature. StarOffice will present you with a splash screen and several dialog boxes, where you will have to provide information and make a few choices. Specifically, you will encounter the following pop-up windows:

- **Welcome**—Note that you can click Cancel to stop the installation, and then click the Next button to continue with the installation.

- **Enter the Key Code**—Figure 15.2 shows this screen, where you enter the customer number and registration key that Star Division provided during your Web registration. Don't use the Company/Campus Key or Media Key options unless you have an enterprise license or other special distribution.

FIG. 15.2
Use the customer number and registration key provided by Star Division to register your application.

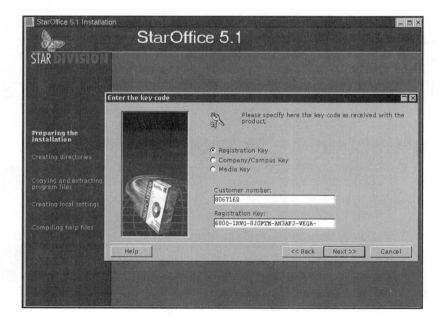

■ **Enter User Data**—Enter all the information you provided to Star Division on the company's home page when you downloaded the software. Every field must match your registration information exactly because these are the values used to generate a valid registration key code. At a minimum, you must enter your first and last name, street address, city, zip code, state (if applicable), country, and email address.

■ **Important Information**—This is a small help file that explains the use of glibc and Java libraries and components. Read the text, and click the Next button.

■ **Software License Agreement**—Read as much as you think you need to, and then click Accept to continue or Cancel to stop the installation.

■ **Select Installation Type**—Choose from Standard (default), Custom, or Minimum installations. Minimum installs only the basic functionality in about 105MB, with few bells and whistles. Standard installs everything but needs 155–175MB of storage space. Custom enables you to pick and choose the specific components you want.

■ **Select Installation Directory**—This enables you to specify where the office51 subdirectory should reside on the system. It defaults to your home directory (`/home/your_name` or `/root`). You will be prompted for the system to create a directory for you, if it doesn't exist, as pictured in Figure 15.3. Click Browse to find a new path, or just enter the full path in the text box.

FIG. 15.3
The installation program is very robust and flexible; you can install StarOffice anywhere on your system you want.

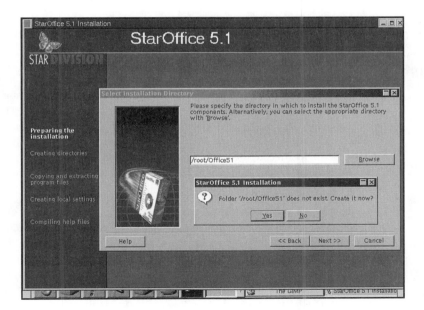

■ **Start Copying**—Click Complete to accept the configuration settings you chose and start copying files.

■ **Java Setup**—If you don't have Java or JavaScript installed and enabled, you will get this window. Click OK to proceed, or click Cancel if you absolutely need to run StarOffice on Java.

■ **Star Division Setup**—This informs you that a StarOffice shortcut was added to the KDE panel.

■ **Installation Complete**—Click Complete to finish the installation.

At this point, if you're running low on disk space, you should be able to use the GNOME File Manager to remove the .tar file and the so51inst subdirectories in the /tmp directory where you temporarily stored the StarOffice archive. However, you may want to wait awhile and make sure that the installation was successful before removing them. You can also compress the tar file using gzip to free up some space, if you need it.

To launch StarOffice in single-user mode, use the GNOME File Manager, and navigate to the /root/Office51/bin directory. You should see a program file there called soffice that you should double-click. Alternatively, you can type /root/Office51/bin/soffice from the command line to achieve the same results.

N O T E Keep in mind that you can install this application as the root user or your individual account name. For brevity's sake, I don't reference the individual account directory (/home/yourname) every time here. Replace the references to /root based on your particular path. ■

Installing StarOffice for Multiple Users

The process for installing with multiple users is similar to the process of single-user operations. However, a few other steps are involved. Primarily, the differences are that the program must be installed to a system or network location using the /net command-line option, and each individual user must run the StarOffice setup command to properly configure his home directory. For example, in the example used so far, you would type /tmp/so51inst/office51/setup /net to install the multiuser, network-capable version of StarOffice.

The network setup program follows the same basic configuration steps as for single users, until you get to the Select Installation Type window. Instead of the Standard, Custom, or Minimum options, you only have a choice of Standard Workstation or Standard Installation (local) (see Figure 15.4). You should normally select Standard Workstation, which will copy only a little less than 2MB of StarOffice files and directories to your home directory. Any time you run StarOffice in this mode, you will actually be using the /net installation as an application server. The drawbacks to this method are that nobody will be able to use StarOffice if the LAN hardware or cabling malfunctions, and LAN traffic may be heavy and slow if many users simultaneously share the application.

FIG. 15.4
Licensed network users can choose to install StarOffice entirely on their own PCs, or they can install a minimum amount of local files and run StarOffice over the LAN.

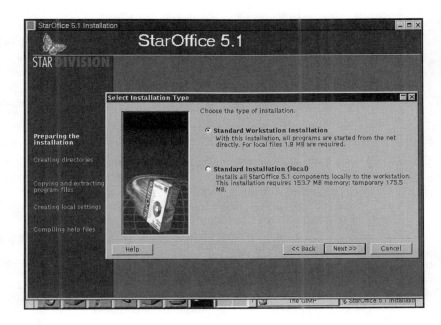

You should use the local installation method only if you have many different Linux workstations and are using the /net installation to share the installation program over the network. In this latter case, the full 155–175MB of files is installed on every drive, and each PC will be running StarOffice locally, not across the network to an application server.

Each user will have to run the StarOffice setup program from the installation directory to install the necessary directories and files in his home directory. Unlike the single-user installation discussed previously, you will want to install StarOffice in a multiuser setting to a more logical directory than /root/Office51. For example, you might want to install to /home/apps/Office51 or /usr/local/Office51 and then share that directory over the network with Network File System (NFS) or Samba. Each user will have to enter the appropriate registration key and user data again as well.

Configuring Internet Settings

Congratulations! If you got this far, then you successfully installed StarOffice. Unfortunately, you still have some mandatory configuration steps to accomplish. When you first launch StarOffice after installation, StarOffice will need to determine how you want to use the Internet with StarOffice. You have the option of disabling Internet use and bypassing this step; if you select to do this, you can just use Netscape Communicator as your email and news program.

Personally, I recommend configuring StarOffice for Internet use (just in case) but using Communicator as a general rule. Netscape specializes in the integration of browser, mailer, and news programs, so its offering is considerably more polished and user-friendly, which explains why it is the most widely used product of its kind on the Internet. You will encounter six configuration windows when configuring StarOffice for Internet use, as follows (you navigate back and forth between the screens using the Back and Next buttons):

- **The Welcome screen**—This window informs you that you can configure StarOffice Internet use by clicking Next, or you can disable it by clicking Don't Use the Internet.

- **The Manual Browser Configuration screen** (see Figure 15.5)—You should enter the IP addresses and ports of any proxy servers you use for HTTP routing. You should check the box indicating you have no proxy server, unless you're in a corporate setting and an administrator confirms that you need it.

FIG. 15.5
Some organizations use proxy servers to route certain types of traffic to the LAN and protect identification of internal LAN IP addresses.

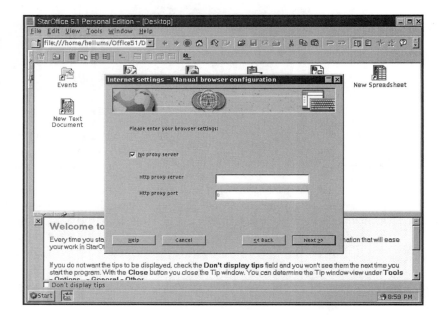

- **The Manual E-mail Configuration screen** (see Figure 15.6)—You can check the box stating Email Settings Are Not Required if you don't want to configure StarOffice email. Otherwise, you should enter the DNS name or IP address of your inbound (POP3) and outbound (SMTP) mail servers, which are often the same server. You should provide your username with that server (usually the same as your Internet account login name). Enter your password if you aren't worried about security and don't want to log in every time you check mail.

FIG. 15.6
If you want to use StarMail as your default mail program, you must provide information about your inbound and outbound mail servers and accounts.

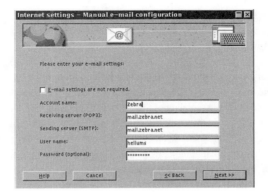

■ **The Manual News Configuration screen** (see Figure 15.7)—You can disable news settings in StarOffice by checking that news settings aren't required. Otherwise, enter a descriptive account name for your news server, followed by the news server's DNS name or IP address.

FIG. 15.7
If you want to use StarDiscussion as your default Internet news program, you must let StarOffice know about your news server and account name.

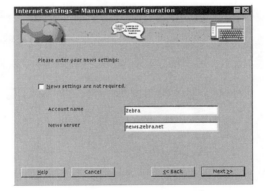

■ **The Overview screen**—This window gives you one last chance to modify settings before configuring Internet use. Click Back to make changes or Create to continue.

■ **The Ready screen**—This is a confirmation window to let you know that StarOffice successfully configured Internet use to your specifications. Click the Thanks button to exit the Internet configuration program, and begin using StarOffice.

Using the StarOffice Configuration Menu

StarOffice comes with default settings that will more than likely suit your needs fine. However, as you use StarOffice, you might find that you need to configure the way certain components operate. To accomplish this, you can select Tools, Configure from the main menu bar. You will have the ability to modify options in five different tabs, labeled Menu, Keyboard, Status Bar, Toolbars, and Events.

N O T E   StarOffice is very object-oriented, so you will find that the individual tabs shown in the Tools, Configure menu will have different subsets or supersets of configurable items and current settings, based on the individual module of StarOffice you are using. For example, the F6 function key is enabled and configured to run a spell-check in StarWriter, but it might have no value (or a different value) in other modules. This section explains the process to follow, but available space precludes covering all the individual module configurations possible. You should familiarize yourself with these different menus and experiment with various settings until you're satisfied that StarOffice meets your individual needs. ■

Configuring Your StarOffice Menu

The Menu tab enables you to associate any menu item with any StarOffice function (see Figure 15.8). To modify your menu functionality, configure the following options:

FIG. 15.8
You can configure menus for each StarOffice application or module to meet your specific needs.

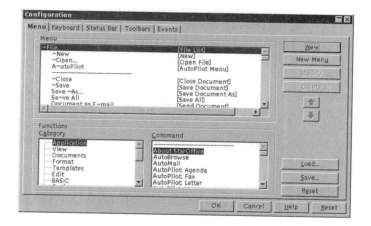

- ■ **Menu**—Click the Menu item you want to modify, delete, or move. If you are adding a menu item, click the menu item immediately above where you want to put the new menu choice.

- ■ **Functions**—Click a category to see the available commands associated with it. Click the specific command you want to perform when you select the menu item in question. The Modify button will be enabled if you select any category/command pair other than the current configuration.

- ■ **New**—Click New if you want to add the selected function immediately below the selected menu item.

- **New Menu**—Click this button if you want to create a submenu immediately below the selected menu item.

- **Modify**—Click here if you want to apply the currently highlighted function to the currently highlighted menu item. Your changes will be reflected in the menu frame.

- **Delete**—Click this button if you want to remove the highlighted menu item.

- **Arrows**—Click the up or down arrow keys to move a highlighted menu item up or down in the menu.

- **Load**—Click this to choose a previously stored menu configuration, if applicable.

- **Save**—Click here to save your current configuration to a file. This enables you to try many different combinations until you find one you like.

- **Reset**—Click this button to clear any changes you have made to this menu over time, and revert back to the original configuration that existed when you first installed StarOffice.

Configuring Your StarOffice Keyboard

The Keyboard tab enables you to change the way Star Office reacts to Control, Shift, and Alt key combinations (see Figure 15.9). To modify your keyboard functionality, configure the following options:

FIG. 15.9
StarOffice enables you to configure how your keyboard reacts.

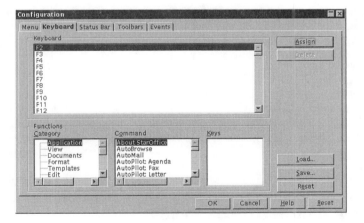

- **Keyboard**—Click the key or key combination you want to modify or delete. StarOffice enables you to assign actions to numerous combination of keys, including function keys and the Shift or Ctrl keys. Notice that the F1 key is unavailable and is reserved for the Help agent.

■ **Functions**—Click a category to see a list of commands available with it. Click the command you want to execute when you press the key or key combination specified in the keyboard frame.

■ **Keys**—Certain categories and commands have specific industry-standard keys or key combinations associated with them, such as Ctrl+C for copy and Ctrl+V for paste. This frame shows you any keyboard items that are currently assigned the function you have highlighted.

■ **Assign**—This applies the highlighted function to the highlighted keyboard item.

■ **Delete**—This removes the function currently assigned to a key.

■ **Load**—Click this to choose a previously stored keyboard configuration, if applicable.

■ **Save**—Click here to save your current configuration to a file. This enables you to try many different combinations until you find one you like.

■ **Reset**—Click this button to clear any changes you have made to keyboard functionality over time and revert back to the original configuration that existed when you first installed StarOffice.

Configuring Your StarOffice Status Bar

Compared to the Menu and Keyboard tabs, the Status Bar tab is relatively small and simple. Basically, it enables you to add or remove a few components from your status bar, which appears at the bottom of your StarOffice application window when you have a file open. To modify your status bar settings, click a status bar item to toggle it on (X will be displayed) or off (X is replaced by a blank box).

When you have the status bar configured as you like, you can click the OK button to store your configuration, or click the Cancel button to ignore your changes. As with the other configuration tabs mentioned previously, you also have the ability to choose Load, Save, and Reset to switch between stored configuration files or to revert back to "factory" settings.

 StarOffice reserves certain sections of the status bar for specific fields. You might not be able to see some of the fields you select unless you have the page maximized or are filling the entire screen width.

Configuring Your StarOffice Toolbar

To access the Toolbar tab, select Tools, Configure from the main StarOffice menu bar (see Figure 15.10). In this tab, you can select the toolbars StarOffice will display and the groups of items that will be displayed under certain toolbars, if applicable. To modify the toolbar settings, configure the following options:

FIG. 15.10
You can customize and view any toolbars you want in StarOffice using the Toolbars tab.

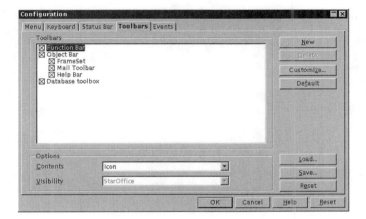

- **Toolbars**—Click any listed toolbar to toggle it on (X) or off (empty). If any options are applicable to the toolbar you have highlighted, they will be shown in the Options frame.

- **Options**—These list boxes might not be available for certain toolbars. If they are available, click the list box by Contents to pick how you want the toolbar items to be displayed; normally, you can choose from Icons, Text, or Icons and Text.

- **Visibility**—This field is available only with user-defined toolbar items. You can determine when, during specific operations or events, a toolbar should be displayed.

- **New**—Click this button to add a user-defined toolbar. The Visibility field will be enabled for user-defined toolbars.

- **Delete**—This button removes a user-defined toolbar.

- **Customize**—This button enables you to pick icons associated with toolbar items or revert back to the defaults. While you are in the Customize window, you can also drag and drop toolbar icons and text within a toolbar back and forth between the toolbar and the Customize window (see Figure 15.11). This enables you to move, add, or remove toolbar items.

- **Default**—This reverts your settings for the highlighted toolbar back to original settings.

- **Load**—Click this to choose a previously stored toolbar configuration, if applicable.

- **Save**—Click here to save your current configuration to a file. This enables you to try many different combinations until you find one you like.

- **Reset**—Click this button to clear any changes you have made to toolbar functionality over time and revert back to the original configuration that existed when you first installed StarOffice. (The top Reset clears changes made to the highlighted toolbar, and the lower Reset clears changes made to any toolbar.)

FIG. 15.11

The Customize window enables you to move, add, or delete any toolbar items with drag-and-drop functionality.

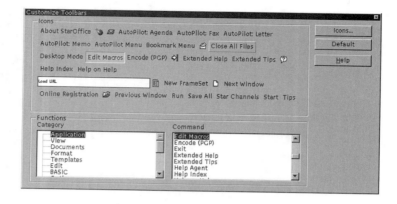

Configuring StarOffice Events

StarOffice enables you to select predefined or custom macros to execute when certain StarOffice events occur. An *event* is just a particular standard action that occurs while you are using an application, such as highlighting, resizing, or minimizing a window, and creating, opening, closing, saving, or deleting a file. Figure 15.12 shows the Events tab.

FIG. 15.12

You can provide additional functionality by assigning macros that execute when specific StarOffice events occur.

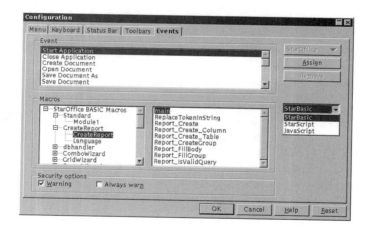

To modify how your system responds to StarOffice events, configure the following options:

- **Event**—Click the event that you want to modify.

- **Macros**—Click the plus sign next to a Macro group in the left frame to expand it and see the available macros. Select the one you want to assign to the highlighted event. The available macros for that category will be listed in the box next to it (for example, about a dozen macro modules are available under the CreateReport Macro). Click the specific macro and macro module you want to execute when the highlighted event occurs.

■ **StarOffice**—This option is usually ghosted out (unavailable), unless you're using a global macro. You can select StarOffice here to specify that it should run at any time the event occurs within StarOffice, rather than just assigning the macro to an application-level event, such as closing a StarWriter document.

■ **Assign**—Activate the changes you made during this session in the Events tab. You will see a second column appear in the Event frame next to your highlighted event, and it will show the name of the macro that is configured to execute.

■ **Remove**—Remove the macro currently assigned against the highlighted event.

■ **Scripting**—Select the type of macros you want to use. You can choose StarBasic, StarScript, or JavaScript. If you select JavaScript, be prepared to enter the actual JavaScript code in a pop-up window.

Click the OK button to accept all the changes you made while in this tab. The Cancel button ignores any changes you made while in this window. If you want to ignore all changes you have ever made to your Event options, you can click Reset; this loads the configuration settings that existed when you first installed Linux.

Setting StarOffice Options

As discussed earlier, you had the option of configuring Internet settings when you first installed and launched StarOffice. However, what happens if you chose not to configure Internet use at that time, but you want to configure it at a later date? StarOffice provides this capability under the Tools, Options item of the main menu (see Figure 15.13).

FIG. 15.13
Some StarOffice options can be configured either within a module or in the Options menu.

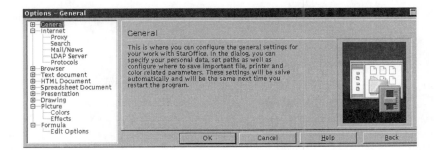

As you can see, this window enables you to tweak many different settings for your StarOffice operations. Available options are grouped under categories, by application, or by service. Most of the settings are peculiar to individual modules, and the default settings are good enough to get you started. This section documents only the items you are most likely to need to configure early on in your use of StarOffice. You will gradually learn how to use the remaining features of the Options menu.

Setting General Options

You are more likely to use some of the General options than others because these are more generic and impact the way StarOffice behaves as a whole. You can modify many settings in the following general categories: User Data, Paths, Spelling/Language, Colors, Print, Font Substitution, View, and Desktop, among others.

Changing User Data   When you installed StarOffice, you had to provide basic information that was used to generate your registration key. However, you can add additional information that will enable StarOffice templates to save you some time from repeatedly typing in basic information, such as your phone and fax number, company name, title/position, or email address, if it changes. To update this data, click the plus sign to expand the option marked General in the Options tab. You will see several subcategories; select User Data, make the changes you need to, and click OK (or Cancel, if you decide not to change this data).

Removing the StarOffice Splash Screen   When StarOffice crashes while you're editing a document, it attempts to restore the document you were working on when you launch StarOffice again. Unfortunately, the dialog box that enables you to do this is hidden behind the default StarOffice splash screen. To stop this problem from occurring, select General, View from the Options window. In the Logo field of the Display section, select Don't Show. The next time you launch StarOffice, you will not see the splash screen logo.

Setting Internet Proxy and Mail/News Options

If you didn't choose to configure Internet use during the initial installation, you can do it through the Options menu. This grants you the opportunity to change any of the settings you provided during installation or to enable Internet use if you chose not to during installation.

To set proxy parameters, follow these steps:

1. Select Internet, Proxy from the Options menu.
2. In the Proxy Server field, select Manual to enable or None to disable.
3. Enter the applicable DNS names or IP addresses and ports of any HTTP, FTP, Socks, or Security proxy servers you use. If you don't already have this information, your system administrator can provide it.
4. Enter the DNS names or IP addresses of hosts or LANs that do not require routing through the configured proxy servers.
5. Click OK to save settings, or click Cancel to ignore and exit.

To set Internet and Mail/News server parameters, perform the following steps:

1. Select Internet, Mail/News from the Options menu.
2. In the Server block, enter the DNS names or IP addresses of the outgoing and incoming mail servers (they're usually the same, but not always). Your system administrator or Internet provider can supply this information if you don't know it.
3. In the User block, enter the account name and (optionally) the password of your email account. This will allow StarOffice to automatically authenticate you when you connect to download or transmit your email.
4. In the News block, enter the DNS name or IP address of your primary Internet news server. You can get this information from your provider or administrator also.
5. In the Text Format block, check the box indicating whether you want to use HTML, Rich Text Format (Windows-compatible), or StarOffice format for email. HTML is probably the safest option for compatibility with mail recipients.
6. In the Messages block, check the box and provide a time delay if you want messages flagged as "read" after a short period of time.
7. Click OK to save settings, or click Cancel to ignore and exit.

Setting Other Options

The remainder of the options that you can configure under Tools, Options are very specific to individual document types or StarOffice modules or applications. The defaults for each of these should serve you fine, but you may find over time that StarOffice behaves differently than you want it to. If so, you can look in one of the following Options categories to see if you can change a parameter to suit your needs:

- Browser
- Text Document
- HTML Document
- Spreadsheet Document
- Presentation
- Drawing
- Picture
- Formula

Configuring a Printer for StarOffice

By default, StarOffice supports the printer you already have installed and configured for your Linux 6.0 system. This is listed as Generic Printer in the Default Printer and Installed Printers section of the Printer Installation window (see Figure 15.14). However, you can add new printers and modify the settings of any installed printers.

FIG. 15.14
StarOffice comes with
a printer manager to
install and configure
additional printers for
use with StarOffice.

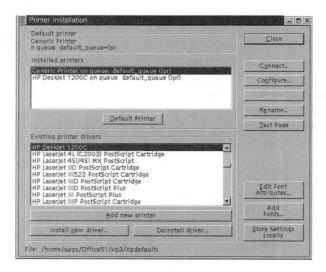

You can access the Printer Installation window by selecting Settings, Printer from the
StarOffice Start menu. To add and configure another printer for use with StarOffice, modify
the following options:

■ **Existing Printer Drivers**—Select a printer from the list of existing printer drivers. A
printer driver is nothing more than a set of instructions the computer needs to interface
with your printer for standard functions, such as italics, bold, graphics, color, page ejec-
tion, and so on.

TIP   If you can't find a driver specific to your hardware, you can try looking in the manual or documentation that came with your printer. Most printers support a short list of industry-standard printer languages, such as HP DeskJet or HP LaserJet. You could select one of those, and it should work
seamlessly with your printer, even though the brand name is different.

■ **Install New Driver** (optional)—Click this button if you need to add an additional driver that supports your hardware. You will be prompted to provide the path and filename
of a driver you received from the printer manufacturer or somewhere else on the
Internet.

■ **Deinstall Driver** (optional)—Click this if you want to remove the highlighted printer
driver.

■ **Add New Printer**—Click this, and the highlighted printer (driver) will be added to the
Existing Printer Driver section.

■ **Connect** (optional)—This enables you to associate your printed documents with a specific queue, where files are temporarily stored while waiting to print. You should have
no reason to change this setting under normal conditions.

- **Remove** (optional)—Click this button to remove an unneeded driver.
- **Rename** (optional)—Select this button to rename your driver to something easier to remember, for example.
- **Edit Font Attributes** (optional)—This enables you to change font settings. During normal operations, there is no reason to change these settings.
- **Add Fonts**—Click here if you have acquired additional fonts from a manufacturer or the Internet. You can install them and make them available by selecting the path and file from the pop-up window.

After you add the printer, you should be able to click Close and make the printer available for StarOffice modules. However, you may want to configure and test the printer you just installed before you try printing a long document and find out that it doesn't work. To configure and test your installed printer, modify the following options:

- **Configure**—Click this button to see a pop-up window that enables you to set such default parameters as paper size, orientation, resolution, margins, and postscript or color capabilities.
- **Test Page** (optional)—Clicking this button will instruct StarOffice to print a test page to the highlighted printer. If the page prints out incorrectly, you will have the chance to try other drivers or settings before printing another test page.

N O T E When you click the Test Page button, you might see a pop-up message saying that you have to save your changes first, even if you didn't make any. Don't worry about this—you didn't do anything wrong. ▓

 TIP You can switch printers and modify a few of these printer settings from within a document by selecting File, Printer Settings from the main menu bar. Choose an available printer, and click the Properties button. This activates a pop-up window, where you can change settings for that particular print session.

Troubleshooting StarOffice

StarOffice is a very good program, with an integrated, polished appearance. However, it is being maintained for multiple platforms, it's not as expensive as competing products, and it doesn't have as large an installed base for trouble reporting and beta testing purposes. As a result, you may find (like I do) that you will have to troubleshoot some bugs in the StarOffice 5.1 suite.

Handling Unrecoverable Error Messages

I frequently encounter the unrecoverable error message shown in Figure 15.15. As you can see, this is fairly cryptic and uninformative. Personally, I usually am more interested in finding out what caused the problem than I am in recovering a few minutes' worth of unsaved data. When this error message occurs, you will be forced to restart StarOffice and attempt what you were trying again. If the program continues to crash, about all you can do is try to determine if you have something related to the problem incorrectly configured. If different configuration settings don't fix the problem, you can document the incident to the best of your ability and provide a bug report to Star Division through their Web page; tech support may be able to help you fix the problem, or it might be fixed in the next release.

FIG. 15.15
StarOffice is a very nice application suite, but it does have its share of bugs that can be difficult to fix on your own.

As with any software that misbehaves a bit, I recommend that you use the functionality you need in it, accept its shortcomings, perform frequent backups, and save your files often. After all, this a very useful and *free* program (for non-commercial, personal use).

N O T E If StarOffice fails to launch correctly and you see a pop-up window saying "Object not accessible. The object cannot be accessed due to insufficient user rights," then you probably installed the single-user version of StarOffice and ran setup as root. This is fine if you intend to always use StarOffice as root, but this will cause permission problems if you try to run it when logged in as someone else. Perform a network installation with the /net option, if necessary for such a working environment (multiple logins or multiple users). ■

Repairing StarOffice Installations

It is quite possible that some application files or programs can become corrupted or unavailable to StarOffice, for whatever reason. If this happens, StarOffice provides a method of performing a self-check to verify that all is well (see Figure 15.16). To perform this self-check, perform the following steps:

FIG. 15.16
If the StarOffice setup program detects a previous installation, it will ask you if you want to deinstall, repair, or customize the number of installed components.

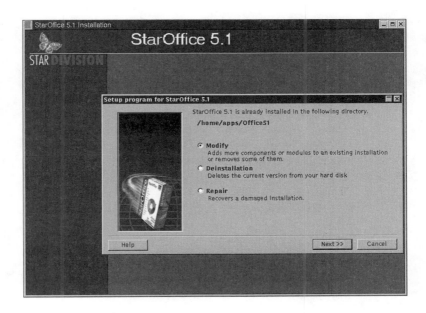

1. From an X terminal, type the full pathname of your StarOffice setup program (for example, `/root/Office51/bin/setup` or `/home/apps/Office51/bin/setup /net`). You will see the window shown in Figure 15.16. The Modify radio button will be unavailable if you performed a network installation but forgot to add the /net command-line option for the repair. If you need to modify your selection, click Cancel and run the program again with /net.

2. Click Repair and then the Next button. You will be prompted to confirm the repair by clicking Complete. The setup program will then try to repair any damaged files it finds.

3. If StarOffice can't repair the problem, you may consider using the Deinstallation option and then reinstalling the application altogether; I wouldn't use this option unless you absolutely have to, though (and preferably after trying to fix the problem with Star Division).

TIP   StarOffice will run and operate with 16MB of memory. However, the published minimum is 32MB. Performance will be unsatisfactory using anything less, especially if you have a relatively slow processor and hard drive. If you need to use StarOffice, you should consider a memory upgrade to at least 32MB, and preferably 64MB.

## CHAPTER 16

Installing the GNU Image Manipulation Program (GIMP)

by Max Cohan

In this chapter

What Is the GIMP?

GIMP, which stands for *GNU Image Manipulation Program*, is a powerful graphics program that is comparable in functionality and capabilities to commercial photo/image-editing programs (such as Adobe Photoshop). GIMP has everything from simple paint tools to complex filters and scripts that automate its functionality. In fact, there are very few things that the commercial programs can do that GIMP cannot. What's more, GIMP contains many functions lacking in other (very expensive) programs.

One of GIMP's big advantages is that its design is highly modular. You can find multitudes of plug-ins and extensions on the Web, and you can use them simply by throwing the binary in the appropriate directories. If you are a programmer, you can use C to create plug-ins and add many capabilities, from reading a new file type to manipulating images without needing to directly modify the main code or having to learn about all the pieces.

To give you a taste of GIMP's capabilities, these are just the main features that the home page (http://www.gimp.org/) highlights:

- Suite of painting tools, including Brush, Pencil, Airbrush, and Clone
- Tile-based memory management so that image size is limited only by available disk space.
- Subpixel sampling for all paint tools for high-quality anti-aliasing
- Full alpha channel support
- Layers and channels
- A procedural database for calling internal GIMP functions from external programs, as in Script-fu
- Advanced scripting capabilities
- Virtually unlimited number of images open at one time
- Extremely powerful gradient editor and blend tool
- Capability to load and save animations in a convenient frame-as-layer format
- Transformation tools including rotate, scale, shear, and flip
- Plug-ins that allow for the easy addition of new file formats and new effect filters

Obtaining and Installing GIMP

GIMP comes with Red Hat Linux 6.0. However, you may want to look at the main GIMP Web site (http://www.gimp.org/) to get the latest version and more information on using and programming GIMP. You will definitely want to visit the GIMP site because it contains tons of reference material and additional tools for GIMP, including plug-ins and scripts (explained later in this chapter).

You can install GIMP when you initially configure the system; it is located in the graphics tools menu. Alternatively, you can install it later from the CD-ROM; simply install it at the command line by mounting the CD and running the following:

```
rpm -Uvh /mnt/cdrom/gimp-1.0.4-3.i386.rpm and
rpm -Uvh /mnt/cdrom/gimp-data-extras-1.0.0-4.noarch.rpm
rpm -Uvh /mnt/cdrom/gimp-manual-1.0.0-5.noarch.rpm  can be also be helpful.
```

Finally, you can download the source or binary from this site: http://www.gimp.org/.

Binaries are much easier to install, but they are usually a little out of date compared to source code. In addition, you can optimize a program compiled from source code to match your exact configuration. I recommend you begin by installing GIMP from your Red Hat CD. If you choose to download the latest version from the Web site, go to http://www.gimp.org/ and select Download. If you plan to compile the source version and are not familiar with the procedure, select Install Help before proceeding. Next, choose a mirror site that is close to you. The details of actually compiling and installing the source code are not covered in this chapter. Install from binaries if you are not comfortable compiling programs.

If you choose to download the binary version, find the binary directory on the download site and then the RPMS directory. The files will be called something like gimp-#.#.#-#.i386.rpm. After you complete the download, install the version with rpm, as described previously.

Part

III

Ch

16

Running and Using GIMP

GIMP can normally be found at /usr/bin/gimp. You will need to run X-Windows before starting GIMP. You can type gimp at the command line to run the program. You can also find it in the GNOME menu under Graphics. Check the previous chapters to learn how to run programs using the various window managers. This chapter is based on GIMP version 1.0.4, so some features may be different if you have a different version.

The first time you run GIMP, it will prompt you to create a directory to hold your personal configuration files. Go ahead and click Install (see Figure 16.1). This creates the ~/.gimp directory and all other files automatically; the program will let you know which files and directories were created. You can safely ignore these messages and click Continue to proceed to the GIMP program.

The toolbox then appears onscreen, as shown in Figure 16.2.

FIGURE 16.1
This screen appears only the first time you run GIMP.

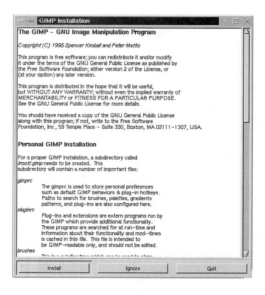

FIGURE 16.2
The toolbox gives quick access to the most common tools.

The Basic Drawing Tools

You will need to begin by creating a new empty image; choose File, New. A window will pop up allowing you to change the attributes (size, color map, background type) of your new image. For now, accept the defaults and click OK. The best way to learn GIMP is to jump right in, and it is easiest to start by using some of the basic paint tools. In addition to selecting tools from the toolbox, you can select any of the following tools (and many more) by clicking the right mouse button in the image and using keyboard shortcuts:

■ **Pencil**—The pencil is one of the simplest drawing tools. It enables you to draw sharp lines in the current color using the current "brush." Select the color you want, and click to start drawing. The pencil tool will not do any anti-aliasing (smooth slightly fuzzy edges), so it can be used to draw sharp, clean lines.

TIP You can draw a straight line from the last point you drew by pressing Shift while you click and dragging the pointer to the endpoint of the line. If you hold down the control key and click on a point in your picture, it will change your current drawing color to the new color.

■ **Paintbrush**—The paintbrush is very similar to the pencil, but the lines it draws are slightly fuzzy. These lines are anti-aliased (blended along the edges) so that the lines look smooth and soft, like the lines a paintbrush would produce. You can double-click the paintbrush icon to open the Paintbrush Options dialog box, which lets you change the amount and style of this blurring effect (see Figure 16.3).

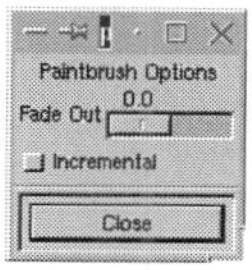

Part
III

Ch
16

FIGURE 16.3
The Paintbrush Options dialog box.

■ **Airbrush**—The airbrush is similar to the paintbrush, but it draws lightly and enables you to make multiple passes to darken the colors. This is very similar to the effect of drawing with an airbrush, hence the name. Double-clicking opens up the Airbrush Options, which lets you adjust the pressure (how darkly the airbrush sprays initially) and the rate (how much it darkens with each pass) (see Figure 16.4).

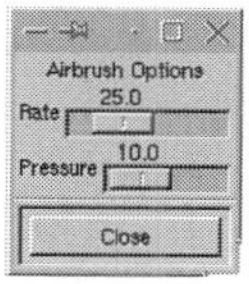

FIGURE 16.4
The Airbrush Options dialog box.

■ **Eraser**—This tools is just what it sounds like: It erases to the current background color. The eraser also enables you to choose options on whether to act "soft," like the paintbrush (which has fuzzy anti-aliased edges) or "hard," like the pencil (which has precise sharp edges) (see Figure 16.5). Just double-click the Eraser icon to open the Eraser Options dialog.

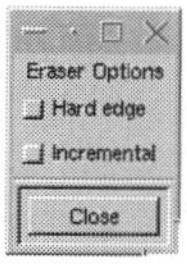

FIGURE 16.5
The Eraser Options dialog box.

■ **Bucket Fill**—This tool fills an area that is surrounded by another color. You can use this to fill the background or the inside of shapes with a solid color or pattern. If the fill doesn't quite fill the inside of the shape, turn up the Fill Threshold a little—if you turn it up all the way, you will fill the entire image. One fun effect is to choose a yellow color and a low opacity, and turn the threshold all the way up to "age" a photograph (see Figure 16.6).

FIGURE 16.6
The Bucket Fill Options dialog box.

 ■ **Blend Fill**—This tool fills the entire image area with a gradient of colors. You can change the mode and opacity to make very interesting effects, ranging from darkening images to making a horizon bluer or redder (see Figure 16.7).

FIGURE 16.7
The Blend Options dialog box.

 ■ **Text**—You can use this tool to add text to an image. After you select this tool, click the image where you wish the text to appear. Once you click, a dialog box appears that enables you to choose the font you want to write with (see Figure 16.8). Enter the desired text in the box at the bottom of this dialog box. If the text did not appear in exactly the right place, you can easily move it by dragging the text that appears.

FIGURE 16.8
The Text Tool options dialog box. Notice that you can see and choose from all the available fonts in this box.

This covers the major drawing tools. Try using them. Select the Pencil tool and draw a rough circle (see Figure 16.9). The circle need not be neat, but it must close completely, so do not leave any gaps. Next, select the Fill tool. Then, double-click the Fill tool, and select a Pattern fill. Lastly, click inside the circle you have drawn—the pattern fills the circle (see Figure 16.10).

FIGURE 16.9
Nice circle... I "cheated" a little and used a circle selection, and then picked Stroke to make it draw a perfect circle.

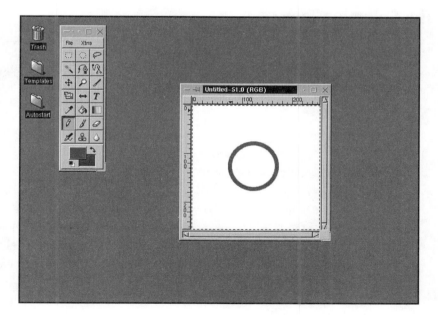

Part
III

Ch
16

FIGURE 16.10
The Fill tool should fill the inside of whatever you drew. If it fills the entire screen, you left a gap.

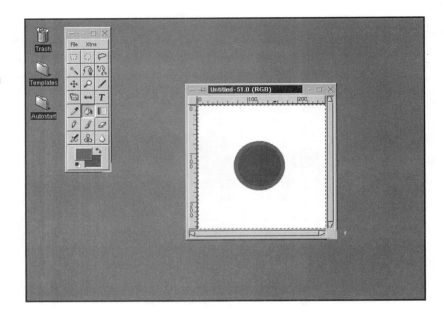

The Selection Tools

The next important set of tools are the selection tools. These tools enable you to select various portions of the image and move them, apply many of the actions only to the chosen areas, and cut and paste sections of images. The only difference among the various selection tools is the shape and manner in which they select portions of the image. All selections are the same, and you can use a combination of the tools to highlight exactly the portion of the image you want to select. You also can draw using selections by right-clicking and clicking Edit, then clicking Stroke after you select an area; this is used to make clean shapes such as circles, squares, and rectangles.

The following are the selection tools:

- **Rectangular Select**—This icon enables you to select a rectangular area. Hold the Shift key and drag as you size the selection to make it a perfect square.

- **Elliptical Select**—Use this tool to select an elliptical (or circular) area. Hold the Shift key and drag as you size the selection to make it a perfect circle.

- **Free-Hand Select**—This icon enables you to select an irregular hand-drawn area (this works like the pencil tool, except it's used for making selections).

- **Fuzzy Select**—Also called magic select, this enables you to automatically select an object by detecting the edges. This tool works very well for sharp objects but poorly for fuzzy or anti-aliased objects.

■ **Bezier Select**—This tool enables you to enclose an area using connected Bezier curves. You can curve the line by dragging the points you entered.

 ■ **Intelligent Scissors**—This enables you to draw a freeform shape around an object. The scissors will close the selection around it.

Several other miscellaneous tools come in useful as well:

 ■ **Move**—This moves all or part of an image. Usually, you use this tool to adjust the placement of one image (or subset) inside another.

 ■ **Magnify**—This enables you to zoom in on the image to perform detail work, or to zoom out to more easily modify a very large image. You click the left button to zoom in and hold Shift while clicking the left button to zoom out.

 ■ **Crop**—This tool enables you to crop a section of the image. This removes everything except the selected area. You can use it to remove unused areas, borders, or even irregular shapes.

 ■ **Color Picker**—This is a simple but very useful tool that lets you choose the current color by selecting a pixel in the image.

 ■ **Transform**—This tool has many modes for manipulating an image. It can rotate, change the scale, shear (twist like a parallelogram), and change perspective (change the angle of an image to make it appear closer or farther).

 ■ **Flip**—As the name would imply, this tool enables you to flip the whole image, or a selected portion, horizontally or vertically. This is also called a mirror effect.

 ■ **Convolver**—This works as a dual-mode tool, You can change whether it is in Blur or Sharpen mode by double-clicking the icon. In Blur mode, this works like a smudge tool to lightly blend colors. In Sharpen mode, this tool brings out fine edges and increases contrast between two edges.

Layer Support

The GIMP's layer support is an extremely powerful feature. GIMP sees all images as a series of layers: Imagine it as a set of transparent sheets one laid over the other. You can modify one layer without changing the rest, you can move one layer in front of another, and you can hide a layer. Layers are also used for masks, texture mapping, and other advanced manipulations of images.

Creating Complex Effects

One of the coolest and simplest features of GIMP is its capability to quickly create complex effects with Script-Fu. Scripts are mini-programs that work only inside GIMP that are used to combine many features of GIMP into a single function. They make very complicated procedures accessible to novices and enable a professional to simplify and streamline their workflow. You should realize there are two different lists of scripts: One is in the menu of the toolbox, and the other is in the right-click menu (see Figure 16.11).

FIGURE 16.11
The open Script-Fu menu. There are many such cascading menus in GIMP.

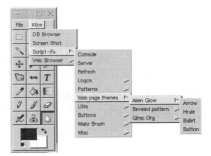

For this chapter's example, let's examine a text effect. From the Xtns drop-down menu, select Script-Fu. Then select logos and click 3D Outline. A dialog box pops up, allowing you to specify the text you want displayed in the text string. Make sure to surround your text in double quotes, as in "GIMP is Cool!" (see Figure 16.12). Next choose a font. You must choose a font that is on your system, or you will get an error. Fonts and related errors are discussed in the "Troubleshooting GIMP" section of this chapter.

FIGURE 16.12
These are just a few examples of what you can do with Script-Fu. All I did was pick a script, then select a font and a few options from the dialog box that appears. These examples all use Helvetica at 100 points.

Using Filter Plug-Ins

The next major feature is the filter plug-ins, which enable you to perform many complex changes on images. The plug-ins are external programs designed for GIMP. With them, you can blur images and create artistic effects and other special effects. You also can download new plug-ins via the Internet.

You can access the filters by right-clicking an image, selecting Filters, and then choosing a filter (see Figure 16.13). Most plug-ins will operate only on the area you select, or on the entire image if there is no active selection. The best way to learn about the plug-ins is to try them out—feel free to change the options to see how this affects the image. Some plug-ins are primarily for photos; others are for drawn images, and most work equally well on all types of images.

FIGURE 16.13
You can access this menu by right-clicking the image area (canvas). You can access almost every tool in GIMP from this menu, not just plug-ins.

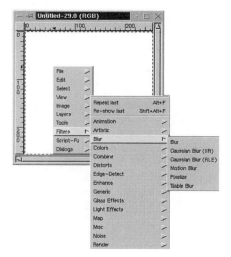

As you can see, the menu of Blur filters is open. These are a good set of filters to start experimenting with because the effects are very obvious and intuitive. You can use these filters to add fog effects, smooth out grainy or jagged images, and add out-of-focus effects. Use them in combination with other tools to create soft shadows and remove blemishes on photos. Try loading a photo or an image you've created. Then right-click, select Filters, and then blur. Finally, left-click one of the generic Blur filters. A dialog box will come up—for now, just click OK. The image should appear to be rather blurry. You can press undo (Ctrl+Z) and try different settings and different filters until you get the effect you want.

Saving Your Images

To save your image, right-click the image and choose File, Save. The Save Image dialog opens. Click the Determine File Type button to open the extension menu (see Figure 16.14). You should normally save images you create in GIMP to the XCF format. XCF is GIMP's native format and preserves the layers, history, and all other GIMP-specific information. However, when you are ready to use the image outside GIMP, you must save it in a format that is compatible with the software that will be using it. The most common formats are JPEG (great for photos and pictures with many colors), GIF (good for pictures with less than 256 colors), and PNG (a newer format that works well with most pictures—however you should still use JPEG for photos). You can also add more image types to save to via file plug-ins, which, of course, are available via the Internet. For example, you can get a PhotoShop plug-in that will enable you to exchange layered images with PhotoShop users.

TIP

You can use gzip (or bzip2) to reduce the size of older uncompressed or poorly compressed image formats such as TIFF, PCX, and others by appending `.gz` (or `.bz2`) to the name (after the type; for example, `image.tiff.gz`). GIMP will automatically compress the file when saving and decompress them upon loading.

FIGURE 16.14

As you can see, GIMP supports a multitude of formats. Generally, the formats that are grayed out are not available in your current color mode.

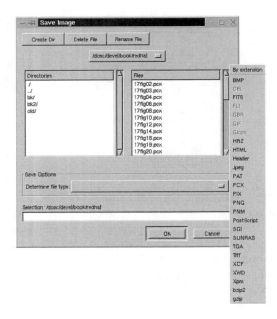

Troubleshooting GIMP

One of the most common problems with GIMP involves choosing a font that does not exist in a Script-Fu extension. This causes an error message, such as the one shown in Figure 16.15. You can use the text tool to browse through available fonts. Your window manager may have additional fonts and font browsers. You can also find more fonts by searching the Internet. Some good places to start are `http://metalab.unc.edu/pub/Linux/X11/fonts/` and `ftp://ftp.gimp.org/pub/gimp/fonts`. For example the `freefonts` and `sharefonts` packages have several useful (and free) fonts. Finally, several fonts that should always be available are Helvetica, which you can find by entering `-adobe-helvetica-medium-r-normal-*-100-*-*-*-*-*-*-*`, and Courier which you can access with `-*-courier-medium-r-*-*-100-*-*`. In both cases, `100` refers to the font size (shown as 10 times the size in points).

Part
III
Ch
16

FIGURE 16.15
If you see this, it simply means you must choose a new font. Many Script-Fu scripts have default font choices that might not be available on your system.

Another important aspect to remember is that there are several image modes: Indexed (fixed palette), RGB (24-bit), and Grayscale (24-bit Gray). You cannot do all actions in all modes. For example, most filters require an image to be in RGB mode, whereas you must be in Indexed mode to save a GIF image. ●

## CHAPTER 17

Installing and Configuring Games

by Jon Konrath

Red Hat Linux 6.0 comes with comprehensive development tools, full communication capabilities, and productivity software. But, when your noncomputer friends come over to see your new Linux installation, you probably won't be showing off the C compiler. What you need are flashy entertainment programs, the kind that will help you take up some of the time that Red Hat Linux is helping you save.

Of course, Red Hat Linux 6.0 comes with plenty of games and other amusements, ranging from simple yet mind-bending puzzle games to multiplayer strategy games. Many games use the X Window system for graphics, and others run in plain text mode. And if the games included with Red Hat Linux aren't enough to help you procrastinate through any amount of work, you can also download or purchase literally thousands of other recreational titles, ranging from old text-based mainframe games to the latest arcade-style shoot-em-ups.

Games Included with Red Hat Linux 6.0

Several games are installed by default in Red Hat Linux 6.0, and many more optional games are included on the CD-ROM. These are largely for use in the X Window environment, but they aren't exactly high-end arcade games. For the most part, these selections were coded by people for fun and were released to the Linux community for free, usually including source code. They might not compete with dedicated gaming systems such as the Nintendo 64 or PlayStation or some of the commercial software for Windows PCs, but Linux games can still be very challenging and a lot of fun.

If you want to install any additional game packages, consult Chapter 11, "Installing and Managing RPM Packages," which explains how to add and update RPM packages. The package names begin with the name of the game and contain the version number. If you scan the RPMs on the Red Hat Linux 6.0 CD-ROM, you should have no trouble finding them. For example, to install the kdegames package, insert your Red Hat Linux 6.0 CD in the CD-ROM drive and type the following commands:

```
mount -t iso9660 /dev/cdrom /mnt/cdrom

rpm -ivh /mnt/cdrom/RedHat/RPMS/kdegames*.rpm
```

In addition to the standard games, the GNOME desktop environment includes a suite of games that is installed by default. The KDE desktop environment also has a suite of games designed for its look and feel. The KDE games package is not installed by default, but it can be easily added. Both of these packages are described in the following sections.

xhextris

You're probably already familiar with Tetris, the addictive Russian block-dropping game. xhextris is similar, with one twist: Instead of squares, the blocks are made with hexagons. This means that the blocks you need to drop to fill the playing field fit together in an altogether more difficult way. It's confusing at first—and then strangely compelling.

To play, type `xhextris` at a shell prompt, and a high score list will appear. Press N and a new game will begin. Keys J and L move falling blocks left and right, and K and I rotate them counterclockwise and clockwise.

This package is named `cxhextris-1.0-15`, but the application itself is named xhextris. If you ever need to upgrade or uninstall xhextris, make sure to use the `cxhextris-1.0-15` RPM name.

fortune-mod

This isn't really a game, but it is a long-running UNIX tradition. When you issue the `fortune` command, a random quote, message, or adage is printed. For example:

```
% fortune
I hate small towns because once you've seen the cannon in the park there's
nothing else to do.
                -- Lenny Bruce
```

Aside from being run on the command line, fortune is frequently used in many places to glue in a random and funny comment. For example, you could put fortune at the tail of your `.bashrc` or `.logout` to print a quote when you log in or out. And it's not hard to configure most email programs to use fortune to generate a random signature file.

Fortune also has many command-line options. Some of the more useful ones are –n, which limits the length of a fortune to a specified value, and –a, which prints fortunes from any of the available databases, including potentially offensive fortunes that are not printed by default.

Note that fortune is installed in `/usr/games/fortune`, which is not in your path in Red Hat Linux 6.0. To add `/usr/games` to the path of all users on your machine, open the `/etc/profile` file in the editor of your choice. You should see a path statement similar to this:

```
PATH="/usr/local/bin:/usr/bin:/bin:/usr/X11R6/bin:/sbin:/usr/sbin"
```

Add `:/usr/games` at the very end, so it looks like this:

```
PATH="/usr/local/bin:/usr/bin:/bin:/usr/X11R6/bin:/sbin:/usr/sbin:/usr/games"
```

After this change, you can run fortune simply by typing `fortune` at the shell prompt.

gnuchess

The folks at GNU have developed a world-class chess program, and this is the result of their labor. Thanks to an openings library and a hashfile containing positions and moves "learned" in prior games played, GNU Chess is a formidable opponent to almost any player.

GNU Chess isn't pretty by default. It uses ASCII characters to draw its board, and you have to move your pieces by entering coordinates. For example, to move Pawn to King's fourth, you'd enter E2E4. The character-based interface can get annoying fast, but luckily, it's not your only option. xboard lets you play GNU Chess with a much nicer X-based interface. See the description in the later section "xboard" for more details.

trojka

Here's another Tetris-with-a-twist puzzle game that's just as compelling as the other block-dropping games for Linux. In this version, you're dropping single rectangular bricks, made of different patterns of letters and other characters (XXXXX, OOOOO, %%%%%, and so on.) The blocks pile up at the bottom of the screen, and they disappear when there are three in a row of the same pattern, either horizontally or diagonally (or both). As always, the game continues until the block pile reaches the top of the screen, and the blocks start dropping faster as the game progresses.

To play trojka, move the falling bricks left or right with the H and L keys, and drop a brick with the Spacebar. If you like this puzzle, try the full-color version for X, called xtrojka.

Note that trojka is installed in /usr/games/fortune, which is not in your path in Red Hat Linux 6.0. To add /usr/games to the path of all users on your machine, open the /etc/profile file in the editor of your choice. You should see a path statement similar to this:

```
PATH="/usr/local/bin:/usr/bin:/bin:/usr/X11R6/bin:/sbin:/usr/sbin"
```

Add :/usr/games at the very end, so it looks like this:

```
PATH="/usr/local/bin:/usr/bin:/bin:/usr/X11R6/bin:/sbin:/usr/sbin:/usr/games"
```

After this change, you can run trojka by simply typing trojka at the shell prompt.

xbill

An evil computer hacker named Bill has created a computer virus in the form of an operating system; without your help, all will be lost! When you start this game, you're in charge of administering a small network of UNIX and Macintosh computers. But soon, swarms of Bills invade, attempting to install their operating system/virus on your machines.

To stop the invasion, use the mouse and squash the Bills in their tracks. If one of them manages to remove an OS from one of your machines, drag the OS icon back to the computer. You're scored on total uptime, so make sure that you keep your machines clean of viruses. As the game speeds up, sparks might start flying around your network cables. Drag the water bucket over them to prevent a fire. When you've safely defended your computers from a wave of Bills, you'll advance to progressively more difficult levels, with more computers and faster Bills.

xboard

In addition to being the X user interface for GNU Chess, xboard can also be used to play chess on the Internet via ICS, the Internet Chess Server protocol. It can also proxy chess games via email, play chess via its own chess program, analyze saved chess games or arbitrary positions, view chess games discussed in Usenet newsgroups, watch a game between two different machines, or pit two different chess programs against each other.

If you're looking for a quick game of chess against the computer, running xboard with no other options will start a human versus computer 40-move game using GNU Chess, with a 5-minute clock. You can also launch xboard with command-line options to change the length of a game. For example, to start xboard with a 65 minute 30 second, 100 move, one move per second game, use the following command:

```
Xboard -tc 65:30 -mps 100 -inc 1
```

To change other settings, select a menu option to change it. A few often-changed options on the Options menu include Bell, which rings a chime after each move; Always Queen, which turns on automatic pawn promotion; and Highlight Last Move, which outlines the piece that changed in the last move, in case you missed it. To change these options, select them from the Options menu, and they will toggle on and off. Options that are currently on have a bullet next to them in the menu.

xboard -ncp enables you to use xboard without a chess program. Use this option if you want to analyze an arbitrary position, or follow games written in portable game notation or algebraic notation. Select Load Game or Load Position from the File menu to enter a new game or position, or simply move the pieces yourself and select Save Position to save the position.

If you want to play others on the Internet, xboard -ics will connect you to chessclub.com, one of the most popular chess servers on the Internet. This enables you to challenge other players currently connected or to watch ongoing matches. For more details on playing chess over the Internet, see http://www.chessclub.com or the man page for xboard.

xboing

If you remember the old breakout game from the Apple II days, you should try xboing II (see Figure 17.1). Enter the command xboing, and you'll once again be moving a paddle back and forth and bouncing a ball to destroy lines of bricks across the screen. Destroy the blocks to earn points, and get to the higher blocks for more points. xboing looks much prettier on your X display than Breakout did on your old 8-bit machine. Plus, there are many bonuses on the board: Some of those blocks explode, teleport the ball, or give you bullets to fire at the blocks.

To start the game, type xboing at the shell prompt. After a title sequence, a list of the possible blocks and their point values will be displayed. To play, press the spacebar. Use the mouse to move your paddle left and right, and use the button to start the ball or fire bullets. Depending on your X window manager, you might keep moving your mouse out of window focus and messing up your game. If you keep "losing" the mouse, try using the key controls instead. The G key toggles between mouse and keyboard. You can also use keys J and L to move left and right, and K to start the game or shoot. If you get bored with the default levels, press E at the opening screen. You will enter into a level editor so that you can create your own xboing II boards.

FIG. 17.1
Try to destroy the bricks in a game of xboing II.

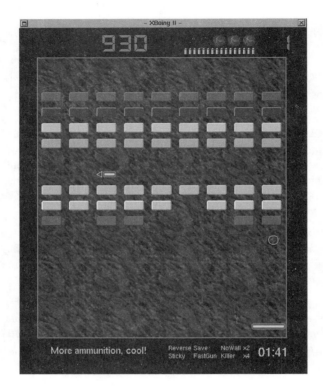

xgammon

xgammon is a version of the classic game of backgammon for X. You can play against the computer or other human players. To play, type xgammon, or type xgammon -otherdisplay somehost:0.0 to play someone at host somehost. Click on the dice to roll, and drag the pieces to move them to new points. You can also undo a move, save the game to a file, or resign if you can't handle the computer. If you can't figure it out, or if you are tired of playing, select Computer vs. Computer from the options menu, and watch the markers fly.

xjewel

There must be some allure to writing a Tetris-like game for Linux. Oddly enough, all of them are so compelling that the rash of dropping-blocks games is very acceptable. This is another such game, with a slightly different puzzle. Each piece is made with three jewels of varying colors. You can move the pieces left and right, or rotate the jewel segments. Jewels vanish from the pile at the bottom of the screen when you line three in a row, and the jewels on top fall in place when others vanish.

To play, use keys J and L to move left and right, K to rotate, and the spacebar to drop. You can also use the numeric keys 4 and 6 to move left and right, 5 to rotate, and 0 to drop. You use the left and right arrow keys to move left and right, and the down arrow key to rotate. The game gets faster as it progresses, and your only hope is to find the infrequent wildcard blocks, which can be used as a jewel of any color in matches. As always, when the jewels reach the top of the screen, the game is over.

xpat2

If you're looking for a solitaire game with many variations, xpat2 is the ticket. This patience game contains many different rule sets and versions of the single-player card game, including Spider, Gypsy, Klondike, Canfield, Baker's Dozen, and others.

To play, choose a rule set from the Rules menu, and then select New Game from the Game menu. If you're not up on your card games, or if you've never heard of some of these solitaire variations, click the Help button to launch the help viewer. From the help viewer's topics menu, select a solitaire version to display its rules. You can also click the Hint key during a game to show an optimal next move. This package is overkill in the pursuit of wasting time, though—be careful how involved you get!

xpilot

If you liked the arcade game Asteroids, you'll love this multiplayer space battle. xpilot pits you against other network players or robots, either in combat or a racing mode. The screen is divided into a playing map, a radar screen, and a message area, all drawn with vector graphics. Moving is tricky at first—when you hit the thrusters, your ship tumbles in zero-g until you rotate and hit the engines again. There's a full arsenal of weapons, ranging from lasers to guided missiles and mines.

Before you run xpilot, you have to find a running xpilot server. For example, if you know a friend who is running a server at `host.server.com` on port 2112 and you want to join the game with the nickname Cartman, start xpilot like this:

```
xpilot -port 2112 -name Cartman host.server.com
```

If you want to play xpilot by yourself, or if your Linux machine is connected to the Internet and you'd like to invite a few friends to play also, you can start your own server. At the shell prompt, enter the following command:

```
xpilots&
```

If you enter xpilot with no arguments, it will search for any xpilot servers running on the local machine and connect to them.

Part
III

Ch
17

After you connect to a running server, you're presented with a command prompt. Type H or ? for a help screen of commands, or press Enter to enter the game. You'll have to remember many keys to navigate your ship; it's best to click on Menu, choose Keys, and read over the list before trying to play. To get started, use A and S to rotate your ship, the Shift key to thrust, the spacebar to raise the shield, and Enter to fire. Remember that once your ship has gained momentum, it won't stop unless you thrust in another direction or hit something. To learn more about the many options of this game, read the xpilot man page or the online help available by clicking the About button.

xpuzzles

This is a set of various geometric puzzles and mind-teasers for X. If you remember the Rubik's cube, you'll probably recognize a few of these. Included in the package are xcubes, xdino, xhexagons, xmball, xmlink, xoct, xpanex, xpyraminx, xrubik, xskewb, and xtriangles.

Although they greatly vary in geometry and complexity, these puzzles work with the same basic mouse movement. Click the right mouse button to randomize the puzzle. To move a piece, click on a square with the left mouse button, and then click on a destination with the left button. You can also solve the puzzle with the middle button.

xtrojka

Just like the text-based version, this is another puzzle game similar to Tetris, but with a new puzzle that's just as compelling as the other block-dropping games for Linux. This time, you're dropping single rectangular bricks that are different colors. As the blocks pile up at the bottom of the screen, they disappear when there are three blocks in a row of the same color, either horizontally or diagonally (or both). The game continues until the block pile reaches the top of the screen, and the blocks start dropping faster as the game progresses.

To play xtrojka, select New Game from the Trojka menu. You can move falling bricks left or right with the arrow keys, and you can drop a brick with the spacebar.

GNOME Games

The GNOME environment includes a suite of games that are installed by default on workstation-class installations of Red Hat Linux 6.0. Although designed for GNOME, these games will also work with other windowing environments. They all feature a uniform look and feel, with similar menus and support for options such as sound.

If you are using the GNOME environment, these games are available from the Games menu located on the system menu, which can be found by clicking the GNOME icon in the toolbar. You can also find the games menu by clicking the middle mouse button on the desktop. Select any game from the menu to start it. Games can also be started by typing their name at the shell prompt. For example, to play gtali, simply type gtali at the shell prompt.

The following are some of the more popular games from the package. For more information on each game, check its Help menu.

freecell

This solitaire game, best known from the Microsoft Windows version, has been ported to X by the GNU team. The object of the game is to move the cards that are stacked in the lower part of the board, in increasing order, to the upper-left part of the board. You can stack cards on each other in decreasing order and alternating color, just like regular solitaire, but to move more than one card, you need free space. There are four open spaces in the upper-left part of the screen, so you can stack cards there. But with the starting arrangement of cards, you'll need to do some careful digging. It sounds hard at first, but pretty soon you'll be seeing free-cell boards in your sleep.

To play, click the New button on the toolbar, and the board will start with eight stacks of cards. Click and drag the topmost cards, and drop them in new positions. If you get stuck, you can click the Undo button to reverse a move, or the Restart button to reshuffle the cards and start again. There's also an exit function, but it can be very hard to use sometimes....

gnibbles

In gnibbles, you and up to three others are worms, zipping across a board that contains diamonds. The object of the game is to capture these diamonds without hitting the walls, other worms, or your own tail. Sound easy? Well, you're moving at a steady pace, and your only control is to move left or right. Your tail grows longer each time you eat a diamond that isn't the same color as you. This means that you're two sharp turns away from knocking into yourself. And when you get other people with growing tails on the same board, it's like a demolition derby. Luckily, grabbing diamonds that are the same color as you shortens your tail. And you can duck into a doorway to transport to the other side of the door, instead of careening into a wall.

To play as a single player, use the cursor keys to move your worm. To play with more than one player, select Preferences from the Settings menu while at the title screen, enter a number of players, and define other keys on the keyboard for their movements. For example, player 1 could use the cursor keys, while player 2 uses the numeric keypad and player 3 uses the A, S, W, and Z keys. Play advances through new levels as boards are completed and continues until one of the worms runs out of lives.

gnobots and gnobots2

A port of a classic text-only UNIX game called robots, gnobots is a strategy puzzle that pits you against a bunch of randomly placed robots (see Figure 17.2). Their only mission is to chase after you and kill you. Luckily, they aren't very smart, and it's not hard to get them to run into each other or collide with other robot wreckage. You also have the limited ability to safely teleport yourself out of a jam, and the unlimited ability to teleport anywhere on the board (which also includes teleporting yourself onto robots).

FIG. 17.2

Escape from the robots in a game of gnobots.

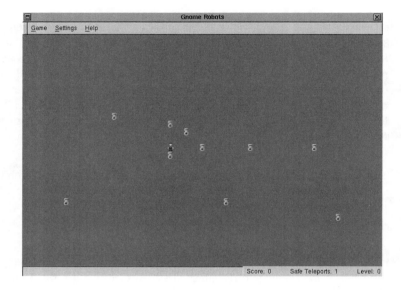

To play gnobots, Select New Game from the game menu. The standard keymap is H and L for left and right; K and J for up and down; Y, B, U, and N for diagonal movement; T for safe teleport; and R for random teleport. You might find it easier to use the numeric keypad keys for movement and the numeric keypad + and - for safe and random teleport.

gnobots2 is more advanced in that it has more sound and a more comprehensive configuration, and it lets you define your own keys and choose from several different variations on the game. It is played the same, except that only one keymap is defined at a time; see the Preferences dialog box for details.

gnomine

Between this and freecell, you might not need WINE for Windows compatibility. Yes, this is a clone of the classic Microsoft time-waster, Minesweeper. You start the game with a field of covered squares and must uncover the squares to find mines. If you uncover a square that is adjacent to mines, the number of mines will be printed in that square. If you think that you know where a mine is, you can flag it with the right mouse button. If you select a square with a mine, the game is over, and all the mines are shown to you. When you've become bored with an 8×8 grid, you can select a medium, big, or custom field size.

gnotravex

In this simple yet aggravating puzzle, you must place nine square pieces in a 3×3 grid. Each side of each square piece has a number on it. When you place square pieces in the grid, the numbers on the sides of adjoining pieces must match. It sounds easy, but the clock is ticking, and there's only one right answer. Luckily there are hints, and you can ask to have the puzzle solved for you. If you think that the standard puzzle is too easy, try a bigger grid; a 6×6 puzzle should keep you guessing for a while.

gtali

Here's a clone of the dice-based board game Yahtzee. In gtali, you must roll the dice and complete a sequence of different poker-like hands to score points and win the game. You can play against other humans or computer players by changing the number of players in the Preferences dialog box.

To play, you're presented with five dice at the beginning of the turn. If they match one of the hands in the scoring column, click the dice and then select the appropriate hand. For example, if you roll all 6's, select all the dice and then select Yahtzee. In addition to poker-like hands such as three of a kind, four of a kind, full house, and so on, you must also complete categories for each number. For example, for the Sixes category, you must roll as many sixes as possible. The total of all the sixes rolled is the point value of that category. The Yahtzee category is a roll of five of a kind.

To re-roll only some of your dice, select the dice you don't want to keep and then click Roll. You can roll only three times, and you can use each hand only once in the game. You can also use the undo feature, and watch the computer's "thoughts" as it goes through its turns.

iagno

This is a beautiful version of the Othello board game for X (see Figure 17.3). It's played on an 8×8 board with black and white pieces. On a turn, the player must put down a piece of his color in such a way that it's opposite another piece of that same color, reversing the color of the pieces in between. As the game progresses, pieces flip from black to white and back until the board is filled.

This version lets you choose from several different tile sets in the Preferences menu. In addition, you can choose from three different levels of computer difficulty, or you can even pit the computer against itself.

mahjongg

Although this game uses colorful tiles similar to those of the old Chinese multiplayer game of the same name, it's actually a single-player solitaire puzzle. You're presented with a stack of mahjongg tiles, and you must remove them by matching pairs of free tiles. A tile is free if one of its horizontal edges is not touching other tiles. Beware—it's possible to get to a point where you've locked all your matching tiles in such a way that there are no more legal moves. This version offers hints and an undo option, in addition to more difficult tile maps and differently patterned tile sets.

FIG. 17.3
Play against the computer in Iagno, the GNOME version of Othello for X.

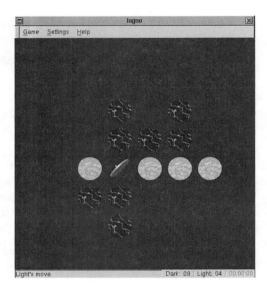

same-gnome

This is one of those games whose premise seems too simple, until you spend eight hours trying to play a perfect game. The game board consists of several beautiful colors of marbles. When you click on a marble, it and all the consecutive like-colored marbles are removed. You can check what like marbles are consecutive by moving your mouse over the playing board; the like colored marbles that are next to each other will swirl and move. When you remove marbles, all the other marbles above then fall down to fill in the gaps. You can't remove a single marble, and two marbles don't score you any points. You get a point for three marbles and additional points for removing more. The game continues until there are no more combinations left. If you get bored with the standard game, you can also select new scenarios in the Preferences dialog box to change the shape and color of the marbles.

sol

This is GNOME's version of the basic solitaire game. Although it starts as classic Klondike, sol lets you chose from almost 30 different single-player card games, including freecell, spider, union square, hopscotch, fourteen, and many others you've probably never heard of.

Luckily, there's online help that explains all these variations. And if you're stuck, undo/redo and hints are available.

KDE Games

The KDE desktop also comes with a suite of its own games. Many of them are similar or identical to the games that are bundled with the GNOME environment, with changes to the look and feel to match the KDE environment. Although they were written with KDE in mind, you can install and run most of these games in any window manager. These games are not installed by default. To install the kdegames package, insert your Red Hat Linux 6.0 CD in the CD-ROM drive and type the following commands:

```
mount -t iso9660 /dev/cdrom /mnt/cdrom

rpm -ivh /mnt/cdrom/RedHat/RPMS/kdegames*.rpm
```

The following are the more popular games of the package. For more information, see the Help file for each application.

Part
III

Ch
17

kabalone

This strategy game is similar to Chinese checkers and is played against the computer. The object of the game is to force six of your opponents' pieces off the board. You can move one, two, or three adjacent pieces in a line by one space. You can also push up to two of a player's pieces if you move a line of pieces greater in number and it runs into theirs.

To play, click on a piece, and then click on a destination to move it. You can move pieces sideways or diagonally. Use the Computer Plays Both Sides options on the Options menu to watch how the game is played if you're not sure how it works. You can also ask for a hint or reverse a position by clicking the hint and reverse icon above the playing board.

kblackbox

In this logic game, you must find several balls hidden in a grid of boxes. To find them, you must shoot rays into the box and investigate how they leave or reflect back at you. Based on your guesstimations, you can also mark the grid to denote where you think the balls might be located.

Game play is simple: Click on the green balls to turn on a laser, and click on the grid to mark a position. When you think you've marked all the positions, click the Done button (with the thumb icon), or click the white flag button to give up. If you're still lost, select Help from the Help menu to read the online tutorial.

kmahjongg

KDE has a solitaire mahjongg game very similar to the GNOME version. Game play is identical: Remove matching pairs of free tiles, where *free* means they aren't bordered on both horizontal sides by other tiles.

Although it's a much simpler version than its GNOME counterpart, several options are available in kmahjongg. If you're bored with the green background, you can select Load Background Image from the View menu to load your own GIF. If you make a mistake, select Undo last move from the Game menu, and the tiles from the last move will be restored. And if you're having trouble, you can also select Demo mode, which shows a sample game; Help me, which shows a possible move; and Show matching tiles, which shows any possible moves based on a selected tile. All these options are also available on the Game menu. If you need more help, you can view the help pages by selecting Help on the Help menu.

kmines

This KDE's Minesweeper clone, which looks and behaves similar to the Windows version. You start the game with a field of covered squares and must uncover the squares to find mines. If you uncover a square that is adjacent to mines, the number of mines will be printed in that square. If you think that you know where a mine is, you can flag it with the right mouse button. If you select a square with a mine, the game is over, and all the mines are shown to you.

When you've become bored with an 8×8 grid, you can select a larger field size. From the Level menu, select Normal or Expert for a larger board, or select Custom to choose your own board size and number of mines. You can also redefine the keys by selecting Keys from the Options menu if you don't like the defaults.

konquest

This multiplayer sci-fi strategy game puts you in charge of a planet, with the goal of taking over the galaxy. Each player can send ships to other planets in an effort to take them over. You'll need to think of a good strategy about offensive attack fleets versus defensive home ships, and you'll need to budget your ships well. You automatically construct new ships, and you can read the planet status indicator to determine the strength of your rivals. The evil overlord who takes over everything wins the game.

To play, select New Game from the Game menu. You must first enter the names of all your players. A window will open, and you can enter everyone's name into a list by typing the names in the name box and clicking the Add button. As you enter more players, a map of the universe is constructed showing where all of the planets will be located. You can also change the number of neutral planets and turns by adjusting the values of Neutral Planets and Turns at the bottom of the window. After you have added all the players, click the Start Game button.

Each player takes turns moving their fleets from planet to planet. When it is your turn, move your fleets by clicking on a source (a planet containing your fleet ships), clicking on a destination, and then entering the number of fleets you want to move in the box at the top of the window. When you are finished, click the End Turn button.

To learn more about the strategies behind konquest, read the online help by selecting Help from the Help menu.

kpat

kpat is the KDE version of solitaire. It's actually nine versions of the solo card game, ranging from Klondike to Ten to Freecell. If you're bored, you can use the Full Auto version to watch the computer play the more esoteric versions of the game.

kpoker

Here's a highly addictive one-player video poker. The beauty of this game is its simplicity. You start with $100 cash, and you click the Draw! button, at $5 a hit. Click the cards you want to keep, draw again, and see if you've won. It's easy to sit down and play one hand or 20; if you don't know your poker hands, you can check the online help for a good explanation of the game by selecting Help from the Help menu.

kreversi

The KDE version of the classic Othello game looks much simpler than the GNOME version, but it's the same idea. To play, you must place your pieces around your opponent's pieces, which reverses them to the same color as your pieces. Click on an empty square to place a piece. It must be opposite a piece of your color, with at least one of your opponent's pieces in between. The person who holds the majority of the board wins.

If you need help playing, you can select Get hint from the Game menu for help with your next move. You can also use the Load game and Save game options on the File menu to save and load unfinished games. And if you're tired of the stock grey background, the Set background image option on the Options menu enables you to select from several stock background patterns to spruce up your game.

ksame

Similar to same-gnome, this puzzle requires you to erase pieces by selecting one that's connected to others of the same color. You must click on a piece that's connected to at least one other piece, and you get points only for erasing three or more at once. The best strategy is to try to remove all of one color at the beginning, to make it easier to score big later. This version doesn't have any options to change the pieces, but it's still a very addictive game.

Part

III

Ch

17

kshisen

If you like mahjongg, you might like this similar game, which is played with the same tiles. It's also a solitaire game, and you must remove all the tiles to finish the puzzle, but the matching system is different. This time, tiles match if they are connected with, at most, three connecting lines. The lines can be vertical or horizontal but not diagonal. Like mahjongg, there is one possible solution; if you remove the wrong pairs, you can mess up the whole game. If you're stuck, try the Get Hint option on the Game menu. You can also change size and level in the Options menu to make the game easier or more difficult.

ksokoban

This Japanese classic is another one of those simple yet compelling logic games. You start in a brick maze, with a bunch of jewels around you and a green area to hold them (see Figure 17.4). Your job is to move the jewels into the holding area. You can push a jewel by standing behind it and pushing against it, but you can't pull, turn, or otherwise manipulate it. This means that you must be careful where you move them because there are plenty of corners and cubbyholes in the maze where you could push a jewel in but never get it out. It's also very easy to push a jewel into place, only to find that you can't run to the other side and push it where it needs to go.

FIG. 17.4
Push the jewels to the holding area in ksokoban.

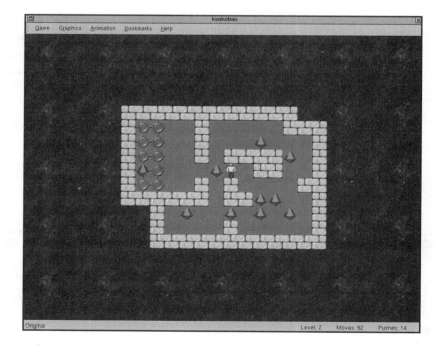

To play the game, use the arrow keys to move through the maze and push the jewels. When you move all the jewels to their proper places, you advance to a more difficult level. You can bookmark your place or choose a different level from a list. As an added touch, there are easy levels for the kids and much more difficult levels if you feel up to the challenge.

ksmiletris

Of course, KDE has a Tetris clone as well. This one uses weird smiley faces in the block design, although you can change them to a few other colorful symbols. Use the left and right arrow keys to move, the up and down arrow keys to rotate the pieces, and the spacebar to drop them. This clone doesn't add anything new to the game, but it is a bit more colorful than other versions.

ksnake

In this game of agility, you're a snake that needs to eat all the apples in the room and then leave without running into a wall or someone else. The problem is that each time you eat an apple, your tail grows longer. And if you spend too much time messing around, more apples appear.

To play, use the arrow keys to move the snake. You can also configure options to change the keys used, start on another level, or introduce more computer snakes by selecting these items from the Options menu. If you tire of the built-in levels, details in the online help, available by selecting Help from the Help menu, explain how to create your own custom levels.

Other Games for X

In addition to the games included with Red Hat Linux 6.0, many games are available for download on the Internet. Most of these are distributed in source form, which means that you need to compile them on your system. Usually, this involves little more than unpacking the distribution and issuing a `make all; make install`. Sometimes, however, games might not work in Red Hat Linux 6.0 without some minor adjustments. For more details, read the documentation that came with the download.

The big repository of good Linux games on the Internet is at `ftp://metalab.unc.edu/pub/linux/games/`. Take a look around, and see what interests you. Maybe you're into text role-playing games or arcade-style video games. Either way, there's a lot of stuff here to download. Following are some of my favorite X-based games that are on metalab for the taking.

Part
III
Ch
17

LinCity

If you've ever played the ever-popular SimCity, here's a Linux clone that's just as compulsively entertaining. In this simulation, you're the mayor of a city, and it's your job to plan everything from the ground up. Build houses, factories, roads—just don't forget the problems of urban decay, pollution, inadequate power grids, and everything else. This is an excellent version, although the author appears to be from England, because sometimes the British English threw me. For example, it took me a few plays to figure out that I needed to build garbage dumps because they weren't called garbage dumps. This game will run under X or SVGALib, and the source is located at `ftp://metalab.unc.edu/pub/Linux/games/strategy/lincity-1.11.tar.gz`.

XEvil

Pure evil is the easiest way to describe this side-view shoot-em-up arcade game. Ninjas and aliens attack you violently with chainsaws, flame-throwers, and other heavy-duty weaponry. It's your job to kill or be killed. Network multiplayer games are also supported. This game isn't for the weak of heart, but it can be a lot of fun.

You can download Xevil from `ftp://metalab.unc.edu/pub/Linux/games/arcade/xevil-1.5.src.tgz`.

Asteroids

Somehow, a good Asteroids clone slipped through the cracks in Red Hat Linux 6.0. There's one listed in the KDE games' RPM information, but it's not there. If you love this Atari classic as much as I do, you can download the source and install it yourself.

There are a few versions of Asteroids, but try downloading `ftp://metalab.unc.edu/pub/Linux/games/arcade/asteroids/xoids-1.5-1.src.rpm` first. The directory in which this is located also holds a few other asteroids games, including the original X consortium version, in case you have problems with xoids.

Character-Based Games

Although many games utilize the graphical user interface of Linux, there are also text-based games as well. Back in the old days of UNIX, not everyone had an X display on their desktop, and a plethora of text-based strategy games and other amusements were written. Many of these classic games have been ported to Linux. Although Red Hat Linux 6,0 does include ASCII games such as GNU chess, fortune, and trojka, many other text-based games can be found on the Internet, usually in source-code format. Although they aren't as impressive as other graphical games, they can still be very challenging and addictive. Also, if your Linux box is on the Internet and accessed by others via telnet, they can play these games without the Linux console.

BSD games

If you're looking for classic UNIX text-based games, the BSD game archive is just the ticket. This is a collected archive of more than 40 games and amusements that were developed for BSD UNIX decades ago. You might recognize some of these programs; many were later ported to MS DOS, the Apple II, and dozens of other operating systems. Highlights of the package include these:

- **adventure**—In this fantasy role-playing game, you explore a dungeon and look for treasure.
- **atc**—This is a real-time simulation of air traffic control.
- **backgammon**—This classic board game also includes teachgammon, an interactive tutorial.
- **cribbage**—This is an ASCII version of the card game.
- **fish**—Go fish! It's you versus the computer in this children's card game.
- **hangman**—Try to figure out the word in six guesses, before all the pieces of the body are assembled.
- **monop**—This is a character-based version of the Parker Brothers board game Monopoly.
- **robots**—This is the robots-chasing-human game from which grobots and gnobots II are based.
- **sail**—This simulates more than 20 different historical naval battles.
- **tetris-bsd**—This is a text-based version of Tetris.
- **trek**—Boldly go where no man has gone before in this text-based Star Trek simulation.
- **wump**—Hunt the Wumpus, a text adventure where you must find the Wumpus and try to kill him with your arrows.

The BSD games package was not included with Red Hat Linux 6.0 but was included with Red Hat Linux 5.2. An information page with a pointer to the BSD games RPM and source is located at `http://www.redhat.com/support/products/rh-linux/package-listing/5.2/i386/bsd-games-2.1-5.i386.html`.

Not all of these games work perfectly with Red Hat Linux 6.0, but many will work fine with a little bit of imagination. Each game has a man page with more information.

MUDs

Multiuser dungeons (MUDs) are much like text-based adventure games where you issue commands to move through a dungeon or a maze, collecting weapons, fighting monsters, and looking for treasure. The big difference with a MUD is that other people are also in the dungeon with you, and you can talk to them in real time. A MUD is run as a server on a computer that's connected to the Internet, and players can connect to it with a telnet program or other client. Once connected, players create fictional characters, explore their surroundings, interact with each other and with computer-generated characters and monsters, and sometimes help design the rooms and objects within the game. Although MUDs originally started as extensions of combat-oriented fantasy role-playing games such as Dungeons and Dragons, many MUD players now are more interested in the social aspect of talking to people from all over the world. Both combat-oriented and social MUDs flourish on the Internet, with hundreds of servers currently running. It's easy to play a MUD using Red Hat Linux 6.0, and it's even possible, with a lot of work, to run your own MUD server on a Linux machine.

Playing Other MUDs   The best way to get started with MUDs is to play one of the hundreds of MUDs available on the Internet. A good source of beginning information is http://www.mudconnect.com/, which has listings of various MUDs on the Internet. Much like Web sites, MUDs are constantly appearing and disappearing on the Internet, although there are also some long-running favorites.

Before you start, you might want to read a beginner's FAQ, such as http://www.mudconnect.com/mudfaq/mudfaq-p1.html. This will not only tell you how to find and connect with MUDs, but it also will tell you what to expect within games. It's easy for a new player to perturb a veteran player, so make sure to observe any appropriate etiquette.

When you find a MUD, you'll usually be given a hostname and a port number. To connect, simply telnet to the host and port, and you'll enter the MUD. For example, if somebody told you there was a good MUD at fredsmud.com on port 4000, use this command:

```
telnet fredsmud.com 4000
```

Inside the game, you're usually presented with some sort of menu, which allows you to read background information about the game, create a character, change your password, or enter the game. The first time you play, you'll need to create a character. This gives you a unique login name and password for the game. After you've created a character, you can enter the game. You'll get a description of the starting room and a command prompt. Commands vary from MUD to MUD, but you can usually type commands or help to view a list. Usually, compass directions will move you through rooms (north, south, east, west), inventory will show you what you're holding, take will let you grab something, and say will let you talk to others. There are many other commands, and each command usually has abbreviations or synonyms, so take a look at the help or ask others in the MUD if you are stuck.

Although you can use a telnet program to connect to a MUD, many client programs also can be used to play. These clients offer features such as macros to enable you to execute sequences of commands with a few key presses and also have text-filtering options that add highlighting or that separate your commands from the incoming messages.

Several MUD clients are available for Linux, ranging from the simple to the esoteric. For a list, along with instructions on their use, see `http://www.mudconnect.com/mudfaq/mudfaq-p2.html`. For the most part, you'll need to download source code and compile it on your Red Hat Linux 6.0 system to get the client running. For more details, see the client's documentation.

Setting Up Your Own MUD   If you've played some other MUDs regularly and you're ready to take the plunge and set up your own server, Linux is one of the most popular ways to get started. It should be stated that running a MUD is very much a labor of love. Expect some initial problems in setting up the server, and be prepared to spend lots of time administering the game. This isn't for the weak of heart or hardware, either. You'll need a fast, dedicated Internet connection (such as Ethernet, xDSL, or a cable modem), at least 100MB of disk space, some knowledge of C, and lots of free time. You should spend a lot of time on other MUDs before you decide to go through with this yourself, and talk to other MUD administrators about their woes before you get started.

Because MUDs are usually distributed as source code and are heavily customized by their administrators, there are scores of different MUD distributions, each a variation of some earlier version. A handful of vanilla distributions have been around for decades and have been modified as UNIX has grown and changed. Meanwhile, many regional variations of these vanilla distributions crop up all over the Internet, with differences ranging from cosmetic to almost complete redesign. In general, most MUD distributions tend to fall into the combat or non-combat categories. The FAQ at `http://www.mudconnect.com/mudfaq/mudfaq-p2.html` provides some information on choosing MUD software. When you're making a decision on what code base to use, be sure to find existing MUDs using the same software, and test-play them or ask their administrators for advice or testimony. Also try to compile a distribution before you fall in love with it; although most MUD distributions were written for UNIX platforms, they aren't always flexible or portable. Some compile with screens of warnings or require significant amounts of recoding, configuration, and playing with things such as makefiles before they will compile and run under Red Hat Linux 6.0.

One of the cleanest and most portable MUDs available for Linux is CircleMUD. Based on the very popular and widely used DikuMUD system, CircleMud is a combat-based MUD that has been refined and made much more administrator-friendly for Linux. It compiles right out of the box under Red Hat Linux 6.0 with no changes, configuration hassles, or even a single warning. It comes with extensive documentation on running and customizing your MUD, and there's a development mailing list with a full archive available on the Internet. Although the software license restricts you from using CircleMUD for profit, it comes with full source code. For more information on obtaining CircleMUD, visit its home page at `http://www.circlemud.org`.

Part
III

Ch
17

Other Character-Based Games

Of course, many other text-based games are available for Linux. One of the biggest archive of text-based games is located at `ftp://metalab.unc.edu/pub/Linux/games`. Many text-based games are available for download in the `dungeon`, `role`, and `textrpg` directories. Recommended titles to look for include empire, nethack, rogue, and moria.

About Quake

Quake is the latest line of 3D, first-person combat games by id Software. A more advanced descendant of Doom, Quake pits you against aliens you must hunt down and kill before they kill you. You must complete levels, find secrets, and pick up new weapons to keep up with the challenge. There's also a multiplayer option where you can fight other players on a LAN or across the Internet.

Quake and Quake II each have a background story, to explain why you're running through caves and shooting monsters. If you have the registered version, you'll see some of it in the form of video clips and more in the included manual. In the original Quake, an enemy code-named Quake used an experimental slipgate device to move troops into military bases, to steal weapons and kill troops. You're the one-man army that needs to stop this at all costs. In Quake II, you're back to fight the aliens, called the Strogg, on their own turf, by traveling in a spaceship to their own planet. The story is interesting, but you don't need to pay attention too much. Although the game does have missions that need to be solved, you'll be spending most of your time in firefights with the half-alien, half-robot Strogg.

Currently, two versions of the game exist: Quake and Quake II, with the latter having a vast amount of new technology, including an updated game engine, better multiplayer gaming, and lots of new weapons, monsters, and levels (see Figure 17.5). Additional Mission Packs for each version also offer additional episodes and adventures. In addition, by the time you read this, Quake III will be released. Although Quake is most popular as a DOS/Windows game, it can be played under Linux with some slight modifications.

This section discusses the installation and play of Quake II. It's the version currently in stores, and it's much more updated than the original Quake. If you are trying to install the first Quake game, most of the steps given are similar.

For more information on Quake, see id Software's site at `http://www.idsoftware.com`, or the LinuxQuake page at `http://www.linuxquake.com`.

Although Quake can be a lot of fun, it's not for everyone. It's rated Mature (17+) by the ESRB for Animated Blood and Animated Violence. Because the overall theme of the game is to destroy your opponents before they kill you, and because the violence is realistically depicted, some people might find Quake offensive. Buyer beware!

FIG. 17.5
A Quake II game is in
progress.

Quake Requirements

Quake is incredibly resource-intensive and requires a fairly up-to-date machine with a fast
audio and video setup. This is no simple puzzle game, but it will shine on any serious PC
hardware. Here are the minimum hardware requirements:

- Pentium 166
- Kernel 2.0.24 or higher
- 200–400MB disk space
- 16MB of RAM
- Double-speed CD-ROM
- A 100% compatible Sound Blaster sound card that works in Linux

Quake will benefit from a faster CPU, and you'll need even more disk space if you want to
install Mission Packs. You'll also get better video performance if you have a 3DFX or
OpenGL-based hardware accelerator, 24MB of RAM, and an optional video renderer.

Obtaining Quake

The Linux versions of Quake and Quake II consist of two pieces: a binary distribution of the
Quake engine program and configuration for Linux, and the platform-independent levels,
sounds, and graphics files that make up the Quake missions. This means that it's possible to
use the Windows version of Quake on Linux after obtaining the necessary binary files.

Download the Demo and Binaries

If you want to try Quake II before purchasing it, you can download a demo version for
Windows and then download the Linux binaries and run it in Red Hat Linux 6.0. Although it's
free, the demo is a 40MB download. Also, it comes with only three levels and no CD audio
soundtrack. Plus, you can't use the demo version with any add-on levels such as Mission

Packs, or other products or modifications, such as QuakeWorld. To download the demo, go to `ftp://ftp.idsoftware.com/idstuff/quake2/q2-314-demo-x86.exe`. If you have trouble reaching id Software's site, the following mirror sites also contain the contents of the idstuff directory:

- `ftp://ftp.cdrom.com/pub/idgames/idstuff` (California, USA)
- `ftp://ftp.gamesnet.net/idsoftware` (California, USA)
- `ftp://ftp.linuxquake.com/pub/idgames/idstuff` (Ohio, USA)
- `ftp://mirrors.telepac.pt/pub/idgames/idstuff` (Lisbon, Portugal)

After downloading the demo, you'll need the Linux binaries. These are available for Red Hat Linux 6.0 at `ftp.idsoftware.com/idstuff/quake2/unix/quake2-3.20-glibc-6.i386.rpm`.

Use a Windows CD-ROM and Download the Binaries

If you've got a Quake II disk for Windows lying around, you're in luck. You can also play the Windows version of Quake under Linux, with a few other additions. This means that you can go to most computer stores and pick up the original Quake II CD-ROM for Windows for about $20, and use it on your PC under Windows or Red Hat Linux 6.0.

If you have the Windows CD-ROM, you will also need to download the Linux binaries. These are available for Red Hat Linux 6.0 at `ftp.idsoftware.com/idstuff/quake2/unix/quake2-3.20-glibc-6.i386.rpm`.

Note that if you have Quake on one computer and you install it with another, you must delete the installation on one computer to honor id Software's licensing agreement.

Buy a Linux Distribution

Linux distributions of Quake II exist, although these might be harder to find. Macmillan Software offers Quake and Quake II distributions for Linux; the Quake II Colossus for Linux includes Quake II, Quake II Mission Pack I, and Quake II Mission Pack II, and all the Linux binaries in one package for about $40. If you can't find this in the store, you can order it on the Web at `http://www.macmillansoftware.com`.

Installing Quake II

First, you will need to determine where you will install Quake II. The standard location is `/usr/local/games/quake2`, which is where the packages for the Linux binaries are installed. If you want to install somewhere else, you'll need to move the binaries after installing them. Before beginning, create the installation directory if it doesn't already exist.

Installing from a Windows CD-ROM

To start the installation, mount the Quake II CD-ROM in your CD-ROM drive with the following command:

```
mount -t iso9660 /dev/cdrom /mnt/cdrom
```

Then, copy the CD-ROM to your system with the following commands:

```
cd /usr/local/games/quake2
cp -r /mnt/cdrom/Install/Data/* .
```

After the copy completes, you can remove some Windows-specific files:

```
rm -f /usr/local/quake2/*.dll
rm -f /usr/local/quake2/quake2.exe
rm -f /usr/local/quake2/baseq2/gamex386.dll
```

If you don't have 450MB for the full install, you can do a partial install without the between-scenes videos that takes about 200MB. Instead of copying the entire CD, do this instead:

```
cd /usr/local/games/quake2
mkdir baseq2
cp /mnt/cdrom/Install/Data/baseq2/pak0.pak baseq2
cp -r /mnt/cdrom/Install/Data/baseq2/players baseq2
ln -s /mnt/cdrom/Install/Data/baseq2/video baseq2/video
```

After copying the files from the CD, skip forward to the section "Installing the Linux Binaries."

Using an Existing Windows Install

If you already have Quake II installed on the Windows partition of your machine, you can either move the files to your Linux partition or create a link from your Windows partition. If Quake on your Windows partition is at /mnt/win/games/quake2/, you can do this to copy the files:

```
cd /usr/local/games/quake2
cp -r /mnt/win/games/quake2/baseq2 .
```

Or, you can simply make a link:

```
cd /usr/local/games/quake2
ln -s /mnt/win/ga,es/quake2/baseq2 .
```

After copying or linking the files, skip forward to the section "Installing the Linux Binaries."

Installing the Downloadable Demo

The 40MB demo distribution comes in the form of a self-extracting zip file, with an .exe extension. You can open this with the Linux unzip program, which is available from `http://sunsite.unc.edu/pub/Linux/utils/compress/unzip-5.31.tar.gz`. To unzip the archive, enter these lines:

```
cd /usr/local/games/quake2
unzip q2-214-demo-x86.exe
```

You then need to remove some Windows-specific files and move some other things:

```
rm -rf Splash Setup.exe
mv Install/Data/baseq2 .
mv Install/Data/DOCS docs
rm -rf Install
rm -f baseq2/gamex86.dll
```

After completing these steps, you're ready for the next section, on installing the Linux binaries.

Installing the Linux Binaries

After you've installed the data files, installation of the Linux binaries is simple. After making sure you're logged in as root, issue the following command:

```
rpm -Uvh quake2-3.20-glibc-6.i386.rpm
```

If RPM complains about a missing library called `libglide2x.so` and you don't have a 3Dfx video card, don't worry about it. Just add `-nodeps` to the previous command, and continue with the installation.

Installing from a Linux Distribution

If you purchased Quake II for Linux, follow the instructions included with the product. Typically, this involves mounting the CD-ROM and then running a setup script, which installs everything in the `/usr/local/games/quake` or `/usr/local/games/quake2` directory. See the instructions that come with the distribution for more details.

Running Quake II

If you have a Quake II CD, put it in the CD-ROM drive before you begin. If you do, the CD audio soundtrack will be used while you play.

To start Quake in X, use the following command:

```
cd /usr/local/games/quake2
./quake2 +set vid_ref softx
```

After a long pause, an animation of the id Software logo will appear, and then a demo sequence will load and begin.

The +set vid_ref softx argument to quake2 sets the video renderer client variable (cvar) to determine which renderer is used by the game. Several options are available for different displays:

Option	Video Display
soft	This uses the SVGAlib library for full-screen play. SVGAlib is a video library that directly supports your VGA display, without using X11. This gives a much better picture, faster video, and more detail—plus, you don't need to run X to use it. If you do use this option while running X in Red Hat Linux 6.0, the screen will momentarily switch from X to a full-screen Quake game. When you exit Quake, your X console will return.
softx	This runs Quake II in a window of your X display. Use this if you want to run Quake, but don't want the rest of your windows in X to vanish.
gl	This uses one of two OpenGL drivers: either Mesa 3-D and Linux GLIDE, or 3Dfx's mini-OpenGL Quake driver.
glx	This uses hardware-based Open GL in X Window.

Part
III

Ch
17

Using the OpenGL drivers requires the Mesa 3-D Library to be installed. See the README file included with Quake for more details.

Also, the following cvars can be set on the command line:

Cvar	Purpose
nocdaudio	Set this to a nonzero value to disable the CD audio. The default value is 0.
sndspeed	Set this to change the sound speed. If set to zero, the default, the sound speed will try to automatically determine the correct speed. Other possible values are 11025, 22051, 44100, and 8000.
sndchannels	Set this to 2 for stereo sound, the default, or to 1 for mono sound.
nostdout	Set this to a nonzero value to disable the output of console messages to standard out. The default value is zero.

Playing Quake II

When you start Quake II, you enter a demo sequence, where a computer-controlled marine runs through the first level. If this is your first time, it might be helpful to watch the computer play, at least until some Stroggs kill it. When you've had enough, press the Escape key to open the main menu. The following options are available:

Game	Start, Save, or Load a Game
Multiplayer	Start a server, join a server, or change your character configuration
Options	Customize your sound, mouse, keyboard, and joystick settings
Video	Change video renderers, size, or other settings
Quit	End the game

Use the arrow keys to move between options, and press the Enter key to select them.

To begin a game, go to the Game menu, press the Enter key, and choose a skill setting. If you have the full version, you'll see an introduction video that tells the start of the story (you can press any key to skip it). After it is complete, you'll be in the alien city of Stroggos and ready to start hunting.

To move, use the arrow keys or the mouse. To run, hold the Shift key while moving. You can also jump with the Spacebar and crouch with the C key. To fire your gun, press the Ctrl key or your left mouse button. To look up or down, use the A and Z keys.

A status bar at the bottom of the screen shows your health, armor, ammunition, and current weapon. As you move around, you'll see items you can pick up. These include other weapons, ammunition, first-aid kits, and armor. Simply move over an item to pick it up. An icon is briefly shown when you take something. You can see all your inventory by pressing the Tab key. To scroll through your inventory of items, use the [and] keys. You can switch to holding another item by pressing Enter or pressing a number key.

At the start of the game, and each time you complete a mission objective, a small F1 icon will start blinking. This means that you need to access your field computer. It details your position, objectives, and kills, and gives you other important information. You can see it at any time by pressing F1.

The following weapons are available throughout the game:

- **Blaster**—This is your default weapon, and you cannot drop it. It doesn't require ammunition, but it doesn't do much unless your target is right in front of you.

- **Shotgun**—The shotgun uses shells for ammunition. It's a great short-range weapon and works okay for long-range targets. The only problem is that it's slower between shots.

- **Super shotgun**—This is slower than a shotgun, and it uses shells faster, but it's worth it. The super shotgun causes great terror, even at longer ranges.

- **Machine gun**—With excellent range and decent damage, this can make a great all-around weapon. Its main problems are that the kickback makes it shoot high, and it's easy to go through 100 rounds of ammo in a panic situation if you're not easy on the trigger.

- **Chain gun**—The machine gun's big brother has some incredible takedown power, but it also eats through lots of ammunition. It has to spin up before it starts firing, so it's not good for short bursts.

- **Hand grenade**—To use one of these, click and then hold it before throwing. The longer you hold it, the farther it'll go. If you want to lay low and attack from a hidden position, the hand grenade is silent, so you won't give yourself away. Well, it's silent unless you forget to throw it.

- **Grenade launcher**—This is a great long-range weapon that combines the grenade's lethal firepower with the accuracy of a rifle. Don't try to use one in a confined area, though.

- **Rocket launcher**—Even better than the grenade launcher, this heavy hitter can do a lot of damage from the next room over. Just don't accidentally point it at a wall and fire.

- **Hyper blaster**—An energy-based version of the chain gun, this weapon starts up automatically and does heavy amounts of damage, but it also drains energy cells in a hurry.

- **Rail gun**—The depleted uranium slugs fired at high velocities by this high-end weapon will slice through anything in its path. Check out the neat spiral trail of blue smoke left in its wake.

- **BFG**—When you absolutely, positively need to kill everyone in the room, this is the guy. The big—well, freaking big gun—is the top-end weapon in Quake II, and you'll never fear walking the streets of Stroggos with one in your hand.

In addition, you'll see military supplies that you'll need to carry. Keep in mind the following information:

- Different weapons require different types of ammunition: shells, bullets, energy cells, grenades, and rockets. There's a set limit on how much of each you can carry. For example, if you're carrying 200 bullets, you won't be able to pick up any more.

- Your health can be restored in a few different ways. In general, health kits (the rectangular boxes with the red cross) will raise it back toward its limit, and stimpacks (the potion-looking bottles) will increase your limit. When you are at your limit, additional health kits will do you no good. But, you can make a note as to where they are, in case somebody knocks you senseless two rooms later.

- Items such as the underwater breather, quad damage, and invulnerability take effect only when you select them.

- You can carry only a limited amount of stuff. If you find a bandoleer or heavy pack, it will let you carry more.

You should now know enough commands to get you moving around and killing things. You should take a look at the user's guide that comes with Quake if you want to progress through the mission without getting killed yourself. You need to complete the mission objectives

Part

III

Ch

17

outlined in your field computer to finish each level. Also, each level has secret areas you'll want to find because they contain caches of weaponry.

Here are a few other hints that might save your skin:

- You'll find many barrel-shaped containers. These contain radioactive explosives, and you don't want to be near one when it gets shot. Although they are powerful, they are light enough that you can push them around—maybe against a weak area in a wall.

- You can swim in the Stroggan water, but if you stay underwater for too long, you'll start to lose health and drown. Press the Spacebar to surface and take a breath, and keep pressing it to tread water. The arrow keys or mouse will move you underwater, but at a much slower rate. If you can't crawl out of the water, press the Spacebar to jump out.

- Watch out for toxic waste, lava, and traps. All three can cause some serious health problems.

The game continues until your health goes below zero. At any time, you can press the Escape key, go to the Game menu, and save the game. Later, instead of starting from scratch, you can load the game from the Game menu and return to the same place in Stroggos, with the same weapons and health.

Quake II Mission Packs

If you're tired of the included Quake II mission and you want more adventure, you can buy the Quake II Mission Packs. The Mission Pack CD-ROM contains two new missions: The Reckoning and Ground Zero. You can buy the Windows CD-ROM of both missions for about $20; it's included with some Linux distributions of Quake II. If you bought the Windows CD-ROM, you need to copy the `rogue` and `xatrix` directories to your quake installation directory. If you have the Linux version, there is a setup script in the root directory of the CD-ROM.

To play The Reckoning, use the following command from the `quake2` directory:

```
./quake2 +set game xatrix
```

To play Ground Zero, use the following command:

```
./quake2 +set game rogue
```

Each new mission contains new levels, weapons, and enemies. Look forward to using ion rippers, traps, particle cannons, chainsaws, and plasma beams to tear apart your enemies. Mission packs also support multiplayer games and even offer new features. You can play cooperative games, where up to four people play against the monsters of Stroggos. There's also a tag game in Ground Zero; pick up the tag token, and you're it. The lucky player that rubs you out gets the token, and the game continues. Ground Zero also introduces some great deathmatch weapons, including a vengeance spear that attacks your opponent when your health drops, and the antimatter bomb, which instantly destroys everything in the room.

Multiplayer Quake

If you're playing only single-user Quake, you're experiencing only half the fun. You can also play Quake with multiple players, either hunting each other in a deathmatch, or playing a game with a common goal, such as Capture the Flag (CTF). Quake has a built-in multiplayer server that enables other people with Quake to connect to your machine via TCP/IP. Their Quake software functions as a client, and yours functions as a client and a server. Or, you can be the client and connect to somebody else's server.

The easiest way to start a multiplayer game is to sneak into work at night with a few friends and get Quake running on a few machines that are connected via TCP/IP. One person needs to run the Quake server, so figure out who has the fastest machine and get that person to do it. Running the server is easy: Go to the Multiplayer menu and select the Start Network Server option. When you start the server, you can pick options for the game, including the initial map, a time limit, a player limit, and many other options to control the game.

When one person has a server going, everyone else should go to the Multiplayer menu and select Join Network Server. Enter the name or IP number of the machine running the server, and then join. You can also select player setup first and change your name, the look of your Marine, or your connection speed.

When you enter the game, you'll be dropped into Stroggos, except that there will be other Marines firing at you. To talk to everyone, use the T key, and then type in a message. Moving through the levels isn't the object anymore—your only task is to pulverize the other players. When the game ends, the server program shuts down automatically when you exit Quake.

If you're interested in keeping a server running without running the client, you can do that, too. Issue the following command to start a standalone server:

```
./quake2 +set dedicated 1
```

You can also start a Quake2 server with a config file, like this:

```
./quake2 +set dedicated 1 +exec server.cfg
```

The server.cfg file should look something like this:

```
set timelimit 20
set fraglimit 25
set dmflags 532
map fact 3
```

If you use a config file, it must contain a map line, or the server won't load a map.

You don't have to get together a bunch of people to play multiplayer Quake; dedicated Quake servers are running all over the Internet. If you know of one, you simply enter its IP number in the Join Network Server menu, and you'll be connected with other Quake players who suddenly want to cut you in half with a rail gun. Practice thoroughly before you start looking for

Quake servers on the Internet—it always seems like everyone else in a deathmatch is bigger, faster, and more deadly at it.

Server Finders

You're probably wondering how to find out about other multiplayer Quake games on the Internet. There isn't a central repository of Quake servers, and by the time you read about a server on the Web, it's probably gone. To solve this problem, many third parties have developed server finders, or programs that scour the Internet looking for Quake servers. Some servers offer more functionality, such as finding servers for multiple games, checking network delay times for faster games, and automatically launching Quake when a server is selected.

Many of these programs were written specifically for Windows. One of the most popular commercial versions is called GameSpy; unfortunately, there is not a Linux port available. However, other free server finder programs are available for Linux.

One of the best graphical server finder programs out there is called xqf. It was written with the GTK+ toolkit for X Window and is actually a front end for another program, called Qstat. It displays lists of known servers, their rules, and player information, and it launches games when you find a server you like.

For more information on xqf, or to download xqf and Qstat, check out `http://www.linuxgames.com/xqf/`.

If you don't play Quake in X and you want a character-based server finder, try the QuickSpy program. It's also a front end for Qstat. It's no longer in production, but you can download a newer version, called QuickSpy2, from `http://www.xnet.com/~efflandt/quickspy2/`.

Troubleshooting Games

Games can be the most complicated software for Linux. They are often resource-intensive and use libraries or hardware features usually untouched by other packages. Also, many of the games mentioned in this chapter were written by individuals and are only occasionally fixed or updated. Most games have a man page you can read to learn more about them and research possible bugs. Also, check the `/usr/doc` directory; in Red Hat Linux 6.0, many software packages have a directory of documentation located there. If all else fails, try a Web search; many of these games, especially the GNOME titles, have more documentation on the Internet.

The following are some other frequently asked questions about Linux games.

Q. Why doesn't audio work on some games?

A. Some games, including many of the X games included with Red Hat Linux 6.0, were designed to run on several UNIX machines. Because of this, they simply dump sound effects audio to `/dev/audio` instead of playing the sound properly. Depending on your sound card and sound drivers, this can lead to garbled or missing audio. Unfortunately, there's no real solution to this, except to report the bug to the author and hope that it's fixed in a later version.

Q. How do I get my joystick working?

A. Joystick drivers are now part of the Linux kernel, which means that it's possible to get them working, but it's not easy. If you have the kernel source, take a look at the file `/usr/src/linux/Documentation/joystick.txt`. If you have an analog joystick, all you usually need to do is recompile the kernel with the joystick driver included or with support for the joystick module. After your joystick is supported, you can use it in many games, such as Quake. For other games, you can install a program called joytokey, which will convert joystick movement into key presses. Details on joytokey are given in the `joystick.txt` file mentioned previously.

Q. I installed more games in `/usr/games` and `/usr/local/games`. Why don't they work?

A. Although `/usr/games` and `/usr/local/games` are standard locations for system and additional games, and although the fortune and trojka packages are installed in `/usr/games`, these directories are not included in your path by default in Red Hat Linux 6.0. Make sure to add `/usr/games` and `/usr/local/games` to your path in your `.bash-profile`, or make the change systemwide in `/etc/profile`.

Q. Why can't I compile a game I downloaded that uses X?

A. To compile X applications, you need several libraries and tools (such as imake) that are included but not always installed with Red Hat Linux 6.0. Using gnorpm, make sure that all X development libraries are installed, and be sure to read the documentation that came with the software to see if it needs any other optional libraries you'll have to download yourself.

Q. Why does key repeat get turned off while I'm playing Quake?

A. For some reason, the X version of Quake turns off key repeat. Sometimes after a crash, it will remain off. To turn it back on, issue the following command:

```
Xset r on
```

Q. In multiplayer Quake games over the Internet, why do things lock up for a few seconds or happen long after I've told them to happen?

A. Although the network play in Quake was designed with the Internet in mind, lag problems plagued people with 28.8 BPS modems. In response, id Software designed a special version of Quake called QuakeWorld, which took care of many modem performance issues in a simple game that offered just multiplayer missions. You can't play single-player missions in QuakeWorld, just multiplayer network deathmatch games on special QuakeWorld servers.

To install QuakeWorld, you must have a registered version of Quake. The software can be found at `ftp://ftp.idsoftware.com/idstuff/quakeworld/unix/qwcl-2.30-glibc-1.i386.rpm`. QuakeWorld servers can also be found by xqf and other server finder software.

For more information of QuakeWorld, go to `http://www.quakeworld.net`.

Q. Why won't Quake II let me use all the video modes in the video menu under SVGAlib?

A. Although the same set of screen dimensions are always listed in the video menu, your SVGAlib configuration might not be capable of creating all these modes. When you start Quake II with the SVGA renderer (`ref_soft.so`), a list of the possible SVGAlib modes is printed to the console. For example:

```
------- Loading ref_soft.so -------
Using RIVA 128 driver, 4096KB.
mode 320:  200 1075253220
mode 320:  240 1075253220
mode 320:  400 1075253220
mode 360:  480 1075253220
mode 640:  480 1075253220
mode 800:  600 1075253220
mode 1024:  768 1075253220
mode 1280: 1024 1075253220
```

These are the only modes you will be able to use from the Video menu. So, in this example, you wouldn't be able to switch to 512×384 mode.

It's possible to define new SVGAlib video modes for some chipsets in `libvga.config`, so you might be able create your own video mode this way. See the SVGAlib documentation for more details on this topic.

Q. Why am I constantly seeing a "POSSIBLE SCAN CODE ERROR 57" message in Quake with the GL renderer?

A. If you're running GLQuake, you probably see this annoying message every time you press the spacebar. It doesn't mean anything, but it appears anyway. Here's a trick using `perl` that will modify the GLQuake binary and replace the error message with a null string so that nothing is displayed. This also backs up your original copy of GLQuake to `glquake.bak`, in case there are any problems.

```
perl -i.bak -0777pe 's/P(ossible unknown scancode)/\0$1/g' glquake
```

Hardware

## CHAPTER 18

Installing and Configuring the Red Hat Linux Kernel

by Robert Napier

In this chapter

Introduction to the Linux Kernel

Most modern operating systems separate low-level functions such as memory management and process scheduling into a *kernel*. These low-level functions are often hardware-dependent. Higher-level functions, such as serving Web pages, communicate with the kernel rather than directly with the hardware, which makes these higher-level functions more portable to other hardware architectures.

The Linux kernel is extremely customizable. You can choose exactly what features you wish to include and leave out features you don't. The advantages of leaving out features are that you have both a smaller kernel requiring less memory and also have a more stable kernel. If a feature has a bug but you do not include that feature in your kernel, that bug can never cause you problems.

The Linux kernel also gives you the options of including features only as they are needed. You do this by creating *modules*.

Understanding Module Support

The Linux kernel is made up of a static part and dynamically loaded parts. The static part is kernel-executable and is always loaded. This includes functions such as math coprocessor emulation and Plug and Play support. The dynamically loaded parts, called *modules*, are loaded into memory as they are required and then are unloaded when they are no longer needed. This includes functions such as support for a particular hard drive and sound support.

When the kernel requires a particular service, it checks to see whether it is already loaded, either statically or via a module. If not, it attempts to load a module that provides the needed service. If it cannot find the service in a module, then it displays an error message.

Modules that are not used for 1 minute are unloaded from memory. This reduces the memory requirements for the kernel, while keeping active modules available. In version 2.1 or later kernels (such as the kernel that comes with Red Hat 6.0), this loading and unloading is handled by a kernel thread called *kmod*. In older kernels (such as the kernel that comes with Red Hat 5.2 and earlier), this functionality is handled by a daemon called *kerneld*.

Because kmod or kerneld is started during the boot sequence, functionality that is required during the early parts of the boot sequence cannot be made into modules. This includes functionality such as support for your boot device, generally your primary hard drive. See the section "Configuring the Kernel," later in this chapter, for more information on how to create modules.

Reasons for Upgrading or Reconfiguring the Kernel

There are many reasons to modify the kernel. The following are some of the most common ones:

- Reconfiguring the kernel to use modules or to remove unneeded functionality can improve system performance and improve stability.

- Reconfiguring or even upgrading the kernel might be necessary to get support for newer or less common hardware.

- Reconfiguring the kernel can significantly improve performance for non-desktop uses of Linux, such as routing or firewall applications.

- Keeping up with the latest kernel developments is interesting and enjoyable for many people.

Installing Kernel Source Code

Red Hat provides the kernel source code as an RPM called `kernel-source`. The version that comes with Red Hat 6.0 is `kernel-source-2.2.5-15`. You also need to install the kernel headers, which in this case are called `kernel-headers-2.2.5-15`. As with all RPMs, the kernel headers are installed as follows:

```
$ su
Password: <your root password>
# cd /mnt/cdrom/RedHat/RPMS
# rpm -i kernel-source-2.2.5-15.i386.rpm
# rpm -i kernel-headers-2.2.5-15.i386.rpm
```

This installs the kernel sources in `/usr/src/linux-2.2.5` and also creates a symbolic link from `/usr/src/linux` to `/usr/src/linux-2.2.5`. This symbolic link is the normal way to find the Linux sources.

Older versions of Red Hat Linux also provide a `kernel-source` RPM. For example, Red Hat 5.2 provides `kernel-source-2.0.36-0.7`. These RPMs install in the same way as with Red Hat 6.0.

Obtaining New Kernel Source Code

Sometimes you might want to upgrade your kernel to a newer version, which may provide new functionality or fix bugs. One of the most common additions is support for new hardware. For example, if you want universal serial bus (USB) support, you will need to upgrade to one of the version 2.3 development kernels. For the latest information on what features, bug fixes, and hardware support are available in each version of the kernel, visit http://www.kernelnotes.org.

TIP If you would like to keep up with the releases of new versions of the kernel, send an email message to `majordomo@vger.rutgers.edu` with the following in the body:

```
subscribe linux-kernel-announce
```

If you are interested in Linux software in general, including the updated kernels, you might consider subscribing to the freshmeat list instead. To subscribe to this list, send a blank message to `freshmeat-news-subscribe@freshmeat.net`, or just visit `http://freshmeat.net`.

Understanding Kernel Numbering

The Linux kernel uses a different numbering scheme than most other software packages: There are stable releases, development releases, "pre" releases, "ac" releases, and other releases. The following sections explore these in more detail.

Stable   Stable versions of Linux have version numbers in the form 2.2.8. The first 2 indicates that this is version 2 of Linux. It is very unlikely that you will encounter anything but a version 2 kernel. The second 2 is even, which indicates that this is a stable release of Linux. *Stable* means that no new functionality will be added. All new versions of a stable release are to provide important bug fixes. The 8 indicates that this is the ninth release of version 2.2 (2.2.0 was the first release). If you are running Linux in a production environment, you should almost always use a stable kernel.

Development   Development versions of Linux have version numbers in the form 2.3.16. The first 2 indicates this is version 2 of Linux. The 3 is odd, which indicates that this is a development release. The 16 indicates that this is the 17th release of version 2.3 (2.3.0 was the first release). The development releases contain new functionality and may not be stable. They may cause system crashes and data corruption, and they generally should not be used in a production environment.

"Pre" Patches   Before a new stable version is released, several release candidates may be released. These have numbers in the form 2.2.0-pre5. This example is the fifth release candidate for version 2.2.0. These releases generally undergo extensive testing and may be released in quick succession. It is usually best just to wait for the actual release unless you are interested in helping in the testing effort.

"AC" Patches   Alan Cox (`http://www.linux.org.uk/diary`), one of the most influential Linux kernel developers in the world, provides unofficial patches to the Linux kernel with numbers in the form 2.2.10-ac3. This example is the third patch by Alan Cox on the 2.2.10 kernel. While his patches are technically unofficial, a large percentage of them eventually become part of the official releases. "AC" patches should be considered extreme cutting-edge and generally should not be run on production systems.

Other Releases   Several other unofficial patches to the Linux kernel are available. Two major providers are The Linux Kernel Patch Archive (`http://linux-patches.rock-projects.com`) and Linux HQ (`http://www.linuxhq.com`). These patches are extremely unofficial and may or may not be integrated into the official kernel. They also are of varying levels of stability and support. If you need a specific driver that isn't supported by the official releases, though, these patches can be a fantastic resource.

Choosing a Kernel Version

When to upgrade, and which version to upgrade to, depends on your situation. Some situations, such as mission-critical production environments, are extremely change-adverse and may not upgrade the kernel unless absolutely necessary. Other groups are interested in testing cutting-edge development and may upgrade their kernel with every release.

If your environment calls for an extremely stable kernel with a long track record, you should consider the 2.0 kernel. This requires downgrading the stock Red Hat 6.0 kernel from 2.2.5, but the 2.0 series kernels are three years old and are incredibly stable. They change very rarely by Linux standards (three times in all of 1998). At this writing, the current version is 2.0.38. Of course, the price of all this stability is a lack of features; in particular, the 2.0 series kernels don't support a lot of newer hardware.

 TIP   If you are interested in running 2.0 series kernels, it is much easier to simply run Red Hat 5.2 rather than Red Hat 6.0. Generally speaking, Red Hat 5.2 is more stable than Red Hat 6.0, although Red Hat 6.0 is stable enough for the vast majority of uses.

Most environments do not need this level of stability, however. The 2.2 series kernels are quite stable and add a lot of important features, particularly in hardware support. The 2.2.5 kernel that comes with Red Hat 6.0 is acceptable for most purposes. You may discover, however, that a particular piece of hardware you have is supported only in a later 2.2 kernel, or only if a known bug in 2.2.5 impacts you.

You should generally let new releases "cook" for a few days before upgrading. By waiting a few days, or even a week, you can see if there are any complaints about the kernel. Check for notes at `http://kernelnotes.org`. This is also an excellent place to find out what changes have happened to the latest kernels so that you can decide whether you want or need a particular kernel. You might decide to take an older kernel that just addresses your needs. Older kernels have been tested longer and have fewer changes, so they may be safer. Of course you should watch out for known bugs by reading `http://kernelnotes.org` first. An old kernel with a known data-corruption bug is not a safer kernel.

Some environments are interested in the latest development versions. The 2.3 series kernels should be installed only on test machines to avoid system crashes or data corruption. If you worked with the last development kernel, 2.1, you may have a false sense of security. The 2.1 series ran for a very long time (with more than 130 releases), and the later releases of 2.1 were quite stable. Linus Torvalds has said that he will not allow 2.3 to run as long as 2.1

did, though, so it is likely that by the time 2.3 becomes stable enough for production environments, it will be moved to the 2.4 stable release.

At the time of this writing, 2.2.11 seems to be a solid kernel with a lot of additions over 2.2.5, so if you really want to upgrade from 2.2.5 without moving to the "bleeding edge," this should be a good choice.

Downloading Full Kernel Versions

Generally, it is better to download kernel patches rather than all the source code. Unfortunately, the kernel sources that Red Hat 6.0 provides aren't exactly 2.2.5, even though they claim to be. They appear to be an intermediate version between 2.2.5 and 2.2.6, with several platform directories removed. Although it is possible to make this version of the sources work with later patch files (mostly by ignoring the dozens of errors), it is a better idea just to download a clean copy of the sources.

The definitive source of the Linux kernel source code is `ftp.kernel.org`. You should avoid using this site, though, because it is extremely busy. Instead, consider using *mirrors*, other sites that provide copies of the same files. The Linux kernel mirrors are much easier to use than most mirroring systems. Instead of accessing `ftp.kernel.org`, just access `ftp.<country-code>.kernel.org`. For the United States, this is `ftp.us.kernel.org`. Accessing this site automatically redirects you to one of the many mirrors in the United States. For a list of other country codes, see `http://www.kernel.org/mirrors`.

After you have chosen the kernel you are interested in from `http://kernelnotes.org`, FTP to the kernel mirror:

```
$ ncftp ftp://ftp.us.kernel.org/pub/linux/kernel
NcFTP 3.0.0 beta 18 (February 19, 1999) by Mike Gleason.
Connecting to 207.33.153.134...
ProFTPD 1.2.0pre3 Server (ProFTPD) [opensource.captech.com]
Logging in...
Anonymous access granted, restrictions apply.
Logged in to ftp.us.kernel.org.
Current remote directory is /kernel/linux/kernel.
ncftp /kernel/linux/kernel > ls
COPYING       SillySounds/   people/       v1.2/        v2.2/
CREDITS       alan@          testing/      v1.3/        v2.3/
Historic/     davem@         v1.0/         v2.0/        whawes@
README        hpa@           v1.1/         v2.1/
```

Now, select the directory for the version you're interested in. At this time, this should generally be `v2.2` or `v2.3`:

```
ncftp /kernel/linux/kernel/v2.2 > ls
LATEST-IS-2.2.12                    linux-2.2.9.tar.gz
README                             linux-2.2.9.tar.gz.sign
linux-2.2.0.tar.gz                 patch-2.2.1.gz
linux-2.2.0.tar.gz.sign            patch-2.2.1.gz.sign
```

```
linux-2.2.10.tar.gz                    patch-2.2.11.gz
linux-2.2.10.tar.gz.sign               patch-2.2.11.gz.sign
linux-2.2.11.tar.gz                    patch-2.2.12.gz
linux-2.2.11.tar.gz.sign               patch-2.2.12.gz.sign
linux-2.2.12.tar.gz                    patch-2.2.2.gz
linux-2.2.12.tar.gz.sign               patch-2.2.2.gz.sign
[...]
```

TIP Some mirrors provide bzip2 (.bz2) compressed files instead of gzip (.gz) compressed files. If you don't have bzip2 yet, you can install it from the Red Hat 6.0 CD:

```
# cd /mnt/cdrom/RedHat/RPMS
# rpm -i bzip2-0.9c-1.i386.rpm
```

If you have the option, use bz2 files because they're smaller and will transfer faster. Not only is this good for you, but it's also good for the server you're downloading from.

In this example, you download and install version 2.2.5, which is the closest to what Red Hat 6.0 ships with. By installing the full version, though, patching will be easier in the future. First download the archive:

```
ncftp /kernel/linux/kernel/v2.2 > get linux-2.2.5.tar.gz
ncftp /kernel/linux/kernel/v2.2 > quit
```

TIP If you have Pretty Good Privacy (PGP) installed, you can verify this package by also downloading the .sign file and checking it with PGP.

Check if there is a /usr/src/linux directory already:

```
# ls -ld /usr/src/linux
```

If this returns a directory, rename it to something else so you won't lose your old version:

```
# mv /usr/src/linux /usr/src/linux.old
```

If this is a symbolic link (you can tell because it will have -> after the name), you can just get rid of the link. You'll be creating a new link later:

```
# ls -ld /usr/src/linux
lrwxrwxrwx    1 root      root        11 Aug 27 14:26 /usr/src/linux -> linux-2.2.5/
# rm /usr/src/linux
rm: remove '/usr/src/linux'? y
```

Now extract the file and rename the directory so that you'll know what you have in the future:

```
# su
Password: <your root password>
# mv linux-2.2.5.tar.gz /usr/src
# cd /usr/src
# tar xfz linux-2.2.5.tar.gz
# mv linux linux-2.2.5
# ln -s linux-2.2.5 linux
```

Part
IV

Ch

18

The symbolic link in the last step provides a standard way to find the Linux source code.

If this isn't the first time you've built a kernel, you might have an old source directory in /usr/src. If so, you should copy the configuration file from that directory to the new directory so that you won't have to reconfigure everything:

```
# cp linux-2.2.4/.config linux-2.2.5
```

The configuration file is called .config and is covered in more detail in the section "Configuring the Kernel," later in this chapter.

Downloading Kernel Patches

If you have a reasonably up-to-date kernel, you will generally want to download patches instead of all the kernel source code. *Patches* are files that contain the differences between one version of a source code distribution and another version. Patches are used for many different things, so the term can be confusing. In this context, we are talking about patches between one release of the Linux kernel and the subsequent release. For example, a possible patch would provide the differences between version 2.2.5 and version 2.2.6.

N O T E This procedure will not work with the kernel sources that are shipped with Red Hat 6.0. While these sources claim to be kernel version 2.2.5, this is not exactly true. Red Hat has applied a number of additional patches and has removed many platform directories from distribution. This means that you cannot patch Red Hat 6.0 sources. Instead, you must download a full copy, as detailed in the section "Downloading Full Kernel Versions," earlier in this chapter. ▪

See the section "Downloading Full Kernel Versions," earlier in this chapter, for an explanation of mirrors. Now FTP to the server and download the patches:

```
$ ncftp ftp://ftp.us.kernel.org/pub/linux/kernel
NcFTP 3.0.0 beta 18 (February 19, 1999) by Mike Gleason.
Connecting to 207.33.153.134...
ProFTPD 1.2.0pre3 Server (ProFTPD) [opensource.captech.com]
Logging in...
Anonymous access granted, restrictions apply.
Logged in to ftp.us.kernel.org.
Current remote directory is /kernel/linux/kernel.
ncftp /kernel/linux/kernel > ls
COPYING         SillySounds/    people/         v1.2/           v2.2/
CREDITS         alan@           testing/        v1.3/           v2.3/
Historic/       davem@          v1.0/           v2.0/           whawes@
README          hpa@            v1.1/           v2.1/
```

Select the directory for the version you're interested. At this time, this should generally be v2.2 or v2.3:

```
ncftp /kernel/linux/kernel/v2.2 > ls
LATEST-IS-2.2.12                        linux-2.2.9.tar.gz
README                                  linux-2.2.9.tar.gz.sign
```

```
linux-2.2.0.tar.gz                    patch-2.2.1.gz
linux-2.2.0.tar.gz.sign               patch-2.2.1.gz.sign
linux-2.2.10.tar.gz                   patch-2.2.11.gz
linux-2.2.10.tar.gz.sign              patch-2.2.11.gz.sign
linux-2.2.11.tar.gz                   patch-2.2.12.gz
linux-2.2.11.tar.gz.sign              patch-2.2.12.gz.sign
linux-2.2.12.tar.gz                   patch-2.2.2.gz
linux-2.2.12.tar.gz.sign              patch-2.2.2.gz.sign
[...]
```

In this example, we're going to upgrade a 2.2.5 kernel to 2.2.12. First download the patches:

```
ncftp /kernel/linux/kernel/v2.2 > get patch-2.2.[6789].gz
ncftp /kernel/linux/kernel/v2.2 > get patch-2.2.10.gz
ncftp /kernel/linux/kernel/v2.2 > get patch-2.2.11.gz
ncftp /kernel/linux/kernel/v2.2 > get patch-2.2.12.gz
ncftp /kernel/linux/kernel/v2.2 > quit
```

Now move all the patch files to /usr/src:

```
# su
Password: <your root password>
# mv patch-2.2.* /usr/src
```

Before you start patching your kernel, be sure to make a backup copy. At this point, you should have a directory called linux-2.2.5 and a symbolic link called linux that points to it. Because all the patch files will expect your tree to be in the linux directory, the best way to make a backup is to remove the symbolic link and copy all the files in linux-2.2.5 to linux:

```
# rm linux
rm: remove 'linux'? y
# mkdir linux
# cd linux-2.2.5
# find . ¦ cpio -pdm ../linux
```

Your linux directory is now an exact copy of your linux-2.2.5 directory, so you can start patching it with the patch files you downloaded:

```
# gzip -cd patch-2.2.6.gz ¦ patch -p0
# gzip -cd patch-2.2.7.gz ¦ patch -p0
# gzip -cd patch-2.2.8.gz ¦ patch -p0
[...]
```

You should not receive any errors. If you do, you probably have a corrupt source tree and should download a new copy of the sources. See the section "Downloading Full Kernel Versions," earlier in this chapter.

Now you should rename the directory and fix the symbolic link so that you will know what version of the sources you have:

```
# mv linux linux-2.2.12
# ln -s linux-2.2.12 linux
```

Part

IV

Ch

18

Configuring the Kernel

However you installed your kernel sources (whether you're using the stock Red Hat 6.0 sources or a copy you've downloaded), you should now have a symbolic link called /usr/src/linux pointing to your source code directory. The source code directory should have a name such as linux-2.2.12. If you do not have this set up yet, see the sections "Downloading Full Kernel Versions" and "Downloading Kernel Patches," earlier in this chapter.

Two common ways are available to configure the Linux kernel. You can use either the GUI interface or the text interface, both of which are nearly identical.

xconfig

To start the GUI interface, first log in as root and then type the following:

```
# cd /usr/src/linux
# make xconfig
```

This displays a menu as shown in Figure 18.1. In this example, the Block Devices button has already been pressed to demonstrate the interface.

FIG. 18.1
The xconfig interface is very user-friendly but can be slow on older machines.

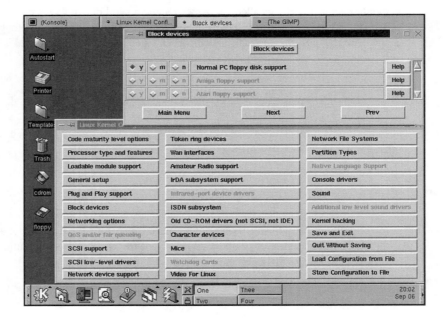

Each entry has a Help button to get more information on the choices. Most options have a Y and N option for Yes and No, and an M option for Module. This is explained in more detail in the section "Making Your Selections," later in this chapter.

TIP If you are logged in as a normal user and you use su to become root, you will get the following error:

```
Xlib: connection to ":0.0" refused by server
```

This is because your current screen (technically your X display) is owned by your normal user account. When another user (root) tries to access your screen, the X Window system prevents it. This security feature prevents other users from opening applications on your display when you aren't expecting it.

To get around this, you can tell the X Window system to allow any connection originating from the local machine.

```
$ xhost +localhost
```

Remember that while this is in effect, anyone logged in to the current machine can open windows on your display. To lock your screen again, type this:

```
$ xhost -localhost
```

menuconfig

Linux also provides a text-based interface called menuconfig. To run menuconfig, enter these lines:

```
# cd /usr/src/linux
# make menuconfig
```

This displays a dialog box, as shown in Figure 18.2.

FIG. 18.2
The menuconfig interface is much more useful on slow machines or over a network. It can also be used without X.

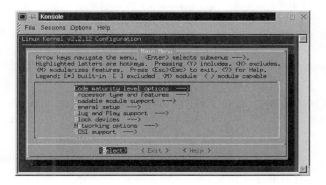

You should notice that the top-level menu options are exactly the same in xconfig and menuconfig. Both read the same configuration files, and anything you can configure with one, you also can configure with the other.

Making Your Selections

In this section, we assume that you are using xconfig, but these instructions work almost identically for menuconfig. The first time you configure your kernel, you should go through every menu. This will familiarize you with what is available and will make sure that you don't miss anything. The few minutes you spend now will provide you a much better understanding of your system. To make this easier, each menu in xconfig has a button marked Next, which takes you to the next menu.

Before changing an option, be sure to read the help information for it. Sometimes there are subtle requirements that may not be obvious. The following sections walk through the menus that you should certainly look at.

TIP In general, you should select M for Module instead of Y for Yes wherever possible. This lets your kernel use less memory. Be sure, however, not to make modules out of anything that you require during booting, particularly support for your primary hard drive. If you're not certain, leave it as Y for now and experiment with it once you have a working kernel.

Code Maturity Level Options   Setting the Prompt For Development And/Or Incomplete Code/Drivers option to yes makes cutting-edge options available to you. Unless you have specific reasons to use these features, such as new hardware or an interest in helping test Linux, you should leave this set to N. Most of the things provided by this option are either not well tested or not fully implemented.

Processor Type and Features   If the kernel you are building is intended for only one machine, then you should set the Processor Family value to your processor type (for example, Pentium or 386). This allows the compiler to optimize the kernel for your computer. If you want this kernel to work on other systems, though, make sure that you set this value to the lowest common denominator. For example, a Pentium will run anything a 486 will, but not vice versa.

The Math Emulation option emulates a math coprocessor. Unless you have a very old computer with a 486SX or 386, you should never need to turn on this option.

If you have a newer processor such as a Pentium Pro, Pentium II, or K6-2, setting the MTRR (Memory Type Range Register) Support option can speed up graphics accesses significantly.

Unless you have multiple CPUs, set the Symmetric Multi-Processing Support option to N.

Loadable Module Support   To get the best use of kernel modules, turn on all three of these options: Enable Loadable Module Support, Set Version Information On All Symbols For Modules, and Kernel Module Loader.

General Setup   If you have a printer or anything else attached to your parallel port, you will want to make Parallel Port Support a module (select M). For PCs, you should also set PC-Style Hardware to M.

If you are running a laptop, you should almost certainly turn on the Advanced Power Management BIOS Support option and look at the options below it.

Plug and Play Support   If you have any Plug and Play devices, you should turn this on. Plug and Play devices are supposed to allow the operating system to configure them automatically without the need for hardware jumpers or DIP switches. Some Ethernet cards and internal modems, for example, have this feature. Sometimes this feature is referred to as *PnP*. Historically, Plug and Play has not worked as well as it should have (both with Linux and with Microsoft Windows). If possible, it is often better to disable the Plug and Play feature and manually configure the device.

Block Devices   The Normal PC Floppy Disk Support option provides access to floppy drives and can generally be made a module.

If you are on a network and want to use protocols such as NFS, you should make Network Block Device Support a module.

Networking Options   Anything that can be set to M here instead of Y should be for desktop machines—for example, Packet Socket and Unix Domain Sockets. Otherwise, the defaults are good for most users.

SCSI Support   Unless you have SCSI drives or a 100MB IOMEGA ZIP drive, you can set all these options to N.

Network Device Support   If you plan to dial up other machines using PPP, you should set PPP (point-to-point) Support to M.

ISDN Subsystem   This section is applicable only if you have an ISDN card in your Linux machine. If you use an external ISDN device (such as a Cisco 800), you do not need to install ISDN support in your kernel.

Character Devices   If you have a printer, set Parallel Printer Support to M.

Saving Your Configuration

After you've looked at all your options, select Save and Exit from the main menu. This returns you to the command line.

TIP   If you've previously configured your kernel and are reconfiguring it due to patches you've applied (see the section "Downloading Kernel Patches," earlier in this chapter), there is an easy way to find out what new options are available. From `/usr/src/linux`, type `make oldconfig`. This only prompts you for new options. Each prompt will have a list of options, with the default option capitalized. Simply press Enter to accept the default, or enter your new choice.

TIP If you are uncertain what option controls a particular feature, look at
/usr/src/linux/Documentation/Configure.help using vi:

```
# vi /usr/src/linux/Documentation/Configure.help
```

This file lists all the configuration options in the kernel. You can search the file by typing / and the string. For example, if you have an Adaptec AHA-1510 SCSI adapter and are looking for support, you could type /Adaptec and press Enter. This would bring you to the following options:

- Adaptec AHA152X/2825 support
- CONFIG_SCSI_AHA152X
- This is a driver for the AHA-1510, AHA-1520, AHA-1522, and AHA-2825 SCSI host adapters.

This won't tell you exactly what menu this entry is on, but it will let you know that this support does exist and is part of a larger AHA152X support system.

Building the Kernel

After you've configured your kernel, building it is simple. From /usr/src/linux, type the following:

```
# make dep clean bzImage modules
```

This makes your new kernel and all the modules. This can take from a few minutes on fast machines to more than an hour on slow machines.

Installing the Kernel

Installing the new kernel is almost as simple as creating it. First, install all the files by changing to /usr/src/linux and typing this line:

```
# make install modules_install
```

This installs your new kernel, but don't reboot yet. If your new kernel doesn't work for some reason, you'll need a way to get back to your old kernel. Assuming that you're using LILO to boot your system, you should reconfigure LILO using gnome-linuxconf. Follow these steps:

1. Log in as root and launch gnome-linuxconf from the main GNOME menu and panel. You will see the gnome-linuxconf window.

2. Select Config, boot mode, Lilo, LILO linux configurations. You will see a tab named LILO Linux Configurations, which has a table listing the currently enabled kernels.

3. If you already have a kernel labeled Old (or similarly labeled), select it and modify the Kernel image file to match your old kernel name. For example, the default Red Hat kernel is /boot/vmlinuz-2.2.5-15.

If you do not already have an Old kernel configuration, click Add. You will see a Linux boot configuration tab, with an empty record. Set Label to `old`. Set Kernel Image File to match your old kernel name. For example, the default Red Hat kernel is `/boot/vmlinuz-2.2.5-15`. Set Root Partition to your root partition, usually `/dev/hda1` (if you're uncertain, check your default LILO configuration). Select Accept to close this window.

4. Click Accept to save your new Linux boot configuration.

5. Click Quit to close the LILO Linux Configurations tab.

Now reboot and make sure your machine still works. If it has problems booting, reboot again and type `old` at the `LILO:` prompt. This brings back your old kernel so that you can work on the new one some more.

After you've installed the kernel and made sure that it works, be sure to make a new rescue disk using `mkbootdisk`. Put a floppy in the drive, and type `mkbootdisk <kernel-version>`. For this example, you would type the following:

```
# mkbootdisk 2.2.12
```

Troubleshooting the Kernel

For simple configurations, everything should work fine, but it is possible to get into a very bad situation when rebuilding your kernel. That's why it's crucial that you keep a backup copy, detailed in the section "Installing the Kernel," earlier in this chapter. Here we will discuss some of the more common problems you may encounter when reconfiguring your kernel.

I Receive Errors While Patching a Kernel, Especially *Hunk FAILED*

You probably have a corrupted copy of the source code. This may be because you've modified files by hand, you're not patching the correct version, or you're trying to patch the sources that come with Red Hat 6.0 (which aren't what they say they are). If you have a backup copy of your sources, restore them. Otherwise, download a fresh copy from the mirror sites.

If a patch fails in the middle, it can be very difficult to undo the damage. That's why it is very important that you make a copy of your sources before you start patching them.

The Kernel Won't Boot

First, boot to your backup kernel. If you haven't made a backup kernel, boot off the Red Hat recovery disk that you made during installation. If you don't have that, you can boot off the Red Hat installation disk, although this requires a lot more understanding of how to work on a Linux system with a very small subset of tools, so it should be a last resort.

If you don't even have the installation disk, you probably won't be able to get this machine to boot. That's why you should always keep a backup kernel that LILO can access.

The most common cause of an unbootable kernel is failing to include support for your boot device (for example, your primary hard drive). This support cannot be a module. In `xconfig` or `menuconfig`, you must specify "y."

I Get *Modprobe can't locate module, XXX* Errors During Startup

These are almost always benign. They simply indicate that something is requesting support that you did not compile into the kernel. The most common versions of this problem are for net-pf-3 (ax25), net-pf-4 (IPX), and net-pf-5 (AppleTalk). If you are running services such as mars-nwe or netatalk but you didn't include these in your kernel, then you'll get these errors. You should probably turn off the services if you're not using them, but you can get rid of the errors by adding the following to `/etc/conf.modules`:

```
alias net-pf-3 off
alias net-pf-4 off
alias net-pf-5 off
```

You can also turn off any other errors of this type by replacing `net-pf-4` with the module listed in the error message. This was particularly a problem in Red Hat 5.2.

If you receive errors about block or character devices, you can look up which device they are referring to in `/usr/src/linux/Documentation/devices.txt`. For example, if you receive errors related to `block-major-3`, `devices.txt` would tell you that this is your "First MFM, RLL or IDE hard drive/CD-ROM interface" (and so is probably a real problem).

I Have Problems Compiling a Recently Released Kernel

Be sure to check `http://kernelnotes.org` to make sure that there aren't problems with the kernel on some platforms. Also make sure that you are compiling with `gcc` and not `egcs` (you'll use `gcc` unless you've tried to trick the system). The Linux kernel doesn't reliably compile under `egcs`.

I Can't Figure Out What Option to Turn On to Support My Hardware

Look at `/usr/src/linux/Documentation/Configure.help`. This is the same file `xconfig` and `menuconfig` use. By reading it directly, though, you can search for things you're interested in and then figure out what option to turn on in the configuration menus.

The LILO Boot Prompt Doesn't Print, or Only Part of It Prints

The LILO prompt prints one character at a time as certain things happen. By noting how many letters printed, you can determine where the failure occurred.

The most common form of this is that "LI" prints and nothing else. This indicates that the first-stage boot loader loaded, but the second-stage loader failed to execute. This is usually due to part of the kernel being above cylinder 1023 on your hard drive. You should make sure that the entire partition that /boot is on resides below cylinder 1023 on your primary hard drive. Otherwise, LILO might not be capable of loading the kernel.

The rest of the boot stages are as follows:

- **Nothing**—LILO has not loaded at all, which probably means that you are not booting the correct device.

- **L**—The first-stage boot loader has been loaded and started, but the second stage cannot load. This usually means that the disk has failed or that your drive geometry is bad. It is unlikely that you would get this during a kernel upgrade.

- **LI**—The second stage loaded but couldn't execute. This usually indicates that it is above cylinder 1023. You can get this when you reinstall the kernel because the old kernel may have happened to fall below cylinder 1023 and the new kernel happens to fall above it. To avoid this, make sure that the entire /boot partition is below cylinder 1023. You can also get this error if you move /boot/boot.b without rerunning lilo.

- **LIL**—The second stage executed but can't load the descriptor table. This can be caused by the same problem of exceeding cylinder 1023.

- **LIL?**—The second stage loaded at the wrong address. The most likely cause of this is moving /boot/boot.b without rerunning lilo.

- **LIL-**—The map file is corrupt. This is usually caused by moving /boot/map without rerunning lilo.

- **LILO**—All of LILO successfully loaded and executed.

Other Problems Not Covered Here

Start by checking http://kernelnotes.org, and make sure there's nothing wrong with the kernel version you're running. Then check the "Linux Kernel HOWTO" (http://www.linuxdoc.org/HOWTO/Kernel-HOWTO.html). Finally, search the newsgroups using http://searchlinux.com. ●

Part
IV

Ch
18

## CHAPTER 19

Installing and Configuring Hard Drives

by Duane Hellums

In this chapter

Hard Drives and Linux

Before you can begin using hard drives effectively with Linux, you must understand many things about them. Luckily, in a typical installation on a standard PC you won't have to worry about many of these issues. For example, it is fairly straightforward to install Linux using a server or workstation installation on an internal enhanced integrated drive electronics (EIDE), or a custom installation on the same drive that has sufficient unpartitioned space. Similarly, you will have few problems with installations on a SCSI (small computer systems interface) drive that is fully compatible and supported by the Linux kernel and Red Hat installation program.

However, in some instances during installation and normal usage you will need to know a little bit more about the interaction between Linux, the basic input/output system (BIOS), your hard drive controller, your hard drive, and its partitions. For all but the simplest installations (in which case you probably won't even need this chapter), planning is key! You'll be much happier with the results if you don't just jump in head first. For example, this chapter will come in very handy if you plan or need to perform the following:

- Buy hard drives and controllers
- Use multiple hard drives
- Use multiple operating systems
- Use SCSI controllers
- Maintain, troubleshoot, optimize, or expand your system's storage

Understanding Hard Drive Technology

To reduce some of the complexity surrounding hard drive technology, this chapter first concentrates on defining and describing many of the different terms you will encounter related to hard drives. These terms are pretty much the same for other operating systems also. Of course, this is not an all-inclusive list of terminology and does not cover every aspect of hard drive technology. If you are using hard drives on an Alpha or Sun system, you should also refer to Chapter 4, "Installing Red Hat Linux on an Alpha," and Chapter 5, "Installing Red Hat Linux on a Sparc." You will find that some terms in this section will be discussed at a fairly high level, while sections later in this chapter will provide additional detail. Specifically, you should become familiar with the following terms and topics:

- Device drivers (for Linux hard drives)
- PC BIOS
- Motherboard peripheral interfaces
- Hard drive controllers
- Hard drive interface cables

- Hard drives
- Hard drive partitions

Device Drivers (for Linux Hard Drives)

This is the operating system software component and link to your hard drive. It is the most critical part of the process because you must have a Linux device driver that is compatible with your particular type of hard drive controller (and vice versa). This is normally an IDE or SCSI device driver for most PCs, but if you have a SCSI controller you also might have to deal with a *PCMCIA* (PC-card) device driver. Linux provides a means for you to pass specific boot-time parameters to the device driver during bootup, if necessary, to change its behavior. This is required sometimes for SCSI controllers that don't have BIOS and must be told what their IRQ (interrupt request) and I/0 (input/output) settings are.

N O T E The Red Hat Linux 6.0 installation program has native support for IDE hard drives. It also probes your system and autosenses most SCSI controllers, then installs the necessary device driver module. If the program doesn't recognize your hard drive controller, you will have the option of picking from the available supported drivers. ■

PC BIOS

Operating systems, Linux included, can get information about your hard drive either from the PC BIOS or from the hard drive itself (if the hard drive supports this capability—most newer ones do). Your BIOS might limit the number of hard drive controllers or hard drives that you use on your system (two IDE controllers and four IDE drives for most newer systems), as well as the size of hard drives used with your controller (8.4GB is a common limit). BIOS also might perform some *address translation*, referred to in BIOS setup as logical block addressing (LBA) or large disk support, between your operating system and the hard drive—this is one way you can get around the 8GB limit (up to a maximum of 139GB based on a 28-bit address).

Part
IV

Ch
19

 TIP If you find that Red Hat Linux 6.0 is not properly recognizing an (E)IDE drive larger than 8GB, you can use boot-time parameters to the kernel driver. For example, if you have a single drive on the first interface, you can pass hda=*cyl*,*heads*,*sectors* (replace the terms with the actual values of your hard drive) during bootup, and this should fix the problem. You might find that some SCSI controllers will not allow you to use more than 8GB, for compatibility purposes with DOS.

Most new BIOS chips can automatically determine drive-related information without your intervention, but on some older versions you will have to enter your BIOS setup program (consult your PC hardware documentation or manufacturer for the proper procedures) and configure it specifically for your hard drive. Some BIOS versions come with only one IDE interface enabled, which requires you to run the BIOS setup program and enable the second IDE interface, if necessary.

CAUTION

Be very careful when you are editing your BIOS options. This is the main intelligence available to your system when you boot up, so incorrect settings could prevent you from booting up properly. Make sure you document existing settings and store this information somewhere safe, so you can reset values if necessary. Be careful when you are navigating around the BIOS setup program, and make sure that you change only those settings that you want to modify. You always have the option to exit without saving changes that you made to your BIOS.

Many different ways exist for entering the BIOS setup program on a PC. This usually is determined by the BIOS manufacturer, but some PC manufacturers come up with their own mechanisms. The basic procedure is to enter a key or combination of several keys simultaneously during the initial power on self-test (POST), which occurs during the first few seconds of bootup and is sometimes accompanied by a cursor or square in the corner of the monitor screen. This is a short list of how to enter some BIOS programs, just in case you can find no other documentation to help you:

- **Del**—AMI BIOS
- **Ctrl+Alt+Esc**—Award and Phoenix BIOS
- **F10**—Various BIOS on some Compaq computers
- **Ctrl+Alt+Enter**—Phoenix BIOS and various BIOS on some Dell computers
- **Esc**—DTK BIOS
- **F1**—Various BIOS on some IBM Aptiva computers
- **Ctrl+Alt+Del followed by Ctrl+Alt+Ins**—Various BIOS on some IBM PS/2 computers
- **Ctrl+Alt+S**—Phoenix BIOS and Mr. BIOS
- **F1 or F2**—Various BIOS on some Packard Bell computers

Some BIOS also come with the *slave device* (second IDE device on an IDE interface, as opposed to *master device*, the first device) disabled for one or both of the IDE interfaces, which you also might have to change, depending on your requirements.

If you use a SCSI system instead of IDE, you can disable the IDE interface in your BIOS and retrieve a few extra IRQ (interrupt request) channels (usually 14 and 15). This can come in handy if you have a high number of peripherals (network cards, modems, video cards, game cards, video capture cards, sound cards, and so on) that can make you run out of IRQ resources very easily. IRQ provides a means for your peripherals and main processor to signal each other that they have information to pass or instructions to execute.

Motherboard Peripheral Interfaces

Technology changes over time, and usually very quickly. As advances are made, they are added to your PC's motherboard as a standard interface. This allows hardware manufacturers to design devices to a standard interface instead of creating a proprietary means of communicating with your system's hardware.

The most common interfaces you'll encounter on your motherboard (mainboard) are ISA (industry standard architecture) and PCI (peripheral component interconnect), which provide a way for your controller cards—in this case, your hard drive controller—to communicate with your PC's processor and memory. If you have a choice, you always should use PCI instead of ISA because it provides increased processing capability and data transfer speed.

A new interface that is being implemented on PC motherboards is the USB (Universal Serial Bus). This interface provides a convenient, external plug-and-play capability for devices such as keyboards, mice, scanners, and cameras. Devices can plug directly into a USB port or into a USB hub that provides multiple ports. However, this interface does not provide high speeds provided by internal PCI and needed by hard drives, so you don't need to concern yourself with it.

Hard Drive Controllers

The hard drive controller serves as the main interface between your hard drive and your PC. It controls interaction between your system and the data storage *bus*. A bus is nothing more than a shared pathway for electrical current that different devices can plug into based on a standard set of (interface) rules—it might help to relate a bus to the electrical system in your house, where you can plug in electrical devices and which is controlled by the fuse box.

The most common controllers (also sometimes referred to as *adapters*) you will use are IDE and SCSI. Your controller card must match your motherboard peripheral interface type (ISA or PCI—another type of bus, incidentally) and hard drive type (IDE, SCSI). For IDE, many newer systems dispense with the card itself and integrate this functionality directly on the motherboard. You will also run into the term *ATAPI* (AT attachment packet interface), which is used by IDE CD-ROMs—essentially, you will be safe using this term synonymously with IDE because the devices use the same interface (IDE standards were extended to include the requirements of CD-ROMs).

SCSI provides considerably more processing power on the controller and the hard drive itself, which explains the higher performance and cost. A SCSI subsystem can perform many disk functions (such as device-to-device file copies, backups, and so on) itself, without requiring interaction with or control from your PC's main processor. Some versions of inexpensive SCSI controllers are intended only for CD-ROMs and similar devices—for hard drives, you should inspect the controller's capabilities and features very carefully before purchasing it or trying to get it to work with Linux.

Part
IV

Ch
19

For example, you should make sure that the controller is bootable, has DMA and bus-mastering capability (for performance), matches the type of hard drive you buy, and possibly supports a floppy (if you need this functionality). Keep in mind that there are several different versions or flavors of SCSI and that your controller might step down the transmission speed on the bus it controls if certain devices on it can't handle that speed. However, some newer SCSI controllers provide multiple channels or segments that allow both speeds to operate on different parts of the bus with the appropriate devices on that SCSI channel or SCSI segment (if you need to mix and match different types of devices without experiencing a degradation in performance).

 Don't be scared off by the fact that SCSI is typically more expensive than IDE and that it is commonly associated with servers and high-end workstations rather than desktop PCs. You might appreciate the improved performance and think it worth the price. Additionally, you can find good deals for SCSI subsystems (controller, drive, and cables), such as a 40MBps 32-bit PCI Ultra Wide SCSI controller and 4.5GB drive from Insight (`http://www.insight.com/`) at a relatively low price of $320. This price is what a 4.5GB IDE hard drive cost just a few years ago. This is just a sample site; you can find others with similar deals, such as `http://www.buycomp.com/`. However, you should make sure that the controller is supported by Red Hat Linux 6.0 and preferably requires the least amount of boot-line parameters and other configuration changes (Adaptec controllers are very popular and widely supported).

Hard Drive Interface Cables

Cables provide a means of arranging your hard drives in your PC's case and efficiently connecting them to the hard drive controller because space and other design considerations prevent drives from being plugged directly into your controller. The cable must have appropriate end connectors that match both the hard drive controller and the hard drive itself. For internal IDE, this involves a flat, 40-pin ribbon cable.

For internal SCSI, you will use either a 50-pin connector or 68-pin connector—these are referred to as *high-density* or *very high-density* connectors, respectively, and contain two parallel rows of 25 or 34 pins for SCSI. For external SCSI devices, the flat ribbon cables are replaced by round, shielded cables that have the same type of 50- and 68-pin connectors as used internally, or a 50-pin connector, sometimes referred to as a *low-density connector*, that looks like a Centronics printer cable connector with flat metal plates and clips instead of pins.

Check your SCSI controller card for minimum and maximum cable lengths between devices on your SCSI bus, if your card or device didn't come with any cables and you must buy some. You can plug up to two IDE devices, referred to as a master and slave, into a single IDE ribbon cable. If you use only one IDE drive, you can ignore the additional IDE connector. SCSI controllers limit you either to 7 or 15 devices, depending on the specific SCSI standard your equipment supports. External SCSI devices are daisy-chained together, end-to-end, instead of all on a single strip, such as you find with internal SCSI devices—each additional external drive requires another cable, in other words. Additionally, each end of the SCSI bus, as it is called, requires a *terminator* or end connector.

Hard Drives

This is where your information is physically stored on disk. Disks are broken down physically into *heads*, *cylinders*, and *sectors* (this information relates mostly to IDE drives because the onboard processor on the SCSI hard drive mostly shields the BIOS and operating system from needing to know this physical configuration). This representation of a hard drive in terms of heads, cylinders, and sectors is also known as the *drive geometry*.

> **N O T E** As mentioned before, LBA addressing translates these physical addresses to logical addresses that do not exceed 1,023 cylinders, 255 heads, and 63 sectors per track (which is caused because partition tables reserve only 10, 8, and 6 bits for these values, respectively). For example, if your hard drive's physical geometry is 8,944 cylinders, 15 heads, and 63 sectors per track, one method by which your hard drive BIOS and Linux will create a valid logical geometry is to halve your cylinder count and double your head count until you end up with a valid C/H/S setting of equivalent size (in this case, 559 cylinders, 240 heads, and 63 sectors per track). Because sectors are normally 512 bytes each, this drive would be 4224MB (4.2GB), which is calculated by (8944×15×632×512)/1024. Another way to calculate this total drive space is by multiplying C×H×S and then dividing by 2 (equivalent of 512/1024). ▨

You should also read the section on disk partitions and understand that some operating systems (Windows, for example) will present a partition to you as if it were a hard drive, which is the intent of having partitions. As a result, you always should confirm visually how many actual physical hard drives you have on the system. Just because you see C:, D:, E:, and F: on your Windows machine doesn't mean that you are out of IDE device connections. Luckily, Linux mounts drives and drive partitions into a filesystem in such a way that it is easy to determine exactly where the physical resource is located.

Of course, your drive type must match your hard drive controller interface (IDE, SCSI), and you must have cables that fit both. IDE drives are the most common on desktop PCs and are cheaper than SCSI drives. A new type of IDE drive, known as UDMA (ultra direct memory access), doubles performance over EIDE drives and nears performance of some SCSI drives at a more appealing price.

SCSI drives have more electronics integrated directly on the drive than IDE drives do. As a result, they tend to be more expensive and more capable, due mostly to the amount of independent processing the drive can do in conjunction with the drive controller, which increases performance of both the SCSI drive and the PC. SCSI drives also seem to last longer and have longer warranties than EIDE drives.

IDE devices are fairly simple to buy and use—just make sure you stay within the maximum capacity (size) and number restrictions of your BIOS and drive controller. For example, some BIOS and drive controllers restrict you to drives no larger than 8GB, and to four (most common) or two (less likely) total drives. If you use more than one IDE drive, you will have to configure the drive as master or slave using a jumper, a small plastic clip with a metal connector inside that makes an electrical connection between two pins on your hard drive (consult your drive label or documentation for the correct setting).

SCSI drives use a slightly different model and give each SCSI device on the bus a unique identification number, ranging from 0 to 6 (7 is reserved for the hard drive controller itself). You must configure the SCSI ID using three binary (on/off) *dip switches* on the device—for example, placing all dip switches in the on position results in SCSI ID 7 (1+2+4); all off results in 0; the first two on results in 3 (1+2); and the last two on result in 6 (2+4). Some SCSI devices even use jumper switches for these settings. Hard drives normally come preconfigured as SCSI ID 0 and receive the highest priority for accessing the bus because higher numbers have lower priority.

You might see hard drives referenced in terms of their spindle or *spin rate*, which refers to the speed in revolutions per minute (rpm, not to be confused with Red Hat Package Manager) and average *access time* or *seek time* in microseconds (which indicates the amount of time required to read and write data on different parts of the drive). Higher spin rates and lower access times indicate a drive capable of better performance and presumably a higher price. Higher-capacity drives, in gigabytes, usually are newer and perform better than older, smaller drives.

N O T E When purchasing and using SCSI devices, you will have to know a little bit more than with IDE, which is relatively more simple. You are likely to run into three main types of SCSI: Fast SCSI (older and cheaper), Ultra SCSI (newer and faster) and Ultra2 SCSI (newest and fastest). These are also referred to as SCSI-2, SCSI-3, and low-voltage differential (LVD) SCSI, respectively. Don't confuse SCSI-2 with Ultra2 SCSI because they aren't the same. Each of these controllers comes in two different processing capabilities: 8-bit (narrow) or 16-bit (wide).

The cheaper 8-bit versions are capable of external data transfers at 10MBps, 20MBps, and 40MBps, respectively. The 16-bit versions can handle twice as many devices (15 instead of 7) and are capable of transmitting twice as fast, or 20MBps, 40MBps, and 80MBps, respectively. Therefore, a 16-bit Ultra2 SCSI (also known as Ultra2 Wide, or U2W) controller and drive can transfer data at 80MBps. You should pick a SCSI model that best suits your processing needs and budget. Although each model is backward-compatible with previous standards, you might force your bus to step down to a lower speed if you mix and match older drives and devices with newer controllers. Your best bet is to make sure all your SCSI components follow the same standard. ▦

Hard Drive Partitions

Many people need to have several different operating systems and file systems on the same drive and the same system, which they can choose to boot up into depending on their needs at the time. This is known as a *dual-boot* scenario. However, operating systems normally don't provide the capability to embed another type of filesystem within theirs, much less the capability to boot from that system. As a result, the only available option would be an additional drive, which at one point in time was extremely expensive (thousands of dollars for 5MB to 10MB, believe it or not). As a result, computer architecture designers came up with the idea of partitions.

Partitions provide a means of logically breaking up a single IDE or SCSI hard drive into multiple sections of variable length that can be represented and handled as separate, individual hard drives. For example, with a single 8GB hard drive, you can create two 4GB partitions (drives), four 2GB partitions (drives), eight 1 GB partitions (drives), or any combination thereof that add up to 8GB (1/4/3, 4/2/2, 4/1/3, 1.5/1.5/1.5/3.5, 2.5/2.5/3, and so on). As mentioned previously, the number and size of partitions can be limited by your BIOS and operating system, especially on older systems.

Generally, other operating systems might not be capable of recognizing changes made by another operating system's programs, and data could be lost or could be difficult to recover as a result. Most operating systems use some version of an fdisk or fdisk.exe utility to partition a hard drive. You should use the partitioning software that comes with each operating system when you create, modify, or delete partitions for that system. Normally, you should not create partitions for Linux using another operating system. The one exception to this is with OS/2, which uses a bootloader that will not recognize and boot to a partition created by Linux's fdisk; for this scenario you should use OS/2 to create the properly sized partition for Linux, and then set the filesystem type from within Linux (and format from within Linux).

You can create three types of partitions: primary partitions, extended partitions, and logical partitions. You are limited to four primary partitions, but you can use one of them as an extended partition, within which you can create many more logical partitions (typically limited to 63 IDE or 15 SCSI partitions). For example, you could have a primary DOS partition for Windows 95, another primary DOS partition for Windows 95 data, a third primary partition for another operating system, an extended partition for the remainder of the disk, and numerous logical partitions (drives) within the extended partition where you can store Linux. Of course, you can also install Linux on a single primary partition, or have a dual-boot system where you have Windows 95 on one primary partition and Red Hat Linux 6.0 on another primary partition.

Part

IV

Ch

19

CAUTION

If you add a second drive to your PC, you might be tempted to partition it in such a way that you can use some partitions for Linux and some for Windows, for example. This can work fine if you have only one hard drive or partition identified in Windows (C:, for example). However, if you have more than one DOS primary partition or drive on the first IDE controller (C: and D:, for example), adding a DOS primary partition on any other IDE controller will cause all versions of DOS or Windows to remap D: (in this example) to another designator. Thus, C: and D: on the first drive, after the addition of what you expect to be E: on the second drive, will result in C: and E: on the first drive and D: on the second drive. This causes no particular problem for Linux, and it might go unnoticed in Windows and DOS, if you're just storing data on these two drives, with no programs or links. However, it also could be dangerous, if you decide at some point to copy all your data off what you think is the second drive (from what you think is E: to D:) and then get rid of your second drive (which you incorrectly think is empty now). With the remapping, you actually would have copied an entire partition of data to the second drive, which you then would have gotten rid of.

Integrating Hard Drives with Linux

Now that you understand most of the basic terminology associated with hard drives, you're ready to move on to the procedures involved with using hard drives with Linux. Specifically, you'll want to know how to add a hard drive to Linux, and then create partitions that you can format, mount, and use with Linux. You also might have to consider the hard drives in relation to any other operating systems you plan to use on your Linux system. The installation chapters (Chapter 1-5) discussed the basics of preparing a single, existing drive for installation of Linux. If you want only Linux on your system, a server and workstation installation will take care of most of the details for you, leaving you very little to know about the hard drive.

Considering Dual-Boot Environments

If you want to use multiple operating systems on the same drive, you have to make room for Linux on that drive. If you are lucky enough to have several partitions, you might be able to move all your other operating system's files and programs off the partitions you need to free up for Linux. This can be a problem because some programs, shortcuts, and links might stop working if you move them between drives (because the drive designator or name will be different). You also might not have sufficient space or might lack two or more partitions to play with because most manufacturers use a single partition (except with very large drives).

In most cases involving an existing operating system, you will have to back up your system, repartition it (leaving space for Linux and its partitions), reformat the partitions for your other operating system using its own fdisk.exe program (or a third-party commercial package), reinstall your recovery software, restore your files and programs, and possibly reinstall certain programs (to re-establish the necessary drive links). When you are finished with that, you will be able to use the Red Hat Linux 6.0 installation and setup program to partition, format, and use the remaining space.

TIP If at all possible, you should consider using an extra hard disk (buy one, if you have to) to run a dual-boot system. This will reduce the complexity of installations for most normal users. It also will reduce the amount of work involved and the probability that you will do something wrong and lose data on your other operating system. You also could try to use the fips program included on the Red Hat CD in the `dosutils` directory; however, even though this is a popular, robust tool, you should perform a backup of your system before using fips. This DOS-based program basically allows you to defragment your existing DOS/Windows file systems and then split the partition into two (you would have to use the DOS fdisk program to delete the new, empty partition to free it up for Linux to occupy). If this is a solution you consider, you should read the documentation in the `fipsdocs` subdirectory fully before trying fips. Finally, you should read the following mini HOWTO documents in the `http://metalab.unc.edu/LDP/HOWTO/mini` directory: `Linux+DOS+Win95+OS2.html`, `Linux+Win95.html`, and `Linux+NT-Loader.html`.

CAUTION

Due to the limitations some older Intel PC BIOS use, the LILO boot loader that comes with Red Hat Linux 6.0 might not work on (and Red Hat won't provide support for) installations of Linux on /boot partitions that are not on the first two drives (IDE or SCSI, or any combination thereof) and completely located below cylinder 1023. As a result, for custom installations you should plan to have a small /boot partition (12MB to 16MB) for storing your boot kernels and associated files. Red Hat's Disk Druid program and the workstation and server installations take care of these details for you, but you'll have to manage this yourself manually if you use fdisk.

Relating Partitions to Mount Points and Device Files

Luckily for new users, Linux really needs only two partitions: the *root partition*, to store files, and another partition for a swap drive (which serves as additional virtual memory to extend your available RAM). Don't confuse the term "root partition" (/, your entire Linux filesystem) with the /root directory (where user files are kept for the root user or *superuser*). If you are performing a custom installation but want to keep the complexity to a minimum, you can just create and use these two partitions.

TIP

As a general rule, you should have at least 16MB RAM and 16MB swap space for the simplest Linux systems, 32MB RAM and 32MB swap space if you plan to use X Window extensively, and 64MB RAM and 64MB swap space. You can add more if you want and even use twice as much swap space as physical RAM. Although virtual memory appears to increase your system's memory (RAM), you should understand the performance issues related to such a practice. Memory modules are on the order of a hundred times faster than typical hard drive access speeds.

For performance reasons, there is no substitution for RAM chips, even though you can save some money and extend the total amount available through swap files. If you are using swap space routinely (running out of physical RAM), you can enhance performance by placing your swap partitions on a different drive than the one that contains your highly active directories (/, /usr, /home, for example).

Part
IV

Ch
19

To Linux, all the files, programs, data, and devices—regardless of which drive or partition they're located on—appear as a single filesystem all existing under the root or / directory (equivalent to c:\ in Windows). Linux uses the concept of *mount points* to achieve this. For example, you can create more than one partition and dedicate each to a different portion of the Linux filesystem. This quickly can be confusing because you can at different times refer to something such as /home as a directory, a mount point, a partition, or even a drive. Many people do this to optimize their system, increase performance, make backups more efficient, maximize their server performance, facilitate file system growth, reduce fragmentation, and reduce chances of conflicts between different parts of your system (logs growing to fill a partition and preventing users from saving their files).

Each partition appears to Linux as a device file in the /dev directory. Device names there are based on the hard drive controller interface (hd for IDE, sd for SCSI) and the position of the hard drive on the interface. For example, you'll see /dev/hda and /dev/hdb for the first and second IDE drives (or ATAPI CD-ROM) on the first IDE bus, then /dev/hdc and /dev/hdd for the two IDE drives (or ATAPI CD-ROM) on the second IDE bus. You'll see /dev/sda through /dev/sdg for SCSI drives (SCSI IDs 0–6) on the SCSI bus (a SCSI CD-ROM doesn't share the same designators as hard drives but appears rather as /dev/scd0, /dev/scd1, and so on). These device files are further extended based on partition number. For example, Linux uses /dev/hda1 through /dev/hda16 for the first 16 IDE partitions on hda and /dev/sda1 through /dev/sda15 for the first 15 partitions on sda. Note that the first four partition numbers (hda1 through hda4) are reserved for either primary or extended partitions, so any logical drives you create in the extended partition will automatically begin with hda5 or sda5.

When you do a file listing (ls -al) and look at device files in /dev, you will not see a file size for controllers, drives, or partitions. You instead will see two numbers that represent the device's major device and minor device numbers. These are what the Linux kernel uses to link or tie into the applicable portions of the software drivers for that device, such as the IDE or SCSI device driver. For example, your first IDE drive should have a major device number of 3 and minor devices of 0 (entire drive) and 1–16 (individual partitions). Your first SCSI drive should have major device number 8 and minor devices of 0 (entire drive) and 1–15 for each individual partition.

One odd thing you might notice is that the next SCSI drive (/dev/sdb) covers minor numbers from 16 to 31, while the next IDE drive (/dev/hdb) skips to minor 64. By default, Red Hat includes filesystem support for only 16 IDE partitions, even though the IDE interface supports 63. You can create additional minor devices using the mknod command. For example, mknod -m 0660 /dev/hda17 3 17 will create another mount point for an IDE partition on that drive. You also will have to chown disk /dev/hda17 to have it belong to the same group as all other hda partitions.

TIP

By using the command more /proc/partitions you can see the major and minor numbers as well as total blocks for all the partitions on your system's disks that were recognized by your kernel. Another useful partition information tool is the sfdisk -l command, which provides a comprehensive table of all your drives' partitions, starting and ending cylinder numbers, and total blocks, similar to the screen you see using fdisk.

You do not have to divide your Linux system up into multiple partitions, but if you want to, there are some general rules you can follow. A popular model (with sample sizes) is to have at least a separate partition for the following directories:

- / (200–400MB, assuming you serve the mount points below on other partitions)
- /boot (16MB)

- ■ /usr (300–400MB or so, depending on how much additional software you install)
- ■ /var (100–400MB or so, depending on how many logs your system generates; some people even create a separate /var/log partition)
- ■ /home (200MB to the remainder of disk, depending on how many users you have and how much information they store. You also can create /home2 and so on for additional users later)
- ■ swap partitions (at least one; 16–128MB or more, if necessary)

As you can see, the recommended minimums would require at least about 800MB. Assuming that you have a 1–8GB drive, there is considerable amount of room to be a little generous reserving space for certain directory mount points, such as swap files, the /home directories, and the /usr directory. It's better to provide extra space now than try to learn how to migrate the information from those partitions to larger partitions later (if you run out of free partition space).

N O T E People who use their Linux PC as a server also sometimes create individual partitions and the corresponding mount points in support of their server files. For example, /home/httpd, var/spool/news, and /home/ftpd might be separate partitions for a Web server, a news server, and file transfer protocol (FTP) servers.

As you can tell, it is okay in the Linux file system to nest or embed partitions underneath other partitions. For example, The / directory might be physically located on /dev/hda1, while /home is located on /dev/hdb3, and /home/httpd resides on /dev/hdb8. As far as Linux is concerned, all these mount points are viewed simply as directories and subdirectories underneath the overall root (/) filesystem. This is different than the DOS and Windows model many users are familiar with, where C:\windows\desktop is located directly on the drive represented by C: (although Windows shortcuts provide a similar functionality as mount points, as well as the capability to map a network drive). ■

Creating Linux Partitions with fdisk

Several methods exist for creating Linux partitions. During a custom installation, you have the choice of using Disk Druid, which is a little easier to use than fdisk, which has a rather terse interface. However, if you performed the necessary planning and already know how many partitions you will use, how large they will be, and what directories you will mount on them, then fdisk can be a relatively simple and powerful (if not pretty) interface. It is also what you are likely to use after you've installed your Red Hat Linux system and need to perform filesystem maintenance, such as adding or removing partitions. Disk Druid is explained later in this chapter in the section titled "Creating Linux Partitions with Disk Druid."

TIP In certain instances fdisk is the only real way to go. For example, if you have created and deleted many different partitions for several operating systems over a period of time, you could have a situation in which you have gaps between primary partitions. The Disk Druid partition program will try to determine the best installation path, but it is not a good replacement for planning and manual configuration sometimes. It is possible for Disk Druid to create an extended partition between two primary partitions that prevents you from accessing the remainder of your disk (above the primary and extended partitions). In such cases, you should use fdisk, create a primary partition that can fill the gap temporarily, create an extended partition above the primary partitions that consumes the remainder of the contiguous, unallocated disk space, and then delete the temporary primary partition.

Other programs facilitate the partitioning of a Linux hard drive, such as cfdisk and sfdisk. The former is intended as a graphical front end to fdisk and is not very mature or stable, so it won't be discussed here (it requires assistance from other formatting tools for new drives and sometimes has trouble reading partition tables). The latter is primarily used to query partition table information and change partition configurations from scripts, so it won't be discussed here either.

The fdisk program probably will be the primary method for partitioning disks for Linux by users reading this chapter. This is because most people pick workstation or server installation methods during the Red Hat setup program and don't have many problems with their hard drives. Therefore, only people performing a custom installation or maintaining a previously installed system are likely to be reading this chapter. Currently, Disk Druid is only an install-time program (executable only during the installation process).

Depending on whether you'll be installing a minimal Linux system or everything on the Red Hat CD, you should plan to have somewhere between 400MB and 1GB of unallocated (unused) disk space. Because of the BIOS restrictions mentioned earlier in this chapter, you might have to reserve at least 16MB of free space, located entirely below cylinder number 1023, for the Linux /boot partition. If you are not able to free up sufficient space for the /boot partition and the rest of Linux, you should add an additional drive (/dev/hdb or /dev/sdb).

CAUTION

Be very careful using any disk partitioning tool of any operating system. This is a low-level tool that can create opportunities for you to make a mistake that will lose data and possibly prevent you from booting your system. You should ensure that you don't change partitions belonging to other operating systems. Make sure you don't overlap any partitions or delete partitions you actually need.

You can use /sbin/fdisk to view, add, remove, or modify Linux partitions on any hard drive. If you have any partitions that were created with other operating systems and you plan to overwrite with Linux, you should use the fdisk utility of that other operating system to remove the partitions in question and update the drive's partition table. After you have freed up enough disk space, you can create the partitions you need for Linux by performing the following steps:

1. As root, run `/sbin/fdisk /dev/hda` from a shell prompt or X terminal to bring up the partition program. Replace `hda` with the appropriate drive (`hdb`, `sda`, `hdb`, and so on). This brings up the main interface. If you do not provide a device name, the program defaults to `hda` for IDE or `sda` for SCSI.

2. Type `m` or `?` at the prompt if you want to see a menu of help information briefly explaining the commands you can use. Type `p` if you want to print a list of the current partitions. If you have a dual-boot system, you will see partitions belonging to other operating systems as well, which you should ignore while using Linux fdisk.

3. To add a partition, type `n` at the prompt. Choose whether you want to create a primary or extended partition. You must create an extended partition if you want to use any logical partitions (otherwise, you'll be limited to four primary partitions).

4. Enter the appropriate partition number that you want to create (1 for `/dev/hda1`, 2 for `/dev/hda2`, and so on). You will be prompted to enter the first cylinder (where you want to start the partition) or to press Enter to accept the default offered to you. Make sure you do not create any overlapping partitions—it helps to choose `p` when you first launch fdisk so you can write down the current beginning and ending cylinders for existing partitions, if applicable. For example, if your 4GB hard drive has 800 cylinders, you can create partitions with cylinder ranges from 1–200, 201–400, 401–600, and 601–800.

5. You are prompted to enter the last cylinder or a value in megabytes or kilobytes to specify how large your partition will be. In the first partition example (1–200) from the previous step, you can enter 200 here. Because it was a 4GB drive being split into four equal parts (in the example), you also can enter `+1000M` and press Enter to create a 1GB partition. If you select `p` again, it will print out the current partition table. Your new partition should show up in the list as a Linux (native) partition.

6. Repeat steps 3 through 5 for the remaining drives until you have allocated all the space you need for your Linux system, including any swap drives you need to create (a maximum of eight swap files totaling no more than 2GB on Intel PCs, 1GB on Sparcs, or 128GB on Alphas). Keep in mind that you will have to create one of the first four partitions as an extended partition if you want to create many logical partitions (drives) inside it—this is the only way to get past the four-partition limit.

7. If you created any swap drives, you will need to change their filesystem type from Linux native to Linux swap. Type `l` at the prompt to view a table of available filesystem types, listed by code. These are the codes you will have to use while in Linux fdisk. From the prompt, type `t` to indicate that you want to change a partition's type, followed by a number indicating which previously created Linux native partition (code 83) you want to use as your Linux swap partition (code 82). When prompted for filesystem type, enter the new code, 82 (you can type `l` again while in the `t` prompt to see the type code list again, if you want). At this point, the partitions exist with the correct types for Linux to use, but you will still have to format and make filesystems on both Linux native and Linux swap drives (discussed in next section) before you can mount them.

8. You must have a partition identified as bootable, using the archive function of fdisk. If you don't already have one, type a and select the partition that you will be using to boot up on. In a dual-boot system, this might already be identified as an existing DOS or Windows disk (which you should leave alone). During all Red Hat installations, including custom installations, this detail will be taken care of for you.

9. If you need to delete any Linux partitions, type d at the prompt. You will be asked to provide the number of the partition you want to delete and to confirm your choice. Be careful that you delete the actual Linux partition (and only Linux partitions) that you want—and don't accidentally delete the wrong one!

CAUTION

Keep in mind that some logical Linux partitions you delete in fdisk might be referenced in some of your configuration files, such as /etc/fstab, if you have used them before as mount points on your Linux system, for example. Adding additional partitions does not cause a problem, but deleting them will cause logical drives to be renumbered automatically. What previously was known to your system as /dev/hda12 actually now might be /dev/hda11. If you plan out your partition changes in advance, you can make the necessary changes to the configuration files even before you use fdisk.

 If at all possible in these types of environments, you should consider booting up into single-user mode (add boot-time command-line parameter single to the kernel name used on the LILO prompt) to make these fdisk changes. If you are already booted into Linux, you can achieve the same result by closing your active files and applications, going to the first virtual terminal window using Ctrl+Alt+F1, logging in on the command line if you're not already, and typing init 1. Depending on the partitions affected, you also might have to unmount certain partitions and turn off your swap devices (discussed later in the section on mounting filesystems).

---

10. If you want to exit without saving changes, type q at the prompt. If you are happy with your choices (maybe you should type p to view your final selections one last time, just in case), you can type w to save your changes and exit to the Linux command prompt.

11. You will be prompted to reboot after your changes are recorded and written to disk. Some portions of Linux will work without rebooting, but others don't, so you should take the small amount of time needed to reboot here. Make sure you have emergency boot disks for any operating systems you have on your system, just in case you made partition changes that cause your system to be unbootable.

Formatting a Partition

When you have freed up sufficient hard drive space and created the necessary Linux partitions to support your planned Linux filesystem, you will have to format them for use with Linux. You must do this using the /sbin/mkfs.ext2 command. You will need to perform this action on any partitions that you created using fdisk and plan to use to store Linux files on. The process is slightly different for formatting regular partitions and swap partitions.

With hard drives, for example, if you created a /dev/hda3 (or /dev/sda3) primary partition, you can put a Linux filesystem (second extended, or ext2) on it by typing mkfs.ext2 -s 1 /dev/hda3 (or sda3—of course, you should replace the device name /dev/hda3 with your actual partition). You also can leave off the -s 1 parameter, if you prefer. It is included here because it is a good option to use with large partitions. Normally, a thing called the *superblock* is copied onto multiple blocks across your new Linux partition. By adding the -s 1 parameter to the command, you reduce the amount of superblock copies that are duplicated across your disk (you'll likely never use them anyway). You can also save some extra space by adding -m 1 after the command and before -s 1. Normally, 5% of a disk is reserved for the root user, which could waste 50MB of a 2GB partition, for example—this option reserves only 1%.

With a swap drive, on the other hand, if you used fdisk to create a Linux swap partition (type 82) on /dev/hda5 (sda5), for example, you would use the command mkswap /dev/hda5 from a shell or X terminal command line. You always can use the -c flag and add the number of blocks used by the partition (check the p option in fdisk or type sfdisk -l to find out this information). This forces mkswap to confirm the integrity and quality of the swap partition. If you receive errors, you should try to create and use another swap partition, or delete and re-create the Linux swap partition again to see if it will work the second time around. If not, you might have a bad hard drive and should replace it.

Mounting Partitions

After you have partitioned your hard drive with the necessary Linux partitions and formatted those partitions for use with Linux, you are ready to mount those partitions and make them part of your overall Linux filesystem. You also can mount partitions formatted by other operating systems and, in most cases, exchange files between them almost seamlessly.

Before you can add a partition to your system, you must have a directory, or *mount point*, where you want to insert the partition (with the exception of swap drives, which are mounted slightly differently). For example, if your Linux installation created a default /home directory on your / partition, but you don't have enough space for your user file space to grow here, you might want to create a new directory called /home2 to add new users. This is where the flexibility of the Linux filesystem comes into play. To help expand your system in this manner, perform the following steps:

1. As root, create the directory using mkdir /home2 (or /home3 and so on for additional space). If there are files in a directory that you mount a partition on top of, you will not be able to see the underlying files—they will not be deleted, but they just will not be visible until you unmount the partition.

2. Set the ownerships and permissions the same as /home using the chown, chgrp, and chmod commands, if necessary.

3. Mount the Linux partition you previously created (hda3 or sda3 for example) using the command mount /dev/hda3 /home2.

4. If you didn't receive any error messages, try using the new directory, which is actually a mounted drive at this point, using commands such as `cd /home2` (to move to the directory), `touch testfile` (to create an empty file there), `ls -al` (to confirm the file was created properly), and `rm touchfile` (to remove the temporary file).

5. If everything worked, you now optionally can make `/home2` the default home directory for any new users, if you want. However, you probably will want to automate the process of mounting this drive; otherwise, you will have to mount it manually every time you boot. To do this, you can edit the `/etc/fstab` file and add a line at the end as follows: `/dev/hda3 /home2 ext2 defaults`. When you reboot, the partition should be mounted automatically.

6. If you just mounted a directory temporarily, or if you need to mount a different partition on a directory already occupied, you will have to know how to unmount the partition. To unmount the `/home2` directory in this example, change to the `/` directory (you can't be in the `home2` directory and unmount it at the same time), and type `umount /dev/hda3` or `umount /home2` (note the different spelling of the `umount` command, without the letter *n*). Then you can mount another partition in its place. You might need to do this, for example, if you need to revert to previous or backup copies of `/home2` on other partitions. The `mount -a` command will remount any currently unmounted partitions that are configured in the `/etc/fstab` file.

In addition to the easy and quick command-line interfaces for formatting and mounting hard drive partitions, there are some graphical tools. Specifically, you can use `/bin/fsconf`, which brings up a color menu from a command line and a filesystem configurator in X window. These give you an Access Local Drives option that enables you to mount `ext2` as well as filesystems of other operating systems (types `iso9660` for CD-ROMs, `fat` for 16-bit DOS, `vfat` for 32-bit Windows FAT32, and `hpfs` for OS/2 or NT read-only). With these tools, you also can add additional parameters to `/etc/fstab`, such as allowing non-superusers to mount or unmount the partition (typically appropriate only for floppy, CD-ROM, and other removable media).

Another very useful utility is the User Mount Tool that you can launch from the main menu and System, Disk Management. With this tool, you can mount and unmount any configured partition or filesystems, including floppy disks—when used by the superuser (root), it allows you to format a drive also.

Finally, you can use linuxconf to automate mounting of directories. When you do this, changes will automatically be made to `/etc/fstab`, so you won't have to make manual additions. This is also the tool you use to configure additional swap drives for Linux. From the main menu in GNOME, select System, Linuxconf, Config, Filesystems, Configure swap files and partitions. Click Add and enter the path of a partition you created previously (with fdisk and `mkswap`). Note that this will only add the proper entry to `/etc/fstab` (specifically, a line such as `/dev/hda2 swap swap exec, dev, suid, rw 1 1`) so that it will be loaded the next time you reboot. To actually activate the swap drive for immediate use, you use `swapon`

/dev/hda2 (in this example) or swapon -a (which mounts any swap files configured in /etc/fstab, similar to the way mount -a mounts all other types of partitions). If you need to unmount a swap device for maintenance reasons, you do so with the swapoff command. For example, swapoff /dev/hda2 turns off the device just configured, while swapoff -a turns off all swap partitions (leaving you running using RAM chip memory only).

Creating Linux Partitions with Disk Druid

The Disk Druid program is used only during initial installation and configuration of Red Hat Linux 6.0. You have a choice of using it or fdisk. If you read the previous sections on partitioning with fdisk, formatting with mkfs.ext2 and mkswap, mounting with mount and swapon, and automating the mount process with linuxconf, you should be able to appreciate the simplistic approach used by Disk Druid.

The functionality of these two partitioning tools is essentially the same as using fdisk, although the interface is much friendlier. If you don't have any special considerations or situations (such as the noncontiguous partition table mentioned earlier in the chapter) that would require the use of the more flexible fdisk, you should use Disk Druid.

Regardless of whether you use Disk Druid or fdisk, you should have all the drives you want to use with Linux already installed on your system and configured in your BIOS, if possible. Adding a drive or partitions to your system later will be considerably harder than doing it all during the initial installation and will reduce the risk of you messing up your system or losing data. This is especially true considering the installation program handles formatting the partitions appropriately and modifying all the corresponding configuration files.

If you choose the Disk Druid approach to partitioning, you will have to know a little bit about the interface and how to use it. All the details on hard drives, hard drive geometry, partitions, and drives (primary, extended, and logical) previously discussed in this chapter still hold true, so they will not be replicated here in detail. The same can be said of mount points and partition types. One thing to keep in mind, though, is that Disk Druid by default will give you a single primary partition, and then stick all other partitions you create in an extended partition (as logical disks). To configure your hard drives for use with Linux using the Disk Druid program during initial installation, perform the following tasks:

Part

IV

Ch

19

1. In the Current Disk Partitions window, you will see a table indicating your currently configured partitions, if they exist. Each partition will be listed as a device with a mount point, a requested and actual partition size, and a filesystem or partition type. Linux drives are listed either as native or swap. In the Drive Summaries box, you can see all the drives installed on your system, with additional information on the drive's geometry and free space. Click the Add button to add partitions to the listed drives. Use the arrow keys to navigate to a specific partition, and then tab down to the Edit button to make changes to an existing partition. Click Delete if you want to remove a partition and mount point. Click OK to accept the current settings and continue with the installation, or click Back to return to the previous screen and select fdisk as your partitioning method.

> **CAUTION**
>
> Make sure you have the correct hard drive selected in the lower frame. It is easy to make a mistake while tabbing and arrowing through this screen to select partition 2, for example, for the wrong hard drive. You don't want to delete or modify the wrong partition because it could result in loss of data or damage your system's operations (especially if you delete a partition used by another operating system).

2. If you selected Add, you will see an Edit New Partition window. If you're creating a swap drive, tab immediately to the Type box and change the value to Swap, which will disable the other settings and allow you to save the changes (otherwise, indicate the type of partition you want to create). For regular Linux partitions, tab to the Mount Point field and enter the directory path (/, /home, /usr, and so on) where you want to mount the partition you are creating, based on your installation plan. Of course, you might be taking the easy route and using only a swap partition and /. In the size field, type the number of megabytes that you want to reserve for the partition in question. You can tab to the Grow To Fill Disk check box and toggle it off or on using the Spacebar if you want to let Linux automatically handle growth of your system across unallocated disk space. If you use only 4GB of an 8GB drive, for example, Linux will know that it can split the remaining disk space and divvy it up among all the partitions that you flagged to grow. Tab to the Allowable Drives frame and flag any drives that you are willing to allow Linux to consider for the mount point you are creating (this enables a little bit of artificial intelligence not provided through fdisk and enables you to let Linux decide where among all the available drives it should put a partition of the size you have indicated). If you want to restrict the partition to a specific drive, you should deselect (remove the asterisk from) all drives listed except for the drive you want to use. Click OK when you are satisfied with your changes, or click the Cancel button to return to the previous window.

3. If you highlight a specific partition and mount point and then click Edit, you will see the same window that you used to add a mount point.

4. As you add partitions and mount points, you will see the Drive Summaries change to reflect the amount of megabytes used and free on each installed disk. The hash marks to the right will also update to show the approximate percentage of disk used (in increments of 10%).

When you are finished making the necessary changes, you can select OK and press Enter to continue with the installation program. You will see an Active Swap Space window, which asks you what partitions you would like to use for swapping (virtual memory). Because this formats the drive for use as a swap device, you will be warned that any information on the drive will be destroyed. Make sure you tab to the Check For Bad Blocks box and press the Spacebar to select it. This tells the installation program to verify integrity of the swap partition before continuing (similar to the mkswap -c command option). This can take a long time for large swap partitions, but it is worth it to make sure that you don't have bad blocks on the swap area, which will be the equivalent of operating a system with faulty RAM chips.

Troubleshooting Hard Drives

Hard drives are extremely reliable, even if you are using a relatively old one. However, lots of things can go wrong with them, especially when you are making changes initially to your system, moving disks around, changing hardware and firmware settings, and so on. The best advice is to make sure you know what the problem is before you make major changes to your physical hard drive. There is no need for repartitioning or changing jumper settings if your problem has to do with permissions, cables, or configuration files.

If you are creating a new system, it can be difficult to debug problems because so many things might be wrong. For example, you might have loose cables, incorrect hardware settings on new drives (jumper or DIP switches), or incorrect BIOS settings. You also might have introduced errors into your system while partitioning or formatting the drive. After you're sure you have configuration files set up the way you need, try rebooting, especially if you have made fdisk modifications. Make sure you have read the appropriate errata and support pages on Red Hat's Web site, if possible, to see if any known problems with Linux are causing your problem. You might need to download new boot images, such as in the case of a SCSI controller that is not automatically sensed or configured by the images you created with the Red Hat Linux 6.0 CD.

When problems occur, systematically check and double-check the components of your system that relate to hard drives. If possible, try to think if there is anything you did recently that could have caused it. Ask yourself if you added a drive, changed BIOS settings, edited a configuration file, deleted a directory, moved some files, and so on. If you can't see files you know should be there, you might have mounted another partition (or an incorrect partition) over the directory in question, or the partition that should be mounted there wasn't for some reason (and you missed the error message about it, if one occurred). Make sure you are staying within the restrictions for maximum cable lengths, disk capacities, and number of disks per controller. Make sure the data and power cables are connected properly to the correct drives and controller interfaces. Make sure you have properly set the master/slave jumpers or SCSI IDs. View man for disk-related commands and utilities in the /bin, /sbin, and /usr/sbin directories, and become familiar with the disk-related information you can gather from files in the /proc directory (such as /proc/partitions, /proc/swaps, /proc/ide/ide0/hda/geometry, model, capacity, and cache).

Attempt to boot up in other operating systems and rule out that it is a total hardware failure or corrupt MBR (master boot record) or partition table. If you're sure this is all okay, launch your BIOS setup program and step through all the options there, looking for anything that might be causing the problem you're encountering. If you don't find any culprits there, boot up using the Linux emergency boot disks and check out your system without any mounted drives or filesystems. Watch the kernel messages that print out during bootup to make sure your Linux kernel is recognizing your IDE and SCSI devices. You might see an error message that can serve as a clue to help you debug and fix the problem. Use any of the utilities mentioned in this chapter or any others that you have read to confirm that you don't have problems in any partition tables or configuration files.

If you just can't find the problem, set the problem aside and come back to it a few days or weeks, if possible. Sometimes attacking the problem in a fresh manner such as this will solve the problem, instead of spinning your wheels and getting you frustrated. If all else fails, try reseating devices (unplugging and plugging back in) the controller cards, cables, and drives. Try moving controller cards to other ISA or PCI slots, if possible. Try swapping power cords between drives and other devices, or swapping cables between controller cards and drives. The key should be to define exactly where the problem is—you don't want to repartition and reinstall if you don't need to, or buy a $200 new hard drive only to find out later that you had a faulty $3 cable or an incorrectly set hardware switch or BIOS setting.

TIP With the popularity of dual-boot systems, you want to make sure that you don't make changes to Linux that prevent you from booting up into your other systems. You shouldn't have to lose data or reinstall both operating systems if you run into problems. For example, make sure you have good backups and recovery disks for other operating systems as well. That way you can boot up in the other operating system and possibly repair the problem. For example, sometimes people make LILO (Linux loader) changes that prevent proper booting. In this case, you can boot to a Windows 95 emergency disk and use the `fdisk.exe` `/MBR` command to overwrite the faulty LILO data and allow your system's hard drive to boot to your Windows partition. Of course, then you'll need Linux emergency boot disks to get back into Linux and repair it, if necessary.

You also can use some techniques to prevent hard drive problems and quickly recover from them if they occur. Most importantly, make sure you have a good set of installation floppies, the Red Hat Linux CD-ROM, and the recovery disk you created during the initial installation. You should also have a printout of your BIOS settings and partition tables for each hard drive in your system. Good, frequent backups of your system can save a lot of heartache if your system gets fouled up. At a minimum, you should have backup copies of your main configuration files and user data. Whenever you need to make changes to hardware or software that involves a configuration file, make a backup copy, such as `/etc/fstab.orig` or `/etc/fstab.bak`, when you add, remove, or modify hard drives and partitions. ●

## CHAPTER 20

Installing and Configuring CD-ROMs, CD-Rs, and CD-RWs

by Kyle Amon

In this chapter

Verifying Hardware Compatibility

One of the things Linux is best known for among free UNIX implementations is hardware support. In this arena at least, it is certainly the king, and there is no exception to be made when it comes to CD drive support. Chances are very good that if you have old hardware of this type lying around, it can be made to work with Linux. An impressive array of newer hardware also works with Linux, but if you're going to spend fresh green on new hardware, it pays to make sure you get something that is already supported.

You are likely to see three basic types of CD-ROM interfaces: ATAPI, SCSI, or a proprietary interface that doesn't follow any common standards. These interfaces support playing audio CDs via an external headphone jack or line level output. Some also enable you to read the data frames from audio CDs in digital form. All CD-ROM drives should work similarly for reading data, although some might not yet provide audio support. If the CDs you use were formatted according to the industry standard ISO-9660 format, you should be able to use them with your Linux CD-ROM. This includes the capability to read from and write to any SCSI- and ATAPI-compliant CD-R (recordable CD) or CD-RW (rewritable CD). Many of these writable drives are also capable of using the new UDF file system format that DVD-ROM drives require for viewing audio and video streams. Unfortunately, at the time of this writing, DVD support for Linux is still in early development.

TIP The various CD technologies and related acronyms are detailed in the later section "Understanding CD Drives."

Currently Supported Drives

On the Alpha platform, only internal ATAPI and standard SCSI CD drives are supported. The Sparc platform supports only standard SCSI CD drives. If your system is one of these, you might want to just read what is relevant to your platform here and move on to the section, "Understanding CD Drives." On the x86 platform, everything that follows is applicable.

ATAPI Drives

Any CD-ROM drives compliant with ATAPI version 1.2 or 2.6 should work fine with Red Hat Linux 6.0. Most drives manufactured today fall into this category. If you purchased your drive recently, it is most likely of this type. The ATAPI interface is basically an extension to the IDE or EIDE (enhanced IDE) standard.

TIP Linux also has an IDE SCSI emulation driver that makes an ATAPI device appear to be a SCSI device. If you have an ATAPI drive for which no native driver has been written, you can use this emulation together with an appropriate SCSI device driver to support your drive. This is also how all ATAPI CD-R and CD-RW drives need to be configured so that you can write to them.

SCSI Drives

Any SCSI drive with a block size of 512 or 2048 bytes should work under Linux. Most SCSI drives on the market fall into this category. Of course, with SCSI drives you will also need a supported SCSI controller to attach it to.

Some SCSI drives come with a proprietary controller that is not fully SCSI-compatible and that might not support connecting additional SCSI devices on the bus. Such cards most likely will not work under Linux. If such a card came with your drive, you will need to replace it with a standard SCSI card to use your drive with Linux. This is not the case if you have an onboard Adaptec 78xx series controller.

Proprietary Drives

A fair number of drives with proprietary interfaces still are floating around, most of which are supported by Linux with special, individual device drivers. These proprietary interfaces are sometimes erroneously referred to as IDE interfaces because, like IDE hard disks, they use a simple interface based on the PC/AT bus. To add further confusion, some vendors, most notably Creative Labs, have offered proprietary, SCSI, and ATAPI interfaces on their sound cards over the years and have shipped drives of all kinds as a result.

Table 20.1 lists every supported proprietary drive and its corresponding driver.

Table 20.1   Linux Proprietary CD-ROM Drivers

Proprietary Drives	Driver
Aztech CDA268-01A	aztcd
Orchid CDS-3110	
Okano/Wearnes CDD-110	
Conrad TXC	
CyCDROM CR520ie/CR540ie/CR940ie	
Creative Labs CD-200(F)	sbpcd
Funai E2550UA/MK4015	
IBM External ISA	
Longshine LCS-7260	
Matsushita/Panasonic CR-521/522/523/562/563	
Teac CD-55A SuperQuad	
GoldStar R420	gscd
Lasermate CR328A	optcd

continues

Part
IV

Ch
20

Table 20.1 Continued

Proprietary Drives	Driver
Optics Storage Dolphin 8000AT	
LMS Philips CM 206	cm206
Mitsumi CR DC LU05S	mcd
Mitsumi FX001D/F	mcdx
Sanyo CDR-H94A	sjcd
Sony CDU31A/CDU33A	cdu31a
Sony CDU-510/515/531/535	sonycd535
Drives attached to an ISP16, MAD16, or Mozart sound card	isp16

TIP For some proprietary drives, alpha or beta drivers are available that are not included in the current Linux kernel sources. These drivers can be found at `ftp://metalab.unc.edu/pub/Linux/kernel/patches/cdrom/`.

Parallel Port Drives

External CD drives that connect to the parallel port have become fairly common. Some older drives utilize proprietary interfaces. These might be standard SCSI drives accessed through the parallel port via built-in, intermediary SCSI controllers. Newer drives, however, are based on standard IDE-type devices that don't require an intermediary controller. These newer drives are identical to internal ATAPI drives with an additional parallel port adapter chip reproducing a small ISA or IDE bus to access device registers and perform data block transfers.

Many newer drives are supported by the Linux parallel port IDE driver, paride, which also supports most compatible no-name and clone drives. Parallel port SCSI drives, however, are not supported in Red Hat Linux 6.0. A kernel patch for ppscsi, a driver that provides this support, is available at `http://www.torque.net/parport/ppscsi.html`. Drives utilizing proprietary parallel port interfaces are not supported either, although a driver is available for at least two of them, the MicroSolutions backpack CD-ROM models 160550 and 162550, at `http://www.torque.net/parport/bpcd.html`. All parallel port CD drives known to work with Linux are listed with their corresponding driver in Table 20.2.

Table 20.2 Linux Parallel Port CD-ROM Drivers

Parallel Port Drives	Driver
Freecom Power CD	paride
Freecom Traveler CD	

Parallel Port Drives	Driver
Hewlett-Packard 7100e and 7200e CD-RW	
H45 Quick CD	
KingByte IDE/ATAPI CD-ROMs	
MicroSolutions backpack CD-ROM (models 163550 and later)	
MicroSolutions backpack PD/CD	
Fidelity International Technology Transdisk CD-ROM/PD-CD	
SyQuest SyJet	ppscsi
MicroSolutions backpack CD-ROM (models 160550 and 162550)	bpmcd

PC Card Drives

PC card drives are supported by David Hinds' PCMCIA Card Services package. This is a relatively large and complex package that contains a set of loadable kernel modules implementing a version of the PCMCIA 2.1 Card Services API (applications programming interface) and a set of client drivers for specific cards. There is also a card manager daemon that facilitates "hot swapping" PC cards by watching for card insertion and removal events and managing the loading and unloading of modules, as appropriate. Chapter 3, "Installing Red Hat Linux on a Laptop," discusses the issues related to using your PCMCIA controller and cards. There are some PCMCIA interfaces on desktop PCs, but they are fairly rare.

PC card CD drives use either an ATA/IDE PCMCIA interface or a SCSI PCMCIA interface. Supported ATA/IDE drives use the ide_cs driver, while supported SCSI drives use one of several SCSI drivers, depending on the controller chip in use. ATA/IDE drives currently supported by the ide_cs driver are listed in Table 20.3. Currently supported SCSI drives and their corresponding drivers are listed in Table 20.4.

Table 20.3   Linux IDE PC-Card CD-ROM Drivers

PC Card ATA/IDE Drives	Driver
Argosy EIDE CD-ROM	ide_cs
Caravelle CD-36N	
CNF CARDport CD-ROM	
Creative Technology CD-ROM	
Digital Mobile Media CD-ROM	
EXP CD940 CD-ROM (some work, some don't)	
EXP Traveler 620 CD-ROM	
Freecom IQ Traveler CD-ROM	

Part
IV

Ch
20

continues

Table 20.3   Continued

PC Card ATA/IDE Drives	Driver
H45 Technologies Quick 2x CD-ROM	
H45 Technologies QuickCD 16X	
IBM Max 20X CD-ROM	
IO-DATA CDP-TX4/PCIDE, CDP-TX6/PCIDE	
IO-DATA CDP-TX10/PCIDE, CDV-HDN6/PCIDE	
IO-DATA CDP-FX24/CBIDE, MOP-230/PCIDE	
IO-DATA CDP-AX24T/CBIDE	
IO-DATA HDP-1G/PCIDE, HDP-1.6G/PCIDE	
Microtech International MicroCD	
Microtech Mii Zip 100	
NOVAC NV-CD410	
Sony PCGA-CD5 CD-ROM	
TEAC IDE Card/II	

Table 20.4   Linux SCSI PC Card CD-ROM Drivers

PC Card SCSI Drives	Driver
IO-DATA CDG-PX44/PCSC CD-ROM	mps110_cs
Logitec LCD-601 CD-ROM	unknown
Panasonic KXL-D740, KXL-DN740A, KXL-DN740A-NB 4X CD-ROMPioneer PCP-PR1W, PCP-PR2W CD-ROM	qlogic_cs unknown
Raven CD-Note 4X	qlogic_cs
Sony CD-ROM Discman PRD-250	aha152x_cs
Yamaha 4416S CDR	aha152x_cs

Understanding CD Drives

As with most things in the computer industry, CD technology involves a plethora of standards. You could certainly become a specialist in the area, but for the average user it all boils down to a few issues concerning hardware capabilities, interfaces, and filesystem types. Of course, a few extensions further complicate the issue.

The following are the hardware categories:

- CD-ROM compact disc read-only memory (CD-ROM) units were the first CD drives on the market. Capable of storing approximately 650MB, they utilize the same format as audio CDs. The first units were relatively slow with SCSI or proprietary interfaces. As usual, speed increased, price dropped, and new standards (such as ATAPI) were formed. CD-ROM changers came along soon afterward.

- CD-R compact disc recorders (CD-R) are essentially CD-ROM drives that allow writing as well. In addition to having the capability to read standard CDs, they can write to special CDs that can then be read by standard CD-ROM drives. These are a write-once read-many, or WORM, medium.

- CD-RW compact disc read-write (CD-RW) drives are essentially CD-Rs supporting the writing of data to CDs multiple times. Although capable of reading standard CDs, these drives use special discs for writing that might not be recognized by some older CD-ROM or CD-R drives, although many multisession CD players sold today can read them fine.

- DVD-ROM digital video disk read-only memory (DVD-ROM) drives expand CD storage capabilities to as much as 17GB. They are generally used for storing full-length motion pictures encoded in MPEG-2 format.

The following are the interface categories:

- **ATAPI**—ATA Packet Interface (ATAPI) is a protocol for controlling mass storage devices. It was designed as a psuedo-combination of the ATA (AT Attachment) interface, which is the official ANSI standard name for the IDE interface used for hard disks and the SCSI interface. This was intended to overcome certain ATA limitations while preserving ATA compatibility. Unlike ATA, it supports the attachment of devices other than hard drives. Due to its low cost and high functionality, ATAPI is currently the most commonly used interface.

- **SCSI**—Small computer systems interface (SCSI) is a bus capable of supporting multiple devices with a high transfer rate. The standard has evolved to include a SCSI-I, SCSI-II, SCSI-III, Fast, Wide, and Ultra myriad mixture of half real, half merely marketing jargon that isn't really essential to this discussion. SCSI is generally considered the interface of choice for high-end systems.

- **Proprietary**—When CD technology first hit the market, the only existing option was to develop hardware utilizing the SCSI interface. Because price was then a barrier to market penetration and because there was no less-expensive standard that could be utilized, many manufacturers developed their own interface protocols. The result was a dozen or so disparate proprietary interface specifications, all obviously requiring specialized drivers. Many older CD-ROM drives have such interfaces, usually provided on a sound card or a separate interface card.

Part

IV

Ch

20

■ **PCMCIA**—Personal Computer Memory Card International Association (PCMCIA) is a trade association (http://www.pc-card.com/) that defines standards for adding memory, mass storage, and I/O capabilities to computers in a rugged, compact form factor. Interface cards based on the technology initially became known as PCMCIA cards, but the industry is shifting toward referring to these cards as PC cards and reserving the PCMCIA acronym for the association only. While PC card devices are a little pricey, they are currently a virtual requirement of mobile computing.

■ **Parallel port**—Many external devices other than printers can be attached to the parallel port of personal computers these days. Such devices often use an IDE interface internally and an external adapter that interfaces the internal IDE bus to the PC parallel port. Flexibility of connectivity, rather than speed of operation, is the selling point for devices utilizing this interface.

The following are the filesystems categories:

■ **ISO-9660**—Formerly called the High Sierra filesystem, the ISO-9660 file system is the most common filesystem format for CD media. Unfortunately, it has MS-DOS file naming limitations. This restricts you to an eight-character name and a three-character extension, and directory hierarchies can be nested only down to eight levels of depth.

■ **Universal Disk Format (UDF)**—Linux support for this format is still in its early stages. Kernel patches are available from http://trylinux.com/projects/udf/, if you need to add support to your existing kernel. UDF is a new filesystem standard intended to replace the ISO-9660 filesystem standard. DVD-ROMs use it for storing MPEG audio and video streams. Support for this filesystem is required to view MPEG movies with DVD-ROM drives. It can also be used by CD-R and CD-RW recorders via something known as packet writing, allowing data to be written more efficiently with such drives.

The miscellaneous extensions are as follows:

■ **Multi-Session CD-R**—Multi-Session CD-R drives with multisession support allow new data to be appended to the end of discs with available space. Although not fully read/write, multisession support adds a modicum of additional flexibility to such drives.

■ **PhotoCD**—PhotoCD (XA) is a standard developed by Kodak for storing photographic images as digital data. With appropriate software, you can view, manipulate, and print such images. With multisession capability as well, information can be added at a later date, thus allowing image modification.

■ **Rock Ridge**—Rock Ridge extensions were introduced to overcome the deficiencies of the ISO-9660 filesystem on Unix machines, where enduring such extreme limitations was unthinkable. It uses undefined fields in the ISO-9660 standard to support longer filenames, a greater directory hierarchy depth, and additional information such as file ownership and symbolic links.

■ **Joliet**—Joliet is a proprietary ISO-9660 filesystem extension that supports long file-names using UNICODE, the successor to ASCII. This supports the new 16-bit character code that can encode characters for every major language of the world. It was defined by Microsoft after the Rock Ridge extensions came into prominence.

■ **El Torito**—El Torito is a specification for making CDs bootable. It defines a method wherein the first 1.44MB of a CD might contain a bootable floppy image. If a computer's BIOS has El Torito support and this floppy image is present, the computer treats it as though it were a floppy and boots from it.

Regardless of what hardware you have, it will be some combination of these listed. You might have an older SCSI CD-R drive with multisession support but not PhotoCD. You might have an external CD-ROM drive utilizing a proprietary protocol via a PCMCIA interface card. You might have an external CD-ROM drive utilizing SCSI via a PCMCIA interface card. You might have an old ATAPI CD-ROM drive with or without support for Rock Ridge Extensions. You might have an old Sony CD-ROM drive and proprietary Sony interface card, or the same Sony CD-ROM drive connected to one of a dozen sound cards utilizing one of half a dozen chipsets. The variety of possible mixtures is so great, in fact, that the number of possibilities alone can daunt a newbie just wanting to add or change a drive. It really isn't that bad, though. Unless you're an old hardware hack with piles of old boards, drives, and chips in the closet, or unless you got some hand-me-down equipment from this nut, chances are very good that you'll be dealing with one of only a few possibilities.

If you have a standalone desktop system, you're probably going to be dealing with a common ATAPI (EIDE) drive or perhaps a slightly less common SCSI drive. If you've got a notebook computer with an internal drive, it will generally fall into one of the previous two categories; otherwise, you'll have an external drive connecting via some kind of PC card or the parallel port. That should be pretty much accurate for about 99% of users.

Although every situation has its own peculiarities, some of which are covered here, no situation is really all that difficult when you realize that what needs to be done is always the same. The only differences are in the details—and, yes, they are important, but only peripherally. In every case, the following steps are all that need to be done:

1. Identify hardware.
2. Install the drive.
3. Add kernel support.
4. Create device files, if necessary.
5. Set boot or module parameters, if necessary.

Part

IV

Ch

20

TIP Although the fundamental steps are always the same, the devil is in the details. As a result, the single most important thing you can do to avoid hours of unnecessary frustration is to identify your hardware. Configuring any piece of hardware is all about a driver for that piece of hardware. Without the proper driver, properly configured and communicating between the hardware and the kernel, you'll get nowhere with hardware every time. Make sure you know exactly what model drive you have and exactly what properties, features, and hardware configuration it uses because this information determines everything else. With more exotic hardware, it is even important to know exactly what chipsets are involved.

Installing CD Drives

Installing CD drives is pretty similar to installing most other hardware. If you have an external model, you get off easy, of course. If not, however, follow the manufacturer's hardware installation instructions for your drive. If you don't have the installation instructions for your drive, don't worry. Barring silly little annoyances such as IRQ (interrupt request) and SCSI ID conflicts, there really isn't that much to it.

If you have an internal ATAPI drive, simply locate an available connector on an IDE controller, jumper the drive to master or slave, as appropriate, and stick it in your machine. Next, connect the data and power cables. You can screw it down or not at this point, but don't replace the system's cover until you verify that everything is working properly. It has been my experience that every time I feel confident enough to replace the cover, wiggle the machine back into its resting place, and hook everything back up perfectly, I have almost certainly made some silly mistake requiring me to rip it all apart again.

The installation process is pretty much the same if you have an internal SCSI drive. The only real difference is that you will be connecting your drive to a SCSI bus and setting its SCSI ID instead of connecting it to an IDE controller and jumpering it as master or slave. If you happen to have a very high-end system with a monster disk subsystem containing multiple SCSI logical unit numbers (LUNs) and/or hardware redundant arrays of inexpensive disks (RAID), you probably know it. If not, you are not likely to need to become a SCSI expert to install a CD drive. Just make sure the drive is set to a unique SCSI ID and is properly terminated.

The only other kind of internal CD drive you might have is a proprietary one. From a hardware perspective, these should also be relatively easy to install. They either will have their own dedicated controller card or will connect to one of possibly several proprietary connectors on a sound card.

If you have a drive with a dedicated controller card, just check the card's jumper settings, locate an available slot of the appropriate type (most likely an 8- or 16-bit ISA slot), and slide the card into it. Then put the drive in, connect the data and power cables, and you're done.

If you need to connect an internal proprietary drive to a sound card, make sure you know exactly what type of drive it is, and be sure to connect the data cable to the proper connector on the sound card. Sound cards with multiple connectors will usually have Sony, Mitsumi, and Panasonic connectors. Make sure you have everything on the sound card jumpered correctly, if appropriate. You might also want to write down any jumper settings on a piece of scratch paper because you will very likely need this information later when configuring driver support into your kernel. Writing down such information is more important with proprietary drives, especially when connected to a sound card, because there are usually more possible settings to remember than when dealing with ATAPI or SCSI drives. While most people can remember something like slave on the secondary ide controller or ID 3 on SCSI controller XYZ for a reasonable amount of time, their short-term memory sometimes fails when confronted with something like base memory address 0x240, I/O address 0x6400, IRQ 5, DMA (direct memory access) channel 1 for 16-bit, DMA 3 for 8-bit, and cdrom at 0x3640. So, write this stuff down now and save yourself the aggravation of having to pull the sound card back out again later to examine its settings. If you need additional help with setting up your sound card, refer to Chapter 23, "Installing and Configuring Joysticks and Game Cards," which covers sound card installation and configuration in detail.

The only other thing you'll likely want to connect in all cases is an audio cable, if you have one. This is usually the easiest part. Even if there is more than one audio connector on your CD drive, sound card, or both (as is often the case), your cable will almost certainly fit in only one place at each end.

If you were weaned on hardware, most of this minutia goes without saying. If you found yourself at all confused, though, and do not have the manufacturer's installation instructions handy for your hardware, I strongly recommend that you enlist the assistance of a friend or relative with a little more hardware experience. After everything is up and running smoothly, you should seriously consider getting and perusing a good book on computer hardware some rainy afternoon.

Installing Hardware Support

After you've installed the hardware, you need to build kernel support for it before it can become available for use. This support comes in the form of a hardware driver, compiled statically into the kernel or dynamically as a loadable module. For now, you should probably compile everything statically into the kernel. When you're sure everything is working properly, you can go back and wrestle with configuring things as modules.

Recall that Chapter 19, "Installing and Configuring Hard Drives," explained how to configure, compile, and install custom kernels and kernel modules. Here, the text explains what needs to be done with the kernel to add support for various CD drives. If you feel that you might need a refresher on the intricacies of kernel compilation, refer to Chapter 19.

Part
IV

Ch
20

In addition to selecting an appropriate driver for your hardware, you must consider a handful of other kernel options if you actually want to do anything with your CD drive. Exactly which of these options need to be enabled depends entirely on the type of CD drive you have and the use you intend to make of it. If you've got a common internal ATAPI or SCSI CD-ROM drive and only want to listen to audio CDs, you're essentially done with this chapter and can consult Chapter 23 to get your sound card configured and working. My guess, however, is that you'd like to do a little more with your drive than listen to music.

The tables that follow summarize what to include in your kernel, depending on the type of CD drive you have and its intended use. These tables include the section of the kernel configuration in which you'll find the options, as well as their descriptions and the name of the resulting module if you choose to compile the option as a module. Fields labeled N/A indicate that the option is not available as a module; fields labeled with an asterisk (*) indicate that you need to select the appropriate driver for your specific card.

For all drives, you will probably want to include both filesystem support options in Table 20.5. Note that the ISO-9660 filesystem automatically includes Rock Ridge extensions, and you can do without the Joliet extension if you don't use Microsoft media.

Table 20.5   CD-ROM Filesystem Kernel Options

Section	Description	Module
Filesystems	ISO 9660 CD-ROM filesystem support	isofs
Filesystems	Microsoft Joliet CD-ROM extensions	N/A

For all ATAPI drives, you will need to include both drivers in Table 20.6. Note that the ide-cd driver requires the presence of the ide driver to function.

Table 20.6   IDE/ATAPI CD-ROM Kernel Options

Section	Description	Module
Block devices	Enhanced IDE/MFM/RLL disk/ cdrom/tape/floppy support	ide
Block devices	Include IDE/ATAPI CD-ROM support	ide-cd

For SCSI drives, you will need to include all the options in Table 20.7, except the one for enabling vendor-specific extensions because this is required only for multisession support with a few specific drives. If you find that multisession doesn't work with your drive and you know that it should, try enabling this option as well.

Table 20.7   SCSI CD-ROM Kernel Options

Section	Description	Module
SCSI support	SCSI support	scsi_mo
SCSI support	SCSI CD-ROM support	sr_mod
SCSI support	Enable vendor-specific extensions (for SCSI CD-ROM)	N/A
SCSI low-level drivers	Select a low-level driver for your specific card	*

For old proprietary CD-ROM drives, locate your drive in Table 20.1 and include the appropriate driver from the kernel configuration section labeled Old CD-ROM Drivers (not SCSI, not IDE). If you need detailed information on any of these drivers, refer to the /usr/src/linux/Documentation/cdrom subdirectory and read the file with the name of the driver you're interested in.

For ATAPI parallel port drives, you will need to include all the options in Table 20.8, except possibly the one for generic ATAPI devices, which is necessary only if your parallel port drive is a CD-R or CD-RW drive and you intend to write CDs with it. You will probably need to create the necessary device files for parallel port drives as well. As root, run the /usr/src/linux/drivers/block/paride/mkd script to create them.

Table 20.8   Parallel Port ATAPI CD-ROM Kernel Options

Section	Description	Module
Block devices	Parallel port IDE device	paride
Block devices	Parallel port ATAPI CD-ROMs	pcd
Block devices	Parallel port generic ATAPI devices	pg
Block devices	Select a protocol driver for your specific card	*

For all CD-R and CD-RW drives except those with parallel port interfaces, you will need to include SCSI generic support because CD-writing software requires this to work. You'll probably also want to include loopback device support for mounting and examining the ISO-9660 filesystem images you create before burning them to CD. These options are listed in Table 20.9.

To write CDs, you'll also want to create the SCSI generic device files if they don't already exist. These are required because CD writing software can't use SCSI CD drives via their normal /dev/sr* block devices. As root, run the command /dev/MAKEDEV sg to create the /dev/sg* devices.

Part
IV

Ch
20

Table 20.9 SCSI CD-R/RW Kernel Options

Section	Description	Module
SCSI support	SCSI generic support	sg
Block devices	Loopback device support	loop

Finally, if you have a CD-R or CD-RW drive with an ATAPI interface, you'll need to enable SCSI emulation support to be able to write CDs with it. If you do this, be sure to disable IDE CD-ROM support; otherwise, there will be a conflict. This option is shown in Table 20.10.

Table 20.10 IDE CD-R/RW (SCSI Emulation) Kernel Options

Section	Description	Module
Block devices	SCSI emulation support	ide-scsi

That was a fairly hefty barrage of information. At this point, you're probably starting to realize why it is so important to know the precise properties of your hardware. If you still aren't sure what to include in your custom kernel, take a minute now to go back over these tables and isolate exactly what is needed for your drive.

Installing Support Software

After you've configured your CD, you need to make sure that you have applicable software support packages installed if you want to be able to do anything with it besides mount and unmount CDs containing ISO-9660 filesystems. Most of this software is contained on the Red Hat 6.0 CD and can be installed or removed easily via Gnome RPM from the Gnome Desktop. The software you're interested in here will be under Packages, Applications, Multimedia, as seen in Figure 20.1.

FIGURE 20.1
Red Hat includes many multimedia packages to use with your CD.

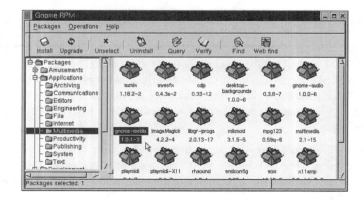

You can find out what a specific package contains by selecting and querying it. If it contains something you want, just make sure you have it installed. That's really about all there is to it. Such applications will then generally be available under the Multimedia tab, unless they are of the command-line only variety.

For a normal CD-ROM, an audio CD player and perhaps a sound mixer application are about all you can use. The only other thing you could possibly use is an application to rip sound-tracks off audio CDs for later listening elsewhere. If you're an MP3 freak wanting to put a Linux-based MP3 player in your car or something, consider cdparanoia, a good "ripper" application available from its home page at http://www.xiph.org/paranoia/.

If you have a CD-R or CD-RW drive, however, you'll probably be wanting software for CD writing. Although such software isn't included in the standard Red Hat Linux 6.0 distribution, it is easily obtainable in RPM format on the Web. The best, most up-to-date resource for information regarding such software, where to get it, and how to use it is probably the CD-Writing HOWTO, a special HOWTO that deals only with writing to CDs under Linux.

No matter what you're doing, there always seems to be a rub—with CD writing under Linux, the rub is that the software for this purpose is so specialized that it doesn't work with all CD-R and CD-RW drives. So, unless you have been careful to get hardware that is known to be supported by this software, or unless you have just plain gotten lucky, you could well have a CD-R or CD-RW drive that will serve you as a great CD-ROM drive, and only that, under Linux. Table 20.11 contains a list of CD-R and CD-RW drives currently known to be compatible with CD-writing software under Linux. If you want to write CDs, do yourself a favor and get one of these drives. However, if you already have a drive that is not shown in this list, it might still work: The only way to know for sure is to try it out. You could also check the latest Unix CD-Writer compatibility list at http://www.guug.de:8080/cgi-bin/winni/lsc.pl to see if anyone has had success with your model drive since this book was published.

Table 20.11   CD-R and CD-RW Drives Supported by Linux

CD-R and CD-RW	Drives
Acer	CDRW 6206A
BTC	BCE 621E
Compro	CW-7502, CW-7502B
Creative	RW 4224E
Dysan	CRW-1622
Elite	Elite b444.41
Grundig	CDR 100 IPW
Guillemot	Maxi CD-R 4X/8X

Part
IV

Ch
20

continues

Table 20.11   Continued

CD-R and CD-RW	Drives
HP	SureStore 4020i, SureStore 6020i, CD-Writer+ 7100, CD-Writer+ 7200i, CD-Writer+ 8100i, CD-Writer+ 8110i
Hi-Val	CDD 2242, CDD-3610
JVC	XR-W2001, XR-W2010, XR-W2042, R-2626
Kodak	PCD 200, PCD 225, PCD 260, PCD 600
Matsushita	CW-7502
Memorex	CRW-620, CRW-1622
Microboards	PlayWrite 2000, PlayWrite 4000RW, PlayWrite 4001RW
MicroNet	MasterCD Plus 4x4, MasterCD Plus 4x6
Mitsubishi	CDRW-226
Mitsumi	CR-2401-TS, CR-2600 TE, CR-2801 TE, CR-4801 TE
Nomai	680.RW
OTI	CDRW 965
Olympus	CDS 615E, CDS 620E
Optima	DisKovery 650 CD-R
Panasonic	CW-7502, CW-7582
Philips	CDD-521/10, CDD-522, CDD-2000, CDD-2600, CDD-3600, CDD-3610, Omniwriter 26, Omniwriter 26A
Plasmon	CDR 480, CDR 4220, RF-4100, RF-4102, CDR 4400
Plextor	CDR PX-24 CS, PX-412 C, PX-R412 C, PX-R810Ti, PleXwriter 412C
Procom	PCDR 4
Ricoh	RO-1420C+, MP 1420C, MP 6200S, MP 6201S, MP 7040A
Sanyo	CRD-R24S
Smart and Friendly	CD-RW226, CD-R1002, CD-R1002/PRO, CD-R1004, CD-R2004, CD-R2006 PLUS, CD-R2006 PRO, CD-R4000, CD-R4006, CD-R4012
Sony	CDU 920S, CDU 924, CDU 926S, CDU-928E, CDU 948S, CDRX 100E
Taiyo Yuden	EW-50
TEAC	CD-R50S, CD-R55S, CDR-55S, CDR-56S-400
Traxdata	CRW 2260, CDR 4120, CDRW 4260
Turtle Beach	2040R

CD-R and CD-RW	Drives
WPI (Wearnes)	CDRW-622, CDR-632P
YAMAHA	CDR-100, CDR 102, CDR-200, CDR-200t, CDR-200tx, CDR-400, CDR-400c, CDR-400t, CDR-400tx, CDR-400Atx, CRW-2260, CRW-2260t, CRW-4250tx, CRW-4260t, CRW-4260tx, CRW-4261, CRW-4416 S

Troubleshooting

The Linux community has battled manufacturers to divulge hardware specifications to facilitate independent driver development from the very beginning. In the early days, developers met with failure more often than not. They were frequently either unable to develop desired drivers, or they managed somehow through reverse engineering, disassembly, guesswork, and persistence. Times have changed for the better. Although there are still some problem companies out there, manufacturer support and development of Linux drivers is increasing steadily.

One of your most important resources will be the Red Hat Linux Hardware Compatibility Lists for Intel (x86), Alpha, and Sparc platforms at http://www.redhat.com/corp/support/hardware/index.html. There you can find the most current information on what hardware is supported and to what degree. If you run into problems not covered in this chapter, you also might have to check out the Linux CD-ROM HOWTO at http://metalab.unc.edu/.

If these documents don't turn up anything on the hardware you're interested in, search Usenet (Internet news) and mailing list archives, and post your problem on the appropriate newsgroups. You might find that someone has already had success with some hardware not yet included in these compatibility lists. The Red Hat site contains errata pages and fixes for known problems, which also might help. Keep in mind that sometimes your hardware just isn't supported by Linux, for whatever reason. In such an instance, you should consider whether it's worth your money to just buy a new CD-ROM that is supported rather than pulling your hair out trying to get yours to work.

Begin by making sure that you have correctly identified all the relevant hardware. Make sure everything is properly connected. Check all hardware configuration settings, jumpers, EEP-ROM, and so on. Watch the console messages that display when you boot up, and make sure everything is properly recognized. If necessary, you should check your BIOS settings also. You can also use commands such as dmesg and lsmod to find out information about what support is supported and configured in your kernel. If you're missing a crucial driver that is not loadable by module, you might have to recompile your kernel. ●

Part
IV

Ch
20

## CHAPTER 21

Installing and Configuring Printers

by Duane Hellums

In this chapter

Understanding Linux Printing

Printing with Linux is similar to printing with other operating systems, although there are a few small differences. Specifically, you will find that you need to know a little bit more detail about the way printers and the printing process works than you do for another OS. In addition, you might find that your printer manufacturer might not provide the necessary Linux drivers for your printer. In some cases, nobody might have written a driver for that specific piece of hardware yet. Luckily, most contemporary printers support a few common printer drivers, so you should have no problem at least getting your printer to provide basic print services.

For the majority of people, printing will involve only connecting the parallel printer cable, powering on the printer, configuring the print driver, and then printing a document from an application or from a shell prompt. Even though it is not necessary to understand all the details about how your Linux print drivers, queues, and background processes work, understanding such details can help if you have to troubleshoot printer problems.

Red Hat Linux uses a standard UNIX style of printing developed by Berkeley Software Distribution (BSD). This method of printing uses a background process (lpd) that "listens for" print requests coming from the local machine or from processes on other network machines (if remote printing is enabled). Each time lpd receives a request, it temporarily creates a new lpd process to transfer and print the data, so you should not be surprised if you see more than one lpd process running in a process listing (ps -ef).

Most PCs come with one or two parallel ports, which typically are enabled and configured in the Basic Input Output System (BIOS). Check the manual that came with your PC or motherboard to find out how to access the BIOS and view or change your current printer port settings. Ordinarily, you will not need to do this, however, because Red Hat Linux auto-detects printer ports using standard parallel port and input/output (I/O) addresses, just as other operating systems do. As a result, the configuration of this port should be transparent to you.

Your BIOS probably will reflect your first parallel port as LPT1 at interrupt (IRQ) 7 and I/O address hexadecimal 378 (0x378), and your second parallel port as LPT2 at IRQ 5 and I/O 278 (0x278). On your Red Hat Linux system, these devices will be designated /dev/lp0 and /dev/lp1. Confirm that these devices are enabled and available in Red Hat by typing ls -al /dev/lp* from an X terminal or at the command-line prompt.

> **CAUTION**
>
> As you add more devices and peripherals to your Linux system, such as a local area network (LAN), sound, multiport serial, game/multimedia, and video capture cards, you will find that limited IRQ and I/O resources quickly become very scarce commodities. This increases the odds of a resource conflict that will require innovative methods of correcting, if you even can resolve the problem (some older cards just demand certain resources). If all else fails, you might have to do without a certain device, find a way of efficiently swapping them when you need to, or buy another device that is more flexible.

Installing and Configuring a Local Printer

More than likely, you connected your printer before you installed Red Hat Linux 6.0, and you configured your printer during the Red Hat installation and setup process. However, you might want to add additional local and network printers to your system, or you might need to make changes to an existing configuration. From a hardware standpoint, your only limitation is the number of parallel ports your system and motherboard support—all you should have to do is obtain another 25-pin parallel printer cable and connect it to both an available port and your extra printer. On the software configuration side, you will be using the Red Hat Print Tool (/usr/bin/printtool).

To add a new printer configuration to a Red Hat Linux system, or to edit an existing printer's settings, perform the following steps:

1. As root, select System, Control Panel, Printer Configuration from the main GNOME panel menu. You also can type /usr/bin/printtool from an X terminal or at the command-line prompt. If you already have a printer configured, you will see it listed in the Print System Manager pop-up window, pictured in Figure 21.1.

FIG. 21.1
Red Hat provides a flexible print manager for configuring your attached or network printers.

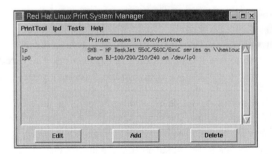

2. (Optional) To edit settings for an existing printer, highlight one of the available printers and click the Edit button. Then skip the next step.

3. (Optional) To add a printer, click the Add button.

4. Choose Local Printer, and click the OK button. You should see the Info box shown in Figure 21.2, which informs you that Red Hat Linux has auto-detected a standard parallel printer port.

5. Click OK to dismiss the Info box and bring up the box pictured in Figure 21.3 that allows you to enter the following information:
   - **Names**—Enter an appropriate name that you want to use when referring to this printer (for example, lp, lp1, laser, hp, canon, inkjet). If you want, you can enter more than one name, separating them with a vertical bar (pipe) character.

Part
IV

Ch
21

FIG. 21.2
Red Hat auto-detects
parallel printers con-
nected to standard
ports.

FIG. 21.3
You select the name of
your printer as well as
the device file and the
location of the print
queue.

- **Spool Directory**—A spool is nothing more than a directory that serves as a queue for temporary storage of files being printed. The directory you name will be created in the default /var/spool/lpd directory with the name you just chose.

TIP Try not to get too confused or worried by the similar acronyms used by all the printing components, such as lp, lpd, lpr, lp0 (LPT), lprm, lpc, lpq, and so on. Although they seem a little cryptic, you will become accustomed to them with time and hopefully will appreciate their brevity and simplicity. If you do make a mistake and use one in place of another, you're not likely to cause any damage or system problems.

- **File Limit in KB**—Leave this as 0 if you don't want to impose a size limit on printed files. Otherwise, enter the restriction you want.
- **Printer Device**—Enter the name of the Linux printer device that is stored in the /dev directory and that serves as the conduit to your printer (the equivalent of the LPT1 or LPT2 device names in DOS/Windows printing). The default is the first parallel port, at /dev/lp0 (LPT1).
- **Suppress Headers**—Check this box if you do not need a banner page printed with each document (sometimes used in a multiuser environment for identification and routing purposes).
- **Input Filter**—Click the Select button. You will see the window shown in Figure 21.4, which allows you to pick your printer driver and associated settings, as follows.

FIG. 21.4
You can choose from a wide variety of supported filters (drivers) to work with almost any standard printer type.

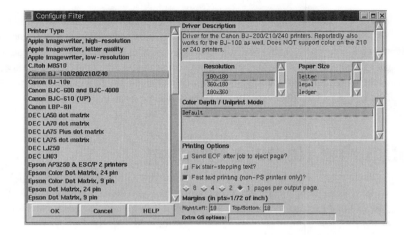

- **Printer Type**—Select the Linux-supported print driver that matches your printer or that is compatible with it. The description, resolution, paper size, and color depth fields will change based on the printer's capabilities.

- **Resolution**—Choose how finely grained you want or need your printouts to be. Larger numbers are better quality because there are more dots per inch printed on the paper.

- **Paper Size**—Indicate what size paper you are using (letter is the default, at 8.5×11 inches). This allows Linux to determine the print area and decide where to break pages.

- **Color Depth**—If you have a color printer, select the color settings you want to use based on the quality you need.

- **Margins**—For 1-inch margins, enter 72; for 1/2 inch margins, enter 36.

- **Printer Options**—These options enable you to tweak the way Linux works with different types of hardware settings and printer capabilities. For example, if your documents just sit in the printer's memory waiting for you to press a button, you can check the box that will send an eject command to your printer each time you print a document. You can also check a box to print multiple copies (1–8) or fix stair-stepping of text.

6. Complete the configuration by clicking the OK button to save your settings. Then click the printer you just added in the Print System Manager window, and then select Tests, Print PostScript test page. A properly formatted and color (if applicable) test page should print. You also can click the Print ASCII Test Page option if you want to see plain text. Click the Edit button and make the appropriate configuration changes, if necessary.

N O T E Stair-stepping of printed text is caused by a UNIX convention (that Linux inherited) that generates only a line-feed character. On some printers, this causes the next line of print to begin in the middle of the next line, creating a stair-step effect. This could also cause lines to print over each other on a single line. In addition to correcting this using the Print tool, you might be able to change the hardware (dip switch) settings on your printer to add a carriage return (CR) to any line feed (LF) characters. Check your printer manual to see if it has this capability. ▪

Configuring Remote Printing

After you have installed and configured Red Hat Linux properly on your PC, you easily can make it a print server for any other Linux PCs you have on the network. When you do this, you can print to a remote Linux printer as if it were connected to your local machine. Assuming that you have TCP/IP networking installed, the file will transfer over the network and automatically print from the other Linux PC.

Red Hat Linux 6.0 also provides the capability of using the same Server Message Block (SMB) protocol popular in Windows networking and file/print sharing. This enables you to use the same configuration tools you used for local printing, but this time to connect to and use a remote printer attached to a Windows-based PC. This leverages your technology investments and bridges the two different operating system environments to meet your specific processing needs. The lower-level SMB networking is transparent to you—all you basically do is tell Linux the name of the Windows machine and printer. Chapter 29, "Configuring NetWare Access," provides the details you need to use a printer that is also shared on a NetWare LAN, which is similar to the model used by Linux for Windows print sharing.

Configuring Remote Linux Printing

By default, your Red Hat Linux PC will not allow other Linux PCs to connect to and use your local printer remotely. If you want to enable this feature, you must edit the `/etc/hosts.lpd` file on the Linux PC attached to the printer. Edit the file with GNU notepad, vi, or any other word processor. Simply create a list of PC names in this file (for example, `hemicuda`, `hemicuda.hellums.com`, `192.168.1.1`), with each new line containing a single PC name.

When you have configured a Linux system to allow printing from remote PCs, you still must configure all Linux boxes to properly connect to and use these remote printing services. This process is similar to configuring a local printer, with only a few small changes. Most of the complicated work will be performed by the native TCP/IP networking capability of Linux and the flexibility of the `lpr` command and `lpd` background process. To accomplish this, perform the following steps:

1. As root, select System, Control Panel, Printer Configuration from the main GNOME panel menu. You can also type `/usr/bin/printtool` from an X terminal or at the command-line prompt.

2. To add a remote printer, click the Add button.

3. Choose Remote Unix (lpd) Queue, and click the OK button. This brings up the Edit Remote Unix (lpd) Queue Entry box pictured in Figure 21.5, where you can fill in the following configuration items:

- **Names**—Enter the name you want to use when referring to this printer (for example, lp, lp1, laser, hp, canon, inkjet). If you want, you can enter more than one name, separating them with a vertical bar character.

FIG. 21.5
You indicate the name of the remote Linux PC and queue, as well as the type of filter or driver.

- **Spool Directory**—A directory will be created in the default /var/spool/lpd directory with the name you just chose for temporary print queue files to be stored.

- **File Limit in KB**—Leave this as 0 if you don't want to impose a size limit on printed files. Otherwise, enter the restriction you want.

- **Remote Host**—Enter the name of the remote Linux machine (or other UNIX host using BSD-style printing).

- **Remote Queue**—Just as you have a local spool directory in /var/spool/lpd, so does the remote computer. Enter the name of that spool here. This is usually the name that is stored in the name field on the other machine.

- **Input Filter**—Click Select to bring up the Configure Filter window, shown earlier in Figure 21.4. As mentioned before, you can select the Printer Type from the available list, as well as Resolution (if applicable), Paper Size, Color Depth (if applicable), number of copies, Margins, and other printing options. Click OK when you are happy with your changes, or click Cancel to ignore any changes you have made.

4. After completing the configuration, click the printer you just added in the Print System Manager window, and then select Tests, Print PostScript Test Page. A properly formatted and color (if applicable) test page should print from the remote Linux printer. You also can click Print ASCII Test Page if you want to see plain text. Click the Edit button, and make the appropriate configuration changes, if necessary.

CAUTION

The print queue on the remote Linux PC will have a specific print filter configured for both local and remote printing. When configuring your local machine to print on a remote printer, you really don't have to select a print filter—lpr will default to the remote printer's settings. Entering the print filter locally, however, will override the remote settings, which might give you unexpected results and complicate troubleshooting. It is best to just leave the filter blank if you're printing to a remote printer.

Configuring Remote Windows Printing

Just as Linux does not allow you by default to print on someone else's printer without that person authorizing it on his local PC, Windows also does not allow remote printing. To do this on a Windows PC that has networking and file and print sharing installed and configured, you must perform the following steps:

1. Right-click Network Neighborhood, and select Properties (or select Network from the Control Panel).

2. Click the File and Print Sharing button.

3. Check the box indicating that you want other people to be able to use your printers.

4. Go to Start, Settings, Printers, and bring up the properties of the configured printer that you want to share (select Add Printer, and follow your Windows instructions to configure new printers).

5. Under the Sharing tab, check the Shared As radio button and enter the Share Name, Comments, and a Password (use this only if you absolutely must because access permissions between Windows and other operating systems normally don't operate as smoothly as they should because Windows is not case-sensitive).

After you have configured the Windows system to allow printing from remote PCs (both Windows and Linux, actually), you still must configure all Linux boxes on your network to properly connect to and use these remote Windows printers. As you might suspect by this point in the chapter, this process is fairly simple and is similar to configuring a local printer and a remote Linux printer, with only a few small changes. Most of the complicated work will be performed by the SMB networking capability of Linux. To accomplish this on your Linux PCs, perform the following steps:

1. As root, select System, Control Panel, Printer Configuration from the main GNOME panel menu. You can also type `/usr/bin/printtool` from an X terminal or at the command-line prompt.

2. Click the Add button, choose SMB/Windows 95/NT Printer, and click the OK button. This brings up an informational warning box explaining that printer passwords are not transmitted as securely as native authentication login passwords and, for that reason, should be different than user account passwords. You will then see the Edit

SMB/Windows 95/NT Printer Entry box, shown in Figure 21.6, where you can fill in the following configuration items:

- **Names**—Similar to local and remote Linux printers, enter the name you want to use when referring to this printer (if you have a local Linux printer already configured, this box will default to lp1). If you want, you can enter more than one name, separating them with a vertical bar character.

FIG. 21.6
You indicate the names and IP address of the remote Windows PC and printer, as well as authentication and print filter/driver information.

- **Spool Directory**—A directory will be created in the default /var/spool/lpd directory with the name you just chose for temporary print queue files to be stored while waiting to be transferred to the remote printer.

- **File Limit in KB**—Leave this as 0 if you don't want to impose a size limit on printed files. Otherwise, enter the restriction you want.

- **Hostname of Printer Server**—Enter the Computer name of the remote Windows 95 or Windows NT machine (or other print server using the SMB protocol).

- **(Optional) IP Number of Server**—This Allows SMB to print directly to the IP address without requiring hostname resolution.

- **Printer Name**—Enter the Share As name you entered in the Sharing tab of the shared Windows Printer Properties window.

- **(Optional) User**—Enter an account or username if you configured the remote Windows printer to require authentication.

- **(Optional) Password**—Enter a password if you required authentication. Keep in mind that this password is sent to the Linux SMB client program in the clear, which opens it up slightly to discovery if your Linux machine has multiple users accessing it at the same time.

- **(Optional) Workgroup**—Enter the Windows networking workgroup name. You can get this information from the Identity tab of the Windows Network Neighborhood Properties window.

Part
IV

Ch
21

- **Input Filter**—Click Select to bring up the Configure Filter window (refer to Figure 21.4). As mentioned before, you can select the Printer Type from the available list, as well as Resolution (if applicable), Paper Size, Color Depth (if applicable), number of copies, Margins, and other printing options. Click OK when you are happy with your changes, or click Cancel to ignore any changes you have made.

3. After completing the configuration, click the printer you just added in the Print System Manager window, and then select Tests, Print PostScript Test Page. A properly formatted and color (if applicable) test page should print on the remote Linux printer. You also can click Print ASCII Test Page if you want to see plain text. Click the Edit button, and make the appropriate configuration changes, if necessary.

Printing to Local and Remote Queues

When you are using an application such as a word processor or a graphics program and you want to print a file, you normally select File, Print. The application in turn sends the file to the default print queue for processing by the line printer daemon or process, /usr/bin/lpd. Applications can do this using the /usr/bin/lpr command. The /usr/bin/lpr command is a very flexible print utility that can be used by applications or by you directly from an X terminal or at the command-line shell prompt. This command uses the BSD-style printing discussed earlier in this chapter to print to both local and remote printers.

Printing Locally to Linux Print Queues

Perhaps the best way to understand Linux printing is through a few examples. On my home network, I used the preceding procedures in this chapter to configure a local Canon BJC-200 printer for use on my machine. I named it lp and canon (lp¦canon) on device /dev/lp0 (equivalent of LPT1) and used the default spooler queue /var/spool/lpd/lp for temporary storage of printed files. This automatically generated a configuration file named /etc/printcap.

To print this configuration file, all I have to do is type lpr /etc/printcap and verify that the output is correct on the printout. If an application is configured to print by default to the lp print queue, the File, Print process should provide the same results (but using the current document or file as output instead). To print on the same printer using the more user-friendly name of Canon, I just type lpr -P canon /etc/printcap, which sends the output to the specific printer (-P) named canon.

Printing Remotely to Linux and Windows Print Queues

If you have a network installed, you don't need a different printer for each machine. You can spread different types of printers (for example, dot matrix, laser jet, laser, and color) around your network so that all machines can get to them easily and conveniently. You can even connect more than one printer to certain machines, if you want to increase their utility as a print server. Part V, "Local Area Networks (LANs)," discusses networking your Linux machines in detail.

Network printing in Linux using `/usr/bin/lpd` and `/usr/bin/lpr` or SMB (for Windows/NT) essentially involves a two-step configuration process. First you must install and configure the network printer locally on the print server, and then you must somehow tell your remote PC or client how to access that printer. In my particular case, I installed and configured networking during installation of both Linux PCs (local and remote) and a Windows 98 PC, so everything was already in place for this capability.

For example, I used the procedures from earlier in this chapter to configure a local Hewlett Packard Deskjet 1120C color office printer on a dual-boot Windows 98/Linux PC named HEMICUDA. On that machine's Linux partition, I configured the printer locally, naming it lp and deskjet (`lp¦deskjet`) on device `/dev/lp0` (equivalent to LPT1), and I used the default queue `/var/spool/lpd/lp` for temporary storage of printed files. I also could have named the queue `/var/spool/lpd/deskjet`. I chose the HP Deskjet 550C/560C/6xxC series print filter, which was the closest match to my newer printer. Networking did not have to be installed to use that printer locally, of course. I used the other process described earlier to configure the Windows 98 partition.

Then I had to configure another Linux PC named CUDA for remote Linux BSD-style and remote SMB/Windows/NT printing over the network. During this configuration process, I provided the remote computer name, HEMICUDA, as well as the remote queue name, `/var/spool/lpd/lp` (Linux/UNIX printing) or printer name and IP address (Windows SMB printing), and print filter (HP Deskjet 550C/560C/6xxC series). On CUDA, I named this remote printer LAN-deskjet so that I could easily remember it.

To test the remote printing capability (and obtain a list of all host names and IP addresses on CUDA, for example) I just had to type `/usr/bin/lpr -P LAN-deskjet /etc/hosts`. From a local perspective, CUDA sent the file `/etc/hosts` over the local area network (LAN) wiring and equipment to HEMICUDA, where it magically printed. From the remote Linux perspective, HEMICUDA received a request to print a file from CUDA, allowed the network file transfer, and then used the `/usr/bin/lpr` command to print the file on the DeskJet printer there. For remote printing to the Windows 98 printer, the Linux print process just handed the print request off to SMB utilities, which completed the network negotiation and file transfer to the Windows PC and printer.

N O T E The basic difference between local and remote Linux printers can be seen easily in the `/etc/printcap` printer configuration file (which Red Hat recommends that you do not edit, but that you modify instead using `printtool`). Local printers, such as a printer connected to LPT1 or `/dev/lp0`, are listed as such in a formatted record marked lp. Remote printers do not have an lp entry; they instead have entries named rm and rp, where the remote machine name and print queue information are stored, respectively. ▪

Part
IV

Ch
21

Printing Directly to a Local Printer

When you configured your local printers on Linux, you had the option of testing your print settings with the `printtool`. If the printer is attached directly to the computer, not over the network, you can also dump plain text directly onto the physical port. For troubleshooting purposes, this can be used to test that the physical link is okay and that your print driver is working.

To perform this direct hardware test, click a local printer in `printtool`, and select Tests, Print ASCII Directly to Port. If your printer is turned on and properly connected, and if the Linux printtool is properly configured, you should see a single line of text print from the chosen printer.

You can also print a plain text file directly to a printer port by redirecting standard output that you see normally on your screen. For example, typing `cat /etc/inittab > /dev/lp0` will have a similar effect as the previous step, if the chosen printer were connected to lp0. Understand that you might have to perform a form feed to force the printer to eject the page, and your printer will behave erratically if you print an executable or non-ASCII file this way (because the printer tries to interpret certain control codes and characters).

Controlling Printers, Queues, and Print Jobs

After you have created all the necessary local and remote printers, at some point you likely will need to control how they function and operate within your Linux system. For example, you can change the default printer used by `/usr/bin/lpr` from lp to another printer name.

To make the printer named laser your default, if you're using the default BASH shell, type the following from an X terminal or at the command-line shell prompt: `PRINTER=laser;export PRINTER` (instead of the semicolon, you can enter both commands on separate lines). You can also add this statement to your `.bash` profile configuration file. Before and after you do this, you can confirm what the default printer is by typing `echo $PRINTER` (Linux will display the name of the current default). This is the printer that will be used any time you use the `/usr/bin/lpr` command without any additional parameters.

If you want an application to print to a different printer than the default local lp printer on /dev/lp0, you might have to modify configuration settings specific to that application. For example, Netscape Communicator defaults to `lpr`, to which I must add the `-P LAN-deskjet` syntax to print on my remote Linux PC.

Using the */usr/bin/lpq* and */usr/bin/lprm* Commands

If you are using Linux in a multiple-user environment, or if you are doing an extraordinarily large amount of printing, you might need to monitor, manipulate, or control the print queues. Two very useful commands for this are the `lpq` and `lprm` commands.

The `/usr/bin/lpq` command provides the status of your print queues for each available local and remote printer. You will see a small table with a rank, owner, job number, filename, and file size. If you just type `lpq`, you will receive information about lp by default. To find information on another queue (such as lp0, for example), you can type `lpq -P lp0`. The `lpq` command will also tell you whether a printer is up or down, whether queuing is enabled, and whether a daemon is running, which can be used for debugging purposes.

If you decide that you don't really want a document to print, even though you've already released it to a print queue, you can stop the document from printing by using the `/usr/bin/lprm` command. To do this, you must be able to reference the print job number for the file in question, information that you can find out from `lpq`. For example, if `lpq` informs you about jobs 20 and 23 on lp and jobs 21 and 22 on lp0, you can delete jobs 23 and 21 by typing `lprm 23` and `lprm -P lp0 21`. This will remove a pair of print-related files from the appropriate print spool directories for those printers.

Using the */usr/bin/lpc* Command

The `lpc` command provides you some capabilities for controlling your printer, the lpd daemon, and your printer's spooling directory. You can use it interactively by just typing `/usr/bin/lpc` from an X terminal or at the command line. This brings up an `lpc` prompt, where you can type commands directly to the interface. Type `help` or `?`, and you will see all the options available. You can also enter the `lpc` command, followed immediately by the specific function you want to perform. For example, you can check status of all printers by typing `/usr/bin/lpc status`, or `lpc stat`, for short. With `lpc`, you can perform the following tasks:

- **status**—Provides the status of the selected printer, queue, and print daemon.
- **disable/enable**—Provides a way to prevent or allow lpr to use certain printer queues and printers (during maintenance or malfunctions, for example).
- **stop/start**—Provides a way to kill the print daemon and start it up again, without actually preventing users from sending print jobs to the queues (useful for debugging purposes or when a configuration change is needed).
- **up/down**—Provides a way to prevent or allow queuing to certain printers, and to start or stop the associated print daemon (the equivalent of disable/stop and enable/start).
- **restart**—Quickly toggles print services off and on again (equivalent to stop/start), which can be useful when printing is acting up and you think it might help to freshen the print daemon processes.
- **abort**—Disables printing and stops the lpd daemon, effectively stopping any current print jobs that are sitting in a queue waiting to print (useful when a large document is printing improperly and you want to fix the problem before printing the file again).
- **clean**—Removes any extraneous files left in the selected queues from previously stalled or cancelled print jobs.

- **topq**—Moves one or more selected job numbers to the top of the queue so that they print sooner (note that you do not need the -P syntax to identify the specific printer—for example, `lpc topq lp0 23` will move job 23 on lp0 to the top of the queue).

Troubleshooting Linux Printing

All in all, Linux printing is pretty mature and robust. If problems occur, you can use a combination of the print utilities just mentioned to help debug printing problems. Specifically, `lpc stat` is a quick way of finding out everything you need to know about the current printing environment. Based on output from this command, you might have to use different combinations of lpc commands to clear up problems with specific printers. If you determine that daemons and queues are functioning properly, you might have to use the `printtool` again to edit default printer settings for local and remote printers. You can also use brute-force printing directly to the printer port, to take spooling and printer daemons out of the equation, for troubleshooting reasons. To do this, type the following command for a printer on LPT1:

```
cat /etc/passwd > /dev/lp0
```

If you have used all the native Linux tools to fix a problem and you still can't get a file to print on one of your local printers, you might have to check the BIOS to make sure that the printer is properly configured and enabled at the PC hardware level. Your next step after that would be to make sure that you have kernel support for line printing and that your lp devices are properly configured on your system (in the `/dev/` directory) and have the appropriate read/write permissions for users and groups to access the printer.

Sometimes a printing problem is not that hard to fix. The daemon might have just gone stale or died, requiring you to restart it. In a multiuser environment, another administrator might have disabled queuing or stopped printing without you knowing. Don't forget to try the obvious and simple troubleshooting steps before looking for more complicated problems. For example, make sure the printer is plugged in, turned on, marked online, and connected firmly to your PC ports. Keep in mind that all the different configuration items mentioned in this chapter, such as text stair-stepping, could be causing certain types of problems. It might just be a configuration problem instead of a system problem. ●

## CHAPTER 22

Installing and Configuring Sound Cards

by Jon Konrath

In this chapter

About Computer-Generated Sound

Previously, one of the greatest criticisms of Linux was its lack of sound support. In the past, sound card drivers were very rudimentary and difficult to configure. Plus, there was support for only a limited number of sound cards. But with Red Hat Linux 6.0, there comes great improvement in sound support. Many new cards are supported, and installation has been greatly streamlined. In addition, other third-party sound drivers, both open source and commercial, have become available. This means more options for audio support and more compatibility for those with lesser-known sound hardware.

Before you begin configuring sound for Linux, it might be helpful to understand exactly what a sound card does and how sound works. Sound itself is an oscillation of air, like the ripples that spread outward when you drop a stone in a pool of water. Similar but much more rapid frequencies are detected by the inner ear and are translated into the sounds you hear. The rate at which these oscillations occur is called *frequency*, and the pattern and repetition of these movements create tonal quality, or *timbre*.

The simplest way for computer hardware to generate sound is called FM synthesis. Back in the golden age of home computers, machines such as the Commodore 64 and Atari 800 had the capability to create sound, mostly utilized in computer games and BASIC programs. To generate sound, these machines used a chip that could generate a few simple waveforms and combine them, giving very basic timbres. These combinations let you play sounds in voices that were decidedly artificial and computer-generated. The timbres created by simple FM synthesis generally sound too perfect because they're exactly the same every time. This might not be realistic, but with FM synthesis, you need to tell the sound chip only what timbre to play and the duration, instead of storing megabytes of sampled sound data. That's why this was the sound generation method of choice back when memory was scarce, and it's still widely used in synthesizers, toys, and video games. Most PC sound cards still support more developed FM synthesis sound, largely for reverse compatibility.

If you want more realistic sound, you must sample it. Sampling occurs when a digital device such as a computer measures the analog property of sound and periodically records these measurements for later playback. Sampling is superior to FM synthesis because it captures every subtlety and nuance of the source sound, instead of trying to imitate it with pure sounds. The downside to this is that it takes space to store all these values. You can change the number of samples per second to save space, but this also lowers the quality of the sound.

Wavetable synthesis is a scheme that combines sampling and FM synthesis. In this, voices are sampled into a library to provide a bank of realistic sounds. They are stored in the sound card's memory and can be played, combined, and changed without the overhead of sampled sound.

Most sound cards also support the Musical Instrument Digital Interface (MIDI). The hardware component of MIDI provides a method to interface synthesizers, sequencers, samplers, drum machines, computers, and other audio equipment. A controller such as a piano keyboard can be used to play the sounds in another device, such as a computer. This communication over the MIDI bus can be recorded and played back or edited later. MIDI files are small, containing just this sequencing information and using sounds from your sound card. Even if you don't have a MIDI instrument or even a MIDI port, your sound card probably plays MIDI files.

Sound cards put all this together on one piece of hardware in your PC. In addition, they usually include ports for input devices such as CD players and microphones, and output devices such as speakers, headphones, or a stereo amplifier. Some sound cards also offer additional hardware, which can range from a joystick port to a CD-ROM or IDE disk drive interface. And many new models contain additional features such as surround sound, digital input and output, and various sound quality features such as simulated surround or Creative Labs' Environmental Audio.

Several different types of sound files exist. The most popular in the UNIX world is the AU file, a format originating on Sun workstations: two-channel, audio, with an 8-bit sample size and 8KHz sample size. This means that when an AU file is recorded, 8 bits of audio are sampled 8,000 times a second. In comparison, the other big sound file type is the WAV file, the standard sound type in Microsoft Windows. Generally, a WAV file has two channels, 8 or 16 bits, and a 22–44KHz sample rate. As far as FM is concerned, there are MIDI files, which aren't sampled, and MOD files, which use sequenced information (like MIDI) but their own sampled sounds (more like Wavetable synthesis). MOD files originated on the Amiga and aren't as widespread, but they are freely traded on the Internet by MOD artists who consider this the format of choice. Many compressed audio file types also exist, the two most popular being MPEG-2 Layer 3, also known as MP-3, and Real Audio.

Now that you have an understanding of how sound works, it's time to explain how sound works in Linux.

Understanding Linux Sound Support

As with any other hardware in your Linux system, a sound card must have some code that recognizes it and lets the Linux kernel properly talk to it. This is a device driver, and many of them exist for the different types of sound hardware available. When it's running, a driver enables the related files in /dev to act as gateways to control the sound card, just like how drivers enable you to use /hda to read and write to your hard drive.

Red Hat Linux 6.0 includes drivers for sound devices in the kernel source. These can be compiled in the kernel or can be loaded as a module. Although the kernel supports many different types of sound cards, the most tested and developed code is for the Creative Labs Sound Blaster family, especially most of the older Sound Blaster cards.

Before you think, "Great, my card works like a Sound Blaster," beware! The first thing you'll quickly find out when configuring sound for Linux is that "100% Sound Blaster-compatible" is one of the largest myths in the computer industry. Although most sound cards claim Sound Blaster compatibility, that's only with a custom Windows driver. In Linux, every different sound card must have its own driver. That's because there's an ever-growing number of sound devices on the market—including PCs with proprietary, built-in sound devices—and the Linux development community has a limited amount of resources. So, even a card that works great in Windows might not work in Linux.

Another problem is that many cards are now Plug and Play. Older Sound Blaster cards used jumpers to configure IRQ and DMA settings. But newer hardware sometimes uses Plug and Play to initialize a card, which won't always work in Linux. Red Hat Linux 6.0 includes support for initializing Plug and Play sound cards.

When the sound driver is correctly loaded and configured, it's possible to interface with your sound card via several device files. The following lists the most standard device files:

Device	Description
/dev/audio	An audio device compatible with the Sun workstation audio device
/dev/dsp	The digital sampling device
/dev/mixer	A mixer device used to mix the levels of various audio inputs
/dev/music	A high-level sequencer interface
/dev/sequencer	The low-level FM synthesis device interface
/dev/midi	Raw MIDI information
/dev/sndstat	A device that displays sound driver status

These devices provide a standard method for sound applications to communicate with your sound card. With this support, applications can play, record, and manipulate sounds using your sound card.

Installing Sound Cards

Before you try to install a sound card for Linux, it's helpful to see how it works in Windows first. If you have a dual-boot machine, or if you haven't installed Linux yet and Windows is still on your machine, install your sound card and get it to work in Windows. Read the manufacturer's instructions, install the hardware, and add the Windows sound drivers. Make sure to connect the cable from your sound card to the CD-ROM drive, and either plug in a pair of external speakers or headphones, or run a line to the amplifier stereo. Try the sound in Windows (Pinball), and play a few audio CDs to make sure that your sound card and CD-ROM are communicating.

When you're sure that the sound card hardware and any related speakers and microphones are all working fine, open the Windows Control Panel for the sound card. The location varies depending on your version of Windows, but lately it's been a tab on the Multimedia control panel. If you have a non-Plug and Play soundcard, a quick look in this control panel will reveal a list of settings, such as I/O Port, IRQ, and DMA settings. Write these down for use later in your Linux configuration.

If you've never installed Windows on this PC, don't worry about it; this is a non-essential troubleshooting test. Make sure to install the card and other related gear correctly, and don't worry about the Windows drivers (or the half-dozen AOL disks that were probably bundled with your new soundcard).

Before you start configuring your sound in Linux, it's helpful to get as much information as possible about your sound system, including the make and model of your sound card and whether it is Plug and Play. Also, if you haven't installed the card or if you can open your PC case, take a quick look at it. Older cards have jumper switches to set the IRQ, DMA channel, and other options. Newer cards have no jumpers or switches; they use PnP or software to change these settings. If your card has these jumpers, write down their settings for use later in your Linux configuration.

Installing Hardware Support

Red Hat Linux 6.0 includes kernel support for several popular sound cards. If you have one of these audio devices, it's not hard to get sound started. If your sound hardware is different, you might be able to configure sound manually to get the kernel to recognize your hardware. If all else fails, some third-party sound drivers, both free and commercial, might do the trick.

Using sndconfig

Red Hat Linux uses the 2.2 kernel, which includes the OSS/Free sound drivers. These are installed as modules by default. To get sound to work for your card, two things must be configured. To do this, a tool called sndconfig is used. Before you run sndconfig, you must make sure to log in as root or use the su command to gain superuser status.

First, if you have an ISA Plug and Play sound card, Linux must be capable of initializing it properly when your system reboots. To do this, you use a tool called isapnp. This tool uses a configuration file located at /etc/isapnp.conf, a file that acts as a dump of all ISA Plug and Play devices on your system. When you run sndconfig, it detects any Plug and Play cards in your system and dumps this configuration into the isapnp.conf file.

If you do not have a Plug and Play sound card, this test will fail. You can continue to the next step, or you can run sndconfig with the --noautoconfig option to skip the autoprobe test.

Next, sndconfig will attempt to identify the type of sound card you have. If it is incapable of doing so, you will be presented with a list of possible options. Use the arrow keys to find the make and model of your sound card, and press Return to select it. Remember, not all sound cards are alike, and sound cards with similar names are not always fully compatible.

After you have selected a card from the list, sndconfig will determine which sound driver to use and will write the configuration to the /etc/conf.modules file. This properly configures Linux to load the appropriate sound driver module for your sound card.

Depending on which sound card you choose, you may be prompted with a Card Settings dialog box. You'll need to enter the values of your I/O Port, IRQ, DMA, and possibly other settings. These are the settings configured by jumpers on your sound card.

Finally, sndconfig will play a sound to test your configuration. Make sure your speakers are connected and turned on before this step. If your configuration fails, sndconfig will tell you. Sometimes you can try again using a different sound card or card settings in sndconfig. But often, this means that you need to move to the next level and start reconfiguring the sound drivers in the kernel.

Configuring OSS/Free Sound

If sndconfig didn't work for you, the next step is to try to configure your Linux sound drivers manually. This requires some knowledge of your sound hardware. Plus, you'll possibly have to rebuild your kernel and most likely reconfigure your module support. This isn't easy work, and you might want to look at getting some help, or at least a commercial product like those mentioned later in the chapter.

Before you proceed, you should make sure that you have the kernel source installed, and be sure to read all the documentation in the directory /usr/src/linux/Documentation/sound. It's also helpful to read the sound HOWTO at /usr/doc/HOWTO/Sound-HOWTO, although the information is slightly dated.

Configuring the Kernel

It's possible that the kernel configuration included in Red Hat Linux 6.0 won't work for your hardware. Some drivers included with the Linux kernel source aren't part of the OSS sound package, which you will need to install and configure manually for some sound cards. It's important to first read any documentation in /usr/src/linux/Documentation/sound that's specific to your sound card.

You can configure sound drivers to be included in the kernel or compiled into modules that are loaded later. With some cards, it's easier to get included support to work and then try to get modular support to work later. This won't work with Plug and Play cards, though, because the card isn't recognized until after the kernel is running. In these cases, configure your sound driver as a module, and then read the following sections on module configuration and isapnp configuration.

The following is a list of sound configuration options in the kernel. To change these options, issue a make config or make xconfig from the /usr/src/linux directory:

■ **Sound card support** (`CONFIG_SOUND`)

If you want to configure sound on your system, you'll need to enable this option. You can either select Y to configure sound into your kernel, or select M and have the kernel load sound support as a module. Usually, you'll be loading sound support as a module.

■ **Ensoniq ES1370-based PCI sound cards** (`CONFIG_SOUND_ES1370`)

Enable this driver if you have a PCI sound card that uses the Ensoniq ES1370 chipset. If you're not sure, look through `/proc/pci` for a card listing Vendor id=1274 and Device id=5000. Because Creative Labs bought Ensoniq, SoundBlaster 64/PCI models use the ES1370 or ES1371 chipset. These drivers aren't part of OSS/Free and vary slightly. Read the documentation at `/usr/src/linux/Documentation/sound/es1370` before proceeding.

■ **Joystick support at boot time** (`CONFIG_SOUND_ES1370_JOYPORT_BOOT`)

If you selected the Ensoniq ES1370 driver, select Y to enable the joystick port. To actually use the joystick, you'll also need to install a joystick driver. See `/usr/src/linux/Documentation/joystick.txt` for details.

■ **Ensoniq ES1371-based PCI sound cards** (`CONFIG_SOUND_ES1371`)

EnableEnable this driver if you have a PCI sound card that uses the Ensoniq ES1371 chipset. If you're not sure, look through `/proc/pci` for a card listing Vendor id=1274 and Device id=1371. Because Creative Labs bought Ensoniq, SoundBlaster 64/PCI models use the ES1370 or ES1371 chipset. These drivers aren't part of OSS/Free and vary slightly. Read the documentation at `/usr/src/linux/Documentation/sound/es1371` before proceeding.

■ **Joystick support at boot time** (`CONFIG_SOUND_ES1371_JOYPORT_BOOT`)

If you selected the Ensoniq ES1371 driver, select Y to enable the joystick port. To actually use the joystick, you'll also need to install a joystick driver. See `/usr/src/linux/Documentation/joystick.txt` for details.

■ **Gameport I/O-range selection** (`CONFIG_SOUND_ES1371_GAMEPORT`)

If you selected the Ensoniq ES1371 driver, select the I/O range of the gameport. The card can use values of 200, 208, 210, and 218.

■ **S3 SonicVibes-based PCI sound cards** (`CONFIG_SOUND_SONICVIBES`)

Enable this driver if you have a PCI sound card that uses the S3 SonicVibes chipset. If you're not sure, look through `/proc/pci` for a card listing Vendor id=5333 and Device id=CA00. You should read the documentation at `/usr/src/linux/Documentation/sonicvibes` before configuring this driver.

■ **Support for Turtle Beach Wave Front (Maui, Tropez) synthesizers** (`CONFIG_SOUND_MAUI`)

Select this option if you have a Turtle Beach Wave Front, Maui, or Tropez sound card.

■ **Have OSWF.MOT firmware file (CONFIG_MAUI_HAVE_BOOT)**

If you select this option, you will need an OSWF.MOT file that's distributed with your sound card's DOS/Windows drivers. If you have this file, select Y.

■ **Full pathname of OSWF.MOT firmware file (CONFIG_MAUI_BOOT_FILE)**

If you said Y to this option, enter the pathname of your OSWF.MOT file. The pathname starts from the root directory (/).

■ **Support for Turtle Beach MultiSound Classic, Tahiti, Monterey (CONFIG_SOUND_MSNDCLAS)**

Select M for this option if you have a Turtle Beach MultiSound Classic, Tahiti, or Monterey sound card. See /usr/src/linux/Documentation/sound/MultiSound for more information about this driver.

■ **Full pathname of MSNDINIT.BIN firmware file (CONFIG_MSNDCLAS_INIT_FILE) and Full pathname of MSNDPERM.BIN firmware file (CONFIG_MSNDCLAS_PERM_FILE)**

If you selected the Turtle Beach MultiSound driver, you will need two firmware files: MSNDINIT.BIN and MSNDPERM.BIN. These files can be obtained from Turtle Beach; see /usr/src/linux/Documentation/sound/MultiSound for more details. Enter the pathnames to the two files in these two options.

■ **Support for Turtle Beach MultiSound Pinnacle, Fiji (CONFIG_SOUND_MSNDPIN)**

Select M for this option if you have a Turtle Beach MultiSound Pinnacle or Fiji sound card. See /usr/src/linux/Documentation/sound/MultiSound for more information about this driver.

■ **Full pathname of PNDSPINI.BIN firmware file (CONFIG_MSNDPIN_INIT_FILE) and full pathname of PNDSPERM.BIN firmware file (CONFIG_MSNDPIN_PERM_FILE)**

If you selected the Turtle Beach MultiSound driver, you will need two firmware files: PNDSPINI.BIN and PNDSPERM.BIN. These files can be obtained from Turtle Beach; see /usr/src/linux/Documentation/sound/MultiSound for more details. Enter the pathnames to the two files in these two options.

■ **MSND Pinnacle have S/PDIF I/O (CONFIG_MSNDPIN_DIGITAL)**

If you have a Turtle Beach MultiSound Pinnacle or Fiji, and if you have the S/PDIF daughterboard, select Y for this option; otherwise, select N. If you have the daughterboard, you will be able to play and record digitally from the S/PDIF port. See /usr/src/linux/Documentation/sound/MultiSound for information.

■ **MSND Pinnacle non-PnP Mode (CONFIG_MSNDPIN_NONPNP)**

If you have a Turtle Beach MultiSound Pinnacle and Fiji sound card, they can be configured either as a Plug and Play card or with a configuration port. Select Y here if your card is not in Plug and Play mode. This enables use of the IDE and joystick ports on the card. If you are using the card in Plug and Play mode, select N for this option, and use isapnp to configure the card.

■ **MSND Pinnacle config port** (CONFIG_MSNDPIN_CFG)

Select the port used for configuring your Pinnacle and Fiji card when not in Plug and Play mode.

■ **MSND buffer size (KB)** (CONFIG_MSND_FIFOSIZE)

Select the size, in kilobytes, of the audio buffers used for recording and playing in the Turtle Beach MultiSound drivers.

■ **OSS sound modules** (CONFIG_SOUND_OSS)

The OSS drivers are the standard suite of sound card drivers included with the Linux kernel. If one of the specialized drivers mentioned here doesn't apply to your sound card, you should select Y or M for this option. You'll also need to select a sound card driver from one of the ones listed later.

■ **Persistent DMA buffers** (CONFIG_SOUND_DMAP)

If you have an ISA sound card and more than 16MB of RAM, you should say Y to this option. ISA DMA buffers must exist below 16MB, and if you have more memory, it might be impossible to allocate the buffers later. If you select this option, the 64KB buffers will be allocated at boot time and kept until shutdown. Say N to this option if you have 16MB RAM or less, if you aren't using the OSS drivers, or if you have a PCI sound card.

■ **Support for Aztech Sound Galaxy (non-PnP) cards** (CONFIG_SOUND_SGALAXY)

Select Y or M for this option if you have an older Aztech Sound Galaxy card that doesn't use Plug and Play, including the Waverider Pro 32—3D and the Galaxy Washington 16.

■ **Experimental Support for AD1816(A) based cards** (CONFIG_SOUND_AD1816)

Select M here if you would like to try experimental drivers for a sound card based on the Analog Devices AD1816(A) chip. See /usr/src/linux/Documentation/sound/AD1816 for more information.

■ **Yamaha OPL3-SA1 audio controller** (CONFIG_SOUND_OPL3SA1)

Select Y or M for this option if your motherboard has a Yamaha OPL3-SA1 sound chip. See /usr/src/linux/Documentation/sound/OPL3-SA for more information.

■ **ProAudio Spectrum 16 support** (CONFIG_SOUND_PAS)

Select Y if you have a ProAudio Spectrum 16, ProAudio Studio 16, or Logitech SoundMan 16 sound card. This driver doesn't work with other Media Vision or Logitech sound cards that aren't PAS16-compatible.

■ **100% Sound Blaster compatibles support** (CONFIG_SOUND_SB)

If you have a Sound Blaster 16, 32, or 64; ESS; Jazz16; or 100% Sound Blaster-compatible sound card, select Y to include it in the kernel or M to compile module support. You should also select this option if you have an IBM Mwave card or a card based on the Avance Logic ALS-007 chip or the ESS chipset. See the ALS007, ESS, and mwave files in the /usr/src/linux/Documentation/sound directory for more information.

- **Generic OPL2/OPL3 FM synthesizer support** (`CONFIG_SOUND_ADLIB`)

  Select Y or M for this option if your sound card has an FM synthesis chip made by Yamaha, such as the OPL2, OPL3, or OPL4. You should always answer Y or M to this, unless you're certain that your sound card uses a software FM emulation scheme. See `/usr/linux/Documentation/sound/OPL3` for more information.

- **Gravis Ultrasound support** (`CONFIG_SOUND_GUS`)

  Select Y or M for this option if you have a Gravis Ultrasound card, including the GUS or GUS MAX. See `/usr/src/linux/Documentation/sound/ultrasound` for more information on configuring this card.

- **MPU-401 support** (`CONFIG_SOUND_MPU401`)

  This option is for true MP401 MIDI interface cards. It's not for sound cards that have MPU401 emulation, such as the Sound Blaster. Select Y for this option only if you have a real MPU-401 card.

- **6850 UART support** (`CONFIG_SOUND_UART6850`)

  If your sound card has a MIDI interface based on the 6850 UART chip, select Y for this option. Unless you have dedicated MIDI equipment, you can usually answer N to this option.

- **VIDC Sound** (`CONFIG_VIDC_SOUND`)

  Select Y for this option if you have an ARM system with a VIDC video controller and 16-bit sound DACs. Unless you're sure that you have this, don't select this option.

- **PSS (AD1848, ADSP-2115, ESC614) support** (`CONFIG_SOUND_PSS`)

  Select Y or M for this option if you have an Orchid SW32, Cardinal DSP16, Beethoven ADSP-16, or some other card based on the PSS chipset. For more information, see `/usr/src/linux/Documentation/sound/PSS`.

- **Enable PSS mixer (Beethoven ADSP-16 and other compatibles)** (`CONFIG_PSS_MIXER`)

  If you have a Beethoven ADSP-16 or compatible sound card, select Y to this option to enable the mixer. For more information see the file `/usr/src/linux/Documentation/sound/PSS`.

- **Have DSPxxx.LD firmware file** (`CONFIG_PSS_HAVE_BOOT`)

  If you have a PSS sound card and have the `DSPxxx.LD` file or SYNTH.LD file for it, select Y to include this file. Without this file, the synth device (OPL) may not work.

- **Full pathname of DSPxxx.LD firmware file** (`CONFIG_PSS_BOOT_FILE`)

  If you selected Y for this option, enter the full pathname of your `DSPxxx.LD` file or `SYNTH.LD` file.

- **16-bit sampling option of GUS (_NOT_ GUS MAX) (CONFIG_SOUND_GUS16)**

  If you have installed the 16-bit sampling daughtercard for your GUS sound card, select the Y option. If you have a GUS MAX, select N because this option will disable GUS MAX support.

- **GUS MAX support (CONFIG_SOUND_GUSMAX)**

  Select Y only if you have a Gravis Ultrasound MAX.

- **Microsoft Sound System support (CONFIG_SOUND_MSS)**

  If you have one of the original Windows Sound System cards made by Aztech or Microsoft, select Y for this option. Don't enable this option simply because your sound card claims to have Microsoft Sound System support.

- **Ensoniq SoundScape support (CONFIG_SOUND_SSCAPE)**

  Select Y for this option if you have a sound card with the Ensoniq SoundScape chipset.

- **MediaTriX AudioTriX Pro support (CONFIG_SOUND_TRIX)**

  Select Y if you have a MediaTriX AudioTriX Pro sound card.

- **Have TRXPRO.HEX firmware file (CONFIG_TRIX_HAVE_BOOT)**

  If you have a MediaTriX AudioTrix Pro, it must be initialized with a TRXPRO.HEX file from its DOS driver directory. If you have this file, select Y for this option. If you don't have this file, the Sound Blaster and MPU-401 modes of your card will not work under Linux.

- **Full pathname of TRXPRO.HEX firmware file (CONFIG_TRIX_BOOT_FILE)**

  If you said Y to this option, enter the full pathname to your TRXPRO.HEX file.

- **Support for OPTi MAD16 and/or Mozart-based cards (CONFIG_SOUND_MAD16)**

  Select Y if your card has a Mozart (OAK OTI-601) or MAD16 (OPTi 82C928 or 82C929 or 82C931) chipset. Also see /usr/src/linux/Documentation/sound/Opti and MAD16 for more information.

- **Full support for Turtle Beach WaveFront synth/sound cards (CONFIG_SOUND_WAVEFRONT)**

  Select Y or M if you have a Tropez Plus, Tropez, or Maui sound card. See the Wavefront and Tropez+ files in /usr/src/linux/Documentation/sound/ for more information.

- **Support MIDI in older MAD16-based cards (requires SB) (CONFIG_MAD16_OLDCARD)**

  Select Y or M if you have a sound card based on the C928 or Mozart chipset and if you want to have MIDI support. You must also enable support for the Sound Blaster driver.

- **Support for Crystal CS4232-based (PnP) cards (CONFIG_SOUND_CS4232)**

  Select Y for this option if you have a card based on the Crystal CS4232 chip set. See /usr/src/linux/Documentation/sound/CS4232 for more information.

■ **Support for Yamaha OPL3-SA2, SA3, and SAx-based PnP cards**
(`CONFIG_SOUND_OPL3SA2`)

Select Y or M if you have a card based on one of these Yamaha sound chipsets. See `/usr/src/linux/Documentation/sound/OPL3-SA2` for more information.

■ **FM synthesizer (YM3812/OPL-3) support (`CONFIG_SOUND_YM3812`)**

Select Y here, unless you know that you won't need this option.

■ **Additional low-level drivers (`CONFIG_LOWLEVEL_SOUND`)**

Some sound cards need additional low-level drivers. To configure these drivers, select Y, and you will be prompted with more options.

■ **ACI mixer (miroPCM12/PCM20) (`CONFIG_ACI_MIXER`)**

Select Y for this option if you have a miroSound PCM12 or PCM20 that supports the Audio Command Interface (ACI) protocol.

■ **SB32/AWE support (`CONFIG_AWE32_SYNTH`)**

If you have a Sound Blaster SB32, AWE32-PnP, SB AWE64, or similar AWE card, select this option. Read `/usr/src/linux/Documentation/sound/README.awe` and `AWE32` for more information.

■ **Gallant's Audio Excel DSP 16 support (SC-6000 and SC-6600)**
(`CONFIG_AEDSP16`)

Select Y for this option if you have a Gallant's Audio Excel DSP 16 card. This driver does not support the III or PnP versions of this card.

The Gallant's Audio Excel DSP 16 card can also emulate either a Sound Blaster Pro or a Microsoft Sound System card, so you should have said Y to either 100% Sound Blaster compatibles (SB16/32/64, ESS, Jazz16) support or Microsoft Sound System support (discussed previously), but not both.

See `/usr/src/linux/Documentation/sound/AudioExcelDSP16` for more information.

■ **I/O base for Audio Excel DSP 16 (`CONFIG_AEDSP16_BASE`)**

Select the base I/O address of a Audio Excel DSP 16 card with this option. Possible values are 220 or 240.

■ **Audio Excel DSP 16 (SBPro emulation) (`CONFIG_AEDSP16_SBPRO`)**

Select Y if you want your Audio Excel DSP 16 to emulate a Sound Blaster Pro. You should also select Y for 100% Sound Blaster compatibles (SB16/32/64, ESS, Jazz16) support and N to Audio Excel DSP 16 (MSS emulation).

■ **Audio Excel DSP 16 IRQ (`CONFIG_AEDSP16_SB_IRQ`)**

Select the IRQ of your Audio Excel DSP 16 card. Possible values are 5, 7, 9, 10, or 11.

■ **Audio Excel DSP 16 DMA (`CONFIG_AEDSP16_SB_DMA`)**

Select the DMA channel of the Audio Excel DSP 16 card. Possible values are 0, 1, or 3.

- **Audio Excel DSP 16 (MSS emulation)** (CONFIG_AEDSP16_MSS)

  Select Y if you want your Audio Excel DSP 16 to emulate a Microsoft Sound System card. If so, you should also select Y to Microsoft Sound System support and N to Audio Excel DSP 16 (SBPro emulation).

- **Audio Excel DSP 16 IRQ** (CONFIG_AEDSP16_MSS_IRQ)

  Select the IRQ of the Audio Excel DSP 16 card. Possible values are 5, 7, 9, 10, or 11.

- **Audio Excel DSP 16 DMA** (CONFIG_AEDSP16_MSS_DMA)

  Select the DMA channel of the Audio Excel DSP 16 card. Possible values are 0, 1, or 3.

- **SC-6600-based audio cards (new Audio Excel DSP 16)** (CONFIG_SC6600)

  Select this option if you have a newer Audio Excel DSP 16 card with a SC-6600 chipset.

- **SC-6600 Joystick Interface** (CONFIG_SC6600_JOY)

  Select Y for this option if you selected a SC-6600-based card and want to enable the joystick interface.

- **SC-6600 CDROM Interface** (CONFIG_SC6600_CDROM)

  Select Y for this option if you selected a SC-6600-based card and want to activate the CD-ROM interface on an Audio Excel DSP 16 card. Enter 0 for Sony, 1 for Panasonic, 2 for IDE, and 4 for no CD-ROM present.

- **Audio Excel DSP 16 (MPU401 emulation)** (CONFIG_AEDSP16_MPU401)

  Select Y for this option if you want your Audio Excel DSP 16 card to emulate the MPU-401 MIDI interface. You should also select Y to MPU-401 support (discussed previously).

- **MPU401 IRQ for Audio Excel DSP 16** (CONFIG_AEDSP16_MPU_IRQ)

  This option selects the IRQ of the MPU-401 emulation of your Audio Excel DSP 16 card. Possible values are 5, 7, 9, 10, or 0, to disable the MPU-401 interface.

- **Rockwell WaveArtist** (CONFIG_SOUND_WAVEARTIST)

  If you have a Rockwell WaveArtist sound system, say Y to this option.

Configuring Isapnp

If you have a Plug and Play card, it must be initialized after the kernel boots so that modular sound support can use it. To do this, you must configure the /etc/isapnp.conf. This is typically done by the sndconfig program, but you can also do it manually if you run into problems.

To produce a isapnp.conf file, you must first use the pnpdump program. When you run pnpdump, it will scan all your ISA Plug and Play cards and then dump information to stdout. This information is in a format similar to an isapnp.conf file, except that all the configuration statements are commented out. To create a working isapnp.conf file, issue the following command:

```
pnpdump > temp-isapnp.conf
```

Then, uncomment the devices you want recognized at reboot. For more information on this, read the `isapnp.conf` manual page or the documentation in `/usr/doc/isapnptools-1.18`. After you configure this file, move it to `/etc/isapnp.conf` and reboot.

If for some reason isapnp doesn't work for your card, two more options might do the trick. If you boot your Linux machine to DOS first, you can load the DOS drivers for your sound card and properly configure it, and then use loadlin to warm reboot Linux. Also, you may be able to use your hardware's BIOS routines to configure your Plug and Play card before Linux boots.

Installing Open Sound System

If the OSS/Lite drivers won't work for you, there's another option: 4Front technologies' Open Sound System (OSS) drivers are available commercially, and operate in many cases when the OSS/Free drivers fail. OSS was developed by the author of the original OSS/Free. However, OSS has been developed as a commercial product. It includes support for many more sound cards, a much simpler installation, and other added features and applications. Furthermore, because it is developed commercially, OSS supports some proprietary sound cards that have not been supported by its open source counterpart.

If you're interested in trying OSS, a trial version is available at `http://www.opensound.com/`. This is the full version of the product, but it will operate for only three hours a day for a week, at which time it will let you use it for only 20 minutes a day. But, if you're unsure about purchasing the drivers, you can try them out first and see if your sound card is supported. If you're happy with the results, a license for OSS costs about $20.

To install OSS, you must first recompile your kernel with no sound driver installed. Then you must download or purchase the version for your kernel and processor configuration. For most stock Red Hat 6.0 installations, this means the glibc version for the 2.2 kernel with single-processor support. When you have the OSS archive, move it to a temporary directory such as `/usr/src` or `/tmp`, and unpack it. For example, if you downloaded the archive `osslinux392s-glibc-2212-UP.tar.gz`, use the following command to unpack it in `/tmp`:

```
mv osslinux392s-glibc-2212-UP.tar.gz /tmp
cd /tmp
tar -xzf osslinux392s-glibc-2212-UP.tar.gz
```

After you unpack the archive, there will be an oss-install executable. Execute this installation program with `./oss-install`. After installation, you can start sound with the `soundon` command. You can also shut it off with the `soundoff` command. If you need to reconfigure your sound setup, use the sndconfig program.

For more information on your OSS installation, look at the files and documentation in `/usr/lib/oss`.

Installing ALSA drivers

Another sound driver option is the Advanced Linux Sound Architecture, or ALSA drivers. This is a project to create an OSS-compatible (but superior) set of sound drivers free to the Linux community. Originally created as a sound driver to support the Gravis UltraSound card, more hardware support was added, and the project took off from there.

Although ALSA is still in very early release (0.4.1a), there are frequent updates. Only a few sound cards are supported, but more keep getting added to the list. If you'd like to check out ALSA, visit the Web site `http://www.alsa-project.org/`.

Installing Sound Blaster Live! Drivers

When I found out I'd be writing this chapter, I decided to test the OSS/Free drivers by running to the store and buying the most current Sound Blaster card, just to see how it would work out of the box with Red Hat Linux 6.0. I thought that people who were building PCs out of new, off-the-shelf components would benefit from knowing how to configure the latest offerings from Creative Labs.

When I got to my local computer store, I found basically three different Sound Blaster cards available: the Sound Blaster 16 PCI, the Sound Blaster PCI 512, and the Sound Blaster Live!. I purchased the PCI 512; the 16 PCI looked like it might have been based on some lite/PnP hardware that wouldn't work, and the Live! cost almost three times as much as the PCI 512— I'd also heard murmuring that OSS/Free didn't support the Live! chipset.

When I got the sound card home, I found both good news and bad news. The good news is that the PCI 512 uses the same EMU10K1 chipset as the Live!, at a third of the price. The bad news is that none of the Linux sound drivers mentioned previously supported this chipset because Creative Labs wasn't freely releasing proprietary programming information needed to access the card's features. Although OSSound is working with Creative Labs to develop some new drivers for the Live! cards in the future, this doesn't help current Live! owners.

Luckily, Creative Labs has been working on a proprietary sound driver for Live! cards and Linux, and a beta version is available free on the developer Web page at `http://developer.soundblaster.com/linux/`. There, you can download the latest beta driver, which works for the Sound Blaster PCI 512 and Live! cards. The EMU10K1 drivers work with only single-processor systems running the 2.0.36–0.7, 2.2.5–15, or 2.2.10 kernels. Also, the driver does not include source code.

After you have downloaded the EMU10K1 driver, unpack the archive in a temporary directory, such as `/tmp` or `/usr/src`. Use the command `tar -xzf emu10k1-0.3b.tar.gz` to unpack the archive. Read the Readme carefully—there are several steps you must follow before you run the included installer program. You must recompile your kernel with some specific options set, such as module support, no SMP support, sound supported in a module, and no sound driver modules. It's also recommended that you have at minimum a 200MHz Pentium with at least 32MB RAM to run the EMU10K1 sound driver.

After you have configured your kernel according to the instructions in the Readme file, make sure you are logged in as root, and run the automated installer with the following command:

```
./install_emu10k1
```

This will automatically install the sound drivers for your Sound Blaster Live! card. If the program displays any error messages, refer to the Readme file for instructions on manually installing the drivers.

The current beta version of the EMU10K1 driver works great but has some problems. For example, the synth device doesn't work, and some older programs that dump au files to /dev/audio either won't work or will produce garbled sound. However, well-behaved sound applications (including sox, GNOME's audio support, and even Quake II) work great.

Testing Your Sound Card

After you've installed your sound driver, reboot your system. If you included sound support in the kernel, watch carefully during the reboot, or use the dmesg command afterward. You'll see the lines Sound initialization started and Sound initialization complete flash by during the startup messages. If your sound card was configured correctly and everything worked, you should see several lines of information stating your sound card type, its IRQ and DMA channel settings, and other sound driver support. If you saw nothing, your sound driver didn't work. Recheck your configuration, or read the troubleshooting section that follows.

After your system has rebooted, the first thing to check is /dev/sndstat. This file gives a complete report on sound driver status. For example, on my system, it looks like this:

```
OSS/Free:3.8s2++-971130
Load type: Driver loaded as a module
Kernel: Linux mungo 2.2.10 #4 Sun Aug 29 18:17:49 EDT 1999 i586
Config options:

Installed drivers:
Type 0: Creative EMU10K1 (0.3)
Card config:
(Sound Blaster Live! at 0xee80 irq 11)

Audio devices:
0: Sound Blaster Live! (DUPLEX)

Synth devices:
Not supported by current driver

Midi devices:
0: Sound Blaster Live!

Timers:
0: System Clock

Mixers:
0: Sound Blaster Live!
```

The next step is to test audio playback on your sound card. The quick way to do this is to redirect a sound file to the dsp device, like this:

```
cat /usr/share/sndconfig/sample.au > /dev/dsp
```

This isn't the best way to play a sound, and you might get badly distorted output from this, depending on your card and driver. Try using the play program (part of the Sox package) instead:

```
play /usr/share/sndconfig/sample.au
```

If you want to play more sounds, you don't need to go download a few megabytes of data. Plenty of sounds are bundled with various Red Hat Linux 6.0 software, if you're willing to dig around for them. Take a look in /usr/share/afterstep/desktop/sounds and /usr/lib/games/xboing/sounds, or just do a find . -name *.au -print from your root directory and see what's there.

Next, check out the capabilities of your CD-ROM drive. Put an audio CD in the CD-ROM, and use cdp or xplaycd to start the CD. Both programs can control the CD, skip forward tracks, and so forth, regardless of your sound card setup. But if your sound driver is working, you'll also be able to hear the music through the speakers connected to your sound card.

While you have a CD playing, you can test sound recording. First you may have to use xmixer to select the CD as the input device. To do this, just launch xmixer and select the button below the CD slider. The quick way to record is by using dd:

```
dd bs=8k count=4 </dev/audio >test,au
```

Then, pause the CD and listen to the results:

```
cat test.au > /dev/audio
```

This probably won't sound very good. Try using the rec command instead:

```
rec test.au
```

And try using play again to listen to the results:

```
play test.au
```

In general, using tools such as play and rec will be sound much better than simply redirecting /dev/audio or /dev/dsp.

Installing Supporting Software

After you've configured sound, you'll need some applications to play, record, and manipulate audio. Fortunately, Red Hat Linux 6.0 contains a full suite of multimedia software, including audio applications. Also, several other titles are available for download on the Internet that will enhance your Linux sound experience.

Sound Applications Included with Red Hat Linux 6.0

The following applications are installed in workstation-class Red Hat Linux 6.0 installs, with the exception of kdemultimedia. If you do not have the following packages, you can install them from your Red Hat Linux 6.0 CD. Consult Chapter 11, "Installing and Managing RPM Packages," for more information on package installation.

Sox   Sox calls itself the Swiss army knife of sound converters. It's a program that can be used to convert sounds from one format to another, but it can also add echo, flanging, reverb, and many other sound effects. For example, to convert a Sun AU file to a Sound Blaster VOC file, use the following command:

```
sox -v 0.5 file.au -rate 12000 file.voc rate
```

The Sox package also includes the play and rec programs for playing and recording audio. These programs can use the same effects as the sox conversion program.

mikmod   The mikmod is a popular MOD player for a variety of UNIX platforms. It uses a curses-based interface and plays many different varieties of MOD file. You can also load several MOD files and shuffle between them, in case you have a large collection you like to listen to for hours.

To run mikmod, issue the `mikmod` command along with the name of a MOD file or several MOD files; mikmod will begin playing the first file. Hit F1 to display possible commands and other help.

Mikmod works only if you have a functional FM synthesizer driver. If for some reason you don't, try the tracker program, detailed later in this chapter.

playmidi   The playmidi is a Linux-based MIDI player with many options. This player uses a curses-based interface; you can also use xplaymidi to play MIDI songs with an X11 interface.

multimedia   This package includes xplaycd and xmixer. The xplaycd is the standard audio CD player software for X. It lets you skip tracks, fast forward and rewind through tracks, and perform other typical CD player tasks. You can also edit the track listing for a CD and store it in a database file. Click the right mouse button on xplaycd to see a command menu, which includes an edit option.

With xmixer, you can set the volume of input devices such as the microphone, the line input, and the CD player. After launching xmixer, you can adjust volume levels by manipulating the sliders below each respective item. You can also designate a recording source by selecting the buttons below each input item.

aumix   If you need a mixer program like xmixer but you're not running X, or if you need to write a script that changes mixer levels, aumix is a text-based mixer program. If you run aumix with no options, you'll get a full-screen curses-based interface. Use the cursor keys to move between input devices, change the sliders, and select a recording source. You can also launch aumix with numerous options to change volumes noninteractively. See the aumux manual page for more information.

cdp   If you're not using X and you liked aumix, you should try the cdp cd player. This also is a text-based program that provides functions similar to xplaycd. The numeric keypad is used to control the program; the Del key provides a help menu of commands. This package also provides the cdplay command, which is a noninteractive way to play audio CDs. With it, you can issue the command cdplay or cdplay stop to start and stop an audio CD.

mpg123   If you've been seeing MP3 files all over the Internet and mentioned in the media, here's your chance to play them on your Linux machine. The mpg123 is a command-line MPEG player with a simple interface but many options for play. You can either download files and play them later, or you can specify a URL and have mpg123 download it and then play it for you. Numerous command-line options are available; see the mpg123 manual page for more details.

x11amp   If you're familiar with the popular WinAmp MP3 player for Windows, you'll recognize the graphical interface of x11amp. This is a full-featured MPEG player that includes features such as a playlist editor, a graphic EQ, and various visualization modes to display while your MPEG is playing. Click the right mouse button on the player to display a menu of options.

For more information on x11amp or MP3 in general, visit http://www.mpeg.org/.

awesfx   If you are using the Sound Blaster AWE 32/64 sound driver, these utilities will enable you to load sound effects into your sound card. The sfxload command is used to load a SoundFont file to your sound driver. For more information, see the AWE32 files in the /usr/src/linux/Documentation/sound directory, or the sfxload manual page.

gnome-media   This package is a suite of audio applications and tools written for use with the GNOME desktop environment. Each program is similar to the programs mentioned previously, but gnome-media has been designed to use the look and feel of the GNOME environment. The package includes gmix, a mixer similar to xmixer; gtcd, a CD player similar to xplaycd; tcd, a text-based CD player; and vumeter, a graphical meter of sound output.

kdemultimedia   This package is a suite of audio applications similar to the gnome-media package. However, these applications were written for the KDE environment. The package includes kmedia, a media player; kmid, a MIDI player; kmidi, a MIDI converter; kmix, a sound mixer; and kscd, a CD player.

Other Sound Applications

Many other sound applications for Linux are available on the Internet. Scores of them are subtle variations on those mentioned previously, such as CD players with different features or more esoteric mixer programs. There are also many other audio players and conversion programs for more obscure audio formats.

The best place to start looking for audio programs is the metalab archive. Take a look at the applications found at the ftp site `ftp://metalab.unc.edu/pub/Linux/apps/sound`. The following sections detail applications from the Internet that you might find useful.

Tracker   If you're having trouble using mikmod to play MOD files, you might want to give Tracker a try. Originally written for the Amiga, this simple program can play one or several MOD files with a text-based interface. You can download tracker at `ftp://metalab.unc.edu/pub/Linux/apps/sound/players/tracker-4.3-linux.tar.gz`.

Wavplay   Sox does a good job playing WAV files, but if you have a lot of sounds from an old Windows machine, you might want a more comprehensive WAV player. Wavplay includes xlt-wavplay, an X interface for playing WAV files, and recplay, a WAV recorder. You can download wavplay at `ftp://metalab.unc.edu/pub/Linux/apps/sound/players/wavplay-1.3.tar.gz`.

Cthuga   You now have several applications that let you hear audio files, but this one lets you see them. Cthuga is a combination of a VU meter's level display and a screensaver's semirandom patterns. When you run Cthuga, it reads audio output and uses it to shape and form geometric patterns and swirls on your screen. There's an X client, along with an SVGALib version, and scores of map, pcx, and tab files that are used to create the different patterns. You can download a copy of the Cthuga source at `ftp://metalab.unc.edu/pub/Linux/apps/sound/lightshow/cthugha-L-1.4.tar.gz`.

Troubleshooting Sound Cards

If you're having trouble with your sound setup, check a few basic things first:

- **Are you running the right kernel?**—Use the `uname -a` command to check the date of the kernel currently running. If you recompiled the kernel a few minutes ago but the date reported is from months ago, you're not running the right kernel. Make sure that you installed the kernel in the right place, edited the `/etc/lilo.conf` file (if required), and ran the `lilo` command to install lilo.

- **Did you build the modules?**—If you installed modular sound support, you need to compile and install the modules. Simply compiling the kernel with `Make zlilo` isn't enough; you need to follow that with a `Make modules` and `Make modules_install`.

- **Did sound start?**—Use dmesg, or look at the end of `/var/log/messages` for any information about the sound card. At the very least, you should get an error message saying that no card was found. Often, this is either because you're using the wrong driver and need to select a different one, or because you configured the driver to look for the card in the wrong place. You could have a plug-and-play card that needs to be initialized with isapnp, or you could have the card configured with the wrong IRQ or DMA channel.

■ **Did sound work in another OS?**—If you also have Windows or DOS on your machine, reboot and see if your sound hardware works there. If not, it could be a problem with your card itself, or maybe your speakers.

Also take a look at the following common questions and problems with sound:

Q. Why do I get No such device or No such device or address errors?

A. No such device means that the kernel doesn't contain a sound driver or the correct sound driver for your hardware. It can also mean that your module configuration is wrong or that you don't have the correct sound module installed or compiled. "No such device or address" means that the kernel couldn't find the sound card at the configuration you specified. Try reconfiguring the sound card's IRQ with sndconfig, or make sure your /etc/isapnp.conf file is correct.

Q. My /dev/dsp and /dev/audio files are missing. How can I recreate them?

A. If you don't have any audio device files, try using the makedev script, which is located at /etc/MAKEDEV. This will make a new device file for any type it knows about.

Q. Why does my Sound Blaster card gives me device busy errors when I use my QIC-2 tape drive?

A. Some Sound Blaster cards use DMA channel 1, which conflicts with the QIC-02 driver. If you are using FTAPE, you do not need the QIC-02 driver; only the QIC-117 driver is required. If you reconfigure your kernel to use the QIC-117 driver instead of the QIC-02 driver, your device busy errors should stop. ●

## CHAPTER 23

Installing and Configuring Joysticks and Game Cards

by Kyle Amon

In this chapter

Understanding Linux Game Device Support

Game device support in Linux is implemented by the Linux joystick driver. Contrary to the implication of its name, however, this is actually a package containing multiple joystick driver modules. The main module is a generic joystick module called, plainly enough, joystick. Instead of directly supporting any devices itself, the joystick module facilitates the capability of various hardware-specific driver modules to support given devices.

Applications utilizing the Linux joystick driver communicate with the main module, joystick, with one of two interface specifications the module implements. Both an older, deprecated 0.x interface and a newer, preferred 1.x interface exist. By default, the module expects applications to communicate with it using the 1.x interface. However, when an application attempts to communicate with it using the 0.x interface, the module detects this and forces use of the old interface for the sake of backward compatibility.

The joystick module then communicates with a hardware-specific driver module, which in turn communicates with and manages the actual attached game device via a character special device, js# (where # indicates which joystick is to be used), in the /dev directory.

Installing Game Devices

The good news is that physically connecting a device to this port couldn't be simpler, in most cases. Merely identify a 15-pin female port on the back of your machine, and plug in your game device. On the other hand, ensuring that all the functionality you want is working properly could be problematic if you're unlucky. There are many reasons for this.

Depending on the type of game device used, you will have to connect it to one of several ports. These include the game port itself, but some devices interface directly with your standard serial (COM) or parallel (LPT) ports. In addition, different manufacturers implement joystick communication with these ports either using an analog or a digital signal. This provides a plethora of combinations that you will have to consider when you try to integrate a joystick or other game device with Linux. Each of these is described in the sections that follow.

PC Game Port

Most game devices will be connected to a PC game port. Although this should simplify matters, what is and what should be are rarely the same. The problem with what would otherwise be a simple PC peripheral port begins with IBM. When IBM designed the PC joystick interface, one of the developers' primary goals was to make it as cheap as possible to manufacture. As a result, even though the circuit itself supported two joysticks, there was only one joystick connector. To use two joysticks simultaneously with the interface, a special Y-cable adapter with connections for two joysticks was needed. Some clone manufacturers later implemented two connectors on their game cards, while others provided inputs for only a single joystick.

Originally, joystick interfaces either were implemented on separate adapter cards or were integrated, often poorly, into multi-IO cards. The situation became even more complicated when Creative Labs integrated a game port and MIDI interface directly on their sound card, also with a single connector. To make this work, they had to deviate from IBM's standard and replace pins 12 and 15 of the PC joystick interface to make room for the MIDI interface pins (output and input, respectively). If you have such a device, you may find that your MIDI devices connected to this interface function problem-free, but certain game devices malfunction because they can't access pins 12 or 15 the way they expect.

 TIP

If you experience trouble connecting game devices to your system, the "Joysticks and Other Game Controllers" section of Tom Engdahl's electronics information page is an excellent resource that can help you resolve any difficulties you may experience—it even explains how to build simple adapters to circumvent known problems, if necessary. This Web page is available at `http://www.hut.fi/ Misc/Electronics/docs/joystick/`, and I recommend you give it a look for fun if nothing else.

PC Serial Port

Devices with this type of connector are in the minority, but there are still a significant number of them out there. If you have such a device, connecting it to your system should be fairly straightforward and problem-free. Simply identify an available serial port, and plug it in. From a hardware standpoint, there is nothing else to do.

PC Parallel Port

This category includes game devices such as Atari joysticks and Nintendo gamepads that were not originally designed for use with PC hardware. Because all these devices communicate digitally, and because the PC joystick interface was designed for analog input only, you can't use the PC game port with such devices. However, the design of the PC's parallel port makes it rather suitable for connecting such devices to PC systems. Getting these types of devices to work with the parallel port is not easy, however. You may have to make relatively simple wiring adjustments (not for the meek or weak of heart, of course), or even make circuit modifications (rarely needed), depending on your individual circumstances.

> **CAUTION**
>
> Devices of this type are not designed to be attached to PC hardware, and doing so is not for the timid. You could damage components of your PC or the device you're trying to attach. If you are not fairly familiar with electronics and PC hardware, secure the assistance of someone who is before attempting anything of this nature. In any case, always do your homework and double-check everything first, to reduce your risk.

If you really need to do this, however, you can find complete instructions on how to attach these devices in the `joystick-parport.txt` file. This file is included with the Linux kernel sources in the `Documentation` subdirectory and with the Linux joystick device package itself. Another good resource is the "Joysticks and Other Game Controllers" section of Tom Engdahl's electronics information page, mentioned previously. Some of the game devices that fall in this category are as follows:

- joy-console—Used with NES, SNES, and clones; supports up to five devices per parallel port.
- joy-db9—For multisystem devices; supports only one such device per parallel port.
- joy-db9—For Sega devices; supports only one such device per parallel port.
- joy-console—Used with multisystem devices; can support up to five plain, switch-based (non-TTL) devices, including NES, SNES, and clones.
- joy-turbografx—For multisystem devices; can support up to seven devices per parallel port (see `http://www2.burg-halle.de/~schwenke/parport.html` for instructions on building the interface).
- joy-console—Used with Sony PlayStation gamepads (PSX); provides experimental and unstable support for one device per parallel port.

Verifying Hardware Compatibility

Linux joystick driver was integrated into the kernel source tree beginning with the 2.1 line of development. Red Hat Linux 6.0 is the first version to ship with a 2.2 series kernel, so it is one of the first distributions to provide out-of-the-box support for a variety of joysticks and similar devices.

TIP

For systems running stable kernels prior to the 2.2 series to support joysticks, it is necessary to download, compile (or patch your 2.0 series kernel), and install the Linux joystick driver yourself. Although most people running Red Hat 6.0 will not choose to downgrade their systems to running pre-2.2 series kernels, in some situations this might be necessary. If you find yourself in this position and still want joystick support, you can download the latest Linux joystick driver from its official distribution site at `http://atrey.karlin.mff.cuni.cz/~vojtech/joystick/`.

Devices supported by the Linux joystick driver fall into several categories. Unless you're a serious game player, though, most likely you'll want to use either a PC analog or digital-type joystick with systems utilizing the x86 (PC) architecture. As a result, you'll need to concern yourself with only one, or possibly more, of the first three categories. The remaining categories are presented primarily for needy, adventurous, or obsessive-compulsive (psycho) gamers.

TIP You are not likely to have native joystick support for anything other than the Intel-based x86 and Amiga (joy-amiga driver) platforms. The exception to this is if you have some luck with PC game port or parallel port compatibility.

PC Game Port Analog Devices

Linux supports analog joysticks and gamepads conforming to the IBM PC joystick standard. It also supports various extensions, such as additional hats and buttons that are compatible with the CH Flightstick Pro, ThrustMaster FCS, or six- and eight-button gamepads. Table 23.1 lists the analog devices known to currently work with the Linux joystick driver. This table also lists additional information, including device-specific driver, parameters, and m value (explained later in this chapter).

Part
IV

Ch

23

Table 23.1   Analog Joysticks and Drivers Supported in Linux

Device	Hardware-Specific Driver	Parameters	m Value
Standard joysticks with two, three, or four axes, and up to four buttons | joy-analog	js_an		
CH Flightstick Pro (compatibles)	joy-analog	js_an	
ThrustMaster FCS (compatibles)	joy-analog	js_an	
Genius Flight2000 F-12	joy-analog	js_an	0x00f3
Genius Flight2000 F-21	joy-analog	js_an	0x08f7
Genius Flight2000 F-22	joy-analog	js_an	0x02ff
Genius GameHunter G-06	joy-analog	js_an	0xf0f3
Genius MaxFire G-07	joy-analog	js_an	0xf0f3
Genius PowerStation	joy-analog	js_an	0xf0f3
Laing #1 PC SuperPad *	joy-analog	js_an	0xf0f3
Microsoft SideWinder Standard	joy-analog	js_an	0x003b
PDPI Lightning L4 gamecard *	joy-lightning	js_l4	
QuickShot QS-201 SuperWarrior	joy-analog	js_an	0x00fb

continues

Table 23.1   Continued

Device	Hardware-Specific Driver	Parameters	m Value
Saitek Megapad XII *	joy-analog	js_an	0x30f3
Logitech WingMan	joy-analog	js_an	
Logitech WingMan Extreme	joy-analog	js_an	
Logitech WingMan Light	joy-analog	js_an	
Logitech ThunderPad	joy-analog	js_an	
Microsoft SideWinder Standard	joy-analog	js_an	

PC Game Port Digital Devices

Some newer devices use proprietary digital protocols to communicate over the game port. Because these protocols are proprietary and therefore vary from manufacturer to manufacturer, not all such devices are supported by the Linux joystick driver. Due to the nature of proprietary protocols and the fact that new protocols and extensions are continually being developed, it is difficult to provide support in a timely manner, if at all. Even so, the Linux joystick driver supports an impressive and ever-growing number of them. Table 23.2 lists devices of this type supported by the latest Linux joystick driver, their corresponding device-specific driver, parameters, and m value, where appropriate.

TIP   At the time of this writing, Linux 2.2 series kernels still contained only version 1.2.13 of the Linux joystick driver. Support for some of the devices listed in this chapter is not available in this version. These devices are indicated by having an asterisk (*) appended to their corresponding device specific driver in the tables that follow. To use one of these devices, you must download and use version 1.2.14 or later of the Linux joystick driver rather than the one included with your system.

Table 23.2   Digital Joysticks and Drivers Supported in Linux

Device	Hardware-Specific Driver	Parameters	m Value
Creative Labs Blaster GamePad Cobra	joy-creative*		
DirectPad Pro parallel port joystick interfaces			

Device	Hardware-Specific Driver	Parameters	m Value
FP Gaming Assassin 3D Gamepads with six and eight buttons	joy-assassin	js_as	
Genius Flight2000 Digital F-23	joy-sidewinder		
	joy-analog	js_an	0x02ff (CHF mode) 0x08f7 (FCS mode)
Gravis Blackhawk Digital	joy-gravis		
Gravis GamePad Pro	joy-gravis		
	joy-analog	js_an	0x00f3
Gravis Xterminator GamePad	joy-gravis		
Logitech CyberMan 2	joy-logitech		
Logitech ThunderPad Digital	joy-logitech		
Logitech WingMan Extreme Digital	joy-logitech		
Logitech WingMan Formula	joy-logitech*		
Logitech WingMan Gamepad	joy-logitech*		
Logitech WingMan Interceptor	joy-logitech*		
MadCatz Panther	joy-assassin	js_as	
MadCatz Panther XL	joy-assassin	js_as	
Microsoft SideWinder	joy-analog	js_an	0x02ff (CHF mode) 0x08f7 (FCS mode)
Microsoft SideWinder Force Feedback Pro	joy-sidewinder		
Microsoft SideWinder Force Feedback Wheel	joy-sidewinder*		
Microsoft SideWinder FreeStyle Pro	joy-sidewinder*		

Part IV

Ch 23

continues

Table 23.2   Continued

Device	Hardware-Specific Driver	Parameters	m Value
Microsoft SideWinder GamePad	joy-sidewinder		
Microsoft SideWinder Precision Pro	joy-sidewinder		
ThrustMaster Millennium 3D Inceptor	joy-thrustmaster		
ThrustMaster Rage 3D	joy-thrustmaster		

PC Serial Port Digital Devices

Some newer devices use proprietary digital protocols to communicate over the serial port rather than the game port. For the same reasons as with PC game port digital devices, support for these devices is incomplete and slow to arrive. Table 23.3 lists devices of this type supported by the latest Linux joystick driver, along with their corresponding device-specific drivers. Notice that all the device-specific driver names contain appended asterisks (*), indicating that support is available only in version 1.2.14 or later of the Linux joystick driver.

Table 23.3   Serial Port Digital Joysticks and Drivers Supported in Linux

Device	Hardware-Specific Driver
LogiCad3D Magellan 3D	joy-magellan*
LogiCad3D Space Mouse	joy-magellan*
Logitech Magellan	joy-magellan*
Logitech WingMan Warrior	joy-warrior*
SpaceTec SpaceBall Avenger	joy-spaceorb*
SpaceTec SpaceOrb 360	joy-spaceorb*

Non-PC (Parallel Port) Digital Devices

Many gamepad and joystick devices designed for various non-PC computers and game consoles can also be made to work with Linux. These include multisystem joysticks and gamepads by Sony, Nintendo, Sega, and several clone manufacturers. Devices of this type supported by the latest Linux joystick driver are listed in Table 23.4, along with their corresponding device-specific drivers.

Table 23.4 Parallel Port Digital Joysticks and Drivers Supported in Linux

Device	Hardware-Specific Driver
Multisystem joysticks (Atari, Amiga, Commodore, Amstrad, and others)	joy-db9
	joy-console
Nintendo Entertainment System (and clone) gamepads	joy-console
Super Nintendo Entertainment System gamepads	joy-console
Sega Genesis (MegaDrive) gamepads	joy-db9 (set to Multi2 mode)
Sega Master System gamepads	joy-db9 (set to Multi2 mode)
Sega Saturn gamepads	joy-db9 (set to Multi2 mode)
Sony PlayStation gamepads (PSX)	joy-console
DirectPad Pro parallel port joystick interface	`http://www.ziplabel.com/dpadpro/construct.html`
SNESKey parallel port joystick interface	
TurboGraFX parallel port joystick interface	joy-turbografx

Installing Hardware Support

As always, installing hardware support is a matter of making sure that the necessary drivers either are compiled statically into the running kernel or are available to it as runtime loadable modules. Although the Linux joystick driver modules can be compiled statically into the kernel, it is more common to compile and use them as runtime loadable modules. This approach keeps your kernel smaller, conserving system resources while the game device is not actually in use. It also prevents a malfunction with your game device from bringing down your entire kernel (and also your PC).

CAUTION

Although the subject here is not Linux kernel compilation and runtime loadable module support, a general understanding of these topics is necessary, and this chapter assumes that you are familiar with them. If you are not, or if you could use a refresher, refer to Chapter 18, "Installing and Configuring the Red Hat Linux Kernel," which covers these topics specifically.

For every type of game device, you must first load the main joystick module into the kernel. This can be done by becoming root and issuing a command such as the following:

```
insmod joystick
```

Next, the hardware-specific driver module for your device must be loaded. In this example, you use the joy-analog module, but you should refer to the appropriate table (Table 23.1 through Table 23.4) to determine which hardware-specific driver module is appropriate for your game device. Replace the examples used here with your actual device driver, and load that one instead.

```
insmod joy-analog
```

 TIP Red Hat Linux 6.0 comes with all possible modules compiled and installed, ready to be loaded into the running kernel if necessary. Therefore, it is not necessary to compile a custom kernel to use game devices. If you do compile your own custom kernel, however, the sections of the xconfig Linux Kernel Configuration menu you'll be interested in are Joystick Support and probably Sound.

To have the joystick modules load automatically when needed, add the following to your /etc/conf.modules file (or, perhaps /etc/modules.conf, for people that have made alternations to their system).

```
#

# joystick driver

#

alias char-major-15 joystick

post-install joystick modprobe joy-analog
```

Although this example is quite basic, it works fine for the Logitech Wingman Light joystick connected to the Turtle Beach Monte Carlo sound card in Sound Blaster mode on a Red Hat system. In fact, configuring the sound card and attached Sony CDU-31A CD-ROM drive is much more complicated than configuring the joystick. If you do experience problems, however, you can refer to the detailed documentation on every type of supported game device and its corresponding driver in the file joystick.txt. This file is included with the Linux kernel sources in the Documentation subdirectory and with the Linux joystick device package itself. Another good source of device-specific information, although relatively technical, is a small text file by Vojtech Pavlik (author of the Linux joystick driver) available from the Linux joystick driver Web site at http://atrey.karlin.mff.cuni.cz/~vojtech/joystick/.

Installing Supporting Software

While Red Hat Linux 6.0 comes with all possible modules compiled and installed, it doesn't include all the utility software provided by the module authors. This support software was designed to help manage and troubleshoot their modules. Because this is the case with the Linux joystick driver, you should download the latest source package from ftp://atrey.karlin.mff.cuni.cz/pub/linux/joystick/ or via the Web site http://atrey.karlin.mff.cuni.cz/. You will have to download the tarballs there a nd then unpack, compile, and install at least the utilities jstest, jscal, and jsattach.

Part

IV

Ch

23

 TIP Version 1.2.14 of the Linux joystick driver package contains some known flaws and will never be rolled into the 2.2 line of kernel development. You should be sure to get version 1.2.15 or later. Version 1.2.15 also marks the first time that man (help) pages for the utilities have existed, so be sure to get this version for these man pages, if nothing else.

The only other supporting software you'll want is games, of course. You will have to find these on CD-ROM or download them off the Internet, although some good games such as DOOM or Quake are included on some Linux distributions. You can find the Linux Quake page at http://www.planetquake.com/linux/. Information on DOOM and how to download it is at http://jcomm.uoregon.edu/~stevev/Linux-DOOM-FAQ.html/. The best way to find what you want to play is to use a search engine such as Yahoo! with a string such as "+games +linux". This will give you several pages of links that you can browse, looking for games to download or purchase. Companies such as Loki (http://www.lokigames.com/) are actively working on porting games to Linux from other operating systems. This trend will continue as more people use and experiment with Linux. You can also check out popular game sites such as http://happypenguin.com/, http://www.linuxgames.com/, more general Linux sites (that often include game-related news, help, and links) such as http://slashdot.org/ and http://www.freshmeat.net/, or popular download sites such as http://www.download.com/.

The joy2key utility uses the /dev/js device interface. Specifically, it enables you to use your joystick in X Window and certain console programs even if you lack the appropriate native joystick support to allow this. You can download the current loadable module from http://www-unix.oit.umass.edu/~tetron/joy2key/. You also can download the source code if you need to make changes to get it to work with earlier versions of the Linux joystick driver.

Troubleshooting

The first thing you should do if you run into trouble is make sure that your joystick is securely connected to your PC's port—it may have come unplugged while you were installing or playing with it. Make sure there aren't any missing or bent pins, and ensure that it works with other operating systems, if possible. If you were moving the interface card around, you might have loosened it, so reseating it (unplugging it and plugging back in) or trying another card slot might help. If all looks well but you still can't get your joystick to work, you can check it using the jstest utility (which should have been installed on your system earlier in this chapter). If this is not working properly, you can try rebooting, reloading the module, or even recompiling your kernel (this should be the last resort, though). Watch the console closely during boot, and look for any error messages or indications that the drivers you need are not being installed. You also can try contacting the game card or device manufacturer and explain the problem, or visit Red Hat's support Web page to see if you can find any known problems or recommendations.

Finally, keep in mind that you probably are not the only person who tried to get your current joystick hardware configuration to work with Linux; check out any game-playing and joystick HOW-TOs you can find, read through Linux- and game-related Internet news threads, and look for people with similar problems and solutions. You can even do a Web search looking for files or messages that include the names of your joystick and possibly the terms Linux or Red Hat.

Of course, in some circumstances you have consulted all available resources, tried all possible combinations, prayed, and everything, only to be frustrated repeatedly. If you find yourself in such a situation with a game device, you can subscribe to a dedicated mailing list for help. This list is monitored by many helpful folks who will be happy to answer your questions about using game devices with Linux. To subscribe to this list, send an email with the following body:

```
subscribe linux-joystick Your Name
```

```
to
```

```
listproc@atrey.karlin.mff.cuni.cz
```

```
joydump ●
```

## CHAPTER 24

Installing and Configuring Backup Support

by John Ray

Types of Backups

You can look at the backup process in two general ways: as a method of performing long-term archiving of important data, or as a way of providing quick access to files that may accidentally be deleted. For example, if you choose to use tape storage as your backup medium, you will probably want to perform incremental backups on a semi-frequent basis. If you wish to have immediate access to information, you can always mirror your data to another drive. You also can choose to use both for your systems, but before you decide what is right for you, take a closer look at these options:

- **Incremental backups**—Traditionally, incremental backups would be performed with a tape drive of some sort. An incremental backup starts with a complete backup of your hard drive to the backup medium. Then, at regularly scheduled intervals you perform additional backups that do nothing more than add what has changed on your drive to the backup. The advantage of this sort of backup is that it is very fast to do (except the first time that it runs) and, other than inserting a tape from time to time, won't require much supervision. The drawback is that you can only access the files through the incremental backup software. You can't access the backup as you are used to currently accessing files on your system.

- **Mirroring data**—There are multiple ways to mirror data to another drive. The method examined in this text is very simple and requires little setup time. "Mirroring the data" means nothing more than creating an exact copy of the data somewhere else. If you have a zip drive or a secondary hard drive, you can use this to hold a copy of your data. Because of the nature of the Unix/Linux filesystem, if a failure occurs on your primary data drive, you can always mount your backup drive in place of your original drive. This gives you the ability to quickly return your system to a working state.

  For example, if you have a critical Web site that needs to be online as much as possible, you could weekly dump the entire Web site to a recordable CD-ROM drive. If the drive containing the site data goes down, you could immediately pop in the CD and mount it in place of the drive that is damaged. You could take this one step further by looking into Linux RAID support for drive mirroring, but this can get a bit complex and should not be attempted by a first-time user.

Verifying Hardware Compatibility

Depending on how you want to perform your backups, you need to check to see that the medium you want to use is supported under Red Hat Linux. If you want to use a second hard drive to back up data, you'll need to be able to access the drive under Linux as with any other drive. If you want to use a tape drive or a CD-Recorder, you'll need to verify that the OS supports them. The quickest and easiest way to see whether your hardware is compatible is to check the Red Hat hardware compatibility list at `http://www.redhat.com/support/docs/hardware.html`. You'll notice that for tape devices, Red Hat currently recommends most SCSI tape drives (attached to a supported SCSI adapter) as supported hardware.

Unsupported, but presumably compatible, hardware includes the following message:

```
The following types of tape drives are compatible with Red Hat Linux, but they
are unsupported. There is no need to build a custom kernel to use these devices
(the driver modules are already part of the kernel-modules package):

        Floppy-controller tape drives.
        IDE tape drives.
        ATAPI compliant parallel port tape drives.
```

If you have a tape drive that meets these criteria, it should work on your Linux computer. Obviously, the most desired type of drive would be a SCSI tape drive. SCSI defines an interface standard on your computer—SCSI tape drives "speak" alike, and SCSI hard drives "speak" alike—so you can easily use and diagnose SCSI hardware on your system. If at all possible, you should run a SCSI-based system—you'll save yourself a ton of headaches in the long run, and you'll have much more consistent hardware support in the operating system. SCSI cards start in the $75 range, and many are supported by Linux. A popular (and inexpensive) chipset is the SYMBIOS SCSI chipset. If you find a good deal on a SCSI card using this chipset, buy it—it will be a good investment.

Although Red Hat Linux offers out-of-the-box support for several types of tape drives, the only supported standard is SCSI, so the examples in the chapter focus on this. If you don't have a SCSI device or a device listed in the "Supported Hardware" page, you aren't necessarily out of luck. Be sure to run a few Web and USENET searches before giving up. You may find that user-contributed drivers and patches are available so that you can configure your machine to work with the device.

Understanding Linux Backup Support

Linux abstracts hardware so that you can use a standardized interface to the devices rather than having to use software that is designed for each individual tape drive or backup device. The basis for most Unix/Linux backups is the command `dump`, which enables you to perform complete and incremental backups of data to a device. The operating system doesn't concern itself with what the device is; it literally just dumps data to it. For example, typically you would use a tape drive as an incremental backup device. Linux enables you to specify any configured storage device to the `dump` command—even standard out (so that your backup would go to your screen).

This hardware abstraction is a very important feature of the operating system. You can create backup scripts that run at certain intervals, and if you ever want to change where the data is being backed up, it's as easy as changing a device name in a configuration file.

If you have been running your system as recommended, you will have been storing software that you have installed in the /usr/local directory structure. One of the benefits of this will now become clear: You will need to back up a limited number of system files. The /etc directory, for example, contains the majority of the configuration files for your machine. The /home directory structure probably contains all your user accounts, and these are obvious targets for backup. If you had these directories backed up and a catastrophic system failure occurred, you could simply reinstall the operating system from the original distribution CD, then restore the backed up directories, and be back up and running in an hour or so. If you've been placing all your added files in the /usr/local directory, you'll also be able to back up and restore your added software. On the other hand, if you've mixed the additional applications with standard system software locations, such as /usr/bin, you'll find that you need to back up these directories as well. If backup space is at a premium, this is going to cause problems. Plan carefully as you build your system—how you choose to set up your computer has implications beyond what you may first believe.

Installing Backup Devices

Backup devices should be installed in your system according to the instructions of the manufacturer. If you have a floppy drive-based tape drive, you'll need to connect it to your floppy controller and similar devices. Chapter 20, "Installing and Configuring CD-ROMs, DVDs, and CD-Rs," demonstrates how to configure CD Recorders on your system; Chapter 25, "Installing and Configuring Zip and SuperDisk Drives," covers configuring these drives for your use. These are all viable backup mediums and can be used to store copies of your data. If you're using a SCSI-based solution and this is your first venture into the SCSI world, you'll want to follow some basic rules to make sure that your devices work as you think they should:

- Make sure that the devices you are connecting have unique ID numbers. If you have two devices with identical IDs, the computer will not be capable of talking to either one.

- Do not use the ID 7. The SCSI adapter itself uses this ID for communicating with the other SCSI devices. If this device is used on one of your tape or disk drives, the entire SCSI chain may not work.

- Finally, be sure to terminate your SCSI chain. Termination is a mystery to many people, but it really is a very simple concept. As an illustration, take a rope, hold one end, and ask a friend to hold the other end. Hold the rope firmly, but allow some slack. Next, create a wave in the rope by moving one end up and down; make sure that your friend keeps his end tightly in place. You'll notice that the wave in the rope reaches your friend's hand and then bounces back up the line toward you. This is precisely what happens with signals on the SCSI bus. If the SCSI chain is not terminated, you'll have stray signals travelling up and down the line. This can result in slow access of your SCSI devices or, even worse, data corruption.

As long as you follow the instructions that come with your devices, you'll be fine. More devices are coming with Linux support, so you may just find instructions on configuring your device for Red Hat support right out of the box.

Installing Hardware Support

The Linux kernel ships with support for SCSI and many floppy-based solutions. SCSI devices are simply plug-and-play: You plug in the device in the SCSI chain, Linux detects it, and you can use it without any further configuration on the system side. IDE-based tape devices should automatically be detected as well. You should be able to see the detected device and see how you should refer to it in the bootup messages.

For example, imagine that you just connected a SCSI tape drive to your system. Your boot messages would now include the following:

```
Sep 12 13:40:44 pointy kernel:    Vendor: ARCHIVE
➥Model: Python 28388-XXX Rev: 4.94
Sep 12 13:40:44 pointy kernel:
➥Type:    Sequential-Access  ANSI SCSI revision: 02
Sep 12 13:40:44 pointy kernel: Detected scsi tape st0 at scsi0,
➥channel 0, id 6,
```

That's all you need to do. Your SCSI tape drive is now accessible as /dev/st0, as the messages indicate.

Floppy-based tape drives and other devices require more extensive configuration. The ftape, for example, requires that you add module configuration information to the /etc/conf.modules file (see /usr/src/linux-2.2.5/Documentation/ftape.txt). These devices require IRQ, IO, and DMA configuration information—and unless you know what these values are, your time is better spent working with a more modern (and better supported) piece of backup hardware.

If you are running a modified kernel version, you may need to add support back into the kernel to support your tape (or other storage medium) device. Chapter 18, "Installing and Configuring the Red Hat Linux Kernel," covers the steps of compiling and installing a new kernel. Pay close attention to these lines as you are configuring the compile using make xconfig, make menuconfig, or make config:

```
*
* Please see Documentation/ide.txt for help/info on IDE drives
*
Include IDE/ATAPI TAPE support (CONFIG_BLK_DEV_IDETAPE) [M/n/y/?]

*
* SCSI support
*
SCSI support (CONFIG_SCSI) [Y/m/n/?]
*
```

```
* SCSI support type (disk, tape, CD-ROM)
*
SCSI tape support (CONFIG_CHR_DEV_ST) [Y/m/n/?]
SCSI generic support (CONFIG_CHR_DEV_SG) [M/n/y/?]

*
* Ftape, the floppy tape device driver
*
Ftape (QIC-80/Travan) support (CONFIG_FTAPE) [M/n/y/?]
Zftape, the VFS interface (CONFIG_ZFTAPE) [M/n/?]
Default block size (CONFIG_ZFT_DFLT_BLK_SZ) [10240]
*
* The compressor will be built as a module only!
*
Number of ftape buffers (EXPERIMENTAL) (CONFIG_FT_NR_BUFFERS) [3]
Enable procfs status report (+2kb) (CONFIG_FT_PROC_FS) [N/y/?]
Debugging output (Normal, Excessive, Reduced, None) [Normal]
  defined CONFIG_FT_NORMAL_DEBUG
*
* Hardware configuration
*
Floppy tape controllers (Standard, MACH-2, FC-10/FC-20, Alt/82078) [Standard]
```

You should fully understand the concepts of configuring the kernel before you activate any of these options. If you are having trouble getting the system to recognize your backup units, you may wish to compile support for your tape devices directly into the kernel rather than load them as modules.

Using Backup Support Software

Everything you need to configure your system for backups is already available on your system. If you're planning to simply back up the files directly to another drive, the process is very simple. Let's take a look at the steps you need to take to perform a simple mirror backup of a portion of your filesystem.

Using *copy* (*cp*) to Back Up Files

First, you must prepare the medium for use on Linux. Assume that you're using a SCSI disk, such as a SCSI Zip drive /dev/sdb as the backup medium for your computer. You'll want to create a new filesystem for the drive by using the mkfs /dev/sdb command. If you want to create separate backup partitions on the drive, you'll need to use the fdisk utility to create new partitions of type 83 (Linux native), write them to the system, then make the filesystem on the partition you want to use for backups. Chapter 19, "Installing and Configuring Hard Drives," covers the information you'll need to create partitions and filesystems on your backup device.

Second, you must mount the device somewhere on your system. For example, you could create a mount point called /mnt/storage to mount your mass storage/backup devices. Do *not* add this device to your /etc/fstab file. The point of doing a backup is so that the data is secure. If you mount your backup device each time you turn on your computer, you risk corrupting the data during normal computer use. Keep your backup medium in a safe place, not connected to your system. For example, you could use the command mount /dev/sdb /mnt/storage to mount your backup drive on the computer.

Third, start copying files. The command cp –av *<source>* *<destination>* creates a mirror of the files you want backed up. The –a option tells copy to recurse through the directory structure and copy the files, preserving the files' original attributes. The v tells copy to be verbose while it is working, and will show you what files are being copied in real time. If you attempt to use copy without this option, you'll end up copying files with your default permissions rather than the permissions that the files have.

For example, if you want to create a duplicate of your /home directory structure to your mounted media at /mnt/storage, you would do this:

```
[root@pointy /]# cp -av /home /mnt/storage ¦ more
/home -> /mnt/storage/home
/home/ftp -> /mnt/storage/home/ftp
/home/ftp/bin -> /mnt/storage/home/ftp/bin
/home/ftp/bin/compress -> /mnt/storage/home/ftp/bin/compress
/home/ftp/bin/cpio -> /mnt/storage/home/ftp/bin/cpio
/home/ftp/bin/gzip -> /mnt/storage/home/ftp/bin/gzip
/home/ftp/bin/ls -> /mnt/storage/home/ftp/bin/ls
/home/ftp/bin/sh -> /mnt/storage/home/ftp/bin/sh
/home/ftp/bin/tar -> /mnt/storage/home/ftp/bin/tar
/home/ftp/bin/zcat -> /mnt/storage/home/ftp/bin/zcat
/home/ftp/etc -> /mnt/storage/home/ftp/etc
/home/ftp/etc/group -> /mnt/storage/home/ftp/etc/group
/home/ftp/etc/ld.so.cache -> /mnt/storage/home/ftp/etc/ld.so.cache
/home/ftp/etc/passwd -> /mnt/storage/home/ftp/etc/passwd
/home/ftp/lib -> /mnt/storage/home/ftp/lib
```

This is another situation where you want to make sure that you're logged into the root account; otherwise, any files that you can't read for lack of permissions won't be copied.

Copying files in this manner is a very simple way of doing backups; depending on your needs, this may be all that your system requires. To restore the files, you simply copy them back to where you want them from the backup media. For your "play" machine, for example, you don't need to do anything complex, so you could simply copy your home directory to a Zip disk from time to time using the procedure just described. If you are running a server, however, you'll probably want to implement some sort of incremental backup system that is updated on a daily basis.

Performing Incremental Backups: *dump*

To perform an incremental backup, you'll use the dump command. This command does exactly what it sounds like: It dumps a filesystem to a device. For the examples of the use of the dump commands, you'll be dumping to the SCSI tape drive that you connected earlier. If you want to perform incremental backups on a ZIP disk or other device, simply substitute the name of your preferred storage device in place of the device name that the example uses: /dev/st0. Note that /dev/nst0 is used rather than /dev/st0. Although st0 is indeed the name of the device, referring to it as nst0 tells the system that it will need to write data to the end of the tape rather than rewinding it. Before you do anything, however, you'll want to erase the tape (you won't need to do this if it's a fresh tape). You can send commands to the tape drive using the mt command. The command to erase a device is mt -f <device name> erase. (Similarly, rewinding a tape is done with mt -f <device name> rewind.) For example:

```
[root@pointy jray]# mt -f /dev/nst0 erase
```

The process of erasing your drive may take a little while. You can also check the device status by sending the status parameter to the mt command:

```
[root@pointy jray]# mt -f /dev/nst0 status
SCSI 2 tape drive:
File number=0, block number=0, partition=0.
Tape block size 512 bytes. Density code 0x13 (DDS (61000 bpi)).
Soft error count since last status=0
General status bits on (41010000):
 BOT ONLINE IM_REP_EN
```

Running dump for the first time requires that the system perform a full backup on the system. To do this, use the command /sbin/dump -0u -f <destination device> <directory to be backed up>. Backing up the user directories to the first SCSI tape device on a SCSI chain is as simple as /sbin/dump -0u -f /dev/nst0 /home, for example:

```
[root@pointy /home]# dump -0u -f /dev/nst0 /home/httpd
  DUMP: Date of this level 0 dump: Sun Sep 12 15:18:35 1999
  DUMP: Date of last level 0 dump: the epoch
  DUMP: Dumping /dev/sda1 (/) to /dev/nst0
  DUMP: mapping (Pass I) [regular files]
  DUMP: mapping (Pass II) [directories]
  DUMP: estimated 6169 tape blocks on 0.16 tape(s).
  DUMP: dumping (Pass III) [directories]
  DUMP: dumping (Pass IV) [regular files]
  DUMP: DUMP: 6064 tape blocks on 1 volumes(s)
  DUMP: finished in 24 seconds, throughput 252 KBytes/sec
  DUMP: level 0 dump on Sun Sep 12 15:18:35 1999
  DUMP: Closing /dev/nst0
  DUMP: DUMP IS DONE
```

The process is quite straightforward. Notice that dump will prompt you for new media if it needs more than one tape. You should eject the tape upon being prompted, replace it with a new tape, and then tell the program that you're ready to go. Backing up to tape can take some time, so after you verify that your computer is indeed talking to the tape drive, you may want to start the dump and then take a break for a few minutes.

You've now successfully completed the first tape in an incremental backup. Subsequent backups will go much faster now. You should now think about planning a backup schedule. Each time you run dump, you specify the level of the backup. The first level dump you created was a level 0 dump, which specifies everything in the directory. Now, if you want to run weekly backups, you would want to use level 1, which copies all the files that have changed since the level 0 backup. You can continue to specify levels, all the way up to 9. Each level backs up only the files that have changed since the level underneath it was executed.

A typical backup schedule may be something like this:

- Monthly, start a new backup set by running a level 0 backup.

- Weekly, run a level 1 backup on the system. This backs up everything that has changed since the level 0 backup at the beginning of the month.

- Daily, run a level 2 backup, backing up all data that has been modified since the beginning of the week.

When you have a backup schedule set, stick to it, and do not immediately recycle your tapes from month to month. Keep a few months' worth of tapes in a safe storage location, and always label the level of the backup on the tape and the date it was created. Number the tapes starting with "1" for the level 0 dump, and increment the tape number starting from there.

Dump keeps track of all the dates of backups. Any time you want to view the backups that have been performed, look at the following example:

```
[root@pointy /home]# dump -W
Last dump(s) done (Dump '>' file systems):
  /dev/sda1     (    /) Last dump: Level 0, Date Sun Sep 12 15:18
```

Restoring Files Backed Up with *dump*   Restoring files that have been written to a tape or other device is simple, but it's not as convenient as simply copying them from one device to another. To restore files, you must use—you guessed it—the restore command. To restore files from the backup just made, you can use the "interactive" version of the restore command. If you'd like to automate the restoration procedure, take a look at the restore man page, which shows several options that can be given to the command. Running in interactive mode provides a friendly command-line interface to the restoration procedure. The following are the basic commands that you'll want to use:

- **add <file/directory>**—«Adds a directory or a filename to the list of files that will be restored. Adding a directory with this command implies that all the underlying directories will also be extracted.

- **delete <file/directory>**—«Deletes a file. If you inadvertently added a directory or file to the extraction list that you don't want to be processed, you can use delete to remove the file.

Part

IV

Ch

24

- **cd**—Changes the directory that you're working in. This works exactly like the Linux shell equivalent cd command.
- **ls**—Shows the contents of a directory. Entries in the directory that are targeted for extraction are preceded by the "*" character.
- **pwd**—Shows the current directory that you are in.
- **extract**—Extracts files that are on the extraction list. This is the last command that you will want to call during the restore operation. You will be prompted for the tape volumes to use for the restoration—start with the most recent tape.
- **quit**—Quits the restore process.
- **help**—Prints a list of these (and a few other commands) for quick reference.

Take a look at a sample restore session from the dump level 0 just created. Start by rewinding your tape and then running the restore command as restore −i −f /dev/nst0. Make sure that you are in the directory that you want files restored to. If you want them to be restored to their original location, be sure that you are in the root directory:

```
[root@pointy /]# mkdir restoredfiles
[root@pointy /]# cd restoredfiles/
[root@pointy /restoredfiles]# mt -f /dev/st0 rewind
[root@pointy /restoredfiles]# restore -i -f /dev/nst0
```

Now, take a look around and see where you are, and navigate to the directory that you want to restore:

```
restore > ls
.:
home/

restore > cd home
restore > ls
./home:
httpd/
```

If you want to restore the httpd directory, you add it to the extraction list. This also adds all the files underneath the directory to the extraction list. The "*" in front of the directory name shows that the directory is indeed targeted for extraction:

```
restore > add httpd
restore > ls
./home:
*httpd/
```

You can also see that the files immediately under this directory are going to be restored:

```
restore > cd httpd
restore > ls
./home/httpd:
*cgi-bin/ *html/    *icons/
```

If you don't want all these files to be restored, you can use the delete command to remove them from the extraction list. In this example, the cgi-bin and icons directories will not be restored. The "*" no longer shows up in front of the items that are not marked to be extracted:

```
restore > delete cgi-bin icons
restore > ls
./home/httpd:
 cgi-bin/ *html/      icons/
```

The command you'll want to use is extract. It performs the extraction of the files that you have marked:

```
restore > extract
You have not read any tapes yet.
Unless you know which volume your file(s) are on you should start
with the last volume and work towards the first.
Specify next volume #: 1
set owner/mode for '.'? [yn] n
```

Finally, you can quit the program and check to see whether the directory structure you've restored has been created. Sure enough—/home/httpd now exists in the restoredfiles directory:

```
restore > quit
[root@pointy /restoredfiles]# ls
home
```

Resetting *dump*'s Data File   If you want dump to forget when a backup was completed, you can manually edit the /etc/dumpdates file to change the information stored in the file. For example, if you changed a large number of files on the system but didn't want them to be backed up, you could change your dump level 0 date to be more recent then the date on which you made your changes. Dump will then assume that the files have already been backed up and won't write them to the backup device.

The /etc/dumpdates file is human-readable and contains what was dumped, the dump level, and the date and time of the dump.

Here's an example:

```
[root@pointy httpd]# more /etc/dumpdates
/dev/sda1         0 Sun Sep 12 16:00:06 1999
```

Using an Easier Way to Back Up Your Files: Taper

If you aren't interested in playing around at the command line, you can look into a few alternative packages. For example, Linux comes with the program Taper, which performs incremental backups through a simple interface. You invoke Taper by specifying the type of device you are using for backups. The three types you'll probably be interested in are these:

Part

IV

Ch

24

s:	SCSI
r:	Removable media
f:	Ftape (floppy-tape drive)

Invoke the `taper` command by calling Taper with the type of backup device you are using: `taper -T <backup device>`. Figure 24.1 shows the initial Taper screen for SCSI devices. If you find that Taper has not been installed on your system, you can install the RPM manually as discussed in Chapter 11, "Installing and Managing RPM Packages." The Taper package is named `taper-6.9-6.i386.rpm` on your Red Hat CD-ROM distribution.

FIG. 24.1

Taper presents an easy control interface to backing up your system.

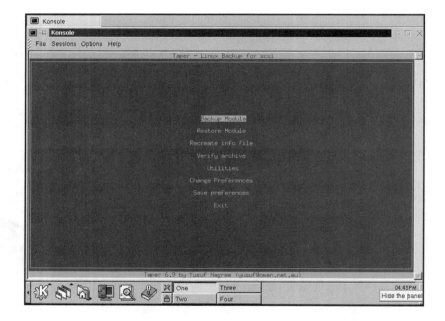

The first thing you'll want to do is make sure that the appropriate backup device is selected on your system. Choose Change Preferences from the main menu, and then choose Tape Drive Preferences from the following screen. The Tape Preferences Configuration screen appears (see Figure 24.2).

When you have determined that the settings correctly match your hardware configuration, you can exit back to the main menu (press Esc to move up one level in the menu hierarchy) and perform a simple backup.

Backing Up Files Choose Backup Module from the main menu to launch the backup system. If you have a tape in the drive with data that Taper cannot identify, it will prompt you to erase that data. After the software has determined that it has a clean tape, it will prompt you for an archive name. Choose whatever you would like that will appropriately reflect the data on the tape. Next, you will be prompted for a volume title. This is a name that will be written to the tape so that the software can verify that you have put the appropriate tape into the drive during a restore.

FIG. 24.2
Taper offers user-friendly configuration options.

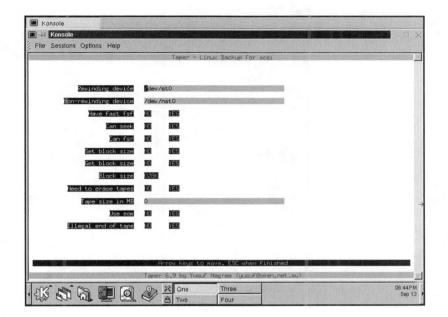

You should now be at the main Taper backup screen, which consists of four windows. The upper-right window displays the file system and enables you to select files and directories for backup. The upper-left section contains the files in the archive. The bottom two windows show files that are selected for backup and files that are excluded from backup, respectively. The basic commands that you'll want to use on this screen are very simple to remember:

- **Arrow keys/Enter**—Navigate through your filesystem. Press Enter to move into a directory tree.
- **I**—Includes a file or a directory in the archive.
- **U**—Unselects a file that has been selected for backup.
- **E**—Excludes a file from the backup. This is useful if you'd like to select an entire directory for backup but want to leave out a few files. Rather than selecting the files you want, you can select the entire directory and exclude the files you don't want.
- **F**—Ends the file selection process and starts the backup.
- **Space**—Hitting the spacebar displays a complete command summary for the program.

Figure 24.3 shows a pre-backup screen with several files selected from the home directory for backup. A few files contained in these directories have been excluded.

Part
IV

Ch
24

FIG. 24.3
The four-pane design of ftape's backup screen makes it easy to determine what you're backing up—and what you're not.

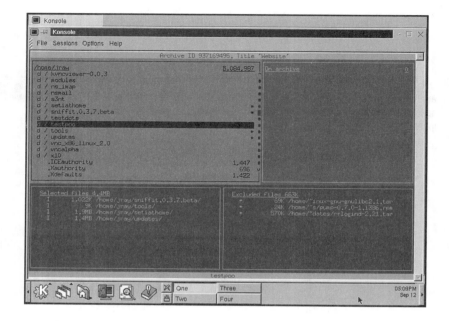

You're now ready to start your backup, so press F. Taper asks if you've finished your selections; select Yes. Taper then displays its status as the files are backed up. Figure 24.4 shows the backing up status screen.

FIG. 24.4
Taper plainly displays its status as it is backing up files.

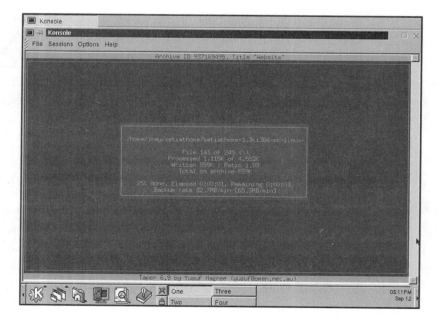

When this is completed, a results screen is shown that displays any problems that occurred in the backup as well as the amount of time it took and various other statistics. Pressing OK takes you back to the main screen. The backup is complete.

Restoring Files   Restoring files using Taper is just as easy as backing them up. Insert a tape with a backup set on it into your drive, then choose Restore Module from the main menu. You will be presented with a screen that displays the available backup sets on the tape and enables you to use the arrow keys to select the one that you wish to restore. Select the set you want, and then push Enter to begin the restoration process.

When prompted for the location to restore files, enter in the directory where you'd like the files to be re-created. If you want to return them to their original locations, make sure that you type in the root directory.

As shown in Figure 24.5, the familiar four panes will be displayed. This screen operates very similarly to the screen where you chose what files you wanted to back up. Use the arrow keys to choose the files you want to restore, pressing I, when the desired file or directory is highlighted. The selected files are shown in the lower-left window.

FIG. 24.5
The restore interface is very similar to the backup interface.

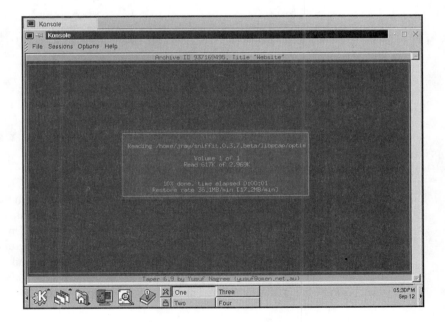

Pressing F starts the restoration after confirming that you have finished selecting your files. As before, a status window is displayed as the files are restored. When the process has completed, a confirmation message is displayed, along with any errors that have occurred.

Part
IV

Ch
24

Taper offers several other easy to use functions, including the capability to test your tape drive and configure the program's default behavior during unattended operation. You'll find that the software is very easy to configure and offers a wealth of options.

Using KDat

One final option that you may want to consider is KDat, KDE's backup tool. KDat provides a KDE-style interface to the backup process and is very simple to use. You can access KDat as Tape Backup Tool from the KDE system pop-up menu, under Utilities.

You'll immediately want to configure KDat to look at the tape device that you plan to use for backups. Choose Preferences from the KDat Edit menu to set your device. You can also configure other default behavior for the application from this window (see Figure 24.6).

FIG. 24.6
KDat offers a simplistic and user-friendly KDE-style interface.

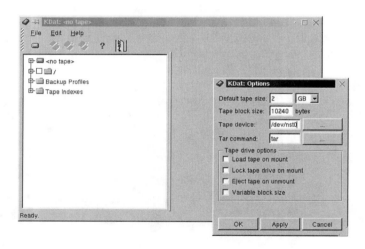

You operate KDat by selecting the files you want to back up and then choosing Backup from the File menu. Restoring files works exactly the same: Pop in the backup tape, choose Mount Tape from the File menu, and choose the files that you want restored. Unfortunately, in its current state, KDat has limited functionality and is at times problematic to use. Taper and dump both provide command-line interfaces to the backup procedure and are strong, stable solutions. If you must use a fancy interface to a backup program, use Taper. KDat is fine for small backups but is lacking as a full-fledged system backup solution.

Configuring Backup Scripts

Automating backups is quite simple given the command-line tools that you have available. Couple the dump and cp programs with the power of cron, and you can set your backups to run whenever it is most convenient.

For example, if you'd like to configure your system to back up files in /home/httpd on a daily basis to the device /mnt/storage, you could add this line to your /etc/crontab file:

```
30 6 * * * root cp -a /home/httpd /mnt/storage
```

This automatically starts the cp procedure at 6:30 AM daily. If you'd like to something similar on a monthly basis, just change the line to look like this instead:

```
30 6 1 * * root cp -a /home/httpd /mnt/storage
```

Now your backup will be run on the first day of every month at 6:30 AM rather than every day.

Extend this reasoning to the dump system, and suddenly you have a very powerful automated backup system, for example:

```
30 10 * * * root dump -2u /dev/nst0 /
30 8 * * 1 root dump -1u /dev/nst0 /
30 6 1 * * root dump -0u /dev/nst0 /
```

Now your computer will automatically start a level 0 dump on the first of each month at 6:30 AM, a level 1 dump every Monday at 8:30 AM, and level 2 dumps every day at 10:30 AM. You'll probably need to work with these settings for your particular situation, but this should give you some idea of what is possible.

Troubleshooting Backups

If errors occur during backup, they are usually due to files that you do not have permission to read. If you are running as the root user, this shouldn't be a problem. You may also end up backing up a file that is in use and end up with corrupted data. One way to avoid this is to boot into single-user mode before attempting to backup or restore files. To do this, supply the single parameter after the name of the kernel you are booting at the Linux LILO prompt. Single-user mode is roughly equivalent to Safe mode on a Windows machine. There are a very small number of services running, and other users cannot connect to the machine (thus, "single-user" mode).

The other common backup problem is that tapes are overused until they are no longer viable. Pay attention to your drive—if it takes longer than usual to write data to your tape drive, try replacing the tape. Tape drives have error correction and will try to fix problems as they occur. This is fine for tapes that are in good condition, but it will work against you when the tapes start to wear out. Replacing tapes on a biannual basis is a good way to ensure that you will be able to restore your data when you need to. If a tape goes bad, there is very little that you can do. Unfortunately, backups are one of those things that either work or don't.

Summary

Now that you've read through this chapter, you should understand what devices you can use to back up your computer and the different methods that can be employed to protect your information. SCSI tape drives are the most common and best-supported backup device in Red Hat Linux. If you have the option of purchasing SCSI equipment, this is the best route that you can take. Red Hat provides several pieces of software to make backing up a breeze. The copy (cp) command can be used to quickly back up files between two devices. The dump command can perform incremental backups from the command line, and Taper and KDat provide a friendly interface to the backup process. When you get sick of backing up files by hand, you can automate the process using the /etc/crontab file. Linux backups shouldn't be a problem or a mystery any longer. ●

## CHAPTER 25

Installing and Configuring Zip and SuperDisk Drives

by Wade Maxfield

In this chapter

The Parallel Port Iomega Zip Drive

The Iomega Zip drive was developed by the Iomega Corporation, in Roy, Utah. The Zip identifier is registered by Iomega Corporation (http://www.iomega.com/).

Until recently, the Zip drive supported only a 100MB disk. However, Iomega has introduced a 250MB drive and disk, called the Zip 250, which supports both 100MB and 250MB disks.

Iomega claims operating system support for Microsoft Windows 95, Microsoft Windows 98, Microsoft Windows NT, Microsoft Windows 3.X, and DOS. Thanks to Grant Guenther and David Campbell, Iomega is also supported by Linux. Grant Guenther wrote the original kernel driver modules, and David Campbell updated them to support the newer disk drives.

Of Mice and Modules

The secret of making the Iomega Zip drive work is modules. *Modules* are the same thing as Windows drivers, except that Linux allows them to be loaded and unloaded into memory while the system is running. For example, if you have a PS/2-compatible mouse, the PC keyboard module should detect it and install support for it into the kernel after booting. This is not an error-free process, but it works most of the time.

The default install of Linux comes with everything you need to support the Zip drive. You simply must load and unload the modules at the proper time.

You must be logged in as root to insert and remove modules in the standard Linux installation. Even if you are logged in as a normal user, this can be done temporarily using the su command if you know the root password. If you type su -1 and press Enter, you will be prompted for a password. Enter root's password at this point. You will be placed in root's home directory and will have root's path set up so that the commands modprobe and rmmod are available to you.

> **N O T E**   If you forget the -1 after the su command, you will not have your path set up or be placed in root's home directory. ∎

The program modprobe looks at the module you want to load and determines what other modules are needed to make that one work. It then loads the other modules for you before loading the one you asked for. Previously, you would have used insmod and would have discovered lots of errors that could be resolved only by patiently going back and loading the modules the system complained about needing.

Attaching the Hardware

The drive comes with a straight-through cable that has a male connector on one end and a female connector on the other end. The male connector is the connector with the pins, and the female connector is the one with the small sockets. The female 25-pin connector on the back of your PC is the parallel printer port connector. Plug the male end into the parallel port on the PC, and plug the female end into the back of the Zip drive.

> **N O T E** Older PCs have a serial port connector that is the same size as the parallel port connec-
> tor. This is a male connector. It is possible to plug the Zip drive cable into the serial port
> and then into the printer port connection of the drive—this can damage the drive and should not be
> done. If you have any doubts, refer to the documentation from Iomega that came with the drive. ▤

Be sure that you have a disk inserted in the drive for the next step. Also make sure you have the Zip drive powered up. If you do not have a disk in the drive, the next step will give you an error message, as discussed in the troubleshooting section.

Getting Linux to Recognize the Drive

> **N O T E** If you have a Zip drive manufactured after August 1998, you will use the command mod -
> probe imm in place of modprobe ppa in the following instructions. See the trou-
> bleshooting section "Modprobe ppa fails," later in this chapter, for more information. ▤

The first time you work with your drive, you should be logged in on a console screen rather than in an X windows session. If you are currently running an X windows session, an easy way to do this is to press the CTRL+ALT+F1 keys simultaneously. This hides the X windows graphic interface and provides you with the first logon console screen. At this point, pressing ALT+F2 through ALT+F5 will give you additional console screens. ALT+F7 will get you back to the X windows graphic interface. Simply log in as root.

If you are currently at a console prompt, you must either log out and log in as root, or you need to run the su -1 command and give the root password when asked. At this point, you are ready to set up Linux for the Zip drive.

Run modpobe ppa from the command line. If this works, you should see something like this:

```
[root@pk75 /root]# modprobe ppa
ppa: Version 2.03 (for Linux 2.2.x)
ppa: Found device at ID 6, Attempting to use EPP 32 bit
ppa: Found device at ID 6, Attempting to use PS/2
ppa: Communication established with ID 6 using PS/2
scsi0 : Iomega VPI0 (ppa) interface
scsi : 1 host.
  Vendor: IOMEGA     Model: ZIP 100        Rev: D.13
  Type:    Direct-Access              ANSI SCSI revision: 02
Detected scsi removable disk sda at scsi0, channel 0, id 6, lun 0
SCSI device sda: hdwr sector= 512 bytes. Sectors= 196608 [96 MB] [0.1 GB]
sda: Write Protect is off
 sda: sda4
```

Here's what just happened:

1. The `modprobe` program looked at the ppa module and went through its list of modules to resolve all undefined items the ppa module needed to operate and loaded those modules first.

2. It then executed the initialization portion of the ppa module, which printed the first four lines of information.

3. The SCSI code in the kernel was then told about the ppa module providing an interface to the Zip drive.

4. The SCSI code then tried to detect the type of drive and the size of the disk in the drive and reported on what it found.

The Zip drive is hosted under the SCSI device sda. If you do an ls on `/dev/sda*`, you will find the following list:

```
[root@pk75 drivers]# ls /dev/sda*
/dev/sda      /dev/sda11   /dev/sda14   /dev/sda3   /dev/sda6   /dev/sda9
/dev/sda1     /dev/sda12   /dev/sda15   /dev/sda4   /dev/sda7
/dev/sda10    /dev/sda13   /dev/sda2    /dev/sda5   /dev/sda8
```

All disk drives follow the same pattern under Linux. Every disk drive can have multiple partitions. The first disk drive is always the "A" (hda) drive. The second disk drive is always the "B" (hdb) drive, and so on. The drive reference without a following number is always the base drive. Each partition on the drive is indicated by a number. Under the DOS partitioning scheme, drives can have only four primary partitions. You may have more than four partitions, but these partitions are logical partitions that are hosted inside a primary partition. When this is done, the primary partition is called an extended partition.

When the Zip drive is recognized, the disk in it is given the primary partition number of 4 if the disk was formatted by Iomega. Therefore, all accesses to the drive are done to `/dev/sda4`. This information is key for mounting the drive under a directory.

Getting Set Up to Use the Disk in the Drive

Here is where personal taste comes to play. Some like to have access to their disk drives under the root directory. Generally, however, storage devices that are not always online are found under the `/mnt` directory. If you do an ls `/mnt`, you should see the following list:

```
[root@pk75 drivers]# ls /mnt
cdrom  floppy
```

This list is just a list of directories. Under Linux, storage devices are mounted under existing directories and become part of the directory tree. This is more convenient than the DOS way of doing things because you aren't limited to the number of letters in the alphabet for your storage devices. In theory, you could have an infinite number of storage devices attached to your Linux system at any one time.

To create a directory for the Zip drive, you use the `mkdir` command:

```
[root@pk75 drivers]# cd /mnt
[root@pk75 /mnt]# mkdir zip
[root@pk75 /mnt]# ls
cdrom  floppy  zip

[root@pk75 /mnt]# ls -l
total 3
drwxrwxr-x   2 root      root          1024 Oct  9  1998 cdrom
drwxrwxr-x   2 root      root          1024 Feb  6  1996 floppy
drwxr-xr-x   2 root      root          1024 Jul 10 07:22 zip

[root@pk75 /mnt]# chmod a+rw zip

[root@pk75 /mnt]# ls -l
total 3
drwxrwxr-x   2 root      root          1024 Oct  9  1998 cdrom
drwxrwxr-x   2 root      root          1024 Feb  6  1996 floppy
drwxrwxr-x   2 root      root          1024 Jul 10 07:22 zip
```

Here the `zip` directory has been created and given permissions with chmod to allow everyone to read and write to the directory. The next step is to allow a standard user to use the Zip drive by creating an entry in the file `/etc/fstab`. (*Fstab* stands for "File System Table," as far as I know. It lists all the devices available for use by the system at boot time or later.)

As root, use your favorite editor in Linux and open the file `/etc/fstab`. It should look something like this:

```
/dev/hda2           /                         ext2     defaults        1 1
/dev/hda1           /boot                     ext2     defaults        1 2
/dev/hda4           /home                     ext2     defaults        1 2
/dev/hda3           swap                      swap     defaults        0 0
/dev/fd0            /mnt/floppy               ext2     noauto          0 0
/dev/cdrom          /mnt/cdrom                iso9660  noauto,ro       0 0
none                /proc                     proc     defaults        0 0
none                /dev/pts                  devpts   mode=0622       0 0
```

You will need to add the following line to the bottom of the file:

```
/dev/sda4           /mnt/zip                  vfat     noauto,user     0 0
```

The entries are separated by tabs or spaces. The first entry is the device you will be using. The value `/dev/sda4` comes from the fact that devices are always found in the `/dev` directory and that the results of the `modprobe` command told you the Zip disk was sda device 4.

The second entry is the directory under which the disk will be mounted. It should be created by root and should have the proper permissions, as previously shown.

The third entry is the type of file system that will be on the disk. Vfat is the long filename directory structure that Microsoft Windows uses, beginning with Microsoft Windows 95 and Windows NT.

The fourth entry consists of two parts. The `noauto` entry indicates to Linux that it is not to be automatically mounted during the boot process. The user entry, a comma separated from the `noauto` entry, indicates to the `mount` command that any user can try to mount the disk in the drive under this directory. After a user mounts the disk, that user is the owner of the files on the disk until the disk is unmounted with the `umount` command.

The last two entries have to do with backup and automatic checking for errors. If the first number is nonzero, the `dump` command assumes that this file system needs to be backed up. If the next entry is nonzero, this indicates that the file system should be checked when mounted at boot time. Neither of these options is necessary, so both are set to 0. Save the `/etc/fstab` file.

N O T E Linuxconf is an excellent tool for editing the `/etc/fstab` file. Look under Config, File Systems, Access local drive, and add the drive information there. Click the User Mountable button underneath the Options tab. ▨

To use the `mtools` commands, you must edit the `/etc/mtools.conf` file. The beginning of the file will look like this:

```
# Example mtools.conf files.  Uncomment the lines which correspond to
# your architecture and comment out the "SAMPLE FILE" line below

# Linux floppy drives
drive a: file="/dev/fd0" exclusive 1.44m
drive b: file="/dev/fd1" exclusive 1.44m
```

Add the following line after `drive b`:

```
drive z: file="/dev/sda4"
```

This entry enables you to address the Zip drive as drive z: when using the `mtools` commands. You cannot mount the Zip drive using the `mount` command to use `mtools`. You also must run the `modprobe ppa` command first.

Finally, as root, you must execute the following command:

```
chmod a+rw /dev/sda4
```

This command changes the permissions to the Zip drive device so that any user can use `mtools` on an unmounted Zip drive. This command is not needed if you always access the drive as the root user. However, if you spend all your time as root user, you may very well make a mistake. The creator of the Linux kernel once erased his whole hard drive and spent many hours with a low-level disk editor getting it back. Be careful when using Linux as root!

To use the Zip drive with Dosemu, you must have installed the Dosemu package during the initial install process, or later from the rpm. For this example, it was installed using the FreeDos option, which provides an immediately bootable DOS package.

The Zip drive was set up to be addressed as disk B: under Dosemu. Edit `/etc/dosemu.conf` using your favorite editor. Search for the line that reads like this:

```
$_floppy_b = ""
```

Then change it to read like this:

```
$_floppy_b = "ATAPI:/dev/sda4"
```

From the command line, run the following command:

```
dos
```

Dosemu will run and will present you with the C:> prompt. At this point, you may access the drive using standard DOS commands; everything works as expected. At the current time, it is best to treat the Zip drive as an unmountable hard drive when using Dosemu. Be sure to exit Dosemu with the `exitemu` command before ejecting the Zip disk.

Note that the FreeDos version is not yet 100% compatible with Microsoft's version of DOS—it is close to 95% at the time of this writing.

Using the Zip Drive

There are a few things to note before examining the details of operating a Zip drive.

All drives must be mounted under directories before they are used. If you fail to mount a drive under a directory, it will be unavailable to any program except for the set of commands known as the `mtools` commands. The `mtool` commands will work only on drives previously formatted by DOS or Windows. In contrast, `mtool` commands are not available to use on mounted drives.

After it is mounted under a directory, the drive is available to any program running under Linux, with some exceptions as to features. For example, DOS or Windows formatted drives contain no security restrictions. If you create a file on that type of drive, anyone can read, write, or delete the file.

Mounting the Drive   After Linux recognizes the drive, and before you use the Zip drive, you must mount it. Because you have created an entry in the `/etc/fstab` file, mounting is simple. As a user, or as root, enter the following command:

```
mount /mnt/zip
```

The mount program determines from the `/etc/fstab` file the proper way to mount the Zip drive. You should see the orange access light come on for a moment. At this point, you can execute the `df` command to make sure that the disk was mounted:

```
[root@pk75 /root]# df
/dev/hda2            1289380   1025802    196950   84% /
/dev/hda1              21438      6590     13741   32% /boot
/dev/hda4             620547      6323    582170    1% /home
/dev/sda4              98078       330     97748    0% /mnt/zip
```

If the disk was successfully mounted, you should see `/dev/sda4` in the list, usually at the bottom. At this point, all the standard Linux commands will work. The vfat module will take care of translating long filenames to short names and will store files on the disk in the proper DOS format so that the disk is readable from any DOS or Windows machine.

N O T E The mount command typed without any arguments will give you about the same information. However, it is not as cleanly formatted, making it harder to read. ■

Ejecting the Disk The `eject` command ejects your disk from the Zip drive. However, note that you must use the `umount` command before ejecting the Zip disk. The command looks like this:

```
umount /dev/sda4
```

This command causes the `sync` command to be run against the Zip disk. `sync` flushes all information that is in memory onto the disk. Linux keeps data that is to be written to the disk in memory until it is convenient to physically write it to the drive. This provides great performance gains, but it also causes some problems if you remove a disk before this information has been physically written.

N O T E If you do not use the umount command before ejecting the disk, you can ruin the file system structure on a disk. Be careful! This warning does not apply to using the mtools commands. ■

Next, you move on to the `eject` command. This command works only as root under Red Hat 6.0. In past releases, making `/dev/sda4` readable, writable, and executable by all users would allow any user to eject the disk.

To use the `eject` command, enter the following on the command line:

```
eject /dev/sda4
```

This causes the disk to come flying out of the drive, especially if it is standing on its side. The first time I used this command, the disk bounded off the desk and onto the floor in one fell swoop! If the Zip drive is laying flat, the disk is less likely to catapult its way out of the drive. Be careful!

Using the *mtools* Commands After Linux recognizes the drive, you can use the `mtools` commands immediately. Because you have created the entry in the `/etc/mtools.conf` file, using the Zip drive is simple. As a user, or as root, enter the following command:

```
mdir z:
```

You will get a formatted listing of the files on the disk.

As evidenced by the mdir command, the `mtools` commands are similar to the DOS commands. Table 25.1 lists the DOS commands and the corresponding `mtools` command.

Table 25.1   DOS Commands the Corresponding *mtools* Command

DOS	mtools	Effect
attrib	mattrib	Changes the DOS attributes of a file
cd	mcd	Changes to a directory
copy	mcopy	Copies a file
del	mdel	Deletes a file
deltree	mdeltree	Deletes a subdirectory and all directories below it
dir	mdir	Lists a directory
format	mformat	Formats a disk
label	mlabel	Labels a disk
md	mmd	Makes a directory
move	mmove	Moves a file from one directory to another
rd	mrd	Removes a directory
ren	mren	Renames a file or directory
type	mtype	Prints the contents of a file to the screen

For example, you would use the following commands to create a directory called ziptest on the root of the currently mounted Zip drive, copy a file named iomega from your local directory into the root directory on that drive, move the file into that directory, and then undo what you did:

```
[root@pk75 /root]# mmd z:ziptest
[root@pk75 /root]# mcopy iomega z:
[root@pk75 /root]# mdir z:
 Volume in drive Z is ZIP-100
 Volume Serial Number is 15F9-2C71
Directory for Z:/

zip-dr~1          33291 07-03-1999  20:40  ZIP-Drive
test                 15 07-10-1999   7:40
50WAYS    EXE    265728 01-30-1998  15:22  50ways.exe
zip-in~1          33668 07-03-1999  20:40  ZIP-Install
ziptest       <DIR>     07-10-1999   8:24  ziptest
iomega             2780 07-10-1999   8:24  iomega
        6 files             335 482 bytes
                        100 087 808 bytes free

[root@pk75 /root]# mmove z:iomega z:/ziptest
[root@pk75 /root]# mdir z:
 Volume in drive Z is ZIP-100
 Volume Serial Number is 15F9-2C71
Directory for Z:/

zip-dr~1          33291 07-03-1999  20:40  ZIP-Drive
```

```
test                   15 07-10-1999    7:40
50WAYS    EXE      265728 01-30-1998   15:22  50ways.exe
zip-in~1           33668 07-03-1999   20:40  ZIP-Install
ziptest         <DIR>      07-10-1999    8:24  ziptest
          5 files              332 702 bytes
                         100 087 808 bytes free


[root@pk75 /root]# mdir z:ziptest
 Volume in drive Z has no label
 Volume Serial Number is 15F9-2C71
Directory for Z:/ziptest

.               <DIR>      07-10-1999    8:24
..              <DIR>      07-10-1999    8:24
iomega              2780 07-10-1999    8:24  iomega
          3 files                2 780 bytes
                         100 087 808 bytes free
[root@pk75 /root]# mdel z:ziptest/iomega
[root@pk75 /root]# mrd z:ziptest
[root@pk75 /root]# mdir z:
 Volume in drive Z is ZIP-100
 Volume Serial Number is 15F9-2C71
Directory for Z:/

zip-dr~1           33291 07-03-1999   20:40  ZIP-Drive
test                   15 07-10-1999    7:40
50WAYS    EXE      265728 01-30-1998   15:22  50ways.exe
zip-in~1           33668 07-03-1999   20:40  ZIP-Install
          4 files              332 702 bytes
                         100 093 952 bytes free
```

Troubleshooting

The following list covers the most common problems you might face in getting your Zip drive to work with your system. If you can't get your drive to work at all, boot into DOS or Windows, and try to use the Zip drive with Iomega's supplied drivers. If you have problems with the Zip drive under Windows or DOS, then Iomega technical support can help you. When you have successfully used the Zip drive under those conditions, you have proven that the computer and the Zip drive work together. Go back over the installation instructions again. If you continue to have problems, check this list of common problems.

Modprobe ppa Fails   You might get a message like this:

```
ppa: Version 2.03 (for Linux 2.2.x)

WARNING - no ppa compatible devices found.
```

As of August 1998, Iomega started shipping parallel port Zip drives with a different interface that is supported by the imm (Zip Plus) driver. If the cable is marked with AutoDetect, this is what has happened:

```
scsi : 0 hosts.
/lib/modules/2.2.5-22/scsi/ppa.o: init_module: Device or resource busy
parport: Device or resource busy
```

If you get this message, it can mean that you didn't plug the drive into the parallel port correctly. Double-check all your connections and make sure that you have plugged the power transformer into the wall and the power connector into the Zip drive. A green power light should be lit on the Zip drive.

This could also mean that your drive was manufactured after August 1998. If so, try using the `modprope imm` command instead. If you still get an error, you could have a hardware problem. Make sure that you have tested the hardware under Windows or DOS. If the hardware does not work there, call Iomega technical support.

The following is a successful example of `modprobe imm` using an early version of `imm`:

```
modprobe imm
imm: Version 0.18
imm: Probing port 03bc
imm: Probing port 0378
imm:      SPP port present
imm:      ECP with a 16 byte FIFO present
imm:      PS/2 bidirectional port present
imm:      Passed Intel bug check.
imm: Probing port 0278
scsi0 : Iomega ZIP Plus drive
scsi : 1 host.
   Vendor: IOMEGA    Model: ZIP 100 PLUS    Rev: J.66
   Type:   Direct-Access                    ANSI SCSI revision: 02
Detected scsi removable disk sda at scsi0, channel 0, id 6, lun 0
SCSI device sda: hdwr sector= 512 bytes. Sectors= 196608 [96 MB] [0.1 GB]
sda: Write Protect is off
 sda: sda1
```

Note that the SCSI device is `sda1` in this example. In this case, you would use `/dev/sda1` as your device for the `mount` command and in the `/etc/mtools.conf` file.

Modprobe Is Successful, But a Read Capacity Error Is Shown

You also might get an error like this:

```
ppa: Version 2.03 (for Linux 2.2.x)
ppa: Found device at ID 6, Attempting to use EPP 32 bit
ppa: Found device at ID 6, Attempting to use PS/2
ppa: Communication established with ID 6 using PS/2
scsi0 : Iomega VPI0 (ppa) interface
scsi : 1 host.
   Vendor: IOMEGA    Model: ZIP 100    Rev: D.13
   Type:   Direct-Access               ANSI SCSI revision: 02
Detected scsi removable disk sda at scsi0, channel 0, id 6, lun 0
sda : READ CAPACITY failed.
sda : status = 0, message = 00, host = 0, driver = 28
sda : extended sense code = 2
```

Part
IV

Ch
25

```
sda : block size assumed to be 512 bytes, disk size 1GB.
sda: Write Protect is off
 sda:scsidisk I/O error: dev 08:00, sector 0
 unable to read partition table
```

This means that the ppa and scsi modules, which were just installed by modprobe, were unable to see the disk in the drive. Typically, the message means that the disk is not fully inserted into the drive. Re-insert the disk into the drive. If that still doesn't work, the disk might be defective and needs to be replaced.

Zip Drive Works with Intermittent Problems   If your zip drive is working but sometimes corrupts data, check your machine's BIOS settings for the parallel port. If the parallel port is set in the ECP mode, put it into the EPP mode. Some of the computer motherboard chip sets do not handle ECP properly.

Zip Drive Fails to Work After Using a Printer   The printer port module (lp) might conflict with the parallel port module and might have to be unloaded before you use the Zip drive. If you have problems accessing the Zip drive, try unloading the parallel port module using the rmmod lp command. When you are finished using the drive, you can run rmmod ppa and modprobe lp to get back to where you started.

If Using a Newer Zip Drive, *modprobe imm* Fails   This can happen due to the failure of modprobe to recognize the need for the parport_pc module. To verify that the parport_pc module has been installed, run the following command:

cat /proc/modules

You should get a listing similar to this:

```
parport_probe    2884    0
parport_pc       5012    0
parport          7092    0
```

If you get this following information along with some other modules, then parport_pc has been installed. If not, read on.

The default install takes care of installing parport_pc by placing the following line in the file /etc/conf. modules:

Alias parport_lowlevel parport_pc

To verify that this line is in the file, you can use the following command:

cat /etc/conf.modules

Even if this line is in the file, it may be that modprobe simply fails to recognize the need for the parport_pc module. You would then have to insert it using modprobe before you run the modprobe imm command:

```
modprobe parport_pc
modprobe imm
```

Problems Occur When Using Zip Drive Under VMWare Version 1.x   VMWare is a virtual
machine that can be installed under Linux and that enables you to run multiple operating systems at the same time. VMWare's Web site can be found at http://www.vmware.com. The IDE
ATAPI Zip drive cannot be used under VMWare's virtual machine as a device. You can put a
virtual disk file on it under the host operating system, and VMWare will be capable of accessing it. However, it will not function properly as a removable media device; although you have
VMWare running the virtual machine that uses a file on the Zip drive, you must not remove
the disk.

The LS-120 Drive

The LS-120 SuperDisk Drive is a 120MB floppy drive manufactured by the Imation company
(http://www.imation.com/) of Oakdale, Minnesota.

Imation also makes various other media and spun off the 3M corporation sometime around
1997.

The LS-120 disk is a 120MB disk that has Laser Servo (the LS part of LS-120) information
encoded in the disk media. This allows a very high density of tracks per inch and a high density of magnetic flux changes per inch to achieve the data storage capacity in the floppy media
3.5-inch form factor. These drives come with an EIDE interface, which means that they look
like a hard drive for a computer. A parallel port version of the LS-120 superdrive on the
Internet also exists; these versions should behave similar to the Zip drive, except that they
would be accessed as /dev/sda rather than /dev/sda4 under Linux.

Unless you have a BIOS dated later than 1998, chances are good that your system will not
allow you to arbitrarily use an LS-120 SuperDisk Drive as a bootable drive. If this drive is
installed as the master drive on the primary IDE controller interface, you might be able to
boot off it if it has a properly formatted 120MB floppy. For older machines, BIOS upgrades
and hard-drive controller cards are sold to solve this problem. Note that you cannot install
Linux using a floppy in an LS-120 drive. The Red Hat install has the floppy drive hard-coded
into it and does not recognize the fact that you are running on an EIDE device.

Under Linux, the LS-120 SuperDisk Drive appears as a hard drive, either as /dev/hda,
/dev/hdb, /dev/hdc, or /dev/hdd. How your computer locates the LS-120 totally depends upon
how you install the drive. Every drive that has an IDE or EIDE interface has a small jumper
block that enables you to instruct the drive on its role in the system.

Two IDE interfaces exist in computers manufactured in the late 1990s. The first IDE interface
is called the primary interface; the other is the secondary interface. Each interface has a
cable plugged into it, with the other end of the cable plugged into a drive. An IDE interface
cable may have a plug in the middle of the drive so that you can accommodate two hard drives on each interface.

Part

IV

Ch

25

Each drive on an interface cable must be specified as either the master drive or the slave drive. On newer systems, the cable may have a twist in it or may be a specially manufactured cable. With this cable, the drive can use the Cable Select feature, which automatically determines whether the drive is a master or a slave.

The jumper block that selects the Master, Slave, or Cable Select options for a drive is usually found on the end of the drive next to the ribbon cable socket. Some disk drives have a jumper block on a circuit board. In almost every case, the jumper block is labeled CS (Cable Select), SL (Slave), or MA (Master). You can have only one master on a cable plugged into the interface on the motherboard. If you already have a CD-ROM drive on the cable, it will be configured as a master. In that case, configure your LS-120 drive as a slave by putting the jumper on the SL pins. If you don't have another operating disk on the cable to which you are attaching the LS-120 drive, configure the drive as a master.

The master drive on the primary interface is /dev/hda under Linux. The slave is /dev/hdb. On the secondary interface, the master drive is /dev/hdc. The slave drive on this interface is /dev/hdd.

All hard drives have partitions. These partitions occupy the very first track of the drive and indicate logical division of the drive. Use of partitions in DOS enables you to break a drive up into drives C:, D:, E:, and so on. Under Linux, use of partitions enables you to allocate chunks of storage space on the drive up into /dev/hda1, /dev/hda2, /dev/hda3, /dev/hda4, and so on. Four primary partitions exist on a disk drive. You may use a primary partition to hold other partitions, called logical partitions. A primary partition holding logical partitions is called an extended partition.

Zip drives with their standard format have the information stored in partition 4. On Mac computers, the partition information is not always used. This means that more data can be stored on the disk. In this case, the disk would be accessed as /dev/sda.

LS-120 drives take this same approach. Data is stored under the disk's identifier. For example, the slave LS-120 drive on the secondary interface would be /dev/hdd. To access data on this drive, you would mount /dev/hdd. A master on the secondary interface would be /dev/hdc.

Neither Modules nor Drivers

After Linux kernels 2.0.31, the LS-120 SuperDisk Drive is recognized without any problems. Support for the ATAPI IDE interface of the LS-120 drive and the ATAPI IDE Zip drive is built into the default kernel.

Attaching the Hardware

If you have a CD-ROM drive already installed in the system, check to see that it is on the secondary IDE interface and that you have a flat ribbon cable without any twists in it. Then move the jumper block currently on the CS pin on the LS-120 drive to the SL pin. Then install the

LS-120 drive. When you plug in the ribbon cable, make careful note of where pin 1 is on the plug. Some ribbon cables are keyed so that you can't plug into the LS-120 drive upside down; some aren't. For the ones that aren't, the ribbon cable has a red or brown strip that runs down one side. That is the pin 1 indicator, and it must plug into the drive where it is closest to the pin 1 indicator.

After installation, if your computer has a newer BIOS, it should recognize the LS-120 drive and report it. If it has an older BIOS, you will not know whether the installation was successful until you boot into Linux.

Getting Linux to Recognize the Drive

After logging into Linux, run the following command on the command line:

```
dmesg
```

You will get a printout much like this:

```
Linux version 2.2.5-22 (root@porky.devel.redhat.com)
(gcc version egcs-2.91.66 19990314/Linux (egcs-1.1.2 release))
#1 Wed Jun 2 09:02:27 EDT 1999
Detected 475874507 Hz processor.
Console: colour VGA+ 80x25
Calibrating delay loop... 950.27 BogoMIPS
Memory: 119924k/122880k available
(996k kernel code, 412k reserved, 1488k data, 60k init)
VFS: Diskquotas version dquot_6.4.0 initialized
CPU: AMD AMD-K6(tm) 3D processor stepping 0c
Checking 386/387 coupling... OK, FPU using exception 16 error reporting.
Checking 'hlt' instruction... OK.
POSIX conformance testing by UNIFIX
PCI: PCI BIOS revision 2.10 entry at 0xfb500
PCI: Using configuration type 1
PCI: Probing PCI hardware
Linux NET4.0 for Linux 2.2
Based upon Swansea University Computer Society NET3.039
NET4: Unix domain sockets 1.0 for Linux NET4.0.
NET4: Linux TCP/IP 1.0 for NET4.0
IP Protocols: ICMP, UDP, TCP, IGMP
Initializing RT netlink socket
Starting kswapd v 1.5
Detected PS/2 Mouse Port.
Serial driver version 4.27 with MANY_PORTS MULTIPORT SHARE_IRQ enabled
ttyS00 at 0x03f8 (irq = 4) is a 16550A
pty: 256 Unix98 ptys configured
apm: BIOS version 1.2 Flags 0x07 (Driver version 1.9)
Real Time Clock Driver v1.09
RAM disk driver initialized:  16 RAM disks of 4096K size
SIS5513: IDE controller on PCI bus 00 dev 01
SIS5513: not 100% native mode: will probe irqs later
    ide0: BM-DMA at 0x4000-0x4007, BIOS settings: hda:pio, hdb:pio
```

```
        ide1: BM-DMA at 0x4008-0x400f, BIOS settings: hdc:pio, hdd:pio
hda: FUJITSU MPD3108AT, ATA DISK drive
hdb: ST38420A, ATA DISK drive
hdc: 4X4X32, ATAPI CDROM drive
hdd: LS-120 VER5 00 UHD Floppy, ATAPI FLOPPY drive
ide0 at 0x1f0-0x1f7,0x3f6 on irq 14
ide1 at 0x170-0x177,0x376 on irq 15
hda: FUJITSU MPD3108AT, 10300MB w/512kB Cache, CHS=1313/255/63
hdb: ST38420A, 8223MB w/512kB Cache, CHS=1048/255/63
hdc: ATAPI 32X CD-ROM DVD-RAM CD-R/RW drive, 1024kB Cache
Uniform CDROM driver Revision: 2.54
Floppy drive(s): fd0 is 1.44M
FDC 0 is a post-1991 82077
md driver 0.90.0 MAX_MD_DEVS=256, MAX_REAL=12
raid5: measuring checksumming speed
raid5: using high-speed MMX checksum routine
   pII_mmx   :   953.262 MB/sec
   p5_mmx    :   862.584 MB/sec
   8regs     :   664.845 MB/sec
   32regs    :   484.251 MB/sec
using fastest function: pII_mmx (953.262 MB/sec)
scsi : 0 hosts.
scsi : detected total.
md.c: sizeof(mdp_super_t) = 4096
Partition check:
 hda: hda1 hda2 < hda5 hda6 > hda3 hda4
 hdb: hdb1 hdb2
autodetecting RAID arrays
autorun ...
... autorun DONE.
VFS: Mounted root (ext2 filesystem) readonly.
Freeing unused kernel memory: 60k freed
Adding Swap: 128516k swap-space (priority -1)
via-rhine.c:v1.00 9/5/98  Written by Donald Becker
   http://cesdis.gsfc.nasa.gov/linux/drivers/via-rhine.html
via-rhine.c:v1.00 9/5/98  Written by Donald Becker
   http://cesdis.gsfc.nasa.gov/linux/drivers/via-rhine.html
eth0: VIA VT3043 Rhine at 0xe800, 00:80:c8:e8:c5:fa, IRQ 10.
eth0: MII PHY found at address 8, status 0x782d advertising 05e1 Link 0000.
Installing knfsd (copyright (C) 1996 okir@monad.swb.de).
nfsd_init: initialized fhcache, entries=256
```

Note that the LS-120 drive is listed in the middle of the list. If you use the following command line:

```
dmesg ¦ grep LS-120
```

you will read just the LS-120 drive information:

```
hdd: LS-120 VER5 00 UHD Floppy, ATAPI FLOPPY drive
```

The drive is version 5 and uses the kernel's ATAPI drive interface. It will be recognized as hard drive device hdd. This tells you that Linux has found the drive.

Getting Set Up to Use the Disk in the Drive

To set up to use the disk in the SuperDisk Drive, refer to the previous section, "The LS-120 Drive." This covers the basics and fills you in on the reasons for the following commands and activities.

To create a directory for the LS-120 drive, you will use the `mkdir` command:

```
[root@pk75 drivers]# cd /mnt

[root@pk75 /mnt]# mkdir ls120

 [root@pk75 /mnt]# ls -l
total 3
drwxrwxr-x    2 root      root      1024 Oct  9  1998 cdrom
drwxrwxr-x    2 root      root      1024 Feb  6  1996 floppy
drwxr-xr-x    2 root      root      1024 Jul 10 07:22 ls120

[root@pk75 /mnt]# chmod a+rw ls120

[root@pk75 /mnt]# ls -l
total 3
drwxrwxr-x    2 root      root      1024 Oct  9  1998 cdrom
drwxrwxr-x    2 root      root      1024 Feb  6  1996 floppy
drwxrwxr-x    2 root      root      1024 Jul 10 07:22 ls120
```

You have created the ls120 directory and given it permissions with chmod to allow everyone to read and write to the directory. Next, you will allow a standard user to use the LS-120 drive by creating an entry in the file `/etc/fstab`.

As root, use your favorite editor in Linux and open the file `/etc/fstab`. It should look something like this:

```
/dev/hda2        /                  ext2     defaults        1 1
/dev/hda1        /boot              ext2     defaults        1 2
/dev/hda4        /home              ext2     defaults        1 2
/dev/hda3        swap               swap     defaults        0 0
/dev/fd0         /mnt/floppy        ext2     noauto          0 0
/dev/cdrom       /mnt/cdrom         iso9660  noauto,ro       0 0
none             /proc              proc     defaults        0 0
none             /dev/pts           devpts   mode=0622       0 0
```

You will need to add the following line to the bottom of the file:

```
/dev/hdd         /mnt/ls120         vfat     noauto,user     0 0
```

To use the `mtools` commands, you must edit the `/etc/mtools.conf` file. The beginning of the file will look like this:

```
# Example mtools.conf files.  Uncomment the lines which correspond to
# your architecture and comment out the "SAMPLE FILE" line below

# Linux floppy drives
```

Part
IV

Ch
25

```
drive a: file="/dev/fd0" exclusive 1.44m
drive b: file="/dev/fd1" exclusive 1.44m
```

Add the following line after `drive b`, assuming that your LS-120 drive shows up as hdd under the Linux kernel report as shown by `dmesg`. If your drive showed up as hdc, then change `/dev/hdd` to `/dev/hdc` in the following command:

```
drive h: file="/dev/hdd"
```

This entry enables you to address the LS-120 drive as drive H when using the `mtools` commands. You cannot mount the LS-120 drive using the `mount` command to use `mtools`.

Finally, as root, you must execute the following command (again changing hdd to the appropriate designator):

```
chmod a+rw /dev/hdd
```

This command changes the permissions to the LS-120 drive device so that any user can use `mtools` on an unmounted drive. This command is not needed if you always access the drive as the root user. Be careful when using Linux as the root user!

Finally, to make ejecting the drive a bit easier, link the LS-120 drive to a device mnemonic that is easier to remember:

```
ln -s /dev/hdd /dev/ls120
```

After you have done this, you can use `/dev/ls120` wherever you would normally use `/dev/hdd`.

Using the LS-120 Drive

There are a few things to note before examining the details of operating an LS-120 drive.

Linux requires that all drives must be mounted under directories before they are used. If you do not do this, the drive will be unavailable to any program except for the set of commands known as the mtools commands, if the drives have been previously formatted by DOS or Windows. The mtool commands are not available to use on mounted drives.

Mounting the Drive   After Linux recognizes the drive, and before you use the LS-120 drive, you must mount it. Because you have created the entry in the `/etc/fstab` file, mounting is simple. As a user, or as root, enter the following command:

```
mount /mnt/ls120
```

The `mount` program looks in the `/etc/fstab` file and determines the proper way to mount the zip drive. You should see the access light come on for a moment. At this point, you can execute the `df` command to see whether the disk was mounted:

```
[root@pk75 /root]# df
Filesystem              1k-blocks        Used Available Use% Mounted on
/dev/hda6                1290167     1058443    165056  87% /
```

```
/dev/hda1              2047936   1270816   777120   62%  /dosc
/dev/hda5              2088128   1088576   999552   52%  /dosd
/dev/hda4              4779452    828945  3703106   18%  /home
/dev/hdd                123006       996   122010    1%  /mnt/ls120
```

If the disk was successfully mounted, you should see /dev/hdd in the list, usually at the bottom. At this point, all the standard Linux commands will work. The vfat module will take care of translating long filenames to short names and will store files on the disk in the proper DOS format so that the disk is readable from any DOS or Windows machine.

Ejecting the Disk   As with the Zip drive, you must use the umount command before ejecting the LS-120 disk, to be safe. The eject command is supposed to flush data to the drive, but don't trust it. The command looks like this:

```
umount /dev/hdd
```

This command causes the sync command to be run against the LS-120 disk. It will flush all information that is in memory onto the disk. This warning does not apply to using the mtools commands.

Now use the eject command. The eject command for the LS-120 superdrive works for all users. To use this command, enter the following on the command line:

```
eject /dev/hdd
```

This causes the disk to eject from the drive. You are now free to insert another disk.

If you have done the softlink (ln -s) to /dev/ls120, then you can run the eject command using the following:

```
eject ls120
```

Using the *mtools* commands   After Linux recognizes the drive, you may use the mtools commands immediately. Because you have created the entry in the /etc/mtools.conf file, using the LS-120 drive is as simple as using the Zip drive.

The mtools commands are similar to the DOS commands. Refer to Table 25.1 for a complete listing of mtools commands.

For example, you will create a directory called ls120test on the root of the currently inserted but not mounted LS-120 drive. Then copy a file named vmware.tgz from your current directory into the root directory on that drive. Afterward, you will move the file into that directory. You also will use the mdir command liberally to make sure that what you just did worked. You will notice that you always get an hdd: hdd1 hdd2 hdd3 hdd4 listing each time you use the mtools commands. This is annoying but harmless.

```
[root@linux1 vmware]# mdir h:
 hdd: hdd1 hdd2 hdd3 hdd4
 Volume in drive H has no label
 Volume Serial Number is F7BD-4EEB
Directory for H:/
```

Part

IV

Ch

25

```
No files
                       125 958 144 bytes free

 [root@linux1 vmware]# mcopy vmware.tgz h:
 hdd: hdd1 hdd2 hdd3 hdd4

[root@linux1 vmware]# mdir h:
 hdd: hdd1 hdd2 hdd3 hdd4
 Volume in drive H has no label
 Volume Serial Number is F7BD-4EEB
Directory for H:/

vmware   tgz   1400298 07-16-1999   9:43  vmware.tgz
        1 file            1 400 298 bytes
                       124 557 312 bytes free

[root@linux1 vmware]# mmd h:ls120test
 hdd: hdd1 hdd2 hdd3 hdd4
[root@linux1 vmware]# mdir h:
 hdd: hdd1 hdd2 hdd3 hdd4
 Volume in drive H has no label
 Volume Serial Number is F7BD-4EEB
Directory for H:/

vmware   tgz   1400298 07-16-1999   9:43  vmware.tgz
LS120T~1      <DIR>      07-16-1999   9:46  ls120test
        2 files           1 400 298 bytes
                       124 555 264 bytes free

[root@linux1 vmware]# mmove h:vmware.tgz ls120test
 hdd: hdd1 hdd2 hdd3 hdd4
[root@linux1 vmware]# mdir h:
 hdd: hdd1 hdd2 hdd3 hdd4
 Volume in drive H has no label
 Volume Serial Number is F7BD-4EEB
Directory for H:/

LS120T~1      <DIR>      07-16-1999   9:46  ls120test
        1 file                 0 bytes
                       124 555 264 bytes free

[root@linux1 vmware]# mdir h:\ls120test
 hdd: hdd1 hdd2 hdd3 hdd4
 Volume in drive H has no label
 Volume Serial Number is F7BD-4EEB
Directory for H:/ls120test

.              <DIR>      07-16-1999   9:46
..             <DIR>      07-16-1999   9:46
vmware   tgz   1400298 07-16-1999   9:43  vmware.tgz
        3 files           1 400 298 bytes
                       124 555 264 bytes free
```

The LS-120 SuperDisk Drive can also read and write to 1.44MB floppies. In the following text, note that the total number of bytes now totals 1.44MB:

```
[root@linux1 vmware]# mdir h:
Volume in drive H has no label
Volume Serial Number is 1550-14F3
Directory for H:/

MINNDTL0 DOC     49664 03-11-1999  16:53
DTLSPEC  ZIP   1047964 03-09-1999   8:23
        2 files          1 097 628 bytes
                           359 936 bytes free
```

To use the LS-120 drive with Dosemu, you must have installed the Dosemu package during the initial install process, or later from the RPM. I installed it using the FreeDos option, which provides an immediately bootable DOS package.

I enabled the LS-120 drive to be addressed as disk B under Dosemu. Edit /etc/dosemu.conf using your favorite editor. Search for the line that reads like this:

```
$_floppy_b = ""
```

Then change the line to read like this (assuming that your LS-120 drive shows up as hdd):

```
$_floppy_b = "ATAPI:/dev/hdd"
```

Then, from the command line, run the following command:

```
dos
```

Dosemu will run and will present you with the C:> prompt. At this point, you can access the drive as drive B: using standard DOS commands; everything works as expected. At the current time, you should treat the LS-120 drive as an unmountable hard drive when using Dosemu. Be sure to exit Dosemu with the exitemu command before ejecting the LS-120 disk.

Troubleshooting

The following list covers the most common problems you might face in getting your LS-120 drive to work with your system. If you have trouble, you should always test your drive using the supplied Windows or DOS drivers. If you have trouble under DOS or Windows, then the manufacturer of your drive can provide technical support.

When you have successfully used the LS-120 drive under those conditions, you have proven that the computer and the drive work together. Go back over the installation instructions again. If you continue to have problems, check this list of common problems.

The LS-120 Drive Is Not Recognized at Boot Up, By Linux, or Your Computer Fails to Boot

The most likely cause of this is that the power connector is not connected or that the ribbon cable is plugged in upside down. If your computer boots but you can't see either the LS-120 drive or your CD-ROM drive, then this indicates that the LS-120 drive is not plugged in properly.

You Can't Store 120MB of Data on the Drive   Make sure you haven't inserted a normal 1.44MB floppy in the drive.

Doing an *ls* of */mnt/ls120* Gives You Nothing   Either the LS-120 floppy is empty or you forgot to mount it. Run the df command to see whether the LS-120 is mounted. If it is, the drive is probably empty. LS-120 disks usually come with no data or files.

You Can't Run Any *.exe* Files   To run Microsoft Win 95 executables, you must use Wine. To run DOS executables, you must use Dosemu.

Errors Occur When Reading the Drive Under Dosemu   If you change the disk in the drive under Dosemu, you will get errors. If you move from a low-density floppy to a high-density floppy, the following error will occur:

```
C:\>dir b: hdd: hdd1 hdd2 hdd3 hdd4

 hdd: hdd1 hdd2 hdd3 hdd4
 Volume in drive B


Sector Not Found error on drive B


Sector Not Found error on drive B
Abort, Retry, Fail or Continue? r
```

If you move from a high-density floppy to a low-density floppy, the following error will occur:

```
C:\>dir b: hdd: hdd1 hdd2 hdd3 hdd4

C:\>dir b:
 Volume in drive B is           .
 Directory of B:\
 hdd: hdd1 hdd2 hdd3 hdd4
 hdd: hdd1 hdd2 hdd3 hdd4
+*<aí%       655,358 01-30-80  12:00a
s                       94 00-00-88  12:00a
Ö                          15-31-207  19:63p
M               1,442,825 00-00-80  12:00a
¢h                       0 00-00-80  12:00a
       5 files    2,098,276 bytes
       0 dirs     1,408,000 bytes free
```

Note that Dosemu did not give you any warnings; it just showed a strange directory listing. Writing to the disk under these circumstances will damage your data beyond recovery! ●

## CHAPTER 26

Installing and Configuring Peripherals

by John Ray

This chapter introduces you to some of the issues with supporting peripherals under Linux and shows you a few different devices that you can plug into your system. All the hardware in this section is currently unsupported in Red Hat Linux, but with a bit of extra installation, you'll soon be using UPSs, scanners, and digital cameras, and even automating your home with your new operating system.

Understanding Linux Peripheral Support

Linux is a rapidly developing operating system that has thousands of devoted followers worldwide. Its development is outpacing other operating systems that have hundreds of paid engineers working on them night and day. Each new version of Red Hat Linux brings a new set of features by which the Linux standard is judged. Red Hat 6.0 brought the latest kernel developments, such as symmetric multiprocessing and IP chains, as well as the latest software—GNOME and KDE—to the end user. With each new software release, and with the increased competition among Linux distribution vendors such as Caldera and Red Hat, the operating system is being pushed inch by inch toward becoming a capable desktop operating system.

Two years ago, if someone had thought about replacing a Windows desktop with Linux, that person would have been laughed at. Today, with Star Office and stable desktop environments, Linux poses a serious threat to the Microsoft marketing machine. The recent Department of Justice/Microsoft trial has soured the public on mainstream operating systems and the practices of their controlling companies. At the same time, an increasing amount of positive press has been generated for Linux in the past year. Developers are flocking to Linux like never before. Commercial software packages such as Oracle and Sybase are appearing. Games such as Quake 3 are also being developed for Linux. Suddenly, the fledgling operating system is being thrust into the limelight.

Hardware Support Trailing Software Support

Unfortunately, for all the developments of the Linux, some areas are still lacking. The operating system is still considered by most to be mainly a network OS capable of running an ISP, for example. Standard desktop activities, such as scanning, require additional software and UNIX expertise that many IT professionals lack. This lack of standardized support for standard computer peripherals is holding Linux back from breaking into the prime-time desktop space. Many peripherals are supported under Linux, but not in the plug-and-play way that they are supported in other operating systems. Most software manufacturers choose to develop software applications for one or two popular desktop platforms and do not pay attention to the Linux crowd. As an example, if you want to use a scanner on a Macintosh, you'd do three things:

1. Plug in the scanner.
2. Install the drivers that came with the scanner.
3. Install the imaging software that came with the scanner.

If you're running Linux, you'd be able to do the first step, but then you'd be left scratching your head. For a peripheral to work under Linux, it must have driver support. Mainstream hardware companies haven't quite jumped on the bandwagon with peripheral support yet, so you have only two options if you want to use a certain piece of hardware with your Linux-based computer: write a driver and application that will talk to your device, or find someone who already has!

User-Developed Hardware Support

Luckily, many people actually have written their own software for controlling peripherals and have made it available for free on the Internet. You might find a single driver for your product, or half a dozen. The downside to using much of this software is that there is, in many cases, a lack of documentation and a lack of a friendly user interface. If you want to use unsupported hardware on your system, you might be in for a bit of a rough ride. Choosing the best item depends on evaluating the choices and your situation, which might not be easy. If you come across a program package that requires a kernel patch to be put in place before use, things can very quickly get dicey.

If you're finding this a bit scary, good! It's best to approach the Linux peripheral situation cautiously. There are hundreds of pieces of software out there—don't go blindly installing something just to try it out. Many hardware support programs require root access to control the peripherals, so you run the added risk of something going wrong. If you want to use something that isn't directly supported by Red Hat, the first thing you should do is check the newsgroups to see if anyone else has used the hardware. You'll find that Deja News (http://www.deja.com/) is an indispensable source for locating Linux wisdom.

If you can afford it, the best advice when dealing with Linux peripherals is to buy what you know works. Don't try to make existing hardware function using three-year-old nonsupported software written by someone who is no longer even accessible by email. Stick to big manufacturers, such as Hewlett-Packard for scanners or Kodak for digital cameras, and you should be able to get what you want done. If you're a veteran Linux user, you can probably interface your computer with a toaster with little difficulty, but first-time users are best advised to take it slowly.

Part
IV

Ch
26

Types of Peripheral Support

There are generally two different types of peripheral support that you will find for Linux: unified driver/software packages, and driver/API packages. There are advantages to each support model—what you choose should be based on your level of comfort with the operating system and, obviously, what is available for the system.

Unified Driver/Software Packages   Packaging the driver directly inside a piece of software that uses it is one way to quickly and easily support a piece of hardware. For example, many different digital cameras are available for desktop computers. A large number of these cameras come with their own proprietary software for downloading the pictures from the camera. You install the software, plug in the camera, and you're done. Running the software speaks to that camera and that camera alone.

The benefit of this model is that it is extremely easy to get a piece of software up and running using this technique; everything is included in a single package. The drawbacks to this approach, however, are significant. If you have three different digital cameras, it is entirely likely that you might need to install three different pieces of software to speak to the cameras. This means that there are three pieces of software that you must maintain and upgrade, and three different interfaces that you also must learn.

From a support standpoint, the driver/software package model can be both a blessing and a curse. If you encounter a problem with the program, you have a simple solution: replace the software and hope that the problem goes away. If it doesn't, you've got a real problem. Depending on the application, though, this might be the best method to use—and in the case of Linux software, it is often the only solution that is available.

The Driver/API Model   The second model (and the one that I personally prefer) offers a greater range of options for the user. Rather than installing one "do-it-all" package, the user installs a driver that speaks to the hardware and can be contacted via a standardized Application Programming Interface (API). With this approach, the user opens up the use of the peripheral to any piece of software using the API. Imagine what Linux would be like if every single video card had its own windowing system rather than the unified X Windows API. With each video card, you'd have your own graphic environment. If you switched a video card, you would need an entirely different piece of software. With the driver/API approach, you can find a single piece of software that supports the necessary API and then stick to that software. If you end up changing devices, all you must do is change the underlying driver of the API. The software itself remains the same and continues to operate exactly as you would expect.

Once again, there are drawbacks to this as well. The installation procedure is usually more complicated, and you must install multiple layers of software before you can start using your peripheral. Drivers tend to be written by different people, and while one driver will perform perfectly, another might behave very poorly. As a result, the software application that uses the driver might seem to be flaky. You might end up in a situation where it is impossible to tell exactly where the problem lies.

Another problem with this technique is that it requires the development of a standard (the API). Because there is no true "controller" of the Linux distribution, it is rather difficult to form a standard. Most of the standards that are already in place come from Linux's UNIX heritage. UNIX hasn't been a big player in the desktop space, so Linux can gain little from it here. The only way that a standard interface to a peripheral can be developed is if the Linux kernel architects (namely, Linus Torvalds) include kernel level support for the devices (as was done with joysticks in the 2.2.x kernels). Another way is if someone manages to gain enough support for another standard—which, in some cases (such as with scanners), is slowly happening.

The Linux standards problem can be seen quite clearly in the ongoing KDE/GNOME battle. GNOME was originally developed to be a completely open source solution to providing a UNIX desktop environment. KDE originally relied on a library that was not open source, but that has since adopted the open source philosophy. Rather than merging the two desktop camps, each has progressed with its own offerings that are very similar. This is a case where competition is not necessarily a good thing for the user. Each desktop product comes out with more features with each new release, trying to outdo the other. The cost is a lack of stability in certain desktop environments (particularly GNOME) and consistency between Linux platforms. This very battle to develop the ultimate Linux desktop might end up slowing the migration of the operating system to the desktop computer role. It's easy to see, then, why individuals may forgo trying to create a standardized API and choose to create driver/software packages.

The Movement to Appliance Peripherals

The days of needing special driver software might soon be coming to an end. The current crop of peripherals uses special protocols and interfaces to communicate with computers. Video capture cards, for example, each require separate drivers and may use different variations on MJPEG or MPEG codecs to compress the video streams. Everything is proprietary. Luckily, however, there seems to be a movement by the hardware manufacturers to develop open interface standards and introduce appliance-like peripherals.

The primary problem with interfacing with peripherals is moving data from place to place. Each device has a different way of doing this. Certain manufacturers, however, have broken the rules on hardware development. Rather than introducing devices that can be used on only one system, these devices can be used anywhere. For example, Zip drives (especially SCSI) are very easy to support on Linux—they're just another drive. Wouldn't it be great if anywhere you have a Zip drive (which, today, is just about everywhere), you could have a scanner? Better yet, how about anywhere you have a 3.5-inch floppy? With devices such as Microtek's ImageDeck (http://www.microtek.com/imagedeck.html), all you need is a floppy or Zip drive. The scanner itself contains built-in Zip and floppy drives. Images are scanned in and stored directly to the removable media, with no PC required. You can then use the stored files anywhere you have a floppy drive. Other devices, such as the Sony Mavica digital camera line, offer direct digital imaging to floppy disk. The latest Mavica camera includes MPEG video support, enabling you to capture up to 60 seconds of digital video in a standard MPEG stream onto a floppy disk. Devices like this are extremely easy to use under Linux because they require no customized support.

Other advances to look forward to are the adoption of standardized I/O ports such as USB and Firewire. USB offers the capability to plug joysticks, keyboards, scanners, and similar devices into a single port. Firewire is a high-speed port that supports hard drives and other high-bandwidth data streams. Digital video, for example, is rapidly taking hold in the consumer video marketplace. Cameras are now including Firewire interfaces standard—you simply plug your camera into a Firewire interface on your computer and download the video stream. This eliminates the need for hundreds of different video codecs to be ported to Linux. Once Firewire is fully supported under the operating system, it won't be long until Linux becomes a player in the digital video field.

Words of Wisdom

No matter what you want, you'll probably find someone supporting it under Linux, but it might not be as easy as you'd hope. As the number of Linux supporters grow, so will the options that are available to the users. If you have a piece of hardware that you'd like to see supported, post on the Linux hardware newsgroup, contact the manufacturer, and express your wishes. The more vocal the users, the greater chance that the hardware will eventually be supported. If you do decide to use a piece of hardware, try to find the software that is most current and well supported. Time will take care of these issues, but for now, dealing with Linux peripherals is a matter of trial, error, and a great deal of patience.

This chapter takes a look at several different types of Linux peripherals and their configuration. The procedures covered in this section might or might not apply to your particular configuration. There is such a wide variation among systems that it would require a book several times this size even to cover all the variations of a single type of peripheral. Instead, you should get an idea of what is possible and some of the ways that you can do it. The next sections cover some of the software packages that appear destined to become a Linux standard, but the end result is entirely up to the Linux users. If you find something you like better, use it. These are just suggestions; your mileage might vary.

As you read through the rest of this chapter, keep in mind that very few, if any, of these peripherals are supported under Red Hat Linux according to the Red Hat support package. You are entirely on your own if you want to investigate these products.

Using UPS Systems Under Linux

One of the first pieces of hardware that you'll probably want to invest in if you're using Linux as a server is an Uninterruptable Power Supply, or UPS. If you aren't concerned with power outage situations, or if you have building backups, you might just want to buy a UPS that will carry your computer through a brief blackout or brownout. These devices are relatively cheap (less than $100) and are installed just by plugging in the power supply of your computer into the UPS backup socket. However, if you'd like a setup where the computer is signaled when a power failure occurs, you'll want to buy a UPS that can communicate with your computer through the machine's serial port.

Determining Compatible UPS Systems

Red Hat does not officially support any UPS systems at this time, so, truthfully, there are no UPS systems that you can expect to be compatible with your system. It's important to understand that before going to buy a UPS; if the UPS doesn't work, you're not going to be able to call Red Hat for support. Nonetheless, a Linux HOWTO document documents the use of several different UPS systems on your computer. The Linux HOWTO is available from `http://www.linuxdoc.org/HOWTO/`.

Two types of UPS systems are available:

- **Smart UPS**—A smart UPS uses standard serial protocols to communicate with your computer through the serial port. These protocols differ among companies and would require different software packages to talk to the UPS. Because these are proprietary protocols, it is difficult for Linux to support them.

- **Dumb UPS**—The dumb UPS communicates with the computer using simple signals over the serial port. Serial ports generally have a few signals that are held in a certain state, such as data carrier detect (DCD). If the UPS wants to communicate a loss of power to the computer, it just needs to drop one of these constant signals, such as DCD. This eliminates the need for the computer to speak specific protocols and simplifies the monitoring process. Several UPS systems are supported using this method.

You should read the Linux HOWTO documents before selecting a UPS. You're best off buying a dumb UPS system, as these are easier to support, are cheaper, and work with a wider range of Linux software. A repository of Linux UPS software is located on many Linux software mirrors, including `http://metalab.unc.edu/pub/Linux/system/ups/`. The currently supported packages include the following:

- APC
- Tripplite
- Merlin Gerin
- Powerbox
- Most dumb UPS systems

After choosing a UPS, you'll also need a cable that has the appropriate connections between your computer and the UPS. With any luck, one came with your UPS when you bought it. If this isn't the case, the supporting documentation should give you some idea of how to create such a cable. The UPS HOWTO has information on creating custom cables if need be.

Installing UPS Support Software

One of the most popular support packages for Linux UPS systems is powerd. This package works with dumb UPS systems and is relatively easy to configure and use. The software is downloadable from the site listed previously in the text. If your UPS is a dumb system, you might want to test powerd as your controlling software. The documentation for your UPS might indicate its signaling protocol so that you can more easily configure powerd to communicate with it.

Be sure to read through Chapter 12, "Installing and Managing Linux Software," before attempting this installation. The UPS software packages do not follow the friendly Red Hat RPM installation and will require compiling before they will run on your system. To install the software, follow these steps.

1. Download the software from one of the Linux software libraries, such as sunsite, or http://metalab.unc.edu/pub/Linux/system/ups/.

2. Uncompress and unarchive the software in a UPS directory:

```
[jray@contempt UPS]$ gunzip powerd-2.0.tar.gz
[jray@contempt UPS]$ tar -xvf powerd-2.0.tar
powerd-2.0/
powerd-2.0/powerd.c
powerd-2.0/powerd.8
powerd-2.0/README
powerd-2.0/Makefile
powerd-2.0/powerd.conf
powerd-2.0/TODO
powerd-2.0/setserialbits.c
powerd-2.0/COPYING
```

3. Now, it's very important to read the README file. This will tell you the necessary steps to take to configure the software for your UPS. For now, assume that the defaults are fine for the system:

4. Next, run make to compile powerd:

```
[jray@contempt powerd-2.0]$ make
gcc -MM *.c > .depend
cc -O3 -fomit-frame-pointer -DPREFIX=\"\"   -c powerd.c -o powerd.o
cc    powerd.o    -o powerd
cc -O3 -fomit-frame-pointer -DPREFIX=\"\"
➥setserialbits.c    -o setserialbits
```

5. Finally, install the software with make install. The man page must be manually copied into the appropriate man directory if you wish to install it.

```
[root@contempt powerd-2.0]# make install
cc -O3 -fomit-frame-pointer -DPREFIX=\"\"
➥-c setserialbits.c -o setserialbits.o
cc    setserialbits.o    -o setserialbits
```

```
install -c -m 755 —strip powerd     /sbin
[root@contempt powerd-2.0]# cp powerd.8 /usr/local/man/man8/
```

The powerd UPS monitor should now be installed on your system. You must edit your system configuration so that it will take advantage of the software.

Editing Your UPS Configuration Files

Different UPS packages have different configuration files. Powerd enables you to specify all its configuration options when it is run, eliminating the need for an extra /etc/powerd.conf file. No matter what UPS monitoring system you're using, however, you will need to edit your startup files to include support for the monitor. If you'd like, you can add a file to /etc/init.d/ that controls the power daemon, or you can edit the /etc/rc.d/rc.local file with the necessary changes. The powerd documentation recommends something similar to the following:

```
if [ -f /sbin/powerd ]; then
    echo "Running powerd"
    /sbin/powerd serialline=/dev/cua0 monitor=DCD failwhen=high &
fi
```

This monitors a UPS on cua0 (COM1) for the DCD signal to become active. When the signal does become active, the UPS is considered to be in power failure mode. You must edit a few more configuration files for the system to be useful. After all, your machine might now be capable of determining that the power has failed, but it doesn't know what to do about it!

Beware of the Serial Mouse

If you are using a serial mouse on your system, it is probably connected to the device /dev/cua0. Be sure that you know which serial port the UPS is connected to; otherwise, you risk shutting down your system by moving your mouse: COM1=/dev/cua0, COM2=/dev/cua1, COM3=/dev/cua2, and COM4=/dev/cua3.

Part
IV

Ch
26

When powerd decides that a situation has occurred, it reads information from the /etc/inittab file to determine what it needs to do. Two situations might occur:

- **Power failure**—When powerd goes into a power failure mode, a timer should start. When a certain time limit is met, the computer should shut down.

- **Power up**—Although it might initially seem that only a power failure is important, it is equally important that the computer recognize a power-up signal. If there is a brief flash in power, you don't want your computer to shut down. UPS systems can maintain computer power for several minutes or the better part of an hour, depending on the load and the supply. Rather than going up and down, it makes more sense to wait a certain length of time after a power failure for a power-up signal. If a power-up signal does occur, the shutdown procedure should be canceled.

The first step in configuring for both of these situations is to edit the `/etc/inittab` file to invoke the necessary scripts. You must be root to edit inittab. You also must be very careful because errors in this file can make your system unbootable.

```
# Handle a power failure
pf::powerfail:/usr/local/bin/powerfail

# Cancel the shutdown if power returns
pg::powerokwait:/usr/local/bin/powerup
```

Now, you'll need the scripts to handle the different power situations. Both of these are easy to create. You may edit these scripts to suit your needs. First, the power failure script:

```
#!/usr/bin/perl
#
# 1999 by John Ray
# Feel free to redistribute and edit

$timetowait=300;                           # Time to wait in seconds
$logfile="/var/log/ups.log";
$timestamp='date';
chop ($timestamp);
system("touch /tmp/powerfailed.tmp");   # Create file to indicate failure

# Log the power failure
open LOG, ">> $logfile";
print LOG "$timestamp — Power failure!\n";
close LOG;
$starttime=time;
while (time-$starttime<$timetowait) {
        if (!(-f "/tmp/powerfailed.tmp")) {
                # The power has returned, no need to shutdown
                $timestamp='date';
                chop($timestamp);
                # Log the power return
                open LOG, ">> $logfile";
                print LOG "$timestamp — Power returned.\n";
                close LOG;
                exit 0;
        }
}
system("/usr/bin/halt");
```

This script logs a power failure to a user-specified file, creates a temporary file to mark the power failure, and then waits a certain number of seconds and halts the system if power hasn't returned. To signal that power has returned, a second script must be written to delete the temporary mark file during the waiting period. This will be sensed, a Power Returned message will be logged, and the computer will resume normal operations.

The powerup script can be as simple as this:

```
#!/usr/bin/perl
#
```

```
# 1999 by John Ray
# Feel free to redistribute and edit

unlink "/tmp/powerfailed.tmp";
exit 0;
```

When you have your configuration in place, you're ready to reboot your machine and put your power protection scripts into place.

Debugging a UPS Configuration

The first time you run your computer with the UPS attached, you'll want to watch it closely. Test pulling the plug on the power, and see if the powerd program responds (watch the `/var/log/ups.log` file). If a power failure is generated before the plug is pulled, you either have a problem with the signals being monitored or the cable that you're using for your connection.

Your UPS manual is the best source for technical information. Check the power failure signal and adjust the powerd configuration appropriately. Again, the HOWTO document is a good source for cabling information as well as other software packages for UPS systems. You probably won't have any problems, but it's best to know the resources that are available in case you have any trouble.

For the UPS itself, it's important to follow the recommended instructions for keeping the battery in top shape. Some systems require cycling the battery: running it down to a state of zero power and then charging it back up. Systems that have been in use for long periods of time might need to have the batteries replaced. Check your instruction manual for battery conditioning and maintenance information.

Part
IV

Ch
26

Using Scanners Under Linux

Another type of peripheral that you might want to use under Linux is a scanner. The development of the GIMP project has pushed Linux forward in the image processing department, but using another computer system to scan in your images seems a bit backward. It would be wonderful to use Linux to handle all your image scanning and processing needs. Red Hat doesn't offer any official scanner support in version 6.0, so once again, you're on your own. This time, however, there is an established base of software to support scanners under Linux.

Determining Scanner Compatibility

As already mentioned, there isn't any hardware support for scanners offered by Red Hat yet. The good news is that there is already a driver/API under development that has garnered much support from the Linux community. The API is called SANE, for Scanners Access Now Easy. There is also a scanner interface called TWAIN that was made to provide a scanner API on other desktop operating systems. SANE was developed because of the inefficiencies in

TWAIN and its lack of operating system independence. The SANE home page is located at `http://www.mostang.com/sane/`.

Table 26.1 lists the current scanners that are supported under the SANE model, as described by the SANE home page. Be sure to check for updates in case your scanner isn't listed.

Table 26.1 SANE Compatible Scanners

Manufacturer	Models
Abaton	Scan 300/GS, Scan 300/S
AGFA	Focus GS Scanner, Focus Lineart Scanner, Focus II, Focus Color, Focus Color Plus, Arcus II, StudioScan II, StudioScan IIsi, SnapScan 300, SnapScan 310, SnapScan 600, SnapScan 1236s
Siemens	S9036, ST400
Apple	Apple Scanner, OneScanner, Color OneScanner
Artec/Ultima	AT3, A6000C, A6000C PLUS, AT6, AT12
BlackWidow	BW4800SP
Canon	CanoScan 300, CanoScan 600, CanoScan 2700F
Nikon	LS-20, LS-1000
Kodak	DC210, DC25, DC20
Polaroid	DNC
Epson	GT-5500, GT-7000
HP	ScanJet Plus, ScanJet IIc, ScanJet IIp, ScanJet IIcx, ScanJet 3c, ScanJet 4c, ScanJet 6100C, ScanJet 3p, ScanJet 4p, ScanJet 5p, ScanJet 6200C, ScanJet 6250C, PhotoSmart PhotoScanner
Microtek	Scanmaker E6, Scanmaker E3, Scanmaker E2, Scanmaker 35t+, Scanmaker III, Scanmaker IISP, Scanmaker IIHR, Scanmaker IIG, Scanmaker II, Scanmaker 600Z, Scanmaker 600G
Vobis	HighScan
Mustek	MFC-600S, MFC-600CD, MFS-6000CX, MSF-6000SP, MFS-8000SP, MFC-800S, MFS-1200SP, MFS-12000CX, SE-6000SP, SE-12000SP
Plustek	Plustek 4830
Qtronix	Sagitta Gray, Sagitta Color
Sharp	JX-610, JX-250, JX-330
Tamarack	Artiscan 6000C, Artiscan 8000C, Artiscan 12000C
UMAX	Vista S6, Vista S6E, UMAX S-6E, UMAX S-6EG, Vista-S8, Supervista S-12, UMAX S-12, UMAX S-12G, Astra 600S, Astra 610S, Astra 1200S, Astra 1220S, UC 630, UG 630, UG 80, UC 840, UC 1200S, UC 1200SE, UC 1260, Mirage, Mirage II, Mirage

Manufacturer	Models
	IIse, Vista-T630, PSD, PowerLook, PL-II, PowerLook III, PowerLook 2000, PowerLook 3000, Gemini D-16
Linotype Hell	Jade, Jade2, Saphir2
Vobis/Highscreen	Scanboostar Premium
Escom	Image Scanner 256
Nikon	AX-210

If your scanner isn't among the SANE supported, there is still a decent chance that software and drivers might be available. There are proprietary drivers and scanner software for several popular scanners. For more information on non-SANE scanners, check out the Linux hardware compatibility HOWTO at `http://www.linuxdoc.org/HOWTO/Hardware-HOWTO.html`.

Installing the SANE Software

The easiest way to install SANE software on your system is from RPM. The SANE distribution is available in RPM format for quick and painless installation on Red Hat systems. The latest version is available from

`http://developer.redhat.com/rhcn/browse/conventional/packageinfo.php3?package=sane`. Follow these steps to install SANE on your Red Hat system:

1. Download the appropriate RPMs. Unless you're going to be doing driver development, you probably just need the main SANE distribution and the SANE client software.

2. Install the RPMs according instructions in Chapter 11, "Installing and Managing RPM Packages." Running `rpm –Uvh *.rpm` should do the trick:

```
[root@contempt sane]# rpm -Uvh sane*
sane                 ##################################################
sane-client          ##################################################
```

After your software is installed, it should be immediately accessible. The SANE software will dynamically detect any of the scanners that are currently installed on your system. If you don't have any scanners installed, there are also two virtual drivers that load PNM files.

Editing Your SANE Configuration Files

Before trying to scan anything, you'll want to make sure that the driver for your particular scanner will be loaded if the scanner is available. The file `/etc/sane.d/dll.conf` contains all the dynamically loaded drivers that you can use. To enable or disable a device, uncomment or comment a line using the # (pound) symbol.

For example:

Part
IV

Ch
26

```
[root@contempt sane-1.0.1]# more /etc/sane.d/dll.conf
# enable the next line if you want to allow access through the network:
#net
#abaton
#agfafocus
apple
artec
canon
coolscan
#dc25
#dc210
dmc
epson
hp
microtek
microtek2
mustek
...
```

In this subset of the configuration file, the net, abaton, agfafocus, dc25, and dc210 drivers are all disabled. If you don't know the name of the driver for your scanner, check the SANE supported scanners page (http://www.mostang.com/sane/sane-backends.html). In some cases, one driver can support scanners from several different manufacturers.

Using SANE

With SANE installed, you should immediately be able to test and use your scanner. To list the available devices that are recognized by the software, use the scanimage --list-devices command.

For example:

```
[jray@contempt jray]$ scanimage --list-devices
device 'apple:/dev/scanner' is an AppleScanner flatbed scanner
device 'pnm:0' is a Noname PNM file reader virtual device
device 'pnm:1' is a Noname PNM file reader virtual device
```

To display the options that are available for a given device, you also use the scanimage command, like this: scanimage --device-name=<full device name> --help. For example:

```
[jray@contempt jray]$ scanimage --device-name=apple:/dev/scanner --help
Usage: scanimage [OPTION]...

Start image acquisition on a scanner device and write PNM image data to
standard output.

-d, --device-name=DEVICE    use a given scanner device
-h, --help                  display this help message and exit
-L, --list-devices          show available scanner devices
-T, --test                  test backend thoroughly
-v, --verbose               give even more status messages
-V, --version               print version information
```

```
Options specific to device 'apple:/dev/scanner':
    --brightness -100..100% [0]
        Controls the brightness of the acquired image.
    --contrast -100..100% [0]
        Controls the contrast of the acquired image.
...
```

All the available options for the device are listed using the help parameter. If your device is recognized, you're ready to scan. The scanimage command is also your interface to the actual process of scanning. Scan at the command line using this syntax: scanimage --device-name=apple:/dev/scanner > output.pnm.

If you don't like using the command line for scanning (after all, you want to scan graphics, so why not do it graphically?) you can use the xscanimage software from within X Windows. Shown in Figure 26.1, xscanimage is very similar to commercial scanning software and should be fairly self-explanatory.

FIG. 26.1
The xscanimage software should seem very familiar to people who have used other scanning packages.

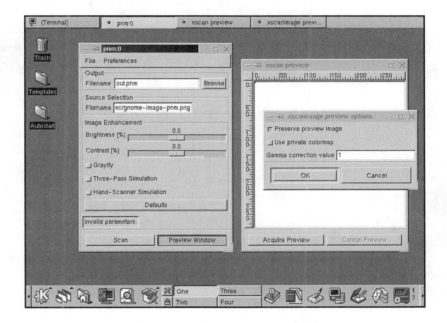

Because Red Hat 6.0 comes with GIMP installed, you might feel more comfortable scanning directly into the graphics package. When you installed the SANE software, you also performed an upgrade on your GIMP packages. Out of the box, GIMP supports the SANE API and automatically recognizes your installed scanners. You can access your scanners by choosing Acquire Image and then the appropriate device from the GIMP Xtns menu. Figure 26.2 shows the GIMP SANE integration.

FIG. 26.2
GIMP provides support
for the SANE API,
enabling you to scan
directly into a
graphics-manipulation
application.

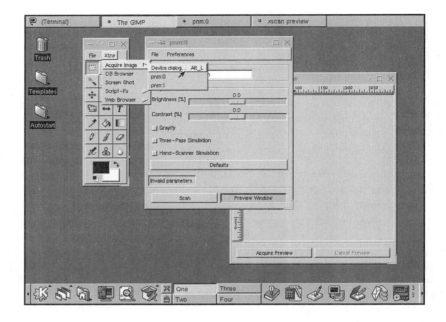

Diagnosing Problems with Your Scanner

Finding problems with your scanner is relatively easy using the SANE model. SANE comes
with two virtual device drivers: pnm:0 and pnm:1. Using these two drivers, you can verify that
your image-scanning software is working. If xscanimage works using the virtual devices, then
you know that your software is working correctly. You should check that the driver for your
scanner is enabled and that your scanner is cabled correctly.

If you are using a SCSI scanner (which is recommended), make sure that the standard SCSI
rules are being followed:

- Use no duplicate SCSI IDs.
- Use no ID greater than 6.
- Always terminate the last device in the chain.

If your scanner is correctly connected to your machine and is supported by the SANE package, you'll have very little difficulty making the software work with Red Hat Linux 6.0.

Using Digital Cameras Under Linux

Digital imaging is one of the fastest-growing peripheral markets today. Cameras are being
introduced in the price range of less than $100, opening the market to people who previously

wouldn't have considered spending several hundred dollars on a camera system. When a digital camera is marketed as part of the Barbie doll line, you can pretty much assume that it has gone mainstream.

Unfortunately, as with the other peripherals that you've looked at so far, there is no built-in support for digital cameras in Linux. Dozens of little applications have been written for the purpose of downloading pictures from a camera to a computer, but it can be very difficult sorting through what works and what doesn't. Until recently, there has been little collaboration in providing a unified interface to digital cameras. However, this is not unlike other operating systems' support for digital cameras: Each different camera uses a different protocol for transferring its images and usually comes with a unique piece of software for accomplishing the task (Sony Mavica cameras being a notable exception). This is all starting to change, however, thanks to a wonderful piece of software called gPhoto.

As with the SANE distribution, gPhoto comes with everything you need to immediately start using digital cameras on your computer. Following the driver/API model, the software provides a unified interface to the digital camera regardless of the model or the capabilities. If you learn how to use the program once, you can switch cameras and keep using the same software to manage your image collection.

Determining Digital Camera Compatibility

As already mentioned, there are many command line utilities that have been written by digital camera owners to transfer pictures from their cameras to their Linux computers. If you do not have a camera that is supported by gPhoto, it doesn't mean that someone somewhere hasn't written a driver for it. The Internet is your best tool for finding software for unsupported hardware. With new drivers being written every day, it is impossible for this text to provide a definitive guide as to what will work on your computer.

Table 26.2 lists the digital cameras that are known to work with the gPhoto system. This list comes from the gPhoto Web site, located at http://www.gphoto.org/. If your camera is not listed, check the site directly because this software is in very active development and is updated quite frequently.

Part
IV

Ch
26

Table 26.2   Current gPhoto-Supported Manufacturers and Camera Models

Manufacturer	Models
Agfa	ePhoto 307, ePhoto 780, ePhoto 1280, ePhoto 1680
Apple	QuickTake 150, QuickTake 200
Casio	QV-10, QV-11, QV-30, QV-70, QV-100, QV-200
Chinon	ES-1000
Epson	PhotoPC 500, PhotoPC 550, PhotoPC 600, PhotoPC 700

continues

Table 26.2   Continued

Manufacturer	Models
Fuji	DS-7, DX-5
HP	C20, C30
Kodak	DC-20, DC-25, DC-200+, DC-210, DC-240, DC-240 USB
Konica	Q-M100, Q-M100V
Minolta	Dimage V
Nikon	CoolPix 900, CoolPix 900S, CoolPix 950
Olympus	D-220L, D-300L, D-320L, D-340L, C-400L, D-400Z, C-410L, D-500L, D-600L, C820-L, C830-L, C840-L, C-900, C1000-L, C1400-L, C-2000Z
Panasonic	Coolshot KXI-600A
Philips	ESP-60, ESP-80
Polaroid	PDC 640
Philips	ESP80
Ricoh	RDC-300, RDC-300Z, RDC-4200, RDC-4300
Sanyo	VPC-G210, VPC-G250, VPC-X350
Sony	DSC-F1HI

If the manufacturer of your camera is listed but the specific model isn't, you might want to try gPhoto anyway. The supported camera list is a list of verified functioning cameras. It's entirely possible that your camera will work but hasn't been verified with the software yet.

Installing the gPhoto Software

The gPhoto software is available from `http://www.gphoto.org/` in both source code and x86 RPM formats. If you are running a Linux distribution other that Red Hat, you might need to download several support libraries that are located elsewhere. The Red Hat Linux distribution, however, includes GNOME and all the associated software that is needed to support gPhoto.

This section covers the installation of the RPMs so that the process of using your digital camera will be as painless as possible. If you haven't already, you might want to read Chapter 11 for more information. Follow these steps:

1. Download the appropriate RPM for from the gPhoto Web site at
   `http://gphoto.org/download.php3`.

2. Install the RPM package using the usual `rpm -Uvh <package name.rpm>` command:

   ```
   [root@contempt gphoto]# rpm -Uvh gphoto-0.3.5-1.i386.rpm
   gphoto          #################################################
   ```

The gPhoto software is now installed and ready to be used.

Configuring gPhoto

Because gPhoto requires access to the serial port, it must be run as root, or you must configure your serial port so that it can be accessed by users in a specific group. If you are going to
want other users to have access to the device, follow these steps:

1. Add a new group to the system using /sbin/groupadd <group name>:

   ```
   [root@contempt gphoto]# /usr/sbin/groupadd serialport
   ```

2. Modify the permissions of the serial port to which your camera is connected so that the
   port is owned by the appropriate group and has group read and write permissions:
   chgrp /dev/<device name> and chmod g+rw /dev/<device name>. This example
   assumes that the camera is connected to COM2, or /dev/cua2:

   ```
   [root@contempt gphoto]# chgrp serialport /dev/cua1
   [root@contempt gphoto]# chmod g+rw /dev/cua1
   ```

3. As a last step, you'll need to add the users of the software into the /etc/group file. This
   file consists of a group name, several group attributes separated by the : character, and
   then a comma-separated list of the members of the group. For example, this is a snippet
   of a group file with several users assigned to the serialport group:

   ```
   [root@contempt gphoto]# more /etc/group
   root::0:root
   bin::1:root,bin,daemon
   daemon::2:root,bin,daemon
   sys::3:root,bin,adm
   utmp:x:11:
   xfs:x:104:
   serialport::503:jray,hlaufman,agroves,graeyling,jackd,kamad
   postgres:x:233:
   agroves:x:500:
   ```

With your system configured for the appropriate group access, you're now ready to connect
and use the software. The first time that you run gPhoto, you must be in X Windows so that
the software can configure itself with information about your camera. After the initial run,
you'll be able to use gPhoto's graphical or command-line interfaces to retrieve photographs
from your digital camera.

Go ahead and start gPhoto from within KDE or GNOME by typing gphoto at a command line.
You should see an initial display very similar to what is shown in Figure 26.3.

Part
IV

Ch
26

FIG. 26.3
gPhoto is started for
the first time.

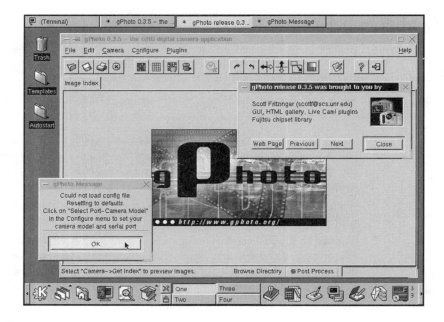

You will immediately be prompted to configure your camera by clicking the Configure menu
and choosing Select Port-Camera Model. The camera/serial-port configuration screen
appears (see Figure 26.4). Choose the model of camera you want to use from the drop-down
menu, and the serial port that it is connected to. When you've made the choices that are
appropriate for your system, click the Save button.

FIG. 26.4
gPhoto offers support
for many popular
camera models.

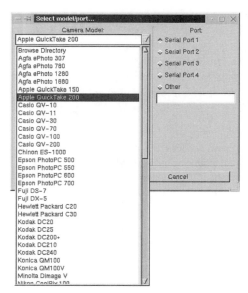

The gPhoto software should now be configured for use. If you'd like to view configuration options for your particular camera, you can choose Configure Camera from the gPhoto Configure menu.

Using the gPhoto Software

After the initial configuration of gPhoto, you (and anyone with access to the serial port that the camera connects to) will be able to download picture information directly from gPhoto's command-line interface.

These are the basic gPhoto options that you can use to retrieve and delete pictures on your camera:

- **-n**—Display the number of pictures that are available for downloading from the camera.
- **-s # <filename>**—Save the picture number (#) to the filename on the Linux host. The picture is not deleted from the camera.
- **-t # <filename>**—Save a thumbnail of a picture number (#) to a filename.
- **-d #**—Delete a picture number (#) from the internal camera storage.
- **-l <filename>**—Save the current live image to a filename. Useful for Webcam applications.
- **-h**—Display the gPhoto version information and a command summary.

Using these commands, you should be able to completely control your camera from the command line. For example:

```
[root@contempt jray]# gphoto -h
gPhoto v.0.3.5 - the GNU digital camera application
Covered by the GNU GPL.  Type "gphoto -v" for details.
Usage: gphoto [-h] [-n] [-s # filename] [-t # filename]
            [-d #] [-l filename]
    -n                  display the # of pictures
    -s # filename       save image # as filename
    -t # filename       save thumbnail # as filename
    -d #                delete image # from camera
    -l filename         save live preview as filename
    -h                  display this help screen
    -v                  display information about the 0.3.5 version
```

You might wonder why command-line access to a digital camera is important. Digital cameras are often used as data-collection devices. Unlike scanners, where the person scanning the image is likely to be the one using it, digital cameras are often used to collect visual data and then distribute it to other people for their use; insurance companies, for example, might employ digital cameras to document claims. Once the camera has been used and it's time to download the images, traditionally it has been a rather slow and cumbersome process of starting the computer, connecting the camera, starting the software, selecting the images, and finally downloading the images to the computer. If the images must be filed somewhere else, the process is generally completed manually.

Part
IV

Ch
26

The capability of command-line control is very important for many Linux applications and can be used to automate digital imaging in ways that are not possible on other platforms. For example, you could create a script that will hotsync your camera after plugging it into the computer, download all the images, time stamp them, and distribute them through FTP, email, NetBIOS (Windows) shares, and so on without any interaction from the user.

However, if you do prefer to run in a graphical user mode, gPhoto offers a very fine interface for digital camera manipulation. gPhoto downloads a thumbnail screen from the camera and then enables the user to select and download individual images from the contact sheet.

The Camera menu provides quick and easy-to-understand commands to handle all the downloading functions. Choose the Get Index option, with or without thumbnails, and then wait a few seconds for the index of camera images to be downloaded to the computer. If you'd like to retrieve one of these images, just click to select it and choose Get Selected from the Camera menu. You will have the option of saving images directly to disk or opening them in a window. If you choose to open them in a window, gPhoto also offers several image-manipulation options in the Edit menu. You can choose to change the image orientation and even modify the color balances of the image through the Edit menu's Color Balance selection. Figure 26.5 shows a drastically altered picture of myself after fiddling with the color adjustments. I can't let my true likeness be seen, now can I?

FIG. 26.5
One of gPhoto's advanced features is color adjustment.

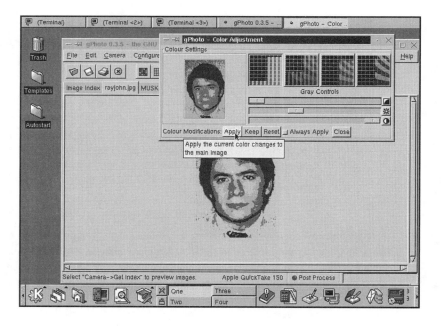

One last nifty feature of the gPhoto software comes as a gPhoto plug-in with the main software installation. Select several images in your camera gallery, and then choose HTML

Gallery from the Plugins menu. The HTML Gallery will instantly create one of the Click the Thumbnail Web site image galleries that are so popular on the Internet. It's a very fast way to put images of family gatherings and special events online, without a single line of HTML being written manually (okay, maybe one or two lines to customize the final page, but you get the idea).

Diagnosing Your Digital Camera

The biggest mistake likely to be made when configuring your digital camera software is the choice of the serial port. If you are using a serial mouse, you might make the mistake of trying to use the same port that your mouse is plugged into. If you read through the UPS section, you already know that this can cause troubles. Before deciding that the software isn't working, first double-check the port that it is plugged into. You also must make sure that the serial port is set up with the appropriate access permissions. Unlike the UPS software that runs as root, you'll probably want several users of the machine to have access to the digital camera.

One of the best options for diagnosing software such as gPhoto is to contact the authors themselves. The gPhoto Web site (http://www.gphoto.org/) offers email addresses to report bugs. It also lists the names and addresses of people who have worked on the individual drivers for the cameras. Contacting the person who wrote the driver module for your particular camera might help determine what is wrong and what you can do to solve the problem.

If you haven't purchased a digital camera yet and want to purchase one that is well supported, be sure to read the gPhoto Web site. The authors provide tips on selecting and purchasing digital cameras and tell which digital cameras offer open protocols that are easy to support.

Using Home Automation Under Linux

Part
IV

Ch
26

This section ends your review of Red Hat Linux peripherals by taking a look at something that can be great fun: home automation hardware and software. For years software has been available for Windows computers that enables you to automate a variety of different electrical appliances in your home. Recently, individuals have ported the software to Linux and UNIX machines. With an investment of roughly $50 to $75, you'll be able to dim lamps, turn on appliances, monitor motion sensors, and many other things, all from your Red Hat Linux computer.

For roughly $40 a month for cable Internet service, I maintain a "mostly" permanent Internet presence with my Linux computer. My computer acts as a server and automation center for my home. If need be, I can remotely connect to my machine, power appliances up and down, and check the status of devices that are being controlled through my machine. If I receive incoming messages on a special "paging" account on my computer, it activates an alarm by my bed so I can tend to issues at work as soon as they arise. My marine fishtank can signal various changes in the condition of the water, and, if necessary, activate CO_2 or ozone generators to correct problems. If you are installing a Linux computer as a server, why not give it control of your surroundings as well?

The standard that makes this all possible is X10. X10 has been around for years, but the control modules have been overly expensive. Spending $25 to turn a light on and off at first seemed a bit outrageous, but pricing has come down in recent months, and control units are available from $5 to $10. The X10 system sends signals from a base unit to multiple control units through your power lines. Each control unit has a unique address consisting of a letter and a number between 1 and 16. Up to 256 devices can be controlled through a single base unit, granting you quite a bit of room for developing your own automated home or apartment. A wide range of X10-compatible devices are available: dimmers, motion sensors, drape openers, thermostats, remote controls, and so on. The best resource for purchasing X10 hardware is http://www.x10.com/.

Determining X10 Hardware Compatibility

As you've probably guessed, there is no Linux support for home automation under Red Hat 6.0. Luckily, there is only one X10 computer interface that is extremely popular, so a large amount of software supports it. The supported device is known technically as a CM11a. Other X10 controller devices are available, but the CM11a has a very important feature that the others lack: the capability to receive events from remote transmitters as well as transmit events on the power line. This means that you can purchase a remote control unit that will enable you to send signals directly to X10 devices; these signals, in turn, will also be received by the CM11a unit, allowing your computer to react to the buttons you push on a remote control.

The CM11a unit is most commonly sold under the name ActiveHome. If you purchase the ActiveHome system from http://www.x10.com, you'll have everything that you need to immediately start automating appliances in your home. The CM11a is also available from Radio Shack as the X10 Computer Interface, for roughly $50. Several other companies, including IBM (which offers the Home Director product) offer the CM11a under different names and packaging.

If you find that the startup costs of the CM11a are a bit much, you can also check out the Firecracker interface offered from the X10 Web site. The Firecracker is a tiny X10 transmitter available with a significantly smaller price tag than the CM11a. The only drawback is that you won't be able to receive events; you can only send them. The focus of this section will be on the CM11a unit, which is the more popular and more capable of the two. If you have Firecracker, check out http://mlug.missouri.edu/~tymm/ for the BottleRocket control software, which provides an easy-to-use command-line interface for accessing the Firecracker control unit.

Installing X10 CM11a Control Software

Many different applications can control your X10 units. One of the newest pieces of software is Penguin Power, or ppower. Penguin Power operates as two separate programs. One is a daemon process that starts when you turn on your computer. The purpose of the daemon is to monitor the serial port for incoming signals from the control unit and then act on these signals. This is necessary for the two-way operation of the CM11a unit. Rather than just having your computer turn things on and off, it can react to your signals as well. The second program is a utility that you can use to issue X10 commands very easily from the command line. You'll find ppower to be a very powerful and easy-to-use piece of software; the X10 hardware and software installs quickly and easily under Linux.

The main Web site for Penguin Power is http://sdcc10.ucsd.edu/~swbrown/ppower/. As of the current release of ppower, an RPM installation also is available. As always, if RPMs are available, they're a wonderful method of installing and managing your software—use them. Follow these steps to install the Penguin Power RPM on your system:

1. Download the current RPM from the Penguin Power Web site
   http://sdcc10.ucsd.edu/~swbrown/ppower/.

2. Install the RPM with rpm —Uvh <filename.rpm>:

   ```
   [root@pointy x10]# rpm -Uvh ppower-0.1.4-1.i386.rpm
   ppower                    ##################################################
   ```

3. Configure your computer so that ppowerd will be activated when your computer boots. The RPM includes an initialization script so that you can just use a runlevel editor or the chkconfig --add <service name> command to add ppowerd to your runlevel startup files:

   ```
   [root@pointy rc3.d]# chkconfig --add ppowerd
   ```

After the software is installed, you'll want to plug in the CM11a unit into your serial power and power line. Be sure to note the serial port that you're using. As stressed previously, it is important to remember that if you're using a serial mouse, you're probably already using COM1.

Configuring the X10 CM11a Control Software

Now that you've installed the software, you'll need to configure the /etc/ppowerd.conf file for any special actions that you want Penguin Power to perform when it receives a signal, as well as what serial port it uses when it starts. This section goes through a condensed version of a configuration file and dissects the different parts:

```
/*
 * The tty the daemon connects to the interface on. This should be a
 * ttyS? device or a symlink to one.
```

Part

IV

Ch

26

```
 */
TTY "/dev/ttyS0"
```

The TTY line configures the serial port that the CM11a interface uses. The device /dev/ttyS0 refers to the same device as /dev/cua0: COM1. Again, be sure that you're really connecting to COM1 when you plug in the CM11a unit. If you're using a serial mouse, it's probably already using the COM1 port:

```
/*
 * The default modes for the command socket. You don't want just anyone
 * turning your power on and off, so make sure you set the permissions
 * right. The arguments here are the mode of the socket and the user
 * & group to own the socket. Access gives the ability to send commands
 * to the daemon.
 */
DAEMON_SOCKET 0660 "jray" "wheel"
```

The DAEMON_SOCKET line lets you define the permissions for who can connect to ppowerd and change the state of devices on the system. Rather than let anyone control your household, it's best if you limit the access. Here, access is included for the account jray and the administrative user group wheel:

```
/*
 * A timeout for programs run by the daemon with 'RUN' to finish
 * by. If the program got stuck for some reason, the daemon will kill it
 * off for you.  A value of zero signifies no timeout.
 */
DAEMON_COMMAND_TIMEOUT 10
```

The Penguin Power software will let you run scripts and other programs when it receives a certain signal. If the external program is taking too long to run, the ppowerd process can kill it. This is a safety feature to make sure that spawned processes don't get away from the ppower system. If you write a program that takes more than 10 seconds to execute, you might want to increase this value:

```
/*
 * The housecode the cm11a listens to by default.
 */
HOUSECODE A
```

The base housecode is an arbitrary letter that is chosen for the CM11a. It doesn't really affect the operation of the software except for a few specific commands. For example, there is a command called All lights on/All lights off that was created to be a quick and easy way to turn all the units in a particular housecode on and off. You'll be able to control other devices in other housecodes, so just choose the housecode that the majority of your X10 remote units are set to:

```
/*
 * Info about type of modules connected to your x10 net. Ppower will
 * track the status of these modules so you should list every dev you
 * have.  If there isn't a type for it yet, choose APPLIANCE.
```

```
*/
DEVICE A1 APPLIANCE
DEVICE A3 APPLIANCE
DEVICE A2 APPLIANCE
```

This section of the configuration file contains a list of all the devices being controlled and monitored by your system. When you request the status of your X10 network, only the modules listed in this section will be tracked:

```
/*
 * 'SIGNAL' type devices are addresses you use that don't have actual
 * x10 hardware on them but still want the daemon to be able to handle.
 * For instance, you could have your remote signal A9 when you want to
 * instruct the daemon to run a macro.
 */
DEVICE B8 SIGNAL
```

The SIGNAL type device is a virtual device that the ppowerd software will monitor. For example, the B8 device isn't connected to anything, but a remote control can send a signal to B8 units. When the B8 signal is received by the Penguin Power software, it executes a special function on the computer:

```
/*
 * Aliases for your devices. The reason for aliases is that it is easier
 * remembering your room lights are 'lights' rather than A1 and A2.
 * These are quite optional.
 */
ALIAS A1 fish
ALIAS A2 lamp2
ALIAS fish,lamp2 lights
ALIAS A3 heater
ALIAS B8 fish_signal
```

In case you'd rather not remember the alphanumeric codes for your devices, you can create aliases for them in the ppower configuration file. The alias lines can link device codes to plaintext names or groups of devices to a single group name (as seen with fish, lamp2, and lights:

```
/*
 * A control for turning the fish tank lights on and off with
 * a B8 signal.
 */
MACRO (fish_signal:OFF) {
        RUN "/usr/local/bin/ppower a1:off"
        /* Writes a log message to /var/log/ppower-signal.log. */
        /* RUN "echo 'date': Signal cought. >> /var/log/ppower-signal.log" */
}

MACRO (fish_signal:ON) {
        RUN "/usr/local/bin/ppower a1:on"
        /* Writes a log message to /var/log/ppower-signal.log. */
        /* RUN "echo 'date': Signal cought. >> /var/log/ppower-signal.log" */
}
```

Part

IV

Ch

26

Here two macros have been created to run when a B8 signal (remember that fish_signal is aliased to B8) is sent to the Linux machine. Each of the macros call the ppower application program, which can send signals to the devices. The ppower application is a user front end for controlling the ppowerd software. You might be wondering why you must intercept these signals and then resend the commands to the A1 devices (the fish tank lights). The reason for this is that an X10 remote control unit can broadcast only to a single housecode (without a bit of reconfiguring). Imagine that the remote is set to broadcast to the B housecode and there's no remote control for the A housecode. To get past this particular problem, just intercept a B8 signal on the Linux machine and then use ppower to rebroadcast an A1 signal to the fish tank lights.

You can do anything you want in the RUN commands. If you wanted to provide an emergency shutdown to your Linux computer, you could add a macro that calls shutdown now when a remote button is pushed. It's just as easy to write a macro that starts up an MP3 player and turns on your stereo. How you choose to intercept and react to signals is entirely up to you. Motion sensors are available for around $25 from the X10 Web site. You could write a very simple script that would use gPhoto to capture a photograph of the area where motion was detected and then send it to you in email—or even dial 911 with your modem. For a minimal investment, your Linux machine can become the ultimate home security device.

When you're finished configuring your X10 software, you can start ppowerd immediately, like this:

```
[root@pointy jray]# /etc/rc.d/init.d/ppowerd start
Starting ppower daemon:                              [  OK  ]
```

Assuming that you ran the chkconfig command earlier, the next time you reboot your machine, the Penguin Power daemon will also be started.

Using the X10 CM11a Control Software

You've just seen how to configure the X10 software to receive and react to signals. Now take a look at how the client package ppower can be used to send commands to X10 units.

The command syntax (as you might have picked up from the configuration file) is very simple: ppower <device>:<command>:<optional value>. The different commands that you can send to the X10 devices are listed in the ppower man page. The most common commands that you'd want to use are probably OFF, ON, BRIGHT, and DIM.

For example, if you want to turn off device A2, you would just use this command:

```
[root@pointy jray]# ppower a2:off
```

Likewise, to turn the device back on, the command is this:

```
[root@pointy jray]# ppower a2:off
```

If the remote device is a lamp module, you should be able to dim or brighten the module by using an extended value in the command line. The DIM and BRIGHT commands require that a value between 0 and 22 be supplied as a change level by which the software will brighten or dim the attached light. For example, if you wanted to turn on and then dim a light to 50%, the command would look something like this:

```
[root@pointy jray]# ppower b1:dim:11
```

Brightening the light to its full strength is nothing more than this:

```
[root@pointy jray]# ppower b1:bright:22
```

If you'd like to monitor the status of your X10 network as signals are sent and received, you can use the --status parameter to view the reception of signals in real time. This can be a great help if you must debug your X10 system:

```
[root@pointy jray]# ppower --status
(Sun Sep 19 17:56:05 1999) Housecode b; Device 8; OFF
(Sun Sep 19 17:56:09 1999) Housecode b; Device 8; ON
(Sun Sep 19 17:56:17 1999) Housecode b; Device 7; OFF
(Sun Sep 19 17:56:21 1999) Housecode b; Device 4; OFF
(Sun Sep 19 17:56:24 1999) Housecode b; Device 3; ON
(Sun Sep 19 17:56:28 1999) Housecode b; Device 4; ON
(Sun Sep 19 17:56:31 1999) Housecode b; Device 8; ON
(Sun Sep 19 17:56:32 1999) Housecode b; Device 8; ON
(Sun Sep 19 17:56:36 1999) Housecode b; Device 8; OFF
(Sun Sep 19 17:56:40 1999) Housecode b; Device 8; ON
```

If you'd like to use the ppower software to turn appliances on and off at certain times of day, you can add entries into your crontab file for the devices you want to control. For example, if you wanted to turn your fish tank lights on at 9:30 AM and off at 9:30 PM, you would just add the following lines to your /etc/crontab file.

```
30 9 * * * root /usr/local/bin/ppower a1:on
30 21 * * * root /usr/local/bin/ppower a1:off
```

This can also be done on an account-by-account basis using the Vixie cron system. If you'd like to keep your X10 events separate from your crontab system events, check the man page for crontab.

By this point, it should be obvious to you that the X10 system and Penguin Power software are very flexible and easy to configure. It is highly recommended that you make this addition to your Linux system because it is fun and mostly inexpensive, and it can actually let your computer do things around the house.

Diagnosing the X10 CM11a Control Software

The X10 devices are generally a plug-and-play system. At times however, they can get out of sync with the system if a power failure occurs. Penguin Power should handle all the power failure situations for you, but in the event that ppower is incapable of sending events, try unplugging the device from your computer and from its main power supply. Remove the internal batteries if they are installed, and then let the unit sit for several minutes. After 5–10 minutes, plug everything back in and try the software again. This usually fixes most weird behavior in the CM11a device.

A more difficult problem to recognize (but one that's very easy to fix) is when the CM11a is plugged into a filtered power supply. If the CM11a is plugged into a UPS or a filtered power supply, it is unlikely that the signal it sends on the supply line will be capable of making it out of the filtering device. The simple solution to this is to make sure that the CM11a base unit is plugged directly into an unprotected wall socket.

Troubleshooting

Linux peripheral support is currently a bit hazy. Much hardware is supported, but very few standard interfaces can access the hardware. Finally, this is starting to change with the introduction of the SANE scanner library and gPhoto digital camera software. If you're willing to spend the time installing and configuring software, there isn't much that you can't get to work with Linux. This chapter demonstrates the configuration of several different peripherals to give you an idea of what is possible with a bit of work. Be warned, however, that much of Linux peripheral configuration is trial and error. If you aren't comfortable working with experimental software, you might want to stick to the Red Hat hardware compatibility list when choosing the peripherals to connect to your system.

For some troubleshooting advice, see the following:

Q I've plugged in my device and it isn't working. What do I do?

A Red Hat Linux does not officially support any devices listed in this chapter; check to make sure that the appropriate software is installed for the device you're using.

Q I've connected my supported UPS/Camera/Home Automation unit and installed the appropriate software from this chapter, but it still isn't working. Help!

A These devices are serial devices and you must have the appropriate serial ports configured for the machine. Remember that COM1=`/dev/cua0`, COM2=`/dev/cua1`, COM3=`/dev/cua2`, and COM4=`/dev/cua3`.

Q I've purchased a SCSI card and connected a scanner, but it isn't working. Why not?

A As with most hardware you install, you can't usually just plug-and-play under Linux. Installed SCSI cards might need kernel nodules configured or installed before they are recognized by the operation system. Before attempting to connect peripherals, make sure the interfaces to the peripherals are installed and working properly (serial cards, SCSI cards, parallel ports, and so on).

Q I can't find my hardware listed as being supported by the software that you covered. Should I just buy new hardware?

A If you have the resources, it is nice to buy hardware that is well supported by gPhoto or the like, but it usually isn't necessary. Search the Internet—chances are, someone has written software that supports your device. ●

Local Area Networks (LANs)

## CHAPTER 27

Installing and Configuring TCP/IP Network Support

by John Ray

The TCP/IP Protocol

One of the scariest parts of configuring a computer, from the user's perspective, is network configuration. Networks are seemingly magical beasts that transmit data from one place to another without any obvious means of finding its way. If you've used other operating systems, you might be experienced with some of the simple peer-to-peer file-sharing network protocols, such as AppleTalk on Macintosh or NetBEUI on Windows. For quite some time, these protocols were all computers needed to get by. Desktop computers were not linked across the country, and you couldn't go home and access your company's data from your easy chair. Times have changed, though. In today's world, connectivity is everything. If your computer cannot exchange data with another computer, it isn't going to be very useful.

The Internet has driven a global revolution in computer communications and has pushed a communications protocol called TCP/IP (Transmission Control Protocol/Internet Protocol) to become the networking standard for both local and wide area networks. The first part of this chapter will help you become familiar with what TCP/IP does and what the different components mean. This will make the process of configuring the computer much easier and will shed some light on an otherwise cloudy topic.

A Brief History of TCP/IP

The TCP/IP protocol was originally commissioned and developed with funding from the Department of Defense. Its purpose was to create links between individual networks across the country that were composed of computers that didn't know how to speak to each other. A computing Tower of Babel had been created, and a method of teaching the machines a common language became a necessity. The goal of TCP/IP was (and is) to transcend differences in hardware and software and to allow computers to exchange information no matter what operating system they happen to be running. TCP/IP bridged the country's networks and formed what was known as the ARPANET. Today, the ARPANET has grown beyond the government installations and universities that it once encompassed. It now includes businesses, libraries, hospitals, and millions of people around the world: This is now known as the Internet.

TCP/IP was developed as an open protocol. Its specifications are freely available and can be freely implemented by any individual who desires to use them. This openness has led to the stable and robust system in use today. Previous networking protocols have needed proprietary standards and have limited adoption to a particular operating system or hardware type. TCP/IP implementations are available on nearly any computing device you find, from the computer on your desktop to the palm-held organizer in your pocket. They can all share information through the TCP/IP protocol.

TCP/IP Explained

For years, TCP/IP existed to me as nothing but a few letters. I knew how to configure machines for a TCP/IP network, but I didn't really understand what all the numbers meant. When I finally got a chance to learn what it was that I was configuring, suddenly everything made a lot more sense. If you're interested in jumping straight into the configuration of your TCP/IP settings, feel free to jump ahead. If you'd like to learn a bit more about what these settings do, read on!

First, let's define a simplistic network, called (creatively) Network A. This network consists of a few computers connected with network cards/modems/and so on, and these computers want to exchange information. For the machines to be capable of communicating, they'll need to know each other's name. Obviously, you can't just start picking names out of a hat, so an addressing system needed to be created—this system is called IP addressing.

IP addresses are 32-bit numbers that represent a unique identification for your computer. When your computer is given an IP address, it is the only computer on the planet that has that address. Rather than being represented as a very large number, IP addresses are stored in your computer in dotted-decimal format, which consists of four 8-bit numbers (0-255) separated by decimal points. For example, the IP address on the computer I'm currently using to write this is 140.254.85.2.

All the computers on a local network share IP addresses that probably look very similar. For example, Network A might contain computers with the IP addresses 192.168.0.10, 192.168.0.15, and 192.168.0.20. As long as computers can identify that they are on the same network, they can communicate directly between themselves rather than having to look in the outside world to find the IP address they want to talk to. To put it another way, if two machines are sitting next to each other, they should be capable of exchanging data without having to search the Internet for each other first. For machines to do this, they must understand the concept of a local network. Computers can't just look at an IP address and guess that a machine is on the same network because it is completely possible that a network could have IP addresses that appear very similar, but, in fact, are not located on the same network. Enter subnet masks.

A *subnet mask* tells the computer what part of its IP address identifies the network it is on, and what part identifies the individual machine on that network. For a computer on Network A with the IP address 192.168.0.15, the subnet mask might be 255.255.255.0. This indicates that the first three numbers—192.168.0—determine the computer's subnet, and the last number—15—is the individual identifier for that computer. Subnet masks are also internally represented in the computer as a 32-bit number. Each bit in the subnet mask matches up with a bit in the IP address. If the bit in the IP address is part of the network, it is designated a 1 in the subnet mask. If it is the computer identifier, it is set to 0 in the mask.

Part
V

Ch
27

For example, this is the binary representation of 192.168.0.15 (the decimal places have been left in just so you can see where the numbers in the IP address come from) and its subnet mask:

11000000.10101000.00000000.00001111: IP address

11111111.11111111.11111111.00000000: Subnet mask

As you can see, a 1 masks each part of the IP address that determines the network that the machine is on. By comparing the masked bits in its IP address to the masked bits in another computer's IP address, a computer can determine whether it can talk directly to another machine or whether it needs to pass the data to another network. This example uses a very simple subnet mask. Subnet masks do not have to neatly match up with the decimal points; they can be rather bizarre, in fact, depending on how the network is configured.

Sending Data to Another Network   To the imaginary Network A, add a second subnet called Network B. The IP addresses on this network are 192.168.99.10, 192.168.99.15, and 192.168.99.20, with the subnet mask of 255.255.255.0. What happens if a computer on Network A wants to send data to a computer on Network B? The subnet identifiers for each computer are different (192.168.0 versus 192.168.99), so the machines know that they'll need to speak outside their own network to find each other—but how do they talk outside their network? To do this, they must use a gateway.

A TCP/IP gateway has nothing to do with a computer in a black-and-white spotted box. It can be a computer or a specialized piece of hardware, depending on the situation. The job of the gateway is to accept outgoing traffic and send it one hop closer to its final destination. A gateway device is given an IP address on the local subnet, the same as every other TCP/IP device. This IP address is then configured in each computer's TCP/IP configuration as the gateway device. With this single piece of data, the computers on Network A will be capable of communicating with those on Network B.

Understanding Domain Name Servers and Hostnames   So far, you've learned what IP addresses, subnet masks, and gateways are. Now, you'll learn the last piece of basic information needed to successfully configure your TCP/IP settings: the IP address of a domain name server, or DNS. The domain name server has a very important job on the Internet. If you've used the Internet before, you've probably typed addresses such as www.etoys.com into your Web browser, not IP addresses. It is the job of the domain name servers to turn IP addresses into hostnames, and vice versa. For example, as mentioned earlier, the IP address of the computer I'm using to type this is 140.254.85.2. I can also refer to this machine on the Internet as `primal.ag.ohio-state.edu`, and a DNS will resolve the name into my IP address. The purpose of the DNS is solely for the benefit of humans—computers would be completely happy dealing with a number. Remembering `etoys.com` is much simpler than remembering `204.71.184.166` (the numeric address of `etoys.com`).

You can think of the different parts of the hostname as being very similar to the subnet and computer identifier parts of an IP address. For my machine's name `primal.ag.ohio-state.edu`, the network (referred to in DNS terms as the domain) I'm part of is `ag.ohio-state.edu`. The part of the name that is `primal` refers to my individual computer. You could say that I have a computer named `primal` that is a part of the `ag.ohio-state.edu` domain.

Sometimes the terminology that TCP/IP applications are expecting when setting hostnames can be a bit confusing. Sometimes, *hostname* refers to just the name of your computer—pointy would be my hostname. *Domain name* is often used to refer to the name of the domain, without the name of the computer attached—or, `ag.ohio-state.edu`, in my case. To tell you that the software is expecting the hostname and the domain name, you might be prompted for a fully qualified hostname or fully qualified domain name. In these cases, enter your hostname and domain name together. If you're uncertain what a program is asking for, it's always best to enter in a fully qualified hostname.

You can tell a bit about the host you're connecting to on the Internet from its domain name. The ending segment of the domain name is called the top-level domain (TLD). The following are the most common TLDs:

- **.com**—Commercial domain
- **.edu**—Educational institution
- **.org**—Nonprofit organization
- **.gov**—U.S. government
- **.mil**—U.S. military
- **.net**—Commercial domain (often ISPs)

Recently, several new public domains were approved for use on the Internet. The approval of these domains upset many people because it was a signal of the complete commercialization of the Internet. Take a look and decide for yourself:

- **.firm**—Businesses and firms
- **.shop**—Businesses that offer online shopping services
- **.web**—Projects related to the World Wide Web
- **.arts**—Cultural/entertainment-related information
- **.rec**—Recreation/entertainment sites
- **.info**—Informational resources
- **.nom**—Anyone wanting a personal site

Later in this chapter, you'll learn how to block access to your TCP/IP services from any IP address or domain. For example, if you are concerned about the U.S. military hacking into your machine, you'll learn how to prevent it.

Part
V

Ch
27

Understanding the TCP (and UDP) in TCP/IP   So just what does the TCP (Transmission Control Protocol) do? The IP portion of TCP/IP defines a method for referring to computers on a network by a numeric address. TCP, however, has a very significant, although behind-the-scenes, role in network communications. On a large network, it's impossible for every piece of information to arrive on time, in order, and error-free. The role of TCP is to make sure that each piece of data being sent over the Internet is received correctly. TCP is a reliable network transport and is used for most of the traffic on the Internet, including email and Web services.

TCP/IP connections take place between two sockets on the two computers that want to communicate. *Sockets* are virtual connection points that are maintained by the TCP/IP protocol. Think of them as simply an imaginary plug on each machine between which a virtual wire (the connection) runs. A different analogy can be conceived by looking at the way in which many programming languages talk to sockets. A socket is like a file on your computer. Data in the file is supplied by the remote computer writing to the socket. When your computer wants to respond, it does exactly the same thing, and the remote machine can read its file to determine your response.

Besides sockets, you might want to become familiar with another important term: the port. *Ports* are another virtual construct, like sockets. Imagine that your computer has thousands of different network jacks in the back for different types of connections. If it is serving email, your computer listens at its email port to see if data is being requested. These ports obviously don't exist in reality, but they do exist in the mind of the computer. When a connection takes place, sockets are opened on a specific port number, which determines the type of traffic to be passed. The file /etc/services lists all the different ports that your computer currently knows about and the protocol that runs on each. The following are some of the more common ports:

- **25: SMTP - Simple Mail Transfer Protocol**—SMTP is responsible for moving mail from one machine to another across the Internet. Each time a piece of email is sent, it travels through an SMTP server.

- **110: POP3 - Post Office Protocol, v.3**—POP is the most common method of delivering email to the desktop. If you have an email account and use a product such as Communicator or Eudora to read your email, chances are that you're using POP.

- **80: HTTP - Hypertext Transfer Protocol**—The protocol of the World Wide Web is HTTP. Web pages are served to millions of people a day from thousands of Web servers running on port 80.

- **20/21: FTP - File Transfer Protocol**—This is basic cross-platform protocol for moving files from machine to machine across TCP/IP connections. FTP uses two ports to do its job: One port accepts commands, and the second port handles all the data transfer.

A similar protocol that is also part of TCP/IP is the User Datagram Protocol (UDP). Unlike TCP, UDP does not guarantee delivery of a piece of information. Instead, it attempts to move information across the network as quickly as possible. If the data gets lost, UDP doesn't care. This might sound like a rather useless networking standard, but in some very specific cases, it is actually much better than using TCP. When transmitting video and sound over a network, what is the most important? The speed of the transmission. If an error occurs in the information being sent, you don't want to wait for TCP to request that the information be resent—you just want to continue viewing the video. Think of UDP as being a television broadcast standard, and a network error as being some static in the broadcast. A little static can be annoying, but it's better than the entire broadcast stopping each time static occurs.

One last protocol that you will find very important when diagnosing network failures is the Internet Control Message Protocol (ICMP). ICMP is useful for returning information about the status of devices on the Internet. Its most common use is pinging computers to see if they are successfully receiving data. A ping is nothing more than a packet that is sent out to a remote computer that requests an echo back. Usually, if the remote computer is online and is properly configured, each ping that your computer sends will be responded to by an echo from the remote host.

Methods of Configuring TCP/IP Settings

Two methods exist for configuring TCP/IP settings: manually (which you'll learn about shortly), and dynamically. Obviously, manual configuration means that you need to type the settings into your computer by yourself. Do not under any circumstances randomly choose your own settings for your computer. You must use an IP address that is assigned to you by your network administrator. Choosing an IP address randomly, or based on a computer on the same network as you, will result in, at best, your computer not working and, at worst, your computer and another computer not working. If you inadvertently use an address that belongs to another active computer, you'll end up causing communication problems for both machines. Even if you are setting up only a local computer network, you should still pay attention to the address you choose. If you mistakenly choose IP addresses that are in use and then later connect your local network to the Internet, you'll be unable to connect to the network whose addresses you've used, and vice versa. With this in mind, several subnets have been set aside that you can use to create your own TCP/IP network. These subnets will never exist on the Internet and therefore are safe to use. These are the private subnets and their subnet masks:

Subnet: 10.0.0.0   Subnet Mask: 255.0.0.0

Subnet: 172.16.0.0   Subnet Mask: 255.255.0.0

Subnet: 192.168.0.0   Subnet Mask: 255.255.0.0

Remember that any bit not masked in the subnet can identify an individual computer on that network. Because only the first 8 bits of the 10.0.0.0 subnet are masked, you can have more than 16 million individual computers on your local private network.

Part

V

Ch

27

The second way that TCP/IP information is assigned is dynamically, usually through the use of a DHCP server. If you are connecting your computer to a cable modem, you'll be using a DHCP server to configure the network information on your machine. DHCP servers eliminate the need for a person to manually keep track of what IP addresses have been assigned. They lease IP addresses to machines based on a time limit that is set by an administrator. If a lease expires, the user's computer requests a new lease or attempts to renew the lease it has.

Using DHCP enables far more efficient use of IP addresses. Imagine a company with 500 employees who each have an individual computer. Now imagine that 250 of the employees work during daylight hours, and 250 work during the night. Using manually assigned addresses, you'd need 500 individual IP numbers for the users (or make sure that there was absolutely no overlap between the employee's shifts). By using a DHCP server configured with a short lease period, you need only half as many addresses. As employees leave work and shut down their computers, their IP leases expire and are made available to the incoming workers. DHCP enables you to create a pool of IP addresses, and whoever needs one at any given point in time can request one. When that user is done using the IP address, it goes back in the pool for the next person to use. All this happens transparently on the user's computer. Red Hat Linux supports DHCP through the use of a very nice client called pump.

Now that you're done learning a bit about the background of the TCP/IP protocol, it's time to move on to the good stuff: getting a network card with TCP/IP up and running on Red Hat Linux.

Verifying Hardware Compatibility

If you are using a modem on a phone line, you're using TCP/IP, but the configuration is mostly automatic and you don't need to worry about hardware compatibility. If you are connecting a network in your home or office, you will want to purchase a network card for your computer. Network cards can be a bit tricky if you try to use an older card; you will need to collect all the IO/IRQ/DMA information available for the card before attempting to configure the device. Personally, I highly recommend using a PCI-based card because these require very little, if any, end user configuration and are so inexpensive that there is little reason to use anything else. As always, the best place to check for updated hardware compatibility is Red Hat's supported hardware page at
`http://www.redhat.com/corp/support/hardware/index.html`.

As of this writing, Red Hat officially supports and recommends the following popular ethernet cards, as stated in its hardware guide (for Intel/x86-based computers). This is a partial list, so check with Red Hat before going out to buy a new card.

- 3Com EtherLink III
- 3Com EtherLink PCI III/XL
- EtherWORKS DE500 10/100 PCI

- Kingston Linksys
- Digital Tulip PCI Ethernet
- SMC EtherPower 10 PCI
- SMC EtherPower 10/100 PCI
- Intel EtherExpressPro 10+/100

Other devices that are supported but possibly problematic include these:

- 3Com EtherLink Plus
- 3Com EtherLink 16
- AMD PCnet32/PCI
- Cabletron E2100 series
- Crystal LAN CS8900/CS8920
- Compaq Netelligent Series
- D-Link Ethernet Pocket Adapters
- Intel EtherExpress 16
- Intel EtherExpress Pro 10/10+
- NE1000/NE2000

Several additional Intel and 3Com cards are also supported in the Red Hat distribution but are not officially supported by Red Hat. Again, this is not an all-inclusive compatibility list. You should always check Red Hat's Web site for the latest compatibility lists. Even if your card is not among the ones listed, check the chipset that runs the card; there is a good chance that the chipset is the same as one of the supported cards, which means that you can use the driver.

Network cards are one of the most popular devices to support under Linux. Linux is a powerful network operating system and is beginning to be recognized by more network card manufacturers as a worthy investment for driver development. If you own a card that isn't supported at all by what is provided in Red Hat Linux, check the Web site for the card manufacturer and see if a driver is available. If you still have no luck, run a few searches. My early experiences with getting my first Ethernet card working under Linux involved downloading a test driver that a Linux-lover in Florida had written for himself! This is obviously not the easiest way to go, but you'll find that if you search hard enough, drivers exist for a much wider range of hardware than you might first believe.

Part
V

Ch
27

Be Aware of the Implications of Your Hardware Choice

Although a device is compatible with Linux, some choices shouldn't be made casually. For example, if you come across a person selling a large number of Ethernet cards (that are supported by Linux) for a fair price, be sure that they offer 10BASE-T or twisted-pair support.

Most cards that are manufactured today offer support for 10BASE-T or thinnet, but several years ago that was not the case. Technology is slowly emerging from the dark ages of networking where a wiring standard called thinnet was common. Thinnet is a long, single network wire that links one computer to another in a chain. If you are networking several machines, this might at first glance seem the way to go, but you'll be setting yourself up for disaster and will have an obsolete setup before you're even up and running. The problem with thinnet is that it works like early strings of Christmas tree bulbs: The computers are networked in a series, so if there is a problem anywhere on the wire, all the computers will stop working. A twisted or loose connector on the back of a computer is all it takes to bring a thinnet network to its knees.

Twisted-pair, or 10/100BASE-T, uses a different approach to networking. Instead of plugging into a chain, each computer has its own piece of wire that plugs directly into a central point, called a hub. If a wire or connection goes bad, that computer is partitioned from the network, and the rest of the computers can continue working normally.

Finally, don't immediately assume that buying a 100 card will be the best investment. The network world is currently in a transition between 10Mb networks (theoretically capable of moving data at slightly at more than 1MBps) and 100Mb networks (capable of more than 12 MBps transmission). If you buy a card that supports 100Mb networks, be sure that the network you are plugging into supports 100Mb or that the card also supports 10Mb networks. Otherwise, you might end up with a network card that can't speak to the network that you're plugging into.

These are just suggestions that you should take into account when selecting your network card. Remember that although Linux is compatible with a large number of cards that are available for $3 at used computer stores, it might be wise to invest in a fully supported card that is current with today's standards.

Installing Your Network Hardware and Configuring Kernel Support

When you've made your choice of network card, you'll need to install it in the computer. This should be done according to the recommended installation instructions of the card manufacturer. If you are installing an ISA card, be sure to note the IRQ and I/O address of the card (and anything else that you can configure). If you have a multiport card that does not support auto port detect, you might need to configure the card on a Windows or DOS machine first.

Module-Based Configuration

If you have one. of the Red Hat supported adapters, you can use the included modules with only a little configuring of the file /etc/conf.modules. Before you can start configuring, you need to understand the naming convention of the Linux network devices. Ethernet devices are named /dev/eth<#>, starting with the number 0. The first Ethernet device in your computer will be /dev/eth0, the second is /dev/eth1, and so on.

Next, you'll need to check the Linux hardware compatibility guide to find the module settings that are appropriate for your card. For example, Table 27.1 shows a few of the settings and configuration options for some of the popular network cards, as taken from the guide.

Table 27.1   Sample Ethernet Module Configuration Options

Device	Module	Configuration
Intel EtherExpres Pro10/10+	eepro.o	io=io_port irq=irq
3Com EtherLink 16	3c507.o	io=io_port irq=irq
3Com EtherLink Plus	3c505.o	io=io_port irq=irq dma=dma_1,dma_n
Compaq Netelligent Series	tlan.o	io=io_port irq=irq speed=10Mbs/100Mbs
NE1000/NE2000 Cards	ne.o	io=io_port irq=irq
Intel i82557/ i82558 PCI EtherExpress Pro	eepro100.o	debug=val
SMC EtherPower Series	tulip.o	debug=val

For your system to recognize your card, you need to configure the system so that the appropriate module will be loaded at bootup. To do this, edit the file /etc/conf.modules and add the appropriate lines for your card. You could choose to skip this step and configure the modules graphically in the section "Editing Your TCP/IP Configuration," later in this chapter. I prefer to have my cards fully configured and recognized by the system before changing any of the TCP/IP configuration.

To install an EtherExpress 16 card (with the IRQ 10 and I/O address 0x310) in your system as eth0, you would add the following lines to your /etc/conf.modules file:

```
alias eth0 eepro
options eepro io=0x310 irq=10
```

If you're using a PCI card, you probably won't need to set any additional parameters beyond a line such as alias eth0 eepro100 for the EtherExpress Pro 100 PCI card. Often you can enable debug settings for cards; these are not necessary for the card to work, but they can log debugging information if set.

Part
V

Ch
27

Kernel-Based Configuration

If you prefer to have your network devices compiled into the kernel, you can easily do that as well. Compiling the device drivers into the kernel gives you a single portable kernel that has all the information necessary to boot your machine with network support. Chapter 18, "Installing and Configuring the Red Hat Linux Kernel," contains the necessary information to configure, compile, and install customized kernels. A brief overview of that process is given here.

To recompile the kernel with specific network card support, cd into the /usr/src/linux directory, and run make config or make xconfig if you'd like graphical configuration support. This sample session shows a few of the supported cards. If you'd like to include the driver in the kernel, just type Y for the card you want to support.

```
*
* Network device support
*
Network device support (CONFIG_NETDEVICES) [Y/n/?]
ARCnet support (CONFIG_ARCNET) [N/y/m/?]
Dummy net driver support (CONFIG_DUMMY) [M/n/y/?]
EQL (serial line load balancing) support (CONFIG_EQUALIZER) [M/n/y/?]
Ethertap network tap (CONFIG_ETHERTAP) [M/n/y/?]
Ethernet (10 or 100Mbit) (CONFIG_NET_ETHERNET) [Y/n/?]
3COM cards (CONFIG_NET_VENDOR_3COM) [Y/n/?]
3c501 support (CONFIG_EL1) [M/n/y/?]
3c503 support (CONFIG_EL2) [M/n/y/?]
3c505 support (CONFIG_ELPLUS) [M/n/y/?]
3c507 support (CONFIG_EL16) [M/n/y/?]
3c509/3c579 support (CONFIG_EL3) [M/n/y/?]
...
```

After you've installed your Kernel-level driver or configured your module, you should see the card recognized when you boot the machine. The following machine has an EtherExpress Pro card installed:

```
Sep 13 18:27:35 pointy kernel: eth0: Intel EtherExpress Pro 10/100 at 0xd800,
    00:90:27:9A:4C:C1, IRQ 11.
Sep 13 18:27:35 pointy kernel:    Receiver lock-up bug exists --
    enabling work-around.
Sep 13 18:27:35 pointy kernel:    Board assembly 721383-006,
    Physical connectors present: RJ45
Sep 13 18:27:35 pointy kernel:    Primary interface chip i82555 PHY #1.
Sep 13 18:27:35 pointy kernel:    General self-test: passed.
Sep 13 18:27:35 pointy kernel:    Serial sub-system self-test: passed.
Sep 13 18:27:35 pointy kernel:    Internal registers self-test: passed.
Sep 13 18:27:35 pointy kernel:    ROM checksum self-test: passed (0x04f4518b).
```

If your card is being recognized, you've made it through the tough part. If your boot messages scroll by too quickly, use dmesg | more after the bootup process to see what has happened. Now you'll get to check out how to configure your TCP/IP and protect your machine from outside intruders.

Editing Your TCP/IP Configuration

In this section, you learn how to configure your network settings in one of two ways: either by using the linuxconf utility to graphically configure the machine, or by editing the configuration files by hand.

Using linuxconf to Edit Your Configuration the Easy Way

The easiest way to edit almost any aspect of your system configuration is to use the linuxconf utility. Because linuxconf is accessible over a Web browser, from the command line, and through an X Windows interface, it is available in whatever environment you happen to be using. Network settings are easily configured in linuxconf.

Setting Your Hostname   To set the hostname of your computer, navigate to Networking, Client Tasks, Basic Host Information in the linuxconf navigation pane. Selecting Basic Host Information reveals a field where you can type the fully qualified hostname of your computer (see Figure 27.1).

FIGURE 27.1

Enter your fully qualified hostname in the Host Name field.

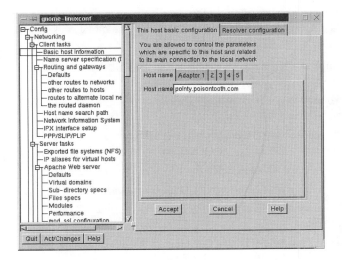

Part

V

Ch

27

Configuring Your Network Card   Next, you'll need to set up any network cards that happen to be in your machine. To do this, select an adapter number from the Basic Host Information. The adapter numbers in linuxconf *do not* correspond to the number scheme of the Linux network devices (that is, Adapter 1 is not necessarily eth1). Figure 27.2 shows the adapter configuration screen for an Ethernet adapter—this is where you'll enter most of the information needed to get your network up and running. If you'd rather get your hands dirty and edit the configuration files by hand, skip ahead to the "Interface Configuration Files" section.

FIGURE 27.2
You can configure your network adapters through the friendly linuxconf interface.

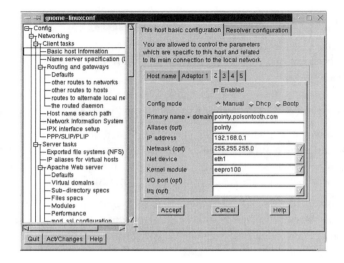

Each setting can be important to the correct operation of your network card. Be sure to set each field if it pertains to your setup. If you're using a PCI card, you'll probably leave the I/O port and IRQ blank. This is entirely normal.

- **Enabled**—If the card is enabled, it will be brought online at boot. Otherwise, it will have to be manually enabled.
- **Primary name + domain**—This is the primary hostname and domain name that this network card will be using.
- **Aliases**—These are other names by which you want to be able to refer to this IP address.
- **IP address**—This denotes the IP address for the adapter.
- **Netmask**—This is the subnet mask for the interface.
- **Net device**—This is the name of the device that will inherit these settings, (eth0, eth1, and so on).
- **Kernel module**—This is the name of the driver module for this device. The drop-down menu to the right of this field shows a list of all available modules.
- **I/O port**—If the module requires an I/O port to be specified, you can do it here. Earlier, you learned how to do this in the `conf.modules` file.
- **IRQ**—Again, if the module for your network adapter requires that an IRQ be set for the card, you can do it here rather than in the `conf.modules` file.

Configuring Nameserver Information   To set up your nameserver, click Networking, Client Tasks, Name Server Specification in linuxconf. You can set up to three nameservers to be used when resolving hostnames. If a DNS fails to look up a name, the request will be passed to the second, then the third. You can also configure search domains for your computer—these are domains that the DNS will look in if you don't specify a fully qualified hostname when connecting to a machine. For example, if you try to Telnet to a computer named www, your machine will assume that you want to look up a computer named www on your local network. If it can't find any machine by that name, it will search the search domains in order until it finds an appropriately named machine, or until the search fails completely. Note, however, that if a hostname exists in more than one of your search domains, you might not know which network you're connecting to. The configuration screen for DNS information is shown in Figure 27.3.

FIGURE 27.3
DNS and domain search paths can also be configured in linuxconf.

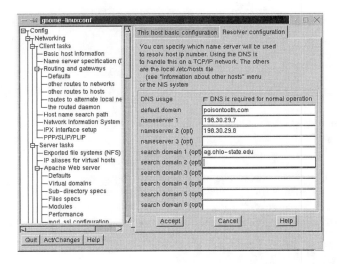

Fill in the necessary fields in this form to configure your nameservers:

- **Default Domain**—This specifies the default domain for the machine. When an unqualified hostname is used, what domain is it assumed to be a part of? This field specifies that domain.

- **Nameserver 1–3**—These are the IP addresses of your nameservers. You may enter up to three.

- **Search Domain 1–#**—These are other domains that you want to search in the event that an unqualified hostname is used.

Configuring the Default Gateway The last piece of information you need to set is the gateway for your network. Click to Networking, Client Tasks, Routing and Gateways, Defaults in linuxconf. As shown in Figure 27.4, there is very little you need to do here; just type in the IP address of the gateway for your network and click Accept. Unless you have two network cards in your machine or are multi-homing on two different networks, there is no need to click the Enable Routing button.

Part
V
Ch
27

FIGURE 27.4

The last step to configuring your network is setting the default gateway.

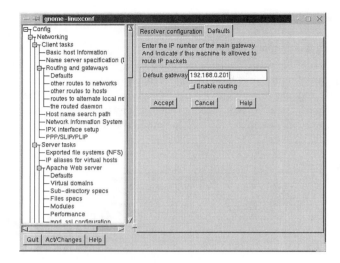

Your computer is now configured for TCP/IP networking. Unless you'd like to make further changes, you can click the Act/Changes button at the bottom of the screen. The changes that you made will be activated, and your network settings will be available instantly.

If you'd rather learn how to configure your Red Hat system manually, continue reading. The next section explains the primary network configuration files that linuxconf writes to. For many network changes, it's easier just to learn what files need to be changed rather than muddle with linuxconf just to change a nameserver or two.

Interface Configuration Files

Each active Ethernet card on your computer can have a TCP/IP configuration file. These files are stored in the /etc/sysconfig/network-scripts directory. If you have an interface called eth0 that you would like to configure network information for, edit the file /etc/sysconfig/network-scripts/ifcfg-eth0. You'll need to add the following lines to the file for a basic configuration:

```
DEVICE=eth0
IPADDR=192.168.0.1
NETMASK=255.255.255.0
ONBOOT=yes
BOOTPROTO=none
```

Obviously, you'll need to change the information to match your configuration, but the settings are very straightforward:

- **DEVICE**—This is the device being configured for network access. The first network card is eth0, the second is eth1, and so on.
- **IPADDR**—This is the IP address that you want the device to have.

■ **NETMASK**—This is the subnet mask for your network.

■ **ONBOOT**—Should the device be configured when the computer boots? Supplying a yes value makes the interface available when the machine boots. If you do not wish the network interface to be online at boot, just specify no. You'll then need to use `ifup eth0` to bring the interface online manually.

■ **BOOTPROTO**—This specifies the protocol that the interface needs to use to boot. The only values you'll probably ever need here are None or dhcp (if you're using a DHCP server). If you are using DHCP, you can leave the IPADDR and NETMASK fields empty.

After the interface configuration file is created, you'll still need to edit one other file that contains the default gateway; otherwise you'll be able to communicate only on your local network. The file that contains the gateway information is `/etc/sysconfig/network`. As with the `ifcfg` files, this file has several name value pairs and should be configured something like this:

```
NETWORKING=yes
FORWARD_IPV4="no"
HOSTNAME="pointy.poisontooth.com"
DOMAINNAME=poisontooth.com
GATEWAYDEV="eth0"
GATEWAY="24.93.96.1"
```

■ **NETWORKING**—If this value is set to no, your network interfaces will not be configured.

■ **FORWARD_IPV4**—Unless you have multiple network cards in your computer, are connected to multiple networks, or are using your computers as a dial-up server, you can leave this value set to no.

■ **HOSTNAME**—This is the fully qualified hostname of your computer.

■ **DOMAINNAME**—This is the domain that your computer is a part of.

■ **GATEWAYDEV**—Unless you have more than one network card in your machine, you'll want to leave this as eth0; otherwise, it would be set to the device that information should be set to in order to talk to the outside network.

■ **GATEWAY**—This is the IP address of the gateway device on your network.

With this file configured, you should be able to reboot your machine, or type `/etc/rc.d/init.d/network restart`, and begin using the network. You might want to look at a few other configuration files first, however, so read on.

Part
V

Ch
27

Creating an Interface Alias

Unlike some operating systems, it's very simple to create aliases to the Ethernet interfaces that you've already configured. An alias interface is like a virtual Ethernet card. It allows one of your Ethernet cards to respond on to another IP address besides the one that is already configured. This can be useful if you want to provide virtual hosting services on your machine. A virtual host pretends to be a unique machine on the Internet, but it is actually a single machine that is configured to respond to a variety of different names or IP addresses.

The easiest way to make an alias of your computer's Ethernet card is to do it manually by copying one of your interface configuration files. For example, assume that you have an interface configuration file called /etc/sysconfig/network-scripts/ifcfg-eth0 and you want to create an interface to it. Alias interface configuration files are named identically to the normal configuration files, but they include :<alias number> at the end of the filename. For example, if you want to create an alias for your eth0 card, follow these steps:

1. Copy /etc/sysconfig/network-scripts/ifcfg-eth0 to a second file, called /etc/sysconfig/network-scripts/ifcfg-eth0:1.

2. Edit the new file. It should end up looking very similar to your original file, except that you have a different IP address and a different device name that corresponds to the name of the ifcfg-eth configuration file.

For example, an alias to the eth0 card looks something like this:

```
DEVICE="eth0:1"
IPADDR="192.168.0.2"
NETMASK="255.255.255.0"
ONBOOT="yes"
BOOTPROTO="none"
```

When the files are edited and ready, you can bring your new interface online with the ifup eth0:1 command. Test your new interface by pinging it. Your computer should now be acting as if it has another Ethernet card installed.

Finding Nameserver and Host Information: */etc/hosts* and */etc/resolv.conf*

The nameserver information on your computer is stored in the file /etc/resolv.conf. This file holds up to three nameservers as well as multiple search domains. You can enter more than three nameservers in this file, but anything after the first three will be ignored. However, nameservers are not the first place that your computer will look to find host information. By default, Red Hat attempts to use the /etc/hosts file to resolve a hostname; if the hostname is not found in /etc/hosts, a nameserver request is made.

Editing the Hosts File   Entering data into /etc/hosts might seem like a bit of a pain (you must enter an IP address and hostname for each machine that you want to be able to resolve without querying a DNS), but it can be very useful in maintaining network connections in the event of DNS failure. If connections must be maintained between computers, each machine must be configured to find the other by IP address or by hostname. By entering in all your frequently used machines in the /etc/hosts file, you eliminate the reliance of the system on a nameserver to make connections to those machines. Another reason that you might want to use and maintain a hosts file is to limit the amount of traffic outside your network. For example, if your network is on a part-time dial-up line that is connected only when there is a need to leave the local network, you might need to talk to a DNS to resolve the name of a machine on your local network.

The /etc/hosts file has a simple structure. Each line has an IP address followed by a space and a list of names that should resolve to that IP address. For example, I have a local network with four machines on it: pointy, bitey, canine, and fang. My /etc/hosts file looks like this:

```
[root@pointy /etc]# more /etc/hosts
127.0.0.1          localhost       localhost.localdomain
192.168.0.1     pointy      pointy.poisontooth.com
192.168.0.60    bitey        bitey.poisontooth.com
192.168.0.61    canine    canine.poisontooth.com
192.168.0.62    fang         fang.poisontooth.com
140.254.85.226     www         www.ag.ohio-state.edu
140.254.86.38    postoffice     postoffice.ag.ohio-state.edu
```

Notice that I've also included a few machines outside my poisontooth.com network. The www.ag and postoffice.ag computers are machines that I use at work. You can enter any IP address/hostname mappings you want; it doesn't just have to be machines on your local network.

Editing the *resolv.conf* File   To add nameserver information to the computer, edit the resolv.conf file. The first line of the resolv.conf file usually contains what is called the DNS search path for your computer. This search path is just a list of domains that should be tried if you happen to ask the computer to resolve an unqualified hostname. For example, if I want to connect to a machine called calendar.ag.ohio-state.edu but I just refer to it as calendar, the computer will think that I'm trying to contact a machine on my local network and will try to talk to calendar.poisontooth.com, which doesn't exist. By setting a DNS search path that includes ag.ohio-state.edu, I can have the machine test for the presence of a calendar.ag.ohio-state.edu and connect to it, even if I just use calendar as its name. The remaining lines of the resolv.conf file are the nameservers that you want to be queried, as in the following example:

```
[root@pointy /etc]# more resolv.conf
search ag.ohio-state.edu poisontooth.com
nameserver 198.30.29.7
nameserver 198.30.29.8
```

This resolv.conf file has two nameservers and two search paths. You can have up to three nameservers listed in this file.

Fine-Tuning pump DHCP Operation with /etc/pump.conf

The DHCP engine of Red Hat Linux offers a few options that you might be interested in configuring. By default, for example, pump retrieves DNS information from the DHCP server and then resets the /etc/resolv.conf file each time a DHCP request is made. This is not always desired, so you can add configuration information on an Ethernet-card basis. You can also limit the number of times that pump will send DHCP requests and the number of retries it will make in the event of an error. To change these options, edit the /etc/pump.conf file. This file is not created by default at installation, so it will be a new file on your system.

```
# sample /etc/pump.conf file

retries 3
timeout 5

device eth0 {
    nodns
}
```

This example file retries DHCP requests three times and times out after five seconds if there is any problem. If the eth0 interface is using DHCP, the DNS information retrieved from the DHCP server will not be used.

Protecting Yourself: Editing the TCP/IP Wrappers and Removing Unnecessary Services

Now that you're fully configured to be a part of the Internet, it's time to take a serious look at protecting yourself from attack. Connecting to the Internet is great fun and is generally a relatively secure action on traditional desktop operating systems. However, because Linux is a multiuser operating system, it allows outside people to connect and potentially attack your computer. If you are connecting in any way to the Internet, you must protect your system from these attacks. Cable modems are putting many people online who never had network access before, and this is also allowing hackers to access computers on a scale far greater than ever before.

Editing Your Runlevel Unfortunately, Red Hat Linux makes it quite easy for intruders to compromise your system. Out of the box, Red Hat installs many extra services that you probably don't need unless you're running a server. For example, do you really need to be running a mail server or a Web server on your desktop machine? If you don't, you'll want to remove them from your startup directory. To view a list of all the ports on your machine that are currently listening for connections, use netstat −l at the command line. This is a portion of the output of netstat −l on my machine, which isn't too far off from a base Red Hat 6.0 installation:

```
[jray@pointy jray]$ netstat -l
Active Internet connections (only servers)
Proto Recv-Q Send-Q Local Address          Foreign Address         State
tcp        0      0 *:389                  *:*                     LISTEN
tcp        0      0 *:imap2                *:*                     LISTEN
tcp        0      0 *:674                  *:*                     LISTEN
tcp        0      0 *:ssl-ldap             *:*                     LISTEN
tcp        0      0 *:smtp                 *:*                     LISTEN
tcp        0      0 *:poppassd             *:*                     LISTEN
tcp        0      0 *:simap                *:*                     LISTEN
tcp        0      0 *:pop-3                *:*                     LISTEN
tcp        0      0 *:netbios-ssn          *:*                     LISTEN
tcp        0      0 *:afpovertcp           *:*                     LISTEN
```

```
tcp      0      0 *:www                    *:*            LISTEN
tcp      0      0 *:734                    *:*            LISTEN
udp      0      0 *:1027                   *:*
udp      0      0 pointy:netbios-dgm       *:*
udp      0      0 pointy:netbios-ns        *:*
udp      0      0 *:netbios-dgm            *:*
udp      0      0 *:netbios-ns             *:*
udp      0      0 *:800                    *:*
udp      0      0 *:1022                   *:*
udp      0      0 *:735                    *:*
udp      0      0 *:1023                   *:*
udp      0      0 *:1026                   *:*
udp      0      0 *:2049                   *:*
```

This is only a portion of the output of the command. Of course, I have added a few features to my machine, such as an AppleTalk server (netatalk) and a Windows NetBIOS server (Samba). With each extra service you run, you open your computer up to one more exploit.

To remove extra services, you'll need to use either a runlevel editor, which is included in the KDE environment, or simply remove the startup files by hand.

If you boot up into a graphical environment such as KDE or GNOME, you're running runlevel 5; if you boot into text mode, it's runlevel 3. Each of the Linux runlevels stores its files in a different directory, so you'll need to remove files from the directory of the runlevel you're using:

- Runlevel 5's directory is /etc/rc.d/rc5.d.
- Runlevel 3 is /etc/rc.d/rc3.d.

Red Hat installs the following runlevel files that you might wish to remove. To delete a runlevel file, you can just cd into the appropriate directory and rm it, or you can use chkconfig —del <servicename> to delete from the current runlevel (You'll need to be root to do this). Deleting the startup files does not delete the actual file on your system. The runlevel startup files are just links to the real files that are stored elsewhere, so don't worry that you're deleting something forever. Here are some services you might want to remove, along with how you can remove them:

The Apache Web server:	chkconfig —del httpd
Sendmail SMTP Server:	chkconfig —del sendmail
LPD print Server:	chkconfig —del lpd
Windows SMB Server:	chkconfig —del smb
PostgreSQL DB Server:	chkconfig —del postgresql
INN News Server:	chkconfig —del innd

If you'd like a "prettier" method of editing your runlevel, use ntsysv—it's the same utility you used to set your starting services when installing the OS. Remove as many services as you can from the runlevel that you're using—you'll end up with a far more secure system.

Part
V

Ch
27

Editing inetd Controlled Services   Not all the services that run on your computer are started when your computer boots. Some software is run only when a request comes into your computer. Rather than having an FTP server running constantly, for instance, the operating system waits for a connection on the FTP command port and then starts the server when needed. The process that controls the monitoring of the ports is inetd, which stores all its preferences in an easy-to-read /etc/inetd.conf file. By commenting out lines in this file, you remove the capability of inetd to start particular services. If you're using Linux as a desktop computer, you might not need a Telnet server or ftp server running. You can edit inetd.conf to eliminate these.

For example, the following is a portion of my inetd.conf file:

```
#
# inetd.conf   This file describes the services that will be available
#              through the INETD TCP/IP super server.  To re-configure
#              the running INETD process, edit this file, then send the
#              INETD process a SIGHUP signal.
#
# Echo, discard, daytime, and chargen are used primarily for testing.
#
# To re-read this file after changes, just do a 'killall -HUP inetd'
#
#echo    stream  tcp     nowait  root    internal
#echo    stream  tcp     nowait  root    internal
#echo    dgram   udp     wait    root    internal
#discard         stream  tcp     nowait  root    internal
#discard         dgram   udp     wait    root    internal
#daytime         stream  tcp     nowait  root    internal
#daytime         dgram   udp     wait    root    internal
#chargen         stream  tcp     nowait  root    internal
#chargen         dgram   udp     wait    root    internal
#time    stream  tcp     nowait  root    internal
#time    dgram   udp     wait    root    internal
#
# These are standard services.
#
#ftp     stream  tcp     nowait  root    /usr/sbin/tcpd  in.ftpd -l -a
#telnet  stream  tcp     nowait  root    /usr/sbin/tcpd  in.telnetd
#
# Shell, login, exec, comsat and talk are BSD protocols.
#
#shell   stream  tcp     nowait  root    /usr/sbin/tcpd  in.rshd
#login   stream  tcp     nowait  root    /usr/sbin/tcpd  in.rlogind
#exec    stream  tcp     nowait  root    /usr/sbin/tcpd  in.rexecd
#comsat  dgram   udp     wait    root    /usr/sbin/tcpd  in.comsat
#talk    dgram   udp     wait    root    /usr/sbin/tcpd  in.talkd
```

The # symbol in front of each line shows that the line is commented out. As you can see, I've commented out all the lines in the example. I recommend that you disable as many services as possible. Certain services, such as talk, are rarely used anymore with the widespread availability of the instant messaging solutions such as ICQ and AIM.

Installing TCP Wrappers   For the services that you do want to run, you can provide additional protect to your machine by configuring TCP/IP wrappers. TCP/IP wrappers do exactly what they sound like: They provide a security wrapper around the selected service. Rather than rely on the built-in security that a server offers, you can limit access to inetd processes by configuring TCP wrappers. Red Hat Linux comes with TCP wrappers ready to go, but not activated.

The TCP wrappers limit the access to a service by an IP address, a subnet, or a hostname. In the case of accessing your machine, you'll probably want to take the approach of locking it down for everyone and then opening it up for the few people that you might want installed. The man pages for tcpd (the TCP wrapper daemon) offer instructions for setting up more complex configurations, but an upcoming section looks at a configuration that you can use immediately to secure your machine.

The two files that you'll need to edit are hosts.allow and hosts.deny. These files not only protect using TCP wrappers, but other software on your system might pay attention to them as well, adding even more security. Check the documentation of your software to verify whether it offers support of the hosts.allow/deny protection system.

First, the hosts.deny file contains the names of the computers you want locked out of your system. My opinion is that it is best to start by locking everyone out of your machine and then opening the computer up for people who should have access.

This is an example of my /etc/hosts.deny file; you can set yours up the same way:

```
#
# hosts.deny    This file describes the names of the hosts which are
#               *not* allowed to use the local INET services, as decided
#               by the '/usr/sbin/tcpd' server.
#
# The portmap line is redundant, but it is left to remind you that
# the new secure portmap uses hosts.deny and hosts.allow. In particular
# you should know that NFS uses portmap!
ALL:ALL
```

Here, all computers are blocked from connecting to the machine. If you have Telnet access enabled on your computer, then add this file—notice that you can no longer Telnet into the system. You'll be able to make the initial connection, but TCP wrappers will verify that the connecting machine is denied, and the connection will be dropped.

Next, you'll need to add access to your computer for the people who should be able to use inetd-controlled services. These people might be your local network, or perhaps the IP address of your computer at home. The file that contains this information is /etc/hosts.allow.

Part

V

Ch

27

My `hosts.allow` file contains my local network, my work network, an ISP that I often dial into, and the IP address of a friend who accesses the machine:

```
#
# hosts.allow   This file describes the names of the hosts which are
#               allowed to use the local INET services, as decided
#               by the '/usr/sbin/tcpd' server.
#
ALL: LOCAL, postoffice.ag.ohio-state.edu, 192.168.0., 140.254.85.,
     199.18.97.68, .erienet.net
```

You can specify addresses in the files in their entirety or partially. If any part of the network or hostname matches the partial IP address or domain name, it will be counted as a match.

If you install software on your computer, it might add lines to your `/etc/inetd.conf` without you knowing it. These services are not necessarily wrapped and will be needed to configured manually to use the wrappers.

For example, installing an upgrade of the Samba Windows server software added this line to my `/etc/inetd.conf` file:

```
swat      stream  tcp    nowait.400      root /usr/sbin/swat swat
```

Wrapped services include the tcpd program in the execution fields. To wrap this service, all that is necessary is to add `/usr/sbin/tcpd` after the field that contains the owner of the process (in this case, root).

The appropriately wrapped line would look like this:

```
swat      stream  tcp    nowait.400      root /usr/sbin/tcpd /usr/sbin/swat swat
```

Using TCP wrappers is a very quick and easy way to lock your computer down. Think of them as a personal firewall for your computer. Be sure to wrap your computer as soon as possible if you're going to be connecting to the Internet. Also, start checking your `/var/log/secure` file. This file contains information about potential break-in attempts on your computer. There are attempted hacks on my machine on a regular basis. Here's a typical few days in my secure log file:

```
Aug 18 14:02:04 pointy in.telnetd[23334]: refused connect from
    ABD0514B.ipt.aol.com
Aug 18 14:02:20 pointy in.telnetd[23335]: refused connect from
    ABD0514B.ipt.aol.com
Aug 18 14:02:35 pointy in.telnetd[23336]: refused connect from
    ABD0514B.ipt.aol.com
Aug 18 14:02:50 pointy in.telnetd[23337]: refused connect from
    ABD0514B.ipt.aol.com
Aug 18 14:03:02 pointy in.telnetd[23338]: refused connect from
    ABD0514B.ipt.aol.com
Aug 20 15:27:33 pointy in.telnetd[27945]: refused connect from
    1Cust160.tnt6.sfo3.da.uu.net
Aug 20 15:27:58 pointy in.telnetd[27946]: refused connect from
    1Cust160.tnt6.sfo3.da.uu.net
```

```
Aug 20 18:33:50 pointy in.telnetd[28227]: refused connect from infoteen.com
Aug 20 18:34:00 pointy in.telnetd[28228]: refused connect from infoteen.com
Aug 21 08:39:59 pointy in.telnetd[29557]: refused connect from
    hh2147242.direcpc.com
```

These are Telnet sessions that were refused by TCP wrappers. If you happen to log any inappropriate access on your machine, do not throw away the logfile; if you choose to follow up on a hack attempt with an ISP or network administrator, that person will want as much information about the incident as possible.

A Brief Look at IP Masquerading   IP masquerading is an advanced use of Linux's networking capabilities that many people can use but that few are aware of. IP masquerading allows a single computer with an Internet connection to act as a gateway to the outside world for an entire network of computers. Unlike proxy servers, a Linux machine acting as an IP masquerading server doesn't require that the client computers have any sort of special configuration to work. If you have a cable modem or a limited number of IP addresses, masquerading is one way that you can get around these problems.

The easiest way to get IP masquerading up and running is to install two network adapters in your computer. One adapter will need to be configured to connect to the outside network; the other will be configured as a private subnet for your internal network. One of these adapters can be a modem, not just an ethernet card.

Here are the example configuration files for a machine with two Ethernet cards: eth0, which is connected to a cable modem, and eth1, the card that is connected to the internal network:

`/etc/sysconfig/network-scripts/ifcfg-eth0:`

```
DEVICE="eth0"
IPADDR="24.93.103.87"
NETMASK="255.255.248.0"
BROADCAST=255.255.255.0
ONBOOT="yes"
BOOTPROTO="dhcp"
```

This device is configured entirely through DHCP, so the only fields that really need to be filled in are DEVICE, ONBOOT, and BOOTPROTO. This device should be connected to the cable modem.

Next, take a look at the configuration for the internal network interface,

`/etc/sysconfig/network-scripts/ifcfg-eth1:`

```
DEVICE="eth1"
IPADDR="192.168.0.1"
NETMASK="255.255.255.0"
ONBOOT="yes"
BOOTPROTO="none"
```

This card will be used by the rest of the computers as the gateway to the Internet. This card can be connected to a hub. The internal network computers should also be plugged into this hub.

Part
V

Ch
27

The last configuration file needed is the /etc/sysconfig/network file:

```
NETWORKING=yes
FORWARD_IPV4="yes"
HOSTNAME="pointy.poisontooth.com"
DOMAINNAME=poisontooth.com
GATEWAYDEV="eth0"
GATEWAY="24.93.96.1"
```

The important lines in this file are the FORWARD_IPV4 line (it must be set to yes for IP masquerading to work) and the GATEWAYDEV line. Enabling IP forwarding allows the computer to move TCP/IP packets between the two network cards.

After you've configured your two cards, you're ready to start masquerading. You must configure the client computers on your network to use your eth0 card as their gateway. In this example, the gateway IP address you would want to set on the internal network computers is 192.168.0.1. You're welcome to use these addresses if you'd like—they were created for precisely this purpose. The IP addresses on the client computers should be on the same subnet that was defined for the internal network, eth1 (that is, 192.168.0.2, 192.168.0.3, and so on are all fine).

The very last step is to configure two networking rules that will turn on the masquerading features in the Red Hat Linux kernel. Type these at any command line (as root), and you're done.

```
/sbin/ipchains -P forward DENY
/sbin/ipchains -A forward -s 192.168.0.1/24 -j MASQ
```

If you'd like masquerading to start at bootup, you can create a startup script and include it in the appropriate runlevel. Here is a sample script that I created that enables you to start, stop, and restart IP masquerading at will:

```
#!/bin/sh
#
# description: Starts and stops IP masquerading
#

# Source function library.
. /etc/rc.d/init.d/functions

# Source networking configuration.
. /etc/sysconfig/network

# Check that networking is up.
[ ${NETWORKING} = "no" ] && exit 0


# See how we were called.
case "$1" in
  start)
        echo -n "Starting masquerading services: "
```

```
        # Flush anything active
        /sbin/ipchains -F
        # Setup chain rules
        /sbin/ipchains -P forward DENY
        /sbin/ipchains -A forward -s 192.168.0.1/24 -j MASQ
        echo "Done."
        ;;
    stop)
        echo -n "Shutting down masquerading services: "
        /sbin/ipchains -F
        echo "Done."
        ;;
    restart)
        $0 stop
        $0 start
        ;;
    *)
        echo "Usage: masquerade {start¦stop¦restart}"
exit 1
esac
```

Copy this file into your /etc/rc.d/init.d directory, and then use a runlevel editor (as discussed earlier) to add it to the services that start when your computer boots. The internal network should now be capable of accessing the outside network. It's that simple. There are no extra charges for IP masquerading because only a single IP address is being used. More information about IP masquerading can be found in the ipchains documentation: /usr/doc/HOWTO/IPCHAINS-HOWTO.

Diagnosing TCP/IP Networking

Diagnosing problems that are occurring on your network can sometimes be a bit confusing. This section looks at some techniques and tools that can be used to figure out what is—and what isn't—going on.

Finding the Simple Problems

The most common network problems are very simple to solve and are usually caused by faulty equipment rather than a faulty configuration. If a computer is no longer communicating on the network, start by checking the computer's connection to the network. Most network cards have two lights that indicate an active link and traffic on the network wire. The link light should be lit immediately after the computer boots and should remain constantly lit as long as the computer is connected to the network. If the light isn't lit, check your hub—the port that the computer is connected to should also have a link light. If this light is also out, check your network cable. You can also try resetting your hub; it might have detected a problem and partitioned the computer from the rest of the network, effectively cutting off its network access.

If the connection between the hub and the computer is intact, the next step is to look for activity on the network wire. There are usually activity lights on both the hub and the network card that flash as network traffic is received. If these lights aren't flashing as you access the network, you might have a problem with your network card; information is not flowing from the computer to the hub.

Testing Network Connectivity

To test whether two computers have the capability to speak to each other, you can use the ping command, which sends out ICMP packets from one computer to another. If the two computers can communicate, a response echo packet will be generated and returned to the original sending machine. The ping command also gives you statistics on network latency and any lost packets. If you're experiencing problems connecting to a remote machine, this might help reveal why. A large packet latency or dropped packets might indicate routing trouble between your computer and the destination. If there is little packet dropoff and a low latency, the problem is most likely due to the configuration of one of the two computers that are trying to communicate rather than the network itself. Use ping in the following format:

```
ping <ip address or fully qualified hostname>.
```

For example, I'll ping another computer on my local network:

```
[jray@pointy jray]$ ping 192.168.0.60
PING 192.168.0.60 (192.168.0.60) from 192.168.0.1 : 56 data bytes
64 bytes from 192.168.0.60: icmp_seq=0 ttl=255 time=0.6 ms
64 bytes from 192.168.0.60: icmp_seq=1 ttl=255 time=0.6 ms
64 bytes from 192.168.0.60: icmp_seq=2 ttl=255 time=0.7 ms
64 bytes from 192.168.0.60: icmp_seq=3 ttl=255 time=0.5 ms
64 bytes from 192.168.0.60: icmp_seq=4 ttl=255 time=0.5 ms
64 bytes from 192.168.0.60: icmp_seq=5 ttl=255 time=0.6 ms
64 bytes from 192.168.0.60: icmp_seq=6 ttl=255 time=0.5 ms
64 bytes from 192.168.0.60: icmp_seq=7 ttl=255 time=0.6 ms
64 bytes from 192.168.0.60: icmp_seq=8 ttl=255 time=0.5 ms
64 bytes from 192.168.0.60: icmp_seq=9 ttl=255 time=0.6 ms
64 bytes from 192.168.0.60: icmp_seq=10 ttl=255 time=0.5 ms
ò
--- 192.168.0.60 ping statistics ---
11 packets transmitted, 11 packets received, 0% packet loss
round-trip min/avg/max = 0.5/0.5/0.7 ms
```

This is indicative of a healthy network because there is zero packet loss and a very low latency. Depending on your type of connection, the response time can vary greatly. This is a local network, with an average of less than a millisecond response time. If you are pinging a machine through a modem connection or one that is located across the country or on the other side of the world, you're going to find much higher response times (in the upper hundreds).

Another useful tool for finding where network traffic is experiencing slowdown or is being lost is traceroute. Traceroute traces the path of network traffic as it moves from one network to another. If you have verified that traffic is leaving your network but isn't reaching its destination, you can use traceroute to find out where the problem is. Invoke traceroute by supplying the hostname or IP address of the computer that you are trying to contact:

```
/usr/sbin/traceroute <ip address or fully qualified hostname>.
```

For example, this is a successful traceroute from one of my machines at work to the etoys.com site. For each hop along the route, you can see the length of time the data took to reach that point in its journey:

```
[jray@contempt jray]$ /usr/sbin/traceroute etoys.com
traceroute to etoys.com (204.71.184.166), 30 hops max, 40 byte packets
 1  kh1-eth1-5.net.ohio-state.edu (128.146.143.1)  2.199 ms  1.735 ms 1.639 ms
 2  kc2-atm0-0s38.net.ohio-state.edu (140.254.58.25)  1.567 ms  1.737 ms
    2.387 ms
 3  krc2-atm0-0-0s1.ohio-dmz.net (199.18.96.5)  1.663 ms  1.780 ms 1.539 ms
 4  tlp3-atm1-0.toledo.oar.net (199.18.202.53)  9.853 ms  10.165 ms 12.673 ms
 5  atm9-0-0-153.br1.CHI1.globalcenter.net (204.246.198.73)  38.521 ms
    38.898 ms  40.349 ms
 6  pos4-1-155M.cr1.CHI1.globalcenter.net (206.132.118.85)  40.623 ms
    39.850 ms  39.001 ms
 7  pos4-0-622M.cr2.SNV2.globalcenter.net (206.132.254.58)  82.193 ms
    76.838 ms  75.078 ms
 8  pos12-0-0-155M.hr1.SNV2.globalcenter.net (206.132.151.62)  76.987 ms
    74.966 ms  77.368 ms
 9  204.71.184.166 (204.71.184.166)  79.003 ms  75.297 ms  73.463 ms
```

Now suppose that you were to run an unsuccessful traceroute. An unsuccessful traceroute shows the path of the data up to the point where the connection fails; this gives you a starting point for trying to find the network fault. You can contact the administrator of the remote network and inquire about connectivity to the network that you were trying to reach.

This is an example of an unsuccessful traceroute:

```
[jray@contempt jray]$ /usr/sbin/traceroute brevardmpo.com
traceroute to brevardmpo.com (24.93.106.47), 30 hops max, 40 byte packets
 1  kh1-eth1-5.net.ohio-state.edu (128.146.143.1)  1.940 ms  1.709 ms  1.709 ms
 2  kc2-atm0-0s38.net.ohio-state.edu (140.254.58.25)  1.538 ms
       1.700 ms  1.542 ms
 3  mciws-fddi6-0.ohio-dmz.net (192.148.245.41)  1.728 ms  1.583 ms  1.559 ms
 4  dub1mcr.columbus.rr.com (204.210.252.70)  9.277 ms  5.023 ms  14.235 ms
 5  * * *
```

The host that the traceroute was trying to reach, brevardmpo.com, is not reachable. If the person running brevardmpo.com verifies that the computer is accessible, then there is a failure between their machine and dub1mcr.columbus.rr.com. You could contact the administrator of the columbus.rr.com network and find out if the network is experiencing problems. Of course, this should be done only if the problem is ongoing. Minor network outages do occur, and network administrators are usually aware of any problems on their network and are already working to solve them.

If you do decide to try to contact the administration of a remote network, you can determine the contact information through the use of the whois command. All public networks must have contact information registered. Technical contacts, network location, and contact phone numbers are all accessible through the use of whois. Another very good use of whois is to look up contact information for computers that might have been logged as trying to illegally access your computer. Reporting attempted break-ins to the administrative contacts for a remote network often results in very prompt and decisive action taken against the user. The equipment is yours—protect it!

For example, here's a whois lookup request on my domain, poisontooth.com:

```
[jray@contempt jray]$ whois poisontooth.com
[rs.internic.net]

Registrant:
John Ray (POISONTOOTH-DOM)
    7879 Rhapsody Drive
    Dublin, OH 43016

    Domain Name: POISONTOOTH.COM
    7879 Rhapsody Drive
    Dublin, OH 43016

    Domain Name: POISONTOOTH.COM

    Administrative Contact:
        Ray, John   (JR10134)    jray@DIFFERENT.AG.OHIO-STATE.EDU
        614-718-9597
    Technical Contact, Zone Contact:
        Singh, David K   (DKS)   dsingh@IWAYNET.NET
        (614)294-9292 (FAX) (614)291-1392
    Billing Contact:
        Ray, John   (JR10134)    jray@DIFFERENT.AG.OHIO-STATE.EDU
        614-718-9597

    Record last updated on 03-Sep-98.
    Record created on 16-Jun-98.
    Database last updated on 13-Sep-99 04:51:13 EDT.

    Domain servers in listed order:

    NS1.IWAYNET.NET               198.30.29.7
    NS2.IWAYNET.NET               198.30.29.8
```

Obviously, this should be more than enough information to contact the administrators of the remote network, for either debugging or security purposes.

Checking Your Current Network Connections

Sometimes it is useful to see what machines are currently connected to your computer. Determining what your machine thinks is happening can help determine whether connections are actually being made or are failing before they go through. The easiest way to do this is use the netstat command, which provides a snapshot of the current network connections and their states on the computer. For example, using netstat on a mail server shows results like this:

```
[jray@poisontooth jray]$ netstat
Active Internet connections (w/o servers)
Proto Recv-Q Send-Q Local Address      Foreign Address        State
tcp        0      0 postoffice.smtp    209.166.42.20.63038    FIN_WAIT_2
tcp        0      0 postoffice.pop     vanw-cas2-cs-21..63611 TIME_WAIT
tcp        0      0 postoffice.smtp    209.166.42.20.39357    FIN_WAIT_2
tcp        0     42 postoffice.smtp    mail.stalker.com.4649  ESTABLISHED
tcp        0      0 postoffice.smtp    199.149.195.243.1033   FIN_WAIT_2
tcp        0      0 postoffice.smtp    tan7.ncr.com.27209     FIN_WAIT_2
tcp        0      0 postoffice.pop     199.149.195.246.1066   TIME_WAIT
tcp        0      0 postoffice.pop     199.149.195.246.1091   FIN_WAIT_2
tcp        0      0 postoffice.smtp    mailhost.webques.2444  FIN_WAIT_2
tcp        0      0 postoffice.8100    firewall-ext.ctc.2703  FIN_WAIT_2
tcp        0      0 postoffice.smtp    192.73.224.2.3094      ESTABLISHED
```

You can see the protocol being used and the local port of the connection (represented symbolically by smtp and pop, in many cases). The connecting machine is shown in the foreign address column, along with the port that that machine is using to make the connection.

The netstat command displays the status of a connection based on the state of the sockets involved. These states are documented in the netstat man page as the following:

- **ESTABLISHED**—The socket has an established connection.
- **SYN_SENT**—The socket is actively attempting to establish a connection.
- **SYN_RECV**—A connection request has been received from the network.
- **LISTEN**—The socket is listening for incoming connections.
- **FIN_WAIT1**—The socket is closed, and the connection is shutting down.
- **FIN_WAIT2**—The connection is closed, and the socket is waiting for a shutdown from the remote end.
- **LAST_ACK**—The remote end has shut down, and the socket is closed and waiting for acknowledgement.
- **TIME_WAIT**—The socket is waiting after close to handle packets still in the network.
- **CLOSED**—The socket is not being used.
- **CLOSE_WAIT**—The remote end has shut down, waiting for the socket to close.
- **LISTEN**—The socket is listening for incoming connections.
- **CLOSING**—Both sockets are shut down, but all the data hasn't been sent.
- **UNKNOWN**—The state of the socket is unknown.

Part
V

Ch
27

You can often determine if there is a problem on your computer based on the status of the sockets. For example, if you are having complaints that your machine is not allowing connections, you can look for sockets that are in the LISTEN state (add the –l option to the netstat command). This gives you a good idea of what services your machine is currently trying to provide and can verify that it is indeed trying to serve the network.

If you've read about Internet hacking, you might have heard of denial of service (DoS) attacks. These DoS attacks can take many different forms, but a common one is called a SYN flood. Now that you've see the states of a TCP/IP connection, it should be pretty clear what a SYN attack is. The SYN state for TCP/IP is the state of actively receiving or sending a connection request. In the case of a SYN attack, the attacker computer sends many connection requests to the computer to be attacked. The victim computer enters a state where it tries to service too many connections and can't keep up. All its resources are tied up, and it won't allow connections from the outside. If you are experiencing complaints from people trying to connect to your computer in vain, look at the states of the connections in progress. If you have a few hundred sockets in the SYN_RECV state, you might very well be under attack.

Compiling and Installing sniffit   If you want to take a more active role in monitoring connections to your machine, you might want to look to a utility such as sniffit. This is a powerful packet sniffer that can watch and analyze traffic on your computer's network. You can use it to determine what machines are connecting to your computer and to other computers on your local network. Being able to monitor connections in real-time is very nice, and sniffit offers a very easy-to-use interface that makes the process completely painless. You can download sniffit from its Web site at http://sniffit.rug.ac.be/~coder/sniffit/sniffit.html.

After you have downloaded the sniffit archive, you'll need to install and compile it. This section covers a very simple installation of the software. If you need further assistance, Chapter 12, "Installing and Managing Linux Software," has extensive instructions on how to compile and install applications.

First, ungzip and untar the source code:

```
[root@pointy sniffit]# ls
sniffit.0.3.7.beta.tar.gz
[root@pointy sniffit]# gunzip sniffit.0.3.7.beta.tar.gz
[root@pointy sniffit]# tar -xvf sniffit.0.3.7.beta.tar
sniffit.0.3.7.beta/
sniffit.0.3.7.beta/HISTORY
sniffit.0.3.7.beta/LICENSE
sniffit.0.3.7.beta/Makefile.in
sniffit.0.3.7.beta/PLUGIN-HOWTO
sniffit.0.3.7.beta/README.FIRST
sniffit.0.3.7.beta/config.guess
...
```

Be sure to check out the README files before continuing; they might have information that pertains to your system or network configuration. When you're ready to continue, run the configure process to customize the program to your system:

```
[root@pointy sniffit.0.3.7.beta]# ./configure
creating cache ./config.cache
checking for gcc... gcc
checking whether the C compiler (gcc  ) works... yes
checking whether the C compiler (gcc  ) is a cross-compiler... no
checking whether we are using GNU C... yes
checking whether gcc accepts -g... yes
checking for main in -lncurses... yes
checking for ncurses.h... /usr/include/ncurses.h
checking for shmget... yes
checking for atexit... yes
checking size of unsigned short int... 2
...
```

You should now be ready to compile the sniffit application, so use the `make` command. You will need to be logged into the system as root for sniffit to work correctly after installation. Running make might take a few minutes, so be patient:

```
[root@pointy sniffit.0.3.7.beta]# make
gcc -w -O2 -c  sn_packets.c -I./libpcap -L./libpcap -DHAVE_LIBNCURSES=1
    -DHAVE_NCURSES_H=1 -DHAVE_SHMGET=1 -DHAVE_ATEXIT=1
    DSIZEOF_UNSIGNED_SHORT_INT=2 -DSIZEOF_UNSIGNED_LONG_INT=4
    -DUSE_32_LONG_INT=1 -DLINUX=1
gcc -w -O2 -c  sn_generation.c -I./libpcap -L./libpcap  DHAVE_LIBNCURSES=1
    -DHAVE_NCURSES_H=1 -DHAVE_SHMGET=1 -DHAVE_ATEXIT=1
    -DSIZEOF_UNSIGNED_SHORT_INT=2 -DSIZEOF_UNSIGNED_LONG_INT=4
    -DUSE_32_LONG_INT=1 -DLINUX=1
gcc -w -O2 -c  sn_interface.c -I./libpcap -L./libpcap -DHAVE_LIBNCURSES=1
    -DHAVE_NCURSES_H=1 -DHAVE_SHMGET=1 -DHAVE_ATEXIT=1
    -DSIZEOF_UNSIGNED_SHORT_INT=2 -DSIZEOF_UNSIGNED_LONG_INT=4
    -DUSE_32_LONG_INT=1 -DLINUX=1
...
```

You're now ready to run sniffit. Several different modes of operation exist, each of which you can learn about in the included documentation. The mode that you'll be able to use immediately is the interactive mode. To enter interactive mode, type `./sniffit -i` from inside the directory where sniffit was compiled.

Watching Your Network Traffic   After initializing for a few seconds, sniffit will start. Your window will be broken into two panes; the upper pane shows the traffic on your network wire. The IP addresses and ports on the left are the senders, and the machines and ports on the right are receivers. Figure 27.5 shows the initial sniffit display with quite a few connections active.

Using your arrow keys, you can move the selection line up and down the screen to a specific connection that you would like to monitor. When you've selected something that looks interesting, press Enter. Any data that is transmitted on that connection will be shown in a new window. This enables you to see precisely what is being sent to or from a particular machine. Much of the data you see will probably look like strange characters because it is binary data, but some data (such as Web connections and Telnet sessions) will show up in plain text.

Figure 27.6 shows a Telnet session being monitored. You can clearly see the commands that the user is typing over the network.

FIGURE 27.5
The sniffit utility displays the active TCP/IP connections on your network in real time.

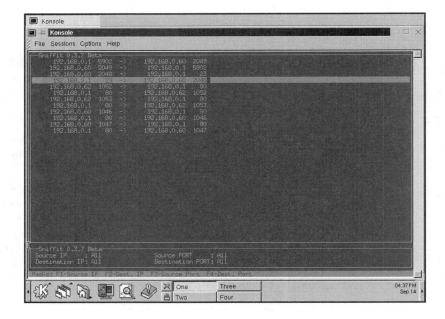

FIGURE 27.6
You can actively watch a connection and see the data being sent.

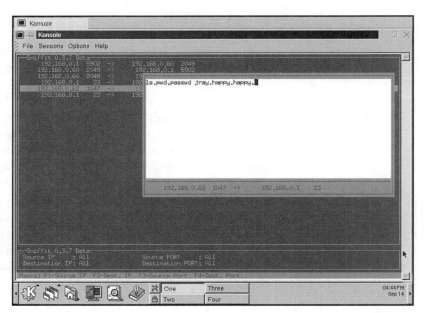

Figure 27.6 also brings to attention an important point. The data displayed in the figure is an actual session in which I have run the `ls` and `pwd` commands and then used `passwd` to change my password to "happy." It's quite easy to see precisely what I changed my password to just by monitoring the connection. Also remember that this can be performed anywhere on the local network as long as the person running the software has root access to the system. How you choose to use network diagnostic tools is up to you, but you should not choose to abuse the power.

You might be wondering why you don't see the responses to the commands in Figure 27.6. This is because I am monitoring one side of the communication, the data being sent from my computer, not the data being received by it. If I wished to view the remote computer's responses, I would have to choose connection represented by `remote machine -> my computer`. This enables you to home in on the data that you want to watch rather than trying to figure out which machine said what.

If you have a very active network, sometimes it can be difficult to find the traffic that you want to watch. If you are trying to watch for illegal access attempts on port 23 (the Telnet port) of a particular computer, you can set sniffit so that it is looking for data being sent only to a particular machine and to a specific port. You can also reverse the scenario and monitor the network for traffic being sent by a machine on a particular port. Any combination of these options is also possible. To set sniffit to watch for specific traffic, use these keys while in monitor mode:

- **1**—Sets the source IP address to monitor. Any connections coming from this source will be shown in the monitor.
- **2**—Sets the destination IP address. Connections to this address are monitored.
- **3**—Sets the source port. If you want to watch for connections originating from a specific port, this enables you to do so.
- **4**—Sets the destination port. This enables you to watch for connections to a specific port and lets you easily sort out different types of network traffic.

If you wanted to monitor all the POP sessions that are connecting on your network, you would push 4, set the port to 110, and then push Enter. If you then wanted to limit the monitoring to a specific server, you could push 2 and type in the IP address of the server that should be receiving the POP requests.

There is absolutely no reason that you can't use this tool to monitor your own computer as well as the rest of your network. If you want to watch the traffic that is directed at you, just specify your IP address as the destination IP address. If you're experiencing bizarre system behavior, it might be that someone is accessing your system without your knowledge. This is one way to find out what they're accessing and who they are.

Part

V

Ch

27

Handling Configuration Problems and Errors

Some of the worst problems that you can face are problems where something sorta works. Often, it is much easier to diagnose problems that are constant and large rather than those that just seem slightly weird. There are a few gotchas that you might want to take note of before giving up on a computer and pulling out a screwdriver and a sledgehammer.

Don't jump to conclusions. If you're reading your favorite Web page and suddenly you can't connect to another site, don't immediately assume that your network is down or that your computer is having a problem. The Internet has its share of hiccups that are resolved within a very short period of time. Before doing anything, stand up, stretch, and come back to the computer in 20 minutes. If the problem still exists, then it might be time to start looking for the trouble.

Gateway Errors   If you can't connect to a computer outside your network, attempt to connect to a computer on the inside. This is a problem that I experience on a very frequent basis. Network administrators in buildings other than the one where I work call me occasionally to report that one of my servers is down. Invariably, I can ask the question, "Have you tried connecting to a machine in your own building?" The answer generally is no. After a bit more probing, they usually discover that the problem is either on the computer that they are sitting in front of or in the connection between buildings. Quickly pinging a machine on the local network takes very little time but can tell you quite a bit. Assume that you're in an office of 10 computers all on the same hub and that your computer can't talk to any of them. There's a good chance that you should be looking for a problem on your machine, not on a server across the street that you just happened to be trying to connect to.

If it turns out that there is connectivity between your machine and the other machines on your local network, take a look at your gateway settings. If your gateway is wrong, you won't be able to send data outside your local network. It's very easy to mistype a number or two. This is the sort of problem that can go undiscovered for a surprising length of time, depending on the user. If a machine spends its time talking to others on the local network, the problem won't be discovered until it decides to speak to a remote machine.

Subnet Mask Problems   Misconfiguring a machine's subnet mask can result in a problem that is almost an exact inverse of a misconfigured gateway. Because the subnet mask determines what machines are the local network, a badly formed subnet usually results in your computer not recognizing the local computers on your network. The symptom of this problem is the incapability of your computer to speak to local computers, but it can talk to remote machines. Luckily, this is easy to recognize and fix.

Duplicate IP Addresses   Duplicate IP addresses can be one of the most annoying problems that you face. A duplicate IP address can disrupt communications in a way that is difficult to diagnosis—this is why it is extremely important for you to obtain your IP address through the appropriate methods (your network administrator). A duplicate IP address will not make anything appear on your screen as it does in Windows or Mac OS. You will get error messages in the log file, but you won't see anything else. Symptoms of a duplicate IP address include network connections that suddenly drop and a general lack of capability to connect at times. The only way to track down a duplicate IP address is to manually check the machines on your network. There is a chance that your network administrator will have the equipment to locate the address, but without it, fixing the problem is a real pain.

Domain Name Server Problems   A very easy problem to diagnose is a misconfigured or malfunctioning IP address. This can manifest itself in several different ways. If you have incoming Telnet services enabled, you will notice that you can connect to the machine, but the login prompt doesn't appear for quite some time. If the computer is trying to resolve the hostname of the computer connecting to it (or its own hostname, for that matter), it will wait for a response from the nameserver or until the lookup process times out.

If you are trying to connect to a remote machine, you'll eventually time out with an error of "host not found" or "no such hostname." The way that you can tell that a DNS error occurred is to attempt to connect to an outside machine using its IP address rather than using its hostname. Because the DNS just translates the name of a machine into its IP address, you can bypass the need for a DNS by just using the IP. If your connection goes through, the problem is definitely in the DNS. This is another situation in which, if the DNS is configured correctly, you might want to just wait a while to see if the problem corrects itself—the DNS server might just need to be rebooted or reset. Always give the network administrator the benefit of the doubt—these are very busy people!

Logging as a Diagnostic Tool

One of your best friends for diagnostics can be your log files. If you want to increase the capability of your logs to monitor your system, you'll need to add a line to your /etc/syslog.conf configuration file. This change is covered in the section "Troubleshooting Linux Software Applications," in Chapter 12, but it will be repeated here.

By default, the /var/log/messages file is set to log what the system considers important messages. However, that isn't all the information that can be logged. You can also request that the system log debug information, which can be voluminous and is not necessarily something that you want to do continuously. To set up the system to log debug information for any process that can, just add this line to the file /etc/syslog.conf:

```
*.debug                                    /var/log/debug
```

After adding the line, you can reboot the machine for the changes to take effect or you can restart the syslog daemon, like this:

```
[root@pointy log]# /etc/rc.d/init.d/syslog restart
Shutting down kernel logger:                        [  OK  ]
Shutting down system logger:                        [  OK  ]
Starting system logger:                             [  OK  ]
Starting kernel logger:                             [  OK  ]
```

Part
V

Ch
27

The file /var/log/debug will start to grow. Certain pieces of Linux software log extensive debug information that can be useful for diagnosing problems. For example, the pump daemon is responsible for making a DHCP request and keeping an IP address. The DHCP process goes through several steps when requesting an address:

1. The computer that wants the IP address broadcasts a discover message to the network.
2. The DHCP server recognizes the discover and sends an offer message back to the client computer.
3. The client machine decides whether it wants the address. If it does, it assigns the address to itself and then asks the DHCP if it indeed can use the address.
4. The server must then respond with an acknowledgement as to whether the client can keep the address. If not, the steps must be repeated.

The entire DHCP process appears almost instantaneous to the user. If there is a problem with the DHCP process, you'll probably just see this message when your computer boots:

```
Bringing up interface eth0:                              [Failed]
```

This doesn't give you much information—how far in the process did the DHCP client get? Was there a response from the DHCP server? If you have enabled the debugging level in your syslog, you can check to see what was logged during the boot process.

For example, this is a severe failure of DHCP, logged in the /var/log/debug file:

```
Sep  8 23:49:09 pointy pumpd[898]: starting at Wed Sep  8 23:49:09 1999
Sep  8 23:49:09 pointy pumpd[898]: PUMP: sending discover
Sep  8 23:49:09 pointy pumpd[898]: breq: opcode: 1
Sep  8 23:49:09 pointy pumpd[898]: breq: hw: 1
Sep  8 23:49:09 pointy pumpd[898]: breq: hwlength: 6
...
Sep  8 23:49:09 pointy pumpd[898]: breq: server_ip: 0.0.0.0
Sep  8 23:49:09 pointy pumpd[898]: breq: bootp_gw_ip: 0.0.0.0
Sep  8 23:49:09 pointy pumpd[898]: breq: hwaddr:
Sep  8 23:49:09 pointy pumpd[898]: breq: servername:
Sep  8 23:49:09 pointy pumpd[898]: breq: bootfile:
...
Sep  8 23:49:39 pointy pumpd[898]: PUMP: sending discover
Sep  8 23:49:39 pointy pumpd[898]: breq: opcode: 1
Sep  8 23:49:39 pointy pumpd[898]: breq: hw: 1
Sep  8 23:49:39 pointy pumpd[898]: breq: hwlength: 6
Sep  8 23:49:39 pointy pumpd[898]: breq: hopcount: 0
Sep  8 23:49:39 pointy pumpd[898]: breq: id: 0x7b1e5308
```

This is actually repeated several times in the file. There is never a response from the server. The DHCP client is sending a repeated discover message but is never getting a response. The capability to log this information for this particular problem eventually led to the replacement of a faulty cable modem. The computer that suffered this failure was indeed sending the DHCP discover message, but the cable modem was not transmitting the response back correctly.

There's no guarantee that any problem you're experiencing will be logged, but Linux does log rather extensively, so it's certainly worth checking.

Keeping Track of It All

You've been given quite a bit of information in a rather short space—don't be worried if it all seems a bit overwhelming. If you're working with a single computer on a network, there's a good chance that you'll never need to diagnose TCP/IP problems. If you're going to be installing several Red Hat Linux machines on a network, you'll get used to the occasional problem, but you'll find that most of them can be solved quite easily.

Summary

A great deal of information was covered in this chapter. When approaching the topic of networking, it's often easier to understand what is being configured if you first understand how it affects the operation of networking in general. If you read the brief introduction to TCP/IP, you now understand the concepts of network masks, IP address, and gateways. The chapter also covered choosing and installing Ethernet cards and their installation and configuration. The chapter then wrapped things up with a look at different ways to monitor and diagnose network problems if they occur on your system. ●

Installing and Configuring Samba

by Duane Hellums

In this chapter

Understanding Linux and Windows Networking

Odds are that if you're running a local area network (LAN), you have one or more Windows-based PCs connected to it. It's even more likely that you will want to share files between your Linux and Windows file systems. Many methods in use today can accomplish this, but a few have evolved as industry standards. You'll be using these standards with Red Hat Linux 6.0.

N O T E This chapter assumes that you have your LAN card and TCP/IP networking installed and properly configured. If you haven't accomplished this yet, proceed to Chapter 27, "Installing and Configuring TCP/IP Network Support." ■

Understanding NFS

Historically speaking, the Network File System (NFS) protocol was used primarily in the UNIX environment. As a result, Linux provides this protocol and the means to use it for NFS file sharing. You might have seen references to NFS in Part 1, "Red Hat Installation," because NFS is one of the main methods used for installing Red Hat Linux over a network. Without getting into too much detail, you should know that NFS has its share of architectural short-comings, primarily related to print sharing, security, and performance.

However, one of the big problems with NFS is that the protocol is not very scalable in an environment that has Windows PCs; this is because the NFS protocol is not native to the Windows operating system. You normally must buy third-party products and install, manage, and occasionally upgrade them on each and every Windows PC.

Understanding SMB

As DOS and Windows have evolved, the Server Message Block (SMB) protocol developed for LAN Manager has evolved as a very flexible and efficient file- and print-sharing standard. Its popularity has spread so much that you can find it standard on almost every contemporary operating system, including Windows, Windows NT, OS/2, Linux, and other flavors of UNIX. One of the reasons for this is that SMB uses a client/server model that enables a server to broadcast its available resources to LAN clients and to easily recognize and access the resources being advertised by other servers.

LAN resources typically appear seamless and transparent to any SMB client on the network, as if they were not being shared by different operating systems. Furthermore, the use of SMB file sharing does not prevent the use of parallel protocols, such as NFS, on the same LAN.

Installing Samba

Although SMB is a published industry standard and relatively open protocol, your system must have a way to recognize and use the protocol. Red Hat Linux 6.0 includes native support for the SMB protocol, but it uses the Samba package in its distribution to provide the behind-the-scenes, client/server SMB file- and print-sharing work.

Samba might or might not be installed on your system already, depending on the installation category you used (server, workstation) and whether you selected or deselected the package during a custom installation. To find out if it is installed, perform the following steps:

1. Select System, GnoRPM from the main GNOME menu. Alternatively, you can bring up an X terminal or a text-based shell prompt to run the `rpm` utility.

2. In GnoRPM, look under Packages, System Environment, Daemons. If you see the Samba package (`samba-2.0.3-8.rpm`), it is already installed.

3. Optionally (command-line only), from the shell prompt, type `rpm -q samba` or `rpm -q samba-2.0.3-8` and verify that you get a message saying that Samba is installed.

If Samba is not installed, you can install it by performing the following steps:

1. Click the Install button on the GnoRPM toolbar, which should bring up an Install window.

2. Make sure that you have a Red Hat CD in your CD-ROM drive; then click Add, which brings up an Add Packages window (if it is configured properly to look in the RedHat/RPMS directory of your mounted CD, usually `/mnt/cdrom`).

3. Double-click the `samba-2.0.3-8.rpm` file, or click it and choose Add.

4. The `samba-2.0.3-8.rpm` file should now appear in the Install window. If it does, click Close on the Add Packages window, and then select the Install button on the Install window.

5. Optionally (command-line only), from the shell prompt, you could type `rpm -i /mnt/cdrom/RedHat/RPMS/samba-2.0.3-8.i386.rpm` to install Samba, assuming that you have your CD-ROM mounted at `/mnt/cdrom`—otherwise, you should replace `/mnt/cdrom` in the filename with the mount point of your CD-ROM (`/dev/hdc/`, for example).

Configuring Samba

Unlike the previous version of Red Hat Linux, not many manual configurations are required for Samba to function properly after you install it. If you performed a Red Hat Linux 6.0 Server installation, all the pieces should be in place for your Linux workstation to serve as an SMB client and server. The kernel and available modules provide the low-level support for the SMB protocol, and the Samba suite provides all the necessary utilities you need to share your resources and to access remote file systems and printers.

Part
V

Ch
28

In one instance, however, you might have to configure the Samba client and server processes. If you performed a Red Hat Linux 6.0 Workstation or Custom installation, you might not have indicated to the setup program that you wanted the SMB daemons (client/server processes) to start up by default. In this case, you will have to go back and tell your system how to start them. To make your SMB processes available to you so that you can share SMB resources in your LAN, perform the following steps:

1. From the GNOME main menu, select System, Control Panel (or type `control-panel` in an X terminal). This should bring up the Control Panel.

2. Click the traffic light icon marked Runlevel Editor. This will bring up the Runlevel Manager window shown in Figure 28.1.

FIGURE 28.1

It's easy to choose which available daemons are started or stopped and in which specific (init) run levels.

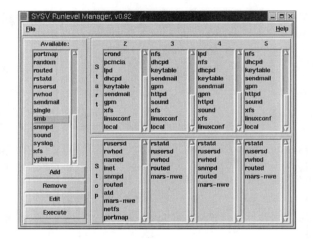

N O T E In the column marked Available, you should see a row labeled smb (if Samba is properly installed). The columns marked 2–5 show all the processes that are configured to run in different init levels. The ones you're interested in are 3 and 5 because these are the multiuser and graphical login multiuser modes. ■

3. If smb is listed in columns 3 and 5, you can close the Runlevel Editor window because Samba should be ready for use. If smb is not listed, click smb in the Available column, and then click the Add button. This brings up a pop-up window called Add smb.

4. Click the pushbuttons marked Start smb and (runlevel) 5.

5. Click the Done button. This brings up the Where pop-up window, which tells you that the standard process number for smb is number 91, which you confirm by clicking the Add button (clicking Done is equivalent to Cancel, unfortunately).

6. Your smb process should now be listed in the 5 column, meaning that it will come up when you graphically log in. You can repeat the process and select Stop smb for specific runlevels (2, for example), but there is no need; the kernel will stop smb when you halt or reboot.

7. Repeat the same steps to Add smb to runlevel 3. If you want, you can remove smb from any Start or Stop runlevel by clicking the smb in the appropriate column and clicking Remove.

TIP

If you want to start the smb processes but don't want to configure your system to start them every time you boot up, click smb in the Available column, and then click Execute. This starts the smbd and nmbd client/server daemons so that you can use SMB network shares during your current login session.

Configuring a Linux Client to Access SMB Network Shares

Let's assume that you want to share a directory or a printer from your Windows 95 or Windows 98 PC and be able to access them from your Red Hat Linux workstation. Of course, for this to work you must have TCP/IP networking and Client for Microsoft installed on your Windows PC. To configure your Windows 95 or 98 PC as an SMB server, you must first perform the following steps:

1. In Windows, select Start, Settings, Control Panel; then double-click the Network icon.

2. In the Configuration tab, click File and Print Sharing.

3. In the dialog box that appears, check one or both of the boxes to indicate that you want to be able to allow others to access your files and print to your printers. If these boxes weren't already checked, Windows will install the necessary file from your CD or hard disk, and then will ask you to reboot to enable Sharing.

4. After rebooting Windows, bring up the Explorer or My Computer, if necessary, and navigate to the directory, file, or printer that you want to share.

5. Right-click the object, select Properties, and then go to the Sharing tab in the Properties window.

6. Click Shared As, and supply a Share Name and Comment, followed by any password protection you want to provide for access to the resource. For files and directories, you can provide three types of access: read-only, full, or password-required (read-only or full).

Leave the Password blank if you do not want to worry about security (in a tightly controlled LAN situation, for example).

Part

V

Ch

28

7. Confirm that your share is being advertised on the LAN by going to Network Neighborhood and clicking your computer. You should see the resource you just chose to share, which should allow your Linux PC to get to it.

TIP

Remember the Share Name that you create in these steps because that information will come in handy when you configure your Linux SMB client. Linux still does not have a convenient, robust, user-friendly, graphical SMB client front-end tool such as Windows' Network Neighborhood to easily browse, find, and access network resources (although some are under development).

Samba comes with the Samba Web Administration Tool (SWAT), shown in Figure 28.2, but it is not discussed here because of a few security and performance issues. If you choose to use it, you will have to uncomment the line in `inetd.conf` that launches SWAT. At a minimum, you should back up your `/etc/smb.conf` file as well because SWAT just writes over any existing settings that you have stored there (which could cause you to lose connections and waste considerable time troubleshooting the default SWAT settings, like I did).

FIGURE 28.2

Samba comes with the SWAT Web Administration Tool that you can use with a browser to configure your Linux network shares.

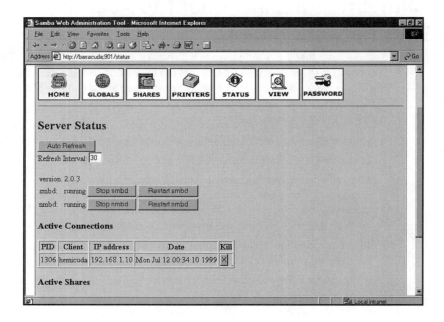

When you have your Windows resource shared the way you want, you can configure your Red Hat Linux 6.0 to access that shared resource over the LAN. Let's use an example in which the Windows Computer Name (located in the Identification tab of the Network settings in Control Panel) is Hemicuda and the Share Name (located under the Sharing tab of the File Properties window) is documents. To make this resource available to your Samba client on your Linux workstation, follow these steps:

1. Use the GNOME File Manager to create a mount point (directory) under /mnt (for example, /mnt/documents). You also can type `mkdir /mnt/documents` from an X terminal, if you choose.

   Placing mount points in the /mnt directory is a convention, but you can actually use any directory as a mount point.

2. Type `mount -t smbfs //hemicuda/documents /mnt/documents`. This uses the Linux mount command to create a link between your local Linux directory (/mnt/documents) and the remote Windows directory using the SMB file system type. Actually, the mount command calls other programs in the Samba suite to do most of the work. You might have to press the Enter key if the command prompts you to do so.

You don't want to have to remount these network shares every time you reboot your Linux system. Instead, you can follow a shortcut, although it is somewhat of a workaround:

1. Select System, LinuxConf from the GNOME main menu. Under Config, File Systems, you'll notice that you can mount local and NFS network file systems, but not SMB.

2. When you select Access local drive, you will see a Local Volumes tab and a table of currently mounted file systems. Click the Add button to see the Volume Specification tab pictured in Figure 28.3.

FIGURE 28.3
You can use LinuxConf to force automatic mounting of SMB network shares, just as it does with NFS resources.

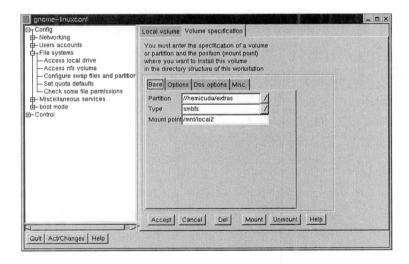

3. Under Partition, you normally can select only local hard drive partitions, and under Type, you are not offered the SMB file system type. However, the information you enter here is stored automatically in /etc/fstab.

   During bootup, the netfs initialization script attempts to mount any NFS or SMB file systems referenced there. So, enter the //system-name/share-name that you want to mount every time you boot in the Partition field, and enter smbfs in the Type field.

Part
V

Ch
28

4. Click the Mount button to save the information (LinuxConf will not mount the network resource, but it will be available the next time you boot).

N O T E Although the same protocol is used for print sharing between Linux and Windows PCs, the instructions for how to configure print sharing are discussed in Chapter 21, "Installing and Configuring Printers." ■

When you have Samba properly configured and have a Windows directory mounted over a local Linux directory, you will be able to share files back and forth between the two systems seamlessly and transparently. The Windows directory will appear to Linux as just another directory. If you perform a directory listing (`ls`) on `/mnt/documents`, you will actually see the files on your Windows shared directory. If you do a move (`mv`) of a file to the `/mnt/documents` directory, the files will be transferred over the LAN and written to the Windows directory (assuming that you didn't share it as read-only).

 TIP If you know the computer name of a remote machine but can't remember what services it is providing over the LAN, you can use the `smbclient -L <hostname>` command from an X terminal (replacing *hostname* with the computer name of your remote system). This provides a listing of all disk-based and printer-based shares (by name) on that machine that you can then mount and access.

Configuring a Linux Server to Provide SMB Network Shares

You use LinuxConf to configure your Samba server and advertise your Linux resources to the LAN. The process is similar to what you just went through to share a Windows resource with Linux, but the interface is a little different. To do this, perform the following steps:

1. Launch LinuxConf by selecting System, LinuxConf from the GNOME main menu.

2. Go to Config, Networking, Server Tasks, Samba file server, Disk Shares (click the plus signs to expand the tree, if necessary). You will see the Share Setup tab shown in Figure 28.4. You will have to click Add to create a new share.

   This tab contains the following options:

   - **Comment/Description**—Enter a simple description that will help you recognize a LAN resource when you see it.
   - **This Share Is Enabled**—Click this button to toggle sharing on and off.
   - **Public Access**—Select this option if you want users who don't have accounts on your Linux machine to still be able to access the network share as guest users.
   - **Writable**—Select this if you think you will need to be able to write to the Linux share at some point. If this option is not selected, the share will be read-only.

FIGURE 28.4
LinuxConf enables you
to configure your Linux
workstation as an SMB
client to access LAN
resources remotely.

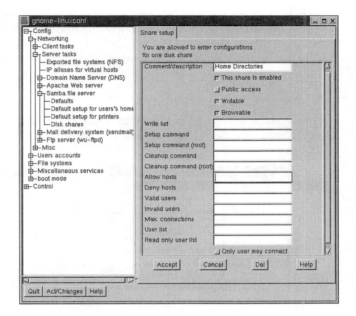

- **Browsable**—Select this if you want the share to appear in an SMB client (such as Network Neighborhood) that supports browsing of any servers that respond to a broadcast query.

- **Write List and Valid Users**—Enter names, separated by commas, of users who are allowed to write to and access the share. If this option is left blank (the default), anyone on the LAN who can browse your Linux PC will be able to do so.

- **Setup and Cleanup commands**—Enter the path and filename of a script or program that you want to run immediately after the share is first mounted or unmounted.

- **Allow and Deny hosts**—Enter the IP addresses, ranges, or machine names of particular machines to which you want to explicitly allow or deny access to your SMB server. Separate multiple entries in a single field with commas, and you can use wildcards (*) for blocks of addresses (192.168.1.*).

- **Valid and Invalid users**—These options provide the same functionality as the previous item, but they involve people instead of hosts.

- **Only User May Connect**—If this option is selected, nobody except people owning a login account on the Linux SMB server will be able to access the machine.

3. Click Accept, and repeat this process for as many shares as you need to configure.

Part
V

Ch
28

TIP Because Linux and Samba are case-sensitive, and not all Microsoft products are, most of the problems involved with using SMB on a daily basis are related to security settings and options. The default security settings are essentially OK for a local area network that has no connection to the outside world. However, you should avoid keeping the security settings wide open if you have Internet connections.

You also can make some server-level configuration changes to Samba. To access the items, click on Config, Networking, Server tasks, Samba File Server, and Defaults (see Figure 28.5).

FIGURE 28.5
You can change the default settings that are applied against new network shares.

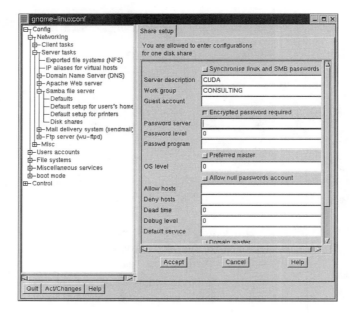

If you don't have certain fields filled in for individual shares, the settings you enter in this default template will take precedence and will be applied to new network shares. To modify the default share values, change the following options:

- **Synchronize Linux and SMB Passwords**—Select this if you want Samba to update your Linux password each time you change your Samba password.

- **Server Description and Work Group**—Type in whatever you want here, understanding that these are the equivalent to Computer Name and Workgroup under Windows 95/98 networking.

- **Guest Account**—Provide the name of the stripped-down user account that will be used for any files created during a remote network connection.

- **Encrypted Password Required**—Select this if you want to enable sending authentication information securely over the network. You will have to select this option if you want your Windows NT, 98, and late-model 95 machines to connect to your Linux server, unless you want to make Registry changes in each Windows client (unlikely).

- **Password Server**—Identify any dedicated password servers located on your network, if applicable.

- **Password Level**—Choose the number of letters in a password that you are willing to attempt to resolve between uppercase or lowercase (higher numbers take longer to resolve).

- **Passwd Program**—Identify the full pathname of your Linux password utility so that Samba can change it when your SMB password changes.

- **Preferred Master and Domain Master**—Select these if you want your Linux workstation to be the overall SMB server in charge of file sharing and name resolution. You must select both options if you want to force your Linux server to become master, otherwise you could have several machines on your network fighting for this role. If this occurs, you might have to make changes to your other servers to tell them not to be master.

- **Allow Hosts and Deny Hosts**—Enter the names of hosts to which you want to explicitly allow or deny access to your network shares.

- **Dead Time, Debug Level, and Default Service**—Set the amount of inactivity time before a connection is terminated, the amount of error information provided, and the location of a network share to offer anyone trying to connect to a nonexistent server resource (to prevent error messages).

Troubleshooting SMB Client/Server Networking

As with most networking issues, lots of things can go wrong, especially if you're in a multi-user environment in which different people are changing the system's settings. Not being able to access a network share is the primary problem you will encounter with Samba. One day you'll be able to access a share, and the next you won't.

If you can't get to data stored on a remote drive, or if the data is different from what you expected, several things could be wrong. It's easy to become confused when you are sharing multiple file systems, directories, and printers across the LAN and different operating systems. It gets even more complicated if you are remotely mounting NFS and NetWare shares.

For example, you might have forgotten to mount the remote directory, or perhaps you mounted it on a different mount point. Confirm the file sharing and actual local location with the mount command from the command line. You also can use the User Mount Tool from the main GNOME menu by selecting System, Disk Management (see Figure 28.6). The mount tool tells you the type and number of devices mounted, as well as on which mount points; it

Part

V

Ch

28

also provides you a simple capability of mounting or unmounting remote resources, or formatting them, if necessary. If you're in a multiuser environment, you should check with a system administrator to find out whether the shared resource in question was made unavailable due to periodic maintenance, backups, or software installations.

FIGURE 28.6

You can easily mount or unmount drive partitions or remote file systems.

If everything looks normal but you still can't get to a network share, you should check to make sure that the SMB daemons are still running. To do this, select Utilities, System Monitor from the GNOME main menu; then confirm that the daemons smbd and nmbd are listed in the rightmost column. If you have to, you can restart them using the Runlevel Editor, as discussed earlier.

To complicate matters, it is very easy to change security permissions or settings on a network share without realizing it. This could make the share inaccessible to other machines. For example, if you keep getting a Windows error message about invalid passwords for the IPC$ resource on your Linux machine, the setting for encrypted passwords in the smb.conf file could be wrong. You should have this value set to yes so that Linux will accept encrypted passwords from Windows machines.

If you can't access files that should be on one of your local directories, it might be because a shared network resource is mounted on top of it. When you mount a remote file system—or a local partition, for that matter—on a mount point such as /mnt/floppy, /mnt/local, or /mnt/cdrom, what actually occurs is that the resource being mounted effectively is overlaid on top of the existing directory. The files that existed in that directory immediately prior to the mount are still there; you just can't see them (until you unmount the file system using the umount command). Type mount from the command line to see what file systems are mounted currently and where the mount point is. ●

## CHAPTER 29

Configuring NetWare Access

by Jim Henderson

In this chapter

Introduction to NetWare

If you are working in a corporate environment with Linux, there is a high probability that your environment includes NetWare servers. For the past 15 years, Novell has provided networking systems and continues to serve as a leader in the PC networking arena.

NCP and IPX

The basis for native connectivity to a NetWare server involves the use of Novell's NetWare Core Protocol, or NCP. NCP, which was developed initially with the first releases of NetWare 2.x in the mid-1980s, is the means of sending requests to and receiving replies from a NetWare server.

NCP is considered by Novell to be a proprietary protocol. As such, it is enhanced with additional capabilities when newer versions are released. Most recent additions include a fragmentation subprotocol that is used to break up Novell Directory Services' requests that exceed the maximum packet size on the network.

In all versions of NetWare, the IPX protocol is the primary protocol used to connect to the server. It wasn't until the release of NetWare 5 that Novell removed the interdependencies between IPX and NCP to allow NCP to be encapsulated in other protocols. In NetWare 5, you have the option of using what Novell calls Pure IP or IPX. Note that connectivity via Pure IP is not yet supported in Linux clients; consequently, this chapter discusses using an IPX client only for NCP connectivity.

NetWare History

The roots of NetWare start with the first versions based on Motorola 6800 processor machines. Novell ultimately moved to the more popular Intel x86 platform and released versions that evolved into NetWare ELS, followed by NetWare 2.x, 3.x, 4.x, and most recently version 5.0.

Most modern NetWare installations use the later releases: 3.11 and 3.12; 4.10, 4.11, and 4.2; and 5.0. These are the versions that this chapter will focus on because earlier versions are not being tested for Year 2000 compliance.

Novell's 2.x and 3.x server products utilized a user database referred to as the *Bindery*. In the late 1980s, Novell created a product called *NetWare Naming Service* (NNS) that was intended to allow NetWare 3.x servers to share their binderies to ease administration of users in a multiserver environment. NNS never did very well except in very large organizations because it was a very complex product. To keep up with the rapid size increase in corporate networks, a different solution was needed. In 1993, Novell announced the next release of NetWare—NetWare 4.0—and the introduction of NetWare Directory Services. A few years after the release of NetWare 4, Novell renamed NetWare Directory Services as Novell Directory Services to reflect that support for NDS would be available on platforms other than NetWare.

In September 1998, Novell announced the newest version of NetWare: NetWare 5.0. As mentioned in the previous section, NetWare 5 introduces the use of NCP over Pure IP without requiring an encapsulation of IPX in IP.

Bindery   The Bindery on a NetWare 2.x or 3.x server is stored in two files on the primary system volume (the SYS: volume): NET$BIND.SYS and NET$BVAL.SYS. These two files formed a basic flat relational database that stored user information such as user ID, username, and a password hash used for authentication.

The password hash algorithm is a publicly known algorithm that is based on the user login ID, password, and password length. By the very nature of hashing algorithms, the hash is not reversible; with these more modern versions of NetWare, the password is never sent over the wire.

The Bindery in a NetWare 2 or NetWare 3 server also keeps track of printing-related objects for the NetWare print subsystem. Printers, print queues, and print servers are all tied together using the Bindery in conjunction with the devices themselves and, frequently, PCs running a program called RPRINTER (for "Remote Printer").

Novell Directory Services (NDS)   In 1993, Novell released NetWare 4.0, which built on the popularity of NetWare 3.11 and added new features in the file system as well as changes in printing setup to make things a bit easier. The most significant introduction with NetWare 4.0, however, was the introduction of NetWare Directory Services. With the release of NDS, Novell opened the door for directory-enabled networking, taking an approach to network resource management based on the proposed X.500 directory standard.

With the release of NetWare 4.11, Novell changed the name to *Novell Directory Services* to reflect the cross-platform support available in NDS. As of this writing, NDS is available on a number of platforms, including NetWare, Windows NT, and Solaris SPARC platforms.

NDS has continued to grow in acceptance in the industry. Shortly after the release of NetWare 5, NDS v8 was announced. NDS v8 is the first full-service directory, providing native LDAP v3 support, utilities for using LDIF formatted files to import data into the tree, and exceptional scalability that has been demonstrated to support up to 1 billion objects in a single tree. Support for LDAP auxiliary attributes makes the definition of the database fully extensible and enhances the capabilities of the directory so that it can store almost any information imaginable.

How to Set Up IPX

At present, NCP-based connectivity to NetWare servers (even NetWare 5 servers) to support the ncpmount and nprint commands requires configuration of the IPX protocol. This is a fairly easy process using the linuxconf utility, but a couple minor changes need to be applied to the configuration files and scripts for things to start up automatically.

Configuration Setup Using Linuxconf

The easiest way to start the configuration process is using the Linux configuration utility, linuxconf. After the utility is started, select the IPX Interface Setup option. This is done using the Config, Networking, Client Tasks option on the menu presented. You will be presented with the screen shown in Figure 29.1.

FIG. 29.1
Configuring IPX with the linuxconf utility.

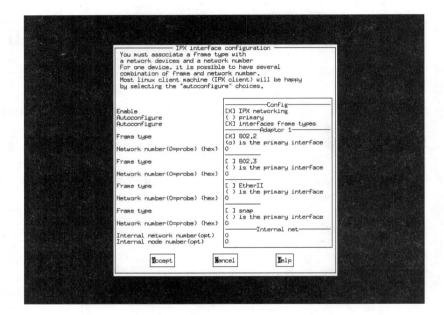

In the IPX interface setup, enable IPX networking under the Adapter 1 tab. As a general rule, you will want to leave the autoconfigure options for the primary interface and interface frame types disabled. There are some cases in which the automatic configuration works, but frequently there are many frame types on the network, and automatically selecting the wrong frame type can make trying to establish consistent communications difficult.

The IPX internal network number and node number are optional, but as discussed in the next section, the default scripts shipped with Red Hat Linux 6.0 assume that these network numbers are used. The internal IPX network number and node number are used only if you are providing NetWare-compatible services with the Mars-NWE package. Otherwise, you will want to leave the internal IPX network disabled.

For the external IPX network number (the network address bound to the network card), an eight-digit hexadecimal number is used. If you know what this address should be, you can enter it; if you do not enter it, however, Linux can automatically detect the address on the selected frame type.

Script Changes

When the IPX networking components are enabled, a few changes are needed in the default scripts to prevent the system startup scripts from having problems with having the IPX internal network disabled.

In particular, a test needs to be added to the network startup script to test for an internal IPX network number of 0 to prevent the execution of the `ipx_internal_net` command. If this command runs during startup, the IPX configuration will fail, as the default is to set the IPX internal network to the primary interface. This setting prevents IPX communications from occurring outside the Linux system.

Listing 29.1 highlights the changes needed in the network startup script, located in `/etc/rc.d/init.d`. Note that these changes must be made while logged in as root, otherwise, you will be unable to modify the script file.

Listing 29.1   Startup Script Changes

```
#!/bin/sh
#
# network        Bring up/down networking
#
# chkconfig: 2345 10 90
# description: Activates/Deactivates all network interfaces configured to \
#              start at boot time.
# probe: true

# Source function library.
. /etc/rc.d/init.d/functions

if [ ! -f /etc/sysconfig/network ]; then
    exit 0
fi

. /etc/sysconfig/network

if [ -f /etc/sysconfig/pcmcia ]; then
    . /etc/sysconfig/pcmcia
fi


# Check that networking is up.
[ ${NETWORKING} = "no" ] && exit 0

[ -x /sbin/ifconfig ] ¦¦ exit 0

# Even if IPX is configured, without the utilities we can't do much
[ ! -x /sbin/ipx_internal_net -o ! -x /sbin/ipx_configure ] && IPX=
```

continues

Listing 29.1   Continued

```
CWD='pwd'
cd /etc/sysconfig/network-scripts

# find all the interfaces besides loopback.
# ignore aliases, alternative configurations, and editor backup files
interfaces='ls ifcfg* ¦ egrep -v '(ifcfg-lo¦:)' ¦ egrep 'ifcfg-[a-z0-9]+$' ¦ \
            sed 's/^ifcfg-//g''
interfaces_boot='ls ifcfg* ¦ egrep -v '(ifcfg-lo¦:)' ¦ egrep \
            'ifcfg-[a-z0-9]+$' ¦
            xargs egrep -l "ONBOOT=[^n][^o]" ¦ sed 's/^ifcfg-//g''

ipv4_forward_set ()
{
    # Turn IP forwarding on or off. We do this before bringing up the
    # interfaces to make sure we don't forward when we shouldn't, and
    # we do it even if networking isn't configured (why not?).
    if [ -d /proc/sys/net/ipv4 ]; then
        # people could have left this out of their kernel, which isn't
        # exactly an error
        if [ ! -f /proc/sys/net/ipv4/ip_forward ] ; then
        echo "/proc/sys/net/ipv4/ip_forward is missing --" \
            "cannot control IP forwarding" >&2
        else
        if [ "$FORWARD_IPV4" = "no" -o "$FORWARD_IPV4" = "false" ]; then
            value=0
            message="Disabling IPv4 packet forwarding"
        else
            value=1
            message="Enabling IPv4 packet forwarding"
        fi

        if [ $value != 'cat /proc/sys/net/ipv4/ip_forward' ]; then
            action "$message"  /bin/true
            echo "$value" > /proc/sys/net/ipv4/ip_forward
        fi
        fi
    fi
}


# See how we were called.
case "$1" in
  start)
    ipv4_forward_set

    action "Bringing up interface lo" ./ifup ifcfg-lo

    case "$IPX" in
      yes¦true)
        /sbin/ipx_configure --auto_primary=$IPXAUTOPRIMARY \
                --auto_interface=$IPXAUTOFRAME
```

```
            if [ $IPXINTERNALNETNUM != 0 ] ; then
                /sbin/ipx_internal_net add $IPXINTERNALNETNUM $IPXINTERNALNODENUM
            fi
            ;;
    esac

    for i in $interfaces_boot; do
        action "Bringing up interface $i" ./ifup $i boot
    done

        touch /var/lock/subsys/network
        ;;
stop)
    for i in $interfaces_boot; do
        action "Shutting down interface $i" ./ifdown $i boot
    done
    case "$IPX" in
      yes¦true)
        if [ $IPXINTERNALNETNUM != 0 ] ; then
          /sbin/ipx_internal_net del
        fi
          ;;
    esac
    ./ifdown ifcfg-lo
    action "Disabling IPv4 packet forwarding" /bin/true
    echo 0 > /proc/sys/net/ipv4/ip_forward
        rm -f /var/lock/subsys/network
        ;;
status)
    echo "Configured devices:"
    echo lo $interfaces

    if [ -x /bin/linuxconf ] ; then
        eval '/bin/linuxconf --hint netdev'
        echo "Devices that are down:"
        echo $DEV_UP
        echo "Devices with modified configuration:"
        echo $DEV_RECONF
    else
        echo "Currently active devices:"
        echo '/sbin/ifconfig ¦ grep ^[a-z] ¦ awk '{print $1}''
    fi
      ;;
restart)
        cd $CWD
    $0 stop
    $0 start
      ;;
reload)
    if [ -x /bin/linuxconf ] ; then
        eval '/bin/linuxconf --hint netdev'
        if [ "$RECONF_IPV4ROUTING" = "yes" ] ; then
```

continues

Listing 29.1 Continued

```
                 ipv4_forward_set
        fi
        for device in $DEV_UP ; do
            action "Bringing up device $device" ./ifup $device
        done
        for device in $DEV_DOWN ; do
            action "Shutting down device $device" ./ifdown $device
        done
        for device in $DEV_RECONF ; do
            action "Shutting down device $device" ./ifdown $device
            action "Bringing up device $device" ./ifup $device
        done
        for device in $DEV_RECONF_ALIASES ; do
            action "Bringing up alias $device" \
                /etc/sysconfig/network-scripts/ifup-aliases $device
        done
        for device in $DEV_RECONF_ROUTES ; do
            action "Bringing up route $device" \
                /etc/sysconfig/network-scripts/ifup-routes $device
        done
        case $IPX in yes|true)
          case $IPXINTERNALNET in
          reconf)
          action "Deleting internal IPX network" /sbin/ipx_internal_net del
          action "Adding internal IPX network $IPXINTERNALNETNUM
            $IPXINTERNALNODENUM"
            /sbin/ipx_internal_net
add $IPXINTERNALNETNUM \
                        $IPXINTERNALNODENUM
          ;;
          add)
          action "Adding internal IPX network $IPXINTERNALNETNUM
                $IPXINTERNALNODENUM"\
            /sbin/ipx_internal_net
add $IPXINTERNALNETNUM \
                        $IPXINTERNALNODENUM
          ;;
          del)
          action "Deleting internal IPX network" /sbin/ipx_internal_net del
          ;;
        esac
        ;;
      esac
    else
        $0 restart
    fi
    ;;
  probe)
    if [ -x /bin/linuxconf ] ; then
        eval '/bin/linuxconf --hint netdev'
        [ -n "$DEV_UP$DEV_DOWN$DEV_RECONF$DEV_RECONF_ALIASES" -o \
```

```
            -n "$DEV_RECONF_ROUTES$IPXINTERNALNET" -o \
            "$RECONF_IPV4ROUTING" = yes ] && \
               echo reload
        exit 0
    else
        # if linuxconf isn't around to figure stuff out for us,
        # we punt.  Probably better than completely reloading
        # networking if user isn't sure which to do.  If user
        # is sure, they would run restart or reload, not probe.
        exit 0
    fi
    ;;
  *)
        echo "Usage: network {start|stop|restart|reload|status|probe}"
        exit 1
esac

exit 0
```

Configuration File Changes

In addition to the startup script changes indicated in the last section, the configuration file for the interface also needs to be changed. The Linuxconf utility does not enable the IPX configuration in the configuration file; as a result, even if the configuration is set up to start automatically, the IPX networking components will not start because this setting is omitted from the configuration file. The configuration file is located at /etc/sysconfig/network-scripts. The configuration file will be named after the interface; for example, if the interface is eth0, the configuration file will be called ifcfg-eth0.

Fortunately, this is a simple matter to remedy, as shown in Listing 29.2. Again, you must be logged in as root to edit this configuration file.

Listing 29.2   Configuration File Changes

```
DEVICE="eth0"
BOOTPROTO="dhcp"
ONBOOT="yes"
IPADDR=""
NETMASK=""
IPXNETNUM_802_2=""
IPXPRIMARY_802_2="yes"
IPXACTIVE_802_2="yes"
IPXNETNUM_802_3=""
IPXPRIMARY_802_3="no"
IPXACTIVE_802_3="no"
IPXNETNUM_ETHERII=""
IPXPRIMARY_ETHERII="no"
IPXACTIVE_ETHERII="no"
```

continues

> **Listing 29.2 Continued**
> ```
> IPXNETNUM_SNAP=""
> IPXPRIMARY_SNAP="no"
> IPXACTIVE_SNAP="no"
> IPX="yes"
> ```

Manual Configuration

If the configuration needed is only temporary, it is not necessary to go through all the steps outlined in the previous sections to provide IPX connectivity. This is one of the true joys of Linux: the ability to change configurations on the fly to provide the services needed at the time they are needed.

All the steps performed automatically by the startup scripts can also be performed manually from within your shell of choice. To manually configure IPX connectivity for file access, three primary commands are involved:

- `ipx_configure`
- `ipx_interface`
- `ncpmount`

By default, the `ipx_configure` parameters for auto primary interface selection and auto interface creation are set to off. If a basic configuration is all that is needed, these parameters need not be changed.

Configuring an IPX interface is an easy task to accomplish. By setting the `ipx_configure` option `--auto_primary=on`, it is not necessary to select the primary interface using the `-p` switch in the `ipx_interface` command.

For example, if you are using device `eth0` for your network interface, Ethernet 802.2 is the frame type you are using, and your connection to server NWFS1 is to be mounted at `/mnt/nwfs1`, the following commands will establish the connection:

```
ipx_interface add eth0 802.2
ncpmount -S nwfs1 -U myusername /mnt/nwfs1
```

This establishes the connection and also enables you to see all the volumes and paths that *myusername* has access to.

In a NetWare 3.x (Bindery) environment, the username is specified as just the username. So, if your login ID that you would use under a DOS/Windows environment is JOHN, you would specify JOHN as the user ID after the `-U` switch.

However, if the environment is a NetWare 4 or NetWare 5 environment, the username should be specified as an NDS fully qualified distinguished name. Thus, if your user ID is JOHN but

JOHN's NDS context is IT.Acme, the username specified after the -U parameter would be JOHN.IT.Acme.

N O T E Those familiar with Novell Directory Services and NDS context settings might wonder why a leading period is not specified as when running under the Novell 32-bit client for Windows. The reason for this is that with the Windows client, a default context is set in the client configuration. In Linux, however, the facilities are not yet in place to provide capabilities such as searching an NDS subtree or to set the current context. A leading period with the ncpmount utility will confuse the utility. ▨

If you are unsure as to which version of NetWare the server is running, you can find out using the nwfsinfo command, discussed later in this chapter.

You may also specify a password on the command line using the -P parameter to ncpmount. It is important, however, to realize that doing so exposes your password to anybody watching over your shoulder and may be considered a security risk.

If you do not wish to specify the password on the command line but also do not wish to be prompted for a password when you use commands, you can create a file in your home directory called .nwclient. This file contains a fileserver and username pair and can optionally contain password information as well. The file is not encrypted, so this feature should also be used with care.

The file format is shown in Listing 29.3.

Listing 29.3   Format of the .nwclient File

```
# This is a comment; format is SERVER/USER [Password ¦ -]
NWFS1/Jim.Home mypassword
# The next line shows a user ID without a password set
NWFS2/Guest.Home -
# The next line shows a user ID that should be prompted for a password
NWFS3/Admin.Home
```

The .nwclient file can be used with any of the NetWare connectivity commands that require an authenticated connection to the NetWare server to provide full functionality. To function correctly, the permissions of this file must be set to 600 using the chmod command.

IP Connectivity Options

If you do not desire to use IPX/NCP to connect to a NetWare file server for file access, you can choose from a few other options. Availability of these options will depend on which products your organization owns and has installed on the NetWare servers.

NFS

The first IP-only option available is presented using the NetWare NFS Services product. This product enables you to export NetWare file systems as NFS-compatible file systems that can be mounted directly on your Linux machine using a standard mount command. Although it is not within the scope of this book to describe the setup and configuration of NetWare NFS Services, it is important that you know that the option is available.

FTP

The second IP-only option available is to use the FTP services included with NetWare 4 and NetWare 5. FTP Services can be installed directly from the NetWare product CD and provides a full FTP server. This option would require you to login to the FTP server and retrieve files from that server.

With NDS-enabled versions of NetWare, the FTP service can be installed on a single server and then can be set up to allow access to any NetWare server within the NDS tree. So, if your network had a single NetWare server called NWFTP01, running FTP services on that server would enable you to access server NWDATA01, as long as NWDATA01 was within the same NDS tree.

Printing

There is probably little need to discuss printing unless you have a specific need to print to a printer that is serviced only by a NetWare print queue. In general, most modern network-aware printers are capable of receiving print jobs from NetWare servers and from IP-based lpd printing at the same time.

Using NetWare print queues from within Linux is also very easy to do. All you need to do is use the `nprint` command to submit your print job to the NetWare queue.

N O T E In an NDS environment, the queue must be defined in the server's Bindery context. The `pqlist` command will tell you which queues are available for printing. ■

To submit a job to a NetWare print queue called TEST_QUEUE on server NWFS1, use the following command:

```
nprint -S NWFS1 -U myusername -q TEST_QUEUE filename
```

Printing from an application would be a two-step process. First, you would print your print job to a file; when that's done, you would use `nprint` to send the job to the NetWare print queue.

If you are already authenticated to the server in question (for example, if you have mounted a NetWare file system on your Linux system), you do not need to specify the –U parameter.

The file will be printed as a stream to the specified print queue; no reformatting is done by nprint because the job can contain embedded binary codes for formatting. If it does, it is up to the program that generates the output to format the text properly and to generate the appropriate printing control codes.

Utilities

Up to this point, a number of utilities for providing NetWare connectivity have been covered. This section contains a quick reference for the most commonly used utilities involved in NetWare connectivity. For complete details on what all the command-line switches do, refer to the online man or info pages. There are many other commands for performing various tasks on NetWare servers that are not covered in this section; for a complete list, execute the command man –k nw at a shell prompt. This will give you a list that contains the NetWare-related commands.

The *ncpmount* Command

The ncpmount command is used for mounting NetWare file systems under a Linux system. The following is the command format:

```
ncpmount [-h] [-S server] [-U user name] [-P password ¦ -n] [-C]
[-c client name] [-u uid] [-g gid] [-f file mode] [-d dir mode] [-V volume]
[-t time_out] [-r retry_count] [-b] [-i level] [-v] [-m] [-y iocharset]
[-p codepage] mount-point
```

The following is an example:

```
ncpmount –S nwfs1 –U user.context /NetWare/nwfs1
```

***fstab* Entries**   The ncpmount utility is also capable of mounting NCP file systems at boot time. It is important to note, however, that the man page and the info page for ncpmount is incorrect with regard to the format of the fstab entries needed to allow the mount command to succeed.

Of particular interest is that the capability to specify the username and password in a secured file is not currently available. To allow NCP file systems to be mounted automatically, the password must be included in the fstab entry. This is a dangerous proposition because the fstab file is readable by any user who logs into the machine. That this file is set up with such low security means that if you do need to automatically mount filesystems at startup, it is advisable that you do one of two things:

- Make sure that the system is secure, and do not install any inetd services that are not absolutely necessary.
- Create a separate, secured startup script for mounting NCP file systems and handle the mount operations in that script.

The *nwuserlist* Command

The nwuserlist command lists the users connected to a server. The following is the command format:

```
nwuserlist [-h] [-S server] [-U user name] [-P password ¦-n] [-C] [-a]
```

Take a look at this example:

```
nwuserlist –S nwfs1 –U user.context
```

The following is sample output from nwuserlist:

```
Conn    User name     Login time
1  :    NWFS1.Home    Thu Aug 12 00:44:27 1999
2:      USER1         Wed Aug 18 11:10:22 1999
3:      ADMIN         Wed Aug 18 19:34:05 1999
4:      ADMIN         Sun Aug 15 21:43:31 1999
5:      ADMIN         Sun Aug 15 23:10:37 1999
6:      NWFS1.Home    Wed Aug 18 18:44:41 1999
7:      USER1         Wed Aug 18 11:10:21 1999
8:      ADMIN         Sun Aug 15 23:10:36 1999
```

The *slist* Command

The slist command lists the servers your workstation sees on the network. The following is the command format:

```
slist [ pattern ]
```

Also look at this example:

```
slist
```

The following is sample output from the slist command:

```
Known NetWare File Servers    Network     Node Address
NWFS1                         84123001    000000000001
```

The *nprint* Command

The nprint command is used to submit print jobs to a NetWare print queue. The command format is as follows:

```
nprint [-S server] [-h] [-U user name] [-P password ¦ -n] [-C] [-q queue name]
[-d job description] [-p path name] [-b banner name] [-f file name in banner]
[-l lines] [-r rows] [-c copies] [-t tab size] [-T] [-N] [-F form number] file
```

Look at this example:

```
nprint –S nwfs1 –U user.context –q HP4SI_QUEUE myoutputfile.hp4
```

The *nwfsinfo* Command

The nwfsinfo command gives you information about a NetWare file server. It is useful for determining whether you need to use NDS-style credentials or bindery-style credentials.

The following is the command format:

```
nwfsinfo [-h] [-S server] [-t] [-i] [-d]
```

Here's an example:

```
nwfsinfo -S nwfs1 -tid

Wed Aug 18 20:17:29 1999
Fileservername    NWFS1
Version    4.11 Revision A
Max. connections    21
Currently in use    3
Peak connections    3
Max. volumes    255
SFTLevel    2
TTSLevel    1
Accountversion    1
Queueversion    1
Printversion    0
Virt.Consolvers.    1
RestrictionLevel    1
    Novell
    NetWare 4.11
    August 22, 1996
    (c)  Copyright 1983-1996 Novell Inc.
    All Rights Reserved.
    Patent Pending - Novell Inc.
```

The *ipx_interface* Command

This command is used to configure IPX network interfaces on the system. The following is the command format:

```
ipx_interface add [-p] device frame_type [network number]
            ipx_interface del device frame_type
            ipx_interface delall
            ipx_interface check device frame_type
            ipx_interface help
```

Here's an example:

```
ipx_interface add eth0 802.2
```

Future Developments

Development of further options to connect Linux workstations into a NetWare network is moving forward at a rapid pace. Several Linux distributions include utilities from various vendors, including the base IPX connectivity components that were developed by Caldera.

In 1999, Novell and Red Hat Software announced a partnership in which Novell invested in Red Hat to further the development of NetWare-compatible connectivity options in Linux. The first fruits of those efforts are to be available in early 2000 with the release of NDS for Linux, a version of NDS that will run natively on Linux as well as integrating Linux authentication through the use of a PAM directly into NDS. For this to happen, other things are also necessary, such as the following:

- A fully developed NetWare client for Linux
- Full NCP support over IPX or TCP/IP

In addition, you may see the following enhancements:

- Enhancement of utilities to support NDS-based queue printing, as well as newer print services from Novell, such as Novell Distributed Printing Services (NDPS) and Novell Enterprise Printing Services (NEPS)
- Creation of management tools to enable you to directly administer NDS from a Linux workstation

With NDS, many features currently available on Windows platforms only may be developed, and with an open API set as well as LDAP v3 compatibility, Linux could certainly emerge as a strong alternative to existing network desktops. ●

## CHAPTER 30

Configuring the Apache Web Server

by Duane Hellums and Neal S. Jamison

In this chapter

The World Wide Web, Apache, and Red Hat Linux

The World Wide Web has become by far the most popular service available on the Internet. Many individuals are taking to the Web to gather information, search for jobs, shop, and even trade stocks. Businesses are flocking to the Web to meet increasing consumer demand. They also are creating intranets that revolve around Web servers and browsers as a standard publishing forum for many types of multimedia documents.

Red Hat Linux 6.0 comes standard with one of the most powerful, secure, and widely installed Web servers on the Internet, the Apache Hypertext Transfer Protocol (HTTP) server. According to the most recent Web server study performed by Netcraft, the Apache Web server accounts for 55% of the total number of Web servers on the Internet—so you know you're running in good company when you use it. This chapter instructs you on installing, configuring, and running Apache on Red Hat Linux 6.0.

Understanding Web Server Terminology

The World Wide Web works largely because of a TCP/IP networking protocol called the Hypertext Transfer Protocol (HTTP). HTTP is a request/response service that allows clients (browsers) and Web servers to exchange information. A Web server is a software program that listens for requests from a browser and provides data in HTML format via HTTP. On Red Hat Linux 6.0, as well as most Linux and UNIX servers, the server process or daemon is known as httpd. A typical HTTP session works as follows:

- The browser, such as Netscape Communicator or lynx on Linux, connects to the server.
- The browser requests a file or some other information when a Web server points to or clicks on a hypertext link.
- The server responds by providing the requested information, then dropping the connection.

By default, HTTP runs on TCP well-known port 80 (this convention provides a shared understanding between clients and servers where certain channels of service, such as HTTP, will be). Of course, you can change this setting to allow httpd to run on another, nonstandard port such as 8080; however, your browser will have to be aware of this change and be configured properly to request services from that port. The well-known port associated with your WWW or HTTP services is specified and controlled in the /etc/services file.

When you first launch Netscape Communicator, it will take you to Netscape's home page, if you're connected, or to a local file on your hard drive. In the latter case, this should not be a sign that your local Web server is running properly. The file is being viewed as if it were in a read-only editor and is not being sent through your Web server software, Apache. To check and make sure it is working, enter http://localhost/ (you can replace localhost with your computer name, DNS name, or IP address also). You should see a message saying that your Apache installation was successful.

This following section explains a few Web server-related terms that you will see either later in this chapter or in other Red Hat Linux or Apache Web server documentation.

Web Server

A Web server is a computer that serves documents (Web pages) over the Internet using the HTTP protocol. The term *Web server* can be used to refer to the computer (a combination of hardware, operating system, and Web server application software) or to the software package itself (the Apache Web server). In addition to Apache, you can download other Web servers for Linux off the Internet and try them out.

Browser

A browser is the client program of the Web. The most common browsers for Linux include Lynx (`/usr/bin/lynx`) and Netscape Communicator (`/usr/bin/netscape-communicator`) or Navigator (`/usr/bin/netscape-navigator`). For Windows PCs, you are most likely to see Microsoft Internet Explorer and the previously mentioned Netscape products.

URL

A URL is the uniform resource locator or address used to reference Web pages and other Internet objects and resources, such as ftp files or Telnet servers. An example of a valid URL is `http://www.apache.org/`. (See the "What Exactly is a URL?" note later in this chapter for more information.)

Server Root

A server root is the location on the computer where the Web server stores its logs and configuration files, by default—for Red Hat Linux 6.0, this is the `/etc/httpd` directory. The Apache `httpd` server executable itself is located in `/usr/sbin`.

Document Root

A document root is the top location on the Web server where all the content and user-produced files are located. This is the directory where the Apache Web server looks for all the files it sends to browsers. In the example used previously, `http://localhost/`, Apache will look in `/home/httpd/` (by default) for a file called `index.html`. Thus if you enter `http://localhost/index.html` in your browser's address box, the file you will receive actually came from `/home/httpd/index.html`. If this file is not there and you haven't made any configuration changes to your Web server, Apache will send a directory listing of `/home/httpd`, allowing people to see all the files located in the document root directory.

Port

TCP/IP services use ports to make connections and pass information. By default, HTTP uses port 80, although it can be configured to use any port number between 0 and 65535. Other common ports are: Telnet (23), SMTP email (25), and FTP (21). If you were to run your Apache Web server on a different port, 8080 for example, you would have to access it using a slightly different URL, `http://localhost:8080/`.

Virtual Host (or Virtual Server)

Most Web servers have the capability to represent more than one domain. This is done using the concept of virtual hosts, in which one Web server can serve multiple sites. Virtual hosts are commonly used by Internet service providers (ISPs) as a low-cost alternative to having a separate Web server for every customer. This is a more advanced topic that you probably will never have to worry about, however.

Secure Sockets Layer (SSL)

This is a protocol developed by Netscape to allow data to be sent over the Web securely. SSL uses public-key technology to encrypt the data passed over the connection. When you are using Netscape Navigator with an SSL link, you will see a small yellow lock symbol on the bottom corner of your browser window. Apache Web servers support SSL technology, but this is also an area that most casual users of Linux will never need to use (on the server side only; you will need it supported on the browser side).

MIME (Multipurpose Internet Mail Extensions)

Multipurpose Internet Mail Extensions (MIME) allows Web servers and browsers to exchange files that are not in HTML or ASCII format, such as Portable Document Format files, graphics images, sound files, and video clips. This enhances recognition of your data by systems at both ends of the link and enables your operating system to determine which application should be launched for you to view or modify the file in its native format.

What Exactly Is a URL?

The Web uses an addressing schema known as the Uniform Resource Locator (URL) to identify Web pages and other resources.

Consider a sample URL:

`http://www.apache.org/docs/index.html`

This URL, which would take you to the Apache Group's documentation page, is broken down into the following segments (separated by double or single dashes, as appropriate):

- Protocol: HTTP
- Domain Name: `www.apache.org`

- Directory: `docs` (Note that sites don't need to have directories; they can also serve files off the root server based on the domain name alone; you might also see a directory with a ~ mark in it, such as `~jones`, which is usually a virtual server belonging to a user's login account, in this case somebody named Jones.)

- File: `index.html` (Note: Depending on your individual browser and server configurations, you might not need to explicitly reference the root Web site document because it is normally assumed to be the default `index.html` or `default.htm` anyway.)

Obtaining, Installing, and Configuring Apache

Most distributions of Linux, including the Red Hat Linux 6.0 CD, include the Apache Web server with the software packages bundled with the operating system. Unless you specify otherwise, it is probably installed on your machine and running already. You can find out by typing `ps -ef ¦ grep httpd` (you should see several instances of this process, which is normal because the server must listen for requests coming from many different people simultaneously). You also can type `/etc/rc.d/init.d/httpd status`.

Keep in mind that you don't always have to upgrade. The benefit of upgrading is to get bug fixes and possibly security patches—you can always check out the version description (CHANGES file on Apache's Web site) to determine what changed and whether it's significant enough for you to take action now or wait for a future release that really gives you something you want or need.

However, you might decide that you want to use a newer version of Apache and upgrade at some point. You should be able to find a newer version of Apache on the Web or another CD you have purchased (or borrowed). Your best bet is to download the most current Apache RPM from `http://www.redhat.com/` (see Chapter 11, "Installing and Managing RPM Packages," especially the section on Webfind [Rpmfind], which enables you to upgrade a package over the Internet). Apache is currently distributing and supporting version 1.3.9; previous versions include 1.3.1 and 1.3.6. If you download from Red Hat or one of its mirrors, you are assured of getting an RPM package, which is considerably easier to install than a `.tar`, `.gz` or `.tgz` file.

However, you might not be able to download the newest version of Apache from Red Hat. Red Hat obviously would be a little behind the power curve on distribution because it must get the software itself, optimize and test it for Red Hat, and prepare RPM packages for distribution on its own home page, CDs, and Internet mirrors.

The good news is that by sticking with Red Hat distributions of Apache you can be assured that the version in question has been extensively and sufficiently tested with Red Hat to ensure it functions properly. Most importantly, you will get a package, including appropriately modified configuration files that are geared specifically toward Red Hat Linux. Many operating systems use different default directories for Web content and Apache server configuration files, for example. You should deviate from the norm and install from another site only if you know exactly what you are doing and can live with the risks involved (typically, this means a high-end user of Linux, such as an Internet service provider, not a normal user).

If you choose to upgrade, there are a few things you should consider first:

- **Disk space**—You will need at least 12MB of temporary disk space. After installation, Apache will require approximately 3MB of space, plus whatever space is required to store your Web pages (this can be anywhere from 2MB to 5MB for a small personal site, to several hundred megabytes or more than 1GB for larger, more complicated sites).

- **Precompiled Apache**—Unfortunately, software applications normally have to be compiled from source code into a series of executables that will work with each and every operating system version that a company wants to support. Often, they will just make the source code available and leave it up to you to compile it. Fortunately, someone usually compiles it for the more popular operating systems, such as Linux, Sun Solaris, HP UNIX, and even Windows and Windows NT. The Red Hat Linux 6.0 CD includes a preconfigured, precompiled Apache Web server that is installed, configured, and turned on by default. You should avoid downloading precompiled versions of Apache from the Internet because of security reasons as well as possible compatibility problems with Red Hat Linux server configurations.

- **ANSI C compiler**—If you want to go the hard route and customize, optimize, and compile a specialized version of Apache for your Red Hat system, you will need to have an ANSI C compiler installed and properly configured (available in the GnoRPM's Development category; see Chapter 11). You also might need to recompile Apache (but not always) if you want to use FrontPage Server Extensions on your Linux Apache server (to facilitate Web site development and management with Windows clients; see Chapter 36, "Configuring Microsoft FrontPage Server Extensions"). The GNU C compiler is recommended and included with the Red Hat Linux CD. See http://www.gnu.org/ to obtain the most recent copy of GCC, if yours is outdated (but this probably will not be necessary).

Downloading Apache Source Code

As mentioned previously, you can download the most recent version of Apache from http://www.redhat.com/ (the preferred method) or directly from the main Apache site (http://www.apache.org/) or any of its mirror sites (which duplicate this service and reduce network bottlenecks by providing copies of the application in several places).

TIP It will be faster to download from a mirror site that is geographically close to you. See `http://www.redhat.com/mirrors.html/` or `http://www.apache.org/mirrors/` for a list of mirror sites. For Red Hat sites, the files will be RPM packages (with filenames beginning with apache) stored in a subdirectory such as `/i386/RedHat/RPMS/` (replace i386 with Sparc or Alpha for other platforms).

If you are downloading non-Red Hat Linux versions of Apache, you will need to decide whether you want to download the full source code to compile yourself or whether you want to skip the compilation step and download the executable files (binaries) and plain-text configuration files (but still get a copy of the source code in case you ever want or need it). Once again, however, it is recommended that you use only Apache RPM packages to prevent conflicts with your installed version of Linux.

NOTE If you absolutely feel you must download a precompiled binary, make sure that you do so from the official Apache site or one of its mirrors. Other binaries out there might be improperly compiled and might even contain security holes or malicious logic that can damage your system and data. ▨

TIP Files with a `.md5` suffix can be used in conjunction with your downloaded file to ensure that you are getting the actual package as intended by the author. This is especially important if you are downloading a precompiled binary. To do this after you download both files, look at the output you receive when you run the following command (the first line is command; the second is output):

```
# md5sum apache_1.3.9.gz
b4114ed78f296bfe424c4ba05dccc643  apache_1.3.6.tar.gz
```

This gives you (on the left) a unique md5 fingerprint or checksum value for this file, based on a complicated mathematical calculation and hash of all the information in the file. Luckily for you, the author of the compilation did the same thing on her end and included the result in the .mdf file for you to compare your results. If they are the same, everything is fine. If they differ, you should attempt the download again.

TIP Some administrators compile an application like this in a directory named after the specific version number, and then create a symbolic link to it (using the ln command) from the standard directory path name. This facilitates upgrading, testing, and recovery at a later date when you can just change the link back and forth between versions.

Downloading Precompiled Apache

As mentioned before, you might prefer to download a precompiled binary and save yourself the added headaches of configuration, compilation, and possibly even the installation of the necessary GNU compiler packages. The Red Hat Apache RPM package includes an executable precompiled for Red Hat Linux. You first should check `http://www.redhat.com/` and see if they have a more current version of Apache that you might want or need. If they do, you either can ftp it down to your Linux system manually or use GnoRPM's Webfind (Rpmfind) feature to download, install, or upgrade it (all in one simple process).

TIP Make sure you have stopped your Apache Web server before you attempt a GnoRPM installation or upgrade. Most installation packages can't overwrite files that are loaded and currently running in memory. Consult the "Starting and Stopping Apache" section of this chapter on how to do this.

Configuring Apache

To get your server up and running initially, Apache configuration files need very little editing, if any at all. Unfortunately, that doesn't mean that you should skip this section and head straight for the instructions for starting and stopping the Apache Web server, either—make sure that you read through this part and take any necessary actions based on your particular environment. Specifically, there are some security aspects of running and configuring Apache that you must be aware of and possibly take action to prevent.

Some of the configuration items, or server directives, that might need editing are detailed in the following sections. The configuration files are very well documented, and you should be able to identify the directives that need to be changed by reading through the files. Refer to http://www.apache.org/docs/ for more information on configuring Apache.

Historically, Apache has used three primary configuration files (which are all located in /etc/httpd/conf on Red Hat Linux 6.0; note that they are located in /usr/local/apache/conf on some other distributions of Linux, though):

- **access.conf**—Controls access to your Web server's resources
- **httpd.conf**—Is the primary configuration file and tells Apache how to run
- **srm.conf**—Specifies which resources you want to offer on your site

N O T E In the most recent version of Apache, the functionality of all three configuration files are collapsed into one file: httpd.conf (even though all three configuration files are still stored on your system). This is in line with the expectations of other HTTP utilities, such as the FrontPage Server Extensions for UNIX (see Chapter 36). ▦

Configuring Basic Apache Options

The httpd.conf file contains the directives that tell Apache how to run. The following are some of the directives that might need your attention:

- **ServerName**—This is the name of your Web server. Example:
  ServerName www.mydomain.com.
- **ServerType**—Options are standalone or inetd. A standalone server runs all the time. A ServerType of inetd causes the server to run only when it is requested. Standalone is recommended for best performance. Example: ServerType standalone.

- **Port**—By default, HTTP servers run on port 80. However, you might want to run your server on a nonstandard port. One reason to do so would be to hide your server from the public. If you were to run your server on a nonstandard port—say, 1234 or 8080—your users would need to know the port and include it in the URL to access your pages. Valid port numbers are 0–65535, although typically the first 1024 are reserved. Example: `Port 80`.

- **User**—Like other Linux processes, the `httpd` process must belong to someone while it executes. This variable specifies which username will be used as the owner of the running Apache `httpd` processes. There are security implications to this directive, as Apache will take on the privileges of its controlling user. Many UNIX systems have a user called nobody just for this purpose. If your system does not have an unprivileged user, you should create one. Example: `User nobody`.

- **ServerAdmin**—This enables you to specify a username where mail containing server-specific error messages can be sent. This value is normally set to the administrative user or an appropriate alias (for example, a user named jones may actually receive system email sent to root, admin, or webmaster. (Assuming this account has been created. This is a good practice because it allows you to assign such responsibilities to a certain person, and you also can tell from the addressee email address who the email was intended for, in this case where the problem is.) Apache will send mail to this user in the event of any problems. Example: `ServerAdmin root`.

- **ServerRoot**—This is the root directory of the Apache installation. All your configuration files and log files will be created (or symbolically linked) here. Example: `ServerRoot /etc/httpd`.

- **ErrorLog**—This is the location and name of the log file where error messages will be stored (relative to the ServerRoot directory). It is a valuable resource when you are trying to debug server problems or security violations. Example: `ErrorLog logs/error_log` (note that this creates the file `/etc/httpd/logs/error_log` because the `ErrorLog` value is appended to the `ServerRoot` value).

- **TransferLog**—This is the location (relative to the ServerRoot directory) and name of the log that records all access to your server and requests for file transfers, along with the results of the request. Example: `TransferLog logs/access_log` (again, this files is actually stored as `/etc/httpd/logs/access_log`).

- **Timeout**—This specifies the length of time (in seconds) that the Web server will wait for a browser to respond before assuming that the connection is dead. The default value is 300 seconds. Example: `Timeout 300`.

Configuring Apache Resources Options

The following directives are used to control Apache's resources. Historically, they were contained in the `srm.conf` file, although newer releases of Apache combine them all in `httpd.conf`. Some of the more commonly modified directives are as follows:

- **DocumentRoot**—This is the root directory of your Web server's documentation tree. Example: `DocumentRoot /home/httpd/html`.

- **DirectoryIndex**—If a user requests a URL from your server that includes only a directory path and no filename, the Web server will attempt to serve a document that matches DirectoryIndex. For example, loading `http://www.apache.org/` results in the file `index.html` being served to your browser. Example: `DirectoryIndex index.html index.htm`.

- **IndexIgnore**—By default, if a user requests a URL from your server that ends in a valid directory path that has no `index.html` file available, the Web server will present the user with a listing of files in that directory to choose from, sort of like a menu. There usually are files there that you don't want displayed (such as `.htaccess` or `README` files). The server will not display files set in the IndexIgnore directive. This directive makes extensive use of wildcards, as you can see from the defaults in this example: `IndexIgnore .??* *~ *# HEADER* README* RCS CVS`.

Configuring Apache Access Options

The `access.conf` file is historically where you would set up access rules to your entire Web server or parts thereof. As with the other files, recent releases of Apache also include these directives in the `httpd.conf` file. The importance of this section can't be stressed enough because this is where you have the opportunity to either close up all your security holes or leave your system wide open to hackers, competitors, disgruntled employees, and so on.

You should pay very close attention when making changes to the security and access permissions for your Web server's directories and files. If you're not careful, you inadvertently could allow visitors to your site to navigate through your system, viewing or editing files they should not be able to, or executing files they should not be executing (see the Caution).

The access rules are broken into chunks or containers where you can place specific information for different resources available on the Web server. For example, consider the following blocks taken from the default Apache installation on Red Hat Linux:

```
<Directory />
    Options None
    AllowOverride None
</Directory>
```

This block is similar to what you might find in a typical `access.conf` file. The `<Directory />` opens the container. Every directive in the file before a `</Directory>` will apply to the directory `/`. Here the scene is set for very limited access permissions for the entire file system. Then you can open up those parts of your file system that you need to for your Web site. The `Options None` directive means that there are no special permissions for the file system (discussed in other blocks). The `AllowOverride None` directive restricts all users from being able to create `.htaccess` files (used for user-specific configurations and access restrictions) that might override the systemwide settings stored in the `/etc/httpd/conf` directory. This assures you than the site operates according to the rules you set up—and *only* to the rules you set up. If you are the only site administrator this is a moot issue, but it is important when there are multiple Webmasters or administrators to deal with.

```
<Directory /home/httpd/html>
    Options Indexes Includes FollowSymLinks
    AllowOverride None
</Directory>
```

With this block the Webmaster controls the permissions of the Web server itself (as it relates to content, anyway), and all underlying files and directories off the `DocumentRoot` directory. Any time you use any of these three options, you should know the potential impact and make sure you don't create any security problems for yourself. Specifically, the `Options` line includes the following capabilities for this Web site:

- **`Indexes`**—Visitors to this site will receive a directory listing of files if they point to a directory that doesn't have a default `index.html` home page, for example. Remove this reference, save the configuration file, and restart the Apache Web server if you want to remove this capability and tighten up security a bit.

- **`Includes`**—Web pages can contain Include commands that imbed one file in another seamlessly during a file transfer to the browser. Some people like to remove this capability because under certain circumstances it can be exploited by hackers.

- **`FollowSymLinks`**—This option tells the Web server that it should feel free to navigate around the file system if it encounters a symbolic link. Because the default configuration file locks down everything from the root directory (/) on, this option listed here only allows visitors to follow symbolic links within the `DocumentRoot` directory (`/home/httpd/html`). Without the / restriction, however, you could have a user on your system create a link to your hard drive, CD-ROM, or printer and allow anyone on the Internet to access it.

```
<Directory /home/httpd/cgi-bin>
    AllowOverride None
    Options ExecCGI
</Directory>
```

In this block for the `cgi-bin` directory, you see a new option: ExecCGI. This directive must be present in any block where you want a visitor to be allowed to execute a CGI executable program. Obviously, you should be worried anytime you think about someone from the Internet executing a program on your server; however, without such programs, there would be very little interactivity, database connectivity, and all the cool tools that people want to provide to site visitors. The only secure server is one locked in a safe and unplugged, and this is not an appetizing option. Basically then, the best thing to do is check your configuration file often and make sure these directives are used only where appropriate and with a level of risk you can accept (for example, you might not have much to fear if your Apache Web server is running on an Intranet only).

```
<Directory /usr/doc>
    order deny, allow
    deny from all
    allow from localhost
    options Indexes FollowSymLinks
</Directory>
```

Here with the /usr/doc directory you see the ability of the Webmaster or administrator to allow explicit access of a limited number of hosts and users to resources located outside the Web server's normal scope. This particular block adds the concept of machine-specific access restrictions. Order deny, allow tells the Apache server to apply any deny rules first, then the allow rules. Deny from all tells the server to deny access to this directory by default. Allow from localhost tells the server that, even though it is restricting access to everyone else, it should allow anyone logged into the localhost machine to access this directory (where Web-enabled user documentation is located).

CAUTION

Be very careful about allowing symbolic links from your Web server. Your Webmaster or system administrator should want to keep tight control over which files are able to be accessed from the outside world. If you allow symbolic links, you potentially open up your entire file system to any hacker who wants to exploit any weakness of your server or the files it is serving to external browsers. There are few reasons to actually provide symbolic link capability, but many different reasons (all scary) why you would not want to allow them. If you allow symbolic links, you will have to worry about the permissions and ownerships of every file on your system, instead of just the files and directories in /user/httpd/html.

You might want to consider testing these important configuration settings locally (while not connected to the Internet) just to make sure there are no unwanted security holes. The Apache documentation includes additional information on using access.conf to control access to your site. If you have a PC with Microsoft FrontPage on it, you also can install the FrontPage Server Extensions against your root Apache Web and any subwebs you create (see Chapter 36). This allows you to further control the security of your Apache Web site.

Starting and Stopping Apache

Several methods of starting and stopping Apache exist, depending on your situation. The long-term solution is to use the system startup files to launch Apache every time you boot up. This is the way Red Hat Linux works out of the box, with /usr/sbin/httpd being launched on bootup (for certain boot modes or runlevels, anyway, if configured to do so) from scripts in the /etc/rc.d/init.d/ directory. However, you don't want to go to all this trouble before you even confirm that Apache is configured and operating properly. This brings on the second method, which involves manually launching the Apache Web server, which is fine on a one-time or infrequent basis. You might have to use the manual method of stopping the Web

server, however, such as when you run into a problem and need to bring the server down
without rebooting or changing init system run levels.

Starting and Stopping Apache Manually

You have several options that you can use to start, stop, and bounce the Apache server. You
can also check the status of any currently running `httpd` process. To perform these actions,
do the following:

Part
V

Ch
30

1. To check the status of your Apache Web server, type `/etc/rc.d/init.d/httpd status`.
   You should see a list of process ID numbers or be told that the server is not running.
   You will see a half dozen or so instances of `httpd`, depending on your configuration.

2. To start your Apache Web Server, type `/etc/rc.d/init.d/httpd start`. You should
   receive a status line saying that the server was started.

3. To bounce the server (bring it down and then back up again with fresh processes),
   type `/etc/rc.d/init.d/httpd restart`. You should see confirmation of the server
   shutting down and then starting back up again.

4. To totally stop the Apache Web server, type `/etc/rc.d/init.d/httpd stop`. The command should tell you that the server is no longer running.

To test your handiwork, using your Lynx or Netscape Communicator Web browser on Linux,
provide a URL pointing to your newly installed Web server to make sure it is working properly. Use the ServerName URL you created, such as `http://www.yourdomain.com/`, or the
default `http://localhost/`. If Apache is properly configured and running, you will see an
Apache test page saying that your content is available for use on the Apache Web server.

Starting Apache Automatically

You can use the `rc.d` system to automatically start Apache for you. This will prevent you from
forgetting to launch it after a reboot, for instance. Commercial and business sites should
always seek this simple, long-term solution. Red Hat Linux 6.0 provides one form of this service via the `/etc/rc.d/init.d/httpd` utility (which also can be used with the `start` and `stop`
options). To automate this process, perform the following steps:

1. Select System, Control Panel from the main GNOME panel menu.

2. Click the Runlevel Editor button. You should see the SYSV Runlevel Manager window,
   which consists of a configuration window on the left and four columns numbered 2–5
   on the right. These last four columns equate to the different boot modes (3 is networked, non-graphical; 5 is networked and graphical; 1 is single user, which doesn't
   have any nonessential daemons running, so doesn't get its own column). If you are running a graphical networked workstation or server (boot mode 5), you will want to get
   `httpd` in column number 5 (it might already be there; you'll have to scroll through to
   see if it is).

3. If `httpd` is not listed in the boot mode category that you want (column 5), click httpd in the Available section of column 1 to select it, and then click Add. You will see a pop-up window that asks you if you want to start or stop `httpd` and in which mode.

4. In this example, you want to add it to mode 5, so click Start httpd and 5, then the Done button.

5. You will be asked where you want to insert the process (in this case 85, which is the default for `httpd`). Click Add to select the default. This should return you to the Runlevel Manager window and pop httpd daemon into column 5, meaning that it will now forever run whenever you boot up into runlevel mode 5. Repeat this process if you want the Apache Web server to run in other modes, such as 3 and 4.

N O T E   If you're interested in knowing what this entire process did, it basically created a link called `S85httpd` in the `/etc/rc.d/rc5.d` directory to `/etc/rc.d/rc.init/httpd`, which by default is executed during bootup (in runlevel 5) with the `start` option, similar to the way you launch the Apache server manually. You can find out more about the Linux runlevels and bootup process by typing `man init` at a command line. ■

Troubleshooting Apache

You Web server might act up even if you haven't made any configuration changes or performed maintenance on your Web server recently (backing up from tape, for example). If it does, your first step should be to look on the console and in the Web server log files (`/etc/httpd/logs`) for any error messages, especially in `/etc/httpd/logs/error_log`. Don't forget to check for email in the account specific by ServerAdmin; Apache might have sent administrative mail to this account stating the problem it encountered. This might give you a hint where the problem is located. If you don't find anything out of the ordinary, try bouncing the Web server once or twice to see if that clears it up. This means that you should stop the `httpd` daemon and restart it again.

If this doesn't work, your next step should be rebooting the PC entirely, if you can afford to do so (without knocking users off or bringing down other critical processes, such as ftp servers). Sometimes a process unknowingly can go stale or become a ghost, and rebooting starts them all up again properly. This is especially true in a multiuser, multitasking, networked environment where many processes are running and a system is often up for weeks or months without a break.

If you just performed an Apache installation, try to rule out networking and domain name problems before you spend too much time tinkering with your Apache configuration files and running processes or daemons. For example, if you created www.yourdomain.com and can't seem to access it, try pinging www.yourdomain.com and make sure that the name-to-IP address resolution is functioning properly. You don't want to waste hours playing with Apache just to find out that your DNS server is acting up (causing you to go back and reintroduce all the configuration changes you just removed from Apache trying to fix the "problem"). Don't laugh—it happens to everyone (too frequently, if you're not careful)!

If you are upgrading, you probably already have a version of Apache or another httpd server daemon or process running; you should stop any Web servers that are running, before you start installing, compiling, and configuring Apache. This will prevent any conflicts for resources such as IP port 80. If you try to install Apache to existing directories that have currently running processes or accessed files, the installation program will not be capable of writing over the files with their newer counterpart.

Part

V

Ch

30

During an upgrade, if you don't stop the currently running Web server processes, the typical result is a haphazard conglomeration of different versions (and the most important ones that are commonly in use won't be updated). As a result, if you try to start your newly installed server, you might find that you're still running old programs with new configuration files and rules, which will be hard to debug (reinstalling and configuring won't help either because you'll do the same thing over again). To reduce these conflicts, always stop the current process and any other processes that might be accessing files in directories associated with that package.

For routine system administration of your Web server and content, you should make a backup copy of any configuration files you want to modify. You also should make sure that backup copies have the same permissions and ownerships as the original file (httpd.conf and httpd.conf.bak or httpd.conf.990910 if you want to use a date to show when you modified it). In this way, you can recover quickly from changes you make by just restoring the original file if you really mess something up and can't figure out what is causing the problem. Swapping out the files and making the problem go away is a surefire way of narrowing down your problem to a configuration item in one of these files. You should also change or restore only one configuration item or file at a time, where it is possible (it isn't always). This practice also helps you debug problems more effectively.

If your domain is operating but Apache won't serve up any files, try verifying access permission within Apache and at the file system level (including ownership). You should get an error message in a log file if this happens. Unfortunately, it's easy to create a file that is owned by root that nobody else can access; it's harder to find the problem, when you can see the file and know the Web server is working. Try using ls –al all the time, regardless of whether you want the additional information for the particular problem you're working on. It's better to have too much information than not enough and possibly miss an important clue that you could see if you were getting a complete file listing. For example, some applications and utilities in an operating system don't generate the error messages they should, such as when a command or word processor tries to save a file to a floppy that has insufficient space. The file might be created, but it could have a zero length because nothing actually got copied. A long file listing (ls -al) would have shown that even though the file existed, nothing was in it.

If you're getting an obvious error message, try to determine if it's related to the operating system, the network layer, or the Apache Web server. This will help you know where to go for resolution of the problem. If you determine it to be the Web server, read over the troubleshooting and help files included with Apache's documentation. If that doesn't work, consider getting on an Internet newsgroup and posting the particulars of your problem (be as specific as necessary, including anything a technician might need to analyze the problem and track a solution). While you might not have seen the exact problem in question or know how to resolve it, odds are that of the millions of people using Apache, several have run into the same problem. You'd be surprised at how willing these people are to share their ingenuity and glory with you.

If your Apache server has stopped functioning for an extended period of time and you can't determine what the culprit is (after applying all these troubleshooting methods), you can always try reinstalling it. However, the amount of work involved here, coupled with the risk to your data, should make this a last resort. Obviously, this would require that you back up all your Web site content and your current configuration files (just in case you can use them again or need to migrate certain settings over). However, it might be the only thing that will get you up and running again. ●

Configuring Email

by Duane Hellums

In this chapter

Red Hat and Email

Since the early days of the Internet, electronic mail (email) has been the most popular online activity, accounting for the majority of the Internet traffic prior to widespread use of the World Wide Web. Staying in touch with friends and family is a driving force behind many people buying PCs for the home in the first place.

Red Hat Linux 6.0 provides all the tools and underlying technologies you need for effective email services at home and in the workplace or small office-home office (SOHO) environment. It is fairly simple to configure these email servers and clients to handle email on a multiuser machine, on the local area network (LAN), or remotely via the Internet. You can even integrate your Linux email server with mail clients on both Linux and other operating systems that support standard Internet mail protocols.

Keep in mind that there is no single correct or perfect email solution (client or server) for any operating system, including Linux. Part of the power of Linux involves having a choice, which naturally leads to many different solutions for you to choose from. The solutions discussed in this chapter are only one way of implementing email and are directed basically at the environment that the majority of readers fall into. However, some extra consideration is given to networked SOHO solutions and environments that tend to use Windows desktop machines and a Linux server. Of course, this is not meant to imply that Linux can't be used in different environments or with other operating systems.

Understanding Linux Email

Before you can correctly install and configure the proper suite of applications that you need for your particular situation, you must understand how Linux handles email. This also will help you troubleshoot mail problems that you encounter along the way.

You should be aware of three different categories of electronic mail protocols when using email on Linux or Windows. These are the Simple Mail Transport Protocol (SMTP), Post Office Protocol version 3 (POP3), and Internet Mail Access Protocol (IMAP). For each of these protocols, there are numerous server processes or daemons to choose from, as well as many different client programs.

Each of these technologies is designed for specific types of network situations, and some email clients (readers) support one, two, or all three of these protocols. The two protocols you will be most concerned with are SMTP and POP3. Regardless of which protocols you use, you also will need to understand the concept of local and spooled mail, the two main mail methodologies used by Linux.

Understanding Local Mail

If you have multiple users on your Linux workstation, each will have a mail store (sometimes called an "inbox" or "post office") named after the login name in the /var/spool/mail directory. For example, root's mail is stored in /var/spool/mail/root. This is an ASCII text flat file where mail programs append incoming mail for root. You can use any of the available Linux mailers for sending and receiving local mail, including the following:

- mail
- pine
- elm
- kmail
- Netscape Messenger

You might wonder how Linux defines local mail versus other types of mail. Basically, if you add a local Linux account name to the To: or CC: line of any of these mailers, they will treat this as local mail and just append the message to the appropriate account mail store. These mailers will also treat it as local mail if you add the local machine host and domain names. For example, the default host and domain name for a workstation freshly loaded with Linux is localhost and localdomain, respectively. Your mailers will handle mail sent to root, root@localhost, and root@localhost.localdomain as local mail. Depending on the program you use and your current system configuration, these programs will use either SMTP directly or hand your mail off to the sendmail program.

You also can use these same mail readers to read your local mail messages. When you first run the pine and elm programs, they create subdirectories in your Linux home directory (mail and Mail, respectively) where you have the option of moving your local mail after reading it. This is also where the programs store such things as configuration settings, alias information, draft messages, sent messages, and named folders for you to categorize, arrange, and store your incoming mail. The mail program also can leave mail in the message store or move it to the user's home directory, where it is stored in a file called mbox (short for mailbox). These three programs are configured by default to check the /var/spool/mail directory for incoming mail, stored by user name.

TIP

You should use kmail or Netscape Messenger as your local and Internet mail program because of their graphical nature. If you choose to use a text-based program for some reason, however, pine is recommended over elm or mail. Pine has a nicer, menu-based interface and is much easier to use than the other programs.

CAUTION

Elm stores your email in a directory with the same name as that used by kmail. If you want to use kmail but have used elm previously, you will have to remove this directory.

Part

V

Ch

31

As you can see, local mail is fairly limited, although it fits in well with certain multiuser system requirements. It can be used quite effectively in situations where a single server supports multiple users who log in simultaneously from text-based terminals through a multiport serial card on the server. It can even be used in a distributed, network environment with other Linux or UNIX workstations using shared Network File System (NFS) directories on the mail server. Individual users can "mount" their home or mail directory on another workstation and can access local mail as if logged in directly on to the mail server PC.

However, most users will be more interested in using Internet mail to exchange email with people anywhere in the world, regardless of whether those other people have a local account. As a result, this chapter focuses on those mail programs that can handle both local and Internet mail protocols (specifically kmail and Netscape Messenger, discussed later). If you want to know more about local mail capabilities, there is plentiful information in the man and other documentation pages for programs such as sendmail, mail, pine, and elm.

Understanding Spooled Mail

The previous paragraphs looked at how Linux handles mail addressed to local account users. What happens, though, when you address mail to an Internet address that is controlled by an external mail server, such as yahoo.com or another ISP? This is where spooled mail comes into play.

I have several accounts on my local Linux workstation, so I can send local mail to duane, hellums, or root (and aliases such as webmaster). I can even include the default host and domain names @localhost or @localhost.localdomain (or @barracuda, because I renamed my Linux host when I configured networking) in the e-mail address. My Linux PC handles all those e-mail services. So, what happens when I tell my email client to send mail to my account at hellums@yahoo.com?

If I am connected and logged in directly to the Internet and have routing and domain name services configured correctly, some mailers can use SMTP to connect directly to the destination mail server in question and transfer my mail to the remote Yahoo! mail server. If I am using a mailer that doesn't support SMTP inherently, however, or if I am not connected to the Internet, the mailer needs a way to process the outgoing mail message. It does this using a spooling technique, where files are stored in an interim "queue" location and processed by another program or process, namely the sendmail daemon.

 You can use the /bin/mail program to send local and Internet mail quickly and easily from the command line. For instance, /bin/mail hellums@yahoo.com < /etc/inittab and /bin/mail root < /etc/inittab will immediately send the inittab file from a PC to a POP3 email account on Yahoo! and a local root account on a Linux workstation, respectively. You can also use cat /etc/inittab ¦ /bin/mail root. This quick messaging capability is used extensively by system daemons to inform administrators of problems. You can add such capability to any shell programs you create to help administer your system.

Understanding sendmail

The `/usr/sbin/sendmail` process or daemon is used to send and receive email using SMTP. This protocol is used primarily to exchange email directly between servers on the Internet (or intranet) that are intended to be live (TCP/IP-networked) the majority of the time. As discussed in earlier paragraphs, outgoing mail is spooled in a directory awaiting a successful connection and transmission to the destination server. Incoming mail is stored for individuals in a "repository" ("inbox" or "post office") on the live server waiting for users to read it with the appropriate client.

The sendmail daemon is used to send mail from a mail client to a mail server at a destination site where the person you are writing has an account. For instance, let's say I prepare an email on my Linux host named barracuda, addressed to my account on Yahoo! (hellums@yahoo.com). When I click on the Send button, my email client will communicate with sendmail to store my outgoing file in a spool directory (`/var/spool/mqueue`). sendmail will attempt to connect and transfer my file to the SMTP daemon running on Yahoo!'s mail server (and listening by default to standard Internet Protocol [IP] port number 25). When Linux mail servers running sendmail receive Internet email, they store the incoming mail in user files under `/var/spool/mail`. Users with accounts on that system then can either use a local or POP3 mail reader to read their mail.

Configuring sendmail for different environments is tricky, complicated, and outside the scope of this chapter; entire books are dedicated to configuration of sendmail. Luckily, the default configuration meets most requirements. If you need to change your sendmail configuration, the configuration file is stored in `/etc/sendmail.cf`. If possible, you should change settings using the servers section of `linuxconf`.

> **NOTE** Due to the overhead involved with repeatedly trying to transfer files in mail queues, the sendmail daemon is intended for exchanging mail between hosts that have constant connections to the Internet. The POP3 protocol was created for hosts that have intermittent connections, such as users that connect to the Internet using Point-to-Point Protocol (PPP) or that frequently power down on a LAN running a Linux server.

Basically, the sendmail daemon will continue to attempt transmission of your queued or spooled email messages at preset intervals. If the originating or destination mail server is not connected or is otherwise incapable of transferring the file for a predetermined amount of time (normally several days), sendmail will remove the queued file and send a message to the originator of the email informing of the problem. The originator will then have to ensure Internet connectivity, verify address information, and re-send the file, if necessary.

Because sendmail was designed for persistently connected hosts, Internet gurus had to come up with an alternate method of sending and receiving email messages between hosts that only occasionally connect live to the Internet. They developed two protocols dedicated to solving this particular problem, (initially) the Post Office Protocol (POP3) and (later) the Internet Mail Access Protocol (IMAP).

POP3 supports the capability to download email messages to a local machine from the Internet or an intranet mail server and (depending on the configuration) alternatively leave messages stored on the mail server. This latter capability is useful if you use multiple machines to check your email and don't want to have your email spread out over several different machines; you can configure your primary machine to download all messages and configure all other machines (such as laptops) to leave messages on the server.

IMAP provides enhanced remote email processing and management capabilities (beyond POP3). For example, you can leave your message store on an IMAP server, download only header information (useful for connections with limited bandwidth), and create subdirectories directly on the server for storing messages. Although IMAP keeps your mail consolidated and reduces the amount of bandwidth required, it requires more hard drive storage space on the server. Most Internet service providers support POP3, but only some support IMAP. For this reason, this chapter discusses POP3 primarily.

Understanding POP3

POP3 is used by client machines that connect to the Internet or an intranet mail server intermittently, such as when home users dial in after work and check for email at an ISP. It can also be used in an intranet environment where a single Linux mail server supports a group of individuals who power down their Linux workstations or Windows-based PCs at night and occasionally download their mail while they work during the day.

Keep in mind that for POP3 to work, both the mail client and the server must support it. You will need to run a POP3 server daemon on Linux and use a POP3-cabable mail client on your networked Windows or Linux hosts. Red Hat Linux 6.0 comes with efficient POP3 clients and servers. By default, the POP3 server daemon distributed with Linux listens to standard IP port number 110 for incoming mail requests. If you have elaborate security requirements and want to change this default port setting, you can do so easily in /etc/services; you will have to make corresponding configuration changes on the POP3 mail client settings, however.

When a POP3 mail client connects to a Linux POP3 server, the user must authenticate using an account name and a password, which may be stored on the client to facilitate future connections. With standard POP3 (without secure shell or any other wrapper), your password is sent using plain text—it is not encrypted in any way. The only people who should have access to this information should be you and superusers at your ISP, but it's something you should be made aware of anyway. When this process is over, all files in the local Linux message store for that person (/var/spool/mail/duane, for example) are downloaded to the client for viewing. As mentioned before, most POP3 clients enable you to leave messages on the server or to delete messages on the server only when they are deleted from the deleted items folders on the POP3 mail client.

NOTE Netscape Communicator comes with Messenger, which provides a powerful and pleasant graphical email interface that supports POP3 and IMAP. It also has built-in support for Internet newsgroups, which function very similar to email. However, Messenger can support only one POP account at a time.

If you receive email only in one Internet account, it might make sense to standardize on Netscape because this is the browser you probably will be using. However, if you receive mail in multiple Internet and intranet POP3 accounts, you should consider using the slightly more capable kmail mail client (which in many ways resembles Microsoft's Outlook Express). The kmail client also requires one third to one half the amount of memory that Netscape needs, so it is more suitable for low-end systems such as laptops. ■

Understanding IMAP

The IMAP protocol is even newer than POP3. It grew out of limitations of POP3 and the incapability of POP3 to support remote management of message stores directly on the mail server itself. For example, remote users want to be able to create subdirectories on the mail server to enable management of email messages. Using this methodology, they can always see the same mail status and environment, no matter where they log in. If you create a directory on your POP3 client, the information is stored locally, not on the server. Consolidation of mail can be a real pain if you have a laptop and a desktop that check mail on the same server.

IMAP is not supported on as many email clients as is the older POP3 protocol, and your ISP account may or may not support it. If you want or need to use IMAP email capabilities, you should consider using Netscape Messenger, which supports IMAP (kmail doesn't). On Windows clients, Microsoft Outlook Express and Outlook support IMAP also. Depending on which version of the IMAP protocol your mail server is running, IMAP will use either standard IP port number: 143 or 220.

Installing and Configuring Linux Email Servers

The sendmail daemon is installed, configured, and enabled by default with Red Hat Linux 6.0. Its operation and interaction with SMTP for local mail should be seamless and transparent to you. sendmail consists of a suite of Red Hat Package Manager files named `sendmail-8.9.3-10.i386.rpm` (executables), `sendmail-cf-8.9.3-10.i386.rpm` (configuration files), and `sendmail-doc-8.9.3-10.i386.rpm` (documentation files). For most configurations, only the executables are required. You can verify that sendmail is installed on your system by typing `rpm —qa ¦ grep sendmail` at a shell prompt or in an X Window terminal. If you do not see a confirmation of these packages, you should follow the instructions in Chapter 11, "Installing and Managing RPM Packages," to install sendmail components.

To get POP3 and IMAP server daemon support, you must install the imap-4.5-3 package. This email suite is available on this book's CD as a Red Hat Package Manager file named `imap-4.5-3.i386.rpm`. You can verify that it is installed by typing `rpm -q imap` and verifying from the output that `imap-4.5.-3` is displayed. If this IMAP/POP3 suite is not installed, follow the instructions outlined in Chapter 11 to complete the installation.

When you have IMAP and POP3 installed, it is fairly easy to configure them for operation on your system. To start these daemons, perform the following steps:

1. As root, edit the `/etc/inetd.conf` (Internet daemon configuration) file with your favorite editor or ASCII word processor.

2. Find the Pop and Imap Mail Services et al section. Uncomment (remove the hash mark in front of) the daemons that you plan to use (for example, pop2, pop3, and imap). You need to uncomment pop2 only if you expect interaction with older email clients that don't support POP3.

3. Find out what process identification number inetd is using, by typing `ps -ef ¦ grep inetd`. For this example, assume that it is PID number 360 (your PID will be different).

4. Force inetd to reload its configuration file by sending it the hang-up signal (SIGHUP) using `kill -1 360` (replace with your particular inetd PID). Alternatively, you can just reboot your machine using `shutdown -y -g0` (shell) or logout, reboot (graphically).

Installing and Configuring Linux Email Clients

There are two main Linux e-mail clients you likely will need to use: KDE mail (kmail) and Netscape Messenger. Both of these programs are available on this book's CD as `kdenetwork-1.1.1pre2.1-i386.rpm` and `netscape-communicator-4.51-3.i386.rpm`. These packages can be installed either during initial Linux installation and configuration, or later. If you have a Windows PC, you likely will be using Outlook Express for Internet mail also.

Installing kmail

The KDE mail client (kmail) is part of the KDE application suite, contained in the KDE networking package (kdenetwork). When logged in as root, you can quickly check to see if kmail is installed by typing `rpm -q kdenetwork` from a shell prompt or X terminal window and verifying the output. If you see a message saying that it is not installed, you can follow t he instructions in Chapter 11 to install kmail. The main package you need to install is `kdenetwork-1.1.1pre2.1-i386.rpm`, but if you don't have any KDE files installed, you may have to install several other packages that kmail depends on.

Installing Netscape Messenger

Netscape Messenger is included on this book's CD as part of the Netscape Communicator package (`netscape-communicator-4.51-3.i386.rpm`). It also requires the underlying

Netscape Common package (`netscape-common-4.51-3.i386.rpm`). Type `rpm -q netscape-communicator` and `rpm -q netscape-common` from a shell prompt or X terminal window to quickly verify that the Netscape packages are installed. As mentioned in the previous paragraph, refer to Chapter 11 for instructions on using GnoRPM to install these packages if they were not installed during initial installation and configuration of Red Hat Linux.

Configuring Kmail for Linux and ISP Email

You do not have to be using the KDE user interface to take advantage of some of the very useful KDE applications and tools. For instance, KDE provides a very versatile mail client that supports POP3 and local mail services. One of its biggest advantages over Netscape Messenger is that you can configure kmail for more than one POP3 and local email accounts (very useful for people that have several accounts). If you don't have more than one account, you may want to try Netscape so that you can use the same program for browsing and email. However, you may want to try kmail even if you have one account because it has a very crisp, user-friendly interface (to use and configure).

Part

V

Ch

31

> **CAUTION**
>
> Although you have to be logged in as root to install your email servers and clients, you should log in as a normal user to receive root mail (to prevent authentication problems). You can easily forward your root email to another user account by editing the `/etc/aliases` file. A configuration line should be there already for root; just uncomment the line and replace the default name with your Linux account. In my case, I used `root: duane`.

To configure kmail for receiving local and Internet email, perform the following steps:

1. From the main Gnome menu, select KDE Menus, Internet, Mail Client. This brings up the main Mail Client window. If this is your first use of kmail, it will bring you immediately to the Settings dialog. If it is not your first time, you can select File, Settings from within kmail. You will see the Identity tab pictured in Figure 31.1.

2. In the Identity tab, provide at least your Name and Email Address. Organization, Reply-To Address, and Signature File are optional. Fill in the Reply-To Address if you want email responses to come to a different server, such as your ISP's. The signature file is a text file you can include automatically in each message with your full name and title. Use an editor to create this file, and then browse from this window to select it for inclusion with each outgoing message.

3. Click the Network tab (see Figure 31.2). For typical configurations, in the Sending Mail section, click the Sendmail option and confirm or update the location of this program on your system (the default should be correct). If your Linux PC and email server are constantly connected to the Internet or intranet, then you optionally can select to use SMTP and provide the server name and IP port number.

FIG. 31.1
You can tell kmail what personal contact information should be included on each outgoing email message.

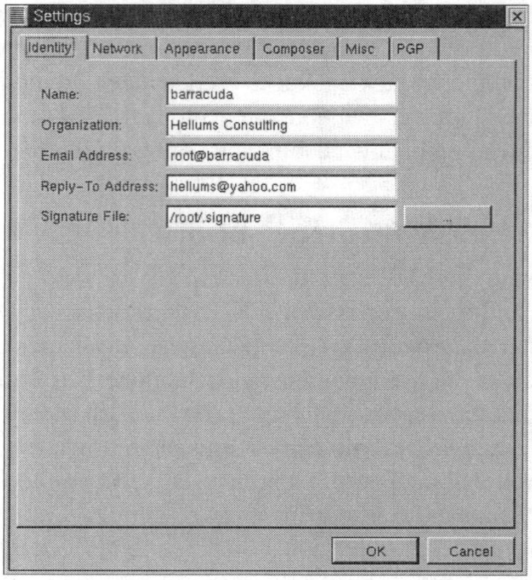

FIG. 31.2
You can choose to send email using sendmail (intermittent connections) or SMTP (persistent connections).

4. In the Incoming Mail section of the Network tab, click the Add button. The Configure Account dialog box appears, which enables you to create either a local mailbox or POP3 account (see Figure 31.3). Both types of accounts enable you to turn on Enable Interval Mail Checking, which causes your Linux system to routinely (every three minutes, by default) go out and download any new mail you've received. To create a local

account, you just have to supply the local mailbox name (`/var/spool/mail/duane` in my case) and the name of a folder you created to move your mail into.

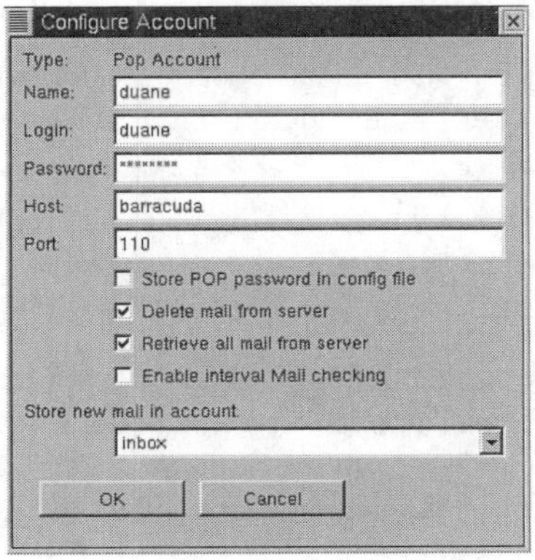

FIG. 31.3
All you basically have to provide is an account name and password, a server name, and an IP port number.

Part
V
Ch
31

5. To create a POP3 account, you will have to fill in the following information. After entering the information, click OK:

   - Enter your Login name and Password (available from your ISP or Linux system administrator).

   - Enter your Host name and Port (localhost or barracuda, and 110 in this case).

   - Check the Store POP Password in Config File option so that you don't have to enter the password each time.

   - Check the Delete Mail From Server and Retrieve All Mail From Server options to delete and retrieve all email from the POP3 server, respectively.

   - In the Store New Mail in Account option, enter the name of a local folder you created to store your POP3 mail to keep it separate from local email or other accounts.

N O T E For all intents and purposes, you have made all the changes you need at this point to send and receive mail with kmail. You should probably send a few test messages now to test your configuration; this will help you narrow down the problem before you make too many changes. Once you have the first few tabs properly configured, you can come back and modify settings in the remaining tabs. ▪

6. In the Appearance tab, you can choose from available fonts for message bodies and listings, and you can determine the layout for lists.

7. In the Composer tab, you can format the phrases used for replies, forwarded messages, and included text. You also can configure the appearance of outgoing messages, such as appending a signature file, using a Pretty Good Privacy (PGP) signature (for

encryption) and wrapping text at a specific width (80 is default). In the lowest section, you can elect to immediately send completed messages or batch process them later manually, and use either 8-bit or MIME-compliant character formatting (some email servers don't support 8-bit, so select MIME unless you have a specific reason not to).

8. In the Misc tab, choose whether you want to delete messages from your trash folder when you exit kmail, and whether kmail should send mail from the outbox folder when you manually check your email.

9. In the PGP tab, you should enter any user identity you have registered (if any) and indicate whether you want to store any pass phrase or encrypt messages sent internally to yourself (such as cc messages).

Before you start sending and receiving email, there are a few other "on-the-fly" configuration changes you can make that change kmail's behavior. Some of these are made from the main menu bar or during normal operations, not from the Settings dialog box. For example, under the View menu, you can change the way you see headers and attachments in received messages. Experiment with the different header options as you begin receiving messages until you find one you like.

From the View menu, you also can choose to view graphical attachments inline as part of your email message, as an icon that you can click on to open, or as a smart attachment, which brings up an appropriate KDE helper program when you try to open the attachment. When you send an email message, you will have to identify a signature file (if you enabled this option in earlier steps). Lastly, you will have to choose how you want to encode binary file attachments, if you try to send them. Either base64 or quoted printable format should work fine, but you may find that certain recipients have trouble receiving one or the other (in which case you should try sending the other format).

Configuring Netscape Messenger for Email

You will recognize many of the same settings in Netscape that you modified to use kmail. Bring up the main Netscape Communicator window from the main Gnome menu by clicking the Netscape icon or selecting Internet, Netscape Communicator. Then, on the main Netscape menu bar, click Edit, Preferences. To configure Messenger for sending and receiving POP3 email, perform the following steps:

1. In the Preferences window, click the Mail and Newsgroups category on the left. This brings up the Netscape Preferences window displayed in Figure 31.4. You can enter the following information:

   - **Plain Quoted Text**—Select the font and color you want to see quoted (included) text in forwarded messages, to differentiate it from regular text.

   - **Remember the Last Selected Message**—Check this button if you want Messenger to return you to the last message you were working on during your previous session.

- **Double-clicking**—Check these buttons if you want to bring up a message in a new window instead of viewing it in the current message window.

- **Confirm When Moving Folders to the Trash**—Check this box if you want to see a confirmation window every time you delete a message and send it to the trash bin.

- **The Newsgroups Menu**—Choose whether you want to see a Messenger window or the Message Center when you click the Newsgroup menu item or button.

FIG. 31.4
You can change the basic way your email and newsgroups interface behaves.

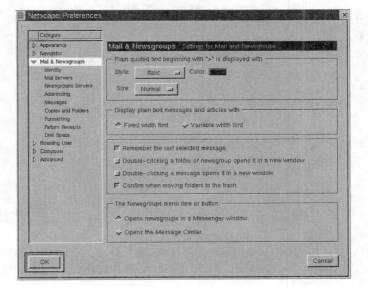

2. Click the Identity category in the left column of the Preferences window. This brings up the window pictured in Figure 31.5, where you can enter the following information:

- **Your Name**—Enter the name you want your recipients to see in the header of your messages.

- **Email Address**—Enter the email address of your POP3 server (certain POP3 servers do not allow relaying and require your actual account address here).

- **Reply-To Address**—If you are sending from an account on one machine but want recipients to reply to another email account, enter the return account here.

- **Organization**—Enter an organization or business name here, if you want.

- **Signature File**—Click Choose to select a text file that you have created with an editor to store your name, address, and any other contact information you want included at the bottom of every outgoing message.

- **Attach my Personal Card to Messages (as a vCard)**—Check this option's box and click Edit Card to enter personal information in a database record that you can attach to outgoing messages (this makes it easy for recipients to add you to their contact manager).

FIG. 31.5
Enter the information you want included in the header of each outgoing message.

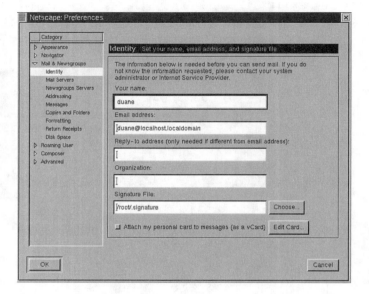

3. Click the Mail Servers category in the left column of the Preferences window. This brings up the window pictured in Figure 31.6, where you can enter the following information:

- **Incoming Mail Servers**—Click Pop and the Edit button to edit the default server, which brings up the window shown in Figure 31.6.

- **Outgoing Mail (SMTP) Server**—Enter the name of your outgoing mail server, which isn't always the same as your incoming mail server (your ISP or system administrator can provide this information) and any account information required by that system, including whether it needs Secure Socket Layer (SSL) for connections.

- **Local Mail Directory**—Use the default mail folder, or click the Choose button and select a new directory path for storage of your messages.

If you chose to add a new POP3 server or edit an existing one, you will see the Netscape popup window shown in Figure 31.7.

FIG. 31.6
You must inform
Messenger where
your mail servers and
message stores are
located.

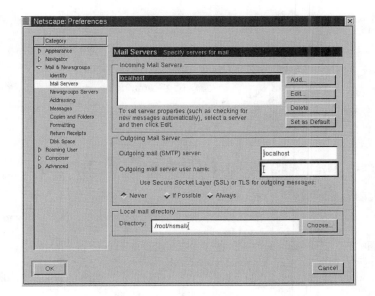

FIG. 31.7
You must modify POP-
and IMAP-specific
settings as well.

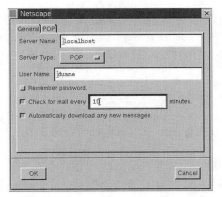

You can modify the following configuration settings in this window:

- In the General tab, enter your email server's name and your account name on that server (which may not be the same as your login account, but usually is), the type of account (POP3 or IMAP), whether you want to store your password to prevent having to enter it each time you login, and how often you want Messenger to check your server for new mail.

- In the POP tab (not visible if you pick an IMAP server), indicate whether you want the server to keep copies of messages you download or delete them when you remove them from your deleted (trash) folder; this is especially helpful if you have multiple machines, such as a combination of laptops and desktops, that access mail on the same server for an individual account (to prevent spreading messages all over the place and not being able to access them when you need them).

■ Test your configuration by selecting Communicator, Messenger from the Netscape menu bar, and then clicking the Get Msg icon or choosing File, Get New Messages on the Messenger menu bar.

Configuring Microsoft Outlook Express for Linux Email

The process for enabling Linux email on Microsoft Outlook Express is no different than the one you used to enable your Internet service provider email account. The basic information you need is the same as well: name or IP address of your incoming and outgoing mail servers, name of your email account on that server, your email account password, type of account (POP3), and the servers' IP port numbers (if different than standard). To enable Windows PCs for sending and receiving mail to your Linux POP3 account, perform the following steps:

1. Launch your Outlook Express program from Start, Programs, or wherever else you have the shortcut installed. This step may be easier if you are already online in Windows; otherwise, you'll have to indicate that you want to work offline. (These steps assume that you have Outlook Express, as well as networking, installed and configured—if not, consult your Windows documentation and accomplish whatever steps are required to achieve that.)

2. Select Tools, Accounts from the Outlook Express menu bar, and then click the Mail tab followed by Add, Mail. This brings up the Internet Connection Wizard window.

3. In the Your Name window, enter the name you want to appear in the From field of your messages and click Next.

4. In the Internet Email Address window, check the box indicating that you already have an email address you'd like to use, and type in your email address (if different than what is displayed already), followed by the Next button.

5. In the Email Server Names window, select POP3 server from the drop-down incoming mail server list, and type the incoming mail server name or IP address of your Linux PC. Keep in mind that if you do not have your Linux system name mapped on Windows to an IP address using Domain Name Services (DNS), Windows Internet Naming Services (WINS), or a local Windows hosts file, then you will have to use the IP address of your Linux server.

6. Enter the Outgoing Mail Server name in the box immediately below the incoming server name. This value will depend on whether you want to send mail to user accounts on your Linux PC or just receive mail from it. You probably want to do both, so you probably should enter the same value as the incoming mail server field. If you want to send mail through your ISP's account, however, you can also enter that (but it won't deliver mail to your Linux account unless your Linux PC has constant or frequent connections to the Internet and is configured to receive mail from the ISP). Click Next.

7. In the Internet Mail Logon window, enter your Account Name and Password for your Linux email account (this should be the same as your login name and password). If you don't want to have to enter your password every time you check your mail, check the box labeled Remember Password. Ignore the box about Secure Password Authentication because you won't be using that on Linux. Click Next.

8. In the Congratulations window, click Finish. You will be returned to the Internet Accounts window and should see your newly created account. Notice that it says Any Available in the Connection column. This parameter allows Outlook Express to check your mail over the dial-up networking account on your modem or on your local area network (LAN). Click Close.

9. To make the remaining changes, select Tools, Accounts from the menu bar again. Highlight the account you just created, and then highlight Properties.

10. In the General tab, you see your Linux mail account name (which you can change if you need to) and your user information. Add an Organization Name, if you want, and a Reply Address (if you want recipients of your Linux email to send replies to a different server than your Linux account). Uncheck the box at the bottom if you don't want the account to be checked automatically and routinely, and would rather have the account perform your mail check manually from the menu bar via Tools, Send and Receive, and your Linux account name.

11. In the Servers tab, you see that this is a POP3 server account, and the names or IP addresses of your Incoming and Outgoing mail servers, followed by your Account name and Password on your Linux email server. Ignore the authentication boxes at the bottom.

12. In the Connection tab, you now can select to force delivery over your LAN if you want. Check the Always Connect to This Account Using box, and select Local Area Network from the drop-down list.

13. In the Security tab, you have the option of identifying any Secure Email setting, such as any digital identifications you have from services such as Verisign. Because you won't be live on the Internet, you don't need to change these settings.

14. In the Advanced tab, you have the option of changing any of the standard IP port numbers for outgoing and incoming email. You don't need to do this unless you change these settings in your /etc/services file on Linux. You also can change the timeout delay in the Server Timeout slide bar—use this if your server times out before you can

Part
V

Ch
31

receive your mail (this shouldn't happen). Ignore the Sending and Break Apart message box. Some people want to download their Linux email to their Windows client but leave the messages on the Linux server for accessing locally there using Linux clients such as kmail and Netscape Messenger. If you want to do this, check the Leave a Copy of Messages on Server box in the Delivery section. This will enable two other boxes, where you optionally can elect to remove files on the Linux server after a specified number of days or when you delete them on your Windows PC (it's a nice way of keeping the accounts synchronized, actually). Check these boxes if you want to. Click OK.

At this point, your Linux email should be properly configured on Windows. You can check it by going to the menu bar and selecting Tools, Send and Receive, and the name or IP address of your Linux email server (or All, if you want to check all accounts). You may have to connect to the Internet to check other accounts.

To send mail to an account on your Linux server, click New Mail on the toolbar, or select File, New, Mail Message from the menu bar. In the From field, select the name or IP address of the Linux account you just created in Outlook Express. In the To field, enter the Linux email account name of your recipient, optionally followed by domain information (I successfully used `hellums@barracuda`, `hellums@localhost.localdomain`, and `hellums@localhost`). You can use any valid address that will be properly resolved on your Linux server based on your DNS and `/etc/hosts` file configurations.

That's all there is to it. You should be able to send and receive email with any of your local Linux server email accounts over your LAN. You may have to tweak the configuration settings you just walked through to suit your individual setting, but it will work (even though you may have to try several different settings).

Double-click the My Computer icon on your desktop and then on the Dial-up Networking folder (if this is not installed, use your Windows setup program and consult your Windows documentation to assist you in installing it—this assumes that you already have networking installed and configured also).

Troubleshooting Electronic Mail

Successful email services rely on so many things, all of which can go wrong. You must have network hardware and cabling installed and properly configured on both your PCs. You must install and configure local and dial-up networking properly on your Windows and possibly Linux PC. You must configure IP naming services properly on both PCs to enable host and domain names to be resolved to correct IP addresses. You must establish the proper user and email accounts on your Linux server, along with installing and configuring the email server software itself. Then you must properly install and configure your Linux and Windows email clients to work with your given hardware, software, and network configuration. When you think about it, that's quite a task, and you almost definitely will encounter problems along the way.

Unfortunately, there are no specific problems and solutions that can be shared with you. Much of the process involves trial and error, attention to detail, and closely following instructions here and in applicable help files. Follow a logical installation and configuration plan that builds on past successes—for example, get local Linux email working first, then Linux POP3, and then Windows email clients. This can simplify the troubleshooting process significantly because you can narrow down where the problem is.

If something doesn't work, try to use a scientific approach to solving the problem. If you can't get Windows to access your Linux POP3 account and email, then check to see if you're getting your messages on Linux before digging into your Windows settings. Check to make sure that the POP3 server is running. Reboot your PCs, if necessary, to make sure that you're working with a fresh, clean, working environment, especially if you just made multiple changes. Try to test one thing at a time before moving on and making other changes; it can be very difficult to debug a problem if you have 5 or 10 things you changed and don't know which is wreaking the havoc.

In the tenuous world of heterogeneous networking, learn to live with a few imperfections, if possible. For example, some well-hidden setting (probably in the Registry no less) on Windows causes Outlook Express to be pretty slow at checking Linux email. However, living with the workaround is more acceptable than spending huge amounts of time trying different configuration settings on all the operating systems, networks, mail servers, and mail clients.

If you purchased the commercial version of Red Hat Linux 6.0, you should try to get email installed and configured very quickly so that you can report problems during your initial technical support contract period. Surprisingly enough, the Internet newsgroups related to Linux are extremely helpful and make for some valuable reading. Subscribe to the appropriate Linux newsgroups related to the problem you're having, and read a few days' worth of messages. If you don't see an archived or new comment on your individual problem, feel free to post a message asking for help. Be as specific as possible regarding your hardware, software, operating system version, network environment, servers, clients, and other factors that people need to recommend a solution. You'll be surprised to find out that many other people may have the same problem, and someone may already have a solution. Be sure to thank such a person for taking the time to solve your problem for free, and then take a little time to appreciate the open systems movement that makes such an arrangement possible. ●

Part
V

Ch

31

Internet

Configuring Modems

by Duane Hellums

In this chapter

Understanding Modems in Linux

Modems rely on the underlying technology of serial ports for their functionality. A serial port is nothing more than a path for your computer to send data down, 1 bit at a time, as opposed to parallel ports, which can send several bits at a time. Because your computer can talk to other devices this way, people also refer to the serial port as a communication or COM port. Your PC motherboard can have from one to four serial ports (commonly referenced by their DOS terms, COM1 through COM4), unless you have a multiport serial card, which is outside the scope of this discussion. Most PCs have only one or two COM ports, depending on whether the system's mouse occupies a COM port or uses its own resource addresses.

You also might want to read the following chapters, which contain additional information related to using modems and COM ports functionally with Linux:

- Chapter 34, "Configuring Dial-In Access"
- Chapter 35, "Configuring Fax Support"
- Chapter 27, "Installing and Configuring TCP/IP Network Support"
- Chapter 33, "Configuring Access to the Internet"

Basically, modems can be used with serial ports and Linux to dial out and communicate with other modems located at your Internet service provider (ISP), on another Linux network, or on a bulletin board system (see Chapter 33). You can send and receive facsimile (fax) documents through your modem as well (see Chapter 35). Modems also can be used to provide dial-in capability to connect to your Linux PC and network from a remote location (see Chapter 34). Linux supports most standard internal and external modems with little or no problem. This is especially true if your modem uses standard settings for serial communication (COM) ports.

Physically, a PC COM port typically consists of a 9-pin male D-connector—this means that there are nine metal pins sticking out of it, and the outline looks like a capital letter D (don't confuse it with your VGA monitor connection, which is a 15-pin female D-connector). Because of the transmission overhead required and certain physical limitations, serial ports can transfer only about 12KB per second, which is roughly 100 times slower than a hard drive or a network connection.

At the logical level, your computer must have a way of differentiating between different data paths, COM ports, and pins. This capability comes by way of two important PC infrastructure or architectural components known as interrupt requests (IRQs) and input/output (I/O) addresses. IRQs merely provide a means for a peripheral such as a COM port to signal the processor that it has some work to be performed or some data to pass to a program. I/O addresses are just low-level memory addresses that devices or cards on your motherboard use to communicate back and forth on with your PC's processor.

At the operating system level, Linux has its own way of referencing these COM ports—namely, a device name (which appears as a file in the /dev directory, as with any other device). Depending on the version of Linux you're using, you will see references to two different devices for each COM port: a ttyS and a cua (or ttyS0-ttyS3 and cua0-cua3). The ttyS device was once used for dialing in, while cua was used for dialing out; however, the tendency is to use only ttyS and phase out cua. You will encounter some older programs that specifically require cua, so don't assume that you can use ttyS always and be successful.

Linux supports standard serial ports COM1 through COM4 on your PC. External modems connect to one of your COM ports and share the same interrupt request (IRQ) and input/output (I/O) settings of that serial port. Internal modems have their own individual settings that you can address, as long as you don't try to use the corresponding hardware COM port at the same time. All this being said, here are the particulars you need to know about each standard COM port device (I/O addresses are listed as hexadecimal numbers, which Linux requires):

- COM1—IRQ 4, I/O 0x3F8, /dev/ttyS0, and /dev/cua0
- COM2—IRQ 3, I/O 0x2F8, /dev/ttyS1, and /dev/cua1
- COM3—IRQ 4, I/O 0x3E8, /dev/ttyS2, and /dev/cua2
- COM4—IRQ 3, I/O 0x2E8, /dev/ttyS3, and /dev/cua3

Of course, these are just the norms that are part of the accepted Intel architecture and standard; they are not hard and fast rules. There is nothing preventing you or a manufacturer from departing from them. It is not uncommon to find that you must work around these restrictions to get the job done. For example, if you have two serial ports in use and install a modem, it might end up on IRQ 5 because IRQs 3 and 4 are already taken.

CAUTION

Keep in mind that only one device can use any IRQ or I/O address at any given time, so make sure you reserve them appropriately and don't create any conflicts. Also note the way counting begins with zero in Linux and UNIX, because you will see it throughout the operating system. Due to this different numbering model between Linux/UNIX and Windows, it's easy to make mistakes and think (incorrectly) that COM1 is ttyS1 or cua1.

Notice also that, by default, COM1 and COM3 share the same IRQ, as do COM2 and COM4. This is okay, so long as you make sure that only one device is using any IRQ or I/O address at any given time. You will have to manage these limited IRQ resources and prevent conflicts as best you can. If your mouse is using COM1 at IRQ4, for example, you should try to use your modem on COM2 or COM4 at IRQ 3. If your mouse uses a dedicated IRQ, then you can use COM1 or COM2 at either IRQ address, if nothing else is occupying it.

Part
VI

Ch
32

Checking COM Port Status

For your COM ports to work, you must have them enabled in your basic input/output system (BIOS). By default, your system should be configured that way, but you might have to check it out if you run into problems. Refer to your PC manufacturer's documentation on how to bring up the BIOS setup program and change settings (or refer to the Tip in Chapter 19, "Installing and Configuring Hard Drives," which includes popular keyboard combinations that different BIOS and PC manufacturers use).

You also must have the proper devices created at the operating system level. By default, the kernels you install with Linux provide the necessary support for standard COM ports. The information located in the man pages for the mknod command is sufficient for helping you create these devices, on the off chance that you don't have them. You should be aware that just because these files and devices exist doesn't mean necessarily that the kernel supports them. For example, it is possible to recompile the kernel and leave out serial port support, even though these files and devices will remain. You can verify that they exist by typing the following commands at the shell prompt and making sure that the output lists the appropriate COM ports:

```
ls -al /dev/ttyS?
```

```
ls -al /dev/cua?
```

 You can find out what IRQs are currently in use by typing cat /proc/interrupts. Some people who find that they never have enough IRQs available decide to standardize on Small Computer Systems Interface (SCSI) devices, which frees up several IRQs (14 and 15, for example) that are normally associated with the typical IDE interface.

 To find out what your current serial port I/O settings are, type cat /proc/ioports ¦ grep serial from the command line. The output will show a range of I/O bit addresses, such as 02f8-02ff. To find out which IRQs are being used by PCI cards (and thus can't be used for COM ports), type cat /proc/pci ¦ grep IRQ. This won't show you what device is occupying which IRQ—you would have to replace the grep IRQ portion of the command with more and sift through the output for that.

 You can find out what your current Linux serial port settings are by typing setserial -ga /dev/ttyS?. If you want a more complete picture of your entire serial environment, including any symbolic links that exist, add /dev/modem /dev/mouse to this command.

If you're using an external modem, you must obtain the proper modem cable (if one didn't come with your modem). If you're not careful, you could get a null modem cable that works well between two PCs but that isn't wired properly for PC-to-modem communication. You should make sure that the cable you buy is a modem cable and has the correct connectors on each end. More than likely, you will need a 9-pin female D-connector for the PC end and a

25-pin female D-connector for the modem end. You also might run into PCs that have a 25-pin D-connector, so you might need to use a 25-pin-to-9-pin converter if you have only 9-pin cable connections. Just plug the appropriate ends of the cable into each PC, and you're ready to start configuring. You also must provide power for your external modem; internal modems are powered by your PC bus.

Red Hat Linux comes with some excellent debugging tools also, if you have an internal instead of external modem (which has lights for you to monitor). Knowing the status of the different modem pins can be very helpful in troubleshooting problems with modems and the underlying COM ports. One of the best tools for this is the `statserial` command. The only shortcoming of this utility is that it works only with certain types of devices that respond to a specific type of query or request. To find out if it works, and to monitor the status of your serial devices, type `statserial /dev/ttyS0` (COM1, for example).

You can do this for each of your ttyS devices, as well as for `/dev/modem`. This can actually help you determine which device your modem is behind because it responds differently (if your modem is attached and turned on, if applicable) for modems and COM ports. The output indicates status of signals on each RS-232 pin (RTS DTR, CTS DSR, and so on). Request to Send (RTS) and Data Terminal Ready (DTR) are on (displayed as 1 in table) for modems and COM ports, but Clear to Send (CTS) and Data Set Ready (DSR) are on only for modems.

Using Plug-and-Play Modems

Plug-and-Play (PNP) devices evolved out of a need to configure devices dynamically instead of manually or statically. The main problem was that too many IRQ conflicts and malfunctioning devices occurred because settings were not correct. Changing these settings was too difficult and required the user to know way too much about the current status of PC peripherals and devices, which was taxing and unpleasant. PNP allows a system to keep a pool of resources such as IRQs and use them as needed for different devices, using some basic rules for reconfiguring them on the fly during bootup to meet changing needs. For instance, if you add a device that can use only IRQ 5 or 7, and both are occupied by other devices, PNP features allow the PC to reconfigure the other devices (if possible) to another resource so that IRQ 5 or 7 will be free for the new device.

PNP can be implemented at the BIOS or operating system level. If it is implemented at the BIOS level, it can cause problems for non-PNP operating systems. The reason for this is that such operating systems expect devices to be where they were last and don't appreciate or understand any changes that occurred since the last boot. Considerable development has gone into the PNP features of Linux, but it is not ready for prime time yet. If at all possible, you should disable PNP in your BIOS (especially if you are adding and removing devices often). Then you can manage your IRQ and I/O resources manually and prevent any conflicts. If your PNP cards have jumper switches (small plugs that create a bridge or an electrical connection between two metal pins), you should use them to force specific IRQ and I/O settings on them, and then make Linux match those choices.

If you are having problems with PNP modems (or other devices) and you have a dual-boot system, you have some other options. One of the things you can do is use Windows (which is fully PNP-capable) to install and set the correct IRQ and I/O parameters, and then perform a warm boot or restart into Linux. This is not a graceful solution, and it doesn't apply to everyone because we don't all use dual-boot systems. However, it might be a solution for certain situations in which you just can't get something you infrequently use to work properly, and don't feel like buying a new, non-PNP device to replace it.

Using the Hayes AT Command Set

Almost all modems use the standard Hayes AT command set for standardization purposes. This provides a simple way of controlling your modem and manually doing many of the things that communications packages such as `minicom` do for you. This section does not aim to teach you the entire command set; instead, it just familiarizes you with the basic commands you need to perform basic functions. Many settings control such things as modem handshaking, error correction, transmission speed, and data compression. However, you won't normally have to change these settings because the factory defaults should provide the most flexible, capable settings.

You can use the simple and straightforward minicom serial communications program to enter modem command mode and manually enter AT commands (you must set the appropriate COM port for your modem using the `minicom -s` configuration menu first). The minicom program also provides a convenient dialing directory where you can add phone numbers to dial, such as bulletin boards or other computers or hosts. Type `man minicom` to find additional minicom information; if you've used communications software in Windows, you will find minicom quite easy to operate. You also can send AT commands directly to your modem by echoing the command in quotes and redirecting the output to the modem port. For example, to perform some basic functions with your COM2 modem, you could use the following instructions from the command line:

- **Factory reset**—You can reset the factory settings of your modem by simply typing `echo "AT&F" > /dev/ttyS1`.

- **Hangup**—You can hang up your modem and terminate the current call by typing echo `"AT&H" > /dev/ttyS1`.

- **Answer**—You can force your modem to monitor the attached phone line and pick up the receiver on the first ring to answer incoming modem calls by typing echo `"AT &S0=1" > /dev/ttyS1` (S0=4 would pick up on the fourth ring).

- **Dial**—You can dial an external phone and have your modem negotiate communications with a modem on the other end by typing echo `"ATDT 5551212" > /dev/ttyS1`. Of course, you would replace 555-1212 with the actual number you want to dial, preceded by a 1 and the area code (or country code), if necessary, for long distance.

- **Reset**—You can reset your modem to its previous status by typing echo `ATZ > /dev/ttyS1`.

If you find the need, you can consult your modem's user manual and see if it supplies detailed instructions on available AT commands and if they deviate at all from the standard for your specific modem. Unfortunately, not all manufacturers or PC vendors include detailed modem manuals.

> **TIP**
>
> You might be able to use the direct modem commands to manually apply flash upgrades to modems that require it. You should check with the manufacturer and have tech support evaluate the effectiveness of this method, however. The theory behind it is to use the specific AT command that sets your modem to receive mode; then, from a command prompt, type `cat <filename> > /dev/ttyS1` (replacing `filename` with your flash upgrade patch and `ttyS1` with your specific modem device). Unfortunately, most manufacturers normally provide patches and instructions only for Windows. If absolutely necessary, you can apply the patch under Windows, and it will be active when you next reboot into Linux (because it is stored in the modem's non-volatile memory).

Changing Linux Serial Port Settings

After you find out what the current Linux settings are for your COM ports and modem, you can use `setserial` again to change those settings to meet your needs. You can change several commonly adjusted settings within Linux to match the physical configuration of your modem. Keep in mind that changing these settings does not actually make any changes to your actual hardware—this must be done at your BIOS level (either manually or via PNP) or hardware level (jumpers on your modem, motherboard, or serial port card). You configure these options for COM2, for example, by adding the following flags to the `setserial` `/dev/ttyS1` command:

- **Speed**—This setting is intended for use with high-speed modems, such as 56K V.90 modems. Add `spd_vhi` if you want to set Linux to use a 115Kbps speed when communicating with a 56K modem. Add `spd_hi` if you want Linux to communicate with your modem at 56Kbps. Use `spd_normal` to communicate at 38Kbps.

- **Port**—This setting affects the I/O channel that Linux uses to communicate with the modem or your serial port. You must enter the desired value in hexadecimal, preceded by 0x. For example, to set COM2 in this example to I/O 2f8, you would add `port` `0x02f8` to the setserial command.

- **IRQ**—This is how you change the IRQ to reflect what your modem currently is set to. To set COM2 for IRQ 3 in this example, you would add `irq 3`.

After you get the correct settings that you need for your individual modem and COM port, you can automate the process. All you have to do is add a line to the `/etc/rc.d/rc.local` file, and the command will be executed every time your Linux PC boots up. For example, if you have a 56K modem on COM3 using IRQ5, you would enter the following line in the configuration file:

```
/bin/setserial /dev/ttyS2 sp_vhi irq 5
```

Part

VI

Ch

32

TIP   If you need a free IRQ address, take a look at IRQ5 and IRQ9, which typically are associated with parallel printers and network cards, respectively. You also might be able to take advantage of IRQs 10, 11, 12, or 15, if they aren't taken by other devices, such as network cards, video graphics cards, or video capture cards.

Your `/dev/modem` device should be a symbolic link to an actual COM port device such as `/dev/ttyS0`. Symbolic links appear with an "l" to the far left of the listing, preceding the user, group, and world rwx permissions. You can check this by doing a file listing with `ls —al /dev/modem`. If `/dev/modem` doesn't exist, you can type `ln —s /dev/ttyS0 /dev/modem`, for COM1 (ttyS1 for COM2, and so on). Or, you can use the graphical feature provided by the Control Panel—select System, Control Panel, and then click the phone icon, followed by the appropriate COM port where your modem is configured.

CAUTION

Use `/dev/modem` or `/dev/ttyS#` designators consistently across all your applications. If you mix and match these references, you probably will run into device-locking problems. For example, the `uugetty` utility running against a COM port uses `uucp` file-locking conventions. Each time you use such a device, a lock file is created in the `/var/lock` directory for that device with an `LCK..` prefix (in this case, `LCK..modem`). Programs and utilities understand how to use and share this file and how to lock and unlock it, but you must use the same naming conventions for your devices throughout. If your other programs use `/dev/modem` and you use `/dev/ttyS0` here, you might find that you can dial in but not out, or vice versa.

Dealing with Winmodems

Winmodems also sometimes are referred to as controllerless modems. These are inexpensive modems that have offloaded some processing (normally controlled by the modem hardware) to the operating system. This makes the modem cheaper to produce and takes advantage of today's faster processors to handle the additional processing. The only major problem with this is that currently these types of modems work only with the Windows operating system. There are some current efforts underway to get drivers written for Winmodems, but it might take a while yet.

If your PC has any version of such a modem (by any vendor), you won't be able to get it to work with Linux. You must either replace the Winmodem or add an additional controller-based modem to your system.

Troubleshooting Modems

Modems rely on several underlying layers of support to function properly. If these layers are not in place or are configured incorrectly, then you will run into problems. First and foremost, you must have BIOS support for your serial ports. If your modem is working at any time after installing Linux, you probably can rule out BIOS settings as the culprit when you run into problems (unless you changed BIOS settings the same time you ran into modem problems). The key thing is to make sure that the BIOS does not have different settings than Linux does. You also must make sure that the PNP capabilities of your BIOS aren't resulting in sporadic changes to the settings of the system's serial ports. If you suspect that the problem might be in your BIOS settings, consult your system documentation for instructions on how to access your BIOS setup program and verify or change serial (COM) port settings.

If you can't get your modem to work at all, you should check to make sure that the serial COM port devices exist on your Linux system. Perform a file listing using `ls -al /dev/ttyS?` and make sure you have either two or four devices listed (ttyS0–ttyS3). Do the same thing for `ls -al /dev/modem`, and make sure this exists as a symbolic link to one of the ttyS devices (usually ttyS1). While you have the file listing available, now is a good time to confirm that the permissions and ownership of the modem and COM port device files are correct for your environment. It is surprisingly easy to end up with security settings that prevent you from reading from or writing to a device or file, including the COM port. If root can use the device and other users can't, it is probably because the permissions are wrong. If necessary, use `chmod 666 /dev/ttyS?` (change the mode of all COM ports, or replace the question mark with a specific COM port if you prefer). If you want root and anyone in the users group to use, but nobody else, you can use `chmod 660 /dev/ttyS?` and `chown root.users /dev/ttyS?`.

You should check to make sure that the IRQ and I/O settings of the modem match what your software is using and what you expect. Use the `setserial -a /dev/ttyS1` command to find out the status and settings of COM2. If you don't see any error messages or anything out of the ordinary, then you can continue debugging other alternatives. If something looks awry, though, you can correct it with the `setserial` command. For example, if you know that your modem on COM2 is using IRQ3 and I/O 0x2F8, but `setserial` reflects IRQ4 and I/O 0x3E8, you can change the modem setting by typing `setserial /dev/ttyS1 irq 3 io 0x2F8`.

It is more likely that your Linux device files (`/etc/ttyS0`, for example) are not configured properly, possibly with the wrong ownerships or read-write permissions. They also might need to be reconfigured with additional options using the `setserial` command. For example, you can use the `speed_vhi` flag to enable the highest transmission rates of 56K V.90 modems. The configuration settings out of the box are usually sufficient to get the job done, if you make the changes mentioned in this chapter. However, sometimes mismatches do occur between these default settings.

Part
VI

Ch
32

If you run into such a situation, use a logical, scientific approach to troubleshooting the problem. Look first for simple solutions, such as cable connections and recently modified configuration files. Make backup copies of any configuration files you change so that you can recover easily from any problems that occur. Often problems in Linux can be traced to ownerships and permissions, so make sure you check those very early in the process.

If you can't seem to get your modem to respond to your commands or applications trying to access it, something might have your modem locked. As mentioned previously, most programs use uucp file-locking conventions, creating a lock file within the file system as a flag for other applications that the device is already in use, to prevent conflicts. It might be possible that the lock file exists but nothing is actually using the modem. If this is the case, you can just remove the lock file by typing `rm -rf /var/lock/LCK..modem` (replace `modem` with `ttyS1` or whatever your modem is actually configured as). You also should check your `/etc/initab` file to see if any programs being launched automatically during bootup use the modem (such as getty or uugetty daemons that provide fax or dial-in access capability). ●

Configuring Access to the Internet

by Duane Hellums

In this chapter

Understanding Internet Connections

If you have a PC, you likely will want to hook it up to the Internet at some time. This is the basic connection you will need to be able to appear as a network node directly on the Internet, send email to friends and family all over the world, read Internet newsgroups, and surf the World Wide Web (among other things). Linux provides all the necessary technology and tools you need for this. You do not need a local area network (LAN) or Ethernet network interface card (NIC) in your computer for such activities. All you basically need is a modem, Red Hat Linux 6.0, and an account with an Internet service provider (ISP).

You might think that you don't need to know anything about networking if you don't have a network interface card (NIC) or a LAN. However, without duplicating much of the valuable information in other chapters here, a few networking topics should be discussed before you begin configuring your Internet connection. If you need additional networking information, Part IV, "Hardware," and Chapters 27, "Installing and Configuring TCP/IP Network Support"; 28, "Installing and Configuring Samba"; 29, "Configuring NetWare Access"; and 30, "Configuring the Apache Web Server," discuss Ethernet client-server networking architecture and components.

Luckily, you don't have to become an expert in TCP/IP to connect to the Internet. However, you do need to be familiar with a few things, if you're not already. This information can help you understand what's going on when you connect as well as contribute to successful troubleshooting of any problematic connections.

Understanding Ethernet Networking

The basic foundation of the Internet is based on Transmission Control Protocol/Internet Protocol (TCP/IP) networking. Each networked PC or hardware device (such as a print server or router) has a specific unique IP address that identifies it to the LAN and the Internet (if connected). Each PC on the LAN can hear the traffic, but it will respond only if the data being transmitted is for that particular PC.

This numeric address is in the form of four numbers, ranging from 1 to 255 (some numbers have special meanings or are reserved, so all are not available or regularly observed). Each of these four numbers is separated by a decimal. This means that numbers such as 204.115.65.9, 114.231.14.158, and 192.168.1.1 are all valid IP addresses that can be referenced by other machines.

N O T E The 192.168.1 group of IP addresses is reserved for private networks that are not connected full-time to the Internet. Such is the case in typical small office/home office (SOHO) environments. This enables you to create an entire LAN without the need to register all your addresses and change them every time you move. Keep in mind though that external (Internet) users cannot route traffic to your 192.168.1 Ethernet address—they must use the IP address of your PPP (modem) link. ISPs drop traffic to these private networks and do not route them because many users on their LAN might be using the same address (and Internet addresses must be unique to be effective). ▪

To receive data, each NIC listens for its own address and ignores information addressed elsewhere. For sending data, information destined for another PC somewhere is broken into small chunks (IP packets) and is addressed using the destination PC's IP address. These packets are then transmitted onto the network with hopes that they will make it to the destination PC, where they will be combined, resequenced (in case they arrived out of turn), and processed.

Some networks use special PCs or dedicated equipment called *routers* that have rules specifying how they should handle packets of information that are not addressed to any of the local network nodes. In this way, your data can traverse the Internet hierarchy, hopping from network to network until it reaches its destination.

If you have an Ethernet card in your Linux PC, you should already have associated an IP address with it. For example, you might have several networked Linux PCs with IP addresses of 192.168.1.1, 192.168.1.2, and 192.168.1.3. Regardless of whether each PC had a NIC, they recognize themselves as the default localhost address of 127.0.0.1 that allows certain network functions to work even without being physically connected to the network.

One final thing to understand regarding internetworking, as it is sometimes called, is the concept of domain name services (DNS). DNS is a mature Internet technology that enables you to use a name instead of a numerical address and to have these names magically mapped to IP addresses. Names such as www.redhat.com, www.harvard.edu, and www.whitehouse.gov are considerably easier to understand, use, and remember than numbers. The DNS naming conventions are hierarchical, just like the routing discussed previously. For example, the redhat.com domain could have (but doesn't have) PCs named pooh.redhat.com and tigger.redhat.com, just like a 192.168.1 LAN has PCs numbered 192.168.1.1 and 192.168.1.2.

For this domain name resolution to occur, your PC must know the IP address of a primary DNS server, which does the conversion from name to IP address. In some situations, you also can specify an alternate DNS server, in case the primary is down. If both are down, your PC won't know how to convert computer and network names to IP addresses and will not be capable of functioning properly on the Internet.

Part
VI

Ch
33

N O T E Your ISP might not want to give you the addresses of its primary and alternate DNS servers. Depending on the exact configuration of your ISP's PPP connection, this information may be provided internally and transparently to your PC, without you having to provide the information manually. You may have to leave it out and see if it works, and then ask for it if you can get to Internet IP addresses but not domain names. It also might help to not mention that you are using Linux—they might shy away from helping you because they might not know the technology involved. Just tell them that your dial-up networking program needs to know the DNS information, and don't give up. ■

Understanding Point-to-Point Protocol Networking

So what happens when you don't have a LAN or a NIC on your Linux PC? How do you connect to the Internet and exchange data with virtually anyone in the world? This is where the Point-to-Point Protocol (PPP) comes into play. You may or may not have a registered IP address and a physical connection directly onto the Internet. To simulate being a node on the Internet, PPP enables you to create a TCP/IP-based link between your Linux modem and a modem located at your ISP. The same technology is used on a Windows PC (dubbed dial-up networking) to connect to the Internet. Chapter 32 provides the necessary information you need to install and configure a modem on your Linux PC if you do not already have one; a modem will be required to connect to the Internet.

Luckily, much of this capability occurs behind the scenes and is relatively transparent to you when using Red Hat Linux 6.0. When this link is created between your PC and a PPP-capable device at your ISP, a registered IP address will in effect be on loan to your PC, allowing you as well as any other PC on the Internet to reference it, locate it, and address information to it.

For example, you could reference a particular PC locally as 127.0.0.1 or 192.168.1.1 to access resources (such as `http://192.168.1.1/` or `http://127.0.0.1/` in Netscape Communicator to view Apache Web server pages), but nobody at your ISP or the Internet could use these addresses to obtain information. When you connect to the Internet and your ISP assigns your end of the modem link a registered address (such as 205.167.5.19), though, anyone can use standard TCP/IP clients to contact your PC, assuming you are running those particular services on your Linux machine (for example, Web browsers, ping, telnet, ftp, and traceroute).

NOTE Some ISPs give you dynamic IP addresses, and others provide fixed IP addresses. If you receive dynamic IP addresses, your address will be different virtually every time you log on because the IP address is merely pulled from a pool of available addresses. If you have a fixed IP address, your address is always the same every time you log on (similar to a phone number, in effect). If you want to publish or list your Web page for friends, relatives, and customers to easily find it, a fixed IP address is obviously the way to go (although you may be charged extra for this service). ■

Installing Internet Software

Red Hat Linux 6.0 provides easy-to-use, automated tools to help you connect to and disconnect from the Internet. As a result, connecting to the Internet is not the chore it once was with Linux. Primarily, you will need the basic TCP/IP networking suite along with the PPP software and necessary TCP/IP clients. PPP is the Point To Point Protocol, which is used to implement TCP/IP networking over a serial communications link, such as your phone line.

If you didn't install the PPP daemon during your initial installation, you can find it on the Red Hat Linux 6.0 CD in the `RedHat/RPMS` directory, named `ppp-2.3.7-2.i386.rpm`. You can confirm that you have it installed either by using GnomeRPM from the main menu under Settings or from the command line by typing `rpm -q ppp`. Use GnomeRPM to install it, or use the `rpm -ivh ppp-2.3.7-2.i386.rpm` shell or X terminal command (assuming you have your CD-ROM already mounted on `/mnt/cdrom`).

Connecting to the Internet would not be very useful if you didn't have a wide range of clients that give you capabilities to access the information on the Internet. You should reference information in the following chapters for Internet, serial communications, and network-related information:

- Chapter 14, "Installing and Configuring Netscape Communicator"
- Chapter 34, "Configuring Dial-In Access "
- Chapter 31, "Configuring Email"
- Chapter 32, "Configuring Modems"

Configuring Dial-Up Connections

You must go through a series of steps after initial configuration and installation of Red Hat Linux 6.0 to be able to access the Internet seamlessly and headache-free. First and foremost, you must get your serial ports and modems working properly. Chapter 32 discusses this procedure.

ISPs can configure their dial-up connections any of a number of ways based on their requirements and the needs of their customers. You may have to adapt the instructions in this chapter slightly to work with your custom situation. Your ISP should be willing and able to provide you the information you need regarding login options, authentication methods, and DNS server information. This section doesn't attempt to discuss every possible configuration and setting; rather, it covers the basic steps necessary to get people in the most common situations connected to the Internet. To configure an ISP connection, perform the following steps:

Part
VI

Ch
33

1. While logged in as root, go to the main GNOME panel menu and select System, Control Panel (or type `control-panel &` from a command line or X terminal window). This brings up the Control Panel window that has a number of icons to choose from.

2. If you haven't done so already, click the Modem Configuration icon to bring up the Configure Modem window. Select the appropriate serial communications (COM) port that your modem uses (from your initial Linux installation settings, hardware documentation, your Windows settings, or trial and error). Keep in mind that COM 1 is `/dev/ttyS0`, not `/dev/ttyS1`—this is a common mistake during configuration. Click OK to save your settings and return to the Control Panel. This also creates a link from the appropriate tty serial device to your modem device (`/dev/ttyS2` to `/dev/modem` for COM3, for example).

N O T E It is important to create this symbolic link for your modem if it doesn't already exist, because certain programs expect to use the /dev/modem device instead of a ttyS device. Having the link also facilitates device file locking so that no conflicts occur between different programs that are trying to access it. ▪

3. Click the Network Configuration icon in the Control Panel. This brings up the Network Configurator window, where you can define Ethernet and Point-to-Point Protocol (PPP) network devices, among others. You also can type netconf & from the command line or an X terminal window. The first time you use this tab, it probably will have only an lo (loopback) and eth0 (Ethernet NIC) device listed.

4. Click the Interfaces tab and then the Add button at the bottom. This brings up a Choose Interface Type window. Check the PPP box and click OK to create a ppp networking device (if you already have one, such as ppp0, this process will create a new one, ppp1). Your ISP may use the older, less capable Serial Line Interface Protocol (SLIP)—if so, you will have to provide just a phone number, SLIP login name, and SLIP password in the Create SLIP Interface window.

5. Assuming that your ISP is using the much more popular and robust PPP interface, in the Create PPP Interface window enter your Internet service provider's phone number (including prefixes and country and area codes, if necessary) (see Figure 33.1). Also enter the login name and password on that system because you probably will want to automate your authentication process. Check the Use PAP authentication box if your ISP requires it.

TIP You could click Done here and then Save in the pop-up confirmation window for a quick PPP configuration and test. However, it makes more sense to proceed with additional configuration options by selecting the Configure button before saving the settings.

FIGURE 33.1
The basic information you need for a PPP connection with your ISP is the phone number, login name, and password.

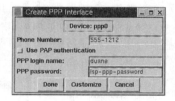

TIP As an alternative to netconf, which is fully documented in the Red Hat Linux Getting Started Guide on the Red Hat CD, you can try the kppp program, which has a nice graphical interface you might find more familiar if you come from a Windows or Macintosh background. The kppp utility is available from the GNOME main panel menu by selecting KDE Menus, Internet, kppp. You might have to remove the lock reference from the /etc/ppp/options file, but when you get the kppp window up, you can click Setup and enter many of the same settings required by the PPP setup portions of netconf.

For example, after creating a new account, you will have to create a name for it, provide a phone number to call, supply DNS addresses, specify authentication methods (PAP, CHAP, script login), indicate your modem device, and enter your login name and password (which you can save to automate future connections). When the program is running, it even provides nice details in a kppp Statistics window, including the IP address of both ends of the PPP link. The good news is that most of the defaults are correct for a simple, error-free Internet connection setup. You should consider using kppp if you run into any problems configuring netconf. The kpppload program is another good utility you can use to monitor the amount of data you transfer and at what speed.

6. Click Customize to expand the Create window into the Edit PPP Interface window (see Figure 33.2), which has additional tabs and entry fields. Leave the Use Hardware Flow Control and Modem Lines option checked, along with the Abort Connection on Well-Known Errors box.

FIGURE 33.2
You can add the capability for local accounts other than root to use the modem's PPP interface, as well as change modem settings.

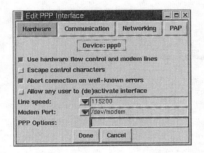

7. In the Hardware tab, also check Allow Any User to (De)Activate interface if you want to change the permissions of the PPP link to allow non-root users to use it. Don't check the Escape Control Characters unless you find that your client encounters problems communicating with the server when it sends 8-bit CTRL characters instead of 7-bit character ESC sequences.

8. Select the appropriate modem connection speed for your modem in the Line Speed pull-down box. Keep in mind that compression can allow effective throughput of up to four times more than your modem's actual physical bandwidth. For a 33.6Kbps or 56Kbps modem, for example, you should enter 115200. Don't enter any PPP Options flags in the last box.

9. Click the Communication tab to see the information displayed in Figure 33.3. Linux assumes that you are connecting to an ISP link that kicks off PPP shortly after you authenticate yourself, so it automatically sets itself up to launch the PPP client on your Linux PC after a five-second pause. This is the most common Internet PPP connection method in use today. If your ISP uses a different script or setup, you should determine what that server expects so you can make the necessary changes here. In this case, use the Insert, Append, Edit, and Remove buttons in the Communication tab to create a

custom login and PPP negotiation script. The first three buttons bring up an Edit Chat Entry window that consists of a simple Expect and Send text box; data you enter here will be shown in the correct spot in the two columns of the Communication tab.

FIGURE 33.3

ISPs require different login sequences or scripts, and you may have to customize the default configuration to work with your ISP.

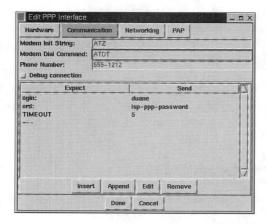

10. Click the Networking tab (see Figure 33.4). If you want your Linux computer to connect to the Internet automatically every time you boot up, check the Activate Interface at Boot Time option. If you have a fixed IP address, your ISP may want you to enter the IP addresses of the local Linux PPP client and the remote Internet server in the Local IP address and Remote IP address boxes. However, in most instances ISPs use dynamic rather than static IP addresses, so you can just leave these blocks blank so that your ISP can provide them during your login. The remaining defaults in this window are sufficient for most connections.

FIGURE 33.4

You can elect to connect to the Internet every time you boot up, and you might have to provide fixed local and remote IP addresses (depending on your ISP and networking needs).

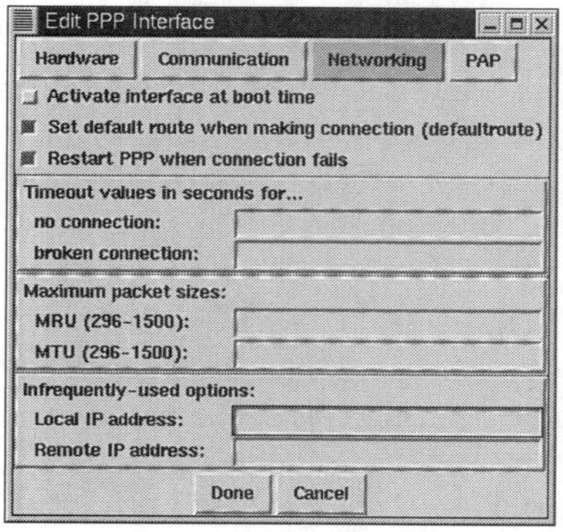

11. If your ISP uses PAP authentication and you checked the box indicating this in Figure 33.1, then enter your PAP username in the Send Username text box. Click the PAP tab and the Append button if your ISP requires you to enter additional PAP-related script settings. You will see the Edit Chat Entry window previously referenced, which enables you to enter an Expect and Send pair for communication with your ISP's PPP connection script.

12. Click the Done button at the bottom of the Edit PPP Interface window (followed by the Save button in the pop-up confirmation window) to save your settings and return to the Network Configurator window, where you should see your new connection (named ppp0 because this is probably the first PPP interface you created).

13. Click Activate to have your modem initiate the call. You should hear your modem dial out (if the modem's volume and speaker variables are set to do so). If your ISP modems are operational, your modems will complete the connection and you will see something to the effect of `Connect 50666/ARQ/V90/LAPM/V42BIS` (your modem connection results will be different), indicating that you have a good link with any configured compression and error-correction capabilities.

When the connection has been successfully completed, you can perform all the normal TCP/IP networking functions. In effect, your system will feel, look, and operate as if you were connected physically with network cables to the ISP LAN. However, you may have to go back and tune the settings you just created to get your PPP connection working properly with your ISP. Unfortunately, some ISPs may not know much about Linux settings, so you may not be able to reference exact windows and screens. However, you should be able to communicate properly with ISP technicians using the generic terms of PPP, PAP, password, username, script, and so on. Just hope that you can speak to a technician and not be promised a pamphlet that documents how to connect your Windows PC to the ISP (often the case).

Part
VI

Ch
33

Troubleshooting Internet Access

There are many interdependent components of an Internet connection, including basic TCP/IP networking, domain name services, TCP/IP server and clients, PPP software and associated devices, modems, and PC serial ports. Any number of these things could misbehave and cause you problems trying to connect to the Internet.

If you run into problems, you should step back and look at the big picture, trying to determine exactly where the problem is occurring. As you mentally step through the different underlying technologies, try to come up with ways of testing each one individually to rule them out as the cause of your problem. Your goal should be to use utilities such as `ping`, `telnet`, `ftp`, `traceroute`, `netstat`, and `ifconfig` to confirm your expected configuration information and look for anything that deviates from your expectations.

Try to make only one change at a time while debugging your connection. That way, you will be able to determine whether individual changes were successful. It will also simplify debugging and troubleshooting because you will be able to determine what changes caused problems (hopefully).

Try to rule out simple problems, such as loose phone cables or connections. Make sure that the phone is not busy when you're trying to call, if you have multiple phones hooked up to the line you are using with Linux. Call your ISP only after you have ruled out all the simple problems you can think of (try rebooting as well, just in case, so that you're working with a clean set of processes). This way, you can save time with your ISP, who naturally will have a troubleshooting process that asks you to do these things anyway. If you show that you're ahead of the game (and save them time for other tasks), you will receive better service quicker. If you have two phone lines, your ISP technician can often help troubleshoot the connection in real-time, listening to your modem signals during the connection and looking at what is happening at the ISP side during your login and PPP negotiation process.

You might have to tweak the modem's initialization strings, if you have an odd, modified, specialized, or nonstandard modem of any sort. You should also confirm that you have the correct modem speeds selected. Most importantly, you must ensure that you have the correct serial COM port identified for your modem. Lastly, make sure that there is not a lock on your modem (possibly left over from an earlier call) by typing `ls -al /var/lock/LCK..modem` (or `/var/lock/LCK..ttyS*`, as appropriate, if you're not using the symbolic link for your modem device). ●

## CHAPTER 34

Configuring Dial-in Access

by Duane Hellums

In this chapter

Although the main purpose of this chapter is to explain how to dial into your Linux system over phone lines, it also discusses how to physically connect another PC to your Linux server or workstation. This allows a remote PC to become either a terminal on your Linux machine or an actual node on your Linux network (through your Linux PC). The process and underlying technologies for establishing both capabilities in Linux are very similar, so it is logical that these topics should be grouped together here. You also may want to read related information in the following chapters:

- Chapter 32, "Configuring Modems"
- Chapter 35, "Configuring Fax Support"
- Chapter 27, "Installing and Configuring TCP/IP Network Support"
- Chapter 33, "Configuring Access to the Internet"

Understanding Remote Access

Many people eventually find that they need to run some of their Linux programs or view data on their Linux systems from a remote location. Linux is suited ideally to this because of its inherent multiuser, multitasking capabilities and support for Internet Protocol (IP) networking. If your Linux PC were a live node on the Internet 24 hours a day, you would be able to access your Linux PC's standard IP applications: Web traffic, email, file transfer (ftp), or Telnet for remote login capability. However, most small business and home users don't have this costly luxury. This chapter discusses three basic methods of connecting to your Linux PC:

- **Cable connection**—Some people have more than one PC in the home or office and want to log into a nearby Linux PC (to remotely manage it from a Windows desktop, for example) but don't have the equipment or the know-how to network them together. You can do this easily and cheaply over standard PC serial interfaces (communication or COM ports) with a single cable and some basic configuration changes (or a legacy green-screen terminal, if you have one lying around). Your remote PC performs the function of a host or terminal, and you normally will be able to access only text-based, command-line applications over such a link.

- **Telephone login**—Other people want to be able to call in over a modem link and log into their Linux PCs for similar reasons. Other than adding the additional hardware of a modem to your Linux system (and remote PC), this is also a very simple process. Again, your remote PC is just a host and you will be able to access only text-based, command-line applications in this manner.

- **Dial-in (dial-up) networking**—Finally, some people want almost full networking capability from remote locations, similar to what they have with their Internet service provider (ISP). When you have the modem and dial-in connection configured properly (from telephone login, mentioned in the preceding paragraph), it is relatively simple to add the necessary Point-to-Point Protocol (PPP) networking capability to your telephone link. Unlike the two previous methods of connecting to your Linux PC, your remote PC in effect becomes a fully networked IP node and can itself run any IP-based client/server applications, such as Windows-based POP3 email clients and Web browsers.

Configuring Cable Connections

You should know some basics about serial ports before you can understand the discussion here and so that you can prevent problems while connecting your PCs. You shouldn't dwell on these details too much or worry about them—just be familiar with them because it is easy to miss a small detail that can cause you some troubleshooting grief later.

Mastering Serial Port Terminology

A serial port is nothing more than a path for your computer to send data down, one bit at a time (as opposed to parallel ports that can send several bits at a time). Because your computer can talk to other devices this way, people also refer to the serial port as a communication or COM port. Your PC motherboard can have from one to four serial ports (commonly referenced by their DOS terms, COM1 to COM4), unless you have a multiport serial card, which is outside the scope of this discussion.

> **N O T E**   Chapter 32 contains a detailed discussion on COM ports, IRQs, serial interface cards, and cables as they relate to the use of internal and external modems. You will be using the same underlying technology here, so you should take some time out to read that chapter if you haven't already (assuming you need a refresher on serial port interfaces). ■

Ensuring Hardware and Linux Support

For your COM ports to work, you must have them enabled in your Basic Input Output System (BIOS). By default, your system should be configured that way, but you may have to check it out if you run into problems. Refer to your PC manufacturer's documentation on how to bring up the BIOS setup program and change settings (or refer to the Tip in Chapter 19, "Installing and Configuring Hard Drives," which includes popular keyboard combinations that different BIOS and PC manufacturers use).

Finally, you must obtain the proper serial cable. If you're not careful, you could get a cable that connects to both PCs fine but which will never work as you expect it to, causing you nothing but headaches. Specifically, you will need a null modem cable, which also sometimes is referred to as a crossover serial cable or a serial printer cable. The difference between it and regular serial cables is that the receive and send pins on one end are switched (both sides can't transmit on the same channel, while both listen on another channel, obviously).

Part
VI

Ch
34

As mentioned earlier, make sure that they have the proper end connection: These should be female ends, to plug into the male PC connectors. You also may run into PCs that have a 25-pin D connector, and you may need to use a 9-pin-to-25-pin converter if you have only 9-pin cable connections. Just plug the appropriate ends of the cable into each PC, and you're ready to start configuring.

Configuring Linux Terminal Settings

As long as you know the correct device names, IRQ settings, and I/O addresses for your COM ports, this process should be fairly straightforward. To enable a remote PC to connect to your Linux PC over a serial interface, you should perform the following steps:

1. **Modify the terminal configuration file**—While logged in as root or superuser, open the /etc/gettydefs file with your favorite editor. This file is where you specify the control parameters for the link you will establish.

2. **Remove modem controls**—Edit only the line in /etc/gettydefs that begins with DT38400, and remove both references in that line to CRTSCTS so that your Linux PC will know that there is no modem attached to the link.

3. **Add a launcher to the startup file**—Open the /etc/inittab file with your favorite editor. This file is where your system initially launches some key system daemons, such as the programs that generate the login prompts you see and use.

4. **Determine the appropriate COM port**—Recall the Linux device name for the port you plugged your serial null modem cable into. Assuming that you are using COM2 (you can use any available), you would be using /dev/ttyS1.

5. **Add a login prompt to the COM port**—Go to the very end of /etc/inittab, and add the following command (for COM2, ttyS1; otherwise use S2 and ttyS2 for COM3, ttyS3 for COM4, and so on):
   S1:23456:respawn:/sbin/getty ttyS1 DT38400

N O T E   The syntax of inittab bears some explanation. The 23456 tells inittab to launch the getty program in all boot modes except single-user mode (1). Respawn tells inittab to run the getty program again if it terminates or is closed by a user for any reason. The s1 and ttys1 refer to COM port 2. You should recognize DT38400 as the name of the terminal type configured in previous steps in /etc/gettydefs. ▦

6. **Reload inittab's configuration file**—You must make inittab recognize changes you just made to its configuration file. From an X terminal or command-line prompt, type init q to refresh the daemon.

7. **Restart existing login prompts (optional)**—If you already have a getty running on a COM port, such as when you're updating or troubleshooting a connection, you may have to restart it. Perform a file listing with ps -ef ¦ grep getty, and note the

process identification (PID) number on the far left of your screen for the appropriate COM port (ttyS1, in this example). Terminate it and restart it by typing `kill -9` and the PID, followed by the Return key.

N O T E The term *login process* is used loosely here to reduce confusion. When you run a getty process on a COM port, it actually only monitors activity on the port. When it initially receives data of any sort, it immediately launches the login process, which authenticates the user by account name and password pair before handing off control to the shell prompt (bash). Because these later stages are automatic and transparent, it's easy to just think of getty as a login process, even though the purist will point out the inaccuracy. ■

At this point your Linux system should be properly configured for serial port logins. However, if you intend to connect your Windows PC to Linux using the serial cable, you must configure it also.

Configuring Windows Terminal Settings

Technically, you can use any green-screen dumb terminal, but these seem to be dying out mostly in preference for PC "smart" terminals. You can use any number of Windows (or Mac) communications software packages to connect to your Linux server. This section discusses only HyperTerminal, which is the standard free package that comes with Windows 95 and 98. It is a simple, straightforward interface with some bells and whistles you can learn to take advantage of later, such as kermit and zmodem file transfers over this simple serial interface.

To configure your Windows PC for connecting to Linux over the null modem serial cable you have connected, you first must make the necessary changes on the Linux side of the link (discussed in previous paragraphs). Then perform the following tasks:

1. Launch HyperTerminal in Windows 95 or 98 by selecting Start, Programs, Accessories, Communications, and the HyperTerminal folder. If you don't see this folder, you may have to use the Windows setup program and documentation to install it.

2. Click Hypertrm to bring up the HyperTerminal program and the Connection Description window. Enter a simple, easy-to-remember name for your serial connection, such as Linux, and pick an icon if you want. Click OK.

3. In the Connect To window, ignore the settings for phone and modem links, and click Connect Using. Pick Direct to Com1 (or whichever serial COM port you attached your cable to). Click OK.

4. In the COM1 Properties window, the default settings are probably 2400, 8 data bits, 1 stop bit, and no parity bits, with hardware flow control. Change only the Bits Per Second value in the drop-down box to 38400 (remember that you set the link speed to 38400 in the previous section of this chapter). Leave the remaining settings as they are, and click OK. This returns you to the HyperTerminal window with a new connection name of Linux.

Part
VI

Ch
34

5. In the Linux HyperTerminal window, press any key to send some data over the link and force the getty process running on Linux to acknowledge the link and initiate a login prompt. If you don't see one, you should check your physical connection on both ends and verify your Linux setup as well as Windows settings. If that still doesn't work, you might try restarting HyperTerminal, Windows, and possibly even your Linux server.

NOTE You will not be able to log in as root over this terminal connection. You will have to log in as a normal user and then use the su command and supply the necessary password to become the superuser (root). ■

6. Provide your login name and password when prompted to do so. If you are properly authenticated, you should receive a shell prompt, which you can use in exactly the same manner as you would if you were at a command-line prompt physically sitting on the actual Linux server. Use any simple commands to view a process or file listing, just to make sure that the link and its speed and timing are configured properly.

If all goes as planned, you should be able to do whatever processing you want, including running programs such as linuxconf. When you are finished processing over the serial link, you can terminate it by typing exit or logout. If you just close the terminal window in Windows without logging out, your Linux server will not know that you are gone and will keep your shell prompt running, which can be a security problem in some locations—anyone that connects a properly configured computer to that port will be logged in immediately as you and can begin processing.

Configuring Telephone Login

Although it's nice to have physical connections and be able to remotely use your Linux server from another PC, you may also need to connect to your Linux server from another type of remote serial connection: a modem. Because both links use a form of RS-232 signaling, the process is very similar for both. Basically, you just have to add a few steps to create modem lock files, force your Linux modem to answer incoming calls, and run a different type of getty (and associated login process). If you haven't physically installed your modem and configured it appropriately, you should log in as root and do that before proceeding. To configure your Linux PC for remote telephone login, perform the following steps:

1. Determine the appropriate COM port: Recall the Linux device name for your modem port. Assuming that you are using COM1 (you can use any available port that doesn't conflict with other devices), you would be using /dev/ttyS0 (or /dev/modem—see the Caution sidebar). You will have to use the long reference ttyS0 and the short term S0 in various places in the steps that follow (change the code included here to reflect your actual situation, as necessary).

> **CAUTION**
>
> Use /dev/modem if that's what other programs such as pppd and chat (for dial-out Internet connections) use; otherwise, you could have device locking problems. The uugetty utility uses uucp file locking conventions. Each time you use such a device, a lock file is created in the /var/lock directory for that device with an LCK.. prefix (in this case, LCK..modem). Programs and utilities understand how to use and share this file (and lock and unlock it), but you must use the same naming conventions for your devices throughout. If your other programs use /dev/modem and you use /dev/ttyS0 here, you may find that you can dial in fine but can no longer dial out, or vice versa. Your /dev/modem device should be a symbolic link to a COM port such as /dev/ttyS0, anyway (appears with an "l" to the far left of the listing, preceding the user, group, and world rwx permissions). You can check this by doing a file listing with ls -al /dev/modem. If /dev/modem doesn't exist, you can type ln -s /dev/ttys0 /dev/modem, for COM1 (ttys1 for COM2, and so on). If you just perform dial-in and not dial-out connections, then you can use either name to reference the device in the /etc/inittab file.

2. Create the dial-in configuration file: While logged in as root or the superuser, use your favorite editor to create a file called /etc/conf.uugetty.ttyS0 (replace ttyS0 with your actual dial-in modem device name, such as ttyS1, ttyS2, or ttyS3, or /dev/modem—see the Caution sidebar). Enter the following information in this file (replacing the DELAY with another number, which represents the number of rings you want the modem to listen to before automatically answering the phone and initiating a data connection with your remote PC):

```
TIMEOUT=60
INIT="" AT\r OK\r\n
WAITFOR=RING
CONNECT=""ATA\r CONNECT\s\A
DELAY=1
```

3. Add a launcher to the startup file: Open the /etc/inittab file with your favorite editor. This file is where your system initially launches some key system daemons, such as the programs that generate the login prompts you see and use.

4. Add a login prompt to the COM port: Go to the very end of /etc/inittab and add the following command. (For COM1, S0 and ttyS0; otherwise, use S1 and ttyS1 for COM2, S2 and ttyS2 for COM3, and so on. Use S0, S1, S2, or S3 in conjunction with conf.uugetty.modem if necessary—see the previous Caution sidebar.)

```
S1:23456:respawn:/sbin/uugetty -d /etc/conf.uugetty.ttyS0 115200
```

5. Reload inittab's configuration file: You must make inittab recognize changes you just made to its configuration file. From an X terminal or command-line prompt, type init q to refresh the daemon.

6. Restart existing login prompts (optional): If you already have a (uu)getty running on a COM port, such as when you're updating or troubleshooting a connection, you may have to restart it. Perform a file listing with ps -ef ¦ grep getty and note the process

Part

VI

Ch

34

identification (PID) number on the far left of your screen for the appropriate COM port (ttyS1, in this example). Terminate it and restart it by typing kill -9 and the PID, followed by the Return key. Also, if you are running any tasks against this port, such as the configuration you would have if you are using a PC smart terminal with your Linux PC (as outlined previously in "Configuring Cable Connections"), you will have to remove those configuration file references (or comment them out with the # symbol at the beginning of the line) before you proceed with the modem configuration.

At this point, the uugetty process will be listening to the incoming modem and will launch a login prompt when it receives an incoming call. It will control all the modem communications, as necessary. If you configured your dial-in and dial-out connections properly, you will be able to use either without interfering with the other (see the previous Caution sidebar). This doesn't mean that you can dial in and out at the same time; you will have to use two phone lines and install and configure two modems in your PC if you want to do that.

Configuring Terminal Emulator Software

You can use any communications package in Windows or Linux to call your Linux dial-in server. However, because you never know where you will be or whether there will be a Linux workstation handy, this section discusses how to use your dial-in Linux configuration with a remote Windows PC and modem. Specifically, the text discusses how to use HyperTerminal, the free communications package that comes standard with Windows 95 and 98.

In Windows 95 or 98, select Start, Programs, Accessories, Communications, HyperTerminal to bring up the HyperTerminal folder. Double click the Hypertrm icon to launch the HyperTerminal communications program. Then follow these steps:

1. In the Connection Description window, enter the name of the connection, such as Linux. Change the icon if you want by clicking an appropriate icon. Then click OK.

2. In the Connect To window, select your dial-in Linux workstation's country code (the default is USA), area code (defaults to your current dial-up networking settings), and phone number. In the Connect Using field, select the appropriate dial-out modem on your Windows PC (the default should be correct). Click OK.

3. In the Connect window, you will see the phone number you are dialing (click Modify if you need to go back and change it) and your location (click Dialing Properties if you need to define specific instructions for your connection, such as turning off call waiting or using a 9 to access an outside line). Click Dial if your Linux workstation is already configured for dial-in and you are ready to test the configuration (you will need two different phone lines, or you must dial from an outside location). Your Windows PC modem will dial out and hopefully connect to your Linux dial-in modem.

4. In the Linux—HyperTerminal window, you should enter your login account name and password. If you are properly authenticated, you will receive a command-line prompt, where you can enter additional commands.

5. Type `exit` at the Linux command line to log out and close the connection. You also can click the hang-up icon in HyperTerminal to log out, and click the connect icon to dial and log back in.

TIP

By default, your Linux PC will not allow a remote terminal to log in as the root or superuser. You will be allowed to log in as a normal user and then use the `su` command to switch user and become root (with full root privileges), however. If you prefer to log in directly as root from a remote location, you can log in as root on the console and edit the `/etc/securetty` file with your favorite editor. Then add a line containing the device name of the devices over which you will allow a remote root login. You may run into a bug I encountered also—after I made any dial-in connections to Linux, I was unable to use any of the GNOME menu items or panel launchers. I unfortunately had to restart my X session by using the Ctrl+Alt+Backspace key combination.

Configuring Dial-in Networking

Text-based computing may not be what you want or need from a remote location, however. With a normal dial-in account, you can use programs such as lynx on the remote terminal to directly access your Web server files, for instance (assuming that you have an address such as localhost correctly configured to your local Linux IP address). However, this puts all the processing on the Linux server, and you cannot use your remote Windows clients, such as Web servers, Telnet, and file transfer protocol (ftp) clients.

Luckily, after you get your modem, TCP/IP networking, and PPP networking installed and configured, and then configure your Linux computer for dial-in, it's an easy task to add this networking capability. Refer to Chapter 32, Chapter 27, and Chapter 33 for additional information in these areas. When you get PPP networking up and running across your dial-in modem link, your Windows PC will not appear as a terminal to Linux, but rather as an actual node on your network. You will be able to easily set the network addresses for both connections of the link after you log in.

The magic that makes this all possible is the same Point-to-Point Protocol (PPP) technology that you use with your Linux and Windows PCs to connect to the Internet and effectively become a node on your Internet service provider's network as well as the Internet itself (if they have routing and domain name services configured and operating properly). Unlike the dial-up networking and PPP client that comes with Windows, your Linux PC comes with a PPP daemon (`/usr/sbin/pppd`) that serves as both a client and a server. This enables you to connect to other networks and allow other PCs to connect to your network.

If you didn't install the PPP daemon during your initial installation, you can find it on this book's CD in the Red Hat RPMS directory, named `ppp-2.3.7-2.i386.rpm`. You can confirm that you have it installed either by using GnomeRPM from the main menu under Settings or from the command line by typing `rpm -q ppp`.

Part

VI

Ch

34

You can configure pppd either directly from the command line or by storing settings in the /etc/ppp/options file. If you store the settings in the options file, this may interfere with your dial-out PPP connections to the Internet. Unless an individual is calling in very frequently, it is just as easy to add the little amount of information you need on the command line.

N O T E By default, you cannot run /usr/sbin/pppd as a normal user; you must become root over the dial-up connection by using the su command. This is no problem if you or only a few people connect, but you wouldn't want to give the root password to too many people. If you prefer, you can allow everyone that dials in to use pppd as the superuser by making the /usr/sbin/pppd file "suid root," although this is a widely acknowledged security hole that can be used potentially by hackers to get into your system as the superuser. Generally speaking, any hacker would need to authenticate to your system, meaning that this person would need someone's password or be able to guess it somehow. If this is not a big concern for you, you can set suid by adding 4000 to the current file settings of /usr/sbin/pppd (if it's rwxr-xr-x, or 755, then as root you would type chmod 4755 /usr/sbin/pppd.) Then any user that properly authenticates and logs in can run it now and initiate the PPP network connection. ▪

After you have logged in and become superuser, you could launch the PPP daemon by simply typing /usr/sbin/pppd on the command line. This will generate some unintelligible characters from the Linux side of the link to your remote terminal, be it Windows or Linux. The problem with this is that you need to initiate PPP on the remote dial-in side also for networking to work. If you are just using HyperTerminal as in the previous section of this chapter, there is no way to kick off PPP on Windows to negotiate the network connection with the pppd running on Linux. To do this in Windows, you need to use dial-up networking, according the following steps:

1. From the Windows 95 or 98 desktop, double-click My Computer (or whatever you renamed this folder), Dial-Up Networking, and Make New Connection.

2. In the Make New Connection window, enter the name you want to call your PPP network connection (something like "Linux" will do), and select the modem you want to use from the drop-down list. Click Next.

3. Enter the area code and country code (if needed) and the telephone number of your dial-in Linux PC. Click Next. You will see a confirmation box showing that your Linux connection now exists. Click Finish.

4. In the Dial-Up Networking window, right-click the network connection you just created, and select Properties. Make sure that no changes are needed in the General tab, and then click Configure. Make any changes that are necessary to your actual modem, such as speed, COM port, and whether you want to listen to the modem dial out. Then click the Options tab and check the Bring Up Terminal Window After Dialing box. This is the most important setting because it forces the login prompt to be visible and allow you to log on, become the superuser, and initiate the PPP daemon. Click OK to save your settings and close the Properties window.

5. In the Server Types tab, uncheck all the Advanced options and all allowed network protocols except TCP/IP. Click Configure and select the radio buttons indicating server-assigned IP address and name servers (you can enter other name server addresses if you have one locally or want to use the remote Linux server—for example, you could use 192.168.1.1 for the primary if that was the IP address of your Linux machine). Uncheck IP header compression and leave Use Default Gateway on Remote Network checked. Click OK to save your settings and close the Linux (dial-up) window.

6. Double-click the icon for the connection you just created. This brings up a Connect To window. Don't worry about entering the password; it is not needed at this point. Click Connect to have your modem dial out and connect to Linux.

7. After the connection is complete and the terminal window pops up, provide your Linux account name and password. After authentication, you will receive a shell prompt.

8. At the shell prompt, log in as superuser using the su command and providing the superuser (root) password.

9. Determine what unused IP addresses you want to use for both ends of the dial-up connection. For example, on your local area network, you might use the 192.168.1 series of IP addresses, like many small businesses and individuals with local networks. Let's assume all machines on that network have IP addresses between 192.168.1.1 and 192.168.1.10, and you decide to use 192.168.1.20 for your Linux PPP node and 192.168.1.25 for your Windows node. You want the remote network to be capable of referencing your Windows IP address, and you also want your Windows PC to be capable of referencing IP addresses on your Linux network. To do this, you need to use the `defaultroute` and `proxyarp` parameters with pppd. Type the following in your terminal window to kick off PPP on Linux:

```
/usr/sbin/pppd 192.168.1.20:192.168.1.25 defaultroute proxyarp
```

10. When you start seeing Linux generate what looks like garbage characters to your terminal screen, click Continue (F7) to have Windows initiate its end of the PPP connection. You will see another pop-up window showing that the connection is being made, and then you will be active on the remote Linux network.

When the connection has been successfully completed, you can perform all the normal IP networking functions you can as if you were connected physically with network cables on the Linux LAN. For example, you can enter `http://192.168.1.20/` in your Windows browser to bring up the default home page on your Linux Web server (if it's configured), `telnet 192.168.1.20` to bring up a text-based login terminal, or `ftp 192.168.1.20` to use your Windows file transfer client with any configured Linux ftp servers. You can do the same thing with 192.168.1.25 to access IP resources and servers on your Windows machine (from both Linux and Windows). Even clients such as your POP3 email reader will be capable of accessing individual IP ports on your Linux server.

Part

VI

Ch

34

Troubleshooting Remote Access

There are many low level infrastructure components that must be in place before you can do the high-level networking functions discussed in this chapter. For example, you must have same settings in your BIOS for your COM ports and modems to work properly. You also must have networking and dial-up networking installed on any Windows clients, as well as some sort of name services configured on Linux and Windows PCs to translate computer names to IP addresses.

If you are having problems with your serial (COM) port connections, you usually can rule out hardware problems, especially if they work properly in other operating systems such as Windows. It is more likely that your Linux device files (/etc/ttyS0, for example) are not configured properly, possibly with the wrong ownerships or read-write permissions. They also may need to be reconfigured with additional options using the setserial command. The configuration settings out of the box are usually sufficient to get the job done, if you make the changes mentioned in this chapter. However, sometimes mismatches do occur between these default settings, especially on the Windows side of the connection equation. If you run into such a situation, use a logical, scientific approach to troubleshooting the problem. Look first for simple solutions, such as checking cable connections and recently modified configuration files. Make backup copies of any configuration files you change so that you can recover easily from any problems that occur. Often problems in Linux can be traced to ownerships and permissions, so make sure that you check those very early.

If your file and process listings print out incorrectly on your screen when using serial cable connections between two PCs, you may be dropping (losing) characters during the transmission. In this case, you may have to play with the baud rate or speed settings for both ends of the link.

One of the most common problems is seeing an error message about a process spawning (attempting to start) too fast. This usually is caused by adding a line to a configuration file, such as /etc/inittab or /etc/gettydefs, that prevents it from performing functions properly. When this happens, edit the file you think is causing the problem (it probably was edited recently) and make the necessary changes. In the case of /etc/inittab, you can comment out a line and then restart using init q. You also may have to stop any processes that are causing problems using the kill command.

If you are having network problems, you can use any of the typical IP clients to test your network connections. For example, the ping command can be used in conjunction with an IP address or a computer name to determine if there is a route to the remote machine. If one works and the other doesn't (address or name), then it's an indication that your /etc/hosts file or Domain Name Service (DNS) is not configured properly. If neither works, then you should check the cable connections, Ethernet hubs, and then possibly even the networking configuration of both PCs. ●

## CHAPTER 35

Configuring Fax Support

by Duane Hellums

In this chapter

Red Hat Linux 6.0 comes with all the software you need to be able to efficiently send, receive, view, and print a facsimile (fax) directly on your computer. As long as you have a fax modem installed, you can install and configure the `efax` and `fax` programs that come with Red Hat Linux 6.0 to use it properly. As with most fax software, `efax` enables you to manually or automatically send and receive faxes. The fax script is located at `/usr/bin/fax` and is a command-line, front-end interface to `efax` and other helper programs for viewing and printing faxes.

Both `efax` and `fax` support Group 3 protocols and most class 1 and class 2 fax modem commands. This covers most popular modems, including those by AT&T, Boca, Cardinal, Digicom, Intel, Megahertz, Motorola, Practical Peripherals, Supra, Telebit, Viva, U.S. Robotics, and Zoom. However, you should consult the hardware compatibility guide on Red Hat's Web site to make sure that Linux supports your specific make and model of modem. Keep in mind also that you may be able to use your modem, even if it is not included on the hardware compatibility list.

Understanding Your Fax Modem

Chapter 32, "Configuring Modems," explained how to install and configure a modem for use with your Linux system. By now, you should have your modem operational and should know how to reference it in your system. For instance, if your modem is set for COM2, it will be available as either device `/dev/ttyS1` or `/dev/cua1`. If your modem is set for COM3, it will be `/dev/ttyS2` or `/dev/cua2`, and so on. You should also have the `/dev/modem` device linked to the appropriate COM port, which you can perform or verify by accessing Control Panel, Modem Configuration.

The difference between the `/dev/ttyS1` and `/dev/cua1` devices is that historically ttyS1 has been used for calling out, and cua1 has been used for receiving calls (data and fax). The reason for having two devices is that both their device drivers were programmed to react to the existence of a Data Carrier Detect (DCD) signal. If you use the wrong one and no carrier signal is detected, any application trying to use that device will just stop processing and wait for a signal that never comes (effectively locking up or *hanging*). The trend is to use `/dev/ttyS1` as both a dial-in and dial-out device, as long as the driver supports such a practice. However, many programs still use the convention of separate device names for dial-in and dial-out devices.

Although `efax` does most of the work for you, you also will need to know some information about your fax, such as the class and speed (most faxes now support the maximum speed of 14Kbps).

Installing *efax*

You can find the `efax` collection of programs on this book's CD as a Red Hat Package Manager (RPM) package. It is stored on the CD as `/RedHat/RPMS/efax-0.8a-11.i386.rpm`.

You can confirm that `efax` is installed by using GnomeRPM, or by typing `rpm -q efax` at a command-line shell prompt. If this program is not installed, follow the instructions in Chapter 11, "Installing and Managing RPM Packages." The `efax` suite actually consists of three main programs, as follows:

- `efix`—The `/usr/bin/efix` utility that handles the necessary file format conversions in support of `efax`
- `efax`—The main `/usr/bin/efax` program that handles all the communications with your fax modem
- `fax`—The `/usr/bin/fax` script that acts as a text-based user interface to `efax` and `efix`

N O T E Eventually, you probably will find that `/usr/bin/fax` is easier to use for all your fax needs. However, that interface merely builds on the lower-level functions of `/usr/bin/efix` and `/usr/bin/efax`. As a result, it is probably more useful to take a stepwise, building block approach to give you a firm understanding of the small manual processes available to you before tackling `/usr/bin/fax`. This should also help you to debug specific configuration challenges in smaller bites that are easier to isolate and troubleshoot. ◼

Preparing Files for Faxing

To send a fax, you will need to convert, either automatically or manually, all pages to the Group 3 compressed TIFF file format for `efax` to process and send. Faxes you receive are also stored in this format, so you will need to have a way of viewing this format. For one-page text and graphics, you can use your favorite application, as long as it saves files in the correct TIFF format (`efax` doesn't support certain types, such as multistrip format). For larger files, it is best to use `efix` and `fax` for these file translations.

Other effective methods and tools, including programs such as the GNU Image Manipulation Program (GIMP) and GhostScript, also will be discussed in this chapter. If you want to use these programs, you will have to make sure that they are installed as well.

Converting Text Files with *efix*

For example, let's say that you have a six-page ASCII text file named `myfile` that you created with Gnotepad or another word processor. The process basically involves converting the six pages in this file into six separate TIFF formatted files for `efax` to process. To convert this text file to TIFF format, go to the directory where `myfile` is located. Type `/usr/bin/efix -nmyfile.%03d < myfile`, and watch to make sure that you don't get any error messages. You should see a copyright notice indicating that the command was successful. This will create TIFF files named `myfile.001`, `myfile.002`, `myfile.003`, `myfile.004`, `myfile.005`, and `myfile.006`. You can then fax these files using `/usr/bin/efax` or `/usr/bin/fax`, as explained later in this chapter in the section on sending faxes. For non-ASCII text in documents—such as what you would see in StarOffice word processor, for example—consult the next section.

Converting Graphics Files

To fax multipage graphics or more complicated documents, you can use several methods. The basic process involves saving, exporting, or printing the file in question to a PostScript file on your system. Then you can use GhostScript (`/usr/bin/gs`) and the TIFF export driver that comes with it to translate that .ps file to the G3 TIFF format required by `efax`.

For example, let's say that you have a three-page document with graphics in the StarOffice word processor and a Web page of similar length in your Netscape Communicator browser, both of which you want to prepare to be faxed. Both applications offer you the ability to select File, Print, and then Print to File. Assuming that you save the files as `document.ps` and `netscape.ps`, respectively, you can type the following lines to convert the two files to multiple TIFF format files:

```
(c1)gs -q -sDEVICE=tiffg3 -dNOPAUSE -sOutputFile=document.%03d \
document.ps < /dev/null
(c1)gs -q -sDEVICE=tiffg3 -dNOPAUSE -sOutputFile=netscape.%03d \
netscape.ps < /dev/null
```

After you run this command, you should see six additional files in your current directory, named `document.001`, `document.002`, `document.003`, `netscape.001`, `netscape.002`, and `netscape.003`. If you type `file document* netscape*` in your X terminal or at the command-line shell prompt, you will be able to confirm from the output that the original .ps files are PostScript and that the converted files are stored as TIFF images.

Configuring *efax* to Send Faxes

By this point, you should be able to prepare some files that are ready to be faxed. This is the point at which it is important to know the proper device name and speed for your modem. Oddly enough, there are no specific configuration files that you must edit before you use `efax`. However, you do have to send the `/usr/bin/efax` command different options and flags when you execute it, based on your desired results. As you can tell by the lack of figures in this chapter, no graphical front-end program is available for `efax`, although the fax script (discussed later in this chapter) is at least an enhancement to this rather laborious fax process.

N O T E This is where you may have to use some level of trial-and-error process with different options to get the `efax` program to interface correctly with your fax modem. Document the configuration settings you use here at the command line because you will need them later when you configure the `/usr/bin/fax` script. ■

You will have to provide at least a few command-line options for `efax` to properly transmit your TIFF formatted files to a remote fax machine. For example, you will have to provide the following information:

- **Device name**—You must provide the path and filename of your fax device. For example, use `-d /dev/cua1` if your fax modem is configured for COM2.

- **Option**—You should tell `efax` whether you have a class 1 or class 2 fax. Use `-o0` if you have a newer, class 2 fax; use `-o1` if you have a class 1 fax.

- **Identification**—FCC regulations dictate that a fax modem identify itself, at least by phone number. If your number is 808-555-1212, for example, you should use `-l "1 808 555 1212"`.

- **Telephone number**—You must tell `efax` the telephone number of your destination fax and whether your phone uses tone dialing. If your phone supports tone dialing and you are faxing to 800-123-4567, for example, you would use `-t T18001234567` to have your fax modem dial the number. If you need to dial 9 to get an outside line and wait a few seconds before dialing the number, you would use `-t T9,,18001234567` with the `efax` command.

- **Filename(s)**—You must tell `efax` which files you want it to send because it sends them one page at a time. You enter them all on the same line after the phone number, without any additional option tags.

Now let's put all these command options and flags together with the text files that prepared earlier for faxing. Let's assume the TIFF files are all in the same subdirectory on your Linux file system, and that you are currently at a command-line prompt or an X terminal in that directory. Assuming that you have a class 2 fax on COM2 that is capable of 14.4Kbps transmission rates, here is the command you would have to type to send the StarOffice word processor files created earlier (the process is the same for other files created) to someone at the local number 123-4567 from your number, 808-555-1212:

```
[1c]/usr/bin/efax -d /dev/cua1 -o0 -l"808 555 1212" -t T123-4567 \
document.001 document.002 document.003
```

When you type this command, you should hear your modem click on and begin dialing the number, and you should see a message from `efax` saying that the program successfully connected to (opened) the modem and is dialing the number that you specified. You will also hear the typical intermittent fax tone that will communicate with the fax on the other end, if that fax is turned on. If the call is completed, you will hear some fax modem negotiation tones; then your modem will send the individual pages, which the remote fax will acknowledge.

Configuring *efax* to Manually Receive Faxes

Receiving a fax is a similar process to sending, although there are a few minor differences. One important difference is whether the phone is already ringing or whether you expect it to start ringing soon (or even later). You must give efax different commands that will change the way it behaves in both these instances: One picks up the phone immediately, and the other waits until it detects that a call is not picked up by a person.

To start the efax program manually and have it answer a call that is coming in at the very moment you enter the command, you will have to add the following options to your efax command:

- **Device name**—You must provide the path and filename of your fax device. For example, use -d /dev/ttyS1 if your fax modem is configured for COM2.

- **Option**—You should tell efax whether you have a class 1 or class 2 fax. Use -o0 if you have a newer, class 2 fax; use -o1 if you have a class 1 fax.

- **Identification**—FCC regulations dictate that a fax machine identify itself, at least by phone number. For example, if your number is 808-555-1212, you should use -l "1 800 555 1212".

- **Capabilities**—This is where you let efax know what kind of modem you have so that it can negotiate the best transmission method. If left off, the default is high-resolution, 9600bps, 8.5-inch page width, and unlimited page length. This default equates to -c 1,3,0,2, but most people have 14Kbps modems and will more likely use -c 1,5,0,2, or -c 1,5, for short. If you don't use all eight number positions, you will get a warning, but efax will work fine.

- **Received Fax File Name(s)**—You must let efax know what you want to call faxes you receive. For example, you can name them inboundfax.001, inboundfax.002, and so on by using the -r inboundfax option.

Putting this all together, the following command would be used to force the Red Hat Linux 6.0 fax modem discussed earlier to answer calls immediately and receive incoming faxes, if applicable:

```
[1c]/usr/bin/efax -d /dev/ttyS1 -o0 -l "123-4567" -c 1,5 -r inboundfax
```

> **TIP** You can run this command while you are in the middle of a voice call, too (similar to the capabilities of standalone or all-in-one office fax machines). If someone on the other end initiates a fax tone, you can just type this immediate command to begin reception of the fax while you are on the phone.

If all goes well, you should hear the fax modem pick up and begin answering the remote modem tones with its own. You should see output from efax that a fax call was answered, along with the identification of the remote fax and some session information, such as speed and page size. After the page(s) of the fax is fully received, efax will indicate that it has received the inbound fax files and then will hang up the phone.

N O T E This method works best when you do not use your Linux PC to receive faxes very often. You may need to manually receive only when you are expecting a fax or pick up and hear a fax on the other end. If your Linux PC is not powered up, it is usually best to just stay on the line until the remote fax hangs up. This will buy yourself more time for booting Linux and preparing to run your manual fax receipt command or shell script. ▪

Configuring *efax* to Receive Faxes on Standby

For obvious reasons, you might not want to have to run a command manually every time you receive an inbound fax. Luckily, efax provides a way to put your fax modem in standby mode and automatically receive an incoming fax when the fax arrives.

If you must have your fax modem wait for an extended period of time for an incoming fax (several hours or all day, perhaps), you can run /usr/bin/efax once as a background process, and it will remain active until it receives a fax or until you stop the process. You can even have your modem wait each time for the fourth or fifth call so that you will have time to pick up first to see if it's a voice call.

To launch the efax program and make it wait for incoming calls, you can add the -w option to the efax command. You add the -iS0 modem register option to indicate how many rings to pause before picking up and playing the tones to negotiate the fax modem link. In this situation, you want to replace the -r option used earlier in this chapter (you don't want to keep writing over the same files) with an option to create filenames dynamically based on the date and time of reception (in the format MMDDHHMMSS). To use the fax modem discussed up to this point for such purposes, use the following command to place the fax modem in standby status awaiting the fourth ring to pick up:

```
[1c]/usr/bin/efax -d /dev/ttyS1 -o0 -l "123-4567" -c 1,5 \
[1c] -w -iS0=4  2>&1 >> fax.in.log
```

If all goes well, you should see efax quickly prompt you that it has opened the fax modem and is awaiting activity. When the phone starts ringing now or later, efax will indicate that activity is detected, but it will continue waiting for the number of rings for which it is configured. If the phone has not been answered for the number of rings set, efax will pick up and initiate the fax link, with a "fax call answered" prompt to your shell or X terminal.

N O T E Using this automatic method, you can receive only one inbound fax per process. After efax receives the fax and saves it to disk, the process will die off and return you to the shell prompt. If you want your modem to wait on another fax, you will have to run the command again. If you need to receive more than one fax during the day and you don't have time to keep bringing up this process, you should consider using the initialization process (init) to run and manage efax processing. ▪

Configuring *init* to Automatically Receive Faxes

Luckily, as mentioned before, there's a way to force efax to run every time you boot up. This requires no intervention on your part, unless you encounter some problems with the program. As you may have guessed, you do this "permanent" configuration using the initialization process (init). The init process not only starts the efax process, but it also has the job of managing it and launching another instance of it if one should die off for any reason.

The initialization process basically is a central repository and manager for other daemons and processes, such as efax. If you configure init to launch another daemon, it will do so on bootup and persistently thereafter, as necessary—in other words, init will start another daemon if one is killed for any reason.

To add efax to the init process, you will need to perform the following steps:

1. Using vi, Gnotepad, or a similar editor, create an ASCII text file by an appropriate name in the /usr/bin directory, such as /usr/bin/efax-init.

2. Change permissions of that file using chmod 700 /usr/bin/efax-init to make it executable.

3. Inside this init script, add the standby command developed in the previous section: /usr/bin/efax -d /dev/ttyS1 -o0 -l "123 4567" -c1,5 -w -iS0=4 2>&1 >> fax.in.log and save the file to disk.

> **CAUTION**
>
> You must be logged in as root (or become superuser with the su command) to edit certain configuration files. You should always make a backup of such important files before you edit them so you can recover from any emergencies. Double-check your syntax before and after saving the files, and verify the permissions are correct for your purposes (you might want to check and document the correct ownerships and permissions of the original file before making any changes, so afterward you can update any new configuration files you create). Recovering from mistakes in these files can sometimes be problematic. Be very careful and more than just a little paranoid—similar to when you perform surgery on (edit) the Windows registry.

4. Using the same editor, add the following syntax to the last line of the /etc/inittab file (that manages which processes will be started during bootup and kept up while the system is working): s1:45:respawn:/usr/bin/efax-init.

5. Close any active programs you have running, and type init 1 from the command-line prompt to go to single user mode. Watch the screen output to make sure that init doesn't generate any error messages after you edited it to add your efax-init script.

6. When the system is in single user mode, type init 5 to come back up into graphic, network mode (or use 2-4 if you typically use other modes). You will have to log back in again.

7. Confirm that the `init` process kicked off the `efax-init` script (which should have kicked off the `efax` command string built in the previous section).

8. Test the setup by sending yourself a fax (if possible), by having someone else send you one, or by calling a faxback service at some company (most companies provide information related to this service on their Web home page). You should receive the fax, with a numeric filename based on the date and time it was received (in the format MMDDHHMMSS). For example, Aug 8, 3:53:14 PM would be saved as 0808155314.001 and 080815314.002.

Configuring the *fax* Script to Automate Faxing

Now that you've learned the hard way of using `efax` manually, it's time to discuss the easy way. The `efax` collection of fax software includes the script file `/usr/bin/fax`, which accepts several command-line options itself. The difference between it and `/usr/bin/efax`, however, is that `fax` operates at a much higher level and hides most of the complexity of faxing, which it in turn hands off directly to `efax` and `efix`. The fax script provides you the following basic capabilities (which you will find similar to those from `efix` and `efax`, discussed earlier in this chapter):

■ **Test**—Run `/usr/bin/fax test` to find out how your configuration settings behave with your modem's hardware settings. You can capture and redirect (> `fax-test.txt`, for example) the output to a file for subsequent viewing and debugging or documentation purposes.

■ **Make**—Run `/usr/bin/fax make netscape.ps` to convert the PostScript files that you saved to file earlier in the chapter to the TIFF bitmap files required by Send. The `.001`, `.002`, and `.003` file extensions are automatically added. You can use `fax make myfile` to convert the ASCII text-based files to TIFF also; `fax` autosenses the file type and makes the necessary translations.

Unlike `efax`, which requires you to convert files using `efix` first, the `fax send` command does both, negating the need to use `make` unless you want to run a few fax preparation batch jobs, for example.

■ **Send**—Run `/usr/bin/fax send 123-4567 document*` to send the three-page file you created earlier and sent using `efax` to the fictitious local phone number 123-4567. If the original source file still exists (named document), you can just type `document`, and Send will handle the conversion during the transmission.

If you've already dialed the number and are talking to someone on a combination phone/fax, you can manually initiate a fax transmission of the files listed here by using the `-m` flag, or by typing `/usr/bin/fax send -m document*`.

- **Receive**—Run `/usr/bin/fax receive inboundfax` to answer an incoming call immediately and save the pages sequentially with a filename prefix of `inboundfax` (for example, `inboundfax.001, inboundfax.002`) in the `/var/spool/fax` directory, similar to what was done earlier with `efax`.

> **TIP**
>
> If you leave off the filename prefix with the `Receive` command, `fax` will automatically generate filenames based on the current date and time, similar to the way you saved files previously in this chapter.

- **Answer**—Run `/usr/bin/fax answer` to put your fax modem on standby waiting for an incoming call that usually occurs later, after you execute the command. The fax program will run in the background until it receives an incoming fax call. Fax pages will be saved sequentially with a filename prefix of `inboundfax` (for example, `inboundfax.001, inboundfax.002`), similar to the way it occurred earlier with `efax`.

> **TIP**
>
> To keep `Answer` running in the background at all times and accepting fax calls, you can add the following line to `/etc/inittab` (see previous caution), replacing the `efax-init` script placed there earlier: `s1:45:respawn:/bin/sh /usr/bin/fax answer`.

- **Print**—Run `/usr/bin/fax print inboundfax*` to print up all the pages you just received using the `Receive` command.
- **View**—Run `/usr/bin/fax view inboundfax.001` to view the first page of your received fax or to preview faxes you intend to send (`document.001`, for example).
- **Rm (Remove)**—Run `/usr/bin/fax rm inboundfax*` to remove all pages of the fax you received and stored on your hard drive.

You should notice by now that `/usr/bin/fax` is considerably easier to use than `efix` and `efax`. Specifically, it hides much of the configuration settings from you and doesn't require you to remember the syntax or the settings for correct placement on the command line as options. However, it doesn't do this by magic. By default, the information that you provided earlier when manually configuring `efix` and `efax` must be stored inside the `/usr/bin/fax` script itself as parameter variables. The configuration settings you normally will be concerned with editing in this script are as follows:

- **DEV**—Enter the device name of your fax modem (`DEV=cua1` for COM2, `DEV=cua2` for COM3, and so on).
- **CLASS**—Uncomment the appropriate class of fax modem you have (mine is `CLASS=2.0`) and comment out the other few classes listed.
- **FROM**—Enter the telephone number identification for your location, in quotation marks (`FROM="1 800 123 4567"`, from the earlier fax).
- **NAME**—Enter the name you want to appear on top of printed faxes, in quotations (`NAME="Red Hat Linux 6.0—Penguins Rule!"`).

- **PAGE**—Uncomment the correct paper size (default is `PAGE=LETTER`).

- **PRTYPE**—Uncomment the correct printer type (`PRTYPE=pcl` or `PRTYPE=ps` for HP or PostScript).

- **PRCMD**—Enter the correct printer command (default is `PRCMD="lpr"`).

- **VIEWCMD**—Uncomment the fax viewer that works best on your system (I had to use `VIEWCMD="pnmtoxwd ¦ xwud,"`, although I usually just use the GIMP or StarOffice word processor to view and print faxes).

- **RES**—Enter high (`RES=204x196`) or low (`RES=204x98`) resolution.

- **PRINT**—Uncomment only one of the efix or gs (GhostScript) print utility sections, whichever you find works best on your system.

- **INIT**—Enter a specific modem initialization string if your fax modem doesn't work with the generic default.

- **SPKR**—Enter a speaker mode and loudness, if you need to hear your fax burp and whistle (while debugging, for example).

- **TXCAP**—Enter the transmission capabilities codes discussed earlier in this chapter (`TXCAP="1,5,0,2,0,0,0,0"` for 14Kbps modems and unlimited page length).

- **FAXDIR**—Enter the desired location of your fax spooling directory (default is `FAXDIR=/var/spool/fax`).

- **ANSRINGS**—Enter the number of times you want your phone to ring before the fax modem picks up and starts playing fax tones (default is `ANSRINGS=1`, but you may find 4 or 5 better).

You should make a backup copy of the original script before you make changes (always a good practice!), just in case you need to recover from changes you make. Do the same thing with any other files, such as `/etc/inittab`, that you might modify to get `/usr/bin/fax` to work. After you have backed up and edited the `/usr/bin/fax` script to your liking, you should save your changes. If you already have `fax` running from `inittab`, all you have to do is "bounce" the process by typing `/usr/bin/fax stop`, followed by `/usr/bin/fax start`, to have the script reload with the new settings you created.

Troubleshooting *efax* and Fax Modems

Fax modems can sometimes be tricky to debug. If you can't get any reaction out of your modem at all, it may be an indication that your settings are wrong. This is especially true if your modem works in Windows but doesn't in Linux. More than likely, you are using the wrong device name or don't have the correct permissions needed to access and use the device. If you've double-checked the hardware and software settings and still can't get the fax modem to operate in any available operating system, you should try reseating the card, or pulling it out and putting it back in firmly and evenly. Double-check the hardware settings, and make sure they are the same as what you have configured your software to use.

Part
VI

Ch
35

Also consider other possibilities, such as whether your modem is supported by Linux; certain modems, such as the U.S. Robotics WinModem, are designed specially for Windows and do not provide sufficient flexibility to get them working (without major surgery) under Linux. Some fax modems also do not have "jumpers" on the card, which are normally used to change hardware settings, such as selecting COM settings 1–4 or the associated Input-Output (I/O) values.

 N O T E You might get one or more errors during fax transmission. This is natural for fax machines, which do not all provide error correction and efficient flow control. However, if the receiving fax records too many problems (defaults to 10 or more), it will ask the sender to resend the page in question. ▪

Listening to the modem's activities and tones can be very helpful in narrowing down your problem. If you are hearing the fax modem pick up the call and send tones to the remote fax, then you can rule out the possibility of a hardware failure or device configuration problem. For outbound calls, if you hear your fax modem access the line, dial, and generate the necessary intermittent tones, but you don't hear anything on the receiving end, it's probably a good indication that the fax modem on the other end is malfunctioning.

 TIP You can run the `/usr/bin/fax test` command to find out loads of information about your fax modem settings and capabilities. This wealth of information might help you solve any configuration or hardware problems as well. For example, it could indicate that you have only a class 1 modem instead of class 2, which would require different configuration settings for you. It could also tell you the speed limitations (maximum baud rate) of your fax modem. Look at the `/var/spool/fax/cua1.log` log file and see if it contains any error messages in that you can't explain as well.

Keep in mind that `efax` is not the only program that uses your modem, and you may not be the only person on the network using it, either. You may notice that your fax modem generates modem commands very sporadically and almost at random during calls or answers. If so, it could be that several programs or daemons may be contending for this resource at the same time. Keep in mind that Linux by nature is a multiprocessing and multiuser system, so just because you're not using the modem doesn't mean it isn't being used. Another thing to consider is that if your modem fails to connect but you continually hear tones before it gives up, you may have bad telephone line quality.

TIP Perform a file listing on the `/var/lock` directory using `ls -al /var/lock`. Make sure that there are no LCK..modem, LCK..cua1, or LCK..ttyS1 (assuming you're on COM2) files that you can't account for. It may be that `efax` is trying to access your modem, but another application or process is using it exclusively. Determine whether you need to free up the fax modem device for use with your `efax` software, or whether you can just remove the lock file. Sometimes when a process goes stale, it is incapable of removing the lock file, which prevents other programs from accessing the resource.

If all else fails, you can always turn to the documentation that comes with efax. The quantity and quality of the help files is pretty good. Type man efax, man efix, or man fax (or the corresponding info efax, info efix, info fax), depending on which program you think you need help with the most. ●

## CHAPTER 36

Configuring Microsoft FrontPage Server Extensions

by Duane Hellums

In this chapter

Microsoft FrontPage 2000 is a suite of Internet Web development and management tools. The client can be used to create Web pages and sites, and runs only on Microsoft operating systems. Certain functionality or components that the client builds into a Web site require direct interaction with the Web server. If the Microsoft FrontPage 2000 Server Extensions (FPSE) are not installed on the Web server, FrontPage still can be used to create and edit Web pages—the developer just can't add any bells and whistles to the pages.

Luckily, these server extensions are available for most contemporary Web servers and operating systems, including Apache and Red Hat Linux 6.0. As a matter of fact, it's a pretty easy process of incorporating FPSE into your Linux server because Red Hat Linux 6.0 comes with Apache preinstalled and preconfigured, with only a few minor modifications necessary. All you have to do is download, install, and configure the FPSE. If you want, you also can optimize the FrontPage 2000 client for use with your Linux-based Web server, but this is not strictly necessary.

Understanding FrontPage 2000 Server Extensions

Many ways exist by which you can create and manage a Web site and the myriad technologies, files, and folders associated with it. For instance, you can edit the text manually in Hypertext Markup Language (HTML) files and learn how to "tag" Web objects such as hyperlinks, graphics, and included files. Then you can transfer the files to your site using File Transfer Protocol (ftp). However, when you remove a local hyperlink on your site, you probably should delete the file it points to. How can you easily and efficiently do this without a management tool? Try as you might, it is likely that you will end up with stranded files that waste server space and complicate management of your site.

If you add hyperlinks and forget to include the files, or vice versa, will you have to wait until you get your first email complaint about it from a customer, if the person even bothers? Even a site of intermediate size and complexity requires several people to maintain it. How do you coordinate with these other people to prevent one of them from writing over files you just updated, and vice versa?

Wouldn't it be nice if you could click a button and have the computer handle many of these administrative nightmares? Microsoft recognized this customer requirement pretty early and developed FrontPage for this purpose. The company then came out with two upgrades: FrontPage 98 and FrontPage 2000 (which doesn't require Office 2000 or Windows 2000, by the way).

N O T E FPSE versions are backward-compatible with previous versions of the client, but certain features available to the client (database connectivity, hit counters, discussion groups, and so on) are available only on your Web site if your Internet service provider (ISP) installs the corresponding extensions on the server. ▨

Microsoft created FrontPage as a means of doing all this work graphically in a WYSIWYG (what you see is what you get), drag-and-drop interface on the Windows platform. Other competing products, including Adobe's Go Live!, are available as well. Each contains its own set of tools and utilities that facilitate Web creation and management.

I don't have to sell you on the product or its features—it pretty much does that on its own. This chapter just acknowledges the popularity and widespread use of FrontPage, and covers how to get it to work with your Linux-based Apache Web server, if you so choose. If you want to know more about features and capabilities, you can check out Microsoft's FrontPage site at `http://www.microsoft.com/frontpage`. For server-specific information, you can read the FrontPage Server Extensions Resource Kit (SERK), located at `http://www.microsoft.com/frontpage/serk`.

 TIP The Server Extensions Resource Kit is also located on your FrontPage 2000 client CD and on your FrontPage-enabled Linux server at `/usr/local/frontpage/version4.0/serk/default.htm`.

Obtaining FrontPage 2000 Server Extensions

Microsoft does not develop or "port" FrontPage 2000 Server Extensions directly to UNIX or Linux. They outsource this job to a company named Ready to Run Software. That company develops and supports the UNIX versions of the FPSE and makes it available for downloading from the Web site `http://www.rtr.com/`. They also have a copy of the SERK available for viewing, in addition to the copy on Microsoft's site.

To download the Microsoft FrontPage 2000 Server Extensions for Linux Web servers, perform the following tasks:

1. Use a browser and Internet connection, and access Ready to Run Software's Web site at `http://www.rtr.com/` (do this directly on your Linux PC, if possible).

2. Find the most current link that takes you to the FrontPage 2000 Server Extensions download page. This is subject to change, of course, but it currently is `http://www.rtr.com/fpsupport`. You can skip directly to the license agreement by going to `http://www.rtr.com/fpsupport/fp2000license.htm`.

3. Fill in at least your email address and first and last name (required) on the licensing form. Other fields are optional.

4. Select the radio button on the form next to the Linux platform that applies to your situation, and then click the Submit button. RTR has only the Intel x86 versions available during this writing. The `tar.gz` file is 9.8MB, which will take a while to download over a 52Kbps modem downlink.

5. When your browser kicks off the download utility, select the location on your hard drive where you want to download the `fp40.linux.tar.gz` file. I recommend the `/usr/local`

directory of your Linux PC, but you can actually store the file anywhere you want, as long as you can get to it from your Linux PC (such as a network share).

6. While the extensions are downloading, click the Download link at the top of RTR's Web page, which brings up the `http://www.rtr.com/fpsupport/download.htm` hyperlink.

7. Right-click the Installation Script hyperlink, and select Save Link As (Netscape Communicator) or Save Target As (Internet Explorer). This will bring up another download window for you to enter the correct directory where you want to save the `fp_install.sh` script. Again, I recommend `/usr/local` on your Linux PC, but you can store it in the same place you stored `fp40.linux.tar.gz`, if different. This is the script you will use to install the server extensions.

Configuring Apache for FrontPage 2000 Support

Apache Web Server version 1.3.6 should have been installed by default during your initial Red Hat Linux 6.0 installation and configuration process. You can verify this using the GnoRPM package manager, or by typing `rpm -q apache` in an X terminal or at the command-line shell prompt (this should respond with a line indicating apache-1.3.6-7 is installed). If it is not installed, you can use the procedures outlined in Chapter 11, "Installing and Managing RPM Packages," to move the necessary files down to your hard drive.

If Apache is installed, you must become familiar with several files or directories. You will have to provide some of this information during the FrontPage 2000 Server Extensions installation process. Specifically, you will deal with the following Apache files and directories:

- `/etc/httpd/conf/access.conf`—A configuration file used for security-related settings for Apache

- `/etc/httpd/conf/httpd.conf`—The main configuration file for your Apache Web server

- `/home/httpd/html/`—The site where all your Web site's HTML pages are stored for Apache to serve to browsers visiting your site

Most importantly, you may be called upon during certain installation scenarios to edit the `httpd.conf` and `access.conf` files. Like most important configuration files, you must be logged in as root or become the superuser by using the `su` command and providing the necessary password. This is because the FrontPage 2000 Server Extensions for UNIX sometimes require a few variables to be configured in a specific manner, which is not the preconfigured setting for Apache when installed from the Red Hat Linux CD. If you do not make these changes now, your FPSE installation script might (but not always) run into problems and terminate, waiting for you to fix them and then run `fp_install.sh` again. To prepare these Apache configuration files for your FPSE installation, perform the following tasks:

1. Edit the Apache `/etc/httpd/conf/access.conf` file with your favorite ASCII text word processor, such as vi or gnotepad+.

2. Find all instances where there is an `AllowOverride None` setting, and change it to reflect `AllowOverride All`. If you leave these references at `None`, the FPSE installation script normally will exit without completing.

3. Edit the Apache `/etc/httpd/conf/httpd.conf` file with the same editor you just finished using on `access.conf`.

4. Add the following two lines at the bottom of this file, which have the purpose of disabling Apache's use of the `srm.conf` and `access.conf` configuration files (if you have made changes to these files prior to installing FPSE, you should migrate this content over directly to the `httpd.conf` file), and then save the file to record your changes:

```
ResourceConfig    /dev/null
AccessConfig      /dev/null
```

You might not have to make these changes to `httpd.conf`, depending on your system configuration. You do not have to make any other changes to your Apache Web server or its associated configuration files. However, you should make a backup copy of the Apache- and Web-related directories and files prior to installing the FrontPage 2000 Server Extensions.

Installing and Configuring FrontPage 2000 Server Extensions

Based on your two downloads earlier in this chapter, including `fp_install.sh` and `fp40.linux.tar.gz`, you have all you need to install the FPSE and configure it to work with Linux and Apache. Most of the configuration on the server extensions is done during the installation process (`fp_install.sh` script).

If these two files aren't located on the same directory, you will be prompted when you execute the installation script to identify where the GNU zip or `tar` file is located. You also have the option of using GNU unzip (gunzip) to expand the file first, which will expand it from about 10MB to 26MB. However, the installation script is much more flexible and robust than the one that came with the FrontPage 98 Server Extensions for UNIX, so you don't have to perform this additional step. If you choose not to use gunzip to expand the compressed file first, you will have to provide the location (directory path and filename) of the `/bin/zcat` utility, which decompresses a file on the fly.

To install and configure the FrontPage extensions, you will have to perform the following steps and provide the following information:

1. As root, execute the `fp_install.sh` script from wherever you downloaded it (for example, I installed mine once from `/usr/local` and another time from

/mnt/local/fp_install.sh, a Windows network share drive). The script will set up the installation environment, including verifying that you are logged in as root.

2. Verify that you are satisfied with your existing backups, if you performed them, by typing Y at the prompt (the default is N, so be careful not to just hit Enter as you can in other parts of the installation script).

3. Agree to install the extensions at /usr/local/frontpage by hitting Enter when prompted for a directory (or enter another directory, if you want, which will be linked to /usr/local/frontpage). If the directory already exists from a previous successful or failed installation attempt, you will have the option to continue (Y) the installation and overwrite the directory, or to cancel (N) the installation.

4. The fp_install.sh script will look in the local directory where it resides for a fp40.linux.tar.gz or fp40.linux.tar file. If it finds a .tar.gz file, it will prompt you to provide the location of the zcat utility (/bin/zcat). If you already used gunzip to decompress the file, the script will begin installing it automatically to /usr/local/frontpage or another chosen directory.

5. Answer Y when asked if you want to install a new root web.

6. Type /etc/httpd/conf/httpd.conf when prompted for the location of the server config filename, unless you have changed the out-of-the-box configuration of Apache (in which case, you should enter the location of the config file).

7. Choose a login name for the FrontPage root web administrator. This does not have to be the same as an existing Linux login account or name; it can be anything—even "administrator" or your name. You will have to provide this name along with an associated password that you create when the FrontPage 2000 client asks you to authenticate yourself to the Server Extensions when trying to open or edit a FrontPage 2000 web.

8. Select the default Linux account name (nobody), or enter an existing account name. It is a good idea from a security standpoint to use the default because the nobody account does not have shell login capability. The local files can be owned by anyone because the FrontPage 2000 client FPSE handles all the necessary web, directory, and file access control lists (separate from the Linux security and authentication mechanisms).

9. Select the default Linux group (nobody) or provide another, such as users.

10. Assuming that you're installing the FPSE with the default Apache Web server, select option 2 (Apache) when asked what type of server you are using.

11. Verify that there are no error messages when the installation script installs the root web on the default port 80 and changes the necessary ownerships and group affiliations of web directories and files. You might get a comment about the DocumentRoot variable not being set in the httpd.conf file, which by default is in the srm.conf file on Red Hat Linux 6.0. If you get this warning, try copying the configuration line from the latter file to the first.

12. Provide a password for the administrator or other named account you established earlier for the root web. You will see several messages indicating creation of the root web and that Web pages and directories are being updated to reflect new access privileges. You should see an Install completed message as well.

13. Select the local character encoding supported by your system, or the default Latin1.

14. Select the default language used by FrontPage Web (default is English).

15. Unless you have specific reasons for doing so, you can answer N to the next two (final) questions, involving the installation of FrontPage 2000 server extensions on per user or virtual webs. These aren't strictly necessary because FrontPage 2000 can perform these functions for you.

At this point, hopefully, you should see a prompt telling you that the installation was successful and is complete. All you have to do now is "bounce" the httpd Web server daemon by typing /etc/rc.d/init.d/httpd stop. Then, to bring the Web services back online, type /etc/rc.d/init.d/httpd start. If you receive an error message related to MIME or the Web server doesn't come back up, you might have to copy or move the TypesConfig line from the /etc/httpd/conf/srm.conf to the /etc/httpd/conf/httpd.conf configuration files. When you bring the server back up, you should be able to test your FrontPage 2000 Server Extensions with Linux and your Apache Web by bringing up the FrontPage 2000 client on a Windows machine and selecting File, Open Web. Type in your machine's domain name, machine name, or IP address in the Folder Name listbox—for example, I can access my machine using http://barracuda.hellums.com/, http://barracuda/, or http://192.168.1.1/. You should be prompted for a login prompt, where you can provide a username and password.

> **TIP**
>
> One of the first things you might want to do is create one or more subwebs on your Apache server using FrontPage. Run the /usr/local/frontpage/version4.0/bin/fpsrvadm.exe program on your Linux server, and select option 15. You will be prompted for a subweb name (your choice), port (80 is default; 8080 is widely used), username (nobody?), and group (nobody?). This utility can be used for checking FPSE installations, enabling/disabling authoring, and changing security permissions.

Configuring FrontPage 2000 Client for Linux and Apache

The first thing that will happen when you attempt to access your new FrontPage web is you will be required to authenticate yourself, as indicated in Figure 36.1. Enter the username and password used during the installation and configuration of the root web in previous steps.

FIG. 36.1
FrontPage 2000 provides good protection of your Web resources.

The next thing you'll want to do is create additional username and password pairs for users other than the administrator. This can be for yourself as well as others who will be helping you. To add the username hellums to the extensions and Web server on barracuda (192.168.1.1), and to give me authoring and administration privileges from hemicuda (192.168.1.10), for example, you would perform the following steps:

1. From FrontPage on Windows, select Tools, Security, Permissions to bring up the Permissions window you see in Figure 36.2. In the Settings tab (visible only for sub-webs), you can choose to use the same permissions as the parent web (the next web up the hierarchy), or use separate settings that are managed as a subset of the overall web; this way different people, or Marketing, Accounting, Sales, and Human Resources, can all have and maintain separate webs within a web.

FIG. 36.2
You can use existing security settings from the root web or create your own.

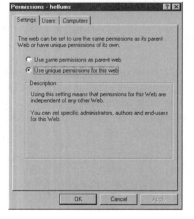

2. You can set permissions for your web by selecting Tools, Security, Permissions, Users. Click the Add or Edit buttons to make changes. In the Add Users window, you can enter a username and password and give administer, author, and browse permissions (in this case, username hellums with administer and author permissions) (see Figure 36.3).

FIG. 36.3
You can set specific privileges you want to give to many different authors.

3. Not only do you need to try to restrict access to your machine to just a few people, but you also want to do the same for specific machines or networks. You can do this using Tools, Security, Permissions, Computers. Click the Add and Edit buttons to bring up a window similar to the one shown in Figure 36.4. You can enter specific IP addresses or a range of addresses (by using the asterisk wildcard).

FIG. 36.4
You can restrict administer and author access to your FrontPage web to only a few machines or networks.

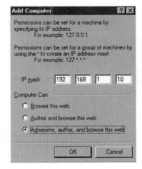

4. Select Tools, Page Options, Compatibility to optimize FrontPage 2000 to use only technologies supported by your Linux clients and servers. You can see these available options in Figure 36.5. If you are in a mixed environment, or if you expect that many Windows browsers will be accessing your FrontPage-enabled web on your Apache server, you can target both Microsoft and Netscape browsers.

FIG. 36.5
FrontPage-enabled webs can be targeted against specific Web server and browser environments.

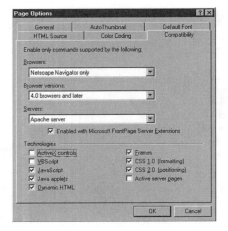

Troubleshooting FrontPage Server Extensions

The FrontPage 2000 Server Extensions themselves work fairly seamlessly and are low maintenance overall. Most of your problems will be related to the Apache Web server daemon or incorrect security settings on a web or subweb you're administering or authoring.

The first thing you should do if you can't get to your FrontPage 2000 web files or folders is to run a process list (ps -ef ¦ grep httpd) to make sure that you have some Web daemons running to handle incoming file requests. You can also test this by "manually" connecting to the Web server using telnet, the server's address, and a port number, such as telnet 192.168.1.1 80 or telnet barracuda 80 (these are my settings, and you will have to replace the IP address, machine name, or domain name based on your environment). If you get a response, it means that your Web server is running on the port that you're testing.

You must make sure that you are sitting at a PC that also has the correct permissions in FrontPage 2000 to allow you to do the type of work you are attempting. If you have checked all your security settings in FrontPage 2000, and you still can't make the necessary changes to your Web directories and files, then you should check to see if your Linux file and folder permissions are correct. Something or someone may have changed them without your knowledge.

If all security permissions appear to be okay and you still can't get through, you can use a few utilities on the /usr/local/frontpage/version4.0/bin/fpsrvadm.exe menu. Specifically, you can choose from among the following:

- **Check and Fix (4)**—This program will check the FrontPage server extension files that are installed against a Web server and running on a specific port (default is 80).

- **Enable Authoring (5)**—This program turns authoring back on for the entire FrontPage 2000 Web if someone has turned it off for some reason, such as for temporary maintenance or a security problem.

- **Uninstall and Install (3 and 1)**—Use this program only if you have tried everything else and think you need to refresh the FrontPage 2000 server extension files running on your web. You will have to renew all your settings and security permissions afterward. ●

Appendix

Internet Resources

by Duane Hellums

In this appendix

This appendix provides you with additional support resources that can enhance your Linux experience. If you find that your specific environment or situation calls for more detailed information than what is provided in this book, you can refer to this appendix and find out if there's another ready reference on the Internet to help solve your problem. Some of the information is related to basic installation and configuration; the rest is aimed at increasing your knowledge of Linux and your ability to optimize it to meet your changing needs. This is obviously not an all-inclusive list, and you'll likely find your own favorites as well.

Many of these are HOWTO documents, which can be valuable references for you if you run into problems or want to perform advanced functions in Linux. The ones included here supplement specific chapters in this book and were updated within the past year. Linux kernels and distributions evolve rapidly, and you should make sure that the HOWTO reflects the most up-to-date information.

You might have a problem-free installation of Red Hat Linux 6.0 and won't need to refer to many of these resources. However, the more you know about Linux, UNIX, and Internet technology, the easier it will be to administer your Linux system. Take a little time after you start using your Linux system to identify some of these resources that look interesting to you. Then when you find time, refer to them and learn more about your system. You will find tools and utilities that help you maintain your Linux PC and increase your enjoyment of it. Many of these sites have almost up-to-the-minute news about Linux kernel and application development, helping you find fresh ways to use and enjoy Linux.

In addition to the World Wide Web, you should consider subscribing to some of the many Linux-related Internet newsgroups, where you can read recommendations of others as well as post your own problems or suggestions. Visit at least the following sites: `linux.redhat.install`, `comp.os.linux.redhat`, `alt.os.linux.redhat`, and `comp.os.linux.portable` (if you have a laptop).

Installation, Configuration, and Administration Resources

Web Site	Description
`http://www.redhat.com/cgi-bin/support?faq`	Frequently asked questions and responses to trouble calls. A great place to start when you run into a problem installing or configuring Red Hat Linux
`http://209.81.8.22/archives/3/80/1999/`	Geocrawler archive of Red Hat Internet news messages (other years are available also)

Web Site	Description
http://www.linuxdoc.org/ HOWTO/Hardware-HOWTO.html	A laundry list of individual components supported by the Linux kernel, and where to find drivers for some hardware
http://www.linuxdoc.org/ HOWTO/Config-HOWTO.html	Extra help with specific Linux configuration areas
http://www.linuxdoc.org/ HOWTO/Bootdisk-HOWTO.html	Extra help for creating floppy boot and root disks
http://www.linuxdoc.org/ HOWTO/BootPrompt-HOWTO.html	Extra help for adding initial boot parameters to get the Linux kernel to recognize hardware it is having trouble autosensing
http://www.linuxdoc.org/ HOWTO/KickStart-HOWTO.html	Information about creating kickstart instructions for automating the Linux network installation process when installing on many PCs
http://www.linuxdoc.org/ HOWTO/mini/Hard-Disk- Upgrade.html	Explains how to create a copy or image of your Linux disk on another hard drive
http://www.linuxdoc.org/ HOWTO/mini/Large-Disk.html	Information on disk geometries and the 1024-cylinder restrictions of the Linux kernel
http://www.linuxdoc.org/ HOWTO/Multi-Disk-HOWTO.html	An all-encompassing explanation of disk drive and partition management as it relates to Linux and other operating systems
http://www.linuxdoc.org/ HOWTO/mini/Loadlin+ Win95.html	Shows you how to boot into Linux directly from Windows
http://www.linuxdoc.org/ HOWTO/mini/Kerneld.html	Explains how to configure your kernel and associated modules to support your necessary hardware and networking environment.
http://www.linuxdoc.org/ HOWTO/mini/Ext2fs- Undeletion.html	Opportunities for you to attempt retrieval of deleted files on Linux
http://www.linuxgeek.org	A portal of sorts for new Linux users seeking information, advice, and troubleshooting assistance

Platform-Specific Resources

Web Site	Description
`http://www.linuxdoc.org/` `HOWTO/Alpha-HOWTO.html`	An Alpha overview and tutorial
`http://www.linuxdoc.org/` `HOWTO/MILO-HOWTO.html`	Explains how to use the Linux Alpha Miniloader to boot Linux on an Alpha
`http://www.linuxdoc.org/` `HOWTO/Laptop-HOWTO.html`	Details on how to get Linux installed on your laptop
`http://www.cs.utexas.edu/` `users/kharker/linux-laptop`	The definitive reference on installation and configuration of Linux on laptops. It includes a supported hardware database
`http://www.linuxdoc.org/` `HOWTO/mini/Saving-Space.html`	Describes how you can minimize the amount of space required for Linux, often helpful for older systems and laptops
`http://www.linuxdoc.org/` `HOWTO/PCMCIA-HOWTO.html`	Describes how to configure PCMCIA support and devices on Linux
`http://www.linuxdoc.org/` `HOWTO/IR-HOWTO.html`	Describes how to configure Linux to support infrared devices

Hardware-Specific Resources

Web Site	Description

`http://www.redhat.com/corp/`
`support/hardware/intel/`
`60/rh6.0-hcl-i.ld.html`
	Details on known compatible and incompatible hardware for Red Hat Linux 6.0 on the Intel i386 platform

`http://www.redhat.com/corp/`
`support/hardware/sparc/`
`6.0/rh60-hardware.sparc.html`
	Details on known compatible and incompatible hardware for Red Hat Linux 6.0 on the Sun platform

`http://www.redhat.com/corp/`
`support/hardware/alpha`
`/6.0/rh60-hardware.alpha.html`
	Details on known compatible and incompatible hardware for Red Hat Linux 6.0 on the Alpha platform

`http://www.linuxdoc.org/` `HOWTO/CD-Writing-HOWTO.html`	Information on getting your CD-R to work with Linux
`http://www.linuxdoc.org/` `HOWTO/CDROM-HOWTO.html`	Information on getting your CD-ROM to work with Linux
`http://www.linuxdoc.org/` `HOWTO/Ftape-HOWTO.html`	Information on getting your tape backup devices to work with Linux

Web Site	Description
`http://www.linuxdoc.org/` `HOWTO/mini/ZIP-Drive.html`	Information on installing and configuring your ZIP drive on Linux

`http://www.linuxdoc.org/`
`HOWTO/Keyboard-and-`
`Console-HOWTO.html`
	Information on configuring your keyboard and text display (console) on Linux

`http://www.linuxdoc.org/` `HOWTO/Serial-HOWTO.html`	Information on configuring standard and multiport serial cards with Linux

`http://www.linuxdoc.org/`
`HOWTO/Plug-and-Play-`
`HOWTO.html`
	Information on configuring Plug-and-Play devices to work on Linux

`http://www.linuxdoc.org/` `HOWTO/Printing-HOWTO.html`	Information on printing with Linux
`http://www.linuxdoc.org/` `HOWTO/Sound-HOWTO.html`	Information on installing and configuring sound cards and getting sound to work on your Linux PC

`http://www.linuxdoc.org/`
`HOWTO/Sound-Playing-`
`HOWTO.html`
	Information on how to play different types of audio sounds on Linux

`http://www.linuxdoc.org/`
`HOWTO/mini/Soundblaster-`
`AWE.html`
	Information on getting your Soundblaster 32 or AWE sound card to work with Linux

`http://www.linuxdoc.org/` `HOWTO/MP3-HOWTO.html`	Information on getting your Linux PC to interpret and play MP3 audio files

`http://www.linuxdoc.org/`
`HOWTO/Text-Terminal-`
`HOWTO.html`
	Information on getting dumb and smart terminals to work with Linux

`http://www.linuxdoc.org/`
`HOWTO/mini/3-Button-`
`Mouse.html`
	Information on getting your three-button mouse to work with Linux

`http://www.linuxdoc.org/` `HOWTO/Modem-HOWTO.html`	Information on getting your modem to work with Linux
`http://www.linuxdoc.org/` `HOWTO/mini/ADSL.html`	Information on using Linux with Asymmetric Digital Subscriber Loop
`http://www.linuxdoc.org/` `HOWTO/mini/Cable-Modem.html`	Information on getting your cable modem to work with Linux
`http://www.linuxdoc.org/` `HOWTO/mini/Software-RAID.html`	Information on using RAID software on your Linux server

`http://www.linuxdoc.org/`
`HOWTO/mini/DPT-Hardware-`
`RAID.html`
	Information on getting hardware-based RAID devices to work with Linux

Graphical User Interfaces, Desktop Environments, and Window Manager Resources

Web Site	Description
http://www.linuxdoc.org/ HOWTO/XFree86-HOWTO.html	Step-by-step procedures on acquiring, installing, updating, and configuring XFree86
http://www.linuxdoc.org/ HOWTO/XWindow-User-HOWTO.html	Explains how a user and administrator can tweak and configure XFree86
http://www.linuxdoc.org/ HOWTO/XFree86-Video-Timings-HOWTO.html	Describes how to manually create an XFree86 mode line for high-performance or custom video card and monitor combinations
http://www.xfree86.org	XFree86 Project home page list of mirrors
http://www.xfree86.org/FAQ	XFree86 Frequently Asked Questions (FAQ)
http://www.xfree86.org/ 3.3.5/ftp.html	XFree86 version 3.3.5 downloads (mirror site list)
http://www.x.org	X Window home page (basis for XFree86; FYI mostly)
http://www.gnome.org	The GNOME Project home page GNOME
http://www.gnome.org/ users-guide/index.html	User's Manual
http://www.gnome.org/ webmirrors.shtml	List of Gnome Web site mirrors
http://www.gnome.org/ applist/list-martin.phtml	GNOME software map, where you can find lots of new goodies to download
http://www.enlightenment.org	The Enlightenment home page
http://www.kde.org	K Desktop Environment (KDE), KOffice suite
http://www.afterstep.org	Home page for the Afterstep window manager (based on the popular NeXTStep)
http://www.windowmaker.org	Window Maker window manager (based on the popular NeXTStep)
http://interpath.linuxberg. com/themes	A place to find new themes
http://www.themes.org	Themes for E, KDE, WM, and other window managers

Networking-Specific Resources

Web Site	Description
http://www.linuxdoc.org/ HOWTO/SMB-HOWTO.html	Details on the SMB protocol and Samba software suite, which are used for Linux to share resources in a native Windows network environment
http://www.samba.org/	List of mirror sites where you can find more information on Samba or download the newest version
http://www.linuxdoc.org/ HOWTO/WWW-HOWTO.html	Details on installing and configuring a variety of graphical and text-based Web servers and clients on Linux
http://www.linuxdoc.org/ HOWTO/NET3-4-HOWTO.html	An all-encompassing tutorial on Linux networking (mostlyTCP/IP)
http://www.linuxdoc.org/ HOWTO/Ethernet-HOWTO.html	A broad explanation of Ethernet networking with Linux, including vendor-specific information
http://www.linuxdoc.org/ HOWTO/Mail-Administrator-HOWTO.html	Lots of helpful information for administering a Linux email system (server and clients)
http://www.linuxdoc.org/ HOWTO/Mail-User-HOWTO.html	Helpful information for installing and configuring your email clients
http://www.linuxdoc.org/ HOWTO/mini/IP-Masquerade.html	Help for organizations connecting many network PCs to the Internet using a single Internet connection and Linux
http://www.linuxdoc.org/ HOWTO/mini/DHCP.html	Discussion of how to configure Linux as a Domain Host Control Protocol (dynamic IP) client and server
http://www.linuxdoc.org/ HOWTO/Firewall-HOWTO.html	A tutorial on firewalls and proxies, with details on how to configure Linux in this capacity
http://www.linuxdoc.org/ HOWTO/IPX-HOWTO.html	Details on configuring your Linux network to interface and share resources with Novell NetWare
http://www.linuxdoc.org/ HOWTO/VPN-Masquerade-HOWTO.html	How to create a secure virtual private network through your firewall with Linux
http://www.linuxdoc.org/ HOWTO/mini/PLIP.html	How to perform IP networking over a Linux parallel interface

Software-Specific Resources

Web Site	Description
http://linuxcentral.com	A place to find and buy Linux products, including distributions, books, and software
http://linuxberg.com	Loads of Linux software
http://www.freshmeat.net	News on new Linux software releases, updated daily
http://www.gnu.org	The GNU Project
http://www.redhat.com/community/list_subscribe.html	Red Hat index of mailing lists you can subscribe to
http://interpath.linuxberg.com/picks.html	Top 20 popular picks of Linux software (10 console and 10 graphical)
http://www.filewatcher.org	A useful search engine for Linux packages, binaries, patches, and so on
http://www.linux.org	A place to find lots of information about current developments in Linux and to buy cool things such as Linux mugs and T-shirts
http://www.linux.org/apps/lsm.html	The Linux Software Map project, where you can find out about all kinds of Linux software applications and utilities you can download (searchable)
http://www.execpc.com/lsm	The Linux Software Map project (non-searchable)
http://www.sun.com/staroffice	Sun's StarOffice productivity suite information page
http://linux.corel.com/linux8/download.htm http://linux.corel.com/linux8/install_instr.htm	Corel WordPerfect 8 download pages
http://home.netscape.com/download/	Netscape Communicator 4.7 for Linux download page
http://www.real.com/products/player/	RealNetworks RealPlayer 5.0 download page
http://www.mpegtv.com/download.html	A site to download pages for streaming MPEG viewer on Linux and Netscape

General Linux-Related Resources

Web Site	Description
`http://www.slashdot.com`	Recent news and information about Linux
`http://www.linuxtoday.com`	More recent news and information about Linux
`http://www.linuxjournal.com`	Web site of the popular Linux magazine, even has some online articles
`http://www.linuxworld.com/lsm`	Useful articles and book reviews on Linux topics, with a wealth of other links
`http://www.linuxdoc.org`	Linux Documentation Project (LDP), with Linux Guides, HOWTOs, man pages, FAQs, newsletters, and links to other resources
`http://linuxdev.com`	Linux development issues and news, and other Linux links
`http://www.linuxdoc.org/ HOWTO/DOS-Win-to-Linux- HOWTO.html`	Document that compares and contrasts Linux, DOS, and Windows
`http://www.linuxdoc.org/ HOWTO/Unix-Internet- Fundamentals-HOWTO.html`	The basics of UNIX and internetworking
`http://www.linuxdoc.org/ HOWTO/Reading-List-HOWTO.html`	A recommended reading list of Linux books and resources
`http://www.linuxhelp.net`	A Linux portal with news, articles, HOWTOs, and advisories
`http://www.rfc-editor.org/ rfc.html http://www.ietf. org/rfc`	Internet standards, Request For Comments (RFC) Documentation, and a search engine (not searchable)
`http://www.linuxdoc.org/ HOWTO/Security-HOWTO.html`	Details on how you can secure various parts of a Linux system

Index

Get FREE books and more...when you register this book online for our Personal Bookshelf Program

http://register.quecorp.com/

 Register online and you can sign up for our *FREE Personal Bookshelf Program*...unlimited access to the electronic version of more than 200 complete computer books—immediately! That means you'll have 100,000 pages of valuable information onscreen, at your fingertips!

 Plus, you can access product support, including complimentary downloads, technical support files, book-focused links, companion Web sites, author sites, and more!

 And you'll be automatically registered to receive a *FREE subscription to a weekly email newsletter* to help you stay current with news, announcements, sample book chapters, and special events, including sweepstakes, contests, and various product giveaways!

 We value your comments! Best of all, the entire registration process takes only a few minutes to complete, so go online and get the greatest value going—absolutely FREE!

Don't Miss Out On This Great Opportunity!

QUE® is a brand of Macmillan Computer Publishing USA.

For more information, please visit *www.mcp.com*

Other Related Titles

What's on the Disc

The companion CD-ROM contains Red Hat Linux 6.0 Publisher's Edition.

Installing Red Hat Linux 6.0 from the CD-ROM

1. Insert the CD in the CD-ROM drive.
2. Restart your computer.
3. You might need to change your BIOS settings to boot from the CD-ROM. Typically, you enter your BIOS setup program with the F2 or DEL keys during the boot sequence.
4. Make your changes (if any) and exit the BIOS setup utility.
5. If your CD drive is capable of booting from CD-ROMs, you will boot into the Red Hat setup program.
6. Follow the onscreen prompts to complete the installation.

Installing Red Hat Linux 6.0 from Boot Floppies

1. Using DOS or Windows, format two 1.44 MB floppies.
2. Copy three files from the CD-ROM to a temporary location on your hard drive, such as C:\TEMP:, D:\IMAGES\BOOT.IMG, D:\IMAGES\SUPP.IMG, and D:\DOSUTILS\RAWRITE.EXE. If your CD drive letter is not D:, substitute the drive letter that corresponds to your system.
3. At the DOS prompt, move to the directory where you copied the three files. Type RAWRITE and press Enter.
4. When prompted to do so, type the name BOOT.IMG and press Enter.
5. When prompted to do so, type the drive letter of the disks you are going to prepare and press Enter. Because you are going to be booting from this disk, it's typically A:.
6. Most CD-ROM drives are supported by the information found on the boot disk. However, you might want to create the supplementary disk just in case. Repeat step 3. When prompted to do so, type the name SUPP.IMG and press Enter.
7. Repeat step 5.
8. If you don't already have the boot floppy in your disk drive, insert it now.
9. Restart your computer.
10. You might need to change your BIOS settings to boot from the floppy drive. Typically, you enter your BIOS setup program with the F2 or DEL keys during the boot sequence.
11. Make your changes (if any) and exit the BIOS setup utility.
12. If your computer is set up properly, you will boot into the Red Hat Linux setup program.
13. Follow the onscreen prompts to complete the installation.

NOTE If Windows 95, Windows 98, or Windows NT 4 is installed on your computer and you have the AutoPlay feature enabled, the START.EXE program starts automatically whenever you insert the disc into your CD-ROM drive. ▪

Read This Before Opening the Software